REPAIR & RENOVATE

yourhome

WARNING

Although the publishers, authors, and editors have made every effort to ensure the accuracy of instructions and advice in this book, they can accept no responsibility for any accident or injury resulting from the use or selection of tools, materials, and methods. Readers should always observe safety precautions, check and follow local codes and laws, and obey manufacturers' operating and use instructions.

REPAIR & RENOVATE
yourhome

BY

Julian Cassell

Peter Parham

Mark Corke

Mike Lawrence

bay books

contents

introduction

Home improvement is fast becoming a national pastime, with more and more people tackling jobs that would previously have been left to the services of professional craftspeople. Taking on a job yourself can be cheaper and more rewarding than using a professional—ensuring that the finished effect is how you envisaged and falls within a budget.

repair & renovation issues

This revolution has been fuelled by a booming DIY retail sector, which tries to convince us that no job is too difficult and any practically minded person can set about full-scale home renovation. Although it is true to say that there is indeed huge scope for applying yourself to home-improvement tasks, it is always important to know your limitations right from the outset. It is best to approach DIY as a learning curve, building up your experience and knowledge before tackling jobs of greater difficulty.

Repair issues can be neatly separated from those of renovation—the former are concerned primarily with making good existing features, and the latter are related to adjusting the appearance of certain areas in your home. Renovation therefore leans more heavily on the creative side of your abilities, whereas repairs generally tend to be dependent on your ability to apply yourself practically to restoring a particular finish or structure.

Most people are able to recognize when a particular area of their home needs adapting or changing, but realizing or envisaging what that change should be exactly can often be more difficult. Therefore, inspiration for change needs to be balanced with the potential options available, which in turn relate firmly to budget, personal choice, your ability to tackle the work, and how much professional advice or input may be required for the task. It is best to try and tackle each of these areas in turn.

The smallest of renovation or home improvement tasks will always cost some money, and therefore it is impossible to begin work without deciding on a budget. Right from the start, budgetary constraints will be the major governing factor in deciding on the extent of work.

Personal choice is clearly of the utmost importance when you come to repairing and renovating your home. Work out your ideal situation, and then compromise as necessary, taking into consideration the wishes of other people who will be affected, and the relative value of your home. Decide whether your plans are to renovate purely to cater for your needs, or whether you are aiming to provide a general level of improvement that will also appeal to others, including potential buyers.

Next comes the question of your ability to tackle home-improvement tasks. This book takes into account a wide variety of options and techniques, covering all aspects of renovation. However, some techniques are clearly more demanding than others. It is always advisable to seek professional advice when needs dictate, even if it is just to provide a guiding hand rather than full-scale employment. The areas of plumbing and electricity are specific examples where professional help will almost certainly be required. There is also a clear safety issue here, and safety is one area where there is no room for compromise when renovating.

LEFT *The wall between these two rooms has been knocked through, allowing more light into both rooms and turning two living rooms into one area.*

The layout of this book has been designed to give project instruction in as comprehensive, yet straightforward, a manner as possible. The illustration below provides a guideline to the different elements incorporated in the page design. Color photographs and diagrams combined with explanatory text, laid out in a clear, step-by-step order, provide easy-to-follow instructions. Each project is prefaced by a blue box containing a list of tools so that you will know in advance the range of equipment required for the job. Other boxes of additional text accompany each project, and are aimed at drawing your attention to particular issues. Pink safety boxes alert the reader to issues of safety, and detail any precautions that may need to be taken. They also indicate where a particular job must be carried out by a tradesperson. Green tip boxes offer professional hints for the best way to go about a particular task involved in the project. Boxes with an orange border describe alternative options and techniques, relevant to the project in hand, but not demonstrated on the page.

difficulty rating

The following symbols are designed to give an indication of difficulty level relating to particular tasks and projects in this book. Clearly what are simple jobs to one person may be difficult to another, and vice versa. These guidelines are primarily based on the ability of an individual in relation to the experience and degree of technical ability required.

Straightforward and requires limited technical skills	*Straightforward but requires a reasonable skill level*
Technically quite difficult, and could involve a number of skills	*High skill level required and involves a number of techniques*

A list of tools is provided at the beginning of each job.

Option boxes offer additional instructions and techniques for the project in hand.

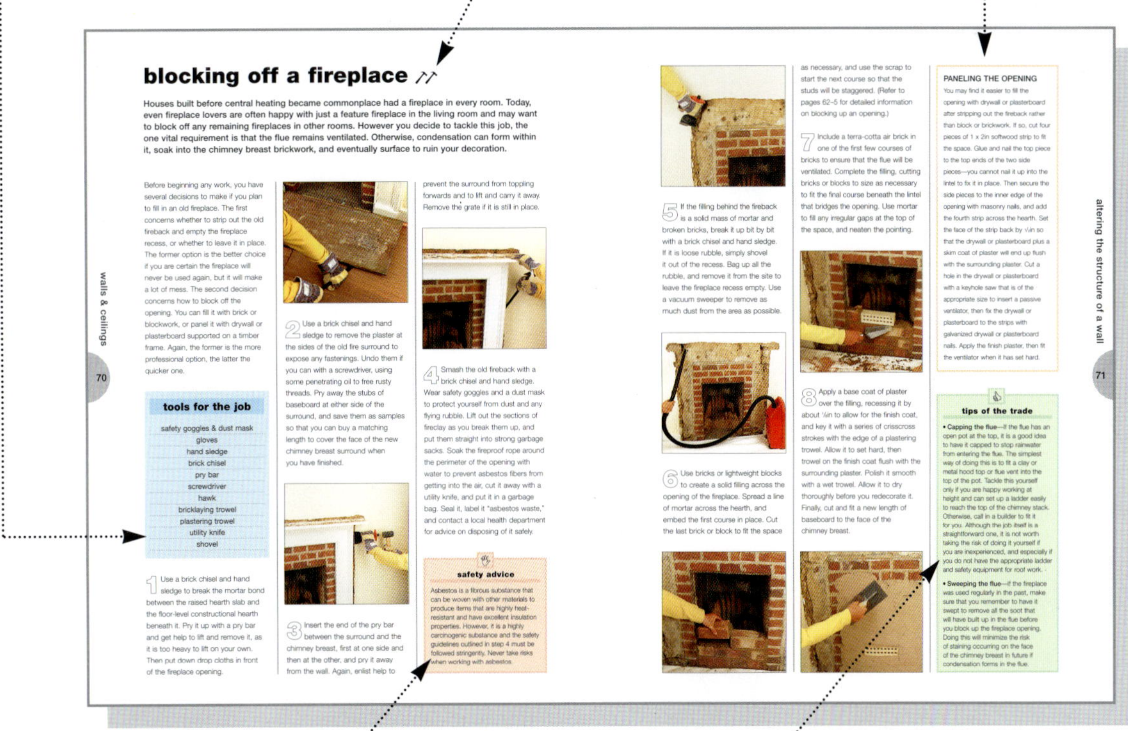

Safety boxes, pink for emphasis, draw attention to safety considerations.

Tip boxes provide helpful hints developed from professional experience or highlight areas where more traditional methods can be used.

planning

Careful planning is crucial for any type of repair or renovation because there are so many issues that need close consideration. In addition to gauging tool and material requirements, it is also important to establish whether planning permission will be necessary, whether you are capable of carrying out all the work yourself, and what the total cost and time frame will be. The extent and nature of a project will be highly dependent on at least some, if not all, of these considerations. This section provides some basic guidelines in all of these areas and helps to provide a framework for decision-making and setting about a renovation project.

The careful use of mirrors, as shown here, can create the illusion of space for your bathroom.

how to start

Before commencing any project, it is important to plan your overall approach to the job and a specific order of work. Simple repairs or minor renovations tend not to raise too many problems, but inadequate planning on larger-scale projects can produce very real difficulties. Even if the physical work itself is organized, issues such as building regulations and planning permission may need to be addressed.

planning permission

Before any construction project can begin, some consideration must be given to whether the particular work will need planning permission. The majority of projects inside the home do not need planning approval, and so this is not an issue for most work that you are likely to carry out. However, there are some circumstances that you should be aware of before beginning renovations.

restrictions

Most restrictions are applied to houses that are historic buildings and/or are in conservation areas, national parks, or areas of outstanding natural beauty or overseen by an association. If your property fits into any of these categories, always call the local authority before commencing any plans. However, even in these cases, formal permission is rarely required for internal alterations, minor improvements, and general repairs and maintenance. Projects that definitely require planning permission are generally those in which an area of the house has a "change of use," normally when business purposes are proposed. For example, if you wish to divide off a section of your home for business use, or you want to create a separate apartment. So in general, in addition to these restrictions, as long as the exterior appearance of the building is not changed, interior work may be carried out relatively free from too many planning obstacles. If in any doubt about what is permissible, it is best to contact your local Department of Planning and Zoning.

Exterior work can often be subject to strict building restrictions. Always check with an appropriate body before embarking on work that may require authorization.

building regulations

While most interior renovation is unlikely to require actual planning permission, all construction work should adhere to building regulations. So whenever you plan to carry out any construction work, contact your Department of Planning and Zoning, who will be able to provide any necessary guidelines for potential work.

making a scale drawing

It is always sensible to make a scale drawing of a proposed construction job, in order to get a firm idea of material quantities. This does not have to be up to architectural standards, but it should provide enough detail to give you a good idea of the effect a project will have, and how it will change the existing look of your home. Graph paper always makes any technical drawing easier, and allows for more accurate measurement. It can often be helpful to add furniture to the diagram, so that you can gauge the effect of the alteration on the overall layout of the room—this can be especially important when dividing an existing room into two separate areas, as the amount of space is obviously reduced.

time

Always consider the time required to complete a project, as this can influence the most convenient time to commence the job. For example, while some projects can be completed in a weekend, other jobs will take longer, causing disruption to the household for several days. Most projects in this book are designed to be completed within a weekend, although the actual finishing may take longer, as you return to the job for final decorating. As soon as you begin to combine a number of projects or work on large areas, completing jobs can become more difficult. This is especially true of projects that run between weekends or evenings, so it is advisable either to break them down into smaller sections, which can be completed as part of an overall larger renovation, or take time away from day-to-day work in order to make headway into the particular task. Otherwise, pressure to finish the job and minimize disruption can lead to inadequate work with poor finishing. Never underestimate the time involved in a project, and consider it an important part of the planning procedure to decide on dates and times when the work can be done, and within what time it can be finished.

Many DIY tasks will cause some inevitable disruption to the household. Bear this in mind when planning a job, and aim to commence work at a time convenient to all of those involved.

Making a scale drawing can help you to visualize the effect of any work on the surrounding environment. Adding furniture to the diagram will also help.

budgeting

The greatest expense in a construction project is usually the price of the labor itself, and therefore by reducing this input, costs are reduced. If professional trades are required, this should be given priority in terms of your overall budgeting strategy. Aside from this, material costs can be calculated relatively easily, so long as accurate measurements are taken. Remember that bulk buying of particular materials should mean financial discounts, and it is always worth shopping around for the best deals. This is especially the case with common items such as general lumber and wallboard because the market is so competitive, and suppliers can vary their prices from week to week. If your planning is comprehensive, you have a better chance of remaining within your budget. However, it is always worth building in a slight surplus requirement to your figures so that if work does take longer—or requires more materials—you are able to complete the project without delay.

dealing with professionals

Before starting any construction work, it is important to establish what work you are capable of doing yourself, and to what extent you will require professional help. Small renovations or repairs are unlikely to require a great deal of assistance, but when tackling any major renovation, it is almost certain that the services of plumbers, electricians, or contractors may be required. In these cases, try to identify the kind of assistance you require and understand how to get the best service.

architects and surveyors

In some circumstances, it may be necessary to draw on the services of architects and surveyors. Although not considered conventional "craftsmen," they supply services that enable the practical side of major renovations to be planned and carried out in the correct manner. Architects really need to be employed only on larger projects where major design features have to be considered. On large projects, architects or surveyors can be employed in a kind of project management role, overseeing general work to ensure it meets building codes (see page 10). Bear in mind that these services are expensive and fees for monitoring work can add a further 10 percent to the original price of drawing plans. There may also be daily or hourly rate charges for site attendance.

Professional advice for major projects is always advisable, particularly for projects that may require building permits. Bear these costs in mind when planning the work.

finding good craftspeople

Finding good, reliable craftspeople can be difficult—there is no point in hiring the best bricklayer in the world if he never shows up for work. The best method is to use personal recommendations, as you can see or hear about the quality of the work from a former client. The other alternative is to contact three or four advertised companies for estimates. However, although this may help to ensure a competitive price, it does not guarantee the quality of the work or the reliability of the craftsperson. Even companies that display particular trade association medallions may be no more reliable than other advertisers, so check the credentials with the association itself and then with an independent body. Always ask to have a look at a person's work, preferably through the property owner, and then perhaps with the builder or craftsperson.

estimates, quotes, and prices

Before allowing any craftsman to begin work in your home, it is essential to know how much the actual job is going to cost. Estimates, quotes, and prices can be a minefield—and are frequently the source of customers' disgruntlement. The main factor to bear in mind at this stage is that if you receive an estimate or a quote, this is exactly the case—they are only estimates or quotes, and therefore the price you pay can inflate considerably. If at all possible, it is best to get an exact price from the craftsperson, which should not fluctuate unless you decide to change the specifications for the work. In some circumstances, an estimate may be necessary, as you may not have made final decisions on specifications and need to see how the project develops. However, the closer you can get to deciding on a price before the work begins, the better position you will find yourself in when budgeting for the job and keeping track of any payments.

You will usually have to make an initial downpayment, especially if the craftsperson is supplying expensive material, but generally speaking there is no reason to pay the full amount until the job is complete and you are happy with the finished product. For long projects, it is fair to stage

Keep the lines of communication open. Although the cost of work may rise slightly as the job progresses, this can be negotiated at each stage, helping you monitor the cost overall.

payments throughout the job, but always leave the largest payment until completion. Finally, treat contractors or craftspeople who insist on cash-only payments with some suspicion. Although there are potential savings to be made in this line, it means you have no recourse in terms of defective work or problems at a later date. Such methods of payment could also suggest illegal transactions in the eyes of the relevant tax authorities.

extras

On making any final payment, the word or phrase "extras," "extra work carried out," or "add-ons" on your bill can add a surprising amount to the figure you were expecting to pay. In many cases, these may be items that you authorized during the overall work. However, it is always best to get a price for extra work before it is done, so that shocks do not occur at the final stage of payment. Alternately, arrange during the initial contract stage that any extra work has to be carried out on your authority and is charged at a specific hourly or daily rate. This makes it much easier to keep a track of expenses and helps you prevent unexpected surprises when you receive the final statement.

avoiding disputes

Disputes can easily be avoided so long as you have a written contract. Over half the battle is won if you have chosen the right craftsperson. Further gains can be made by ensuring that the price you are quoted is written and detailed in terms of the work to be carried out. This therefore acts as an accurate referral document for all parties. Aside from this, the only problems that generally arise concern the standard of work compared to what was initially agreed. Most of these problems can be sorted out through discussion and compromise, and it is best to avoid legal wrangles unless absolutely necessary. However, if you are that unhappy with the work that has been carried out, your only option may be to withhold payment and hand the matter over to a lawyer.

In following these simple guidelines, you should be well equipped for employing the services of various craftspeople. Simply remember that, in all occupations, there are both good and bad operators and that the building business gets more than its fair share of criticism. However, if you do have reliable craftspeople at your disposal, pay them in full on time and recommend them to friends—in looking after their interests, you will almost certainly be looking after your own.

Professional craftspeople will do a good job for a fair price. However, before agreeing on the terms and conditions of the contract, establish the length of time and expense of the project.

tools & equipment

The range of tools and equipment necessary for completing DIY tasks can be vast and expensive. Yet many of the basic tools are in fact multi-purpose and make up what might be called a "household tool kit." Once this strong base of essential tools has been established, you can go on to purchase more specialized tools as and when they are required. Although it is not necessary to spend a fortune on equipment, it is generally a good rule to buy the best tools that you can afford. Top-quality tools tend to last longer and give better results, time and again.

household tools

This general household tool kit contains the essential tools for carrying out any number of small jobs and tasks around the home. Although the kit will not cope with every situation you encounter, it provides a good starting point to which you can add more specific tool requirements.

power tools

Power tools are designed to make jobs easier and less time-consuming. For most enthusiasts, mid-range tools are ideal, as the very expensive equipment is designed for everyday work, and the very cheap equipment for the occasional DIY person. Even so, the cost of power tools has dropped considerably, and it is possible to buy quality products relatively cheaply. For some tasks, it can even be worth buying cheap tools for limited use before discarding.

construction tools

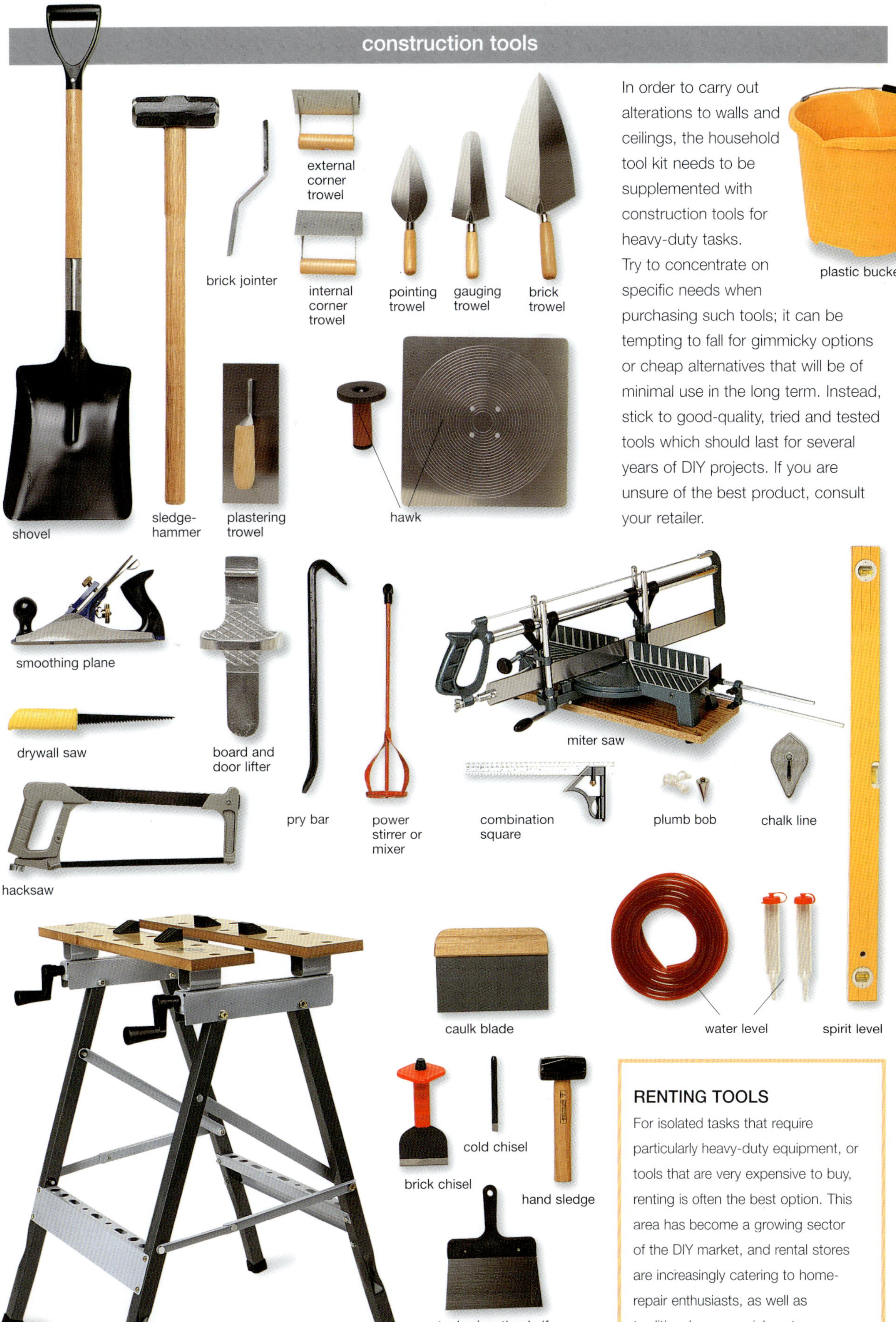

In order to carry out alterations to walls and ceilings, the household tool kit needs to be supplemented with construction tools for heavy-duty tasks. Try to concentrate on specific needs when purchasing such tools; it can be tempting to fall for gimmicky options or cheap alternatives that will be of minimal use in the long term. Instead, stick to good-quality, tried and tested tools which should last for several years of DIY projects. If you are unsure of the best product, consult your retailer.

RENTING TOOLS

For isolated tasks that require particularly heavy-duty equipment, or tools that are very expensive to buy, renting is often the best option. This area has become a growing sector of the DIY market, and rental stores are increasingly catering to home-repair enthusiasts, as well as traditional commercial customers.

renting specialist equipment

Certain projects described in this book will require the use of specialist tools and equipment, which are often large and expensive. If the equipment is only needed for the occasional job or one specific task it can be uneconomic to purchase it outright. Renting a piece of equipment for a week, a day, or just a few hours is a viable alternative, and the market now caters for this growing practice amongst DIYers. Knowing that you have access to an almost unlimited range of specialist equipment will allow you to plan far more ambitious projects.

when to rent

When planning any job, however large or small, thought should be given to the skills and tools that will be needed. In many cases, the projects shown in this book can be completed successfully with a basic set of household tools. As your skill levels increase with experience and confidence, you will be amazed at just what can be achieved without recourse to a vast armoury of tools, but at times this is just not enough, and a particular task will call for the aid of a specific piece of equipment. Just about any tool can be rented these days, but it can be difficult for the amateur to know what is available and recognize when a piece of equipment is a candidate for renting. Throughout this book you will see references to different tools. A basic tool kit, sufficient to complete most projects, is anatomized on page 14. Where larger pieces of machinery are shown, then it is safe to assume that these can be rented. That said, if you will be using such equipment for an extended period of time, or on a frequent basis, you should consider buying, because there may come a time when the total cost of the rental will be greater than the price tag of the tool.

RIGHT *A small-scale cement mixer can be rented for relatively little cost and will greatly contribute towards a professional finish.*

what to rent

Equipment such as carpet cleaners are popular rental items, but there are plenty of others, of which the average person may be unaware. Concrete mixers and floor sanders speed up the work magnificently, putting professional results within reach of the amateur. A small compressor and nail gun can be used to fix a large amount of floorboards down very quickly, while a powerfloat will give a smooth, glass-like finish to concrete and screeds.

LEFT *Although this damp-proof fluid injection machine is highly specialized, it is possible to rent one to do the job yourself.*

at the rental store

Once the preserve of the professional builder, rental stores are increasingly catering for the DIY market, and many stores even offer a home-delivery service at little extra charge for tools too big or too bulky to transport yourself. Before you start using an unfamiliar machine for the first time, it is vital that you fully understand how it operates, so make sure you have this explained to you before leaving the store. Do not be afraid to ask for a demonstration if you are at all unsure. Staff in rental stores are usually very knowledgeable, so do not be afraid to ask for advice. Often they will be able to suggest different methods for completing a task, and direct you to tools that you might not know. Explain to them clearly what your project is, what tools you have already, and ask them what tools they would suggest you need to hire to complete the job most efficiently. Many stores will have a catalog, though do not expect this to explain how each piece of equipment works. It is more likely to give details of cost, minimum periods of rental, and so forth.

In addition to the machine itself, you may need to buy some consumables. In the case of a floor sander, this will mean the sanding sheets. Often the shop will give you a selection of these ,and only charge you for those you

ABOVE RIGHT *You may need to rent a good-quality grinder to sharpen tools in your existing tool kit.*

RIGHT *A heavy steel roller is a vital tool for ensuring full adhesion of vinyl flooring, but for just this one job it is best to rent.*

BELOW *An electric floor sander will make light work of an otherwise daunting task. Large, edging, and corner versions are available.*

actually use when you return the machine. The store should stock and offer you all the necessary safety gear, such as goggles, kneepads, and ear protectors, though it is likely you will be obliged to purchase these.

Finding the nearest tool-rental store should be as simple as looking in the yellow pages our local telephone book. Most reputable companies belong to the RSA (Rental Stores Association). If you have difficulty finding an outlet, call the RSA and they will be able to tell you the location of your nearest member store.

safety considerations

When undertaking any projects around the home, safety should be the number one consideration. There is an element of risk to almost any job, and it is vital to minimize such risks by taking all necessary precautions. For example, safety equipment should be considered a vital element of your general tool kit, and you will also need to maintain a top-quality first aid kit. Above all, never carry out any task that common sense indicates will be dangerous.

ladder safety

Ladders and steps are invaluable for gaining access to higher levels. Although simple tools, they are often abused and can lead to nasty accidents if used incorrectly. By obeying the following rules you will minimize the risk of injury.

- The distance from the base of the wall or skirting board to the foot of the ladder must be a quarter of the height the ladder rests at.
- The base of the ladder must rest on a level, nonslip surface.
- Both foot pads must touch the ground—you may shim with plywood pads, but keep the ladder level.
- Ensure that the top of the ladder has total contact with the wall surface.
- Before mounting a ladder, check that all rungs are secure and have not been damaged in any way.
- When using a ladder out of doors, watch out for overhead powerlines and cables.
- Never overstretch—if you cannot reach comfortably, move the ladder.
- When working at any height, have a helper hold the bottom of the ladder to prevent it moving.

safety advice

The over-enthusiasm of children and curiosity of animals can lead to accidents. Try to keep these "elements" clear of the working area!

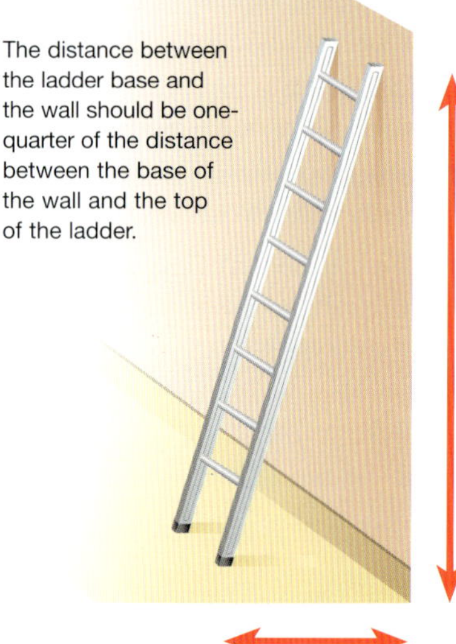

Careful ladder positioning is vital for the safety of its user.

safety equipment

A range of safety equipment is available for various DIY tasks. Some items are intended for particular jobs, but many, such as goggles, work boots, and protective gloves, should be worn in most situations. It is also essential to have a well-stocked first aid kit to deal with grazes and abrasions.

protective gloves

work boots

lead test kit

latex or plastic gloves

hard hat

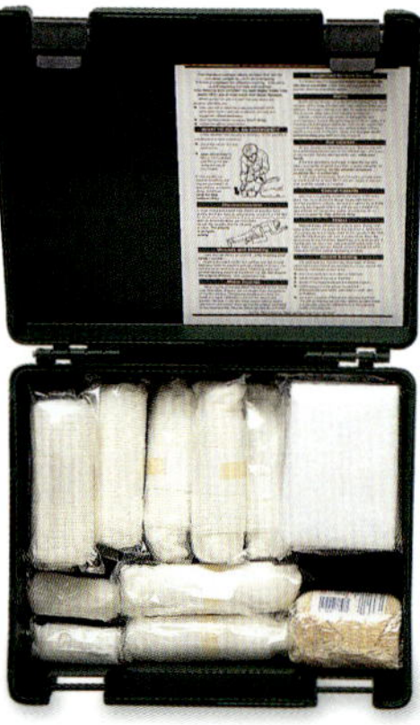

first aid kit

goggles

ear protectors

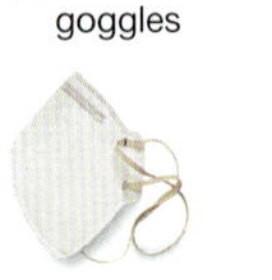

dust mask

respirator mask

knee pads

looking after your health

lifting

Get help when lifting boards and joists. Do not lift more than you can safely carry, and when lifting bend your knees, not just your waist. Wear gloves to protect your hands from rough concrete and wood splinters.

dust

Dust can be deadly so always wear a good-quality dust mask. Some cheaper masks available offer little or no protection against certain dusts. Cut tiles and sheet wood outside wherever possible, particularly when using power tools.

drilling

Never drill into an area of a wall, floor, or ceiling where there are likely to be electric cable wiring or gas and plumbing pipes behind. Use a stud finder to locate the exact position of such services before starting work.

Never assume that wiring or plumbing is only to be found on a plumb or horizontal line—diagonal services are not unknown in older houses, so a stud finder should be used always before starting any work that involves drilling or nailing into a wall or even ceiling.

fire risk

Some of the procedures described in this book utilize heat-producing tools, most notably hot air guns that are used for the removal of old paint. Always have a bucket of water or fire extinguisher close at hand when working with such tools—a small fire can quickly turn into a big fire if it is not quickly put out.

It is also worth making periodic checks on all power tools, as the wiring can deteriorate.

electric cutoff

If using electrically operated power tools, it is a good idea to invest in a special cutoff device. In the event of the cable being accidentally cut, the device will shut down the electricity supply to the tool. This is commonly called a ground-fault interrupter (GFI), and is a secondary line of defence after the circuit breakers or fuse boxes installed at the main power supply for the house.

You can have an electrician install ground-fault interrupters to replace standard electricity sockets anywhere in the house. Most GFIs have "Test" and "Reset" buttons, and manufacturers recommend that you check the operation of each GFI regularly—usually every month.

toxic materials

Some older properties may contain asbestos products or insulation. If you come across suspected asbestos, get it removed by a specialist contractor.

Lead was added to paint until fairly recently and can be released into the atmosphere if an old finish is burnt off. Remove lead-based paints with paint stripper before recoating, rather than with a blow-lamp or hot air gun. Modern paints and varnishes are far less toxic, but it is still important to follow the instructions on the can, particularly concerning brush cleaning and disposal of excess paint.

Remove paint from skin with a proprietary hand cleaner, not mineral spirits, which strip essential oils from the skin and can lead to dermatitis in extreme cases.

Avoid breathing the heavy vapor from adhesives, and work in a well-ventilated space whenever possible. If you start to feel light-headed, stop work immediately and go outside into the fresh air.

GENERAL TOOL CARE

- Before using any unfamiliar tools, read and fully understand the manufacturer's instructions. Tools from rental stores should come with an instruction booklet but if you are in any doubt ask for a demonstration before you leave with the tool.

- Chisels, planes, and cutting equipment must always be kept as sharp as possible. More accidents are caused by blunt tools slipping on the surface than by sharp tools. An oilstone is ideal to keep tools such as chisels razor-sharp.

- Power tools require additional precautions. Unplug any tool before changing bits or blades, and never operate with safety guards removed. Regularly inspect cables and wires to ensure they are in good condition. If frayed or damaged, replace them to prevent the risk of potentially lethal electric shocks. Although just about every power tool is double insulated for safety, never let a cable trail in water or use a power tool outside in the rain. Power tools in general may also require periodic servicing, and accessories, such as bits and blades, should be renewed when necessary, as old ones can strain the motor and drive of the tool.

- Hammers can often slip off nail heads when you are attempting to hammer them in. To avoid this, sand the striking face of the hammer to clean it and provide a fine key. This technique may be applied to all types of hammers, and is useful for any hammering procedure.

walls & ceilings

Many factors affect the anatomy or make-up of the walls and ceilings in your home. Some relate to age, with practices that were once common building practice or regulation now being out of date or superseded by improved design and modern materials. Architectural preference can also make a significant difference, which means that even buildings of the same age can have entirely different wall or ceiling structures. So before embarking on a renovation project, it is important to try and recognize the different types of house structure, so that you can make informed decisions on the extent and type of work that will be required. This section considers the most common varieties of walls and ceilings, and how they are constructed.

house construction

Ceilings and walls are, quite obviously, major components in a house's structure. So before embarking on any alterations, it's important to examine the makeup of your house in its entirety. This will help you to recognize some of the main design features and form a greater understanding of the structure of your home and its particular characteristics.

safety advice

Houses constructed, remodeled, or redecorated before 1978 may include building materials that contain lead or asbestos. Before beginning work, check with your local health department or environmental protection office for information on how to test for and safely handle these health hazards.

Most modern houses are referred to either as brick and block or wood-framed. However, there are wide variations on this theme, and older buildings may include a number of different structures and features. Understanding the principles of house construction can help with recognizing some of your home's characteristics.

It's important to remember that, regardless of house design, the role of walls can be isolated to one key feature—whether they are loadbearing or non-loadbearing. Non-loadbearing walls act as a partition and do not bear any of the house weight, whereas loadbearing walls play an integral part in support and bearing the weight of floors. This theme is common to all house structures and is the starting point for deciding on any alterations.

tips of the trade

It can sometimes be difficult to identify a wall that is loadbearing. The following points may help.

- Consider that all exterior walls are loadbearing.
- Check to see where floorboards run parallel with a wall. This implies that the joists run in the opposite direction (ie, at a right angle), and are supported by the wall.
- Look in the attic to see if roof timbers sit on top of the wall. If so, support for the roof is being supplied by that wall.
- Cut a small hole in the ceiling at the top of the wall to allow you to inspect the wall construction, to see where joists are running and to see how much support the wall is creating.

understanding wood & block

The majority of houses combine wood, blocks, or bricks in their construction, and any of these components can have a loadbearing role to play. In other words, a wall that is wood-framed is as capable of being loadbearing as a wall that is made from block or bricks. Similarly, a wall made of brick or blocks does not, necessarily, have to be loadbearing.

The common misconception that a wood-frame wall has less of a loadbearing capability than one made from solid block or brick must therefore be totally dispelled. Instead of judging walls by the material they are made from, it is more useful to think of walls in terms of the role they play within the total house structure (see the illustration on page 23).

brick & block houses

Modern brick houses are based on a cavity wall construction, with an outer layer of brick or block and a secondary, inner layer of brick or block. The cavity between the two walls is usually around 2in wide. These houses should not be confused with older brick and block properties, where the characteristics are more likely to be those specified under "solid wall construction" (right).

To ensure structural strength, the cavity between the outer and inner brick walls is spanned by special ties. If the internal wall is loadbearing, it will be made from block or brick. If it is non-loadbearing, the interior wall may again be built with blocks, or less heavyweight stud partitioning (wood frames) may be used.

wood-frame houses

As the name suggests, the main structural elements of these houses are built using timber frames, though they are also built on a cavity structure comprised of two walls. The interior, wood wall framework is erected first, and the outer wall is then built from brick, block, or wood cladding. As with brick and block houses, the exterior walls are generally loadbearing. However, because the interior walls are made from wood, it can sometimes be difficult to determine whether these walls are loadbearing or not.

solid wall construction

This type of construction features in older houses, where there is no cavity and therefore not a two-layer system. Walls in these houses tend to be thicker than in modern ones, often with the stone or brick makeup extending from the outer to the inner face of the wall. Interior walls are either made of similar materials to the exterior walls, or they may be constructed from wood partitioning, demonstrating lath and plaster characteristics (see page 29). Loadbearing walls in these houses are nearly always the same stone or brick structure as the exterior walls.

supports

Entrances in loadbearing walls, such as windows and doors, reduce the strength of the wall. For this reason, additional support will be needed over the window or door, to bear the structural weight of the wall above. (Non-loadbearing walls do not always need this additional support.) These extra supports are referred to as lintels, which are made of concrete or steel, or headers, which are made of wood.. The type of material is dependent on the age of the house, the wall construction, and the size of the opening. Modern techniques favor engineered wood framing members (such as LVL), whereas reinforced concrete lintels are generally used for doors and windows. Exterior cavity walls may combine lintel types with concrete on the outer wall and wood on the interior.

house structure

To understand the role and function of ceilings and walls, it can be useful to put them in the context of an entire structure. The cross section of a house shown below demonstrates the integration of walls and ceilings, and highlights those areas of the house that bear weight or help to support the weight of the building.

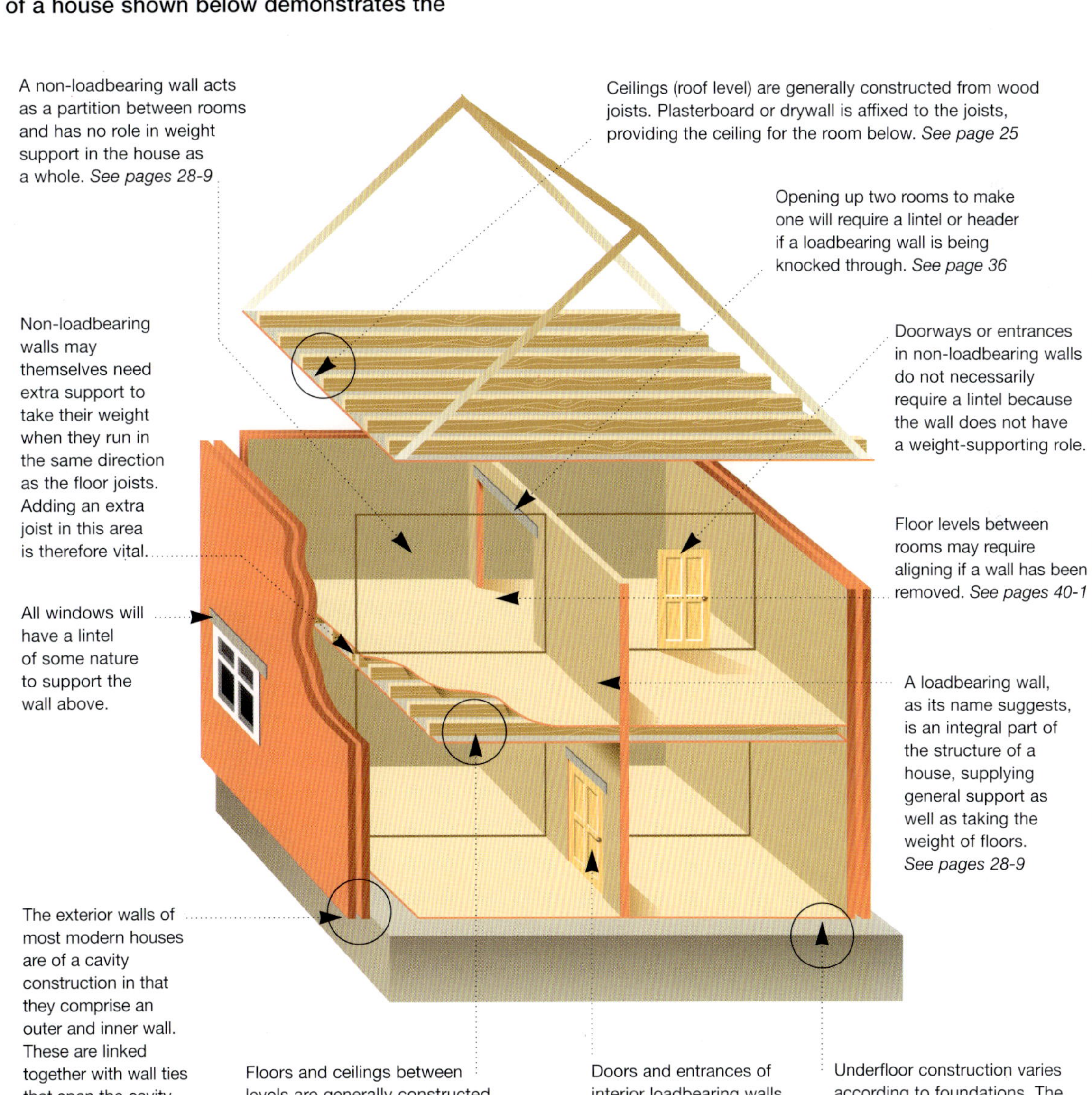

A non-loadbearing wall acts as a partition between rooms and has no role in weight support in the house as a whole. *See pages 28-9*

Ceilings (roof level) are generally constructed from wood joists. Plasterboard or drywall is affixed to the joists, providing the ceiling for the room below. *See page 25*

Opening up two rooms to make one will require a lintel or header if a loadbearing wall is being knocked through. *See page 36*

Non-loadbearing walls may themselves need extra support to take their weight when they run in the same direction as the floor joists. Adding an extra joist in this area is therefore vital.

Doorways or entrances in non-loadbearing walls do not necessarily require a lintel because the wall does not have a weight-supporting role.

Floor levels between rooms may require aligning if a wall has been removed. *See pages 40-1*

All windows will have a lintel of some nature to support the wall above.

A loadbearing wall, as its name suggests, is an integral part of the structure of a house, supplying general support as well as taking the weight of floors. *See pages 28-9*

The exterior walls of most modern houses are of a cavity construction in that they comprise an outer and inner wall. These are linked together with wall ties that span the cavity. *See pages 26-7*

Floors and ceilings between levels are generally constructed from wooden joists whose weight is supported by the exterior walls and interior loadbearing walls. *See pages 24-5*

Doors and entrances of interior loadbearing walls will always have a lintel above them to provide support for the wall above.

Underfloor construction varies according to foundations. The floor surface will normally consist of concrete or wood joists with some type of wood subfloor.

ceiling & floor construction

The structure of a house dictates that the ceiling of one room will quite often combine to make up the floor of the room above. Since alterations to one room can thereby affect the structure of another, it is vital to consider both ceiling and floor anatomy when planning changes. All the structures shown here have wooden joists that make up the framework of the ceiling. Quite a few modern homes, however, incorporate solid concrete ceilings—so there will be some variation on the themes outlined below. As with most designs, trends vary with time and the basic ceiling structure will be very dependent on the age of the building.

lath-and-plaster ceilings

An old design, lath-and-plaster ceilings are now avoided in modern techniques of construction. However, they are still commonly found in older houses and may well feature in a house that is intended for renovation.

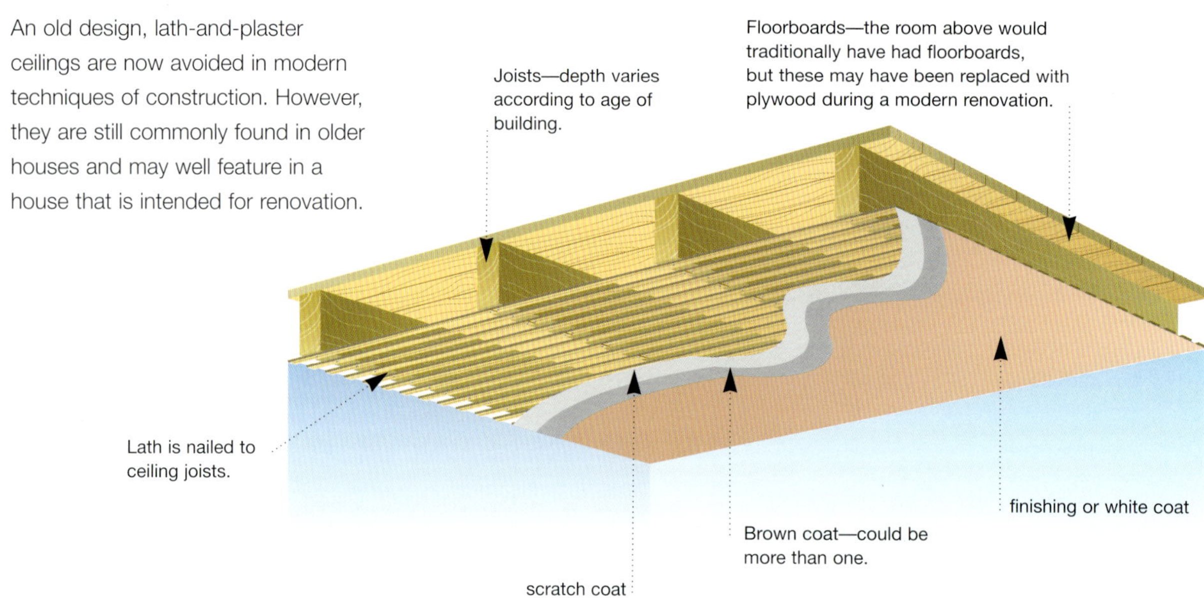

plasterboard and plaster ceilings

The invention of plasterboard made lath construction an out-of-date and time consuming method for building ceilings. Therefore, most modern ceilings have a plasterboard base, which is plastered as shown here, or a drywall base, as shown on page 25.

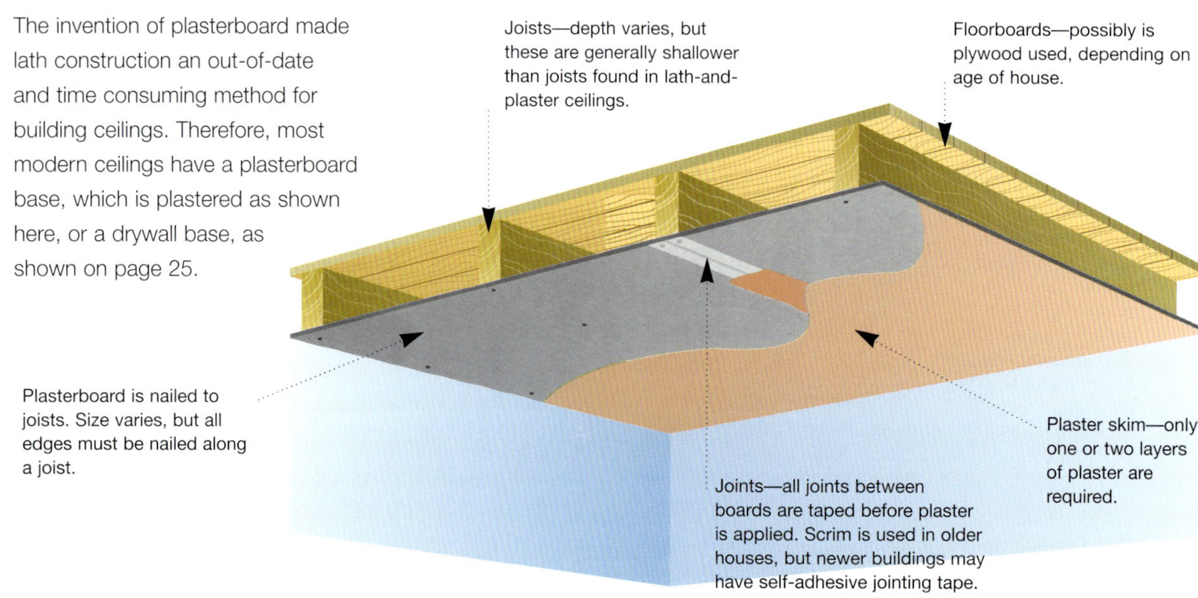

drywall ceilings

Although similar to plastered ceilings, drywall ceilings are finished using a slightly different technique. Drywall tape over the tapered edges seals the joint and produces a smooth surface ready to paint. This is probably the easiest ceiling structure for a home-improvement enthusiast to tackle.

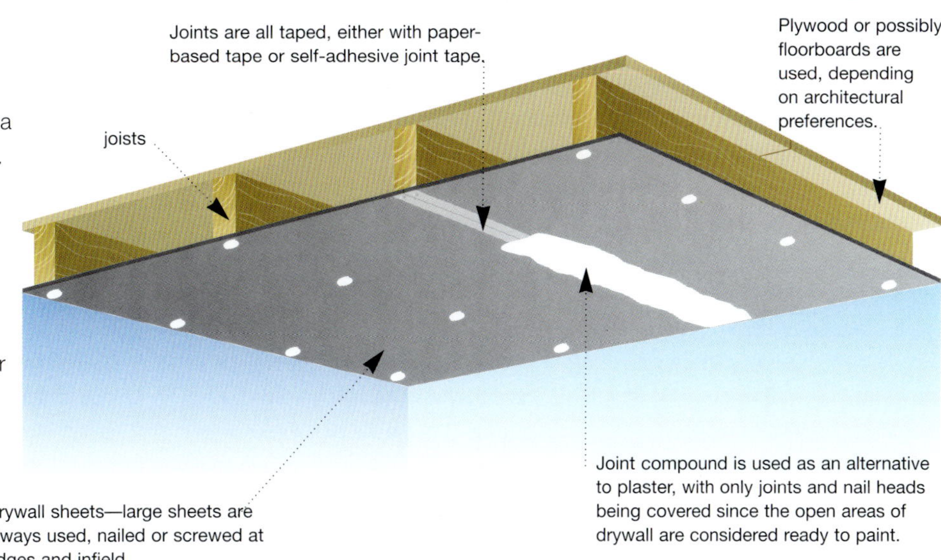

wooden ceilings

Not all ceilings have a drywall or plaster-based finish. Wood is a common alternative. Be aware, though, that wood ceilings may constitute a fire hazard unless they are installed over a drywall ceiling, because air can mitigate between the room and the joist bays.

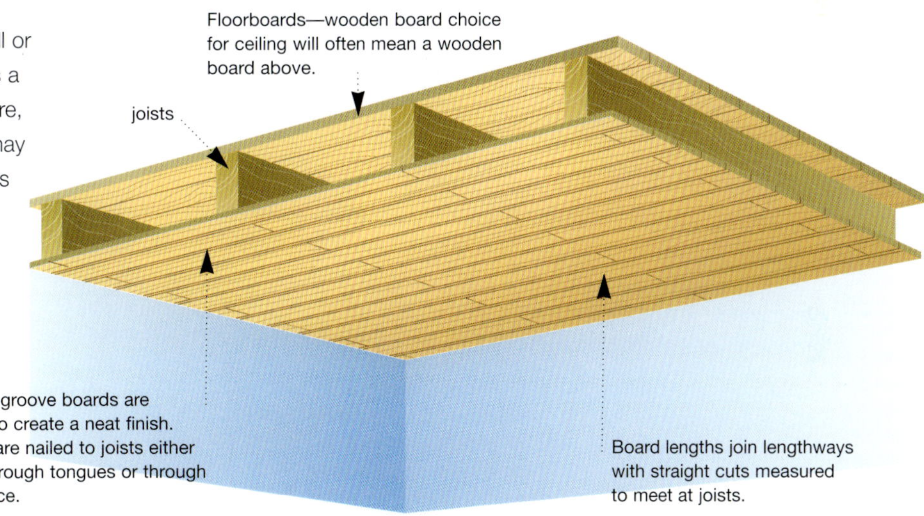

top floor ceilings

The ceiling between the top floor of a house and the attic space is often slightly different in makeup from the other ceilings in the house. The overall structure will depend on the age of the building, and may therefore look like any of those already shown. The main difference will be the presence of an insulating layer between ceiling and attic, and a basic plywood floor may be fitted on the upper layer.

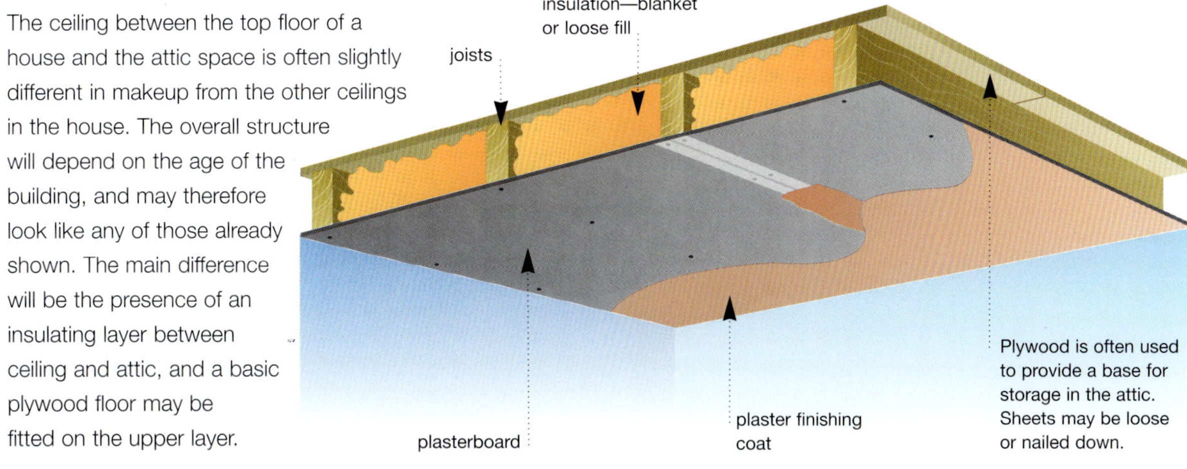

exterior walls

Wall purpose and structure can be categorized as to whether the wall is interior or exterior. Much like ceilings, the age of the property can affect the type of structure considerably, as can architectural or design considerations. This is particularly the case for exterior walls, which are visible as a finished product, whereas interior walls are constructed to provide a flat surface ready for paint or wallpaper. That said, exterior walls can generally be identified by two simple categories —whether they are of a solid or cavity structure.

solid walls

Solid exterior walls, or those with no cavity, tend to be found in older buildings. Depth and makeup is varied, but most show similar characteristics to the examples outlined below.

cavity walls

Nearly all modern houses have exterior walls constructed with a cavity. This means that the exterior wall effectively consists of two layers, with a void or cavity between the layers for insulation.

There are many possible combinations for how these two layers are constructed, but the examples on the following page demonstrate the most common variations that occur.

brick/block solid wall

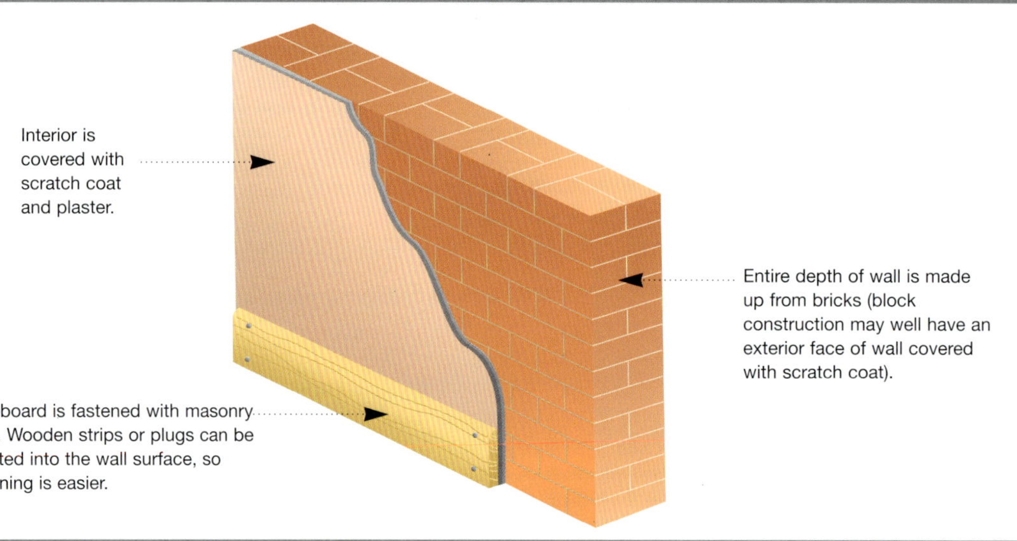

natural stone solid wall

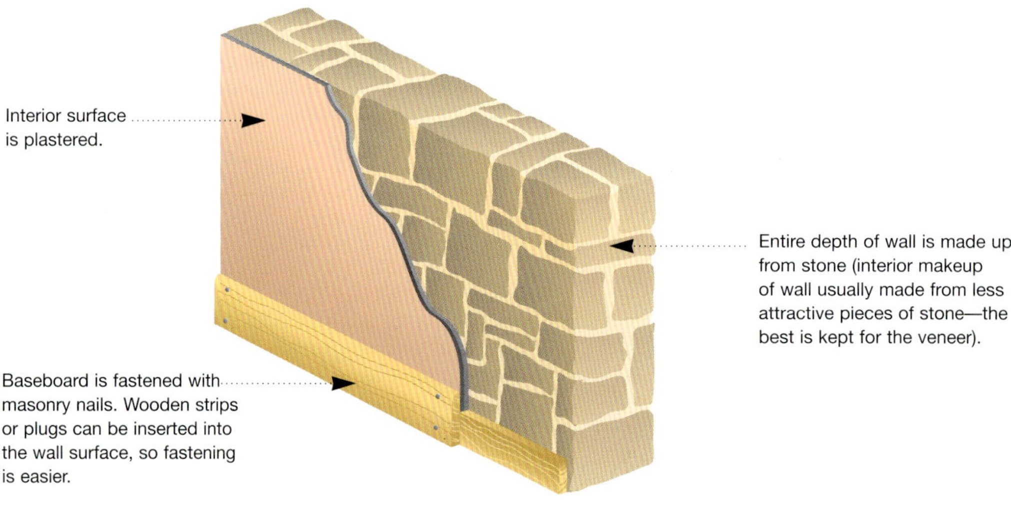

brick/block cavity with scratch coat & plaster

This type of cavity wall employs solid-wall construction materials to provide a brick outer layer for the finished exterior of the house, and a block inner layer that requires additional coatings before paint can be applied.

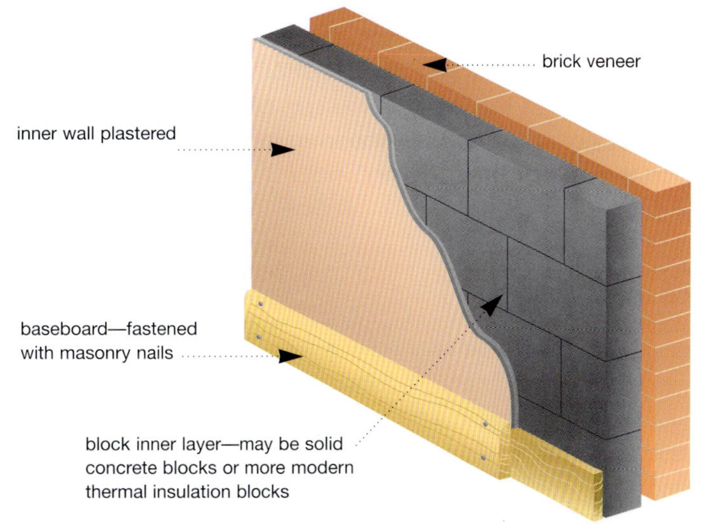

brick/veneer

This is a popular form of construction in modern houses, where the exterior wall layer is made from a solid facing material such as brick, and the interior layer takes the form of a wooden framework.

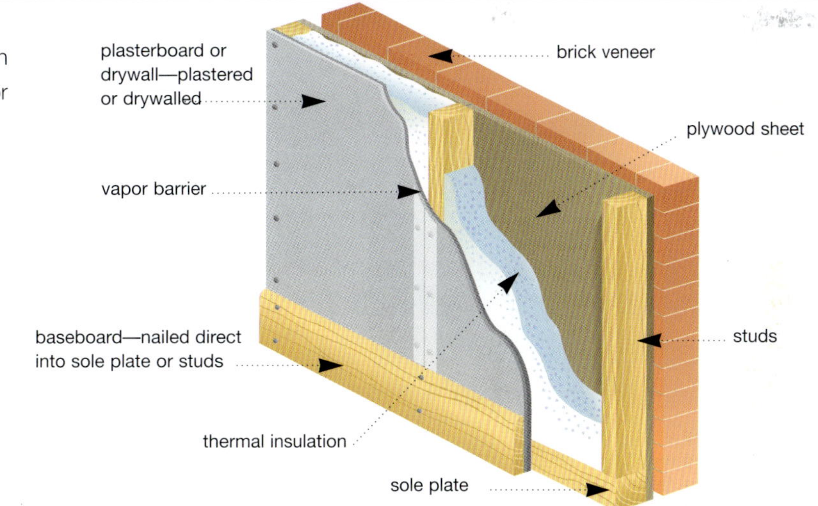

brick/block cavity—drywalled

This example shows that block walls can be combined with drywall techniques for finishing purposes. Outer and inner wall construction is similar to that shown for the first example of cavity walls, but the interior finishing is clearly different.

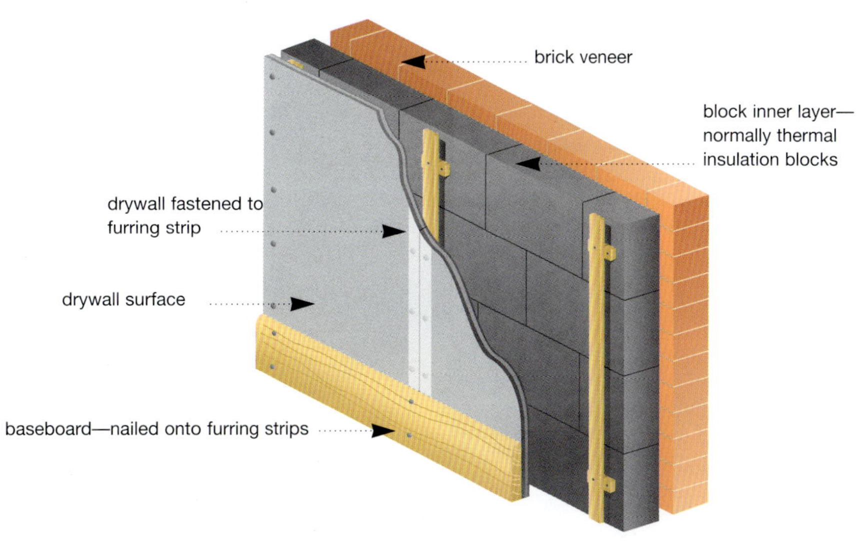

interior walls

Interior walls are usually constructed as a single layer and therefore do not have the same depth as exterior walls. Many characteristics are similar, but there tends to be a wide variety of structure in terms of the interior makeup of the wall itself. Much is dependent on whether the wall is loadbearing or non-loadbearing, and therefore what structural requirements it has in relation to the rest of the building.

solid construction

As the name suggests, these walls are made from solid materials, blocks or bricks. The main structural differences depend on how the outer faces of the wall are finished.

hollow construction

Hollow wall construction is very common in modern houses, with most homes containing some form of "hollow" wall. However, this does not necessarily mean that the wall is non-loadbearing, and it is important to check such issues out before beginning the work. The examples on the page opposite illustrate the most common types of interior hollow walls.

block

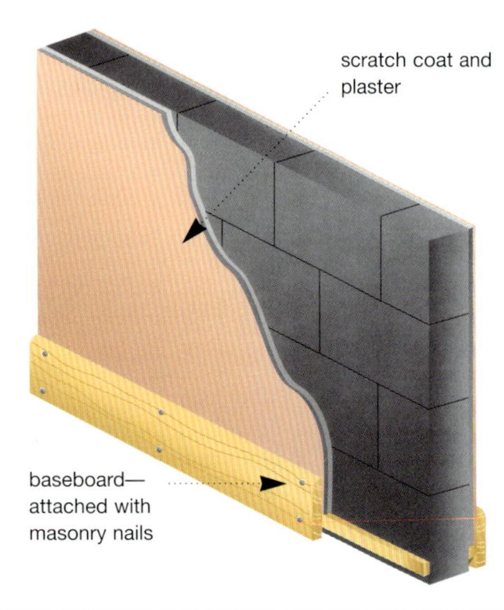

brick

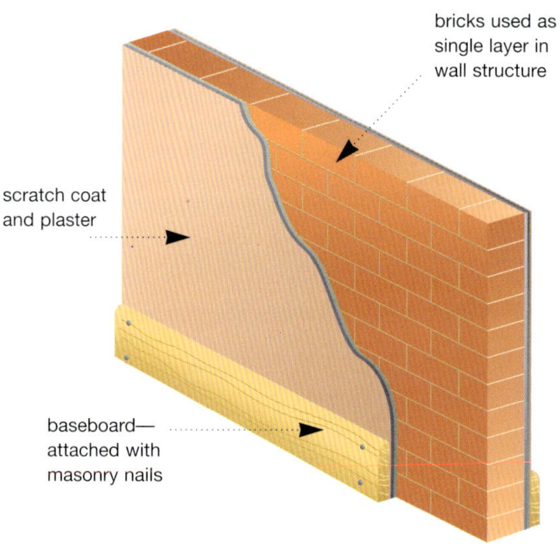

block/drywalled

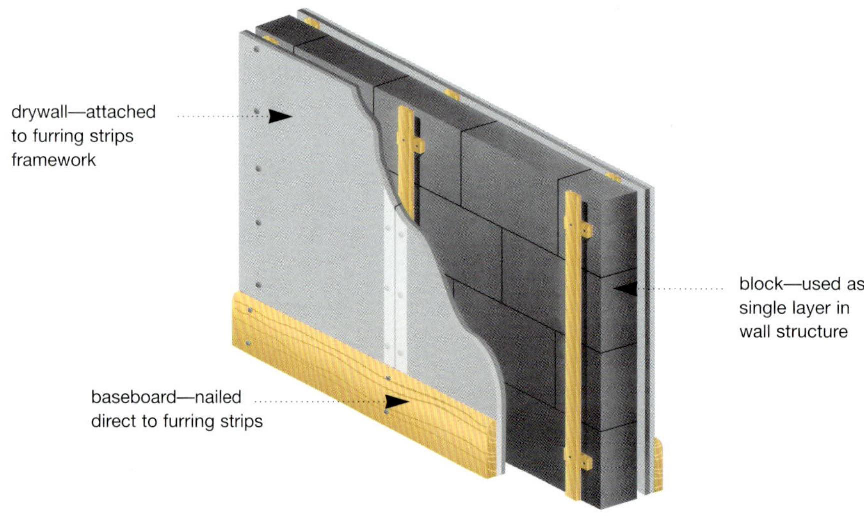

drywall/stud partition

Probably the most commonly occurring of all modern inside hollow walls. Easy to build and adaptable to most circumstances.

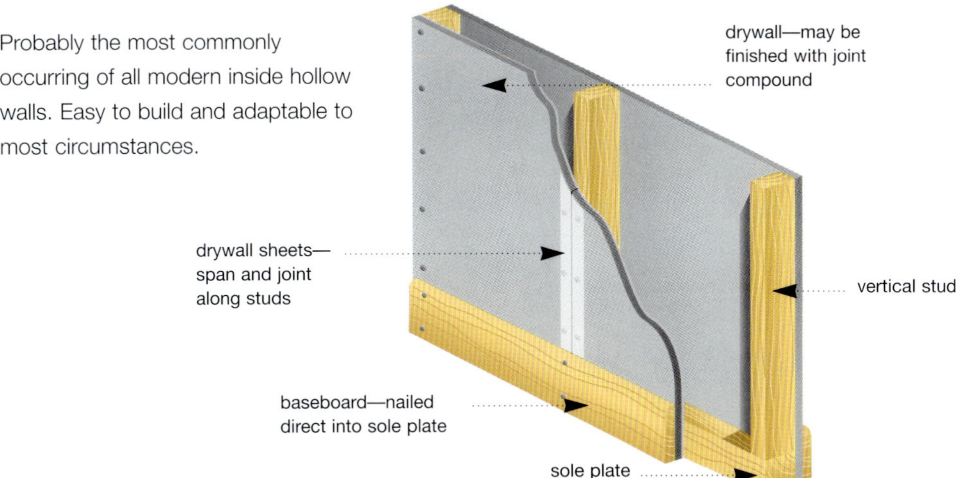

dry partition wall

A lightweight and simply built wall. Its makeup still provides a rigid finished product.

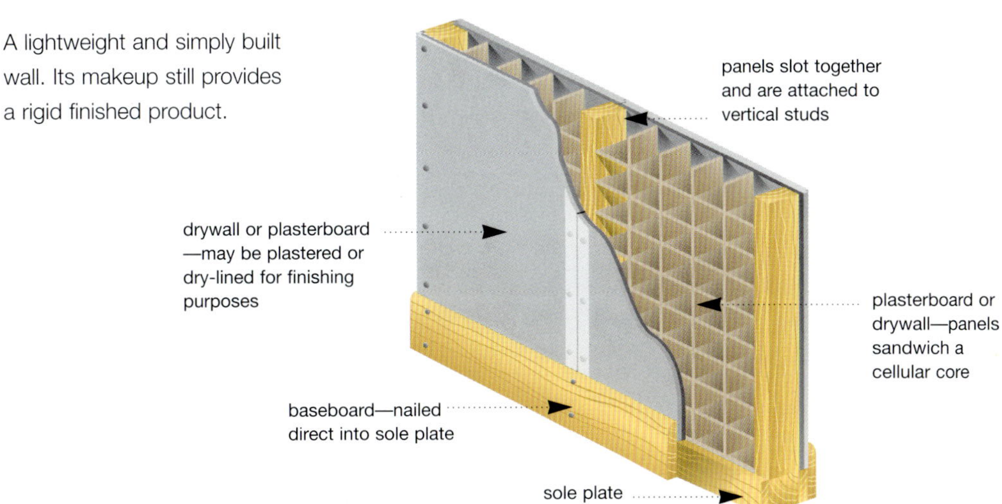

lath-and-plaster partition

As with ceiling structures, lath and plaster dates back to older houses before the advent of plasterboard.

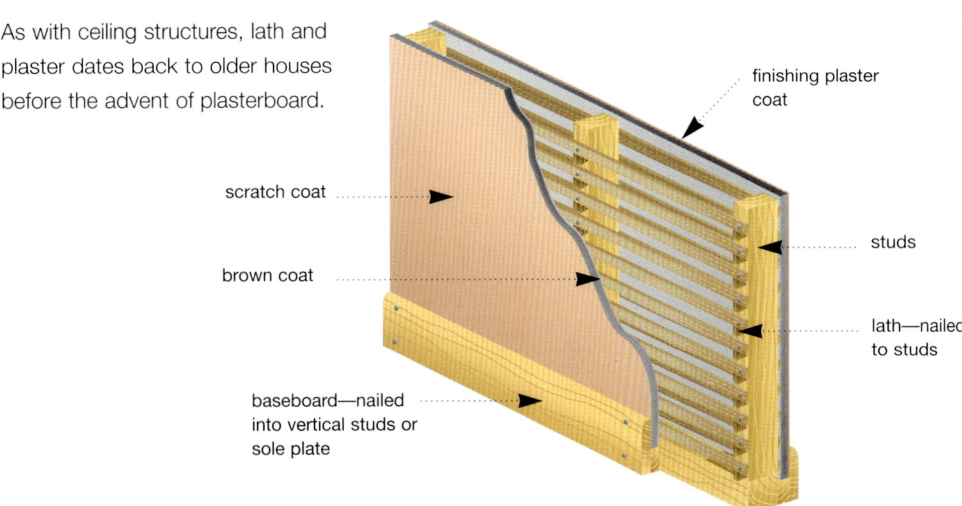

altering the structure of a wall

The type and extent of work required to alter a wall structure will largely depend on the existing structure. Before deciding on the exact changes you would like to make, it is important to identify the kind of wall you currently have, so that you can gauge the best procedures for transformation. As always, the key issue is whether the wall is loadbearing or non-loadbearing—only once this has been established can planning begin for alteration. This chapter covers a range of projects, some with more structural implications than others, but many of the outlined tasks deal with the more aesthetic aspects of altering the structure of walls within your home.

Open plan dining and living areas create a very relaxed and comfortable feel for your home and surroundings.

recognizing problems—1

Cracks and faults in wall and ceiling surfaces can often look more problematic than they actually are. However, while the main concern may appear to be aesthetic, cracks should also be seen as signs of potential structural problems—such as movement—so it is important to try to determine their cause. Many cracks form for particular reasons and can easily be identified and categorized. The diagram below shows common areas where cracking occurs.

testing cracks and movement

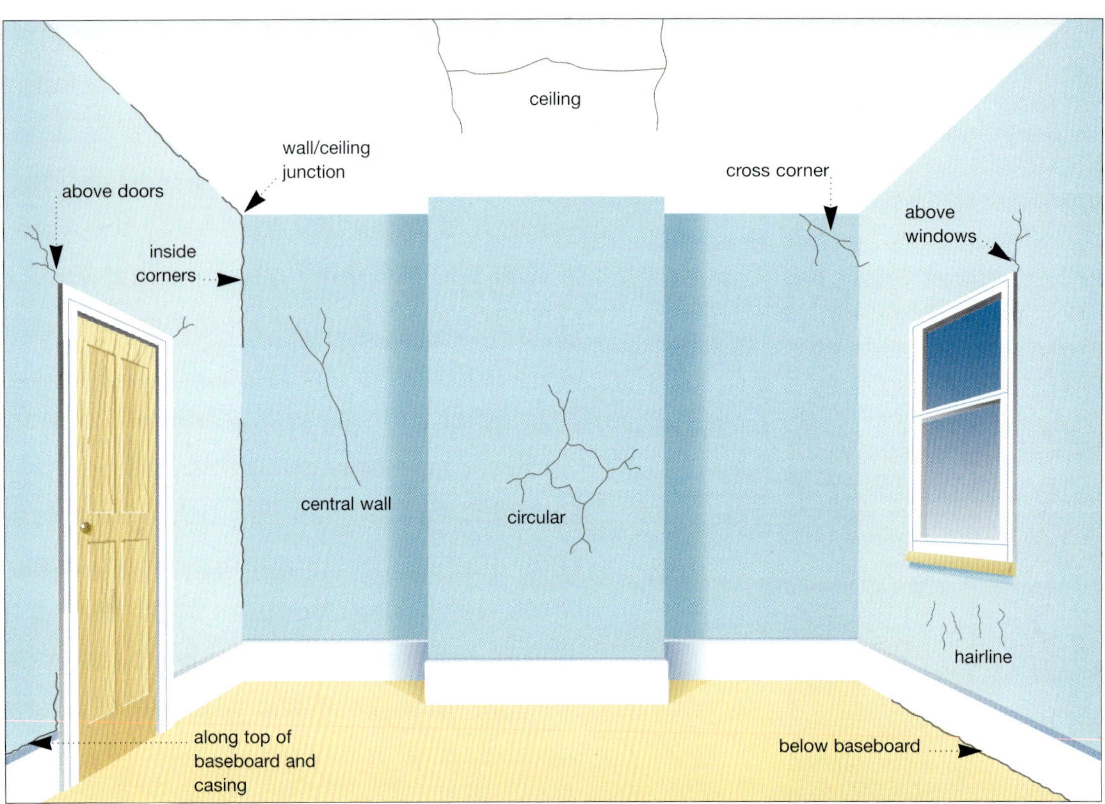

Determining the movement and development of cracks—if any—can obviously be difficult. Such movements tend to be slight and take time to develop, making it virtually impossible to monitor accurately. For this reason, crack-monitoring systems can now be bought that enable accurate measuring of any movement. Although manufacturers' guidelines do vary, the general principles of use for these systems remain the same for most commercial brands. If in doubt, contact the product manufacturer or a structural surveyor for further assistance and advice.

1 Screw the detector in place, with the detection scale roughly positioned over the crack. Do not overtighten the screws at this stage.

2 Shift the scale on the detector so that it sits precisely in line with the crack. Tighten the screws when you are happy with the position.

3 Remove the plastic lugs from the edge of the detector to free the two-plate mechanism. If movement occurs, the scale on one plate will move in relation to the other, thereby making it possible accurately to observe the extent and duration of any movement. Detectors, of slightly varying designs, can also be used across corners or at ceiling and floor level.

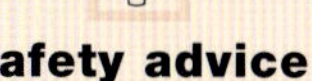

safety advice

Always seek professional advice about cracks that may represent structural problems. Detecting subsidence or structural faults is a skilled profession, and should never be underestimated. Failure to gauge the gravity of the situation could present long-term dangers to both the structure of the house and the health of its inhabitants.

type	causes of cracks & remedies
inside corners	These cracks are often a result of settlement in new homes and therefore can be filled and painted. Persistent cracking should be monitored.
ceiling	Ceiling cracks that are very directional, in that they have a relatively straight course or turn at a right angle, tend to result from slight board movement in the ceiling structure. These can be filled and painted or, if they persist, taping can normally prevent them from reappearing.
cross corner	Cracks that extend across a corner from one wall to another can represent a subsidence problem, especially if lines of brick or block work can be picked out. In such cases, seek professional advice.
above windows	Cracks are often visible extending from the corners of windows up toward ceiling level. So long as they are relatively small, they generally represent slight settlement or movement. However, large cracks that show a vertical shift should be investigated further.
hairline	These cracks are common, multidirectional, and suggest slight movement of a plaster surface. Numbers tend to increase with the age of the building. Most are superficial and do not represent any cause for alarm. However, if new plaster surfaces display a number of persistent cracks, this could suggest that the plaster was poorly mixed or has not bonded correctly to the wall. In such cases, replastering may be necessary.
below baseboard	Gaps below baseboard tend to suggest that the baseboard was poorly fitted. However, cracks that continue to develop could reflect floor problems or some subsidence. Those which continue to grow should be investigated by a professional.
circular	Cracks that form irregular, circular shapes tend to reflect areas of plaster delaminating from the wall lath or substrate. This is common in old lath-and-plaster walls, where age has taken its toll and the plaster surface has become unstable in localized areas. The affected area can be removed and patch-plastered.
central wall cracks	These may occur for any number of reasons and should simply be monitored to check that they do not grow wider. Seek professional advice in extreme cases.
along top of baseboard and casing	Cracks occur in these places either because of age and slight building movement, or because the materials are new and take a little time to settle to the atmospheric conditions of the particular room environment. Unless the cracks persist or grow after filling and repainting, there is generally no cause for alarm.
above doors	See explanation for cracks above windows.
wall/ceiling junction	These cracks commonly occur during settlement in new houses, and as a result of age in older ones. Small cracks can be filled and repainted, whereas larger types should be monitored to check that they do not expand, thus requiring structural repair.

recognizing problems—2

In addition to movement, structural areas of the home can also be affected by damp and insect or fungal infestation. Many such problems are easily remedied, but others can have wider consequences and be extremely damaging to the building structure, especially if they are left untreated. These sorts of problems can take many forms and affect different areas of the home, but the diagram below outlines many of the key areas to look out for.

moisture and infestation

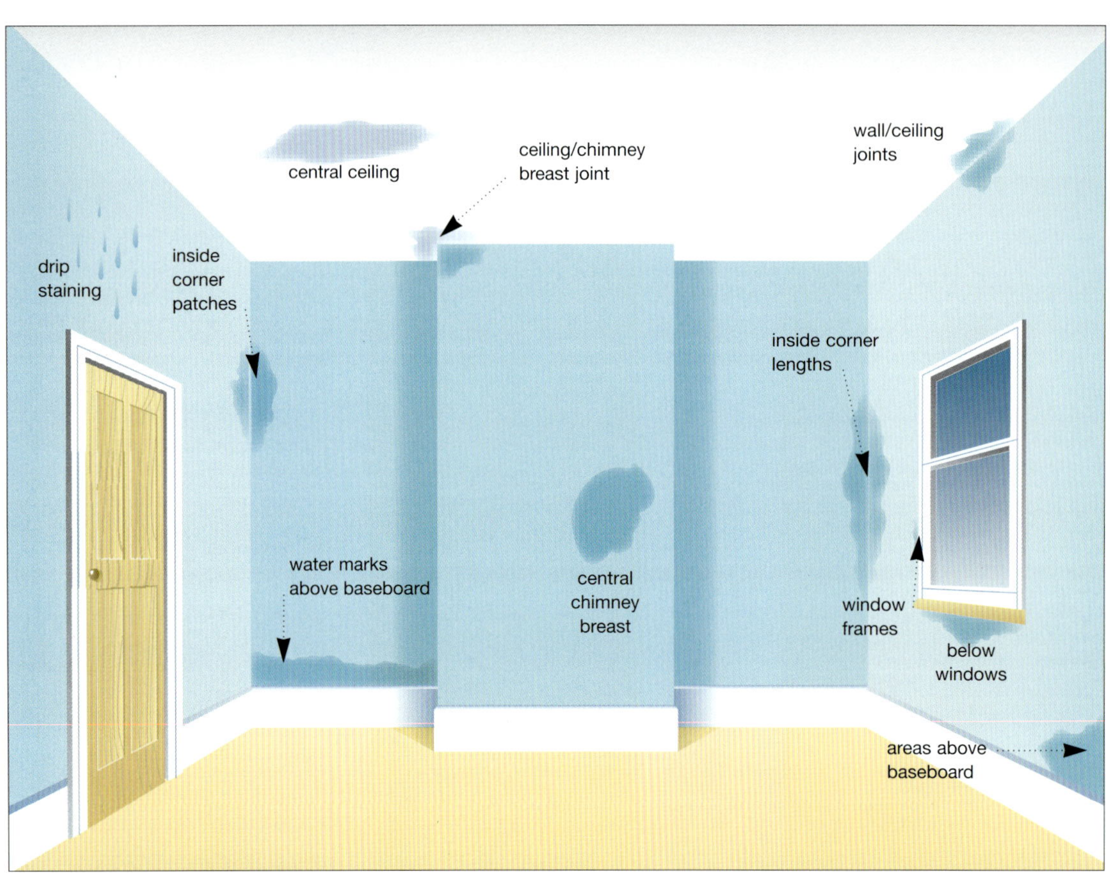

other problems of infestation

Aside from those problems usually associated with moisture, there are other potential problems that can be linked to insects and fungal attack.

dry rot

This is an exceptionally damaging form of decay that mainly affects timber but also spreads across masonry. While identifying and counteracting the source will remedy the problem, dry rot attacks with actual fungicidal spores which spread the disease very quickly, making it difficult to eradicate. Dry rot does initially take hold in areas of moisture and poor ventilation. It is identified by thin, white strands which spread along surfaces, rather like a spider's web. The effect breaks down building structure irreparably. Treatment should therefore be fast, involving the cutting out and destroying of all infected areas. New wood and materials should be treated to protect them against dry rot infection.

woodworm

These are basically the larvae of particular beetles, and so there are two methods for discovering if you have the problem. Either the appearance of the beetles provides evidence of their presence, or more commonly, the actual flight holes are visible, indicating their existence in the household woodwork. Action against woodworm must be swift, as the parasite can quickly break down wood and spread throughout the entire house. Spray infected areas with the appropriate insecticide and any unaffected woodwork nearby, to prevent further spreading. When replacing any wood, always ensure that the new material has been preserved properly. If in any doubt, seek professional advice.

type	causes of damp & remedies
central ceiling	These patches tend to be a result of leaking pipes in the ceiling, or at top floor level they may be a roof leak dripping on to surfaces below. Consult a plumber for fastening pipework, and make any necessary tile repair work at roof level.
ceiling/chimney breast joint	Damp patches that develop in these areas may be a result of a gap in flashing around the chimney. Therefore inspect the area and effect a repair if required.
wall/ceiling joists	At top floor level, this is often a result of a blocked gutter. Unblock the gutter to eliminate the resulting moisture penetration. This sort of moisture may also result from a lean-to building, where the flashing at the point where it joins the main building has deteriorated. Check the flashing and repair if necessary.
inside corner lengths	Elongated damp patches along internal corners often indicate a blocked or cracked downpipe on the exterior of the building. Dripping water therefore gradually penetrates, causing a persistent damp wall stain. Unblock or replace the downpipe as required.
window frames	Moisture penetration is common around the edges of windows due to a buildup of condensation or because of a break in the seal around the edge of the window frame itself. Check that the window is sealed correctly and reapply silicone sealant if necessary. If the problem is more condensation-based, install better ventilation systems for the room, or simply open windows more often.
below windows	Seals beneath windows may be damaged or the drip guard below the sill may be blocked. Check both areas, and clear or re-seal as required.
areas above baseboard	Large damp patches above baseboards are often a result of the buildup of material, such as piles of soil, on the exterior side of the wall surface. This bridges the foundation coating and causes damp penetration. Simply remove the obstructive material, and ensure soil levels are kept below the foundation coating.
central chimney breast	These patches commonly develop in disused chimneys where the chimney and fireplace have been blocked off. The disused chimney void therefore has no ventilation, causing the moist damp air to penetrate through the chimney breast. To cure this problem, install an air vent in the chimney breast in order to improve air flow and circulation.
water marks above baseboard	If these are not a result of the foundation coating being bridged on the other side of the wall, then it may be straightforward rising damp. This is common in older houses with no foundation coating or in houses where the foundation coating is damaged and therefore allowing water penetration. Various damp-proofing injection systems are the most effective cure. These systems are always best carried out by professionals.
inside corner patches	Small damp patches in walls often result from patches of damaged pointing or base coat on the exterior of the building. Simple repair of the appropriate material should cure the problem.
drip staining	Visible stains from drips or running moisture on the walls tends to point in the direction of a condensation problem. This commonly occurs in kitchens and bathrooms. Simply install better ventilation systems and open windows more often.

removing a loadbearing wall

Removing a loadbearing wall is not a project that should be tackled lightly, and professional advice and instruction should be sought before carrying out this procedure. Total wall removal is rare, and it is more common to knock through a loadbearing wall in order to open up the floor layout and convert two rooms into a single area with a more open plan design. The work involved is strongly based around supportive measures.

The most important factor when taking on work of this kind is to ensure that there is adequate support, both while the area of wall is being removed and when the work is complete. Whether removing a masonry wall (shown here) or a wood-framed wall, you must set up a temporary support to hold the weight of the ceiling during demolition. It is also crucial to install a lintel or a header for permanent support. The size and makeup of this support beam depends upon the structure of the wall and the span of the opening. Both these factors require serious calculation, and the beam type and construction should be decided in consultation with a structural engineer. Once these precautions, procedures, and planning have been finalized, the is manageable. First, the opening must be made, and second, the supportive beam must be inserted. In a masonry wall, as shown here, a steel I-beam serves as the lintel—in a wood-framed wall, a header is used.

making the opening

Preparation and planning is essential for this procedure, and because the nature of the work is relatively demanding in a physical sense, two people are much better than one in this instance. Also keep the working area clear of any obstacles as much as possible, as this will help to reduce the likelihood of accidents.

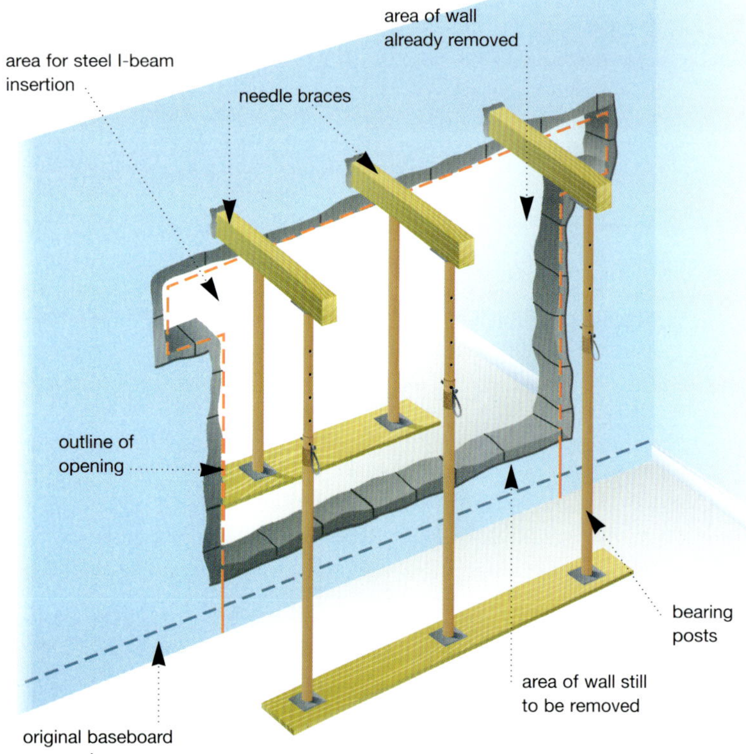

1 Mark out the size of the opening on the wall surface.

2 Knock holes through the wall above the proposed opening.

3 Insert needle braces through the holes.

4 Support the needle braces with bearing posts on both sides of the wall.

5 Use a stone cutter or hand sledge and brick chisel to cut around the edge of the opening.

6 Remove the blocks or bricks by first loosening them with a hand sledge and brick chisel, and then levering out with a pry bar or lifting by hand.

7 Continue to remove blocks until the entire area is clear.

inserting the lintel

Two people or more will definitely be required for this stage of the project, as even the smallest lintels are surprisingly heavy. It is also a time-consuming process when setting the I-beam in position. Make sure that you check the level of the I-beam because problems will be difficult to rectify later.

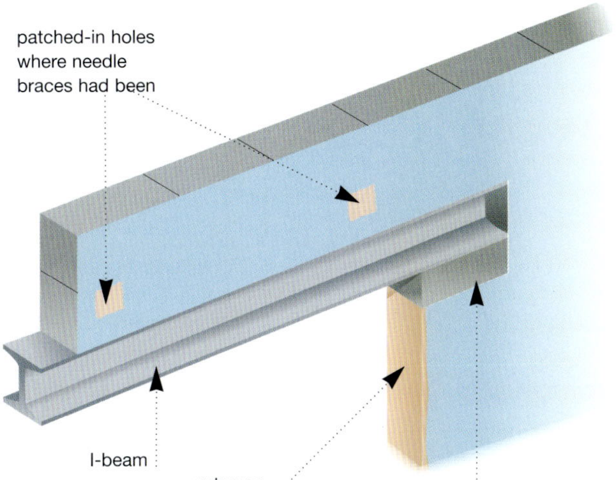

1 At the top corners of the opening, take out bricks or blocks to accommodate the I-beam ends.

2 Check and recheck measurements to ensure that the lintel will fit into the required space.

3 Apply a bed of mortar to the area before lifting the I-beam into place.

4 Check that the I-beam is level. Use cut bricks or blocks, wedged beneath the end of the I-beam to rectify if necessary.

5 Apply more mortar around the I-beam ends to ensure it will be held securely in place.

6 Frame around the I-beam to allow for drywall to be installed.

7 Remove needle braces and patch in holes.

factors to consider

In addition to the practical considerations of how to support your wall, there are also a number of other issues that should be carefully addressed.

needle brace requirement

The number of needle braces that you will require for the support will depend on the width of the opening that you plan to create. The actual needle brace dimensions should not be less than 4 x 6in, but you should consult a structural engineer in order to establish the exact needle brace requirements of your wall.

bearing

Steel bearing posts can be rented at a relatively low cost, and their adjustable nature makes them ideal for these supporting purposes. Make sure that the bases of the posts are positioned on scaffold planks so that the weight distribution is evened out. Most post bases have nail holes so that they can be nailed into the scaffold planks to eliminate any risk of them moving.

I-beam support

In many cases the new I-beam may be accommodated in the existing wall structure with no extra support below it. However, in some cases it may be necessary to install extra concrete support. Consult a structural engineer for the correct requirements in your specific circumstances.

safety equipment

This sort of work requires close attention to safety, and all the necessary precautions must be taken. Make sure to wear protective gloves, goggles, and a hard hat when taking down the wall. A dust mask may also be needed, especially when clearing away the rubble and dust caused by wall removal. The work area must be kept as clear as possible from obstructions, and rubble should be removed regularly. (See page 18 for more practical health and safety advice.)

removing a non-loadbearing wall

Before embarking on this project it is vital to ensure that the wall is definitely non-loadbearing. Once this is established, removal requires little more than a simple methodical approach. However, it is important to bear in mind that there will undoubtedly be a certain amount of making good to do once the wall has gone, so try to minimize the amount of damage caused to the ceiling and other wall surfaces when you try to remove the wall.

The techniques required for removing a non-loadbearing wall will largely depend on whether the wall is of a stud construction or built from solid bricks or blocks. Once this has been established, ensure that electrical sockets, switches, and pipework have been removed and rerouted as necessary by an electrician or plumber.

tips of the trade

Never underestimate the amount of mess and dust that can be generated by projects such as wall removal. Plan the task to fit in conveniently with your busy household (such as at a weekend, when disruption will not be a problem) and take the time to remove all furniture and floorcoverings from the room(s) in which you will be working.

removing a stud wall

The lightweight construction of stud walls means that their removal tends to be a fairly straightforward job, so long as you follow an organized, basic order of work.

tools for the job

- pry bar
- stud finder
- hand saw

1 Begin by removing any features on the wall surface such as picture rails, cove, and baseboards. A pry bar is the ideal tool to pry baseboard

away from the wall. Try not to damage the baseboard, as it can be saved and possibly reused on another wall.

2 Locate a central stud in the wall, either by using a stud finder or by tapping along the wall surface with the head of the pry bar—areas between studs will sound hollow, whereas stud positions will make the noise of a dull thud. Dig into the wall

by the stud with the end of the bar and lever the drywall away from the stud framework.

3 When all the drywall has been removed, begin to take out the wooden studs by sawing through

each one in a suitable place. Cut slightly above the plate or firestop—if you cut too tight to the joint, the saw may catch the nails or screws in the studs.

4 To remove the floor plate, it is often easier to saw it into separate sections. This helps to reduce the strength of its bonding power with the floor surface.

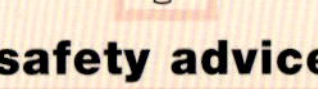

safety advice

When carrying out any sort of demolition job, wear gloves, goggles, and a hard hat to protect yourself from any flying debris or sharp edges.

5 Use the pry bar to lever the sections of the plate away from the floor surface. A similar technique may be used for the ceiling plate and wall plates as required.

part removal of a solid block wall

Non-loadbearing block or brick walls may be totally or partially removed to create a larger room space. Partial removal can provide a more aesthetically pleasing finish because, instead of producing a completely open room, it creates two areas with character and interest.

tools for the job

- pencil or chalk line
- pry bar
- hand sledge
- brick chisel
- corner bead
- hacksaw
- plastering trowel
- level

Removal of blocks can be harder work than that of a simple stud wall, and you will need additional tools such as a hand sledge and brick to break down the joints. It is always best to start at the top and work down, removing single blocks if possible. When partially removing a wall, draw guidelines directly on the wall surface using a chalk line or pencil and level. A stone cutter can be used to make an accurate cut down these guidelines, but in most cases it is easy enough to follow the line using the hand sledge and brick chisel.

1 Once the main area of wall has been removed, straighten up the block edges as much as possible, and remove any loose mortar.

2 Use a hacksaw (see page 113) to cut some corner bead to the required height of the wall edge and position it along the edge using bonding plaster to hold it in place. It may be necessary to use a level in order to gain a truly vertical position for the bead. Position another corner bead on the adjacent edge. Hold the corner beads in position while the bonding plaster dries.

3 Apply bonding agent to the edges of the trimmed blocks. Make sure to work the solution into every crevice, and allow to dry to a tacky consistency.

4 Then apply more bonding plaster along the entire wall edge. A perfect finish is not required at this stage, so just ensure a good coverage of the whole edge. Score the bonding plaster (see page 111) before allowing it to dry.

5 Mix and apply finishing plaster over the top of the bonding coat, creating a smooth, flat finish. Use the rigid frame of the corner beads on which to rest the edges of the plastering trowel so that the finish is flush. Apply plaster along the adjacent edges of the corner bead, feathering it with the original wall.

aligning floors

Once a wall has been removed—whether totally or partially—it can be common for the floors between what were once two rooms to vary slightly in level. This happens most often in older houses, where either there has been some slight subsidence, or an addition has been built with slightly different floor levels to that of the original house. The reasons for variation in levels is not that important, but making good the situation is vital in order to obtain a suitable floor joint.

Even when floor levels are similar, it is likely that you may need to fill the gap left by the old wall. This is often the case when a block wall has been removed—either the blocks break off at ground level, producing a rough surface, or the blocks drop below the floor level, leaving a gap to fill between the two rooms. The techniques required for such tasks will be mainly dependent on whether the floors are concrete- or wood-framed.

concrete floors

tools for the job

- dust brush
- brick chisel
- hand sledge
- paintbrush
- gauging trowel
- wooden batten
- plastering trowel

After removing a stud wall, little repair is normally required because the wall would have been built on top of an existing concrete screed. However, when removing a block wall, it can be common to find that the concrete screed was laid after the block wall was erected. This means the block removal either leaves a large hole along the line of what was the wall base, or the blocks are broken away leaving a rough, unfinished joint across the floor. In either situation, some repair work will be required.

1 Dust away as much debris and loose material as possible from the old block wall base. Ensure that none of the broken block edges protrude above the surrounding floor surface. Trim such protrusions using a brick chisel and hand sledge.

2 Apply a bonding agent generously along the entire broken block joint, allowing the solution to overlap the edges of the concrete screed on both sides of the joint.

3 Mix up some mortar (5 parts building sand to 1 part cement) and press it firmly into the joint. Use the edge of a gauging trowel to

"chop" the mortar in, thus ensuring it gets into every area along the length of the joint. Allow the mortar to protrude slightly above the surrounding concrete.

4 Cut a length of wood, slightly longer than the width of the joint, and position it across the joint. Slowly push it along the length of the joint, moving the wood in a side-to-side sawing motion so that it gradually removes the excess mortar, to create a flush join between the existing screed

and the new mortar. This process may need to be repeated two or three times to produce a finish that is totally smooth and flat.

5 Once dry, mix up some self-leveling compound and apply it along the joint, allowing a large overlap on to the surrounding screed. Gently spread the compound using a plastering trowel. Allow it to settle and dry, providing a perfectly smooth and level joint.

making a slope

Where floor levels vary slightly, a slope or step may need to be constructed. Slopes can be created by simply feathering the edges of the self-leveling compound to produce an even drop between the two levels. Alternately, the floors can be evened by applying a greater depth of compound to the entire surface of the lower concrete screed level.

wooden floors

tools for the job

- cordless drill/driver
- claw hammer
- pry bar

One of the key considerations when working on a wooden floor is whether the surface will be exposed—thus making aesthetic considerations important. If it is to be covered, a firm, level joint is the only major concern, but exposed floors need more care.

repairing a covered floor

1 Attach lengths of 1 x 2in wood strip to the wooden joists on either side of the old wall joint. Ensure that the top edge of each length of batten sits directly flush with the top of the joist and therefore precisely below the subfloor or flooring.

2 Filling the gap will depend on its dimensions. Ideally, nail a new floorboard in position along the joint, allowing the nails to go through the board and into the battens that have been attached to the joists. Different gap dimensions may require you to cut a board such as particle board to the appropriate size before nailing it in position along the gap.

repairing an exposed floor

Most exposed floors are made up of traditional floorboards, so filling gaps may also entail adjusting the original board position.

1 Attach lengths of 1 x 2in wood strip to the wooden joist on the floorboard side of the old wall joint. Use a pry bar to lift every other board carefully along the joint junction and to lift the chipboard flooring. (You can use the same tool to lift sheets of particle board flooring.) Alternately, the boards may need to be unscrewed.

2 Use a claw hammer to remove any old nails that are protruding from the floor joists.

3 Cut boards to length and use them to fill in across the floor surface, creating a neat finish.

building a stud wall—1

Stud walls are built in two main stages, and the following four pages explain each step. Before any work can begin, however, you must first establish the direction of the ceiling and floor joists—this will determine whether the top and sole plates are to run parallel or at a right angle to them. Use a stud finder or density detector for this task. These simple tools contain sensor pads that trigger a light every time they pass over a joist.

When the wall runs parallel to the joists, it is best to position the sole plate directly above a joist and the top plate below a joist. On second floors, use an additional joist below floor level to provide extra strength (see page 23).

When the wall is to run at right angles to the joists there is greater flexibility because fixings will be made on subsequent joists across the span of the room. So be prepared to find a compromise between your desired position for the wall and the most practical location.

making the frame

tools for the job

- stud finder
- hammer
- chalk line
- level
- pencil
- hand saw
- cordless drill
- tape measure
- board lifter (optional)
- plumb bob (optional)

Studs may either be 2 x 4in or 2 x 3in in dimension, and are generally made from sawn softwood. Traditional-style buildings utilize sturdy, thicker studs, whereas most modern buildings will contain the smaller ones. The distance between the studs is vital—if you are covering the frame with plasterboard that is ⅜in thick, the studs must be a maximum of 1ft 4in apart. However, if you are using ½in plasterboard for this procedure, the studs should be no more than 2ft apart.

1 Use a stud finder to trace the position of joists and any wiring or pipes that may be above the ceiling surface.

2 Having decided on the wall position, hammer a nail into the ceiling close to the wall joint, at what will be the center of the top plate position. Do the same at the opposite ceiling/wall joint.

3 Attach a chalk line between the two nails and snap a guideline on to the ceiling surface. This line will help to provide the exact position for the top plate.

4 Use a level and pencil to continue this guideline down both walls at each end of the ceiling guideline. Continue the lines down to floor level.

5 Hold a stud section at baseboard level, and direct the wall pencil guideline so that it bisects the stud. Make a pencil guideline on either side of the stud, thus marking the baseboard. Remove the stud and cut out this section of baseboard in order to accommodate the sole plate. Repeat this process on the opposite wall. The guidelines should now indicate the various positions of the

top plate (ceiling), sole plate (floor), and wall plates.

6 Cut a plate to the exact length between the opposing walls. Position it, allowing the cut baseboard sections to accommodate each end of the plate length. Mark on this piece of plate (the sole plate) the exact position of any doors that may be required. Remember to allow for the door jamb and the skimming space.

7 Nail or screw the sole plate into the floor at 1ft 4in intervals. For concrete floors, drill and plug the holes first.

8 Cut a plate to the exact length between the opposing walls at ceiling level, and make a pencil mark bisecting the center of the joists at each end. Align this mark with the snapped ceiling line, then screw the plate to each joist crossing.

9 Cut two studs to the exact length between the top and ceiling plate on each wall. Crown the studs, pointing the natural curves in the same direction, and fasten them.

10 Mark along the sole plate at 1ft 4in intervals to indicate the positions for the vertical studs. If a door position has been marked, skip any studs in the doorway, but continue marking along the sole plate at the same intervals.

11 Cut small blocks of wood and nail them in position at the side of each stud guideline. This is not essential, but it will help to make fastening the vertical studs in place much easier. The frame is now complete and ready to be filled in (see page 44 for the next stage).

USING A PLUMB BOB

It is also possible to create guidelines using a plumb bob or line. Once you have established the ceiling guideline (steps 1–2), attach the plumb bob to each of the nails in turn and mark along, and at the bottom of, the line to gain a vertical guide. The plumb bob may also be used from a central ceiling position to mark sole plate guidelines along the floor. Ensure that the plumb bob is stationary and not touching anything before marking off.

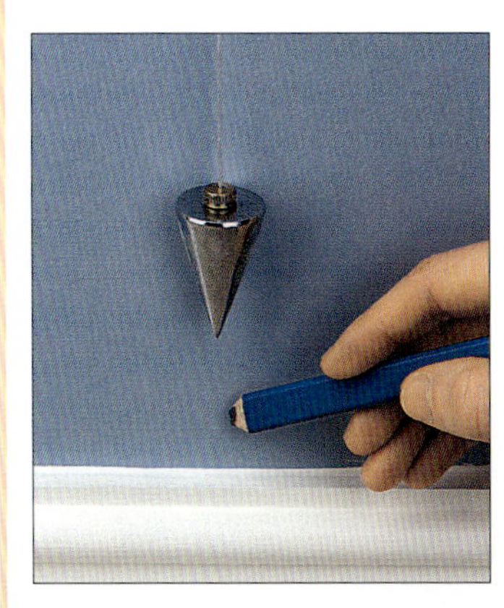

building a stud wall—2

Once the outer framework of the stud wall has been installed, attention can be turned to filling in the framework and drywalling. Make a final check on the plumbness of the frame and its positioning, because any slight adjustments are best made at this stage rather than later. See page 42 for a list of tool requirements.

studding the frame

1 Measure each stud and cut the required lengths. Fix them at the base, holding them against the block supports to prevent them from moving. Use sinker nails and toenail them in at an angle on both sides of the stud, so that the nails penetrate into the sole plate.

2 With the stud fastened at its base, hold a level against the length to find the precise vertical fastening position in the top plate. Drive toenails into each side of the stud and into the top plate.

3 Keep checking the level and adjusting the stud until it is precisely vertical, before securing it in place.

4 To make the door frame, cut a header to the exact size between the two studs on either side of the door opening. Remember to check the correct height measurement for the door (including the door jamb), and nail the length in place, ensuring that it is level.

5 To add strength, install cripple studs vertically between the door head and the top plate. Nails may be inserted in the base of the vertical stud, whereas at ceiling level the nails must be angled through the vertical length into the top plate.

6 Blocking can be added between the studs in order to provide extra rigidity. These blocks should be positioned halfway between the sole and top plates. Secure them in place with nails.

7 On completion of the framework, work on providing access for any services or electrical cables that may need to run through the wall. Drill holes through studs and blocks as required.

8 Thread cables through the holes drilled in the studs. (Check with a qualified electrician the exact wiring requirements for the services you require.)

attaching the drywall

As discussed on page 42, ensure that you are using the correct thickness of drywall according to the spacing of the studs. Bear in mind that if you are planning to use joint compound, the drywall should also have tapered edges (see page 96).

Invariably, sheets of drywall need to be cut to fit, so careful measuring is required. As most ceilings or wall surfaces are neither perfectly flat nor completely square, the edge of drywall sheets will often need to be "scribed" in order to produce a precise fit. This is most important at ceiling level and in corners because the joint needs to be as tight as possible, whereas at floor level there is some leeway because the baseboard will cover the joint.

tips of the trade

Although it is often easier and more practical to have two people hanging or installing drywall, it can be achieved while working on your own with the aid of a drywall "T". This allows you to lever drywall sheets into position on the wall surface, while leaving your hands free for fastening purposes.

1 Holding the drywall sheet as close to the ceiling as possible (so that it touches), slide a small wooden block and pencil along the sheet, keeping the block resting against the ceiling surface. The pencil guideline produced will mimic the profile of the ceiling, providing a guideline to cut the drywall for the perfect fit.

2 Use drywall nails or screws to fix the sheets in place. Fastenings should be made between ½in to 1in from the board edges and at 6in intervals or centers along all edges and studs. Fasten drywall around a door opening so that the joint is above the center of the door. Although this is technically more difficult to measure and cut, after the process of taping or finishing a central board join such as this will be less likely to crack than joints that run vertical from the door opening corners.

3 When one side of the wall is completely covered, drill the necessary holes in the drywall for any electrical wiring. Then, before drywalling the other side of the stud wall, install insulation blankets between all the studs. Finally, finish the drywall (see page 96) and trim the door opening.

tips of the trade

- **Blocking**—Fix extra blocks between studs where heavy items are to be fixed on the wall surface. For example, ensure that an extra block is positioned to accommodate fastenings for sinks or basins.
- **Flush joints**—When positioning all the studs and blocks, take extra care to ensure that the surfaces of all the particular joints are flush. Uneven joints may cause bows in the drywall, making installation difficult and causing weak spots.
- **Secure nailing**—When installing fasteners or nails, ensure that their heads sit slightly below surface level for a secure fastening, but not so far that the head of the nail causes the drywall to crumble and reduces the strength of the installation.
- **Screwing alternative**—Drywall screws instead of nails can be used to fix sheeting. This can often be easier when working on your own and reduces the risk of damaging drywall with hammer blows.
- **Marking off**—It can be difficult to locate the exact position of studs when drywalling, as the wallboard itself is covering them. So when the stud framework has been completed, mark off where the center of each stud is located on the floor with a pencil. Then use a level to draw a pencil guideline on each board from floor to ceiling as you work.

pass-throughs

Pass-throughs provide ideal access for serving food from a kitchen into a dining area. Although they are still used for this purpose in many cases, they can also make attractive decorative features and may be constructed in a range of different styles. Building a pass-through in a solid block wall or a loadbearing wall will require greater effort (see opposite page). However, carrying out such a project in a non-loadbearing wall is a very straightforward exercise.

pass-through in a non-loadbearing stud wall

tools for the job

- stud finder
- pencil
- level
- tape measure
- drywall saw
- hand saw
- hammer
- cordless drill/driver
- miter block or miter saw

1 Work out your preferred position for the pass-through, then use a stud finder to find stud positions in the wall, and to check for services such as wiring and plumbing. Be prepared to make some small adjustments according to the position of the wall studs and these services. (It is almost certain that you will need to cut through some studs, but try to adjust your measurements so that the sides of the opening correspond with the edges of the studs.)

2 Use a pencil and level to draw a guideline on the wall to show the exact size of the pass-through. It is essential to get dimensions and measurements as plumb and level as possible at this stage—this will help to make constructing the pass-through quite simple when the necessary hole has been made.

3 Use a drywall saw to cut around the pencil outline. (This type of special saw is used for this process instead of a back saw because its sharp point is able to pierce the drywall easily.) If you come across a stud obstruction, use the very end of the saw to score the drywall until you penetrate through to the stud surface.

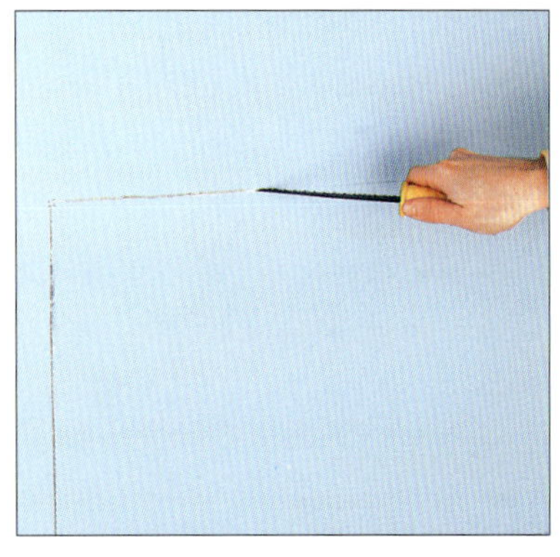

Once the wallboard panel has been cut around, it may be removed and discarded. Next, repeat this procedure for the other side of the wall. If the wall was insulated, remove the insulatory blanket as required.

4 Remove blocking by first sawing through it with the back saw. Then lever out the blocks with a pry bar or hammer. If you try to saw too closely to the vertical stud, it is likely that you will come into contact with nail or screw fixings, which can damage the saw blade. Instead, remove all such fastenings using a hacksaw.

5 Leaving the central stud in place, cut and fit blocks to either side of it at the top and bottom of the opening. It is best to use screws for this purpose, because trying to angle in nails with a hammer can push the blocks below the edge of the opening, making them difficult to pull out of the wall and back into the required position. Provide pilot holes for the screws first, as this will help to avoid applying too much pressure on the blocks when fastening them in place.

6 Cut out the central stud, keeping the saw blade flush with the top and bottom of the opening.

7 Trim out the opening with 1 x 5in dressed softwood. Nail measured lengths in position, beginning with the base followed by the top of the opening and finishing with the two sides. Trim nails are best for this situation, and their heads can be filled before painting the trim around the opening.

8 Use the miter saw to cut casing and fit it around the opening on both sides to finish off the project.

Trim nails can again be used for fastening purposes. In addition to nailing the casing through the front, use one smaller nail at each corner of the opening going through one section of casing and into the adjacent section. This will help to pull the corner joints together and reduce the risk of any movement, which can potentially cause cracking.

LOADBEARING WALLS

The illustrations shown here provide instruction for inserting a pass-through in a non-loadbearing stud wall. However, if the opening is to be inserted into a loadbearing wall, or a block or brick wall, the technique will need to be modified. In fact, the procedure is very similar to that for removing a loadbearing wall (see page 36). Clearly, the scale of the project will be reduced because you are dealing with a much smaller opening for a pass-through. However, a lintel of some nature will be required to fit the opening. Before making the opening, create the proper support for the wall—for a masonry wall use a needle brace (see page 42), and build a temporary wall for a wood-framed wall.

A pass-through provides a useful and attractive access point between two rooms. It can also draw light into dark areas of the home and makes a handy display area.

soundproofing walls

The best time to soundproof a wall is during its construction, but unless you are physically building a new wall yourself, this option does not often arise. Manufacturers have now come to recognize this rather basic problem and have, accordingly, developed a number of systems to make soundproofing existing walls a feasible and effective procedure, including better insulation slabs, which are now tested to a much higher standard.

By far the greatest need for wall soundproofing tends to arise with walls that you share with a neighbor.

soundproofing a common wall

tools for the job

- pry bar
- tape measure
- pencil
- hand saw
- cordless drill/driver
- level
- protective gloves
- dust mask
- hacksaw
- caulk gun

Traditionally, soundproofing a common wall would usually mean building a new stud wall in front of the existing party wall, and using insulation blankets to fill the gap. The dimensions involved would almost certainly mean losing a sizeable area of your own room, as well as requiring some fairly major construction. However, the method below only encroaches 2–3in into the room space, and is therefore rarely noticeable in terms of the overall room dimensions. Proprietary drywall panels are used for this technique—these consist of two different thicknesses of drywall joined together, with another soundproofing layer sandwiched in between. Although this is the ideal material, for the procedure, you can use normal drywall sheets so long as the bottom layer is of a greater thickness than the top layer. (This adheres to a basic soundproofing theory—when layering similar materials, never use the same depth of material twice.)

1 Score the caulk joint on top of the baseboard before prying it away from the wall with a pry bar Try not to damage the board, which can be re-used when soundproofing is complete.

2 Starting at floor level, use a pencil to make a series of measurements along the corner of the wall at 2ft intervals. It is unlikely that the height of the wall will fit exactly into divisibles of 2ft, so simply make the last mark directly at ceiling level.

3 Cut a resilient channel to the exact length of the wall you wish to soundproof, and fasten it in position at floor level. Make sure that the open side of the channel is facing up, and that the fastenings are made just above the floor level. Screw the bottom edge of the resilient channel into the framing.

4 Position a second channel at the next measurement, this time ensuring that the open side of the channel is facing down to floor level. Use a torpedo level to ensure that

the bar is positioned precisely level. Continue to fix resilient channel at the marked-off intervals right up to ceiling level. All channel from the second one up should have the open side facing down.

5 Fit sound insulation, beginning at floor level. Lip the bottom edge of the slab into the open side of the floor level resilient channel, and fit the top edge of the slab into the open side of the resilient channel above. So long as your measurements have been correct, a precise fit should be achieved. Wear protective gloves for this process, because the sound insulation fibers can be irritating to the skin, and the channel edges can be sharp.

6 When the bottom section of the wall is complete, progress to the next level, inserting slabs in a similar fashion. Bear in mind that at this and subsequent levels, it is not possible to lip the bottom edge of the slab into the channel. However, the top edge will be lipped into the bar, allowing the bottom edge of the slab to rest flush on the top edge of the bar below. Continue to fit slabs until the entire wall is covered.

7 Once trimmed and cut to fit, attach the double plasterboard or drywall panels to the wall. Using plasterboard screws, fasten through the lower level of the panels and into the resilient channel. Screws should be long enough to fix the board firmly to the channel, but not so long that they reach the original common wall. Otherwise, an automatic channel for sound transference will be created.

8 Lip the staggered edge of the next panel over the first, butting it up tightly to create a flush join. It may be easier to put marks along the previous sheet, identifying the exact position of the last fastening. These will indicate the position of the resilient channel and therefore allow you to position the next fastening exactly. Continue to fit panels as required, fixing along the channel at 6–8in intervals.

9 Finally, apply a bead of caulk around all the new joints made between the plasterboard or drywall panels and the existing floor, walls, and ceiling. The wall may then be plastered or taped and finished, its baseboard reapplied, and painted.

CARPET SOUNDPROOFING

Bear in mind that soundproofing efficiency will benefit from laying good-quality padding and carpet in the room. This situation may be improved by using a specially designed acoustic flooring underlayment system. Although padding and carpet are more generally concerned with the floor of a room, they will indirectly assist the soundproofing of a wall. This is especially the case if the floor is suspended, which enables noise to travel more easily from one room to another level. So deal with floor soundproofing issues at the same time as dealing with walls.

tips of the trade

Different tools will be required for marking and cutting different materials. Resilient channel should be marked with a fiber-tip pen before cutting with a hacksaw or aviation snips. Sound insulation should be marked with chalk and cut with a utility knife—a dust mask is also vital for this process. Plasterboard or drywall panels can be marked with a pencil and cut with a utility knife.

building a block wall

Although stud walls (see pages 42–5) are easier to construct than solid block walls, there are some instances when a block structure may be more appropriate or even preferred. For example, in a house where all existing walls are of a block or brick construction, a stud wall may be out of character. Block walls also provide better soundproofing qualities and are better suited to supporting heavy objects or multiple fastenings.

tools for the job

- torpedo level
- pencil
- tape measure
- cordless drill/driver
- adjustable or plier wrench
- hammer
- gauging trowel
- bricklaying trowel
- hand sledge
- brick chisel
- goggles
- protective gloves

1 Use a torpedo level and pencil to draw a vertical line on the wall from the floor to the ceiling. This will be the line on to which the wall profile is attached, helping to "tie in" the blocks to the existing wall structure. Profiles vary slightly in design, but most will require holes to be drilled for the fasteners. (Use the masonry bit specified by the manufacturers of the profile.) Hold the profile steadily in position on the wall surface and carefully drill through it into the wall surface beneath.

2 Plug the holes and insert the supplied fasteners. Coach screws are often provided for this purpose, and are used in combination with a large washer to add extra strength and rigidity. Position them by hand and tighten with an adjustable or a plier wrench. Continue to add coach screws up the entire length of the profile. Once the profile is fixed in place, repeat steps 1 and 2 to fix the second profile to the opposing wall.

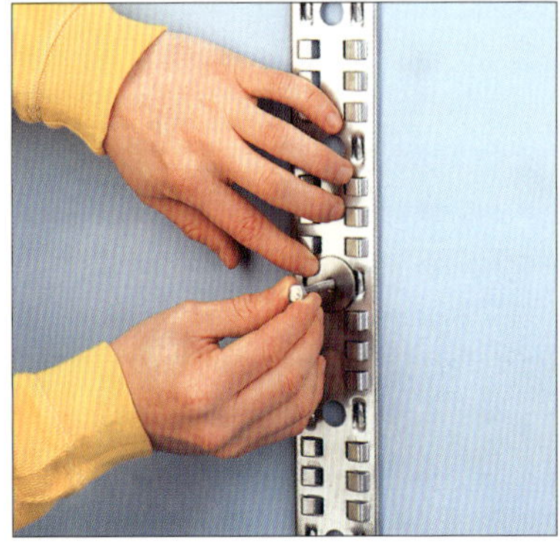

3 Attach a string line to the wall to one side of the profile. It should be in such a position that when the first block is positioned, the line will

correspond to the face of the block and slightly below its top edge. A block may be positioned "dry" to gain the appropriate fastening point. Attach the other end of the line to the corresponding position next to the other wall profile. This line will help with positioning the first layer.

safety advice

Block walls are quite heavy, so it is important to check that the weight is supported by the floor below. At ground level this is less of a problem, especially on a solid concrete base, but building on a suspended wooden floor is a different matter and you should seek professional advice. When building on second floors or above, similar approval should be sought because joists may need additional strengthening.

4 Apply a strip of mortar to the floor, extending away from the profile, and of a width and length slightly wider than a standard block. Try to keep this mortar base a consistent but uncompacted level.

5 Take the first block and mold a cap of mortar on to one end using a gauging trowel. This process

is known as "buttering" and is an integral part of the block- or brick-laying technique.

6 Lift and position the buttered end of the block tight up against the wall profile, while settling the base of the block into the mortar bed. The block weight will force mortar out from underneath it while finding a good, solid resting position.

7 Tap the block with the butt end of the bricklaying trowel to help it settle, and check that the front face of the block just rests against the string line, and that it is level.

8 Use a torpedo level to make any final adjustments, ensuring that the block is both level and vertical across the appropriate dimensions as required. After final positioning, continue along the floor adding blocks, checking levels, and adjusting as necessary until the entire first course of blocks is complete. Trim excess mortar with a trowel as you progress and use it as the base for the next block, together with any extra fresh mortar that is required.

9 Apply a layer of mortar along the top of the first course of blocks to a similar depth as used at ground level. Also, use the ties provided by the profile kit to link into the profile itself and bed into the mortar layer.

10 The most essential rule of block wall construction is to ensure that mortar joints on adjacent levels never coincide. Therefore, before starting the second layer, cut a half block using a hand sledge and brick chisel. Always wear goggles when carrying out this

procedure to protect your eyes from flying debris. Use a sturdy surface to prevent the block from toppling.

11 Add the half block before continuing along with full blocks for the remainder of the course. Keep checking levels at regular intervals and move the string line up to correspond with the next block level. Never lay more than five courses of blocks in one session, and allow them to dry before progressing with further courses.

openings

It is likely that an opening of some sort will be required in the wall. Simply mark out the dimensions on the floor and build up to these guidelines, leaving the area of the opening free. Once you have reached the required height for the entrance, a lintel or header will need to be installed over the top of the opening before you can continue adding blocks, then building up to ceiling level can be completed.

installing wall ventilation

Effective ventilation is an essential part of any household construction, both for general efficiency and health and safety. Before double glazing and improvements to insulation, installing ventilation systems was rarely necessary because drafts were a "natural" feature of most houses. However, increased efficiency of insulation in most modern houses means that artificial devices must be installed as substitutes for what was once an automatic system.

AREAS FOR VENTILATION

Key areas for ventilation include:

- **Bathrooms and kitchens**—Bathrooms are an environment in which moist air is pervasive. Adequate ventilation is therefore vital to prevent mold or dry rot, and condensation that can ruin decoration. Similarly, kitchens can be exposed to steam and condensation, as well as cooker fumes, that need good ventilation. Both rooms tend to require mechanical ventilation, such as an exhaust fan that actually takes air out of the room and to the exterior of the house.
- **Crawl spaces**—Crawl spaces require ventilating beneath them using air bricks in the exterior wall. Failure to install air bricks or allowing them to become blocked can cause problems such as dry rot.
- **Chimney breasts**—When a fireplace has been blocked off, it will be necessary to install a vent in the chimney breast to allow air circulation in the chimney void. The same ends can be achieved by installing air bricks on the exterior wall into the chimney void. However, the interior method tends to be easier to carry out and is equally effective.
- **Furnaces and solid fuel fires**—These systems must be vented correctly to ensure that fumes are not allowed to build up inside the house. Always seek professional advice from a qualified engineer and have appliances checked regularly.

installing a through-wall vent

tools for the job

stud finder
tape measure
pencil
hole saw and bit
protective gloves
goggles
dust mask
hacksaw
caulk gun

1 Mark off on the wall the center point for the ventilation shaft. Check for any wiring with the stud finder and ensure that the height and position of the hole adheres to any relevant building regulations.

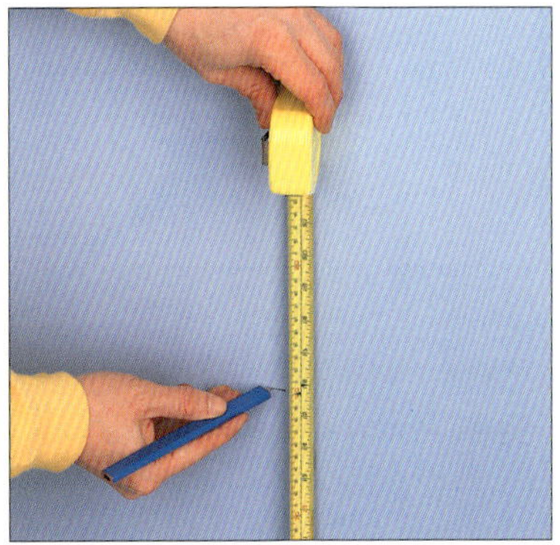

2 Attach the hole saw bit to the main drill body, ensuring that it is correctly fitted in place. Read the guidelines provided by the manufacturer for this process as techniques vary with heavy-duty tools.

3 Position the pilot drill point on the marked wall point and start drilling. The pilot drill will make the initial hole in the wall to secure the hole saw in place and allow the larger round hole saw bit to begin cutting the hole in the wall surface. Be sure to hold firmly on to the drill as it is both heavy and can "kick" as it bites into the wall surface. Goggles must be worn to protect eyes from flying debris, and a mask is also important as the drill can generate a lot of dust. Ear plugs may also help.

When the drill reaches the other side of the wall, there is a danger that it will blow out the exterior finish or bricks, thus causing a larger hole than required, which will need repair. To prevent this from happening, the core drill can be used from both sides of

safety advice

It is important to get professional advice before installing or changing ventilation systems. This is vital when dealing with the requirements for fuels such as gas, oil or solid fuels as failure to vent correctly can endanger life.

the wall, so that the breakthrough point is inside the wall itself. Advance the pilot bit so it penetrates through the wall well before the hole saw does. When it has pierced the other side, finish drilling from the opposite side.

4 Remove the cut core by hand. It should come out in one or two large pieces, depending on the wall makeup. If you are drilling through a cavity wall, ensure that no large pieces of the core fall into the cavity.

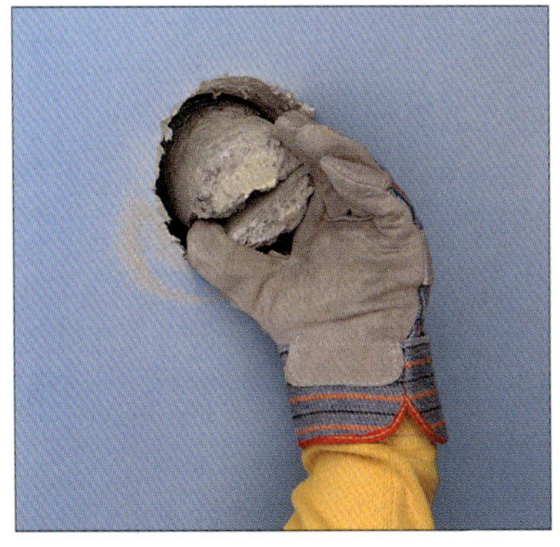

5 Line the hole with some duct pipe, cutting it to the right size with a hacksaw. The ductwork can be

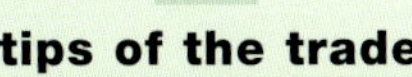

tips of the trade

Installing a passive ventilator in an exterior wall is straightforward, so long as you have the correct equipment and tools. It will be necessary to rent a hole saw and bit from your local rental store—such equipment is expensive to buy, and not worth purchasing for small jobs such as this.

normally bought as part of a kit, and the manufacturer's guidelines for positioning should be included.

6 Seal around the edge of the ductwork with silicone, ensuring a good unbroken seal. Carry out this process on both the interior and exterior of the wall. (If areas around the edge of the hole broke away or became damaged while drilling, repair them with mortar followed by all-purpose filler, before applying sealant.)

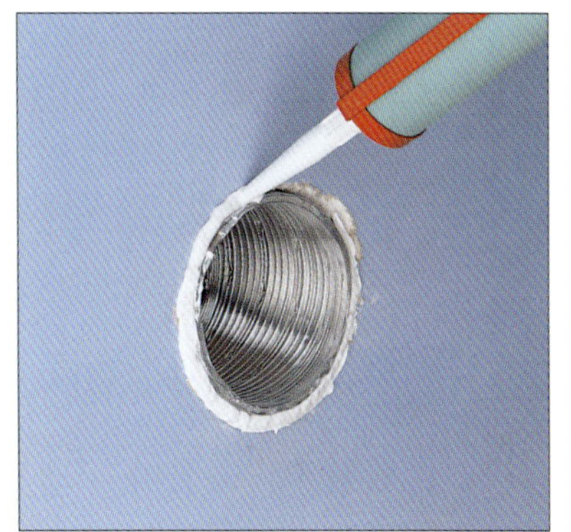

7 Inside, fix a louver vent to cover the hole. This must be a passive ventilator made of metal or

plastic so that it cannot be closed off and inhibit ventilation. Plastic vents may be painted to match and therefore blend with the wall color, making them a less noticeable feature.

8 On the exterior, fit an exhaust cover over the hole. This enables a good flow of air while limiting strong gusts of wind. It also prevents rain from penetrating through the vent into the room.

9 Again, seal around the exhaust cover with more silicone sealant to ensure a good seal.

tips of the trade

Where electrically operated ventilation fans need to be fitted, it will be necessary to seek the help of a qualified electrician in order to ensure that the fan is wired safely and to code. An electrician will also be able to provide advice on the positioning and type of ventilation required to provide sufficient air flow and circulation for the room in question.

installing a doorway—1

Installing a doorway in a loadbearing wall is not a task that should be taken lightly because of the structural nature of the work. It is important to follow the correct procedures and techniques when tackling a project such as this. It is always advisable to seek some professional guidance before beginning work, because the procedure will vary slightly depending on the makeup of the wall and its exact position in the house structure as a whole.

The work involved depends strongly on supporting the wall. This means supplying the necessary temporary support while the part of the wall for the doorway is removed, and supplying the necessary permanent support for above the doorway in the future. For the permanent support you will need to use a lintel or heading to act as the permanent support. Its size and make-up will depend on two factors—the structure of the wall to be removed and the span of the proposed opening. Both of these require serious calculation, and the question of lintel type and construction should be decided in consultation with a structural engineer.

Once all the necessary safety precautions and procedures are in place, and planning permission has been gained if it is required, the work itself is perfectly achievable. The project can be divided into two stages: first, the opening has to be made and second, the lintel has to be inserted.

making the opening

A methodical approach is required for this procedure and it is important to follow guidelines in the correct order. The work will produce a lot of dust and rubbish, so use drop cloths and arrange for the rubble and broken masonry to be disposed of.

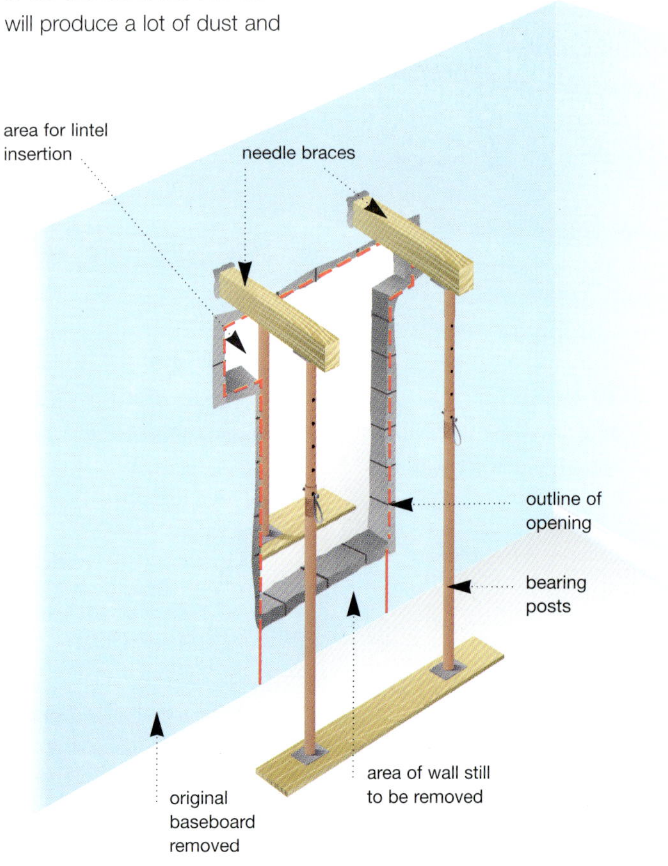

1 Mark out the size of the opening on the wall surface.

2 Knock holes through the wall above the proposed opening.

3 Insert needle braces through the holes.

4 Support the needle braces by bearing posts on both sides of the wall.

5 Use a stone cutter or hand sledge and brick chisel to cut around the edge of the opening.

6 Remove the blocks or bricks by first loosening with a hand sledge and brick chisel, and then levering them out with a pry bar, or lift by hand.

7 Continue to remove blocks until the entire area is clear.

installing the new lintel

It is essential for two people to be involved when inserting lintels, as they are surprisingly heavy. It is also much easier to carry out this procedure while working from some sort of access platform, rather than using stepladders.

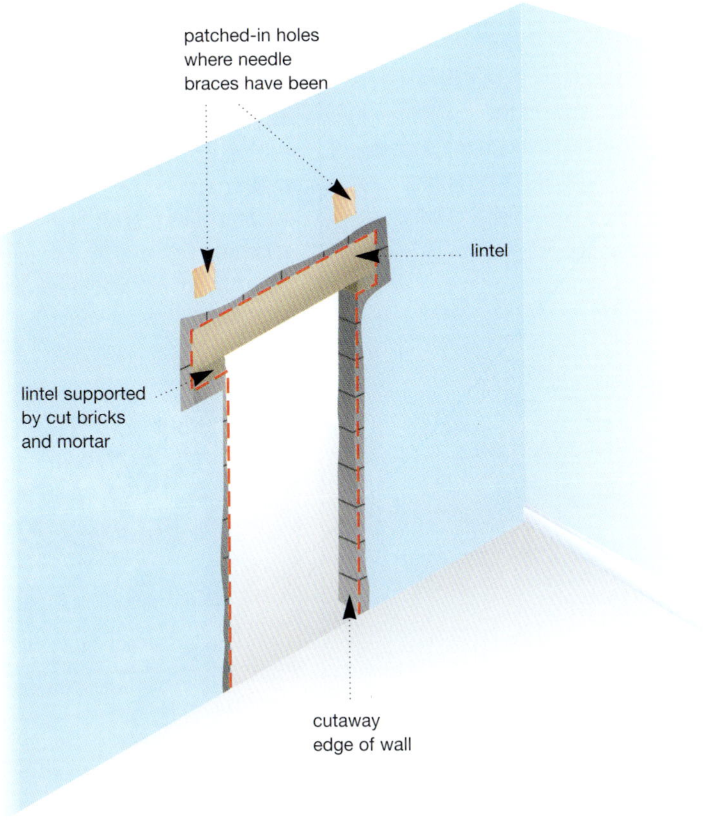

1 At the top corners of the opening take out bricks or blocks to accommodate the lintel ends.

2 Check and recheck measurements to ensure that the lintel will fit into the required space.

3 Apply a bed of mortar to this area before lifting the lintel into place.

4 Check that the lintel is level. Use cut bricks or blocks, wedged beneath the end of the lintel to rectify this if necessary.

5 Apply more mortar around the lintel ends to ensure it will be held securely in place.

6 Make good with drywall and/or scratch coat, and plaster around the lintel.

7 Make good with drywall and/or scratch coat, and plaster around the cut blocks or bricks that make up the sides of the opening.

8 Remove the needle braces and patch in the holes.

factors to consider

In addition to the practical considerations of how to support your wall, there are also a number of other issues that should be carefully addressed.

needle brace requirement

The number of needle braces required for support will depend on the width of the opening. Needle brace dimensions should not be less than 6 x 4in, but consult a structural engineer on exact requirements.

bearing posts

Bearing posts can be rented at low cost, and their adjustable nature makes them ideal for supporting purposes. Make sure that the bases of the posts are positioned on scaffold planks so that weight distribution is evened out. Most post bases have nail holes so that they can be nailed into the scaffold planks to eliminate any risk of them moving.

lintel support

In many cases the new lintel may be positioned in the existing wall structure with no extra support below it required. However, in some cases it may be necessary to install extra concrete support. Consult a structural engineer for the correct requirements in your particular circumstances.

safety equipment

This sort of work requires close attention to safety, and all the necessary precautions must be taken. Wear protective gloves, goggles, and a hard hat when taking down the wall. A dust mask may also be needed, especially when clearing away rubble and dust caused by wall removal.

installing a doorway—2

Installing a doorway in a non-loadbearing wall is much easier than the technique used for a loadbearing wall. However, before work begins, you must be certain that the wall is non-loadbearing and it is always best to take professional advice to check this. For solid-block, non-loadbearing walls, a lintel is generally required, and the procedure is similar to that shown on pages 54–5. The example shown here deals with cutting an entrance into a non-loadbearing stud wall.

safety advice

Make sure that there are no services running through the stud wall, which will otherwise require rerouting before work can begin.

tools for the job

- stud finder
- awl
- pencil
- level
- drywall saw or hand saw
- tape measure
- pry bar
- cordless drill/driver

1 Use a stud finder in order to locate the position of the vertical studs in the wall. It is essential that you locate a stud close to or directly where the hinge side of the door will eventually come to hang. Once the position of this stud has been located, all your other measurements should be taken from this point and will help to guide the process.

2 On the main stud, locate the exact edge of the stud by inserting an awl through the drywall or plasterboard at the detection points that you determined using the stud finder.

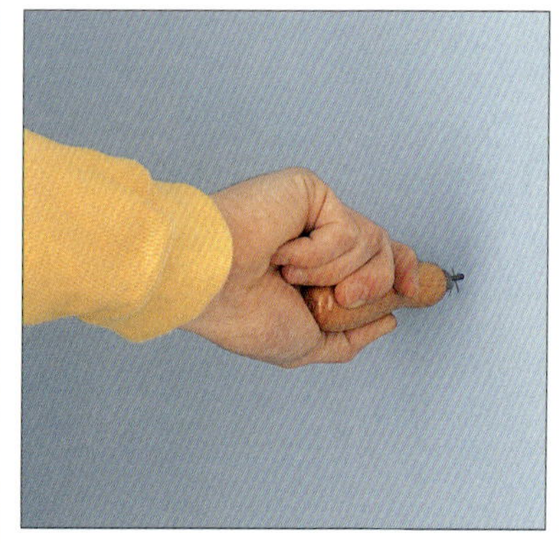

3 Join up the line of holes with a pencil and level. A well-constructed stud wall should show this line to be exactly plumb. If this is not the case, the stud may require slight repositioning once exposed.

4 Measure out the rest of the opening dimensions on the wall surface. For a standard interior door and doorway, remember to allow for the dimensions of the door plus the thickness of the door jamb, leaving an additional 1/4in to allow for a gap between door and frame. Remove the section of drywall or plasterboard by accurately sawing along the guidelines with a drywall saw.

5 The other side of the wall will require cutting out as well. From the interior of the wall, use an awl to pierce the drywall or plasterboard at the corners and positions corresponding to the initial opening. It is then possible to join these markings with a pencil on the other side of the wall, and again cut out the area with a drywall saw. Remember to keep the edge of the saw tight against the stud.

tips of the trade

When using a back saw to saw through existing studs, there is always the possibility that you may come across screws or other fasteners, so keep a hacksaw at hand to deal with such an eventuality.

6 Remove any vertical studs or blocks from the entrance with a back saw, trimming back precisely to the drywall or plasterboard edge.

7 Cut away the sole plate with the back saw, back to the edge of the drywall or plasterboard. If the sole plate is fixed in the entrance, it may be necessary to use a pry bar to free it. It is also recommended to add some fastenings into the sole plate at the bottom corners of the opening. In this way, the cut sole plate will be secured firmly back in position.

8 Although the stud creating the hinge side of the opening is precisely aligned with the edge of the drywall or plasterboard, it is unlikely that your measurements will have allowed the stud on the opposite door to align as accurately as possible. Therefore, it may be necessary to insert a stud along this edge. Cut the framing to size and angle screws in at the bottom of its length, which will make fastening easier and help to secure the stud.

9 Angling the screws before the stud is positioned makes it easier to tighten the screws once the stud is in place. Depending on the wall structure, it will then be necessary to fix the stud at the top of the opening. Usually, there will be an existing wall block to help you. Alternately, you may find it necessary to install another block for secure fastening purposes.

10 Fill in the top part of the frame by cutting lengths of wood to the required size. Again angle screws into these lengths before tightening and driving them into position once the length is in place. Ensure that the screwheads are countersunk into the wood, so that they are below surface level.

11 Where studs extend down to the top of the opening, it is necessary to add further fastenings to ensure rigidity. Fit another length on the other side of the vertical length to finish off the opening frame.

STUD WALL ISSUES

- **Dimensions**—Stud walls are generally constructed from wood that is either 2 x 4in or 2 x 3in in dimension. Before purchasing or reusing any wood to make the entrance, make sure you know which stud dimensions will be required.
- **Use**—Doorways may be left open, doors installed, or other features such as arches added. When measuring for the entrance, calculating specific size requirements is very important, especially for doors, because sizes vary so much.

installing a door jamb

A door jamb houses the hinges and closing mechanism, and provides the general perimeter for a door when positioned in a wall surface. Jambs can be found in a simple kit form, and are then fitted to the precise opening. Although this is a very straightforward procedure, accuracy is essential because any deviation from plumb and level positioning will cause major problems when it comes to hanging a door.

tools for the job

wooden mallet
hammer
tape measure
pencil
hand saw
level
cordless drill/driver

door jambs

The sections that make up a jamb are often referred to by different terms. For our purposes, the top part of the lining is called the head, and the side sections the stiles.

1 Assemble the three parts of the jamb on the floor. Put the stile ends into the premade slots in the head. They should fit relatively snugly, but may need one or two blows with a mallet to ensure the joint is tight.

2 Secure the stiles in place by nailing through the top of the head into the stiles. Screws may also be used for this purpose. Make sure that each stile is secured with at least two fasteners.

3 Measure the exact distance between the stiles at the head end of the jamb. Transfer this measurement to the floor level of the jamb and nail a length of strip wood between the stiles, securing them in position at this required width. Make sure that the strip does not extend past the outer edge of the jamb, as this will hinder fitting the jamb when it is positioned in the wall opening.

4 To ensure that the jamb is totally square, it is necessary to make further measurements and fastenings at the top of the jamb. Measuring away from the top corner of the jamb, mark off one point at 12in along the head, and another at 16in along the stile. Then adjust the distance between the 16in mark and the 12in mark on the head, and make sure that it is exactly 20in. With these three measurements checked to be exact, this means that the jamb will be totally square.

5 Cut a length of wood strip to fit across the angle of the head and stile. Nail it in place, checking to be sure that the diagonal measurement of 20in is maintained. The jamb is now firmly braced at both the top and bottom.

6 Use a back saw to cut off the excess head. Make sure that you cut right back to the corners of the jamb, since leaving any excess will hinder positioning it in the wall.

7 Lift up the jamb and position it in the wall opening. Concentrate on the hinge side of the door. Use a level to check that the jamb is plumb, and that the front edge is level with the wall surface on both sides.

8 Fasten the hinge side of the jamb in place with screws, through the stile and into the framing beyond.

9 Depending on the precision of your measurements, it is likely that there will be a small gap between the stile and wall on the opposite side of the jamb. Before trying to rectify this situation, make the correction easier by inserting screws at intervals along the stile. Allow them to penetrate into the stile, but not through to the other side.

10 Cut some wooden shims from scrap and position them in the gap between the stile and wall. Position shims at the screw fixing points. The best technique is to apply two shims in each case, inserted from the opposite sides of the wall., so when the shims meet, they can be gradually pushed in together to form a rigid support between the stile and the wall.

11 When all the shims have been inserted, you can then secure the frame in place in the door opening by tightening the screws, so that they go through the shims and into the wall. Again, as you tighten the screws, continue to check the position of the jamb with a torpedo level.

12 Use a back saw to cut off shim excess as required (trim back flush). Add final fasteners to the head, screwing through into the horizontal header above. Use scrap to shim out any additional spaces.

SOLID BLOCK WALLS

The technique for installing door jambs into solid block or brick walls is exactly the same as that shown here except that there are different fastener requirements. In order to deal with masonry, concrete anchor screws or frame fasteners should be used for securing the jamb in place.

- **The right jamb**—Jambs are sold in kit form and so are, to a certain extent, standardized to correspond to modern wall and door dimensions. In older houses it may be necessary to make your own customized jamb.

making an arch

Arches can be used as an alternative to traditional doors or square openings, providing more of a feature between rooms. In the past it would have been a highly skilled procedure to produce a framework for an arch and finish it with subsequent coats of plaster. Today, however, manufacturing innovation has made the process much easier. Arch forms made from plaster or drywall can be bought, positioned, and finished to create perfect profiles.

making an arch in a stud wall

tools for the job

- cordless drill/driver
- screwdriver
- hacksaw
- hammer
- tape measure
- putty knife
- drywall knife or plastering trowel

Although arches may be built onto existing wall openings, beginning from scratch and building them into a new stud wall is by far the easiest procedure. A new wall, if erected correctly, is more likely to be true and square compared to older walls, thereby making the process of fitting the arch much more straightforward.

1 Most arch forms have predrilled holes for fasteners. Hold the form in position while drilling four pilot holes into the studs. Make sure that the front lip of the arch form corresponds to the manufacturer's guidelines in terms of encroaching up to the level of the drywall or plasterboard on either side of the wall.

2 Secure the form in place with wood screws. Use a screwdriver rather than a cordless drill/driver to tighten the screws, since overtightening could crack the form. Greater control of movement can be achieved by using a simple hand tool in situations like this.

3 From the base of the arch form to the floor, it will be necessary to cut and fit drywall or plasterboard so as to cover the wooden stud and bring its surface up to the same depth as the base of the arch form. Fasten this strip in place with drywall or plasterboard nails, taking care not to damage the wall finish.

4 Cut corner bead to the correct length (form base to floor) and attach it on both edges of the opening using drywall or plasterboard nails as appropriate. Make sure that the apex of each corner bead aligns precisely with the respective bottom corners of the form.

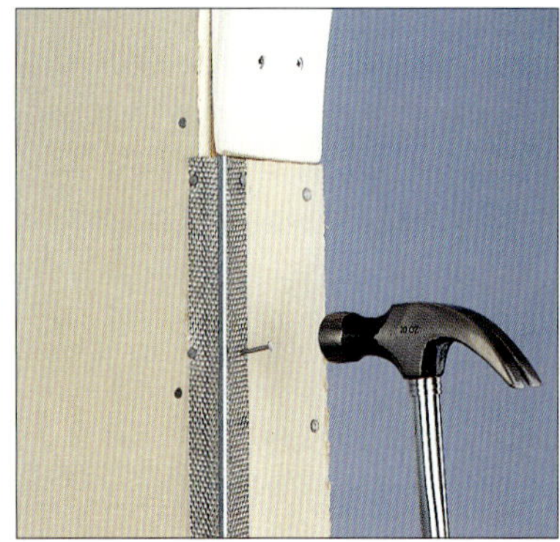

5 Repeat steps 1–4 to fit the second form and entrance jamb. It is rare that the dimensions of the forms will join exactly, and therefore it is almost certain that there will be a gap between the top edges

tips of the trade

Instead of using corner bead along the vertical edge of the arch, apply corner tape and joint compound to achieve a smooth, even finish. The interior area of the arch form can also be filled with a bonding coat plaster before being finished with joint compound.

of the forms. Use the same technique as for the studs on each side of the entrance to fill the gap between the forms—in other words, fill the gap with drywall or plasterboard and use corner bead to form the edges.

6 Once the forms, jamb, and corner beads have all been positioned and aligned, fill the arch form holes with all-purpose filler or bonding coat plaster.

7 Tape the drywall or plasterboard joints with self-adhesive joint tape, and also the joints between the drywall or board and the arch forms.

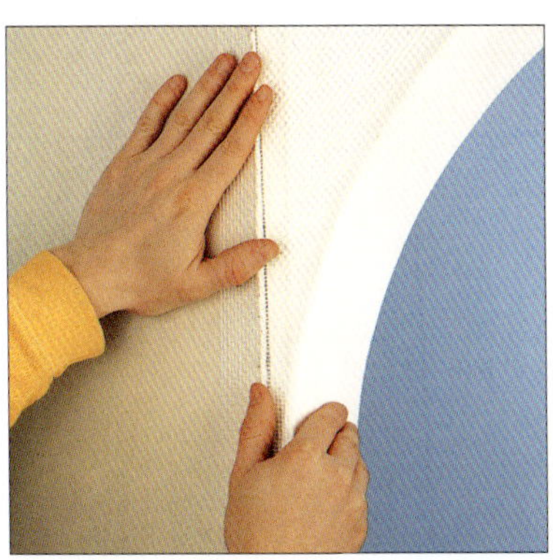

8 If you have used drywall for the arch, push joint compound into the joints with a drywall knife, then smooth the compound with a damp sponge. Apply a broad, even band of compound over the surface of the joints, then sand lightly when dry. If you have used plasterboard, apply plaster over the walls and onto the arch forms, then polish and leave to dry. The arch can now be painted.

tips of the trade

- **Blending**—Where the smooth form face meets the original edge of the entrance, it may be necessary to feather the joint with fine filler in order to provide a perfectly smooth arched profile. Once filled, use a fine-grit sandpaper to finish the joint.
- **Dealing with cracks**—In most cases, as long as the forms have been securely positioned and the joints have been filled correctly, joint cracks are unlikely to appear. However, if cracks do appear, and are not repaired by refilling and painting, it is worth lining the arch with lining paper, thus covering any hairline cracks should they try to reappear in the surface. This technique can only be used to cover small cracks, however—anything larger suggests that the arch forms have not been fitted correctly, and in this case it may be necessary to begin the fitting procedure again from the beginning.

Arches add shape to rooms and soften edges, producing a relaxed and comfortable atmosphere. They also help to link decoration between two living areas.

closing up a doorway—1

When a doorway needs to be blocked up, the first consideration is whether the wall itself is of a solid block or brick construction (shown below), or is composed of a stud framework. In either case, the project will always be much easier to complete if you use similar materials to those that were used in the construction of the rest of the wall, because the dimensions of the materials will be the same.

tools for the job

- pry bar
- cordless drill/driver
- screwdriver
- hammer
- trowel
- level
- plastering trowel

1 The first task is to remove the door and frame from the entrance. The door may simply be unscrewed from its hinges, but the frame, or the door jamb, will almost certainly need to be pried away from the surrounding blockwork. A pry bar is the ideal tool for this purpose and should be able to pry the jamb away along with any fastenings.

2 The blocks that are inserted will require some form of tying in to the existing wall for strength and stability. There are a number of different frame tie designs, and the types used here require screwing into the blocks in the entrance. Drill a series of holes for the plugs at the mortar levels, so that the ties will be inserted at the same level for tying into the new mortar between the blocks used in the entrance.

3 Insert the plastic wall plug into the drilled hole and screw in the wall tie tight up to the collar. You may need to use some sort of lever mechanism to make the last few turns of the tie. Holding a screwdriver across and between the V-shape of the tie design and using it to rotate and lever the tie into position should produce a firm fastening.

4 Mix up and apply a bed of mortar along the floor between the two sides of the entrance. The mortar should be laid at about the block width and be generous enough to provide a good bedding for block placement.

5 Butter the end of the first block with mortar, giving it a good "cone"-shape coverage. Be fairly generous with the mortar, without applying too much of an excess so that it keeps falling off and away from the top of the block. Use a gauging trowel for this purpose, smoothing around the edge of the block to form good adhesion between the mortar and the block. This is also a good test to see if your mortar mix is of the correct consistency. It should hold a firm but pliable shape on top of the block.

filling the aperture

1 Remove door, door jamb and casing.

2 Build up blocks in the opening, using frame ties to tie them in with the surrounding blockwork or by removing blocks at alternate levels on either side of the opening so that new blocks are tied in with the existing wall structure.

3 Fill area between the top level of blocks and the lintel with bricks.

4 Apply plaster scratch coat.

5 Apply final plaster skim.

6 Fill in with missing section of baseboard or replace entire section of baseboard along length of wall.

7 Sand new plastered area and paint as required.

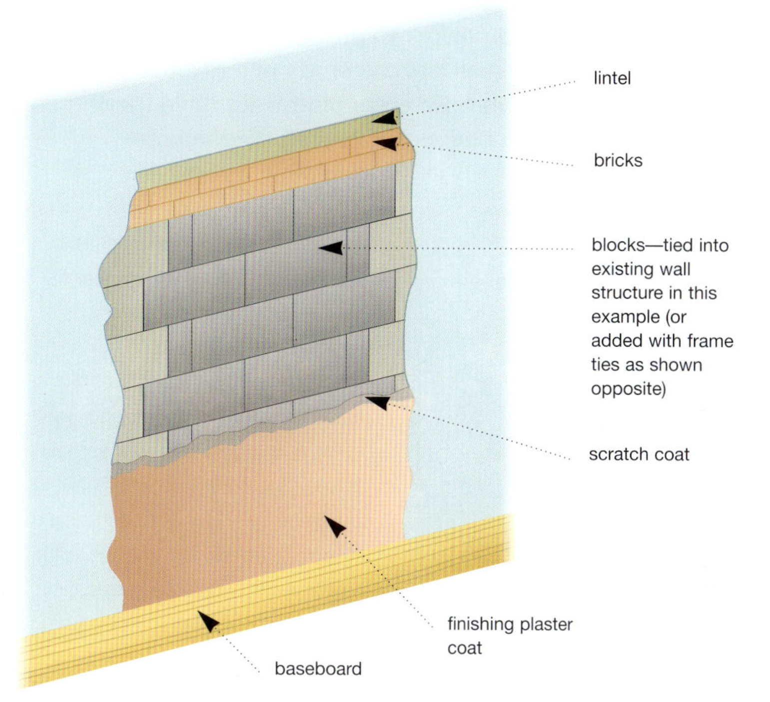

6 Position the block on the bed of mortar under the first frame tie, forcing the buttered end of the block tight up against the entrance surface. Use a spirit level to ensure the block is correctly positioned. Continue to build up levels until the entrance is filled. Remember to insert frame ties at each level to ensure that the new blockwork forms a strong bond with the existing wall. Also make sure that the vertical joints between successive levels of blockwork are staggered.

POINTS TO NOTE

• Frame tie alternatives

Instead of using frame ties, you could simply remove the first block on every other course. Then tie in new blocks, as they will be staggered into the old wall.

• Cutting blocks

Concrete blocks may either be cut with a stone cutter, which you will probably have to rent, or using a hand sledge and brick chisel. For either method, be sure to wear goggles for safety reasons.

• Wooden floors

When closing up an opening on a wooden floor, you will need to insert a wooden sole plate across the bottom of the entrance, which will help to provide a more rigid base, and build up your blockwork on top of this. Otherwise, the flexibility of a wooden floor may fracture the joints in the blockwork as you progress.

• Neat joints

Because of the weight of brick or block walls, it is unsafe—and typically a violation of building codes—to build these walls over a wood floor supported by a joist system. If working on the ground floor, brick or block walls must be built on a concrete footing. On the second story and above, the wall must be built over a steel lintel. In each case, existing wood flooring must be removed before building the wall.

• Improving the finish

However proficient your blockwork and plastering skills are, making a blocked-up entrance in a wall completely invisible after redecoration is a difficult task. Make sure that after plastering you undertake some fine filling and sanding along the joint between the new and old walls. You might also want to consider lining the wall before painting, as this will again make any joints less noticeable.

closing up a doorway—2

When closing up a doorway in a stud wall, the work becomes a case of filling in the wood and drywall or plasterboard framework to provide as flat a finish as possible. One of the most important considerations is making sure that the studs and drywall or plasterboard you use are of similar dimensions to the actual wall. Different stud walls have varying depths, depending on the house and its age, so check carefully before purchasing the materials.

tools for the job

- screwdriver
- pry bar
- hand saw
- cordless drill/driver
- hammer
- utility knife
- straightedge or level
- scraper
- drywall knife or plastering trowel

tips of the trade

Remember that when you fill in or close up an old entrance, it is likely that services will need rerouting. For example, light switches—which are normally found close to doorways—will look out of place once the opening has been closed up. You should therefore make the appropriate arrangements before starting the closing-up project, to have a professional move switches and any other services whose positions may require adjusting.

1 Unscrew the door from its hinges and remove it from the opening. Use a pry bar to pry the casing away from the wall surface. Take care not to allow the pry bar to dig into and damage the existing wall surface.

2 Once again use the pry bar to move the door jamb away from the studs. The ease with which the jamb comes away will depend upon whether it is fastened in position with nails or screws. If nails have been used, jamb removal tends to be a much easier procedure.

3 Fill in the missing section of sole plate by cutting a piece of stud to length and fitting it at the base of the entrance. Drill a pilot hole and screw it securely in position.

4 Cut a vertical length of stud to the height of the frame and secure it in position, again with screws. Add another length on the other side of the frame, and then a central stud running from the middle of the new section of sole plate up to the center of the header that was above the door frame.

5 Add extra rigidity to the three new studs by fitting blocks between each one. Angle screws through the blocks and into the vertical studs in order to provide extra strength. Nails may also be used for this purpose as long as they hold the blocks very securely in position.

6 Rather than using a large drywall or plasterboard sheet, which would require accurate cutting to fit into the framework opening, use smaller sheets fitted horizontally. These are easier to handle and trim to size. Hold a sheet in position at the top of the opening and mark the cutting requirement using a pencil.

7 Lay the sheet flat on the floor and use a utility knife to score a line in the sheet between the pencil guidelines. A level provides an excellent straightedge to guide the blade of the knife. Once scored, turn the sheet over and snap it upward to break it along the scored line.

8 Place the cut sheet back in the opening and carefully nail it into position. Continue to measure and fit more sheets until the opening is filled. Carry out the same procedure on the other side of the wall—you may wish to fill the void with insulation before this second part of the process. If you do choose to insulate the wall, remember to wear protective gloves and a rated insulator, as the insulation fibers may cause skin irritation.

9 Apply self-adhesive joint tape along all the joints, both between the sheets and the existing wall, and along the joint between each sheet. Smooth the tape to be sure there are no wrinkles.

10 If you have used drywall sheets, use a drywall knife to push joint compound into the joints, then smooth the compound with a damp sponge. Apply a broad, even band of compound over the surface of the joints, then sand lightly when dry. Repeat this procedure on the other side of the wall. If you have used plasterboard sheets, fill along all the taped joints with some bonding plaster to provide a good base for the plaster. Once this has dried, apply a skim of finishing plaster to the whole area, feathering a joint with the existing wall surface. Repeat this procedure on the other side of the wall. Once all the drywall finish or plaster has dried, the missing baseboard can be replaced and the walls painted.

PREPARING TO DECORATE

To achieve a good finish and make the closed-up area as invisible as possible, there are a few final procedures that will improve its effect.

- **Fine sanding**—Although a standard procedure for preparation, sanding is even more vital when trying to blend in an old doorway. The application of some fine filler, followed by more sanding, will improve the smooth nature of the final finish. Always wear a safety mask to avoid inhaling hazardous dust.

- **Closed doorway painting**—When painting a stud wall, even if you are using a color identical to that of the rest of the wall, the old doorway will still show up. It is therefore best to prime the newly finished area, apply a first coat of finishing paint, and then apply the top coat over the entire stud wall. This may sound extravagant, but it does make such old doorways less noticeable in the overall finish.

- **Lining**—The best option is to line the entire wall after the old doorway has been closed up. The thickness of the lining paper (1000–1200 microns is ideal) helps to further smooth the wall surface and reduces the likelihood of the closed-up area remaining apparent. Once lined, all the walls may be painted.

building a glass-block wall

Glass blocks provide an unusual alternative to more traditional wall structures, and produce a highly decorative finish that adds character to any room surroundings. They cannot be used for structural support, but they do fulfill the majority of roles required by most walls and make ideal shower walls or room dividers. Extremely versatile, they can even be used to construct curves—thus adding further interest to a wall surface and providing attractive, translucent properties.

tools for the job

- torpedo level
- pencil
- nail and line
- hammer
- cordless drill
- gauging trowel
- sponge

1 Use a torpedo level and pencil to draw a plumb line on the wall surface, extending from ground level to the finished wall height. As with block walls (see pages 50–1), attach a string line at a height just below the top of where the first course of glass blocks will be, and where it will touch the face of the blocks. You may wish to hold a glass block in position to obtain the correct height and position measurements. Secure the line in the corresponding position on the opposite wall.

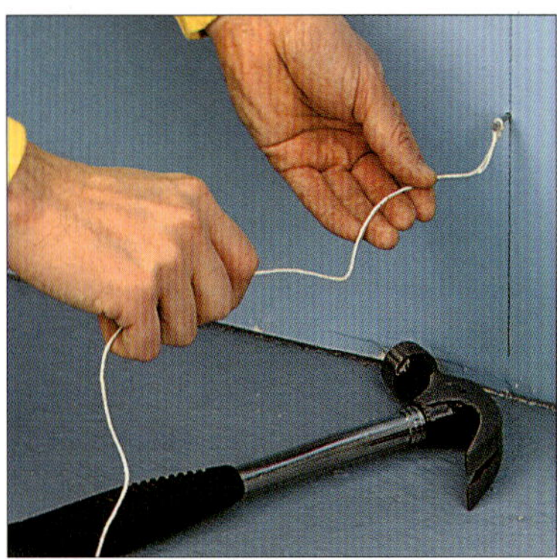

2 To add strength to the finished wall, it will be necessary to build a rigid steel framework inside the glass block structure. These steel rods need to be positioned every four to five courses (depending on the manufacturer's guidelines). In order to get the bottom course position for these rods, hold a block "dry" in position at the base of the wall—on top of spacers—to ensure that it is at the correct height. Hold a steel rod on top of the block and mark the position at which it touches the wall surface.

3 Remove the block, spacers, and rod, and drill into the wall surface at the marked-off point. Measure the area required for the block and spacer, and mark off further points at which the rods will be inserted. Drill these holes at this stage, rather than leaving them until later.

4 Mix up mortar as recommended by the manufacturer. (White cement produces a more pleasing finish with translucent bricks than the other, traditional types of mortar.) Use the spacers to position a block. Remove the brick and apply mortar to the area between the spacers.

5 Take a glass block and butter one side with some mortar, ensuring a good, even coverage, while trying to keep the mortar off the glass faces of the block.

6 Position the block back on the spacers so that the buttered end is against the wall, with the adjacent edge bedding down into the mortar

on the floor level. Ensure that the block is level and vertical using the spacers—the block should rest against the edge of each spacer.

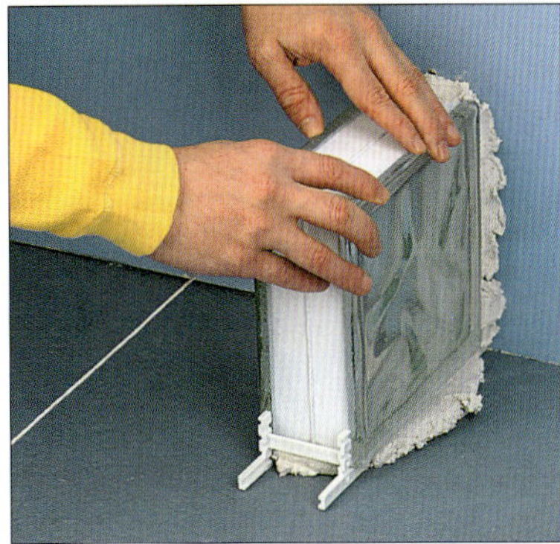

7 Position spacers and add blocks until the entire first course is complete. Use a torpedo level to ensure that the block positions are precise. The top edge of each block should also rest against the string line. Insert a steel rod into the predrilled hole at the top of the first course of blocks.

8 Add courses in this way until the wall is complete. Remove the face plates of the spacers.

9 Once the blocks have dried out, they can be grouted using a similar mortar mix as used for the building process. Work mortar into any gaps in the joints and smooth to a finish with a clean, damp sponge. The blocks will need wiping over several times to remove all mortar residue and leave a clean, bright glass-block surface. If the wall is to be used in a shower stall, use waterproof tiling grout, and seal the edge of the wall with silicone sealant.

wooden floors

When building on wooden floors, fix a wooden sole plate to the floor to act as the base for the block wall. Ensure that the wood is the same width as the glass blocks.

spacers

The spacers provided with glass block walls are designed so that they can be adapted to make both T and L shapes, and therefore deal with all requirements in a block wall construction. Simply snap off the parts of the spacer that you do not require.

Glass-block walls make a very distinctive feature, helping to lighten rooms and creating an attractive, decorative finish.

opening up an unused fireplace

If your house has a fireplace that was blocked off the last time fireplaces went out of fashion, reinstating it is a relatively straightforward job. The amount of work involved depends on how the fireplace opening was blocked off, and on whether the old fireback was removed or left in position. Opening up a fireplace is very messy, so remember to roll back the carpet and put down a drop cloth before you begin work.

removing the filling

Tap the face of the chimney breast to discover if the filling is solid or hollow. Pry away the baseboard across the face of the chimney breast, saving it for later reinstatement at either side of your new fireplace. There should be an air brick or ventilator in the face of the chimney breast to ventilate the flue. Start work by removing this—remove a masonry brick from a solid filling, and unscrew a metal or plastic passive ventilator from a board filling. Then shine in a torch to see if the old fireback is still in place. If it is, you will only have some making good to do once the recess is reopened. If it is not, you will have to buy and fit a replacement, or get a builder to do the job for you.

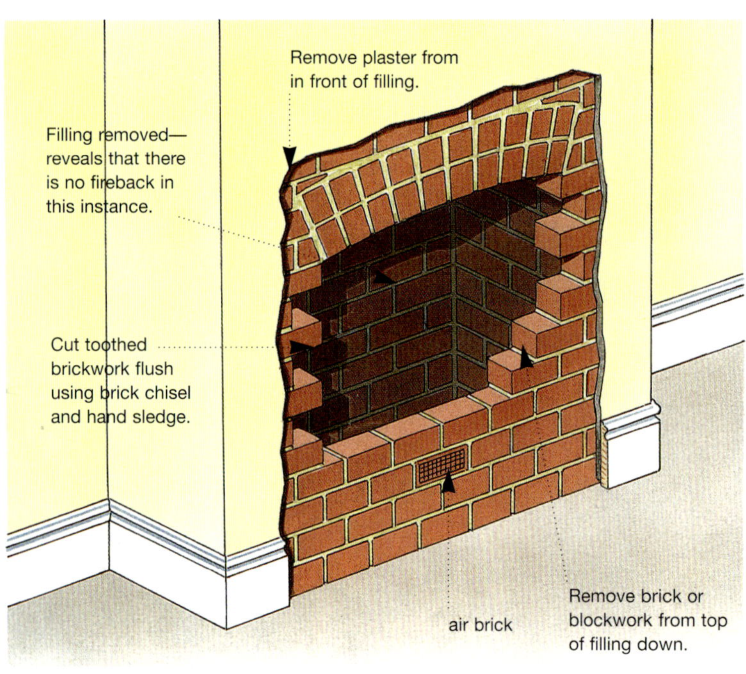

1 With masonry filling, remove the plaster at baseboard level, working from the center of the chimney breast out. This will reveal the edges of the filling.

2 Remove plaster up the sides of the filling until you reach the top, where the filling will have been butted up against the lintel spanning the original fireplace opening.

3 If there was no air brick to break out earlier, remove a filling brick or block at one top corner of the filling. Chisel out its mortar joints after drilling a series of almost-overlapping holes into them with a drill and masonry drill bit, and pry it out.

4 Work across and down the filling, remove one brick or block at a time. If the fireback is still present, take care not to knock pieces of masonry in against it or you might crack it. Clear away the rubble as you proceed.

5 If filling bricks have been toothed (bonded) into the masonry at each side of the opening, cut them flush with the original brickwork with a sharp downward blow using a brick chisel and hand sledge.

REMOVING BOARD FILLING

With board filling, make a test drilling to see if drywall, plasterboard, or a manufactured wood board has been used. If it is drywall or plasterboard and there was no air vent to remove, make a hole in the center of the panel with a hammer and simply pull the pieces of drywall or plasterboard away. If plywood or another type of board was used, insert a keyhole saw or power jigsaw blade into the drilled hole and cut out toward the edges of the filling. Pry the cut sections of board away. Then look to see how the supporting framework of furring strips has been attached to the edges of the recess, and undo any screws you can locate. If there are no screws to be found, you can assume that masonry nails have been used, and then pry the battens away carefully with a pry bar.

replacing the fireback

If the original fireback remains, you may have to patch it up in places. If it is missing, you will obviously have to buy a replacement one and install it. Start by measuring the width of the opening and order a new fireback to fit the space. Standard fireback widths tend to be 16 and 18in, but larger sizes are available if you want a more impressive fireplace. You will also need some lightweight mortar (made with vermiculite and lime), some corrugated cardboard, fireproof rope, brick rubble (use the filling you removed earlier), and fire cement.

PATCHING UP AN OLD FIREBACK

If an existing fireback is sound but cracked, you can repair it with fire cement. Let the fireback cool for a couple of days if it has had a real fire in it. Brush off soot with a wire brush and rake out the cracks with an old screwdriver, undercutting the edges. Wet the cracks to help the cement to stick, then fill them flush with fire cement. Smooth the filler with a wet paintbrush, and allow it to harden for several days before relighting the fire.

safety advice

Wear safety gloves, goggles, and a face mask when removing filling to prevent dust inhalation and injuries from flying debris. This is particularly important when working with masonry filling. It is also a good idea to enlist advice from a professional builder if you intend to have a real or fuel-effect fire installed, to ensure that the flue is sound and safe to use.

1 Separate the two halves of the fireback by tapping along the recessed cutting line with a hand sledge and brick chisel.

2 Mix some mortar using four parts vermiculite (a lightweight granular insulation material) and lime, and place a bed of it where the base of the fireback will sit. Set the fireback in place, then pull it forward and trap lengths of fireproof rope between it and the edge of the fireplace opening.

3 Cut two strips of corrugated cardboard to match the height of the fireback and place them behind it, held in place with dabs of mortar. This will burn away when the fire is lit, to leave an essential expansion gap behind the fireback. Then fill the space behind the fireback with mortar, bulked out with broken brick—you can use the remains of the masonry filling for this.

4 Bed some mortar on top of the lower half of the fireback and stand the top half in place on it. Neaten the joint and carry on filling behind the fireback.

5 Once the filling is level with the top of the fireback, add more mortar to form a slope up to the rear face of the flue. This forms a narrow throat that draws the smoke from the fire up into the flue.

6 Use fire cement to seal the edges of the new fireback to the fire surround, and to cover the fireproof rope.

blocking off a fireplace

Houses built before central heating became commonplace had a fireplace in every room. Today, even fireplace lovers are often happy with just a feature fireplace in the living room and may want to block off any remaining fireplaces in other rooms. However you decide to tackle this job, the one vital requirement is that the flue remains ventilated. Otherwise, condensation can form within it, soak into the chimney breast brickwork, and eventually surface to ruin your decoration.

Before beginning any work, you have several decisions to make if you plan to fill in an old fireplace. The first concerns whether to strip out the old fireback and empty the fireplace recess, or whether to leave it in place. The former option is the better choice if you are certain the fireplace will never be used again, but it will make a lot of mess. The second decision concerns how to block off the opening. You can fill it with brick or blockwork, or panel it with drywall or plasterboard supported on a timber frame. Again, the former is the more professional option, the latter the quicker one.

tools for the job

- safety goggles & dust mask
- gloves
- hand sledge
- brick chisel
- pry bar
- screwdriver
- hawk
- bricklaying trowel
- plastering trowel
- utility knife
- shovel

1 Use a brick chisel and hand sledge to break the mortar bond between the raised hearth slab and the floor-level constructional hearth beneath it. Pry it up with a pry bar and get help to lift and remove it, as it is too heavy to lift on your own. Then put down drop cloths in front of the fireplace opening.

2 Use a brick chisel and hand sledge to remove the plaster at the sides of the old fire surround to expose any fastenings. Undo them if you can with a screwdriver, using some penetrating oil to free rusty threads. Pry away the stubs of baseboard at either side of the surround, and save them as samples so that you can buy a matching length to cover the face of the new chimney breast surround when you have finished.

3 Insert the end of the pry bar between the surround and the chimney breast, first at one side and then at the other, and pry it away from the wall. Again, enlist help to prevent the surround from toppling forwards and to lift and carry it away. Remove the grate if it is still in place.

4 Smash the old fireback with a brick chisel and hand sledge. Wear safety goggles and a dust mask to protect yourself from dust and any flying rubble. Lift out the sections of fireclay as you break them up, and put them straight into strong garbage sacks. Soak the fireproof rope around the perimeter of the opening with water to prevent asbestos fibers from getting into the air, cut it away with a utility knife, and put it in a garbage bag. Seal it, label it "asbestos waste," and contact a local health department for advice on disposing of it safely.

safety advice

Asbestos is a fibrous substance that can be woven with other materials to produce items that are highly heat-resistant and have excellent insulation properties. However, it is a highly carcinogenic substance and the safety guidelines outlined in step 4 must be followed stringently. Never take risks when working with asbestos.

5 If the filling behind the fireback is a solid mass of mortar and broken bricks, break it up bit by bit with a brick chisel and hand sledge. If it is loose rubble, simply shovel it out of the recess. Bag up all the rubble, and remove it from the site to leave the fireplace recess empty. Use a vacuum sweeper to remove as much dust from the area as possible.

6 Use bricks or lightweight blocks to create a solid filling across the opening of the fireplace. Spread a line of mortar across the hearth, and embed the first course in place. Cut the last brick or block to fit the space

as necessary, and use the scrap to start the next course so that the studs will be staggered. (Refer to pages 62–5 for detailed information on blocking up an opening.)

7 Include a terra-cotta air brick in one of the first few courses of bricks to ensure that the flue will be ventilated. Complete the filling, cutting bricks or blocks to size as necessary to fit the final course beneath the lintel that bridges the opening. Use mortar to fill any irregular gaps at the top of the space, and neaten the pointing.

8 Apply a base coat of plaster over the filling, recessing it by about ⅛in to allow for the finish coat, and key it with a series of crisscross strokes with the edge of a plastering trowel. Allow it to set hard, then trowel on the finish coat flush with the surrounding plaster. Polish it smooth with a wet trowel. Allow it to dry thoroughly before you redecorate it. Finally, cut and fit a new length of baseboard to the face of the chimney breast.

PANELING THE OPENING

You may find it easier to fill the opening with drywall or plasterboard after stripping out the fireback rather than block or brickwork. If so, cut four pieces of 1 x 2in softwood strip to fit the space. Glue and nail the top piece to the top ends of the two side pieces—you cannot nail it up into the lintel to fix it in place. Then secure the side pieces to the inner edge of the opening with masonry nails, and add the fourth strip across the hearth. Set the face of the strip back by ½in so that the drywall or plasterboard plus a skim coat of plaster will end up flush with the surrounding plaster. Cut a hole in the drywall or plasterboard with a keyhole saw that is of the appropriate size to insert a passive ventilator, then fix the drywall or plasterboard to the strips with galvanized drywall or plasterboard nails. Apply the finish plaster, then fit the ventilator when it has set hard.

tips of the trade

- **Capping the flue**—If the flue has an open pot at the top, it is a good idea to have it capped to stop rainwater from entering the flue. The simplest way of doing this is to fit a clay or metal hood top or flue vent into the top of the pot. Tackle this yourself only if you are happy working at height and can set up a ladder easily to reach the top of the chimney stack. Otherwise, call in a builder to fit it for you. Although the job itself is a straightforward one, it is not worth taking the risk of doing it yourself if you are inexperienced, and especially if you do not have the appropriate ladder and safety equipment for roof work.
- **Sweeping the flue**—If the fireplace was used regularly in the past, make sure that you remember to have it swept to remove all the soot that will have built up in the flue before you block up the fireplace opening. Doing this will minimize the risk of staining occurring on the face of the chimney breast in future if condensation forms in the flue.

installing a faux fireplace

Fireplaces have always had a dual function—in addition to providing heat, they provide a focal point and therefore contribute decoratively to the room as a whole. The advent of central heating meant that many fireplaces were blocked up, but they are now enjoying a revival. Solid-fuel and gas fires require professional installation, but building a fireplace for aesthetic or ornamental purposes is relatively straightforward.

fitting a surround

This fireplace was made from pieces of marble and wood from various sources. Marble is a heavy stone, so make sure that your subfloor can handle the weight. (It should be at least 1 1/8in thick.) Marble is a fragile material that can shatter easily, so provide plenty of support while it is being positioned, and while the mortar is drying. The surround is made from stained softwood.

tools for the job

- pencil & tape measure
- gauging trowel
- sponge
- level
- pointing trowel
- screwdriver
- caulk gun
- sponge

1 Having chosen your location for the fireplace, mark its central position on the wall surface.

2 Measure from the marked point on the wall surface and draw in the dimensions of the hearth on the floor. Use a gauging trowel to apply a number of mounds of mortar within the confines of this hearth guideline. Make sure the mounds are of a consistent size, so that when the hearth is positioned, it will bed down as evenly as possible.

3 Lift the hearth into place and check that it is centered on the wall mark with a tape measure. Allow the hearth to bed down into the mortar. Check for any mortar squeezing out from under the hearth edges and remove with a clean, damp sponge before it dries.

4 Use a level to check the hearth positioning across all dimensions—side to side, front to back and diagonally—as it will not be possible to make adjustments later.

5 Add mounds of mortar to the back panel and position it centrally on the hearth. Allow the panel to secure to the wall, but do not press it finally into position. Check it is sitting plumb by using a level.

6 Carefully lift the fire surround into position, pushing the back panel onto the wall until the surround is flush against the wall surface. This will also help to force the back panel into its correct position.

7 Remove the fire surround and seal around the edges of the back panel using some more mortar (a pointing trowel is ideal for this process). However, take care not to get any mortar on the marble face—if this happens, remove it immediately with a clean, damp sponge before it dries.

8 Reposition the fire surround on the back panel. Secure it in place using glass plate fastenings, which will help it to sit level on the wall surface. Attach the fastenings under the mantel shelf so that they will not be too conspicuous.

9 Finally, attach the internal brass surround to the back panel with some silicone sealant. The surround can be pressed into position by hand. Before it sets, be sure to remove any excess silicone that squeezes out with a dry cloth.

MORTAR CHOICE

Mortar made from white cement is ideal for marble fireplaces because of its aesthetic qualities. Fireplaces may also be positioned using bonding coat plaster, but when using light-colored marble, bear in mind that marble can stain easily. Also, some marble types have transparent characteristics which will mean that the fixing material may be visible in places. For this reason, a light-colored mortar is best as it should be less noticeable than many of the darker types. Modified white marble mortar has latex added for better performance and is available from home-improvement outlets.

Once blended into the rest of the decoration, a faux fireplace can make a stunning impact on the look and feel of a room. Painting the internal "fireplace" matte black creates the impression of an authentic old fire instead of a newly installed reproduction.

altering the structure of a ceiling

When redesigning a room layout or planning a new color scheme, it can be common to neglect ceilings or assume that their finish will be led by other design elements in the room. However, this does not have to be the case, and entering any renovation project should include close consideration of ceiling improvements and potential alterations. Therefore, appropriate heights, soundproofing, access, and insulatory properties are all considered in this chapter, together with ideas for finishing.

Different patterns and designs make suspended ceilings an unusual alternative to traditional ceiling finishes.

lowering a ceiling—1

The most common reasons for lowering a ceiling are to install new ductwork or plumbing, or to reduce the height of a room for decorative or soundproofing purposes. High ceilings are most common in older properties, but ceiling levels can be adjusted in any room—regardless of age—provided the practicalities of head clearance and final appearance are considered. This is a two-part process: the first step is to construct a framework for the plasterboard or drywall.

making the frame

Before focusing on the ceiling itself, it is important to consider the existing wall construction. The new ceiling will be supported primarily by fastenings to the walls in the room, and so the strength of these fastenings is vital. For solid block walls, concrete anchors or frame fasteners can be used with confidence, because the strength of the fastener will be consistent on all wall areas. If you are fastening to stud walls, however, it will be necessary to locate the studs before you begin. Wall plates can then be fastened directly into the studs, rather than the surrounding, weaker plasterboard or drywall. Joist hangers, brackets used to support the ends of joists, are recommended for all applications.

ensuring accuracy

Taking extra time to ensure accurate measurements, and that the joists are correctly aligned, will be highly beneficial when it comes to applying plasterboard or drywall to the framework. Even small discrepancies between joist levels will be accentuated once the panels have been applied. It is also vital that the joists are not fixed in the hangers in a twisted position. Otherwise, when panels are applied they will not fit flush against the bottom of the joist, resulting in weak fastenings along the entire joist length.

joists set at 2ft centers

joist hangers hold joists in place

joists span shortest dimension of room

tools for the job

- tape measure
- pencil
- level
- hand saw
- cordless drill/driver
- hammer

1 Having decided how far you need to lower the ceiling level, for whatever purpose, use a pencil and level to mark out a guideline around the entire perimeter of the room. Never simply measure the distance at different points and join them together, as slight variations in most ceiling surfaces mean that these measurements do not provide a true level. It is a better working procedure to mark off height at one point and use that to draw your guideline.

tips of the trade

Modern ceilings are normally 8ft high, and manufacturers make most building boards according to these dimensions. This is a good guideline to follow when you come to deciding on the height to set your ceiling. The joists used for the frame shown on these pages are 2 x 4in, which is the minimum that should be used in such cases.

For ceiling spans that are greater than 6ft, joists should be 2 x 6in or even wider still. Plasterboard and drywall thickness can affect the positions of joists. When you are using standard drywall, aim to position the joists in position at 16in or 24in intervals.

2 Fix lengths of 2 x 4in framing to each wall width dimension. Fasten with the bottom edge of each plate running precisely along the pencil guideline. In this example, the wall plates are being attached with concrete anchors because the walls are solid-block construction. If you are attaching to stud walls, you will need to use a stud finder to find the studs and therefore the ideal positions for fastening the wall plates.

3 The joists for the frame should always span the room across its shortest dimension, so mark off 2ft intervals along the appropriate opposing wall plates, or whatever intervals you are using, to denote the position for the metal hangers, which will be used to support the joists.

4 At each marked-off point on the two wall plates, partially nail a hanger in place—leave it free enough to adjust when the joist is in place.

split-level ceilings

Some people choose split-level ceilings as an alternative to a complete ceiling level change. This is ideal for rooms in which high windows prevent the possibility of lowering the entire ceiling, or for people who want variation in the room height. The same basic system can be used to construct the frame, with some slight modifications to the main structure.

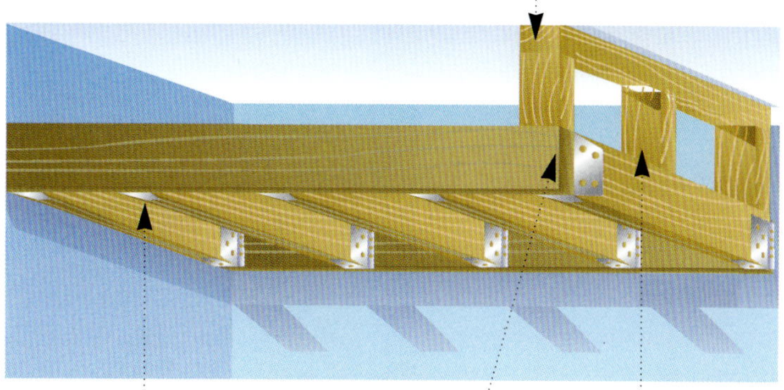

5 Cut joists to the exact size between the opposing wall plates, positioning the cut joist inside the hangers. First, use hanger nails to nail the hanger into the sides of the joist to clamp it in place. Then nail the hanger into the wall plate face for a secure, final fastening. Continue to attach joists to hangers across the rest of the ceiling framework.

6 For extra rigidity, add blocking between joists. The blocking should be staggered on either side of the midline of the joists. The ceiling is now ready for fixing plasterboard or drywall.

lowering a ceiling—2

Once the frame of your lowered ceiling is in place, plasterboard or drywall needs to be fixed in position, before plastering or finishing can begin. Large sheets of plasterboard or drywall can be difficult to handle (see below) but lath is an ideal option since it comes in smaller sheets. This is also the point at which additional features, such as soundproofing or lighting fixtures, should be considered. All of these tasks are quite straightforward, provided you plan ahead.

PLASTERBOARD/DRYWALL

If you are using regular-sized plasterboard or drywall, you will need help lifting and maneuvering the boards. Nail plasterboard sheets at 6in intervals along all the joists, and drywall at 12in intervals. The joints between each sheet should be made halfway across the width of the joists. This will ensure that the edges of two sheets join along a single joist.

plasterboarding with lath

Lath is much smaller and easier to handle than large sheets of plasterboard, which makes it better for maneuvering and enables you to work alone. Lath is also ideal to use when joists are set at 2ft centers, because the sheets of lath tend to be supplied in 2 x 4ft dimensions, which means that lath does not require cutting, except for around the perimeter of the ceiling.

tools for the job

- hammer
- screwdriver (optional)
- hand saw
- protective gloves

1 Starting in one corner of the room, attach a single lath across three ceiling joists. Plasterboard nails are ideal for this process, or alternately, drywall screws can be used.

2 Continue to add lath to the joists, staggering the joints so as to create a brick bond pattern. This means that as you reach the perimeter of the ceiling, you will need to measure and cut lath to fill the various gaps.

soundproofing

Lowering a ceiling also provides the perfect opportunity to add some soundproofing to the room. By inserting sound insulation into the ceiling space before plasterboarding or drywalling, you can make a substantial difference to the amount of noise audible from the room above. (An alternative soundproofing technique is shown on pages 82–3, where lowering the ceiling level is not an option.)

1 Weave 2 x 4 x 4in insulation between the top of the joists and the existing ceiling. If you have not been able to bring the ceiling down this far, use sound insulation of the same size but with a 2in depth instead of 4in. Rest the batts in position, so that they are loosely joined but wedged securely above each joist.

2 Nail plasterboard or drywall sheets to the ceiling (see box). Bear in mind that it is important to use large sheets in this case, rather than

lath, as the fewer the joints, the greater the soundproofing effect. Then apply a second layer of plasterboard or drywall (see step 5 page 82).

fixture canopies

safety advice

Before beginning any work on or around the fixture canopy, turn off the power at the main panel, and place a strip of tape over the tripped breaker/fuse to prevent anyone from turning it on.

Ceilings tend not to have too many obstacles, and therefore lowering one can be a fairly trouble-free task. The main exception is a fixture canopy, which needs to be adjusted or lengthened in order to be of use for the new ceiling level. This work should be carried out after the new joists have been positioned, but before drywalling has begun.

tools for the job

- screwdrivers (various)
- cordless drill
- hammer
- pencil
- tape measure

1 Unscrew the fixture canopy by hand, allowing the cover to slide down the wire to the fitting itself.

2 Unscrew the retaining screws that are keeping the canopy secured to the old ceiling. Put the screws safely to one side as they will be needed again later.

3 Release the electrical wires from the canopy by unscrewing the relevant terminals, allowing the wires to drop free. The pendant should now be separate from the electrical cable, and can be put to one side.

4 Use insulation tape to tape up each wire in the electrical supply cable. Ensure that each wire is completely separated from the others.

tips of the trade

It may be worth changing light fittings for recessed spotlights, which will generally be less intrusive. However, always consult a qualified electrician before starting work.

5 Drywall the ceiling until you come to a point where the old electrical cable is about to be covered. Drill through the drywall directly below the cable, using a bit that is wide enough to accommodate the cable.

6 Pull the cable through the hole before continuing to apply drywall across the rest of the ceiling. If the cable is too tight in its original position and does not have the required excess to pull down to the new ceiling level, it will be necessary to add some extra cable to the existing one, joined with a junction box. Once the ceiling has been plasterboarded or drywalled, the fixture can be reconnected.

building a suspended ceiling

Suspended ceilings are traditionally linked with offices and commercial buildings. However, such ceiling structures are becoming increasingly popular in private dwellings. They are an ideal option for lowering ceilings, and require less structural work than alterations using joists and plasterboard or drywall. The tiles provided for suspended ceilings also tend to have both thermal and sound-insulating properties, and therefore make a useful alternative to traditional ceilings.

The construction of a suspended ceiling is a straightforward exercise so long as sufficient planning time has been allowed. It is worth drawing a scale diagram of the room in order to work out tile positioning and thus the ideal location for the main tees in the framework (see diagram below).

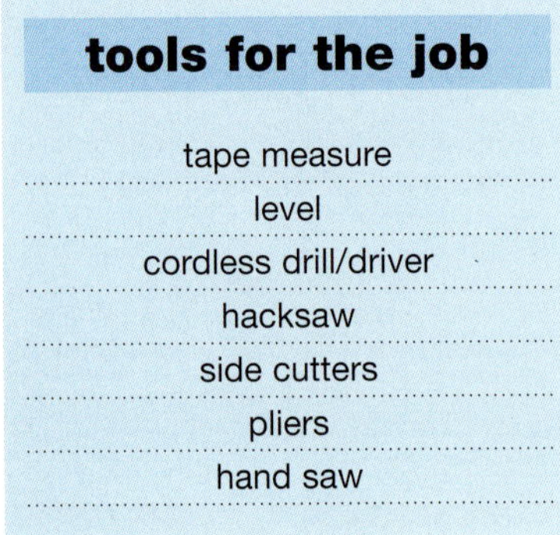

tools for the job

- tape measure
- level
- cordless drill/driver
- hacksaw
- side cutters
- pliers
- hand saw

1 Draw a level pencil line around the perimeter walls at the suspended ceiling height. Fix wall angle sections along this line at 1ft 4in intervals. Attaching to solid block walls should be quite easy but you will need to follow the stud pattern (see page 76) on stud walls.

2 Fix angle brackets into the existing ceiling at measured intervals above the position where the main tees will be.

3 Cut a section of hanger wire to a manageable length for working—6–10ft is suitable—and secure one end to a heavy object such as a workbench. Push the other end of the wire into a cordless drill and tighten the chuck until it is held securely in position. Slowly start the drill, causing the wire gradually to tighten until it is completely rigid. This will ensure that the wire has no slack and will make a rigid support when joined between the tees and the ceiling.

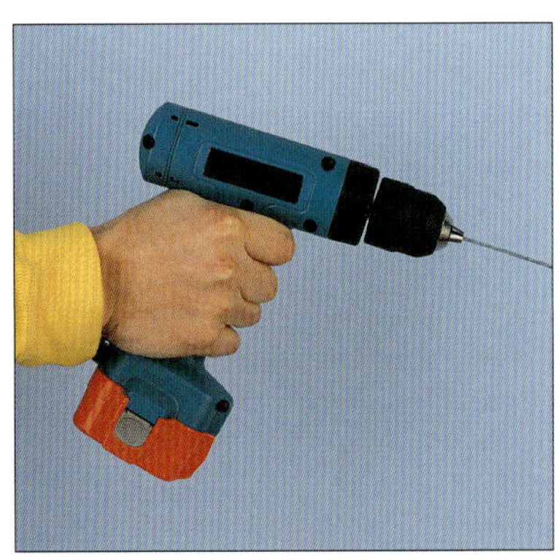

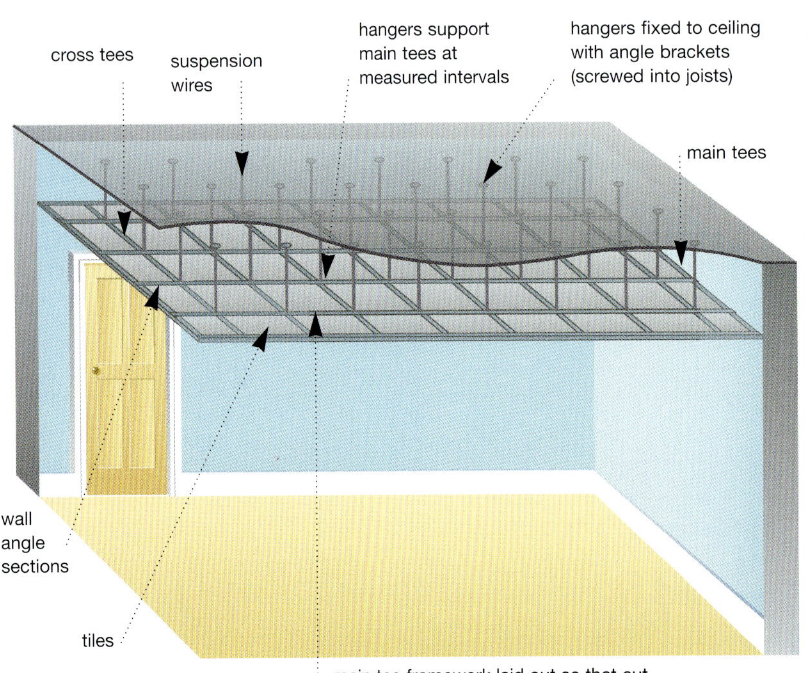

4 Use side cutters to cut the wire down to the required lengths. Allow an excess of 4in at each end of the length for attaching to the main tees and angle brackets.

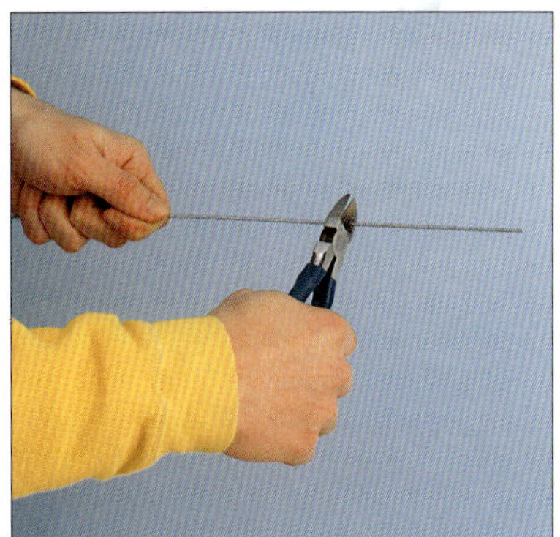

5 At each angle bracket, thread a section of wire through the bracket hole and tighten it in position by wrapping the end of the wire on to the main vertical section with pliers.

6 Position the main tees on the angle sections. Thread the end of the hanger wires through the appropriate holes and wind the ends back on to the vertical length.

7 Fit the smaller cross tees in position, at the appropriate intervals between the main tees. The intervals should correspond to the tile dimensions.

8 Simply drop the tiles in place, feeding them above the suspended ceiling level first and then lowering them into position between the tees. There is no particular insertion order, but it is always best to position the full tiles first before working around the edges. (The edge tiles may be cut using a back saw or utility knife before they are fitted in place.) Some manufacturers provide clips that fit on top of the tees to hold the tiles down in position.

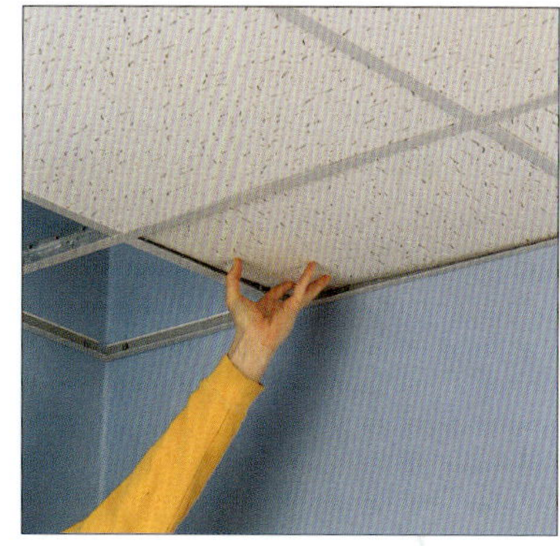

tips of the trade

Main tees need to be cut so that they can fit precisely between the angle sections on opposing walls. Mark off the length requirement on the tee, and cut using a hacksaw.

Different patterns and designs make suspended ceilings an unusual alternative to traditional ceiling finishes.

soundproofing a ceiling

If you are unable to combine soundproofing with lowering a ceiling (see page 78) it may be necessary to use other techniques for minimizing sound. One method is to lift the floor above and soundproof from above the ceiling in question. Alternatively, it is possible to work from below, taking the existing ceiling down and starting from scratch.

working from below

Soundproofing from below requires the removal of the old plasterboard or drywall. Once you have broken through the first piece, the task becomes a straightforward case of removing sections and sheets with a hammer or pry bar.

tools for the job

- claw hammer
- pry bar
- cordless drill
- protective gloves

1 Carefully remove the old ceiling with a pry bar. Then check between the joists for the presence of wiring or plumbing. Remove any remaining nails with a claw hammer—all joists must be free from obstructions before work begins so that new fasteners can be inserted.

2 Starting on one side of the ceiling, attach resilient channel across the joists at 1ft 4in intervals. Attach the bars in place using drywall screws, ensuring that the screws are inserted into the joist.

3 Place soundproofing insulation above the resilient channel and between the joists. Try to ensure that the insulation meets and joins above the channel. Continue to position insulation until the whole area is covered. Wear protective gloves for this process, as the fibers in the slabs can cause skin irritation.

4 Hang ½in plasterboard or drywall sheets to the ceiling using drywall screws. Fix the screws through the sheets and into the resilient channel at intervals. Allow the screws to bite sufficiently to hold the sheets securely in place, but without the screwhead breaking into the surface and creating a weak installation.

5 Attach ⅜in plasterboard or drywall sheets over the first layer of plasterboard, staggering joints so that none of the second layer joints correspond with the first. Longer drywall screws will be required to penetrate both layers and attach into the resilient channel. The ceiling may now be finished or plastered in the usual way.

tips of the trade

Cove molding is a useful way to introduce an additional soundproofing seal around the edge of the ceiling (see pages 100–1).

working from above

If possible, working from above a ceiling is an easier option for adding sound insulation. Although this involves lifting a floor in order to gain access to the ceiling space, it tends to be less messy than taking a whole ceiling down. Sound insulation is therefore slotted between joists from above, before the floor is relaid. However, where joist depth or the ceiling space is particularly large, sand may be combined with sound insulation slabs to create a more effective soundproofing system.

tools for the job

- brick chisel
- back saw
- hammer
- cordless drill/driver
- dust mask
- protective gloves

1 Strip the floor back to the subfloor and remove the boards using a brick chisel or pry bar. Take care not to damage any of the boards, as they will be repositioned once soundproofing is complete.

2 Cut sections of 1 x 2in wood strip with a back saw. Attach the lengths in place along the bottom of the joists, just above the plasterboard or drywall ceiling.

3 Cut and install ½in plywood strips between the joists, attaching them by nailing through the plywood and into the strips.

4 Line the face of the plywood with a plastic membrane sheet. Tuck the membrane into the corners and allow it to encroach up to the top of the floor joists. Nail in position only at the top of the joists.

5 Carefully pour kiln-dried sand onto the plywood between each joist, spreading out the sand into a layer about 2in deep. A small piece of wood strip cut to the width of the

space between the joists makes an ideal tool for spreading the sand across the area, and will produce a consistent level.

6 Fit sound insulation in between the joists and on top of the sand. The insulation may need to be cut to fit—use a back saw and wear a dust mask when cutting. Protective gloves should also be worn when installing the insulation. Finally, replace the subfloor—using a thick padding and good-quality carpet will also add to the overall effect of the soundproofing.

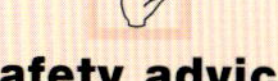

safety advice

Remember that sand adds a great deal of weight to the ceiling, so check with a structural engineer that your ceiling will be able to cope with the load. Furthermore, this technique should not be used in ceilings containing water pipes. Any small leaks soaking into the sand over time will increase the weight further and could result in ceiling collapse.

insulating a ceiling

Trying to make your home as energy-efficient as possible provides benefits on a financial level and contributes towards protecting the environment. One of the simplest ways to increase energy efficiency is to ensure that you have adequate attic insulation. This is easy to install, but requires some thought about how to deal with any obstacles.

tips of the trade

When installing attic insulation, do not cover any ventilation access. Most roof spaces are ventilated through grills or openings in the attic, or at the junction between the roof and exterior walls. Covering these areas can lead to damp and condensation problems, so keep filling safely away from them.

blanket insulation

Blanket insulation is the most commonly used form of attic insulation material as it is the simplest to handle and can be laid very quickly. Roll-length measurements provided by the manufacturer make it easy to estimate the amount required. When measuring, be sure to choose rolls that are the same width (or slightly wider) than the joist bay in your attic. This will help to avoid extra cutting.

tools for the job

protective gloves & dust mask
utility knife

1 Roll out the insulation blanket between the joists. Do not compress it, because much of its effectiveness is provided by maintaining its depth. Carefully cut the insulation with a utility knife whenever a division is required.

2 Greater efficiency can be achieved by laying a second layer over, and at right angles to, the first. This technique obscures all the joists, so if you choose this option you may need to build access bridges in your attic.

loose-fill insulation

Loose-fill insulation offers an alternative to blankets. Although it can be used in most situations as a direct alternative, it is mainly used in attics where there are a number of awkward spaces to fill, making it a more practical option than blanket insulation. It is made of similar material to the blankets, but has been shredded into smaller pieces.

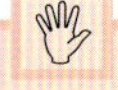

safety advice

Always wear gloves and a dust mask when handling attic insulation, as the fibers in its construction can be irritating to both skin and the respiratory system.

1 Pour the loose fill directly from the bag into the bays between the joists.

2 Use a piece of wood strip, cut to the same length as the width of the bay between the joists, to even the loose fill out in the joist bay.

tips of the trade

Just as ventilation inlets must be kept clear of insulation, recessed electricity fixtures must also be given clearance, so that they do not overheat. Cut around recessed fixtures, leaving plenty of clearance between the insulation material and the fixture.

3 Insulation must always be on top of obstacles rather than below, so make some cardboard bridges for plumbing, before covering over them with the loose fill.

attic access

Attic access panels must be movable, so it is not possible simply to install insulation over the top of them. However, insulation is still necessary if it is to be effective throughout.

tools for the job

- back saw
- hammer
- protective gloves
- dust mask

1 Cut four pieces of 1 x 6in dressed softwood to the dimensions of each side of the attic access. Nail them in position to create a shallow box.

2 Insert a section of blanket insulation inside the box. Loose fill insulation can be used.

3 Cut a piece of plywood to size, attach it to the top, and position the box as the access panel.

DEALING WITH PIPES

Pipes situated between and below joist level are best dealt with as shown left. However, pipes situated above the joists need another method of insulation.

Fit pipe insulation over and around any exposed pipes, butt-jointing sections as required.

Where a junction is required, miter the insulation so that a precise joint is achieved. Insulation can be cut using a utility knife or scissors.

insulating water tanks

The growing popularity of combination boilers means that modern houses are less likely to have attic-situated water tanks. However, some older houses still have water tanks that feed the various systems in the house. It is therefore important to ensure that the tank is insulated correctly.

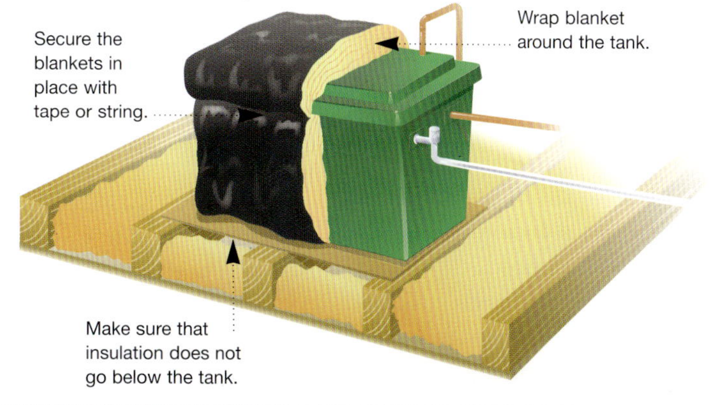

building an attic access panel

Many homeowners find the thought of converting their attics into extra rooms, or into special storage areas in order to free up other rooms, an attractive option. Most attics have some sort of access built into the design of the house, but renovation may make it necessary to install a proper access panel.

cutting in an access panel

tools for the job

- stud finder
- tape measure
- pencil
- level
- drywall saw
- back saw
- cordless drill/driver
- hammer

Before installing a new access panel, make all the necessary calculations and judgements about its position. If you wish to install a built-in, fold-up ladder, instead of using a stepladder, ensure that your chosen site has suitable provision for storing and/or supporting it. Also check to see what is directly above the proposed access panel, as all precautions must be taken to ensure that services will not be interfered with or disrupted.

The panel must be large enough to allow access for both yourself and any items that need to be passed through the opening. The structure of the ceiling is vital because some joists will have to be cut in order to make room for the access area. Note that this cutting technique can only be used through conventional framing, and not through trusses or engineered materials. It is advisable to seek professional advice before starting, in order to ensure that the ceiling structure will sustain an access panel. In older homes, where joist depth tends to be more substantial, this is rarely a problem. In newer homes joists tend to be thinner, and so you need to check the structural strength.

1 Use a stud finder to pinpoint the joist position on the ceiling. Mark out the proposed position of the panel, ensuring that two of the opposing sides are directly below the edges of two joists. In this way, it will only be necessary to cut through one central joist to create the opening.

2 Wearing a dust mask, use a drywall saw to cut around the pencil guideline. On the two sides of the square that run in the same direction as the joists above, try to rest the saw against the joists. This should help to achieve an exact cut to the precise joist width.

3 Having removed the plasterboard or drywall, use a back saw to cut out the central joist. This will now provide access through the hole and into the roof space. Trim back the cut joist (from above) a further 2in at either side of the panel, so that when blocking is inserted to create the opposing sides of the panel, it will be positioned back from the ceiling opening to supply a more rigid structure.

4 Use the back saw to cut blocking to size, and then screw the blocking in place to form the panel frame. In addition to attaching blocks centrally to the cut joists, it will also be necessary to fasten the corners. Angle screws through the blocking and into the joists at all four corners of the access panel frame with a cordless screwdriver.

5 Cut 1 x 6in dressed softwood to the inside dimensions of the opening. Fasten it in place by nailing or screwing directly through the lengths and into the joists and blocking. Make sure the bottom edge sits level with the ceiling to produce a smooth jamb upon which to attach the remaining features.

6 Cut a ⅜ x 1in stop to the inside dimensions of the jamb. Make a pencil guideline around the jamb, halfway up its height. Then nail the stop in place, so that the bottom edge sits precisely on the pencil guideline. This stop will act as the ledge upon which the finished access panel will rest.

7 Measure and cut casing to fit around the jamb. Allow the casing front edge to bisect the edge of the jamb, in order to create a neat and balanced finish.

8 Tighten the mitered joints of the casing by inserting additional nails at each corner, thus pulling the miter together.

9 Cut a sheet of medium-density fiberboard (MDF) or finish-grade plywood to the dimensions of the panel and drop it into place above the ledge created by the stop. This can now be primed and painted.

attic ladders

Access through an access panel can be made by means of a portable ladder or by a permanent, custom-designed ladder. Many manufacturers provide easy-to-install ladder systems, but make sure that your ladder is accessible and that the attic has enough clear storage capacity, without obstructing joists. If possible, choose your ladder design before building a panel, because many manufacturers stipulate particular dimensions and positioning in order to achieve the best access results.

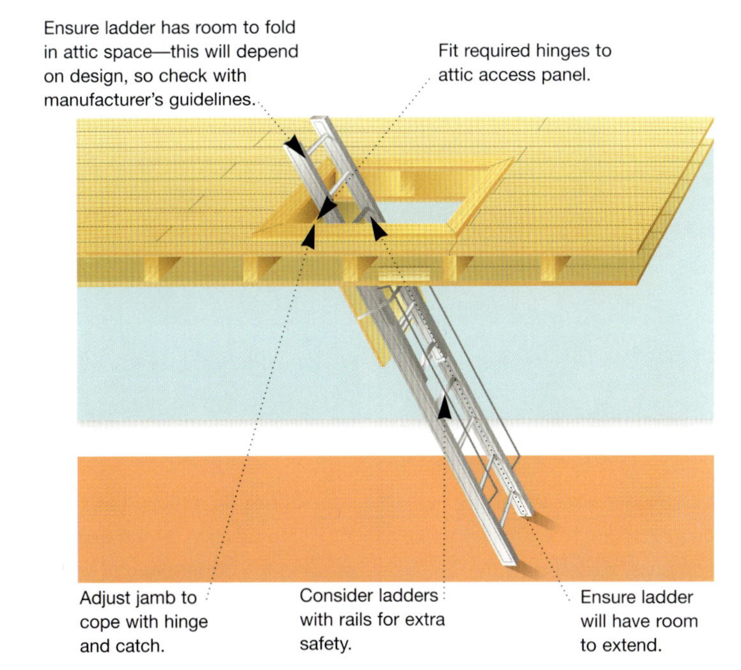

constructing a framed ceiling

Framed ceilings offer a purely decorative option to traditional ceiling structure. They can be useful when trying to lower a particularly high ceiling, and require less structural consideration than lowering the ceiling in its entirety (see pages 76–9). However, framed ceilings do require a large quantity of wood, and the jointing mechanism and measurements used in their construction need to be accurate, in order to achieve the best possible effect.

tools for the job

- pencil
- level
- hand saw
- combination square
- miter saw
- chisel
- wooden mallet
- cordless drill/driver

1 Draw a level guideline around the perimeter of the room using a pencil and level. This line will be the bottom edge of the framed ceiling, and therefore its positioning should be considered carefully. Height suitability is really determined by the existing ceiling height in your home. Older, more traditional houses vary in ceiling height but modern houses tend to be about 8ft.

2 Cut a piece of 1 x 4in planed or dressed softwood to the length of the longest wall dimension. Use a combination square to make guidelines at 6in intervals along the length.

3 Pencil in a central bisecting line through a small scrap or gauge block of 1 x 4in prepared softwood. Hold the gauge block next to each guideline on the full length in turn, marking a second guideline across the length to denote the width of the beams. Then, using the penciled bisecting line on the gauge, mark where this line meets the penciled guidelines on the full length on either side of the gauge.

4 Use a miter saw, set at a 90-degree angle, to cut down to the marks on each guideline on the length. Be exact with this cut, not allowing it to encroach further than the marked-off points.

5 Use a chisel to cut out each sawn section of the length. Ensure that the chisel blade dimensions fit exactly between the sawn cuts so as to produce a precise, accurate finish. One light tap with a mallet on the chisel is usually enough to remove this small section of wood. Repeat steps 2–5 for the length of wood required for the opposing wall. It may pay to sand the cutout area lightly to remove any rough edges.

6 Screw the notched lengths into position on the wall, allowing the bottom, uncut edge of the lengths to run along the pencil guideline. Fasten wood screws at every stud crossing—for a masonry

wall, use plugs and screws. On the two opposing walls—as yet untouched—attach full lengths of 1 x 3in dressed softwood between the notched lengths, level against the wall.

7 Measure exactly between the opposing notches on the two opposing lengths of softwood (from wall to wall). Cut lengths of 1 x 4in dressed softwood accordingly. At the ends of these lengths, measure in exactly the thickness of the plate—1in as shown in this case—and bisect the width of the plate to produce an L-shape pencil guideline. Cut this portion away at each end.

tips of the trade

Dropping the ceiling level will mean that ceiling-installed lighting will also need adjusting. This may require the lengthening of pendants or fluorescent fixtures. Alternatively, a switch to wall-mounted fixtures could be an option. Consult an electrician before embarking on this work.

8 Position the length between the appropriate notches, allowing the length to drop down into position.

9 A couple of knocks with a mallet may be required finally to position the length—fasteners should not be necessary. Repeat this process across the entire ceiling.

tips of the trade

For ceilings where the beam length is more than 10ft you may need to add extra support. Attach a length of 2 x 2in dressed softwood across the top of the beams, and attach it to the ceiling with straps.

Painting the original ceiling above the beams can enhance the desired effect. The beams themselves can also be used as a system from which to hang decoration.

plastering & lining

Before walls and ceilings can be decorated with paint, wallpaper, or other finishes, they have to be given a smooth, flat surface. On brickwork and blockwork walls, plaster does the job. This is a powder based on gypsum that is made into a plastic mix with water and applied to wall and ceiling surfaces, where it dries to a hard coating. On timber-framed walls, a rigid sheet material called drywall or plasterboard is used to clad both sides of the wall structure. Drywall or plasterboard is also used to form ceilings beneath timber floor joists, and to line the inside of exterior walls as an alternative to plastering. There are several other plaster-based products that are used around the house for their decorative effect, including cove, fixture canopies, and panel moldings. This chapter tells you how to use them.

Ornate cove complements the elegant grandeur of this room, but plain cove would suit a more modern decor.

plastering masonry

The type of plaster most widely used for masonry is a mix based on a mineral called gypsum. This is usually applied as a two-coat system, with a thick undercoat applied first and a thinner finish coat on top. Different types of plaster are used for undercoats and finish coats, and there are different undercoats for different backgrounds such as brick, aggregate blocks, and thermal blocks. Ask your supplier for advice to ensure that you select the correct plaster for the job.

The job of the plaster undercoat is to smooth out any irregularities in the wall surface and even out differences in the rate at which the masonry and scratch coat absorbs water, thereby allowing the thin finish coat to dry out evenly and without cracking.

A professional plasterer will plaster a wall in one continuous operation, gauging the thickness they are applying as they work. However, the amateur plasterer will find it easier initially to divide the wall surface up into a series of bays using slim timber strips called grounds. These act as depth guides to help you apply an even thickness of plaster to each bay. They are removed once the plaster has set, and the narrow channels are then filled with more plaster, ready for the finish coat to be applied.

tools for the job

- tape measure
- back saw
- claw hammer
- level
- bucket
- power drill & mixing attachment
- spot board
- workbench
- garden spray gun
- hawk
- plasterer's trowel
- stepladder
- wooden rule (5ft length of 2 x 3in dressed softwood)
- wooden plasterer's float
- angle trowel

1 Nail ⅜ x 1in dressed timber strips to the wall you are plastering at roughly 3ft intervals, using 1in long masonry nails. Check that they are plumb using a level, and insert cardboard or masonite packing behind them if the wall surface is uneven. Fit a strip right in the angle of inside corners, and fasten on a length of expanded metal corner bead at outside corners—this acts as a depth guide during plastering, and remains in place when the wall has been plastered to reinforce the corner.

2 Mix your first batch of plaster. As a guide to quantities, 110lb of undercoat plaster will cover around 86sq ft of wall surface in a layer about ⅜in thick. Half-fill your bucket with clean water, then sprinkle handfuls of dry plaster into it, stirring as you do so by hand or with a power drill and mixing attachment. Add more plaster until the mix takes on the consistency of oatmeal. Tip it out onto your spot board, which should be set on a portable workbench, close to the wall you are plastering.

3 Wet the surface of the masonry in the first bay using a garden spray gun. Wetting the masonry will cut down substantially the absorption rate of the wall, thus preventing moisture from being sucked out of the undercoat too quickly, which will result in poor adhesion and cause the plaster to crack.

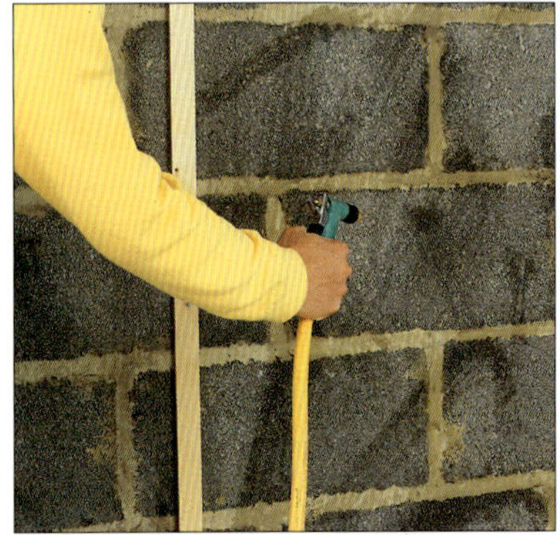

4 Hold your hawk under the edge of the spot board and scoop a trowelful of plaster onto it. Then transfer the plaster off the hawk and onto your trowel, tilting the hawk so that it is nearly plumb as you slide the almost horizontal trowel upwards across its surface. This procedure may take a little practice.

5 Resting the right-hand edge of the loaded trowel against the right-hand batten at floor level, tilt the blade until it is at an angle of about 30 degrees to the wall. Push the trowel up to press the plaster against the masonry, gradually tilting the blade plumb so that the plaster is squeezed out between its lower edge and the wall. The blade will be plumb when the plaster runs out. Load and apply a second band of plaster to the left of the first. Work your way up the bay to the next strip, applying parallel bands of plaster and blending them together. Overfill the center of the bay so that the plaster protrudes above the strips. Use steps to reach the top of the bay.

6 When the bay is complete, hold a wooden rule across the guide strips at floor level and slide it up, at the same time moving it from side to side with a sawing motion. This will remove any high spots from the plaster. Fill obvious low spots with more plaster, and then move the rule across the bay again.

7 Hammer five or six wire nails through a wooden float in a line 1in in from one end of the blade, so that they protrude by about ⅛in. Use this to key the surface of the fresh plaster. Wet the base of the float and hold it flat against the plaster. Then move it around in a circular motion so that the nails make shallow marks.

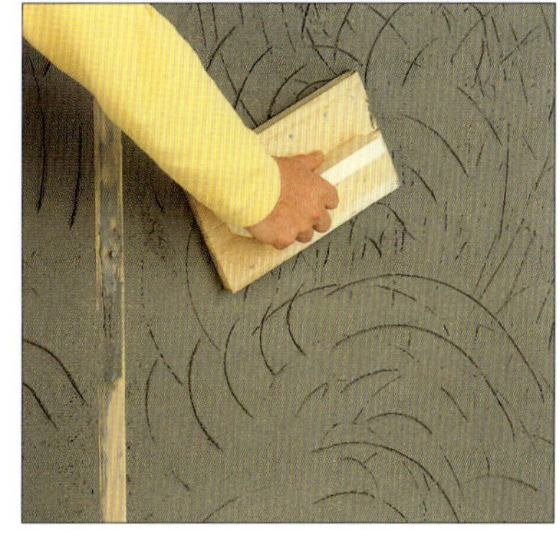

8 Repeat steps 3 to 7 to apply undercoat to the remaining bays. Pry away the strips and fill the channels with plaster. Use an angle trowel to plaster inside angles. Plaster outside corners using a strip and the corner bead as depth guides.

9 Undercoat plaster takes about two hours to set hard, so you should be able to start applying the finish coat to the first bay by the time you have completed the undercoat for the final bay. Mix up a quantity of finishing plaster to the consistency of melting ice cream. Load your hawk and trowel as before, applying a coat with a maximum thickness of ⅛in. Start at the bottom of the wall and work up, again with broad sweeping arm movements. Cover about 22sq ft, then apply another, even thinner, coat over the top of the first. Use a trowel to remove any ridges and splashes, and repeat the process until the entire wall is covered. Finally, wet the trowel and polish the finish plaster with the blade held flat against the surface.

MOVING WOOD STRIPS

As you become more proficient at plastering and gain in confidence, try using the moving strip technique. Put up two strips about 4ft apart, and plaster the area between them. Then remove both strips and reposition one on the wall 4ft away from one edge of the plaster, which will act as a depth guide at one side of the next bay. Plaster this next section, then reposition the strip to the same distance again. Continue working around the room, bay by bay. When you return to your start point, the edge of the plaster in the first bay will act as your final depth guide.

using drywall or plasterboard 

Drywall or plasterboard is a rigid sheet material used for covering the surfaces of wood-framed partition walls, and for surfacing ceilings. It has a lightweight plaster core, sandwiched between two sheets of strong paper that also cover the longer edges of the board. Gray-faced sheets are intended to be plastered over, while ivory-faced sheets can be painted or wallpapered directly—the latter's tapered edges allow the joints to be taped and filled flush, ready for painting.

types of board

Standard drywall, also known as wallboard, has one gray and one ivory face and is the most widely used type. It comes in standard 8 x 4ft sheets and a range of smaller sizes useful for repair jobs. You can also get longer sheets for rooms with high ceilings. Drywall is available with square or tapered edges, in 3/8in and 1/2in thicknesses.

Base board is used for lining ceilings, and is then given a skim coating of finish plaster. It is available only as a square-edge board and has gray paper on both faces. The most common size is 4 x 3ft, and base board comes only in 3/8in thickness.

Both types of wallboard are available with a vapor barrier. These vapor-shield boards are used mainly for top-story ceilings (to prevent condensation in the attic) and for dry-lining exterior walls (see pages 98–9). Thermal board has a layer of rigid insulation bonded to one face and also incorporates a vapor barrier. It is used for walls where extra insulation is needed.

storing drywall

Drywall is fragile until it is fixed to a supporting framework. Always carry sheets on edge—they may snap if you carry them flat. Store them on edge, closely packed against each other and leaning against a wall at a slight angle. If you are using ivory-face boards, stack them with these faces together. Take care not to damage the paper-covered edges as you handle the sheets.

fixing drywall

To line a partition wall or ceiling, drywall sheets are nailed to supporting studs and horizontal top and bottom plates in a wood-frame wall, and joists in a ceiling. These are usually positioned at 16in centers so that the edges of 4ft wide boards can be butt-jointed over the center of every third stud and nailed to the intermediate ones. They are fastened with galvanized drywall or plasterboard nails, which have a jagged shank to grip the wood and a flat head that should be hammered so that it dimples the face of the board. These dimples are then filled with plaster to conceal them. Nails should be placed every 6in, 3/8in in from paper-covered edges, and 1/2in in from cut ends.

cutting drywall

You can cut drywall with a fine-tooth saw, resting it on saw horses to leave the cutting line clear. However, it is easier to cut through the paper and into the plaster core along the cutting line, and then to snap the board over the edge of a length of wood. Cut through the paper on the other face to separate the two pieces. Use a keyhole saw, jigsaw, or knife to make cutouts for light switches, socket outlets, and so on.

MAKING A FOOT LIFTER

A foot lifter is a double wedge used to lift drywall or plasterboard sheets tight against the ceiling. Make one from a short length of 2 x 3in wood, tapered into a wedge shape from the center toward each end so that it rocks like a teeter-totter. Rest the sheet on one end of the wedge, then press down on the other end with your foot to lift the board into position. The small gap at the bottom of the board is concealed with baseboard later.

building a partition wall

With the wall framework in place, fasten the first board beside the doorway if the wall has one, as in this example, or in a corner if not.

tools for the job

- tape measure
- pencil
- long straightedge
- fine-tooth saw
- utility knife
- foot lifter (see box above)
- hammer

1 Measure the floor-to-ceiling height and subtract 3/4in, then cut the board to length. Offer it up to the frame with one edge aligned with the door stud, lift it tight against the ceiling using a foot lifter, and mark the position of the door head on this

edge. Cut a 1in wide strip off this side of the board between the mark and the top edge. This cut edge will be centered on the upper section of the stud above the door opening.

2 Set the board back in place and nail it to the framework. Repeat the process for the board at the other side of the door opening.

3 Fix more whole boards in place, working from the doorway toward the corners. Butt tapered-edge boards together, but leave a ⅛in gap between square-edge boards (to be plastered later).

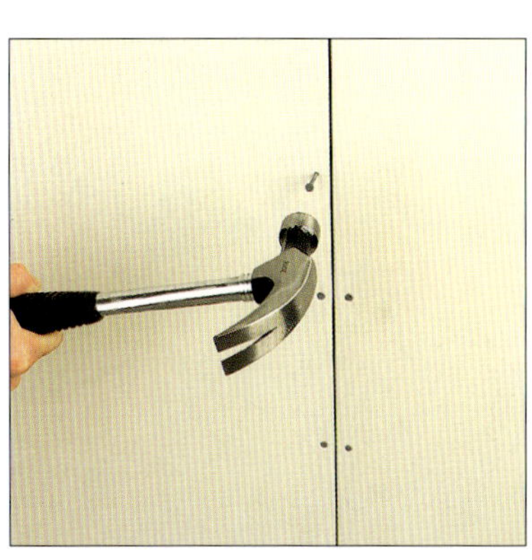

4 Cut the last boards down in width to fit the space at the room corners, and nail them in place. See pages 96–7 for how to fill joints and plaster drywall or plasterboard.

building a ceiling

When building a ceiling, the boards should be fixed with their long edges at a right angle to the joists, and with board ends meeting at the center of a joist. To support the long edges, attach 2in thick supports—called blocking—between the joists along the side walls, and across the room at centers to match the board width. You will also need steps or a platform of scaffold boards to work from, plus a spare pair of hands to help support the boards while each is fixed.

1 Position the first board in one corner of the room. Nail it to the joists and to the blocking, working out from the center of the board. This stops the board from sagging as you hammer in the nails.

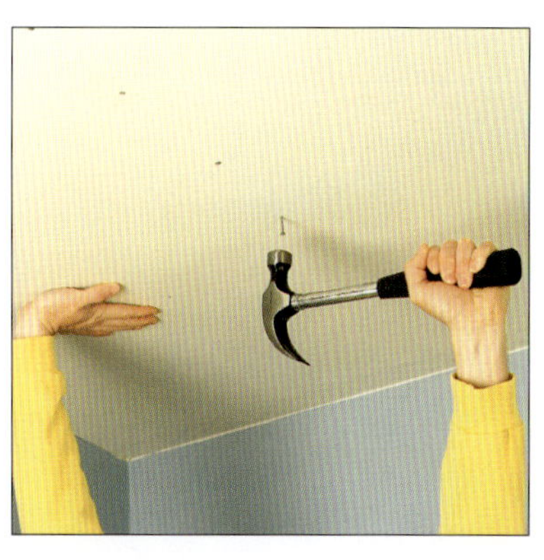

2 Complete the first row of boards, trimming the last one to fit if necessary. Butt-joint tapered-edge boards, but leave a ⅛in gap between square-edge ones.

3 Start the next row with a board trimmed to reach the center of a joist. This avoids having all the joints between boards aligned along just one joist. Continue in this way.

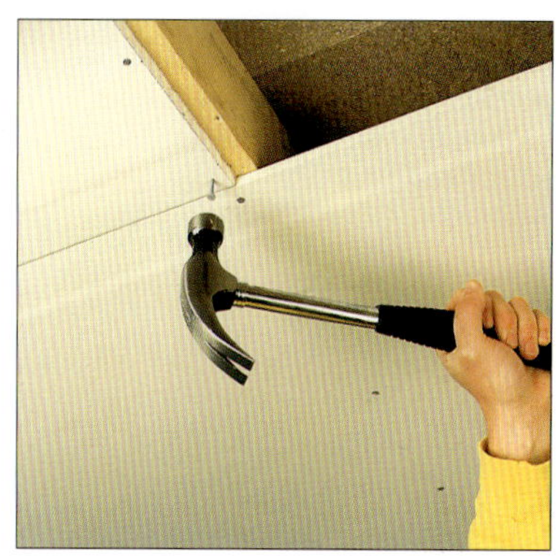

4 Finish the ceiling with a row of boards cut down in width to fit between the last row of boards and the wall. See pages 96–7 for how to fill joints and plaster wallboard.

plastering wallboard

Drywall or plasterboard can be given a thin overall coat of finish plaster if it is fixed with the gray side facing out. If tapered-edge boards are fixed ivory side out, however, only the joints need filling before the boards are painted or papered. In both cases it is vital to tape all the joints first, using paper joint tape or self-adhesive joint mesh, to avoid the risk of the joints opening up in the future due to movement of the ceiling structure.

safety advice

The step-by-step sequences on these two pages demonstrate how to apply a plaster or taped finish to a plasterboard or drywall wall. Exactly the same techniques are used to finish a plasterboard or drywall ceiling, the only difference being that you are working above your head. This has certain safety implications, however, since it is essential that you have a safe working platform so that you can reach the ceiling surface comfortably and without stretching. Scaffold boards or staging set on adjustable trestles, or a low mobile work trolley on lockable casters, are all ideal. Check out what your local rental company has available.

tools for the job

- stepladders & boards for working platform
- bucket & mixer
- spot board
- plasterer's trowel
- hawk
- scissors for joint tape or joint mesh
- angle trowel (optional)
- garden spray gun
- filling knives
- close-texture sponge

plastered finish

Set up a working platform, ensuring that it is steady, and mix some finish plaster in a bucket to the consistency of melting ice cream.

1 Apply a thin band of finish plaster with a trowel along each joint line, then cut joint tape to the required length and bed it into the plaster band, using the end of the trowel to press it into place. If you are using self-adhesive joint mesh, dispense with the plaster band and stick the tape directly onto the board surface. Repeat for all the joints.

2 Spread a thin layer of plaster along each joint, wide enough to cover the tape or mesh. It should also be just thick enough to hide the tape or mesh completely. Smooth the plaster out on either side of the joints with the trowel held flat against the surface of the drywall or plasterboard.

3 Repeat steps 1 and 2 to embed tape or mesh into the wall/ceiling angle all around the room. Embed tape or mesh into the outside and inside corners of the room in the same way. Do not be tempted to omit any of these angles—if you do not tape these joints, you are sure to get cracks opening up there as time goes by.

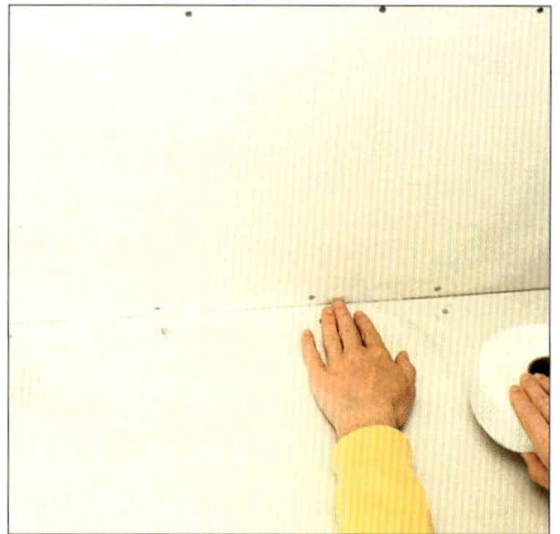

4 Apply finish plaster to the bays between the joints, working up from the bottom if you are plastering walls, and out from one edge if you are plastering a ceiling. Use the same technique as for applying finish plaster over undercoat (see pages 92–3).

5 Return to your starting point and apply a second, thinner coat of plaster over the entire surface. Work with the trowel held almost flat to the surface to control the plaster thickness and ensure a flat finish.

6 Neaten the angles between wall and ceiling and in inside corners by running the edge of the trowel along each surface in turn. Alternatively, use an angle trowel.

7 Wet the blade of the trowel and the plaster surface using a garden spray gun, and polish the surface of the plaster until smooth.

tape finish

Use joint filler instead of finish plaster to fill the joints between tapered-edge boards. You can use either paper or self-adhesive mesh tape—the former is embedded in a band of joint filler, the latter is stuck straight to the plasterboard or drywall surfaces.

1 If you are using paper tape to fill the joints, apply a narrow band of filler down the joint line and embed the tape into it with a putty knife, making sure that you exclude any air bubbles. Then apply another band of filler over the top with a wider knife to fill the tapered edges of the joint level with the board surfaces at each side.

2 If you are using mesh tape to fill the joints, stick the tape in place and fill the joint using the same technique as for paper tape. If you have to make a joint in the tape, butt the ends rather than overlapping them.

3 Finish all the joints with a thinner, wider band of filler, applied with a plasterer's trowel or a coating knife that will bridge the tapered edges of the boards. Then smooth out the edges of the filler with a slightly damp sponge.

WALLBOARD FINISHES

- **Sealing plasterboard or drywall**—To even out differences in porosity between the sheets and the filled joints, you should seal the wall before it is decorated, to prevent paint or wallpaper paste from drying too quickly as water is sucked into the board surface. To seal the drywall or plasterboard, use a thin coating of joint filler, applied and rubbed into the surface with a sponge. Alternatively, apply proprietary plasterboard primer with a brush or roller, or use latex paint diluted with 10 percent water. Use two coats of paint to ensure uniform surface porosity.

- **Tiling plasterboard or drywall**—Wallboard has very little strength if it gets wet, which can happen if a wall is covered with ceramic tiles and the grouting is not waterproof. If you intend to tile an existing plasterboard wall, treat its surface with a coat of solvent-based paint first to seal the surface against water penetration. On a new wall, use special waterproof tile backing board instead of plasterboard or drywall to provide a surface that can withstand water penetration.

dry-lining walls

This technique involves lining exterior masonry walls with plasterboard or drywall as an alternative to traditional plastering. It is used mainly in older properties to improve the insulation performance of solid walls. The sheets are nailed to a framework of sawn furring strips fixed to the wall surface at centers to suit the sheet widths. Standard vapor-shield wallboard is commonly used for this purpose, with glass-fiber insulation batts sandwiched between the sheets and the masonry.

Dry lining can be installed over existing plaster if this is sound, but crumbling or damp plaster should be removed and, if damp, the problem must be treated and the wall allowed to dry out before dry lining is installed. The space between the dry lining and the masonry can be used to conceal wiring runs to switches and sockets.

The wood used for wall furring strips should be pretreated with wood preservative. It should be 2 x 2in if glass-fiber insulation is to be placed behind the plasterboard, and 1¼ x 2in if thermal board is being used. Attach the strips with masonry nails long enough to penetrate the masonry by at least 1in, or with nail wall plugs.

If you are using insulation batts, wedge them in place between the furring strips all around the room before you start cutting and attaching plasterboard or drywall. Insulation is not used at the sides and heads of door and window openings.

Alternatively, thermal board with a layer of polystyrene or polyurethane insulation and a vapor barrier bonded to the rear face can be used to combine wall lining and insulation.

tools for the job

- tape measure & pencil
- straightedge
- hand saw or power saw
- level
- plumb bob
- cordless drill/driver
- foot lifter (see box page 94)

1 Cut the furring strips that will be fixed plumb to a length about 6in less than the room height and then fasten them in place, leaving a 3in gap above and below each furring strip. Space the strips at 16in centers for ⅜in thick drywall or plasterboard in sheets 4ft wide, and at 2ft centers for ½in thick drywall or plasterboard in sheets of the same width. Start fastening the furring strips at door and window openings, and work out from there toward the room corners.

2 When attaching furring strips at the corners of the room, fasten a strip on each wall about 2in away from the inside angle.

3 Cut and attach the horizontal strips at floor and ceiling level, fixing them in the gaps above and below the plumb strips.

4 Add short horizontal wood strips above doorways, and above and below window openings. Finally, fit short plumb strips above these openings, offset by 1in so that they will support the edges of plasterboard or drywall sheets that are fixed level with the edges of the opening below, as well as the filling panel above the opening.

5 Start fastening sheets beside a door or window opening if there is one, otherwise in a corner.

Cut the sheet to the required length, then use a foot lifter to hold it tightly up against the ceiling. Once it is in the correct position, drive in the fasteners. Repeat the process at the other side and above the opening.

6 Cut strips of plasterboard or drywall to size to line the sides and head of the reveal opening around any windows or doorways. Place plaster mounds on the reveals.

7 Fix the sheets to the sides of the reveal so that their paper-covered edges lap the cut edges of the wall lining.

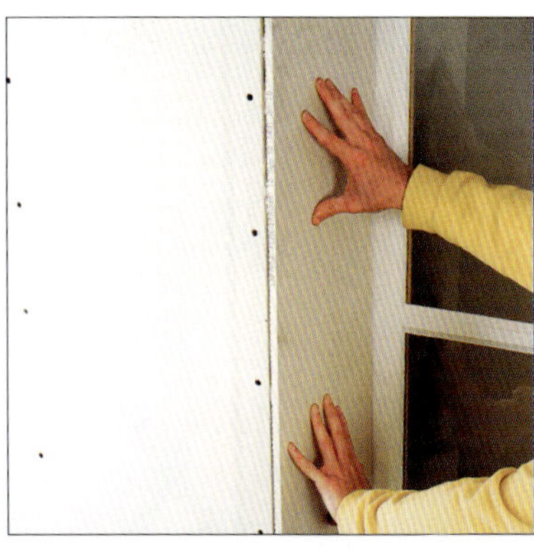

8 Support the piece lining the head of the reveal in place with wooden strips until the plaster sets.

9 Work toward each corner of the room, fastening as many whole sheets as possible. Cut the last sheet ¾in narrower than the distance between the last whole sheet and the next wall. Attach it in place with its cut edge facing the corner.

10 Start the next wall with a whole sheet, butting the sheet against the face of the sheet already in place (but repeat from step 5 if there is an opening in the wall).

11 At outside corners, fasten one sheet with its cut edge level with the face of the strip on the other wall. Then attach a sheet with a paper-covered edge to this wall so that the edge laps the cut edge of the first sheet. If using thermal sheet, you will have to cut away some of the insulation from the back of the sheet to allow sheet-to-sheet contact.

tips of the trade

If there are any switches or socket receptacles on the wall that you are dry-lining, make cutouts in the drywall or plasterboard to fit around them. If these are flush-mounted, remove the faceplates after turning the electricity off at the source and draw the wiring forward through the cutout. Fit a plastic cavity wall box in the cutout, feed in the wiring, and connect the faceplate to the new receptacle.

FASTENING SHEETS WITH ADHESIVE

If the existing wall surfaces are flat and plumb, you can fasten drywall or plasterboard directly onto the wall surface using panel adhesive applied with a cartridge gun. Thermal sheet can be fixed with special adhesive applied to the wall in bands behind the center and edges of the sheets. This method reduces slightly the amount of floor area lost by dry-lining a room, and saves the cost and time of attaching furring strips.

installing cove

Cove, sometimes known and marketed as cornice, forms a decorative joint between walls and ceilings. Traditional types are made from fibrous plaster, but most modern, simple designs are made from gypsum plaster or polystyrene. Polystyrene moldings are cheaper, lighter, and faster to install than traditional ones, but plaster-based cove tends to produce a more attractive finish.

Cove or cornice is usually sold in lengths of 2 or 3yds, which are then butt-jointed along each wall of the room. Cove is mitered at inside and outside corners, although some molded plastic cove has preformed corner pieces. Plaster and plastic cove are fastened in place with adhesive, but the weight of fibrous plaster moldings makes attaching them with screws and wall plugs essential. Old wallcoverings must be removed from the area beneath the cove so that the adhesive can bond to solid plaster or plasterboard. There is no need to fill cracks in the wall-ceiling angle—the cove will hide them.

fixing plaster cove

Measure the perimeter of the room and calculate how many lengths of cove will be required. Allow for the loss of about 6in of cove for every miter joint. Buy enough adhesive to fasten the quantity of cove. Plaster-based cove is fastened with either powder or ready-mixed tub adhesive, while plastic cove usually has its own special adhesive.

MAKING A MITER BOX

If you cannot find a miter box that will cope with standard 4 and 5in plaster cove, make one from scrap wood using a combination square to mark the 45-degree cutting lines. Cut the saw guides right down to the base of the box so that you can saw the miters cleanly.

tools for the job

- tape measure
- pencil
- long straightedge
- level
- utility knife
- wallpaper scraper
- putty knives
- miter box (see box below)
- hand saw
- stepladders
- hammer

1 Hold a length of cove in place in the wall/ceiling angle and mark pencil lines on the ceiling and wall along its top and bottom edges. Use a straightedge (plus a level for the wall lines) to extend these lines around the room. If there is wallpaper on either surface, cut along the pencil lines with a utility knife and dry-strip as much wallpaper between the lines and the wall/ceiling angle using a scraper. Soak any patches that remain to soften the paste, but take care not to wet the wallpaper outside the guidelines.

2 Use the edge of a putty knife to score the plaster surface with a series of crisscross cuts in between the guidelines on the wall and ceiling. This will help the cove adhesive to bond well to the plaster and thus achieve a secure enough fastening to hold the cove in place.

3 Start work on the longest wall in the room. Refer to the guidelines for cutting miters on the opposite page to ensure that you cut the first miter in the right direction—mistakes are wasteful and expensive. Place the cove in the miter box with the ceiling edge in the base of the box, and cut with a fine-tooth hand saw. Smooth the edges with sandpaper.

4 Use a wide putty knife to butter a generous amount of adhesive along the rear faces of the cove. Draw the knife towards the outer edge of the cove so that excess adhesive will mainly be squeezed into the triangular space between the cove and the wall–ceiling angle.

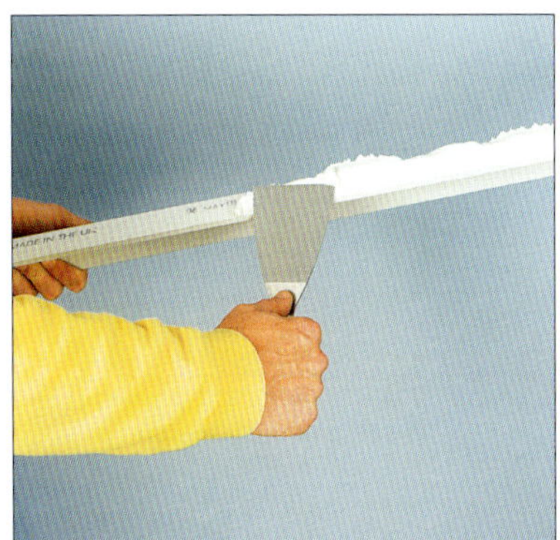

5 Align the bottom edge of the cove with the pencil line on the wall, slide the tip of the miter into the corner, and push the cove firmly up and back to compress the adhesive and ensure a good bond to the wall. This is a job for two people if you are working with 3yd lengths of cove. Scrape off excess adhesive along the wall and ceiling edges of the cove, and check that it is lined up with the pencil lines. The adhesive should grab strongly enough to support the weight of the cove, but if you want to reinforce it while it sets, hammer two or three masonry nails through its lower section and into the wall. Only drive the nails partway in so that you can remove them and fill the holes in the cove later.

6 Measure the distance from the square end of the first length to the next corner. If it is more than one length away but less than two, cut a miter on the next length to fit the corner and stick it in place as in step 5. If it is less than one length away, cut the miter as before, then hold the length in position and mark where it meets the first length. Cut the cove squarely at this point and position it, filling the joint between the two lengths with cove adhesive.

7 If you need a short filling piece to bridge a gap left between two full lengths, measure the gap and cut a piece of cove to fit it. Attach in place, filling joints with cove adhesive.

8 Move to the next wall and cut the correct miter to fit into the corner, then repeat steps 3 to 7 to attach cove around the rest of the room. Fill all joints with adhesive and remove any masonry nails you used to support long lengths of the cove.

CUTTING MITERS

Take care that you cut miters in the correct direction. The cutting diagrams below show the order of miter cuts needed to cove a chimney breast (right), when working from left to right.

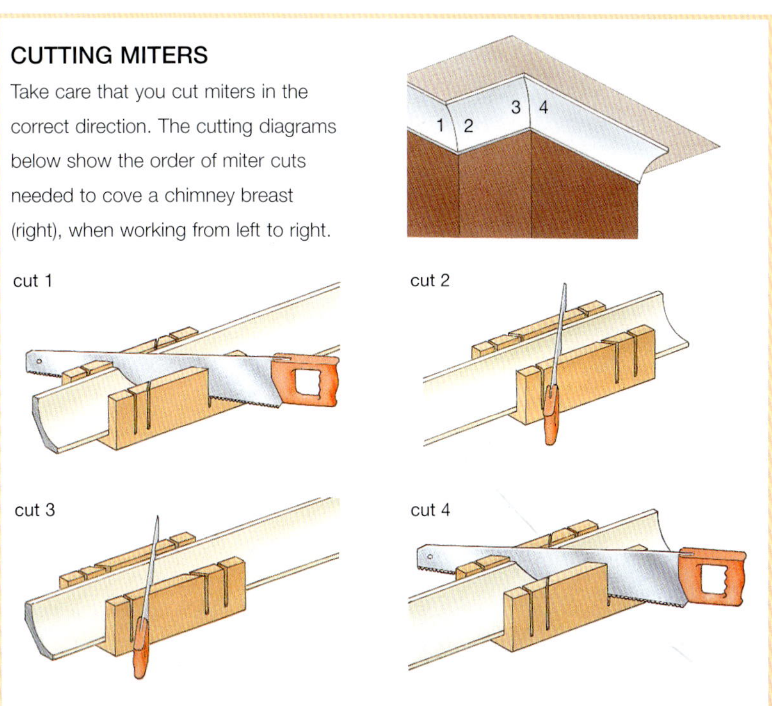

adding plaster features

There are several other types of plaster feature that you can add to a room to complement the effect of cove (pages 100–1). These include decorative ceiling roses, wall plaques, corbels to support door heads, panel moldings to frame areas of wall or ceiling, and even decorative plaster niches to display a favorite ornament. There is a wide range of styles available, from traditional to modern, formed in fibrous plaster or foamed plastic resin.

Ceiling roses are widely available. They are produced in a wide range of different styles to suit every budget and taste, from traditional, ornate examples to simpler, more modern varieties. Their function is twofold—they provide visual adornment to a ceiling, and also conceal the electric wiring connections to a pendant light or chandelier. The smallest, lightest types can be stuck to the ceiling in the same way as cove, but large, heavier roses—especially those that are made from fibrous plaster—need to be attached to the ceiling joists.

Wall plaques, because they are smaller and lighter than ceiling roses, are generally stuck in place, as are panel moldings. Corbels fitted to support a door head or flat arch between rooms need screws driven into wall plugs, while plaster niches are generally attached using mirror plates or similar fasteners. Check the manufacturer's instructions when you choose the plaster feature you plan to install.

tools for the job

- tape measure
- string
- thumbtacks
- pencil
- wide putty knife
- wallpaper scraper
- awl
- power drill & twist drill bits
- screwdriver
- hand saw
- stepladder

attaching a ceiling rose

1 If your room has no central pendant light, the first step is to find the center of the ceiling—a ceiling rose will look odd if it is not carefully positioned. To do this, find the midpoints of opposite walls and tack string lines between them. Where they cross is the ceiling center. With the string lines still in place, hold the ceiling rose over them so that you can position it precisely central. Draw a light pencil line on the ceiling around its perimeter, then take it and the string lines down. (See the sequence on the opposite page for what to do if there is a central pendant light.)

2 If the ceiling is painted, use the edge of a putty knife to roughen the surface inside the line in a criss-cross pattern and provide a key for the adhesive. If there is wallpaper present, cut along the pencil line and scrape off as much of the wallpaper as you can. Soak the remains with a wet sponge and scrape them off too. Then key the plaster as before.

3 If the ceiling rose you are fitting is lightweight to mediumweight, simply fasten it in place with adhesive. Apply a generous band of adhesive all around the edge of the ceiling rose with a putty knife, and add a mound in the middle too. Offer the ceiling rose up to the marked outline and press it firmly upwards against the ceiling surface. Hold it for a few seconds to give the adhesive a chance to hold, then scrape off excess adhesive around the perimeter and use it as a filler in any gaps between the rose and the ceiling.

4 If you are installing a heavy plaster ceiling rose, follow steps 1 and 2 to position it, then locate the

joist positions at either side of the ceiling's central point. Use an awl within the pencil outline to probe for solid wood, and mark the joist positions at the perimeter of the outline. Hold the ceiling rose in place and mark where to drill holes for screws that will pass into the center of the joists—use at least two, but preferably four, screws.

5 Take down the ceiling rose and carefully drill countersunk holes through it at the marked points. Spread a generous layer of adhesive on the back of the ceiling rose as described in step 3, then get a helper to hold the ceiling rose back in place while you drill pilot holes into the joists and screw in the fastening screws. Press the ceiling rose tightly against the ceiling as you do this, but take care not to overtighten the screws or the plaster may crack.

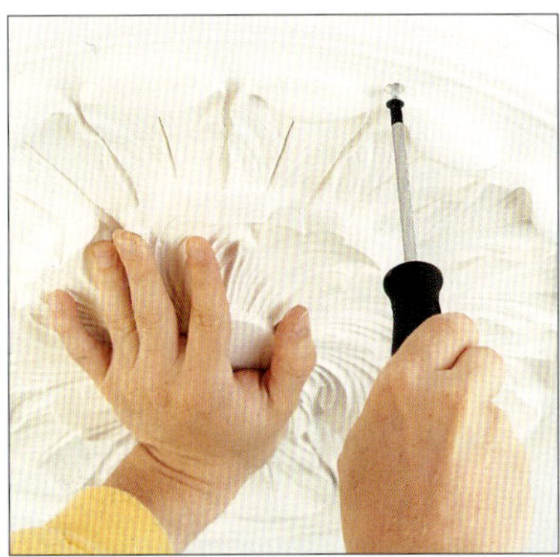

6 Fill any gaps around the edge of the ceiling rose with adhesive, then wipe away the excess with a damp sponge for a smooth finish.

7 Finally, fill the fastening screw holes with a little adhesive and sand it smooth when it has set hard.

coping with a pendant light

1 Turn off the electric power and disconnect the pendant cable from its terminals, making a sketch of which cable cores are connected to which terminal on the baseplate first. Poke the wires up through the hole in the ceiling. Gain access to the ceiling space and connect the cables to the terminals of a four-terminal box, referring to your sketch to see which cables go to which terminal. This will restore the electricity supply and switch control to the light when the power is restored later. Screw the base of the junction box to the side of a nearby joist. Drill a hole in the middle of the ceiling rose for the pendant cable, and fit the ceiling rose as described on the opposite page.

safety advice

Always consult a qualified electrician if in any doubt about carrying out wiring and electrical work yourself.

2 Pass the end of a new piece of cable down through the ceiling. Connect the cores to the neutral, hot, and grounding terminals of the box. Fit the cover on the box.

3 Return to the room below and connect the cable to the new baseplate. Screw this to the ceiling rose, connect the cable, and fit the canopy. Restore the power supply.

installing baseboards

Baseboard is the most effective material for finishing the junction between walls and floors. It helps to protect the bottom of the wall from dents and knocks, but it also provides a decorative feature. This means that, like cove, there is a wide range of designs available, and profiles can be chosen to match similar designs for casing around doors, chair rails, and even picture rails. Once the correct design has been chosen, it's important to spend time fitting it properly.

MITER CUTTING

If the baseboard is to butt up against a straight edge such as plinth block or casing, a simple, straight saw cut at the correct measurement along the length is all that is required. However, when lengths need to join at a corner it is necessary to make a more complicated cut.

- **Mitered cuts**—Either a miter block and hand saw or a specially designed miter saw can be used for cutting 45-degree angles in baseboard. The miter saw locks in place to allow a perfect cut to be made at the correct angle through the baseboard. The direction of the cut will also be dependent on whether a miter for an inside or outside corner is required.

tips of the trade

Most manufacturers now produce baseboard with different profiles on each side. This saves wood but can make measuring and cutting confusing. For this reason, keep checking your board as you measure, cut, and fasten, to ensure that the correct profile is always being used.

coping

This method should be used exclusively on inside corners. In a simple square corner, allow the first length of baseboard to butt straight up against the wall surface. The second length must now be cut to fit against and around the profile that the first length creates in the corner junction.

tools for the job

- tape measure
- pencil
- hand saw
- jigsaw
- plane (optional)
- hammer
- cordless drill/driver
- miter saw

1 Measure the length of baseboard required. Then take a scrap section of baseboard, position it over the length, and draw around its outline with a pencil.

2 Cut the baseboard along the pencil guideline using a jigsaw or coping saw, which makes it easy to follow the curve of the guideline, producing an accurate cut.

uneven floors

In some instances, an uneven floor can make fixing baseboard a more difficult task. This is because the bottom edge of the board is machined to a straight edge and any dips or bumps in the floor will either show as gaps or push the baseboard up. This means that the board will be out of alignment when it comes to meeting the next length in a corner. In such circumstances, it is necessary to scribe the bottom edge of the baseboard so that it will sit flush against the floor surface.

1 Cut the board to the correct length and temporarily position it at the base of the wall. Take a scrap of wood whose depth is the same as the largest gap between the bottom edge of the baseboard and the floor. Holding a pencil on top of the scrap

piece, start in one corner and drag the block and pencil across the floor, next to the skirting, allowing the pencil to draw a guideline on the baseboard's surface. This guideline reveals the line to cut along, so that when the board is fitted, it will follow the profile of the floor without leaving any gaps.

2 Remove the baseboard and attach it to a workbench. If a substantial amount of wood needs to be removed, cut along the guideline using a jigsaw. If it is only a small amount that needs to be taken away, shave off the unwanted material with a block plane.

attaching baseboards

When it has been cut to fit, the baseboard needs to be attached in position. The type of fastener will depend on the wall structure. For stud walls, go through the wall, into the bottom plate and vertical studs. With masonry, the fasteners can be anywhere, so long as they are secure.

nail attachments

Finish nails are ideal for nailing into studwork as their heads are easily concealed, and they tend not to split wood. If hammering into block or brickwork, masonry nails should be used. The number and frequency of nails required will be dependent on the strength of each fastener—nails hammered in about every 24in will usually suffice.

screw attachments

Screws are often better for attaching baseboard to masonry walls. This is because there can be a tendency for nails to bounce the baseboard away from the wall as subsequent nails are inserted. In other words, you may gain a good attachment with one nail, but the vibration caused by hammering the next nail can weaken the first, thus pulling it away from the wall. So use screws, first drilling pilot holes and fastening in place with concrete anchor screws or plugs with tightly positioned screws.

difficult joints

In addition to normal, inside corners, there are other areas of the wall where baseboard requires a different approach to fastening, to ensure that the baseboard is secure.

outside corners

Miter joints at inside corners using a miter saw. Once nailed in position on the wall, insert finish nails through the face of one piece of baseboard and through the miter joint with the second length. Applying wood glue to the joint is recommended.

lap joints

Rather than butt-jointing lengths on open walls, it is always best to make a mitered joint because butt-joints tend to crack quickly after painting, leaving an unsightly joint. Instead, miter the joint and apply some wood glue, before nailing the joint with two finish nails through the miter.

repair & restoration of walls & ceilings

Not all construction projects involve the complete rebuilding of entire ceilings and walls. Indeed, most jobs are concerned with repairs and alterations to small areas, such as restoring surfaces and areas of damage. This type of work is often quick to carry out, but nevertheless important in maintaining or restoring the appearance of walls and ceilings. This chapter covers many of the more common repair projects that occur around the house, and provides instruction on the best means of dealing with damaged areas. Many of the methods used have been briefly mentioned in earlier chapters, but slight variations are often required when it comes to finding the best techniques for repairs.

Whether painted or stained, tongue and groove provides an attractive and durable finish to an entire room.

making minor repairs to plaster

Plaster wall surfaces can be damaged by accidental impacts that leave dents and scrapes, and may develop other defects with age. Ceilings are less prone to damage, but can suffer from popping nail heads and from cracks developing along board edges, at the wall/ceiling junction or in line with the lath in an old lath-and-plaster ceiling. All can be repaired quickly and easily, and are well within the capabilities of even those who are less experienced in home improvement.

tools for the job

- nail set
- hammer
- pliers
- putty knife
- utility knife
- old paintbrush
- caulking blade
- coating blade
- belt sander

ceilings

The two main causes of ceiling defects are vibration caused by traffic on the floor above, and movement in the structure that supports the ceiling surface. Trouble can also arise if the joints in a plasterboard or drywall ceiling were not properly sealed when the ceiling was first put up.

popping nail heads

If you have drywall or plasterboard ceilings, you may find tell-tale discs of plaster on the floor—evidence that one of the nails used to fix the boards to the joists has popped and dislodged the plaster covering it. This happens if the nail was not driven fully in when the ceiling was put up, so that the sheets have moved slightly and loosened it.

1 Use a nail set and hammer to drive the nail in until its head just dimples the surface of the plasterboard or drywall. If it has popped far enough for you to grip the head with pliers, pull it out and drive it in again just next to the original hole. Make sure its head is indented in the plaster.

2 Apply a little joint compound over the nail head with a putty knife, leaving it slightly above the ceiling surface. When it has set hard, sand it down flush and paint over the patch.

cracked ceilings

Cracks in plasterboard ceilings generally follow the edges of the sheets, and are caused by movement in the ceiling structure as temperature and humidity change. In lath-and-plaster ceilings, the cracks may be irregular or run parallel to the lath to which the plaster is bonded. See pages 118–19 for larger-scale repairs.

1 Draw the blade of a utility knife along the crack, undercutting each edge slightly so that the filler will be locked in place when it sets. Then use an old paintbrush to brush any dust from the crack. On lath-and-plaster ceilings, brush some water along the crack to stop the dry plaster from sucking moisture out of the filler and causing it to dry brittle and crack as it sets.

2 Load up a putty knife with joint compound and press it well into the crack, drawing the blade across it as you work. After filling a short section of crack in this way, draw the knife blade along the crack to smooth the compound level with the surrounding surface. Carry on in this way until you have filled the whole crack. Allow the joint compound to set hard, then sand the repair smooth and paint to conceal it.

tips of the trade

If cracks open up repeatedly along plasterboard joint lines, apply self-adhesive mesh joint tape along them and cover the tape with a wide band of joint compound applied with a caulking blade (see joint cracks below). Alternately, apply a flexible textured coating to bridge and disguise the cracks, or put up lining paper.

walls

The main problem with walls is damage caused by collisions with the plaster surface. The cause could be anything—carelessly moved furniture, boisterous children playing, or general wear and tear. Solid walls can also suffer from hairline cracks in the plaster, while hollow walls can develop cracks along the joints between the plasterboard sheets. All are relatively easy to rectify.

dents and divots

All you need to repair small-scale surface damage to walls is joint compound and a putty knife, or a caulking blade for hairline cracks.

1 Remove any loose material from the damaged area using an old paintbrush. Then fill it slightly proud of the surrounding surface with joint compound, and allow it to set hard. Sand the repair flush with the surface using fine-grit glasspaper, then paint.

2 Where an area of wall is suffering from extensive hairline cracks tap the surface with your knuckles to check that the plaster is still sound. If it sounds hollow, its bond to the masonry beneath has probably failed (see pages 110–11 for how to repair it). If it is sound, use a caulking blade to apply joint compound over the affected area, working it in different directions so that all the cracks are filled. Allow it to set, then sand smooth as before.

joint cracks

Long, straight cracks often appear in drywall or plasterboard walls along the lines of the joints between adjacent plasterboard sheets—a sure sign that they were not taped before the plaster coat was applied. The best solution to this problem is to tape these cracks and apply a coating of joint compound over them.

1 Use a belt sander to sand off 1/16in of plaster along the joint line, as wide as the sanding belt. This ensures that the tape and joint compound lie level with the wall surface when the repair is complete.

2 Stick a length of self-adhesive mesh joint tape down the cracked joint. Press the tape firmly into position, butt-jointing lengths if necessary to cover the crack.

3 Use a coating or caulking blade to apply compound over the tape, running the blade down the wall at an angle so that the compound is finished level with the surrounding wall surface. Allow it to set hard, then sand and paint for an invisible repair.

patching plaster

If you discover areas of plaster on solid walls that sound hollow when tapped, or areas of plaster that have fallen away from the wall completely, the solution is to patch the affected area with new plaster. This is a relatively easy job to tackle, even if you have never used plaster before, because you have a solid base onto which to apply it, and the surrounding sound plaster to act as a guide to enable you to achieve a smooth, level finish.

tools for the job

- hand sledge
- cold chisel
- work gloves
- safety goggles
- old paintbrush
- bucket & mixing attachment
- hawk
- gauging trowel
- plastering trowel
- length of wood strip to use as straightedge

1 Use a hand sledge and cold chisel to cut away all of the unsound plaster back to a sound edge. It is important to wear gloves to protect your hands and safety goggles to protect your eyes from any flying chips of plaster. Make sure that you remove any plaster that remains stuck to the masonry within the area you are stripping.

2 Use an old paintbrush to remove the remaining dust from the hole, especially along the bottom edge where the majority of falling dust will collect. If this is not done, the new plaster will not bond properly to the masonry surface at the base of the hole and will eventually fail again.

3 Mix up some bonding agent and use an old paintbrush to brush a coat of this solution liberally onto the masonry, making sure that you reach right to the edges of the hole. This has the effect of sealing the surface, preventing it from sucking moisture out of the new plaster too quickly, which would cause the plaster to crack as it set. Allow the bonding agent to dry before proceeding with the next stage of plastering.

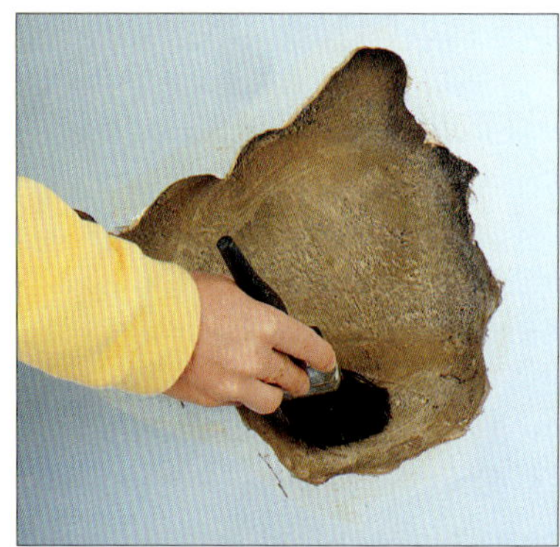

4 Mix up some bonding-coat plaster in a bucket until it is the consistency of thick oatmeal. Follow the manufacturer's guidelines regarding quantities, but remember that it is worth mixing a little more than you think you will need, to ensure that you have a sufficient amount. Make sure that you stir the plaster thoroughly so that it is free from lumps—adding the plaster to the water rather than the other way around helps to avoid lumps in the mix. Scoop some of the plaster onto a hawk and use a gauging trowel to press the plaster into the hole. Start work at the edges of the hole, gradually filling the entire area to within ⅛in of the surrounding surface.

5 When you have filled the hole evenly, lightly score the plaster surface with the tip of the gauging trowel in a crisscross pattern. This process is called keying and is used to give the finish coat of plaster a better chance of bonding well to the underlying surface. Leave the undercoat plaster to dry for a couple of hours before applying the finish coat.

6 Mix a small quantity of finish plaster, this time to the consistency of melting ice cream. Once again, make sure you stir the plaster thoroughly to remove any lumps. Load some onto the hawk, scoop it off with the plastering trowel, and apply it over the patch with a smooth, upward movement of the trowel. Tilt the blade almost upright as you finish the application, to squeeze the plaster out between trowel and wall. Apply a second or third coat if necessary, with the end of the float resting on the surrounding plaster to help you finish the patch level with it.

7 Cut a strip of wood long enough to span the hole and use it as a rule to scrape off any excess plaster that is sitting above the surrounding wall surface. This will also reveal if there are any hollow areas in your patch. If there are, apply an additional layer of finish plaster to fill them, then scrape the wood rule across the patch once more to remove any excess.

8 Leave the repair to dry for a few minutes. Wash your plastering trowel clean, then use an old paintbrush to wet it with clean water, ready to give the repair its final polish.

9 Hold the trowel flat to the wall surface and use it to flatten and polish the patch to a smooth, hard finish. Flick more water onto the wall with the brush as necessary to keep the trowel wet, and do not be afraid to press hard with the trowel as you work. Leave the plaster to set hard, then sand off any flecks of plaster from the patch or the surrounding wall surface, ready for painting.

tips of the trade

- **Ready-mixed plaster**—Unless you have a fairly large number of patches to repair, it is not usually worth buying separate supplies of bonding and finish plaster, since the smallest size generally available is 22lb. This quantity of bonding plaster is enough to cover about 16sq ft, and the same quantity of finish plaster will cover approximately 54sq ft. It is therefore more economical to buy a tub of ready-mixed, lightweight, one-coat plaster and use this to fill the patch in one go. This type of plaster contains latex and other additives that are designed to prevent the plaster from falling out of the hole when applied relatively thickly. Overfill the patch slightly, leave the repair to set hard, then sand back with fine-grit sandpaper until the repair is level with the surrounding wall surface.
- **Storing plaster**—If you are using dry plaster rather than a ready-mixed variety, store any leftover plaster in a tightly sealed plastic bag to prevent it from becoming damp and setting hard in the bag. Date the bag, and throw it away after six months if you have not used it by then—plaster does not keep well once opened.

CHECKING FOR MOISTURE

One possible cause of failed plaster is moisture in the masonry. This may be the result of penetrating damp due to defects in the house structure—typical problems are water penetration around door or window frames, or roof defects allowing water to penetrate ceilings or down chimney breasts. Damp patches low down on downstairs walls may be caused by rising damp, due to defects in the foundation coating. Whatever the cause, it is essential to put the defects right before patching the plaster, as continuing moisture will only cause the repair to fail again (see pages 132–3). If you are unsure as to whether a wall is damp, rent a moisture meter from a rental store and use it to check all suspect areas.

repairing corners

The most vulnerable parts of any plasterwork are outside corners, especially in doorways where the angles are most likely to be dented and damaged. Older homes are especially vulnerable, because the original plaster is often both thicker and softer than modern plasterwork and is also not likely to have been reinforced. Inside corners are less likely to suffer damage, which is generally limited to cracking in the angle due to differential movement in the house structure.

repairing small-scale damage

If the damage is superficial, restoring the corner is a simple two-stage job. If the wall is papered rather than painted, first strip the wallpaper off in the region of the repair.

tools for the job

- old screwdriver or small cold chisel
- old paintbrush
- back saw
- power drill & masonry drill bits
- hammer
- putty knife

1 Chip away any loose plaster from the damaged area with an old screwdriver or a small cold chisel until the area has a clean, sound edge. Then brush away any dust from the area with an old paintbrush.

2 Cut a strip of wood twice as long as the damaged section and at least 2in wide so that the nails fastening it to the wall do not break away more plaster from the corner. Drill pilot holes near each end of the strip and push in a masonry nail. Hold the strip against one face of the corner with its edge level with the other face and hammer in the nails far enough to hold the strip in place. Leave the heads projecting so that you can remove them easily later.

3 Mix joint compound and use a putty knife to pack it into the hole between the damaged edge and the strip on one face of the wall. Run the blade along the wall and strip surface so that the compound is level with them. Press the knife firmly so that the compound bonds well.

4 Allow the joint compound to become touch-dry, then carefully remove the strip and reposition it on the other face of the corner, covering the section you have just filled and with its edge level with the surface of the adjacent wall. Fill the rest of the hole as before, again running the knife on the wall and strip surfaces to leave a smooth, level finish to the repair.

5 When the compound has set, carefully pry off the strip and remove the nails from it. Fill the nail holes with more compound, then lightly sand the repair with fine-grit glasspaper, aiming to round off the repaired section slightly to match the profile of the rest of the corner angle.

complete corner repairs

Where the corner is extensively damaged, it is best to repair the corner from floor to ceiling, incorporating a strip of metal corner bead beneath the repair plaster to make future damage less likely. Unless you have powder plaster available, buy ready-mixed repair plaster for this job.

tools for the job

- tape measure
- portable workbench
- hacksaw
- brick chisel
- hand sledge
- hawk
- gauging trowel
- plastering trowel
- corner trowel (optional)

1 Measure the height of the corner. Clamp the corner bead in a portable workbench and cut it to length using a hacksaw. Saw through the bead first, then cut the expanded metal mesh wings that flank either side of the bead one at a time.

2 Use a brick chisel and hand sledge to chip off a band of plaster about 1½in wide on each side of the corner. Draw pencil guidelines on each wall and cut along each line first, then remove the plaster from the corner.

3 Apply mounds of plaster at 12in intervals on both sides of the corner using a gauging trowel.

4 Press the corner bead into place until the plaster squeezes through the mesh wings. The wings should almost touch the masonry to ensure that the bead is at the correct level.

5 Use the tip of the gauging trowel to flatten the extruded plaster over the mesh and to remove excess. Check that the bead is vertical and make any necessary adjustments. Allow the plaster to dry for an hour before proceeding any further.

6 Next, fill the gap between the bead and the existing plaster. Work from the bottom up on one side of the corner, holding the plastering trowel at a 45-degree angle as you push it upwards and force plaster into the space between the bead and the existing plaster. Repeat the process on the other side of the corner.

7 Wet the float of the trowel with water and polish the repaired plaster to a smooth, flat finish. When the plaster has dried hard, complete the job by using a damp cloth to wipe any plaster off the exposed quarter of the corner bead.

making hollow wall repairs

Hollow walls are found in houses of all ages—modern homes often contain stud walls, while older properties tend to have walls constructed of lath and plaster. In both cases, there is a void inside the wall that can cause problems when it comes to effecting a repair. When filler or plaster is applied to a hole in the outer drywall or lath-and-plaster layer, it tends to fall directly into the wall void unless some kind of support can be provided until it dries.

minor lath repairs

As long as the laths are not damaged, repairing is a straightforward job because the lath supports the plaster. If any lath is broken, you need to provide support to prevent the plaster from falling into the void behind it.

tools for the job

- utility knife
- old paintbrush
- pencil
- scissors or aviation snips
- cordless drill/driver
- bucket & mixer
- hawk
- gauging trowel
- plastering trowel

1 Use a utility knife to cut away loose plaster from the edge of the damaged area, until it is surrounded by plaster that is still bonded to the lath behind. Poke any lumps of plaster trapped between the lath into the void behind.

2 Use an old paintbrush to remove dust and remaining debris from the hole and the lath. Take care that you dust the area thoroughly because loose material left in the hole will prevent the new plaster from bonding to the lath properly, and may lead to premature failure of the repair.

3 Hold a piece of fine metal mesh over the hole and draw a pencil line on it just inside the perimeter of the hole. Cut it to size with scissors or aviation snips, hold it in place, and drill several slim pilot holes through the mesh and into the lath. Secure the mesh to the lath with short, slim countersunk screws.

4 Dampen the edges of the hole with water to prevent the repair plaster from drying out and cracking. Mix some bonding plaster and press it into the hole with a gauging trowel, working from the edges in. Fill the hole to within ⅛in of the surrounding plaster. Press the surface of the wet plaster with the tip of the trowel in a crisscross pattern to provide a good key for the finish coat.

5 Allow the bonding coat to dry hard, then mix some finish plaster and use a plastering trowel to coat the patch and leave it level with the surrounding wall. Allow it to harden, then dampen the trowel and polish the surface to a smooth finish.

tips of the trade

When repairing lath-and-plaster walls, buy a tub of ready-mixed one-coat plaster if you do not have powder plaster available. Apply a single thick coat to the hole with a plastering trowel, pressing it firmly against the lath so that some plaster squeezes between them to form a key. Finish the repair level with the surface and leave it to dry hard before redecorating.

stud wall repairs

If you have a hole in plasterboard or drywall, there will be nothing behind it to support the repair plaster. The solution is to insert a piece of plasterboard or drywall in the hole and bond it into place, then to fill the hole in the usual way.

tools for the job

- pencil & ruler
- utility knife or drywall saw
- hand saw
- cordless drill/driver
- putty knife

1 Draw a square or rectangle around the hole and cut along the lines with a utility knife. Use a drywall saw to cut ½in thick plasterboard, which is too thick to cut easily with a knife. Remove the cut section.

2 Cut a scrap piece of plasterboard, drywall, or masonite to the appropriate size—about twice the height of the hole in one dimension, and a fraction less than its width in the other. Drill a hole in the center of the board and thread a doubled-over length of string through the hole. Tie the cut ends of the string around a nail and pull the string until the nail lies flat up against the face of the patch of board.

3 Apply some all-purpose adhesive to the other side of the patch along the two shorter edges. This will bond it to the inner face of the wall board when it is installed in the hole.

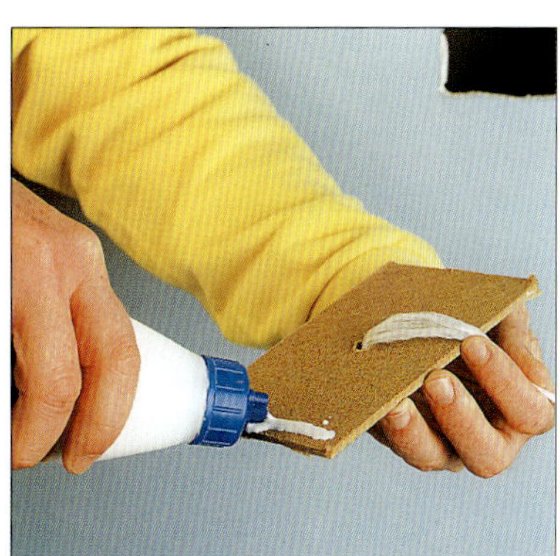

4 Carefully feed the patch into the hole while holding the string in your other hand so that you do not lose it in the void. Maneuver it so that the two short edges press against the inner face of the wall board above and below the hole. Pull hard on the string to bond the patch in place. With all-purpose adhesive it should stay safely in place after a minute or so. Allow it to set for the time recommended on the tube.

5 When the adhesive has set, cut off the string. Mix joint compound and fill the hole in two stages—to about half its depth and then, when this layer is touch-dry, to just above the surrounding surface. Allow it to set hard, then sand it level.

tips of the trade

If the hole in a plasterboard of drywall wall is larger than about 4in across, it is better to use the technique for patching damaged ceilings (see page 118). Make horizontal cuts in the board above and below the hole, back to the adjacent studs at either side, then cut down the center line of the studs to leave a rectangular hole. Cut wood blocks to fit between the studs behind the top and bottom edges of the hole, and attach them to the studs with screws at a 45-degree angle. Cut some plasterboard of drywall to fit the hole, nail it to the studs and blocks, then apply a finishing coat of plaster over the repair.

making solid wall repairs

In many ways, solid wall repairs are easier to carry out than equivalent damage in hollow walls. This is because you do not need to worry about providing support while the plaster or filler dries. However, it can still be challenging to produce a finish that blends with the surrounding wall area. Whether the damaged wall is brick, stone, or block based, the same technique may be used for repair.

tools for the job

- hand sledge
- cold chisel
- protective gloves
- safety goggles
- dusting brush
- old paintbrush
- gauging trowel
- plastering trowel

1 Remove any loose debris from the hole. Use a hand sledge and cold chisel to knock off any rough areas of old base coat or plaster. Always wear safety equipment such as goggles and gloves during this process, to protect yourself from bits of debris that tend to fly away from the wall surface.

2 Use a dusting brush and vacuum sweeper to clean the hole as thoroughly as possible. Pay particular attention to the area around the edges, where dirt and dust tend to collect. Before any work can begin, all loose material must be cleared away so that the hole is totally dust-free.

3 Mix up some bonding agent and use an old paintbrush to apply the solution liberally in the hole. Again, make sure to pay particular attention to the edges of the hole, allowing the solution to extend slightly onto the surrounding wall.

4 Mix up some bonding-coat plaster, and press it firmly into the hole using a gauging trowel. Be sure that the bonding coat is molded into all areas of the hole, and that it is brought up to a level slightly below that of the surrounding wall surface. You may find it easier to combine use of the gauging trowel with a plastering trowel to ensure an even surface finish.

5 Before it dries, score the surface of the bonding coat, using the edge of the gauging trowel. At the same time make sure that none of the bonding coat is pushed above wall level, as this will affect the finish when you apply the top plaster coat.

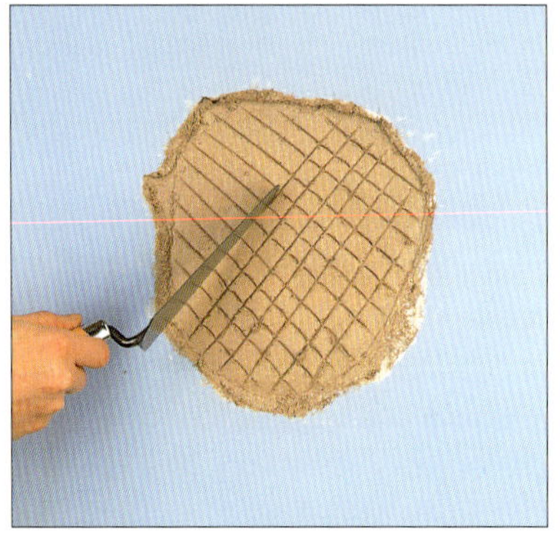

tips of the trade

If you do not have bonding coat and multifinish plaster, it is possible simply to build up the patch with layers of one-coat plaster. This will not produce the same totally smooth, level finish as that of multifinish plaster, but its slightly rougher surface may be more appropriate on wall surfaces of very old houses.

6 Mix and apply a coat of multifinish plaster, using a plastering trowel to press it firmly into position. For holes of this size, rest the edges of the plastering trowel on the wall to the sides of the hole, enabling you to produce a neat finish.

HOLE TYPES

- **Deep holes**—Where depth is greater than that shown above, it is necessary to apply a base coat to the hole before plaster can be applied. As always, it is better to apply thin layers rather than try to speed up the process with thicker ones. Over-application simply causes the base coat or plaster to bulge and makes it impossible to achieve a smooth finish when applying subsequent coats.

- **Shallow holes**—Where the top layer of plaster has come away from the layers underneath, it may only be necessary to apply a single finishing coat. In such cases, however, it is common to find that if one area of top layer plaster has come away, this may be the case for most of the rest of the wall surface. Tapping the surface with the butt end of a trowel and listening for hollow reverberations will give some indication as to the stability of the surface. If the plaster is indeed loose, it is better to remove and replaster at this stage rather than paint and face a similar patching problem in the near future.

7 This finish can be leveled more by cutting a piece of wood strip to slightly longer than the hole diameter, and gradually drawing the strip across the plaster surface, again making it as level with the surrounding wall as possible.

8 Allow the plaster to dry off slightly. Then use an old paintbrush to wet the surface of a plastering trowel with some clean water.

tips of the trade

Plastering is always a messy job, so it is important to keep surfaces and tools clean at all times. When applying plaster or base coat to a hole, keep a clean sponge handy so that you can wipe away any excess material that gets on to the surrounding wall surface. It is always better to clean such messes off the wall while they are still wet—if the base coat or plaster is allowed to dry, its removal will be much more difficult and may require a combination of sanding and scraping to attain a flat surface.

9 Smooth, or polish, the plaster patch with the wet trowel until a totally even and level finish is achieved. Once the plaster dries, light sand will be necessary to smooth the surface before you can begin to paint.

FINISHING OFF

- **Drying naturally**—The temptation when patching a small area of wall is to try to force the drying process to speed up by applying heat directly to the patch. This can have the effect of cracking the base coat and plaster, which will then require further repairs in order to achieve the desired finish. Subsequent cracking can be avoided by allowing the patch to dry naturally at room temperature.

- **Priming**—Once it is completely dry, ensure that the newly plastered area is primed before any further coats of paint are applied. Use a primer specified for use on plaster for this purpose.

- **Lining option**—On walls that may have a number of patch repair requirements, it may be necessary to consider lining the wall after repairs are complete, in order to smooth the surface further. On particularly uneven walls, woodchip or textured paper is a further possibility for providing a more even wall finish.

patching a ceiling

Ceilings can be damaged by water leaks, or sometimes on an old lath-and-plaster ceiling the plaster can simply come away from the lath if the plaster key fails with age, but the most common cause of damage to a ceiling is when someone's foot slips off a joist onto an unboarded area of the attic and ends up poking through—the stuff of many a TV comedy sketch! After the comedy of the moment, however, there is no need for panic, as a simple patch repair will return the ceiling to a finish as good as new. Whatever has caused the damage, the best solution is to cut away the affected area and to fit a plasterboard or drywall patch.

tools for the job

- stud finder
- pencil
- straightedge
- safety goggles
- drywall saw
- utility knife
- claw hammer
- tape measure
- hand saw
- power drill & twist drill bits
- screwdriver
- self-adhesive mesh
- joint tape
- putty knife
- plastering trowel
- hawk

1 Locate the joists on either side of the hole, either by using a stud finder or, if the attic is unboarded, by making holes down through the ceiling alongside the joists so that their positions are visible in the room below. Draw a pencil line along the center line of each joist, extending beyond the damaged area.

safety advice

You must also check whether there are any services, such as water pipes or electricity cables, in the immediate vicinity of the hole before drawing guidelines for cutting. If the ceiling is below the attic these checks can be made manually, otherwise a stud finder can be used.

2 Draw two more lines at a right angle to the first, joining up the joist lines to form a rectangle outline of the area you plan to cut out. Use either a long rule, a wood straight-edge or a level.

3 Cut out from the hole towards one of the pencil guidelines using a drywall saw, then cut along the line in each direction until you reach the joists. Repeat the process at the other side of the hole. Use a utility knife to cut the plasterboard along the guidelines indicating the joist centers. Look out for concealed nails or fasteners as you do this.

4 Pull down the cut-out section of board, and use the claw of a hammer to pry out the old fasteners from the undersides of the joists. Pry them out with the hammer head against the joist, not the plasterboard.

5 Cut two lengths of dressed softwood so that they form a tight fit between the joists on either side of the hole. These will act as blocks to support the edges of the plasterboard patch. They should be at least 2 x 2in in cross section, but 2 x 4in is ideal. Hammer them in until they are half-concealed by the edge of the hole.

6 To secure each block in place, you will first need to drill a clearance hole through one end at 45 degrees to the joist, then screw in a long screw to secure the end of the block to the joist it butts up against. Repeat the process to fix the other end of the block to the opposite joist. Don't worry if the blocks move slightly as you screw them in place—there will still be enough exposed wood to which the plasterboard patch may be nailed.

7 Measure and cut a piece of plasterboard or drywall to fit the hole. Test its fit and cut the sides down to size with the aid of a utility knife. Lift the piece of plasterboard or drywall into place and nail it to both the joists and blocks with 1¼in galvanized plasterboard nails. Position the nails a distance of at least ⅜in from the edges of the plasterboard or drywall, and drive them into the wood until their heads just dimple the paper. Nail the existing board to the blocks along the edges of the hole too.

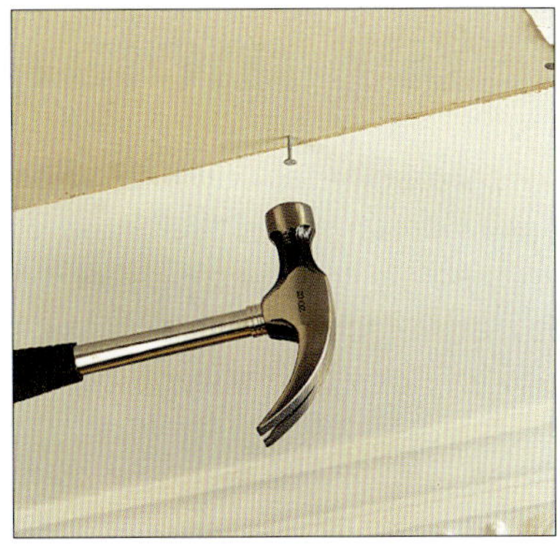

8 Stick lengths of self-adhesive mesh joint tape over the joints to stop future cracks. Then use a putty knife to apply a band of joint compound over the tape, to conceal it and to fill the gaps around the patch.

9 Plaster over the patch with a coat of finish plaster if you have it, or use a one-coat ready-mixed plaster. Feather out the edges of the plaster onto the surrounding ceiling surface to make the patch less noticeable. Wet the trowel and use it flat to the ceiling to polish the repair, leaving a smooth finish. Leave to dry and then paint to match.

WATER DAMAGE

If part of a plasterboard or drywall ceiling has been soaked by penetrating moisture or a plumbing leak, the surface finish will still be badly stained by the water even if the actual plasterboard has remained intact. It is not enough simply to reapply water-based paint, since the stains will keep bleeding through. The solution is to seal the stains in with a proprietary stain-block spray, or to cover them with a coat of any solvent-based primer or paint. Once the stains are sealed you can then paint over the area with water-based paint to match the rest of the ceiling.

LATH-AND-PLASTER

If the ceiling is of a lath-and-plaster construction, the technique for making the repair is slightly different:

1. Pull down as much loose material as you can to begin with, then mark out the area to be removed as for plasterboard ceilings.

2. Make the saw cuts parallel to the lath first, inserting the drywall saw between adjacent lath and cutting through the plaster. Dislodge as much plaster as possible between these cuts and the hole to expose the lath that needs to be removed.

3. Simply pull broken lath down so that the pieces snap where they are nailed to the joists—they are usually very dry and brittle. Saw through the center of any undamaged lath and snap the pieces off in the same way.

4. Clean up the broken ends of lath beneath the joists with your utility knife, then cut and fit the plasterboard or drywall patch as normal.

If a patch of plaster breaks away because the key to the lath has failed, the rest of the ceiling may be close to failure too. If this is the case, the best solution is to pull down the entire ceiling and replace it with a plasterboard or drywall ceiling.

repairing plaster moldings

Many older properties have highly detailed plaster cornices and other ceiling and panel moldings as original features. These would have been molded in fibrous plaster and then screwed into place —most are too heavy to be supported solely by plaster adhesive. Unfortunately, years of repainting will often gradually obscure the fine detail. Many may also have been damaged by the building of partition walls to subdivide large rooms. However, restoration is usually possible.

cleaning moldings

If you have moldings that are clogged with layers of old paint, be prepared for some slow and fussy restoration work. The first thing you have to do is to find out what sort of paint you have to contend with. In an unrestored property it will probably be distemper, but in renovated ones you could find anything from eggshell to modern latex paint.

tools for the job

- work platform
- garden spray gun
- improvised picks & scrapers
- old toothbrushes
- soft-bristle brush

1 The first thing to try on old moldings is water applied as a mist with a garden spray gun. This will soften distemper, but will have no effect on other types of paint. Soak a test area and leave it to penetrate for 10–15 minutes.

2 If the water works, use an improvised pick, scraper, or toothbrush, as appropriate, to remove the old distemper bit by bit. This will be time-consuming and fussy work, so tackle just a short section at a time and make sure you are working at a comfortable height—ideally off a work platform rather than a stepladder.

3 After removing as much paint as possible, scrub the surface of the molding gently with a soft-bristle brush to remove flecks and specks left behind by the picks and scrapers. Repaint it with a thinned coat of latex to act as a sealer, followed by a full-strength coat.

safety advice

Always wear latex work gloves and safety goggles to apply any form of chemical paint stripper.

4 If water fails to make any impression on the old paint, you will need to experiment with chemical strippers. Look for products that come in paste form rather than as sloppy liquids. The former will stay put on the surface of the molding as they soften the paint, while the latter will splash everywhere and make a thoroughly unpleasant mess. Brush the stripper on freely, then work it into the recesses of the molding with a stippling action of the brush.

5 Some strippers are designed to be used in conjunction with special fibrous tissue strips that you bed into the layer of stripper. These not only help to prevent the stripper from drying out too quickly, they also allow you to peel strip and stripper away in one go after the stripper has done its work, making the restoration job much less labor-intensive.

restoring damaged cove or cornices

If the damage to the cove or cornice is minor, you may be able to make it good with filler or plaster of paris, molding the repair material to match the originals. However, if this is not possible, the best option is to replace the damaged section with a new piece of cove that matches the original as closely as possible.

There are several manufacturers who produce modern replicas of traditional cove and cornices in fibrous plaster, so unless your particular cove is very unusual you may be able to find a suitable replacement from one of these suppliers. Another possible source of matching cove is architectural salvage companies, who rescue and sell period details from old houses. Both solutions are expensive, however.

tools for the job

- safety goggles
- work gloves
- brick chisel
- hand sledge
- hacksaw
- plastering equipment (see pages 110–11)
- cordless drill/driver
- screwdriver
- putty knife
- paintbrush

1 If you are able to obtain a length of suitable replacement cove or cornice to match the damaged one, remove the damaged section by carefully cutting it away piece by piece with a brick chisel and hand sledge. Remember to wear protective gloves and safety goggles to protect you from dust and flying rubble. Depending on how the cove was put up, you may find wall and ceiling plaster coming away as you work. Look out for fasteners and screws buried in the cove. Break the plaster away around them, then cut them off level with the wall or ceiling surface with a hacksaw.

2 When you have removed the damaged section of cove, clean up the newly exposed wall and ceiling surfaces so that the new cove or cornice can fit closely against them. Cut the new cove to length and offer it up to check the fit—this is a job for two pairs of hands. If the old cove was put up after plastering, you will then have to replaster the areas that came away in step 1.

3 Make sure that any replastering has fully hardened before installing the length of replacement cove or cornice. When it is ready, drill fixing holes through the cove at the spacings recommended by the manufacturer. Hold the cove back in place and mark the corresponding hole positions on the wall. Drill the holes and insert wall plugs, then apply the adhesive recommended by the manufacturer to the rear faces of the cove and offer it up to the wall and ceiling surfaces, pressing it firmly into place. Secure it with long screws countersunk beneath the surface of the cove or cornice.

4 Insert joint compound into the screw holes and the joints between the old and new sections of cove, then make good the wall and ceiling plaster alongside the repaired section. Finally, paint the cove with a coat of dilute latex paint to seal the surface, followed by a full-strength coat. Brush the paint out well so that you avoid the clogging that overpainting can cause.

improving ceilings

Making sure that a ceiling has a good surface for decorating may require more work than simply minor repairs. Severely sagging old ceilings can require demolition and reconstruction, but some surfaces have other potential options. For example, applying a new plaster skim over a rough ceiling surface is one way of restoring it to a flatter finish. Alternatively, the projects considered below may be more appropriate to your needs.

old textured ceilings

Textured ceilings suit some people more than others. For this reason, you may find it desirable to restore a textured or patterned ceiling back to a flat surface. One technique for removing textured coatings is to use a wallpaper stripper. However, when using such appliances, pay close attention to the manufacturer's operating instructions and adhere to all the required safety procedures—goggles and gloves are essential protective equipment.

Alternatively, if the coating is firmly stuck to the ceiling surface, it can be easier and less time-consuming to simply plaster over the top of it. To do this, refer to the plastering techniques described on pages 92–103—but you may also need to adopt the refining technique described below.

tools for the job

- scraper
- large paintbrush or pasting brush
- plastering trowel
- mixing equipment

1 Use a scraper to knock off all the high points from the textured coating. The degree to which you have to do this will depend on the depth of finish but, generally, removing as much texture as possible will make the plastering process much easier later on.

2 Brush a coat of bonding agent onto the textured surface to seal it and stabilize it in readiness for the plaster.

3 Mix up plaster (see page 92) and apply it to the ceiling with a

plastering trowel. A fairly thick plaster coat is required in order to take up the roughness or texture on the ceiling, so two coats of plaster may be needed.

THE TEXTURED OPTION

On badly cracked or rough ceilings, there is an option to use textured paint to help take up the roughness or undulations of the ceiling surface. The texture produced is not the finish of standard textured coatings, but it is enough to fill minor cracks and provide a more even-looking finish, without going to the expense or time of replastering. Bear in mind, however, that plastering a ceiling is by no means a job for a beginner, and so using textured paint is a serious and economic option for people with less experience.

using textured paper on ceilings

Just as lining paper can be used to smooth a ceiling surface, textured paper can be used to add pattern and interest to the ceiling surface.

The structure of this type of paper is three-dimensional, so some care is required when hanging it. It may be necessary to line the ceiling first to achieve the best possible results.

tools for the job

- chalk line
- pasting brush
- paperhanging brush
- scissors
- pencil
- utility knife or scissors

1 Use a chalk line to gain a precise guideline across the ceiling surface. Secure the paper in the wall/ceiling joint, making sure that the edge of the length runs precisely along the chalk line.

2 Brush out the paper in the usual manner, applying enough pressure to secure it in position and to remove air bubbles from beneath, but not so much pressure that the pattern texture becomes crushed. Continue along the length to the other end.

3 Draw a pencil guideline along the wall/ceiling joint, peel the length back, and cut along the guideline with a utility knife or scissors. Brush the end of the paper back in place and repeat the process at the other end of the length.

4 When joining lengths, take care not to crush the relief with the brush. Wipe off excess paste from the wall and paper surfaces as you work.

tips of the trade

Remember that textured paper needs a stronger mix of paste than normal paper because of its weight.

Textured paper offers a uniform, patterned finish that gives a greater focus to the ceiling and helps to conceal an uneven surface.

repairing wood trim

Wood trim often needs repairs and requires different techniques of restoration from those for walls or plaster surfaces. Wood, whether in the form of paneling, baseboard, or any other feature, tends to suffer from general wear-and-tear such as bumps, scrapes, and splits. Minor damage can be treated with the relevant filler, but more serious damage may require replacement sections of wood in order to restore the surface to an attractive finish.

baseboards

The function of baseboard is to add a finish at the wall/floor junction, and to protect the base of the wall from any damage. Unsurprisingly, the baseboard itself can become damaged over time and in need of repair. For short sections of damaged board, the most economical technique is to replace the entire length. However, on long stretches of baseboard this can be seen as wasteful, and inserting a replacement section is better.

tools for the job

- pry bar & protective gloves
- hand saw
- miter box
- hammer
- tape measure
- damp cloth
- nail set

1 Ease the baseboard away from the wall using a pry bar to pry a gap between baseboard and wall. (Wear protective gloves for this process.) Position two pieces of wood strip behind the baseboard and pry the baseboard free from the wall surface.

2 Position a miter box in front, and to one side, of the damaged section of baseboard. Cut down through the baseboard with a hand saw. Move the miter box to the other side, and then cut on the opposite miter angle through the baseboard. Remove the damaged section.

3 Nail the baseboard back in position on either side of the gap you have created. Take accurate measurements for the new piece of baseboard you require and cut a length to fit, mitering each end correctly to fit snugly in the gap.

4 Before securing in place, test to see that your new section fits. Apply some wood glue along the cut edge of the new piece and position it, removing any excess adhesive with a damp cloth.

5 Attach the section permanently in place by nailing finish nails through the mitered joint at either end of the new section of baseboard. Three nails along each side should be sufficient. Set in the nail head before painting the baseboard.

repairing tongue and groove

Damaged tongue-and-groove paneling presents a different set of problems because removing the panels—which have blind fasteners—can be tricky. Some ingenuity is therefore required so that boards can be replaced without causing any further damage to the surrounding panels.

tools for the job

- cordless drill
- keyhole saw
- pry bar
- claw hammer or pliers
- hand saw
- wooden mallet
- chisel

1 Drill a hole to the side of the damaged tongue-and-groove board and along the joint it makes with the adjacent board. Choose a drill bit large enough to accommodate a keyhole saw.

2 Use a keyhole saw to cut through the joint. Work up and down along the joint, until total separation between the two lengths has been achieved. Accuracy is not vital, as the aim is simply to gain access to the damaged board in order to make your repair.

3 Use a pry bar to lever out the damaged board. You may also need to work a little on the other side of the board, because there will be nails holding the panel in place. However, with one edge loose, a combination of levering and easing should result in the board coming free. It is also worthwhile to remove the board adjacent to the broken one, as the damage caused during cutting is likely to be noticeable.

4 After both boards have been removed, use a claw hammer or pliers to take out any nails that may still be present in the exposed furring

strips beneath the tongue-and-groove paneling. Failure to remove them will hinder progress later.

5 Cut two new lengths of tongue and groove to size. Use a mallet and chisel to trim the tongue off one of the lengths—this is because damage caused in removing the old lengths may have affected the actual interlocking mechanism of the tongue-and-groove system. By removing the tongue on one length, it should then be possible to insert the strip into the existing paneling.

6 Interlock the two new sections into the paneling, and secure them in place with finish nails. The new paneling may then be primed and painted.

tips of the trade

Tongue and groove is supplied in a range of thicknesses, so always check your requirements before purchasing replacement strips.

pointing brickwork

The mortar joints between bricks—known as the pointing—is the weakest link in any exterior wall. If it fails for any reason, water can penetrate the bricks and winter frosts can lead to their faces splitting off—a condition known as spalling. The problem may have been caused by poor workmanship, by use of the wrong mortar mix, or simply by rain erosion. Make a point of inspecting your brickwork each spring, and tackle any areas showing signs of deterioration.

tools for the job

- safety goggles
- work gloves
- cold chisel
- hand sledge
- stiff brush
- bucket & mixer
- garden spray gun
- hawk
- pointing trowel
- profiling tools

1 If you find an area of pointing that is loose and crumbling, the first job is to chip it out back to sound mortar—to a minimum depth of about ¾in—using a sharp cold chisel and a hand sledge. Wear work gloves and safety goggles to guard against flying rubble. Work along the horizontal joints first, then along the vertical, plumb ones.

2 Use a stiff-bristle brush—but not a wire one, which will mark the bricks—to clean dust and rubble from all the joints you have worked on. Then mix a small batch of mortar and allow it to dry to see how well it matches the existing mortar. Use a ratio of 1 part cement to 5 parts soft sand, and experiment with different colored sands to get as close a match as possible.

3 When you have a suitable mortar formula, mix about half a bucketful at a time—pointing is slow work, and unused mortar that has begun to dry out cannot be resuscitated by adding more water. Then spray water from a garden spray gun onto the area where you plan to start work. This helps to cut the suction of the brickwork, and prevents the mortar from drying out too quickly.

tips of the trade

- **Tackling large areas**—If you have a large area of wall to point, you can speed up the chopping out process by hiring a power tool called a mortar raker. This has a tungsten-carbide cutter that grinds out the old mortar to a preset depth in a fraction of the time the job takes by hand. Wear safety goggles, a dust mask, and ear protectors when using this equipment.
- **Access equipment**—Pointing brickwork is a slow job, and working off steps or a ladder can make your feet and back ache. Work off trestles and staging instead for areas up to about 10ft above ground level, and use a slot-together platform tower for work higher up. Not only do these access options enable you to stand or kneel in comfort, they also provide a surface for placing tools and materials conveniently to hand. Both types of equipment can be hired.

4 Put some mortar onto a hawk, and take a sausage shape of mortar off it with a pointing trowel. Press the mortar firmly into one of the horizontal joints, and draw the tip of the trowel over it to bed it in and bond it to the underlying mortar. Point all the horizontal joints first.

5 Use the same technique to fill the vertical joints, one at a time. Press the mortar in well, leaving it almost flush with the surface of the bricks. Trim off excess mortar as you work, but leave any that gets on the face of the bricks to dry. You can then remove it with a dry brush and avoid staining the wall face.

6 When you have completed about 10sq ft of wall, it is time to finish the pointing to match the existing brickwork's joints. In a weathered joint, the pointing has a slope out from top to bottom, with the top recessed by about ¼in and the bottom level with the face of the brick below. Form this type of joint by drawing the tip of the trowel along the newly filled joint, with the flat of the trowel resting on the top edge of the brick below the joint.

7 To match a V-shape recess, drag the tip of the pointing trowel along the center of the new mortar joint, removing some mortar to leave a neatly shaped recess.

8 A joint with a concave profile is one of the most common joint finishes, and is easy to match. Simply draw a rounded object such as an offcut of garden hose along the joint, leaving it with a semicircular cross-section. A recessed joint is set back from the face of the bricks by up to ⅜in. It is formed by drawing a scrap piece of wood or similar implement along the joint to rake out the mortar to a uniform depth. This type of joint should not be used on brickwork in exposed locations.

tips of the trade

If you are having trouble matching the color of your existing pointing, try adding a mortar pigment to your mix. These powders are available in black, brown, green, yellow, and red, and come in 3lb packs that will tint around 110lb of cement. Make a few trial batches first using different amounts of pigment, allowing them to dry out before you compare the final color. Measure the ingredients accurately—too much or too little pigment will change the color of the finished mortar noticeably.

Identify the type of joint in the existing brickwork, and try to match it as closely as possible. The recessed joints in this brickwork are formed using a scrap of wood.

replacing damaged bricks

If failed pointing has allowed rainwater to penetrate behind the face of your brickwork, and subsequent frost has split off the faces of some of the bricks, the only way you can restore the appearance of the wall is to chop out the damaged bricks and replace them. The job itself is a relatively straightforward one. The biggest problem lies in finding replacement bricks that are a good match for your existing ones.

tools for the job

- safety goggles
- work gloves
- cold chisel
- hand sledge
- hammer drill & masonry drill bits
- brick chisel
- bucket & mixer
- spot board
- hawk
- bricklaying trowel
- pointing trowel
- profiling tools

1 Cut out the pointing all around the damaged brick using a sharp cold chisel and a hand sledge. Make sure that you wear work gloves to protect your hands, and safety goggles to keep flying rubble out of your eyes.

2 To make it easier to remove the damaged brick from the wall, drill a series of closely spaced holes down the middle of the brick to a depth of about 4in using a hammer drill and a large masonry drill bit. Take care when drilling that the drill bit does not slip onto any of he surrounding bricks and cause any more damage.

3 Try to split the brick in half by cutting along the line of the drill holes with a brick chisel and hand sledgehammer. When you have done this, hold the chisel on this central split at an angle towards the ends of the brick and cut out sections one by one, taking care not to damage the surrounding bricks. Take care on cavity walls not to drive pieces of brick into the cavity, where they could drop and act as a bridge for moisture between the inner and outer parts of the wall.

tips of the trade

It can be difficult to remove whole bricks from solid walls, especially walls in which the bricks are laid end-on (known in the trade as headers). The best way of repairing a damaged header is to drill it as described in step 2, and then to chop it out to a depth of about 4in—or roughly half the length of the brick. Cut the replacement brick in half and test its fit in the recess, cutting it down further in length if necessary to allow for a mortar bed behind it. Butter mortar into the base of the recess and onto the top, sides and back of the replacement brick, and slide the brick into place. Check that it is centered in the recess, adjust if necessary, and then tap the brick gently home until it is level with its neighbors. Point all around it, matching the existing pointing as closely as possible, to complete the repair.

4 When you have removed the damaged brick, cut away as much of the remaining pointing as possible from the top, bottom, and sides of the recess. Once again, if you are repairing a cavity wall, take care not to let any debris drop down into the cavity.

5 Mix a small amount of mortar and let it dry to see how well it matches the color of the existing pointing. See the tips of the trade box on page 127 for more information on matching the color of mortar. When you have a satisfactory formula, mix another small batch and place it on a spot board—a piece of scrap plywood or similar board close to where you are working. Place a bed of mortar on the base of the recess using a bricklaying trowel, and butter more mortar onto the top and ends of the new brick.

6 Carefully slide the new brick into place in the recess, centering it and then tapping it back with the handle of the hand sledge until it fits flush with its neighbors. Check that the new brick is horizontal and that the joints around it are an even thickness, repositioning it slightly if necessary to achieve this. Use a pointing trowel to add mortar as necessary to the joints around the new brick, then finish the pointing to match the rest of the wall.

MATCHING BRICKS

Unless your house is relatively new, the brickwork will have weathered and changed color over the years to the point where a new brick—even if it is a close match to the originals—will look very noticeable next to its aged neighbors. Look out for advertisements in local newspapers that offer second-hand bricks, which may be a closer match to yours. Architectural salvage firms may also be able to help. If all else fails, tour your area looking for demolition work in progress—you may well find the bricks you want lying in a container somewhere.

Once you have found an appropriate secondhand brick, you will need to clean it if any mortar is stuck to its surface. To do this, use a brick chisel and hand sledge to chip off the old mortar. Make sure you wear appropriate safety goggles and work gloves to protect yourself from flying rubble when you do this.

Try to match the type of pointing on the existing brickwork. Refer to steps 6–8 on pages 126–7 for more details on how to create different pointing profiles.

repairing scratch coat

Many houses have a scratch coat finish applied to their exterior walls, either to make poor-quality masonry more weatherproof, or simply as a decorative feature. It is a layer of mortar applied to the surface of bricks or blocks using a two-coat system to give a final layer up to 1in thick. The surface may be troweled smooth or textured. It may have pebbles or other fine aggregate pressed into the surface to create a finish known as pebbledash.

Weathering and slight movements in the masonry can eventually cause scratch coat to crack. This allows water to penetrate and seep down behind the scratch coat, and if it freezes it can cause patches to lose their grip on the masonry. These sound hollow when tapped, and may break away as time goes by.

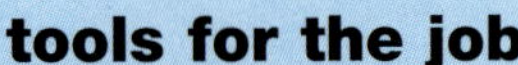

tools for the job

- safety goggles
- work gloves
- claw hammer
- chalk
- brick chisel
- hand sledge
- stiff brush
- old paintbrush
- bucket & mixer
- hawk
- pointing trowel
- wooden straightedge
- plastering trowel
- texturing tools

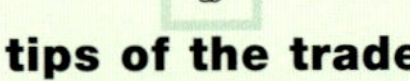

tips of the trade

If your scratch coat is in generally poor condition, with a number of blown or missing areas, it will take forever to patch up, and the apparently sound areas are probably on the verge of failing, too. Your best bet is to hack off all the old scratch coat, and to call in a builder to apply a fresh coat. This job is beyond all but the most dedicated DIY enthusiast because of the large quantities of materials involved, and the need for scaffolding to provide safe access for the work to be carried out.

1 Identify areas of scratch coat that have blown—lost their bond to the masonry behind—by tapping the surface with a hammer handle. Mark around any areas that sound hollow with chalk. Use a ladder to reach scratch coat at second-story level.

2 Wearing safety goggles and gloves, use a brick chisel and hand sledge to chop away the scratch coat until you reach a sound edge. Undercut the edges of the hole slightly to help key the new mortar patch to the old scratch coat, then brush all loose material out of the hole, paying particular attention to the bottom edge where most of the rubble will collect.

3 Apply bonding agent mixed with PVA (polyvinyl) adhesive, using an old paintbrush to apply this sealant onto the masonry and the cut edges of the old, cut-out scratch coat. Doing this will help the patch of new scratch coat to bond well to the masonry, and will also help to stop the scratch coat from drying too quickly, which brings the risk of cracking as it does so.

4 Mix some mortar in the ratio 1 part cement to 4 parts coarse (concreting) sand, and add some liquid plasticizer to the mix to improve its workability. For small repairs, buy a bag of dry, ready-mixed mortar for scratch coats, and just add water.

Load some mortar onto a hawk and start troweling it into the hole. Fill the edges first, then the center, aiming to leave the first coat about ¼in below the surface of the surrounding scratch coat. Score the surface with the corner of the trowel in a crisscross pattern to provide a key for the second coat of scratch coat.

5 Apply the second coat so that it finishes a little above the surrounding scratch coat, then use a wooden straightedge to rule off the excess mortar. Hold its edge against the wall just below the patch and move it slowly up, while at the same time moving it from left to right in a teeter-totter action. This removes excess mortar without any risk of disturbing the underlying patch.

6 Fill any hollows revealed by the ruling off with a little more mortar, then sweep the surface of the repair smooth with a plastering trowel, wetting it first to stop the mortar from sticking to it as you work. Make the mortar as smooth as possible. If the existing surface has a texture, imitate it on the patch using whatever tools are appropriate—perhaps a stiff brush, a sponge, a textured paint roller, or a pointing trowel. If the house is pebbledashed, load some matching pebbles onto a hawk and push them off it and into the wet coat with a plastering trowel. Use the flat of the trowel to embed them well into place.

PAINTING SCRATCH COAT

If you have bare scratch coat, it will be much more weather-resistant—and look better—with a coat of masonry paint applied to it. Kill any green algal growth on north-facing walls with a proprietary fungicide, then apply a coat of stabilizing solution to the scratch coat to seal its surface and reduce its porosity. You can then apply the paint, using a brush, a long-pile roller, or a spray gun. The last is the quickest method, but you need to employ special spraying equipment—the fillers used in masonry paints will clog an airless spray gun. You will also have to spend time masking doors, windows, eaves, woodwork, and downpipes, but the effort will be worth it, especially if you have pebbledash or heavily textured scratch coat, which takes a long time to paint by brush or roller because of the need to work the paint into all the crevices. If you do not have time to paint the whole house in one go, try to do it wall by wall rather than stop in the middle of a wall, since the join may show up in the finished surface.

Finish the patched area of scratch coat to match the existing surface. This could mean using a sponge to texture the surface, as shown here, or applying pebbledash.

solving moisture problems

Most brick houses built since the late 19th century have a waterproof layer called the foundation coating built into their walls just above ground level to stop ground water from being absorbed into the masonry. In older houses, the coating is either a double layer of slate or a couple of courses of dense water-resistant engineering bricks. In modern houses it is a strip of strong plastic. A similar vapor retarder is incorporated in the structure of solid concrete ground floors.

tackling foundation coating bridges

Rising moisture shows up as damp patches on interior walls, usually rising to a height of about 3ft above floor level. However, finding this type of moisture does not necessarily mean that the foundation coating has failed. It could have been bridged in some way, allowing ground water to bypass it and rise into the wall structure. The illustration below shows some common causes of such bridges. The step-by-step sequence at the bottom of the page outlines how to tackle them.

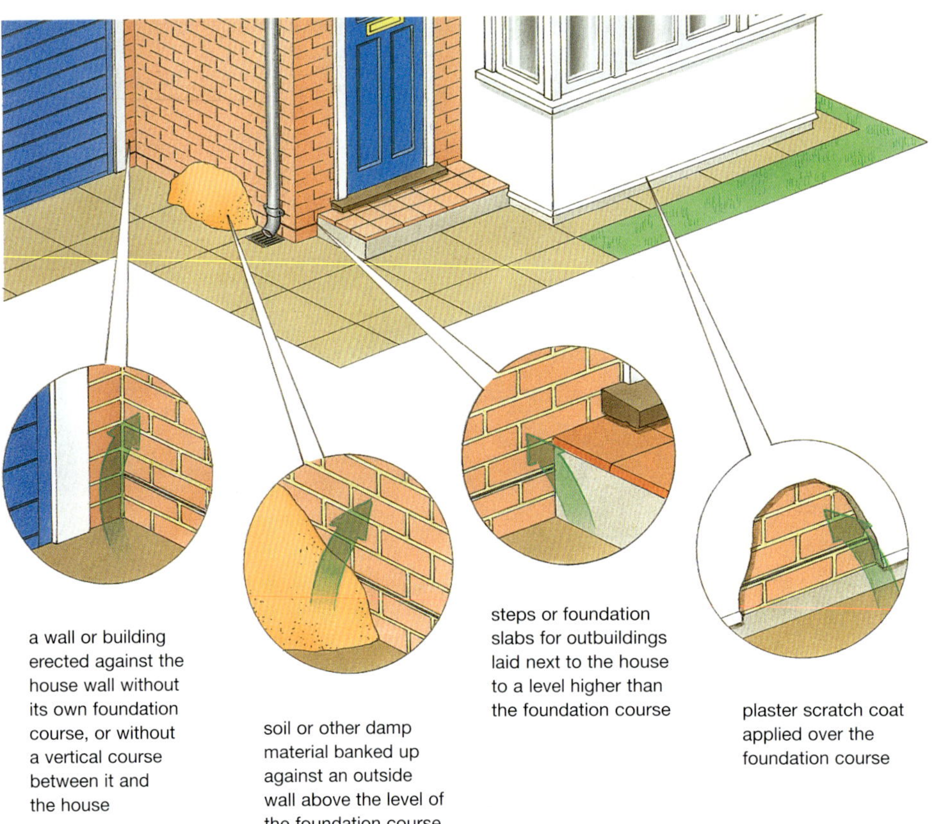

1 Clear soil or other material that has been piled against the walls above foundation course level, and make sure that air bricks have not been blocked. These are essential for providing ventilation to suspended wood floors, which can develop rot if they become damp.

2 Where walls or slabs have been built against the house and they bridge the foundation course, chisel out the mortar or concrete between the two and insert a plumb course. Then seal the joint with non-setting caulk.

3 Treat brickwork above a path or patio that is less than 6in below foundation course level with two coats of clear silicone water-repellent sealer to stop it from absorbing water. Alternatively, lift one row of slabs next to the house and replace them with a layer of gravel.

4 Cut away plaster to just above the level of the foundation course with a brick chisel and hand sledge. The course is usually visible in the mortar joint in which it is embedded. Fix a steel and expanded metal external plaster stop bead to the wall, level with the course, and plaster down to it to leave a neat horizontal edge.

dealing with a failed foundation coating

If your moisture problem persists despite tackling any possible moisture bridges, then it is likely that the course has actually failed. You can call in a moisture-treatment firm to install a new course for you, by injecting waterproof chemicals into the masonry. However, since the work is very labor-intensive and you can rent the same injection equipment the specialists use, it makes sense to do the job yourself. The tool-rental companies that supply the equipment also stock the chemicals you need—you buy them on a sale-or-return basis when you rent the equipment.

To find out whether you have solid or cavity walls, start by examining their structure—if brickwork is exposed and it consists entirely of bricks laid end to end, it is a cavity wall. If the bricks are not visible, measure the wall thickness—it will be around 9½in if it is solid, and about 11½in if it is a cavity wall.

tools for the job

- injection machine (rented)
- hammer drill
- long masonry drill bits
- depth stop
- pointing trowel

1 Rent the injection machine and at the same time collect enough fluid for the job—you may need up to 5¼ pints per 10sq ft of wall if the brickwork is very porous. Rent a professional-quality drill, too—you may well overload a DIY model during this process. Buy masonry drill bits in a diameter to match the size of the injection nozzles and long enough to drill to a depth of 8in. Make sure the rental company shows you how to operate the machine.

2 Carry out the first stage of the injection process by drilling holes 3in deep at about 6in intervals along the wall at foundation course level. The injecting may be done from the inside or outside. Insert the shorter nozzles supplied, secure them in place, and start injecting the fluid. When complete, move the linked nozzles along to the next set of holes and repeat.

solid wall—stage 1

cavity wall—stage 1

3 When you have injected all the holes, drill through the same holes to a depth of 6in in solid walls and 8in in cavity ones. Repeat the injection process using the longer nozzles supplied with the machine. When injection is complete, fill the holes with mortar.

solid wall—stage 2

cavity wall—stage 2

tips of the trade

- **Inside walls**—If solid inside walls also show signs of moisture, lift floorboards alongside them and inject fluid using holes about 2in deep in a one-brick thick wall.
- **Damaged plaster**—If plaster has been damaged by moisture, chip it off and replace it with a waterproofed cement scratch coat. Cover this with a coat of finish plaster when the wall has dried out.

floors & stairs

Floors and stairs are used every day, with little thought given to how they are constructed. To some degree, their design will be determined by the building codes and regulations in force at the time the house was built, and the materials that were available. Within these parameters, however, there is substantial scope for variation in construction to satisfy different purposes and functions, while the preferences of the architect and the relationship of the building to its surroundings will also have an impact.

estimating quantities

Once you have decided that you are going to go ahead with a home-improvement project, one of the most important things you will need to work out is the overall cost of the project, so that you can plan your budget and assess whether it is financially viable, then place orders for materials. To do this you will need to make accurate estimates of the quantities required of each component.

planning quantities

In the rush to get started on a new project it is all too easy to miss out sensible planning. Carefully estimating the amount of materials that will be needed is a vital element of the planning stage, so that you can then place an accurate order—standing in the builder's stores or a DIY store is not the time to be working this out. With expensive items, such as stone floor tiles and carpet, it is especially important not to overorder or you will be left with costly surplus. Some projects are easier than others when it comes to working out the amount of materials you will need. In the case of a floor in a square or rectangular room, for instance, simply multiply the width by the length to get the total area. Working in three dimensions is only slightly more complicated—just remember to multiply width by length by depth. The best way to plan for quantities is to take accurate measurements and transfer these to a scale plan, from which you can calculate the amounts.

tips of the trade

Always add about 10 percent to the final figure when calculating quantities—this will account for cutting and waste, and will leave you with a little spare material for future repairs.

SPECIAL CONSIDERATIONS

- **Patterned floors**—Plan for more waste being left over when laying patterned floor coverings, so that you can match up the design as it is laid.
- **Built-in furniture**—If laying the floor covering in a room with built-in furniture, for example in a kitchen or bathroom, you can cover the entire floor prior to installation, or cut around the furniture, leaving a short margin that will run underneath. If the latter, then either incorporate the built-in elements into your plan, if you have an accurate idea of their dimensions, or measure up after installation.

MAKING CALCULATIONS

Depth of joists

The capacity for a joist to support weight is more dependent on depth than thickness, which tends to remain constant at about 2in. Follow the formula shown below to work out the depth of joist you will need.

The number of joists that you require will depend on the size of the room and the center-to-center spacing

Formula for calculating depth of joists: Depth in units of 1in = $\frac{\text{Span of joists in units of 1ft}}{2} + 2$

Example for room span of10ft: 10ft divided by 1ft = $\frac{10 \text{ units}}{2}$ = 5 + 2 = 7 units

7 units x 1in = 7in

Floor covering

To calculate the amount of floor covering that you need, multiply the width by the length then add 10 percent for cutting and waste.

Example for a room measuring10ft x 23ft: 10ft x 23ft = 230sq ft + 23 = 253sq ft

making a scale drawing

In order to make an accurate calculation of the amount of floor-covering material needed, it is a good idea to formulate a detailed two-dimensional diagram of the room with measurements for each of the different areas indicated. Even craftsmen will make a scale drawing of the room, showing the location of principal features. If the room includes permanently built-in furniture, or will do so, these should be included on the diagram, especially if it is not your intention to lay floor covering underneath. Using graph paper to draw the plan will help ensure accuracy. If you take the plan along when going to buy materials, with all the measurements marked on, this will enable you to place an accurate order so that you do not end up with too little or far too much material.

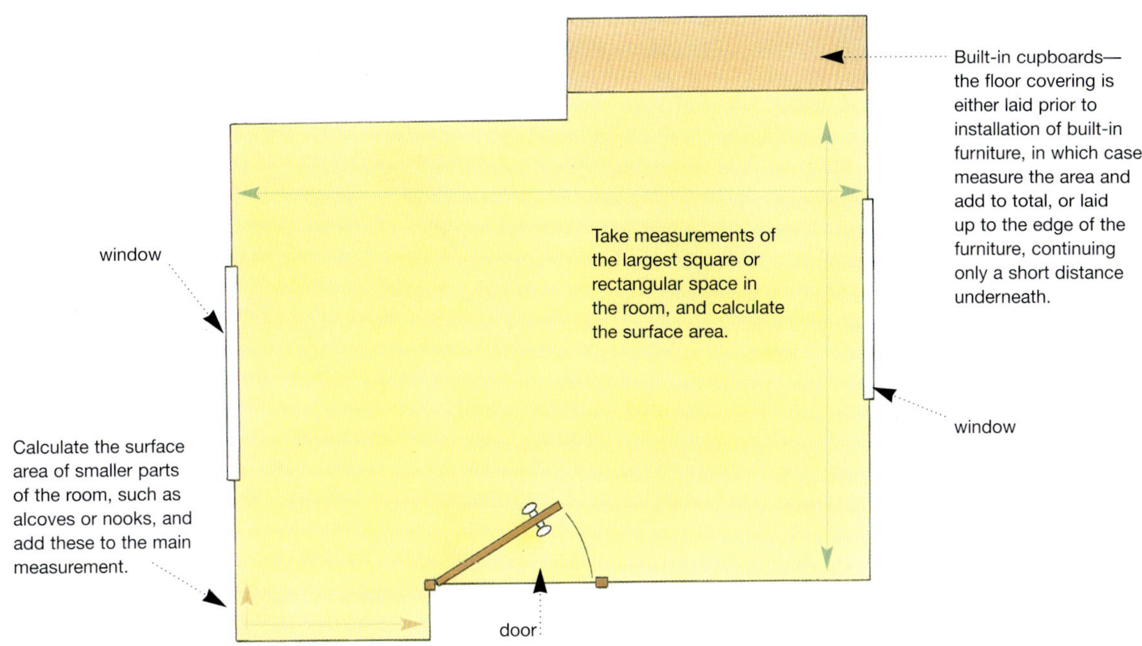

calculating floor covering for stairs

To work out the amount of floor covering needed for a staircase, add together the total run (the sum of the depth of each step) to the total rise (the sum of the height of each step). The total run and total rise can be calculated either by measuring the total width and height of the staircase, or by taking measurements for one step and multiplying this by the total number of steps. This will give the length of material required, but you will need to mulitply this by the width of the steps to give the total surface area. If laying trim, where strips of the staircase are exposed on both sides of the covering, adjust the width measurement accordingly. Add 5 percent to the total for waste.

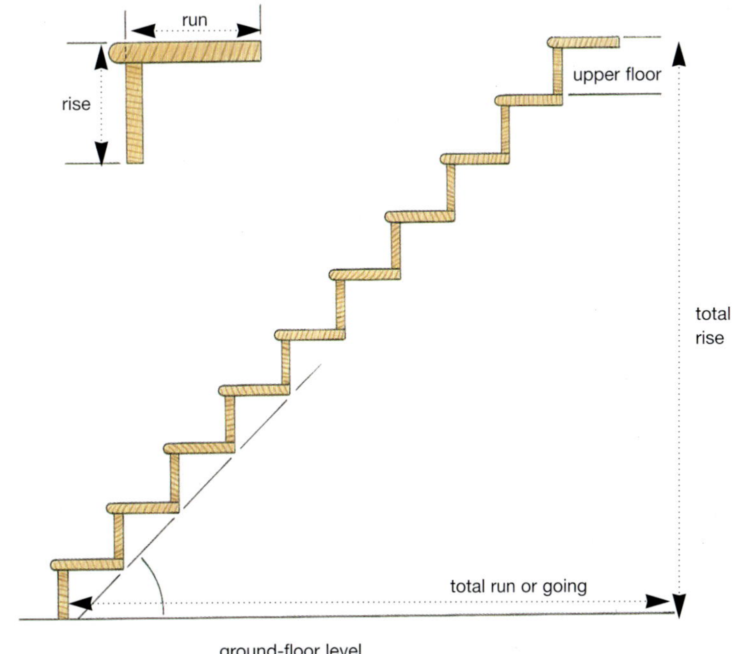

wooden floor construction

In the vast majority of homes the floors will be constructed from wood. Until quite recently a wood floor meant just that—a floor constructed out of solid wood floorboards nailed on top of solid wood joists. However, technological advances have altered many of the traditional methods of construction so that chipboard and plywood are commonly used instead of wood. The age of the property will have a bearing on the method of construction, with newer houses tending to make use of sheet flooring, which provides a smooth base over which to lay a floor covering.

traditional wooden floor

The diagram below illustrates the traditional method of constructing a wooden floor. Floorboards may be either square-edged or jointed to each other with the aid of a tongue-and-groove joint, which helps to cut down on drafts. New houses tend not to have floorboards, as it is a much slower and more expensive process to lay floorboards than laying sheet floors. Where renovations have taken place, often you will find that floorboards have been ripped out and chipboard sheets laid instead, although recently there has been a vogue for plain, exposed floorboards in interior design. Where an upper-story floor has been constructed using this traditional method, it is likely that the ceiling below will follow the old-style lath and plaster construction.

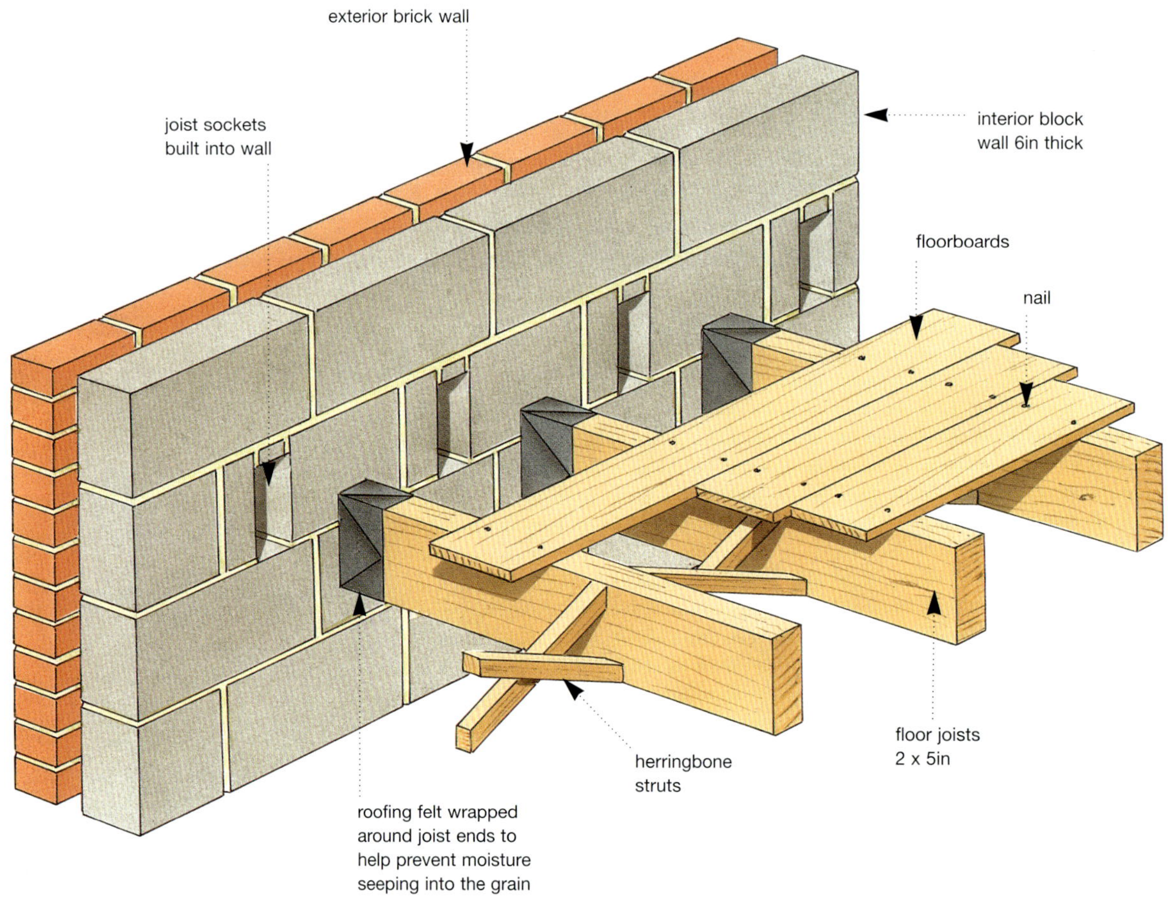

floor supported by joist brackets

Suspended floors in modern houses are commonly supported by joist brackets. These prevent the wooden joists from coming into direct contact with the brickwork or blockwork, so that moisture cannot seep into the ends of the joists. The joists will often be thinner than those used in traditional construction, and sheet chipboard in place of floorboards acts as a stressed component tying everything together. Where the floor forms a ceiling for the room below this will be of plasterboard or drywall finished with plaster coat.

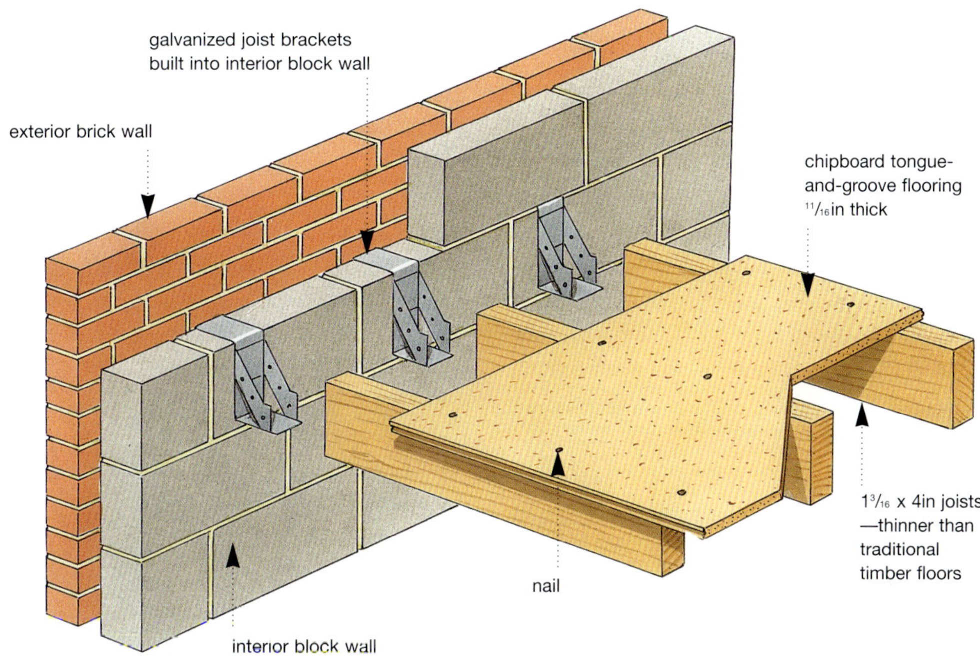

modern I-beam construction floor

This type of floor is regularly found in homes that utilize wooden framing for structural walls. It may look inferior, but in actual fact I-beam construction is extremely strong and rigid. The beams can be made on site, but are most often manufactured under controlled conditions and bought in. As with floors supported by joist brackets, sheet materials will usually be employed as floors and ceilings for beam floors.

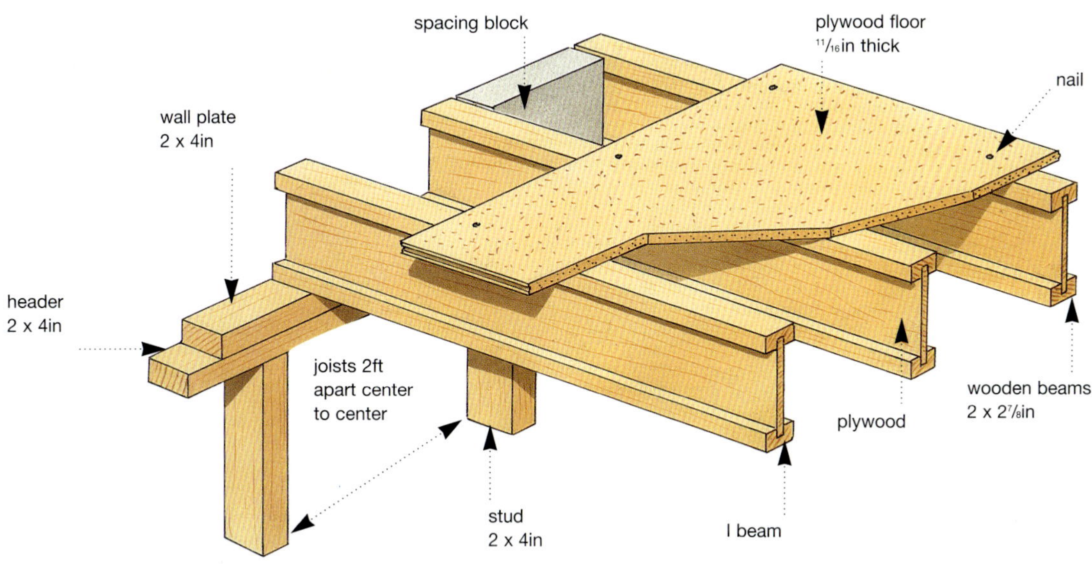

wooden staircases

Most staircases in homes are manufactured from wood. If the stairs are in particularly bad shape, then replacing them entirely is often a more economical option than attempting to repair or renovate them. With most older stairs you will find the structure is sound but there are just a few creaks. These can be effectively repaired and given a new finish by being sanded and then painted or stained, and when this is combined with a new set of balusters and newel post, or paneling under the stairs, a total new look can be achieved for relatively little cost.

closed tread

Closed-tread stairs are the simplest to make and are undoubtedly the most common—most modern homes include a staircase with a single straight flight of stairs of closed-tread construction. More traditional closed-tread stairs tend to be made from solid wood, but with the invention of relatively inexpensive manufactured building boards, on many modern staircases treads and risers will often be made from MDF or plywood. Some local building codes state that a staircase with over a certain number of treads must incorporate a landing. Few domestic staircases have more than twelve treads, but they may include a landing if they turn a corner.

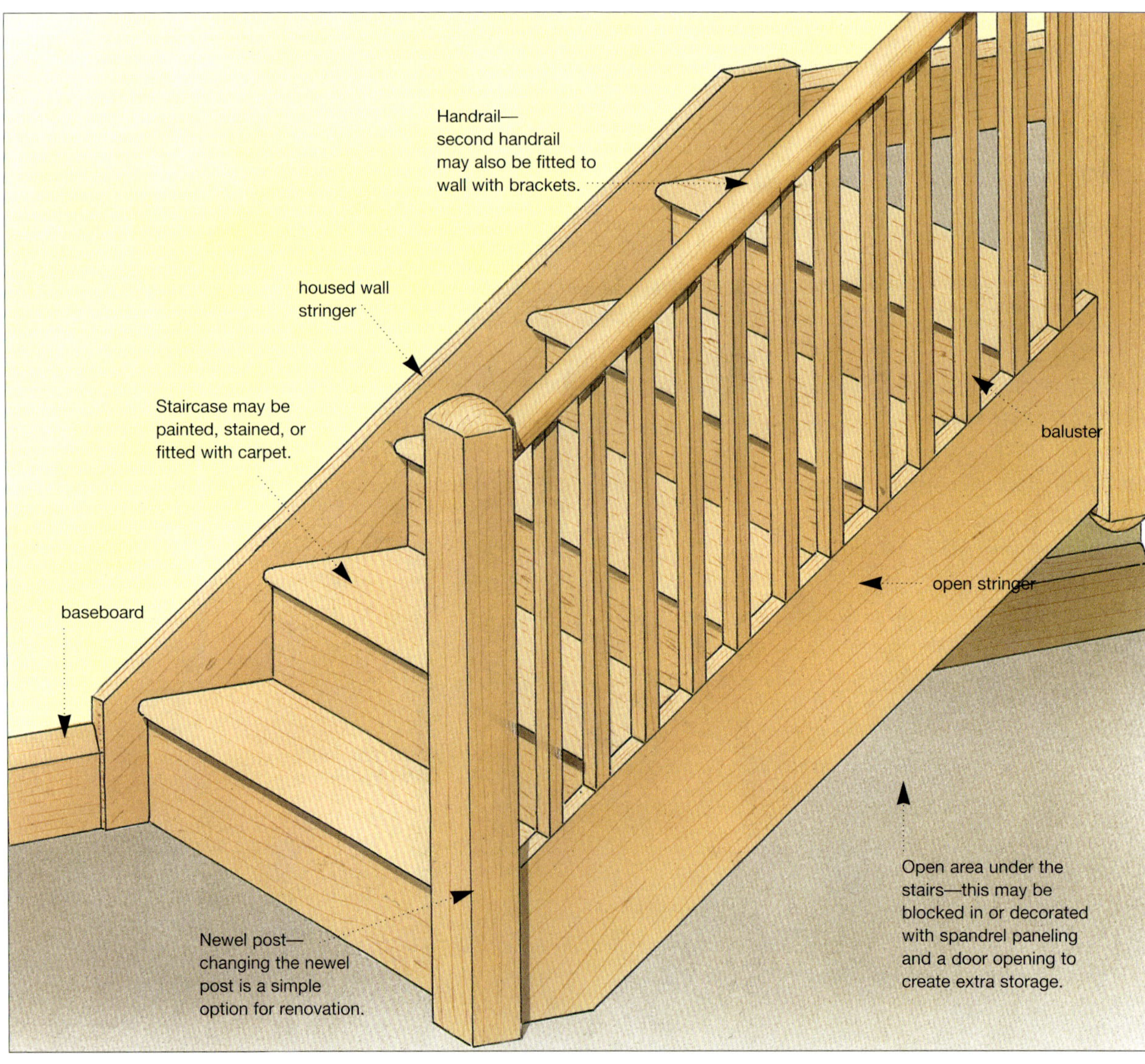

open tread

Open-tread stairs are similar to closed-tread stairs except that more of a feature is made of the staircase. Although once very popular, these days domestic staircases are seldom built with an open-tread construction, partly because of changing trends and fashions, and partly because of the increased cost of production. Lacking the support of risers, the treads must be more stoutly constructed to be able to cope with the loads placed upon them without bending. For obvious reasons open-tread stairs are not usually covered with carpet, but the treads tend to be made of hardwood that can be stained, varnished, polished, or painted. The absence of risers means that these stairs cannot be boxed or paneled in with any great success. Indeed, the very idea of the open tread is to allow the eye to see other parts of the room and the structure of the building.

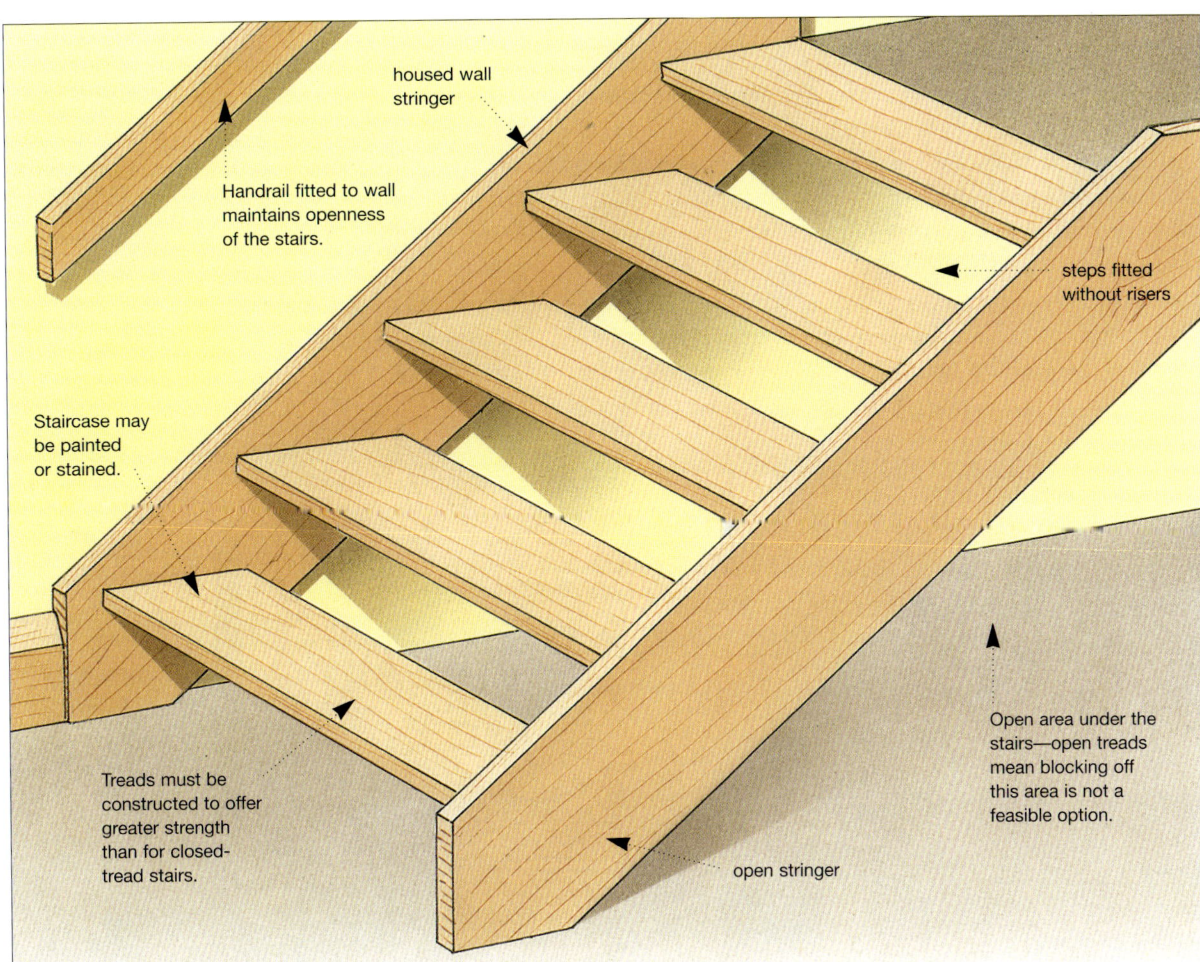

CHOOSING WOOD

Stairs can be so much more than just a means to travel from one level to another. There is a huge range of wood suitable for stair construction if you are considering installing a new staircase, or completely replacing an existing one. You may buy a pre-constructed stairway, or you may choose to have one custom-built.

The cost depends on the type of wood you choose. If you select a hardwood such as oak, be prepared to pay a premium price. Conversely, a softwood such as oregon pine will be far more affordable. You can always use cheaper wood or manufactured boards if the stairs are to be painted, but a pine stair will look good stained or varnished.

RENOVATING A STAIRCASE

Another option is to dress up the stairway you already have. Many DIY stores offer stair-part kits to transform the look of a staircase. Without touching the treads and risers it is possible to remove the existing newel, balusters, and handrail, replacing these with something better suited to your taste and the surrounding decor.

concrete & cast-iron stairs

Concrete stairs are usually seen in commercial properties, but they can be found in residential properties too. Popular in the 1930s, they have recently seen something of a renaissance. Stairs constructed from cast iron are more often located outside a property, as an exterior fire escape or as a means of accessing an upper-story apartment. If cast-iron stairs are inside, it is most often in the form of a spiral staircase.

concrete stairs

If you are aiming for a minimalist, functional interior style, then concrete stairs will contribute greatly to such a look. However, it is possible to soften their harsh appearance with wooden covering or carpet, clever use of wooden handrails, and other details. Concrete stairs can be produced off-site and then installed by a builder, but for a single job it is more economic to construct the stairs in place. The usual method of construction is to construct wood formwork to act as a mold for the wet concrete, which is then removed once the concrete has set.

Concrete stairs are durable, but not without their problems. Spalling occurs when moisture gets into minute cracks in the surface and then freezes in cold weather, causing the surface of the concrete to break away. Spalling can be difficult to stop, for once the surface has broken off more water can find its way in. Another problem is the corrosion of reinforcing rebars or lath embedded into the concrete, which can cause serious structural failure. This problem is rare, but when it does occur the entire staircase will have to be replaced.

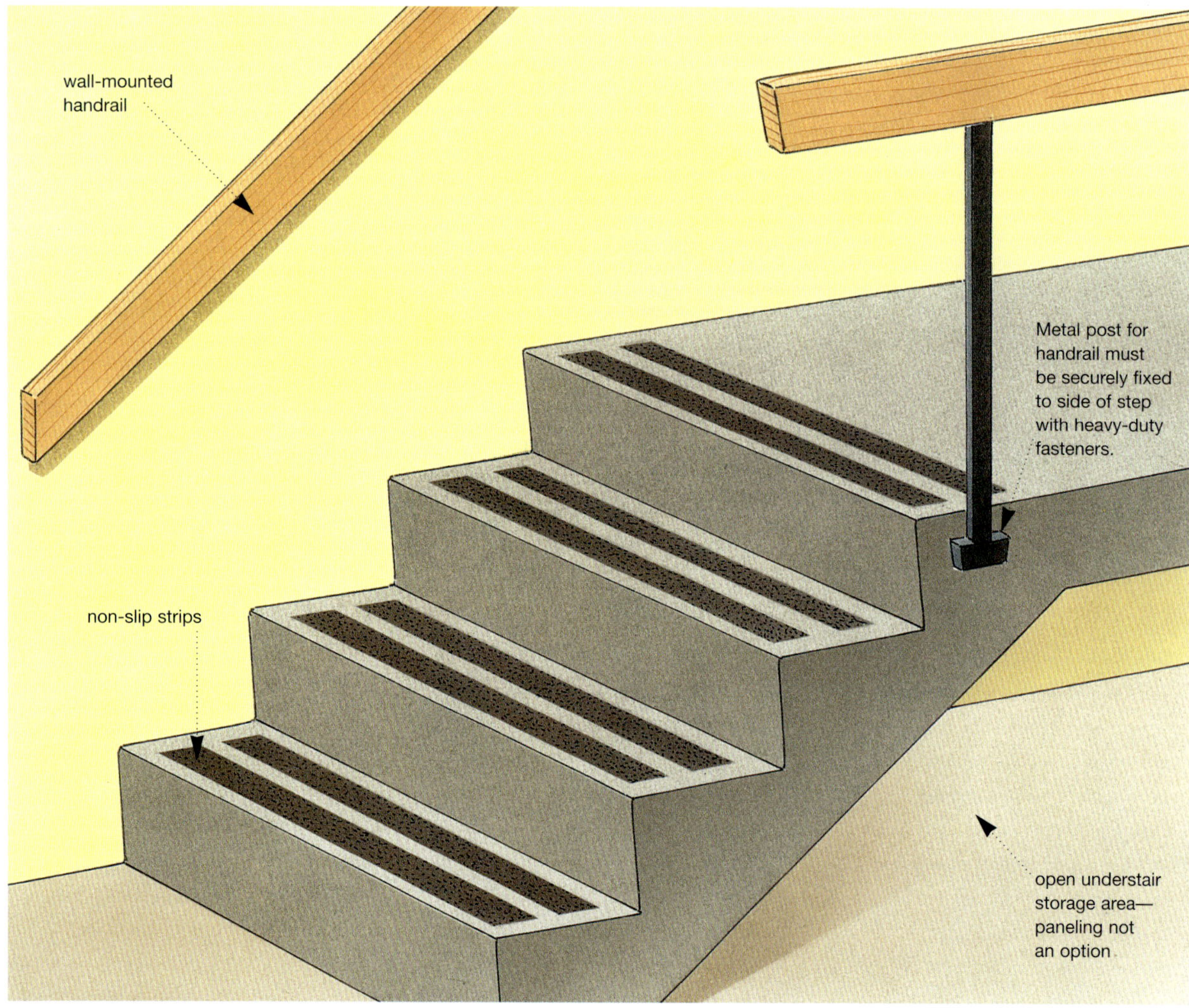

cast-iron stairs

A newly built cast-iron staircase can be expensive to buy, but if you are very lucky you may be able to buy a secondhand example. Old 19th-century industrial buildings often contain cast-iron spiral stairs, so it is worth asking at reclamation yards to see if they have anything that might be suitable. Cast-iron stairs are constructed the same, whatever their shape and size, from sections bolted together. They are almost maintenance-free, so the only thing you may have to do is tighten or replace some of the nuts and bolts, particularly at handrail junctions.

spiral stairs

Installing a spiral staircase will make an unusual and impressive addition to a house, opening up new possibilities in the use of inside space. Spiral stairs rise in their own space and so take up much less floor area then any other type of stairway, so one of the prime reasons for installing such a staircase is the need to cope with a lack of space.

The idea of installing spiral stairs rarely occurs to homeowners, and when it does it is usually dismissed out of hand. Certainly, as the main staircase linking the ground and second story, spiral stairs are not really a practical option, especially in a household that includes children, the elderly or people with disabilities. Yet for a secondary staircase when space options are limited, spiral stairs will make an original and ornate feature. In a small home that does not have space for a straight-flight staircase, a spiral staircase can be used to gain access to the attic space. Not having to use a ladder each time makes this space much more user-friendly, and the fact that a previously uninhabitable room has been made usable means the cost of the staircase is easily recouped. One of the main disadvantages is that, with the steepness of the rise and the continuous turn, moving larger items of furniture to upper stories is a real problem. Spiral stairs may be constructed from wood, metal, or concrete. They can also be built against a wall, in which case the outside edge will be supported by the wall structure, or they may be built freestanding, with all structural support deriving from the central post.

BELOW *Strips of carpet attached to each tread make it easier on the feet and less noisy to ascend and descend these spiral stairs.*

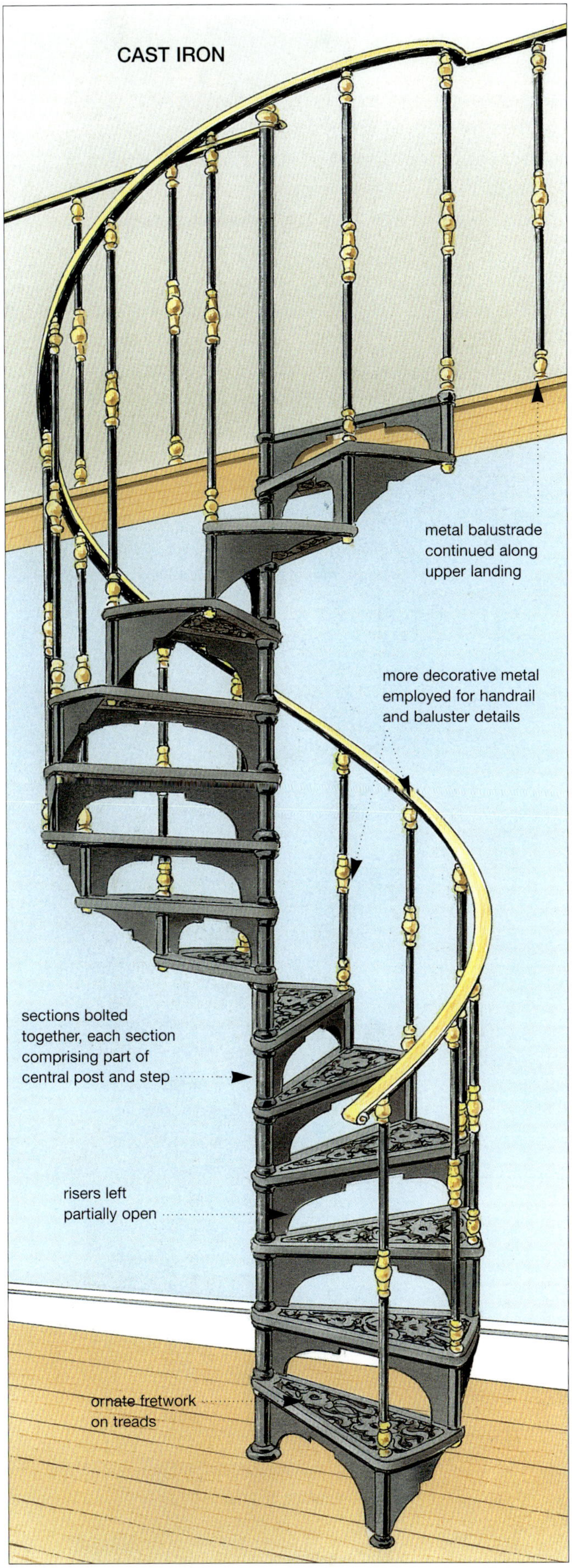

CAST IRON

metal balustrade continued along upper landing

more decorative metal employed for handrail and baluster details

sections bolted together, each section comprising part of central post and step

risers left partially open

ornate fretwork on treads

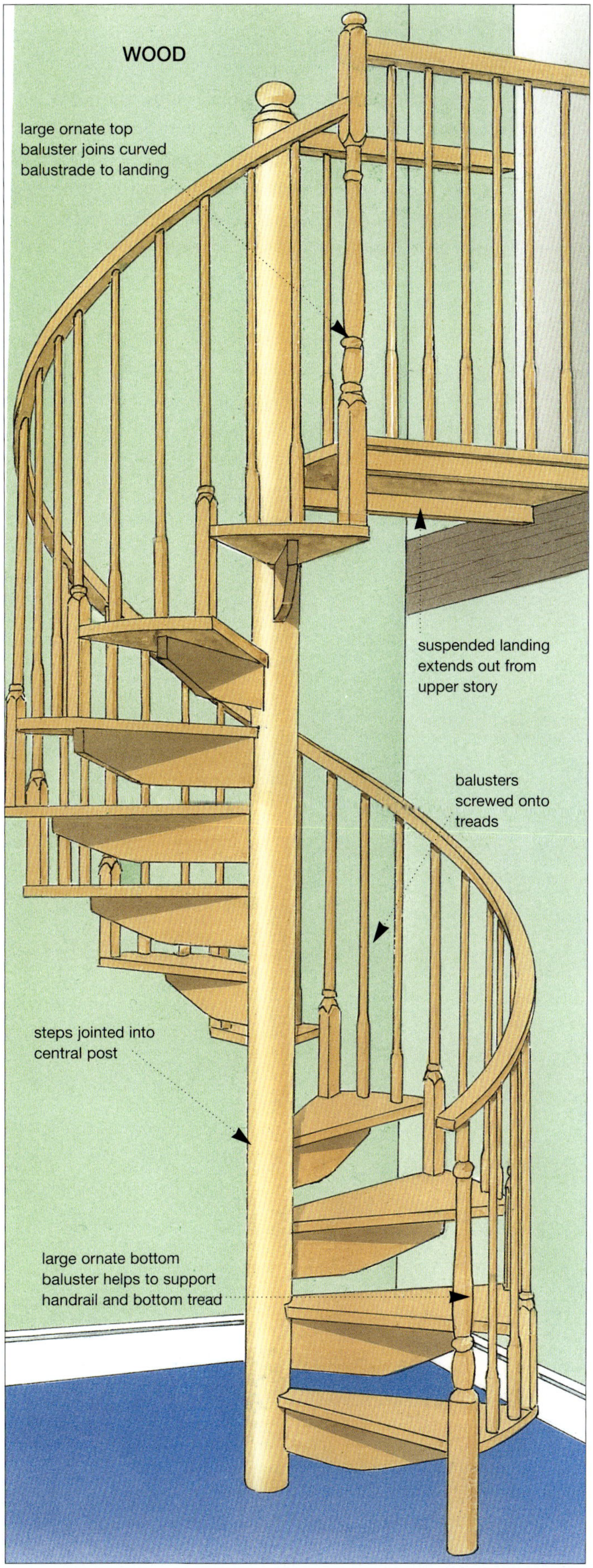

WOOD

large ornate top baluster joins curved balustrade to landing

suspended landing extends out from upper story

balusters screwed onto treads

steps jointed into central post

large ornate bottom baluster helps to support handrail and bottom tread

landings

The term landing traditionally describes the area created by extended treads at a point where there is a turn in the staircase, but is also used to describe the part of an upstairs hallway immediately adjacent to the staircase. Where landings form an integral part of the staircase, their construction will be similar to the rest of the stairs, although there are occasions when they will have been built as part of the structure of the house, particularly where they form short hallways between separate flights of stairs.

Landings perform several different functions. Where space is limited they may be installed to allow the stairs to change direction. They may also be installed into the staircase purely as a design feature, forming a visual break to the run of the stairs. The landing of your staircase is a good place to establish the decor of your home.

The upstairs landing is the first place you arrive at when you reach the top of the stairs, and it leads on to the other rooms. As such it can be used to good effect, either to set the tone for the decoration in adjacent rooms, or to offer a contrast. Generally people match landing and downstairs hallway decoration—but not always. Older homes often have large windows that give good natural light to landings and stairways, something that may be lacking in newer properties. If your landing is dark, try lightening the color scheme and installing additional light fixtures. A more radical approach would be to make an opening in a bulkhead wall to allow more light in.

LANDING TYPES

There are different types of landing for each kind of turn in staircases with more than one flight. A quarter-space landing is the most common, which is where the second flight continues up at a right angle. A quarter-space landing is a small square landing, equal in width to the stairs. Half-space landings allow a 180-degree° turn in the flights, and their length is equal to two flights. A variation of these two is the half-turn open-well staircase with two quarter space landings. This allows for a 180-degree turn but over three flights, often with a shorter flight between two landings. The least common is a flying landing where the stairs continue straight. In between landings and steps are winders, which are really extended, wedge-like steps that describe a short turn at the top of a staircase.

LEFT *The staircase carpet has here been extended along the landing hallway and into the adjacent room to provide continuity of decoration.*

safety advice

Like those on the main staircase, for safety reasons, new or replacement balusters on landings may be subject to building codes. Older properties are not subject to these rules, but if handrails and balusters are being replaced, then you will need to comply. As with all home-repair or renovation projects, check with your local building codes regulator before starting work, as this can save money and frustration in the long term.

RIGHT *A chair and desk have been installed in what would otherwise be unused landing space to create a bright study area.*

BELOW *Rather than having two quarter-landings, this staircase combines a landing with winders to make the 180-degree turn between flights.*

making changes to floors

Making changes to an existing floor, or replacing the floor altogether, is often the first step towards more general renovation of a room. For example, if you are converting an upper-story room into a bathroom you will need to consider strengthening joists to cope with the weight of a bathtub filled to capacity. You may be forced to make changes due to adverse circumstances, such as moisture penetration in a suspended floor, the best remedy for which is often to replace it altogether with a solid concrete floor. Prevention is the best cure, however, and another project described in this chapter is how to add ventilation to the underfloor area in order to avoid damage from moisture.

By installing a plywood floor over the concrete subfloor, this garage has been transformed into a comfortable workroom.

laying floors in bathrooms

If you feel confident about laying floors in any other room in the house, then the bathroom should present no particular problem. However, there are a few special considerations, most of which relate to all the water involved in the day-to-day activities that take place—bathrooms can be extremely wet, and measures need to be taken to minimize the amount of moisture damage to the floor. The damp air, leaking pipes from bathtubs and basins, and the weight of the bathtub all can cause damage to both the subfloor and floor covering.

dealing with moisture

To ensure the longevity of flooring in a bathroom, an adequate ventilation system is essential to eradicate the presence of condensation. Care over plumbing work and regular inspections will make sure that all plumbing connections are tight and leak-free. Laying bath mats will go some way to minimize the damage due to splashes from bathtubs and basins, but more important is to ensure the floor covering is waterproof or resistant to moisture, and that all areas where moisture can penetrate are adequately sealed. Before laying any new floor covering, inspect the existing subfloor for water damage and rot. Remove the bathtub panel and check below the bathtub. Leaking pipes should be obvious and need to be rectified immediately. A musty smell is a sure sign of problems and must not be ignored, and sections of the floor that are soft or rotted will need to be replaced. If you are buying sheets of manufactured board, tell your supplier that these are being laid in a bathroom, as there are special water-resistant grades that are better suited to the damp environment.

ABOVE RIGHT *Naturally water-resistant, hard tiles are a good option for bathrooms, but make sure you seal the grout joints.*

the bathroom fixtures

If the flooring is being replaced or relaid as part of an overall bathroom refurbishment, the fixtures are probably also being replaced at the same time. If not, then before the floor can be replaced you will need to remove the bathroom fixtures and any other cabinets and panels attached to the floor. Elsewhere in this book you will find instructions on renewing the subfloor, and provided you follow these closely you should encounter few problems. When flooring is to be replaced as part of a much larger refurbishment program, it can be a good idea to lay the floor covering before the installation of toilet, bathtub, bidet, and basin pedestal. Though not always practical, where it is you avoid having to lay the floor covering in what is often a tight space that will require exacting cutting.

LEFT *A neater job will often result if floor coverings can be laid before the installation of the bathroom fixtures.*

By using whole sheets the lack of cutting means you are able to put down the floor much faster and will end up with a neater finish. Moreover, because the fixtures sit on top of the flooring there will be less chance of water finding its way onto the subfloor. The only drawback is that you need to be careful not to damage the floor during the installation of the fixtures and when the plumbing and decoration is carried out, but even then the floor may be protected with just a few sheets of masonite.

weight considerations

If you are installing a larger bathtub you will need to take into account the stresses this may impose on the floor. Replacing a standard bathtub with a jacuzzi will add about an extra 500lb when the tub is full. It is very likely that you will need to add some local strengthening to the joist, and the floorboards may be too thin to support the weight of the feet. If you are at all concerned then you should consult a structural engineer, who will be able to assess the risks and recommend a course of action. You will have to pay for this, of course, but it is better than having the bathtub end up in the downstairs living room!

ABOVE RIGHT *A bathroom looks far neater when plumbing is concealed behind wall panels and under floorboards.*

MIDDLE RIGHT *A bathtub holds a considerable amount of water, which puts an enormous load on the floor and may mean you need to add extra strengthening around large bathtubs.*

BELOW *If you are leaving exposed wooden floorboards in a bathroom, you will need to apply a water-resistant finish.*

types of flooring

Almost any type of flooring can be used in a bathroom—even hardwood floors can be treated with a water-resistant finish. Check with your supplier whether the flooring you intend to buy is suitable for bathrooms. Carpet is best avoided, as water can soak through and rot both the carpet and the subfloor underneath, although there are varieties of carpet specifically designed for bathrooms that are water-, mildew-, and stain-resistant with a backing that does not allow water to seep into the pad. Tile and sheet vinyl floors are probably the best choices, as they are easy to clean and effectively resist staining and moisture penetration. Whatever flooring you choose, always use waterproof adhesives and grout, and seal holes with silicone where pipes come through the floor. Moisture-resistant flooring and MDF have a green tinge to them, so can be identified against standard products, which are usually biscuit color.

laying floors for garages & workrooms

Most garage floors are made from concrete, which is fine for an automobile but can be hard on feet and legs. Moreover, a concrete floor tends to be cold and damp, and this is liable to cause tools or machinery to rust. A plywood floor will make for a drier, more comfortable room.

Garages are often used for hobby rooms and children's play areas, but without some modification they can be cold and uninviting. By adding a plywood floor the garage can be transformed into a comfortable activity area. Plywood floors are easier on the knees and allow for a floor covering. They are simple to lay, and since they are not fixed to the subfloor, they can be removed at a later date.

tools for the job

- hand sledge & brick chisel
- mixing equipment
- broom
- tape measure & pencil
- utility knife
- handsaw
- cordless drill/driver

1 Use a hand sledge and brick chisel to knock off any high points on the concrete that could puncture the vapor retarder. Fill any large indentations with a concrete or mortar mix. Sweep the floor to remove any dust and debris.

2 Lay down the vapor retarder, allowing it to lip up the wall by at least 6in. Trim off any excess with a utility knife. If you need to attach two sheets of vapor retarder together, tape along the join with duct tape, then fold the second sheet over on itself three or four times so that you end up with a seam 4in wide, before taping again.

3 Starting at one wall, place 2 x 4in sleepers side down on top of the vapor retarder at 2ft intervals. Use a handsaw to cut them to length. Then cut some blocks to provide support at the end joints and between sleepers, attaching them at 4ft intervals.

4 Cut some insulation board panels to fit between the sleepers and lay them in position: 2in thick panels will sit level with the top of the sleepers and provide additional support for the flooring. You can omit the insulation if you wish, but it does make a big difference to the warmth of the room and provides some measure of sound insulation.

5 Take sufficient sheets of 3/4in shuttering plywood and, with its best side uppermost, drill pilot holes at 8in intervals, 2in in from the edge and across the center of the board. Screw down the boards using 5/16in -gauge screws. Unless the room is completely square, you may find that you have to trim the edges of some of the boards.

safety advice

When cutting the heavy plywood sheets, make sure they are well supported on a sawhorse, workmate, or trestles. You will be able to cut more accurately, and the sheets are much less likely to slip and cause an injury.

6 Shoe molding or baseboards provide a neat trim and help to hold down the edges of the floor. Screw through the baseboards and vapor retarder into the wall. Fold, but do not cut the plastic at the corners of the room, tucking it neatly behind the baseboard as you reattach it.

7 Run a sharp utility knife around the top of the baseboard to trim off any excess plastic flush. If you do not like the look of the vapor retarder sandwiched between the baseboard and the wall, this can be disguised by running a bead of caulk along the top of the baseboard.

8 At door openings, fit a threshold to hide the edges of the plywood. If the new floor is higher than the floor level in the adjoining room, then you will need to make a shaped threshold and cut the bottom of the door to suit. With garage swing-up doors, screw or nail a thin strip of wood to cover the joint between the wood and plywood. Make sure the plastic is sandwiched in between, then trim the plastic level with the finished floor.

FLOOR COVERINGS

If the room is to be used for a children's play area you could cover the plywood with vinyl floor tiles or vinyl sheets. For a deluxe finish, a piece of carpet will offer a measure of thermal and noise insulation.

tips of the trade

Cutting insulation board can be messy, as the white lumps stick to everything. Rather than use a saw, which generates large amounts of static, use a sharp, serrated bread knife, which is almost as fast.

Sturdy and damp-proof, a plywood floor is ideal for transforming a garage into a workshop, and a further covering of vinyl will add extra warmth and comfort.

replacing a wooden floor with concrete

There may be several reasons for replacing a wooden floor with concrete. One of the most likely scenarios is when the original floor has suffered from rot or infestation and must be replaced. In older homes unprotected by a foundation coating, a concrete floor might be installed as part of the overall damp-proofing measures in the property.

tools for the job

- tape measure & pencil
- level
- pry bar
- hand saw
- bolster & chisel
- shovel
- ram
- scissors
- small cement mixer
- tamping board
- plasterer's trowels

1 Before stripping out the old flooring, make a pencil mark 3ft up the wall. Draw a line around the room at this height with a level—this is your datum mark.

2 Remove the old floorboards and joists. Joists are easier to handle cut into sections, especially on older floors, where they will need to be pulled out of wall sockets. Make sure all traces of the old joists have been removed—this is especially important if dry rot has been present.

3 Shovel in a layer of rubble so that its top level is 4ft 3in below the level of the datum mark on the wall. Use a ram to tamp it down and break up any large lumps.

4 The next stage is to lay on the sand layer. Shovel coarse sand on top of the rubble to a depth of 4in, all the time checking the height against the datum marks on the wall. You may find it helpful to cut a wooden strip to 4ft rather than keep measuring each time with the tape measure. Smooth it down with the back of your shovel as you go, and use a long board to make certain that the sand lays as flat as possible.

5 Lay a sheet of plastic vapor retarder on top of the sand, taking care not to puncture the sheet. Make sure that it lips up the wall by about 1ft. Use some strips of duct tape to hold the vapor retarder against the wall.

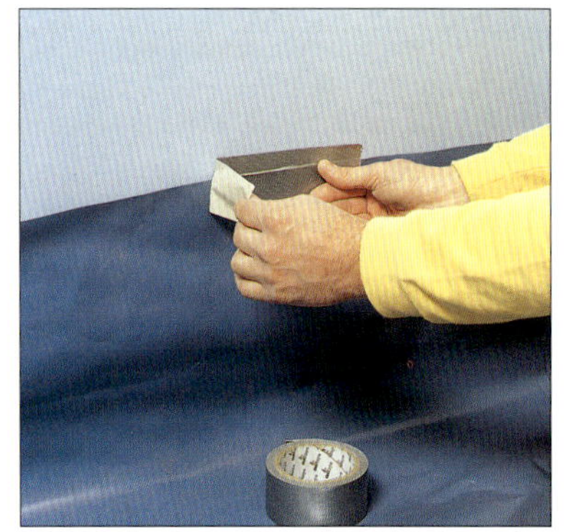

6 Reinforcing rebars strengthen the concrete and prevent it from cracking. Place the rebars raised up on concrete garden slabs. Make a crisscross pattern at 1ft 4in centers, tying any joints with garden wire. Keep the rebars at least 4in clear of any wall. Once finished, the grid should be fairly rigid and should not sag if you walk on it.

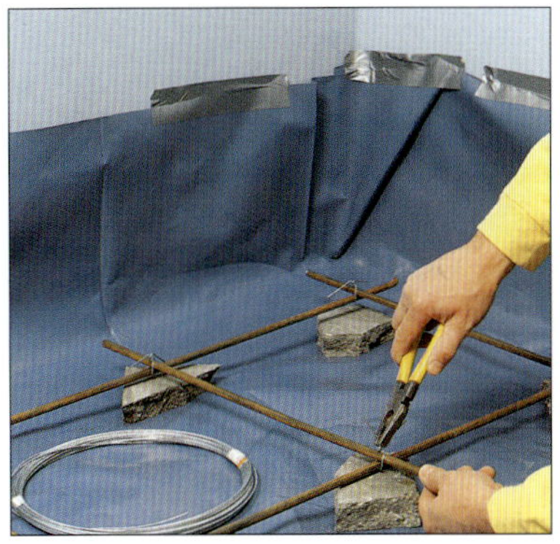

7 Provided another person helps, in a small room it is perfectly feasible to mix the concrete yourself with a small mixer. Use a mix of 1 part ordinary portland cement, 1 part coarse sand, and 3 parts aggregate. There is no need to be too precise, just measure each of the components out by the shovel-full. Do not make the concrete too wet—add just enough water to mix the components into a gray, creamy consistency.

safety advice

Keep cement away from skin and eyes. Wash off splashes as soon as possible, and if you get any in your eyes, flush it with plenty of water and seek medical advice.

8 Rather than simply spreading the concrete in a random fashion, start in one corner of the room and work back towards the doorway. Use the shovel to work the concrete down between the reinforcing rebars, forcing out any trapped air.

9 Check the top level of the concrete against the datum with a guide strip cut to 3ft, to make sure the finished floor will not be lower than adjacent rooms.

10 Tamp the concrete surface with a board or piece of ¾in thick plywood. Starting at one end of the room, work the top of the concrete with the tamp edge. Do not apply great force, but simply stipple the surface slightly. If the room is over 8ft wide you will need a helper. If you work towards the doorway, tamping as you go, the holes left by your boots will refill.

11 After a couple of hours water will have come to the surface before it starts to sink back into the concrete. At this point you can trowel the surface to a smooth finish with metal plasterer's trowels. Spread your weight on two plywood boards about 2ft 7in square. Gently lift the leading edge of the trowel to stop it digging in as you drag it across. Work back toward the doorway, moving the boards as you go.

tips of the trade

When troweling the concrete surface it helps to have two trowels, one for smoothing, and the other to spread the weight of your other hand so you do not damage the surface.

12 You can walk on the concrete the next day, but leave at least three days before trimming off the plastic and fitting baseboard. If laying carpet, wait at least three weeks, as moisture in the concrete will rot the backing.

installing joist hangers

On many modern houses the ends of the joists are supported on metal brackets called joist hangers. Even if you are replacing the entire floor in an older house where joist hangers were not originally fitted, you can still fit them using the method described below. There are several different types of hangers and each type comes in different sizes, so make sure you fit the correct joist hangers for your application.

The most common reason for installing joist hangers is when a new floor is being built, either for a new room or because the original joists need replacing. Joist hangers are typically fixed to either masonry or wood. In some new homes the joist hangers are built into the wall, or if the house is wood-framed special hangers are nailed to the studwork. In older homes where joists are fitted into sockets in the wall, by installing joist hangers the ends are kept away from potentially damp brickwork and masonry. Joist hangers also allow you to space the joists so that the joints of sheet flooring fall directly onto the center line of a joist.

tools for the job

- tape measure & pencil
- level
- cordless drill/driver
- hand saw
- hammer
- utility knife

1 Allow for the width of the wallboard by measuring up ½in from where the underside of the ceiling will be, then mark a level line at this point all around the room using a long level. Mark out the center spacing for the joists along this line no more than 1ft 4in apart center to center. You may need additional joists close to the wall in order to support the edge of the boards.

tips of the trade

- **Positioning joists**—Joists typically run across the shortest span of the room, but loadbearing walls must always support the ends. If you are replacing a floor the new joists should run the same way as the original joists. Consult an architect or structural engineer for advice if you are unsure.
- **Spacing joists**—The spacing of floor joists is always quoted as center to center. This is the spacing between the imaginary center line of each joist. To gain the actual distance between joists, deduct the total thickness of one complete joist.

2 To ensure the finished floor ends up level, nail or screw a temporary wooden strip to the wall so that the top edge is level with your datum mark. Hold the joist hangers on top of the strip at the center line reference marks, and screw or nail them to the wall. If using screws you may find it easier to mark the screw position before drilling the hole and inserting a wall plug. Use a hammer or percussion drill fitted with a bit specifically designed for masonry when drilling into brick or blockwork. If the hole has been drilled correctly, you should be able simply to push in the wall plug for a snug fit.

3 Get a helper to hold the end of the tape measure while you check the length of the joists. Measure by holding the tape across the room and checking the distance between the back plates of the joist hangers. As it is unlikely that the room will be completely square, and thus lengths will vary slightly, do not just measure the first joist and assume all the others will be the same length. Deduct $^{3}/_{16}$in from the overall measurement and mark this on the joist before cutting to length with a hand saw.

safety advice

The chemical used in pressure-treated wood for joists can be poisonous if ingested. Wear gloves if possible, and always wash your hands after work and before eating and drinking.

4 If you have cut it correctly, the joist should drop in without the need to hit it with a hammer. If the joist wobbles from side to side slightly in the hanger, you can make a better fit by wrapping roofing felt around the end and securing the joist in place with nails. Packing the end in felt also has the added advantage of preventing moisture from seeping into the end grain of the joist.

5 Nail the joists into position through a couple of the holes on either side of the hangers. Galvanized nails have a better grip due to their rough finish and are more resistant to rust than conventional finish nails. The nails should be no more than half the thickness of the joist, or there is a risk of splitting the wood. Do not drive them right home at this stage. Place the level across all the joists and check for level, repeating this at several places in the room. If any joists are high, pull the nails and either trim a little from the underside of the joist where it sits in the hanger, or reposition the hanger. When you are certain of the fit, drive home the temporary nails and hammer nails through the remaining holes in the sides of the joist hangers. To avoid splitting the wood, try blunting the ends of the nails with light hammer blows.

6 For any span more than 10ft, attach steel bridging between each of the joists to add extra strength and to prevent twisting (see pages 208–9). The joists are now ready to receive the flooring and ceiling, but before doing this run in any cables and plumbing.

LATERAL RESTRAINT STRAPS

For extra stability in the completed floor you may want to add lateral restraint straps. These come in the form of galvanized steel straps, fitted and screwed to the wall, and are available from any good builder's supplier. Such restraint straps are intended to be attached at a perpendicular angle to the joists.

Provided they are fitted with care and accuracy, joist hangers will form a sturdy suspended floor with the added benefit of providing a moisture-resistant barrier.

cutting an access hatch

There can be lots of reasons for wanting to gain access to the area underneath a floor, but the most common is for the repair or installation of services such as plumbing or wiring. Before the introduction of chipboard and plywood floors, accessing was usually a simple matter of lifting and replacing a few boards. Sheet materials, which cover larger expanses, make access a more complicated affair, since removing sections is not really an option and small access hatches need to be cut into the floor instead.

Using the speed and versatility of an electric router, cutting an access hatch in a chipboard, plywood, or laminated floor need not be complicated. The techniques demonstrated here allow access to be gained with a minimal amount of disruption to the overall floor. Cutting permanent hatches also means that the area under the floor can be easily accessed whenever the need arises.

chipboard & plywood floors

tools for the job

- tape measure & pencil
- screwdriver
- electric router & circular jig

1 A circular jig is a type of jig specially made for use with an electric router. It is fast and easy to use for those with some previous experience with routers. First, mark the position of the access hatch on the floor. Attach the electric router to the special base plate, then loosely screw the plate to the floor, directly over the area you wish to cut. Rotate the router around the screw until the disc is cut all the way round.

2 Remove the disc and drop in a special plastic ring, which is supplied with the circular jig.

3 Finally, drop the cut disc so that it rests on the plastic ring. No glue or fastener of any kind is required, and the area surrounding the hatch is almost as strong as the floor prior to the hole being cut. Access to the underfloor area is available at any time by simply lifting out the disc.

laminated floors

When a laminated or solid wood floor has been laid over a plywood or chipboard subfloor, it is vital to be as neat as possible. The cut-out section can be any size, but making it as small as is practicable will mean it is ultimately less obtrusive.

tools for the job

- safety equipment
- tape measure & pencil
- carpenter's square
- fine-toothed panel saw
- double-sided tape
- router
- wood chisel
- handsaw

1 Mark out a square on the floor 1ft along each side. Check each corner is a perfect right angle with a carpenter's square. Two of the sides must also be parallel with the line of the laminated strips.

2 Prepare some furring strips 2½in wide and no less than ½in thick. Stick the furring strips to the floor with double-sided tape, making sure that the inside edges exactly align with the pencil marks.

3 Insert a ½in thick straight cutter into the router and attach the template guide bush to the base plate. Keeping the base plate down on the furring strips with the bush against the inside of the strips, cut through the laminated floor and the subfloor.

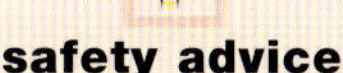

safety advice

Using a router is noisy and dusty, so wear always a dust mask, goggles, and ear protectors.

tips of the trade

Make sure that the router cutters are sharp to avoid splintering the top surface of the laminate.

4 Remove the section of floor and put to one side. Carefully peel off the strips and double-sided tape. Change the router cutter to a bearing-guided cutter and run a rabbet around the inside of the opening, cutting down to the same depth as the thickness of the laminate.

5 Use a sharp wood chisel to square up the rounded inside corners of the laminate left by the circular router cutter.

6 Form a section of flooring from some scrap laminated sheet that is at least 1in larger all round than the hole in the floor. Glue the tongues together with wood glue, then glue this in turn onto the section of chipboard or plywood subfloor that you saved. Put a heavy weight on top and allow the glue to dry.

7 Make a paper or cardboard template so that it just drops into the rabbeted opening in the floor, then clearly mark the positions of the joint lines onto the top edges. Transfer the template to the replacement floor section, noting the position of the joints but keeping it as near the center as possible. Mark around the outside before finally cutting with a fine-toothed hand saw. Sand the edges to remove any rough spots.

8 Provided that the cutting and marking have been accurate, the panel should simply drop into position and require no further fastening. If you are confident that you will never need access later, it could be glued in place. If the panel is quite large, you may want to use small brass screws at each corner to retain it.

soundproofing a floor

Noise pollution can be a cause of friction between neighbors, especially in apartment blocks and properties that have been divided into separate apartments, though the problem can be just as bad within a family home. Adding some soundproofing to a floor helps to cut down noise transmitted from above and will go some way to solving your noise pollution problem. Using the technique shown here, almost any floor can be soundproofed.

Noise is either transmitted through the air or through the materials used in the construction of a house. With the method of soundproofing shown here, sand and insulation batts combine to form an effective barrier against the transmission of noise throughout the house. A floor can be soundproofed from below, but this means destroying the ceiling, and working above your head is tiring on the arms and neck. Moreover, by soundproofing from above, sand can be used as an insulating material, which is both an inexpensive and effective sound-deadening medium.

safety advice

The soundproofing method shown here will increase the weight of the floor. Before starting any work you must check that this will not adversely affect the structural integrity of the property. If you are in any doubt, contact a structural engineer.

tools for the job

- stud finder
- crayon
- circular saw
- utility knife
- gloves
- pry bar
- flooring chisel
- hammer
- hand saw
- cordless drill/driver
- dust mask

1 Unless they are immediately obvious, use a stud finder to check the position of plumbing and electricity wiring. Then mark their positions on the floor surface with a crayon, so that when cutting into the floor you will be able avoid damaging these services.

2 If the floor is constructed of chipboard or tongue-and-groove boards, run a circular saw set to the thickness of the flooring down the joints between boards. Do not cut round more than one or two boards at this stage, for once you start lifting the first couple of boards you may find that the rest can be removed without cutting off the tongues.

3 Use a pry bar and flooring chisel to gently lift the floor, trying not to damage too many boards. Remove any nails that remain poking out of the joists with the claw end of a hammer.

tips of the trade

With all the floorboards removed it can be difficult to move around the room. Have a couple of loose boards to hand that you can position across the joists to walk on as you work in the room.

4 Screw 1 x 2in wooden strips to both sides of the ceiling joists. Make sure the bottom edge is just clear of the ceiling below.

5 Cut ½in plywood strips to sit on top of the wooden strips. Fix the plywood in place with nails.

6 Cut polyethylene membrane material to line the troughs, pressing it into the corners and allowing it to lip the sides of the joists. Nail or staple it into position using a minimum of fastenings near the top edge. Trim off excess plastic so that it is level with the top of the joists.

7 Pour in kiln-dried sand to about 2in deep. Cut a piece of plywood so it rests on top of the joists with the bottom edge 2in higher than the bottom of the trough. Use this to achieve consistent results when leveling out the sand.

8 Place insulation batts on top of the sand. They should not be any higher than the top of the joists, or refastening the boards will be difficult. To cut the slabs, use a fine hand saw, and wear a dust mask.

9 With the two layers of insulating material in place, you can refasten the floor on top of the joists. Any split or damaged boards will need to be replaced. When refastening boards, make sure that all joints are tight and there are no gaps. Covering the floor with thick, good-quality padding and carpet will enhance the soundproofing properties.

If appropriate to the type of floor covering, thick padding stapled to the subfloor will further enhance the sound-insulation properties of the floor.

adding ventilation to floors

Ventilation is essential in any floor space. Stagnant air can lead to rot, unpleasant smells, and moisture, which can destroy floor finishes and carpets, and in some cases the floor itself, if left untreated. Some floors suffer from a lack of ventilation more than others, such as those in bathrooms and kitchens. Before starting on major work it is worth checking that poor ventilation is not simply a case of existing air bricks being blocked by soil and dirt.

installing a floor grille

Though not as effective as an exterior air brick, a grille fitted into floorboards will allow air to circulate in the floor space, which might otherwise be a potential breeding ground for rot and infestation. If the grille is installed under a window or a radiator, the convection currents will help to draw air into the room.

tools for the job

- stud finder
- tape measure & pencil
- cordless drill/driver
- jigsaw or keyhole saw
- awl or small drill
- screwdriver

1 Determine the positions of the joists. These are often indicated by the position of the floor fasteners or you can use a stud finder. Measure and draw a parallel line 6in out from the baseboard. Place the top edge of the grille on this line and draw a pencil line round it, keeping the ends equally spaced between the run of joists where these run at a right angle to the wall.

safety advice

When determining the position of the grille, use a stud finder to locate plumbing and wiring to avoid cutting through these services by accident.

2 Set the grille to one side and draw another line ½in inside the grille outline. Drill a hole at each corner with a ½in drill bit, making sure that the edges of the bit stay inside the second guideline.

3 Cut out the waste area inside the second guideline, using a jigsaw or keyhole saw. Work from each drilled hole. At the last hole the waste section is liable to fall through into the ceiling area. To prevent this, particularly if the grille is so small that you will not be able to get your hand into the hole to remove the cut-out section, partially screw in a large wood screw to give you something to hold when the block is cut away.

tips of the trade

When a grille is to be fitted into a polished floor you will want to get the best finish possible. Special jigsaw blades are available that cut on the down stroke and prevent splinters on the floor surface.

4 Remove any rough edges from the hole with abrasive paper before screwing on the grille. Align the edges of the grille with the pencil guideline. Use an awl or small drill to make a pilot hole for the screws, and fasten the grille in position. For a neater appearance, align all the screw slots so that they face the same way.

5 Where carpet is to be fitted, cut out the hole in the carpet before fitting the grille in place. Then screw down the grille so that the carpet is sandwiched between grille and floorboards. If the carpet has a thick pile, you may find that you need to use slightly longer screws than those that were originally supplied with the grille.

installing an air brick

Exterior air bricks are the traditional means of ventilating the space under wooden floors at ground level. Alterations to the house or garden may mean that the original bricks are no longer performing their function. As a general rule there should be an air brick every 8ft along an exterior wall. If there are less air bricks in the walls of your home, or if you have signs of mold or moisture due to lack of air movement, you should consider installing additional bricks. Air bricks come in a variety of sizes, but the easiest to fit are the smaller ones, used here, which have the same overall dimensions as a standard house brick.

tools for the job

- cordless drill/driver
- hand sledge & brick chisel
- protective gloves & goggles
- pointing trowel
- jointing trowel

1 To install an additional air brick, or replace one that is missing, first select a suitable standard brick to remove, 6½–8ft from the nearest existing air brick. It should also be at least one course below the foundation coating, and below the level of the floor inside. Drill lots of holes to break up the brick, using an electric drill with a large masonry bit.

2 Remove the rest of the brick with a hand sledge and brick chisel, taking great care not to damage the adjacent brickwork. Most of the mortar holding the brick in place will probably come away with the brick. Remove any remaining mortar so that you have a clean hole ready to receive the air brick.

safety advice

When chopping out old bricks with a hammer and chisel, make sure you wear gloves to protect your hands and, more importantly, goggles to protect your eyes from flying chips.

3 Mix up some mortar using 3 parts sand to 1 part cement. Cut a couple of strips of wood 2in long with a square section the same thickness as the existing mortar courses in the brick wall. Place the strips in the bottom of the hole and hold them in place with a little mortar. Damp down the new brick and spread mortar onto the top and ends.

4 Slide in the brick, making sure it stays level with the existing brickwork. Check with a straightedge that the brick is not too far in or sitting proud. Work in additional mortar to the joint with a pointing trowel, if necessary. After about an hour, when the mortar has just started to harden, finish with a jointing trowel.

tips of the trade

When pointing brickwork, leave the mortar to "go off" a little before finishing. In this way you will not drag mortar out of the joint, and the finish will be smoother.

floor finishes

There are probably more choices of floor covering available today then there have ever been. Improvements and innovations in manufacturing mean that materials previously deemed unsuitable are now commonly used for flooring. Many homeowners still make carpet their first choice, and it is easy to see why—luxurious underfoot, a carpet will lend any room a warm and cosy feel. Other types of floor covering are also finding their way into homes. Laminated flooring, which has always been popular in Scandinavia, is now common throughout the USA and Europe. Many people still tend to avoid sheet flooring, but this too has had something of a renaissance in recent years, and a huge range is now available that has little in common with the linoleum of old.

Floor finishes need not start and end with carpets—floor tiles, for example, can make a stylish and original flooring option.

comparing floor coverings

When planning alterations to a room it is essential to know which types of floor covering are appropriate for the particular subfloor, what are the specific qualities of each type, and how much it is all likely to cost. The following table examines each of the main types of floor covering available, listing the cost, positive and negative aspects, suitability, and how difficult it is to install, so that you can easily compare types and make your choice.

PROS & CONS	COST	DURABILITY	INSTALLING	SUITABLE SUBFLOORS
CARPET				
Pros Warm and soft to the touch. Luxurious look. Vast range of colors and patterns to suit any color scheme. Helps to keep down drafts. Available in wide rolls. **Cons** Not waterproof, but special carpets are available for bathrooms. Can mark and stain easily.	Wide range of costs, from cheap to very expensive.	Moderately durable. Carpets with a high wool content last longest and can be cleaned.	May be undertaken by a skilled amateur, but more expensive carpets are best left to a professional. Cheaper foam-backed carpet is glued to double-sided tape at the edges. Woven-back carpet is attached to tackless strips at the edges of the room.	Concrete screed, plywood, chipboard, and solid wood floors are all suitable, but carpet is generally laid on top of padding.
WOOD BLOCK				
Pros Very durable. Easy to maintain. Can be stained or bleached to give different look. **Cons** Limited range of options as not all woods are suitable for floors.	Expensive, but some modern equivalents are slightly cheaper.	Very durable—ideal for high-traffic areas. When worn, scuffed, and dirty can be refinished to bring back to a condition that is good as new.	Laying proper wood block flooring is a professional job requiring hot pitch. An experienced amateur can install small areas using a latex adhesive.	Concrete screed. Not suitable for upper floors or for installing on wood floorboards.
VINYL TILES				
Pros Durable. Easy to maintain and keep clean. Waterproof when correctly laid. Ideal for kitchens and bathrooms. **Cons** Not suitable for living areas, as they can look rather clinical. Cold and hard.	Costs are moderate, considering the life-span and compared to other coverings.	Very durable—ideal for high-traffic areas. Mopping or wiping with a cloth is all that is required in the way of maintenance.	Easy to lay, provided the subfloor is in good condition and the setting-out is correct. Self-adhesive tiles are the cleanest and easiest to lay for the amateur. Others are set into adhesive.	Concrete screed. Plywood or chipboard. Cover solid floorboards with plywood or masonite before laying.

PROS & CONS	COST	DURABILITY	LAYING	SUITABLE SUBFLOORS
SHEET VINYL				
Pros Durable. Easy to maintain. Waterproof when correctly laid—ideal for kitchens and bathrooms. Available in wide rolls. **Cons** Not as resilient as tiles. Not suitable for living areas, as it can look uninviting.	Moderate, considering the life-span and compared to other coverings.	Very durable—ideal for high-traffic areas. Mopping or wiping with a cloth is all that is required in the way of maintenance.	Not as easy to lay as tiles, as it can be unwieldy. Often best to make a template first. Some can be loose-laid, but others are glued to the subfloors with special adhesive.	Concrete screed. Plywood or chip-board. Cover solid wood floorboards with plywood or masonite.
LAMINATE				
Pros Durable. Easy to maintain. Look of solid wood without the expense. Does not need to be laid by a professional. **Cons** Difficult to affect an invisible repair. Can be noisy and slippery. Limited range of finishes.	Moderate, considering the life span and in comparison with other coverings. The cheaper laminates are better suited to low-usage rooms.	Durable. Ideal for high-traffic areas. Mopping or wiping with a cloth is all that is required in the way or maintenance.	Straightforward to install. Some of the new versions clip together and do not require glue, making them even easier. All should be laid on a thin underlayment that varies according to the type of subfloor.	Concrete screed. Plywood or chip-board. Solid wood floorboards should be covered with plywood or masonite before laying.
PLYWOOD				
Pros Durable. Best suited for workrooms and garages. **Cons** Dusty if not coated. Fastenings cannot be concealed.	Cheap to moderate depending on the thickness and grade of plywood chosen.	Very durable. Ideal for high-traffic areas. Waterproof when a suitable paint or varnish is applied.	Simple, with no complicated joints, but take care fitting around pipes. Nailed or screwed to the subfloor or joists.	Laid directly onto joists or flooring. Use a vapor retarder underneath if floor is liable to be damp.
STONE TILES				
Pros Durable. Easy to maintain. Waterproof when correctly laid and sealed. Ideal for kitchens and entrances. **Cons** Noisy, hard, and cold. Slippery when wet. Crockery dropped onto it will smash.	Highly expensive.	Very durable. Ideal for high-traffic areas. Unsealed tiles need to be sealed periodically with a proprietary product in order to retain their appearance and prevent the surface staining.	Not a suitable job for novices. Tiles are laid in wet mortar rather than an adhesive.	Concrete screed. Plywood or chip-board. Solid wood floorboards should be covered with plywood or masonite before laying.

installing chipboard & plywood floors

Chipboard or plywood may be used as a cheaper substitute for floorboards for a subfloor. Plywood is dimensionally stable and makes an ideal base for other floor coverings such as laminated floors and tiles. While it is possible to lay chipboard and plywood over existing flooring, bear in mind that this could make access to underneath the floor difficult in the future.

tools for the job

- tape measure & pencil
- cordless drill/driver
- hammer
- pry bar
- hand saw or circular saw
- carpenter's square
- nail set

chipboard floors

Flooring-grade chipboard is generally ¾in thick and comes in 2 x 8ft sheets . Tongue-and-groove joints provide extra support to the edges. Using larger sheets makes chipboard much faster to lay than standard wooden floorboards.

1 Chipboard floors are most likely to be fitted directly to joists. Lay down one or two boards without fastening them to walk around on.

2 Lay the first board at a right angle to the run of the joists, starting in one corner. Make sure that the board is placed with the tongue facing away from the wall—all boards should be laid printed side down.

3 Screw or nail the board in place. Screws should be 1in longer than the flooring thickness, so a floor ¾in thick will require 1¾in screws. Drive these in at 8in centers. Make fasteners no closer than 2in to any edge.

4 Run a bead of wood adhesive into the end groove of the next board and push this up to the first board. Make sure the joint is tight, with no gaps showing on the face where the two boards meet. If hand pressure alone is not enough, tap the end of the board with a hammer, with a scrap of wood between the hammer and board to protect the tongue.

5 Continue until one row is finished then start on the next. If the last board of the first row was cut to length, start from this end on the second row in order to stagger joints. Do not worry if joints do not occur on joists, as the tongues provide support.

6 Cut the last boards to width ½in less than the overall measurement. Run glue into the groove of each board and place them onto the joists tight against the wall. Force the board onto the tongue of the next board with a pry bar.

safety advice

If using a circular saw to cut flooring, wear appropriate safety equipment. Safety glasses or goggles keep dust and splinters out of your eyes. Wear a dust mask if working in enclosed spaces, or, better still, cut the boards outside if you can.

plywood floors

Very popular in the USA, plywood is often used as a quick method of covering a floor. It provides a very stable and strong subfloor over which tiles, carpet, and almost any other floor covering may be laid. Stronger than chipboard, it is better suited to damp environments and can withstand greater weights. If good-quality plywood is used, it can even be varnished and left without any additional floor covering.

1 Make sure the plywood is laid to best advantage. If sheets are being installed over an existing floor, where the joints fall will not matter. Where plywood is installed directly onto joists, the joints must fall onto a joist. Lay down a few sheets, orienting them in different directions to check.

2 Newer homes have joists placed at close spacing. In older houses floors tend to be constructed using joists with a larger section but spaced farther apart. Fit blocks to reinforce plywood edges where necessary, providing additional support. Use 2 x 3in wood on edge cut to fit between the width of the joists. Angle nails on each side, through the top of the block and into the side of the joist. Keep the top of the blocks level with the joists.

3 Boards can be fixed down by hammering finish nails into the joists and setting the heads below the surface. Alternatively, by drilling pilot holes and screwing them down, gaining access below the floor will be that much easier. Place screws at 8in centers, with no screw closer than ⅝in to any edge.

4 Install the remaining boards, maintaining a ⅛in gap along all joints to prevent the boards from squeaking and to allow for any slight movement. Cut a couple of pieces of scrap wood ⅛in thick and place these between the boards to keep the gap consistent as you fit. This also saves having to keep checking the measurement repeatedly.

5 Replace the baseboard if this was removed, or install it new. Press it down to the floor as you fix it to the wall, but do not insert fasteners into the floor. If the baseboard was left in place, install a small quadrant or shoe molding to hide the joint between plywood and baseboard.

tips of the trade

Running a small bead of caulk around the room will seal the joint between any baseboard or molding and the floor. This helps to prevent dirt and dust from finding its way into the room and soiling carpets or other floor covering.

laying a laminated floor

Until recently the materials available for laying a wooden floor were limited to parquet and other solid woods, which required a healthy bank balance to buy and specialist knowledge to fit. The recent innovation of laminated wooden flooring, which comprises strips of decorative wood bonded to a cheaper backing, has addressed both these points, providing an easy-to-fit and relatively cheap wooden flooring that looks good, is durable, and with minimal care will outlast many other floor coverings.

The general principles of laying a laminated floor are the same irrespective of the manufacturer, but there are subtle differences between makes, so do not mix types. Some of the most recent types have tongue-and-groove joints that require no glue and simply snap together. If you use this type, then follow the instructions shown below, omitting the stages that refer to adhesives. Strips should be installed up and down the room, and it often looks best if they run in the direction of the longest dimension. If the room is square, run the strips away from the strongest light source.

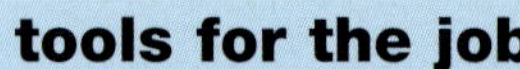

tools for the job

- tape measure & pencil
- pry bar
- claw hammer or screwdriver
- straightedge
- bucket
- metal plasterer's trowel
- mallet
- hand saw

1 If installing on a concrete screed, carefully remove any protruding nibs that might prevent the floor from being level. On wooden subfloors, nail or screw down any sections that are loose, and make sure that all raised nail heads are set below the surface. Lay a straightedge across the floor at several points checking for bumps and hollows—if any are greater than ¼in the floor will need leveling. Mix up latex leveling compound in accordance with the manufacturer's instructions and, using a metal plasterer's trowel, spread it across the entire floor. It sets fast, so do not mix too much at once or try to spread it on too thickly.

2 Once the compound has dried, roll out the recommended underlayment, which will provide an even, soundproof cushion. This material is usually either polystyrene or thin cork. Lay it across the room at 90 degrees to the eventual direction of the laminated strips, holding it in position with sticky tape. Do not overlap joints, instead butt them and attach them with a little more tape.

3 Lay the first row of boards with the grooved side toward the wall. Place the wedges behind this first strip, if supplied, otherwise use some waste wood to give a ½in expansion gap at the wall.

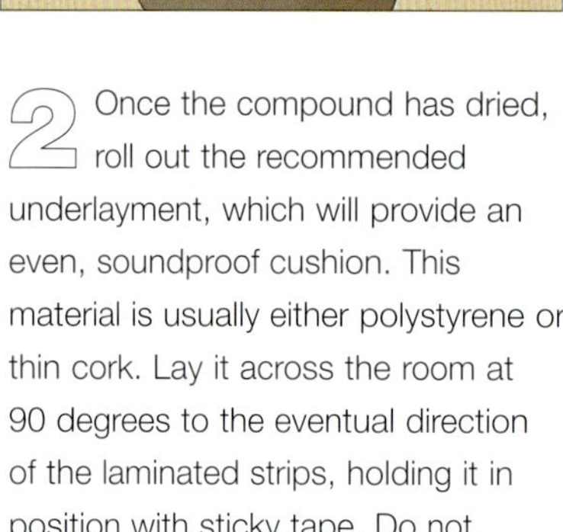

4 Run a bead of white wood glue into the end groove, then push it by hand onto the tongue of the board already laid. If there is still a gap, place a waste strip of flooring against the edge of the board and tap home. Use a plastic, rubber, or wooden mallet, and be careful not to damage the edge of the boards. Continue until you have laid a complete row of strips down one edge of the room.

tips of the trade

Kneeling on the section of floor you have just completed will hold it in place and make tapping in the new sections just that little bit easier. If you bought the fitting kit, the manufacturer should have supplied a hammering block to protect plank edges as you knock them together. Otherwise use a piece of waste wood.

5 The edges of the boards are glued in the same way, but make sure that joints with adjacent boards are staggered brickwork fashion for strength and appearance. No joint should be any closer than 6in to any other joint. Wipe off any glue that squeezes out of the joints straight away with a damp cloth.

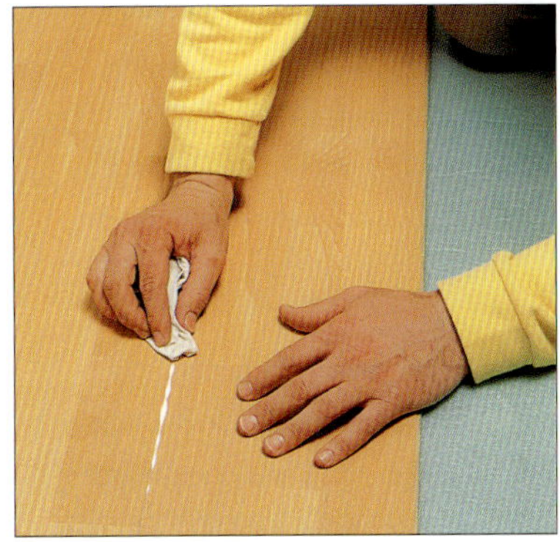

6 Use a sharp hand saw to cut any boards to length. When cutting to size, remember to maintain the ½in expansion gap. Provided the piece of cut-off board is more than 6in long, it may be used to start the next row.

7 You may need to cut the last row to width. Check the distance from the wall to the face edge of the last full board, and transfer these marks to the closing board, measuring from the grooved edge. Deduct ½in for the expansion gap, and cut to size. Run glue into the joint, drop the board into the gap, and use a pry bar to force the tongue into the groove.

8 Leave the room for a minimum of 12 hours, during which time you should try to avoid walking on the laminated flooring to give the glue a chance to set. The final step is to cover the expansion joint with strips of molding. Do not nail the molding into the floor, rather fix it into the wall or baseboard to allow for expansion and contraction of the new flooring.

Laminated flooring is easy-to-clean, durable, and soft underfoot, which makes it an ideal floor covering for use in a nursery or children's playroom.

laying vinyl tiles

Vinyl tiles have undergone something of a revival in recent years, and are now available in a variety of styles and sizes. Some tiles come with a self-adhesive backing, otherwise they are laid by being embedded them into a special adhesive. The quality and longevity of the finished floor will depend on the thoroughness of your preparatory work, so make sure any necessary repairs to the subfloor are carried out before you start to lay your tiles.

tools for the job

- tape measure & pencil
- hammer or cordless drill/driver
- jigsaw or keyhole saw
- chalk lines
- carpenter's square
- serrated adhesive trowel
- hot air gun or hairdrier
- utility knife
- vinyl roller
- wallpaper roller

1 Vinyl tiles are ideal for laying on concrete and masonite, but cannot be laid on floorboards. Cover floorboards over with masonite or plywood before laying vinyl. Cut around any pipes or other obstructions. Nail or screw the boards every 6in in every direction. Ensure fastenings finish below the surface.

2 Jumble up the tiles from several boxes so that slight variations in color will not be noticeable. Lay a few out for a trial run—you can often vary the look of the floor by alternating how the surface pattern or texture flows.

3 Lay out dry two rows of tiles between opposing walls to form a cross. Leave an even gap between the tile and wall at each end. Mark round the tile at the center of the cross—this is your key tile.

4 Remove the tiles and, using the key tile marks as a guide, make a chalk line along the length of the floor. Make sure the line is at a right angle to any main doorway or window. You might need to adjust the line a little, but provided the temporary layout was correct, any adjustments will be minimal. With the aid of a large carpenter's square, mark another chalk line at a right angle to the first, using the pencil marks as a reference.

5 Spread out a quantity of tile adhesive with a serrated adhesive trowel. Cover an area large enough to lay down the first eight or nine tiles, including the key tile. Work from the intersection of the chalk lines, keeping all the adhesive restricted to one quadrant of the room for the moment. Do not apply the adhesive too thickly—spreading rates are generally given on the tub.

safety advice

Many tile adhesives are petroleum-based and give off heavy vapors. Work in a well-ventilated room, and extinguish all naked lights.

6 Embed the key tile, exactly lining up the corners with the right angle of the chalk lines. Then lay tiles adjacent to the key tile, keeping each tile tight to the next. Twist the tiles as you push them into the adhesive—this helps them to bond properly and ensures an even coating of adhesive.

7 Continue laying tiles, one quadrant at a time, wiping away adhesive that squeezes out through the joints. End with full tiles, leaving a gap at the edge of the room.

8 Lay down the last complete tile, then align another tile on top so that it touches the wall. Cut through the bottom tile using the top tile as a straightedge. Discard the waste, then swap the tiles around before gluing.

tips of the trade

Vinyl tiles remain stiff when cold. Warming them with a hairdrier or hot air gun makes the tiles more flexible and easier to cut, and improves bonding.

9 To fit the tiles around pipes, start by making a card template, then copy this onto a tile with a china marker and cut out. Cut just one slit down to a pipe hole and spring the tile open as you embed it into the adhesive. Tiles cut in this way should fit perfectly, with little trace of the cut.

10 Immediately you have finished tiling go over the floor with a heavy steel roller to ensure full adhesion. Proceed slowly, moving left to right and up and down the length of the room. Wipe up adhesive that oozes from the joints. Press down any tiles that the big roller cannot reach with a wallpaper roller.

These tiles have been laid at 90° degrees to each other according to the direction of the "grain." For less obvious joins, lay the tiles with the pattern in the same direction.

laying vinyl sheet flooring

Vinyl sheet flooring is ideal for kitchens and bathrooms, since it is easy to keep clean and resistant to moisture. Many modern varieties of sheet flooring have a cushioned back, which makes them easy on the feet and legs if working in the kitchen for any length of time. Making a template is by far the easiest method for laying sheet vinyl, as it avoids costly mistakes. As with tiles, getting the subfloor in good condition is of paramount importance.

tips of the trade

- **Vinyl care**—Never fold sheet vinyl, as this puts permanent puckers into it. Avoid walking on it and make sure that nothing sharp is trapped underneath.
- **Heating**—Laying the vinyl sheet out flat, pattern side up, for an hour or two in a warm room, makes it easier to cut.
- **Paper template**—Building paper is ideal as it is reinforced, but you can use almost any thick paper.

tools for the job

tape measure & marker pen
utility knife
serrated adhesive trowel
vinyl roller
wallpaper roller

1 Cut and join together sheets of building paper to form a template of the floor space 6in bigger than the overall size of the room. Joint sheets with painter's tape, allowing a good overlap and applying tape to both sides of the joint to prevent it from moving.

2 Cut some windows near the edge of the paper about 2in square. Attach the template to the floor through these windows with painter's tape. The spacing is not crucial, but make sure that you have enough windows to hold the paper template in position so that it does not slip around.

3 Press the paper into the edges of the room. Trim off the excess with a utility knife where it lips up the baseboard or around built-in pieces of furniture. You may find that you have to cut a series of "darts"—plumb relieving cuts—up from inside and outside corners to get the template to lay on the floor properly.

4 When you are happy with the fit, slowly peel the template from the floor, being careful not to tear the paper. Lay the template on top of the sheet flooring and orient it to best effect, noting the position of any lines or pattern, then tape it in place.

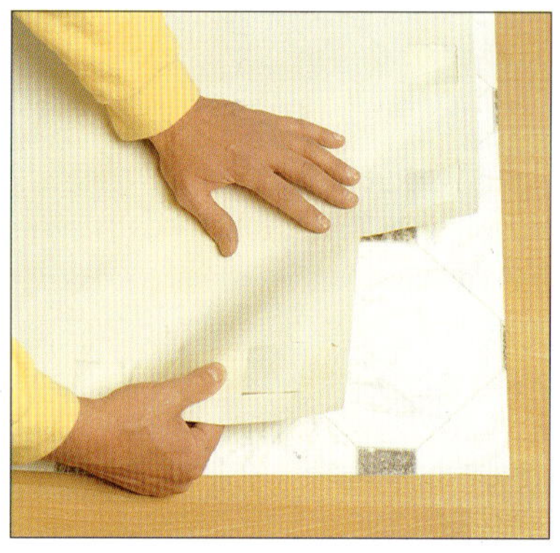

5 Draw around the template onto the vinyl with a marking pen. Discard the template and cut the flooring with a knife. Place a piece of waste masonite or plywood under where you are making cuts to avoid damaging the floor below. Even if you are doing this on a garage floor, the board saves the knife edge from dulling. When you have cut the vinyl to size, roll it up and carry it to the room.

6 Roll out the flooring, then gently fold back the vinyl from the longest wall to uncover a 3ft wide strip of subfloor. Spread adhesive onto the exposed area of subfloor with a serrated adhesive trowel.

7 Press the flooring into the adhesive, smoothing it down with the heel of your hand to force out any air bubbles. If you need to make small adjustments to the fit, now is the time to do it, before the adhesive sets. Roll the rest of the flooring back on itself and spread on the remaining adhesive. Smooth the flooring into the adhesive from the center to the edges to force out any trapped air.

tips of the trade

If you have to join two sections of flooring together, overlap one on top of the other and cut through both pieces at the same time to ensure a perfect butt seam. Peel back the top sheet, remove the waste from the bottom sheet, then fix to the subfloor with adhesive in the usual way.

8 Once the vinyl is in place, ensure full adhesion by pressing down on the flooring with a vinyl roller. Move slowly over the floor, making passes in different directions. Employ a wallpaper roller against the edges of the room and in any hard-to-reach areas, using firm hand pressure.

9 Wipe away the inevitable splashes of adhesive from baseboards, fitted furniture, and the surface of the flooring, using the solvent recommended by the manufacturer and a clean rag.

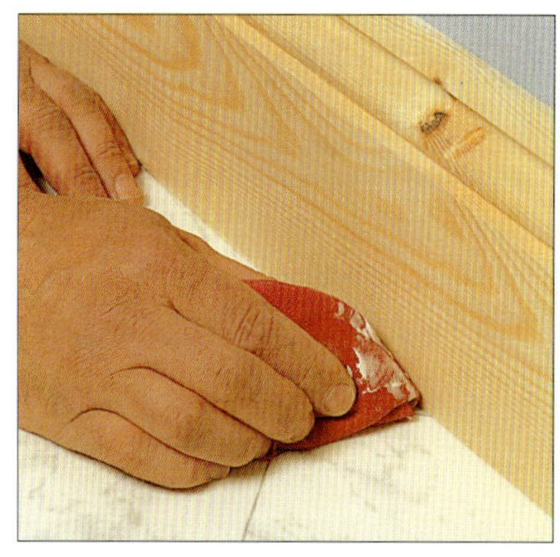

SEALING THE VINYL

In bathrooms and kitchens, seal the vinyl with a bead of clear silicone caulk around the edge.

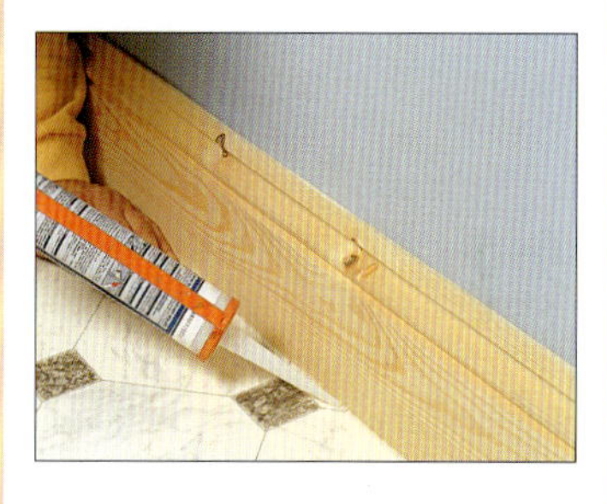

Vinyl is especially good for bathrooms, as it produces a watertight floor surface. Soft underfoot and easy to clean, it is also a good option for a children's playroom.

laying ceramic tiles

Ceramic tiles are ideal for wet areas because of their durability and looks. However, you need to plan work thoroughly and use the correct techniques in order to maximize both these qualities. If the tiles are unglazed, it is important to seal them with a proprietary sealing solution, otherwise their surface can become ingrained with adhesive and grout, which can be difficult to clean off. The majority of floor tiles are supplied with a glazed surface, which makes application simple.

where to start

Most rooms are not totally square, so starting by laying full tiles along a baseboard/wall junction is not usually an option, since slight imperfections in wall alignment will become magnified as the tile design progresses across the floor. You should therefore start by finding the center of the room. Attach a chalk line between center points on opposing walls, pull it tight, and snap the line onto the floor surface to provide a guideline. Repeat this process on the other two walls. The point at which the lines bisect is the center of the room. All tiling designs should be planned from this point. Lay the tiles dry first in order to determine the best starting point, ideally on a wall with few obstacles. You can then draw another guideline to show the starting line for the first full row of tiles. This line should be adjusted so that any cut tiles needed around the edge of the room are balanced.

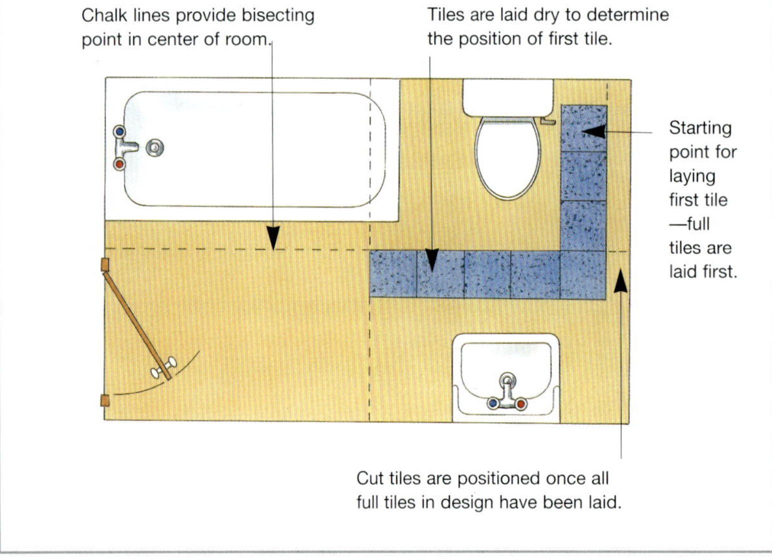

laying the tiles

tools for the job

- adjustable wrenches
- sink wrench
- tile cutter & tile saw

1 In this example, standard tiles are being laid onto a plywood subfloor (see pages 150–1 for more on laying bathroom floors). Secure wooden strips along the starting guideline and at a right angle to this line to provide a good edge to butt the tiles against. Apply adhesive with a notched spreader in the area where the first tiles are to be laid.

2 Position the first tile, allowing it to bed into the adhesive before pressing it firmly in place.

3 Add tiles, keeping consistent gaps between each tile, using pieces of cardboard as spacers.

4 Every now and again use a level to check that all surfaces are flush. Make sure that no tile edges protrude above surface level or sink below it.

5 When all the whole tiles have been laid, fill in around the edge of the room with cut tiles. It is best to let the main body of tiles dry overnight before completing the edge, since you will have to stand on the tiles when measuring.

6 Draw guidelines on tiles that need to be cut. Use a tile cutter to score and snap along the lines.

7 A tile saw is the ideal tool for cutting curves. First, make a paper template of curved shapes, such as the toilet pedestal, and use it as a guide for cutting.

8 Once all the tiles have been laid and the adhesive is dry, mix some grout and fill the joints between the tiles. Press the grout firmly in place, and wipe away any excess.

Ceramic tiles can also be applied to the walls and boxed-in areas of a bathroom for an integrated, watertight, and easy-to-clean finish. See pages 420–1 for tiling walls.

laying mosaic tiles

Some manufacturers now produce mosaic tiles suitable for floor use. They are supplied in sheets, which allows a large number to be laid at any one time—single-tile application would be a very labor-intensive and time-consuming project, even for the smallest of rooms. When laying mosaic tiles, your first concern must be to make sure that they are laid as even and flat as possible so that they are comfortable underfoot.

tips of the trade

If the edges of mosaic tiles lift above floor level, their small size means that they will be uncomfortable underfoot, so it is vital that the surface onto which they are laid is level. Concrete or plywood subfloors are ideal, as other types rarely provide enough rigidity. Make sure there are no protruding nails or bumps in the floor surface.

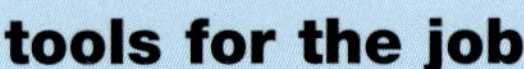

tools for the job

- tape measure & pencil
- hammer
- notched spreader
- mini roller
- grout spreader
- scissors
- tile nippers
- sponge

1 Choosing a suitable starting point when tiling with mosaics is vital and varies slightly from the approach taken when laying larger floor tiles. However, unlike larger tiles, it is important to start laying the mosaics from one wall in the room, using a wood strip to act as an initial supporting barrier to butt the tiles up against. Position the strip close to the wall, ideally about two or three tile widths away from the baseboard. (When the wood strip is removed it will be easy to fill the remaining gap with the small tiles.)

Tile sheets are not applied directly next to the baseboard because, if the room is not totally square, even a small angle of difference will become exaggerated in the finished tile design. The second strip shown here (fixed at 90 degrees to the first) provides a good guideline for producing a square design that will appear balanced and in alignment with the walls of the room, even if they are not totally square. Spread adhesive onto the subfloor in the area where the first mosaic sheets are to be positioned.

2 Remove the backing from the first sheet of mosaic tiles. This backing may be made of plastic or paper, and its only function is to make the sheets easier to handle before being laid in place.

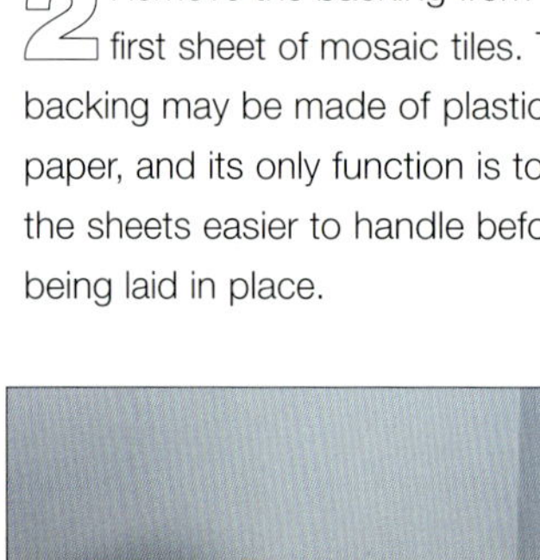

3 Position the sheet of mosaic tiles, adhesive side down, so that the edges of the tiles on two sides of the sheet rest against the right angle formed by the wood strips. A mosaic sheet is not rigid like a standard floor tile, so pay particular attention that each tile edge is in the correct place and that none is angled out of position. Fix any that are misaligned before the adhesive has a chance to dry.

4 Run a mini roller over the surface of the sheet. Apply even pressure across its expanse to embed the mosaic tiles into the adhesive, and make sure that each tile is as flat as possible.

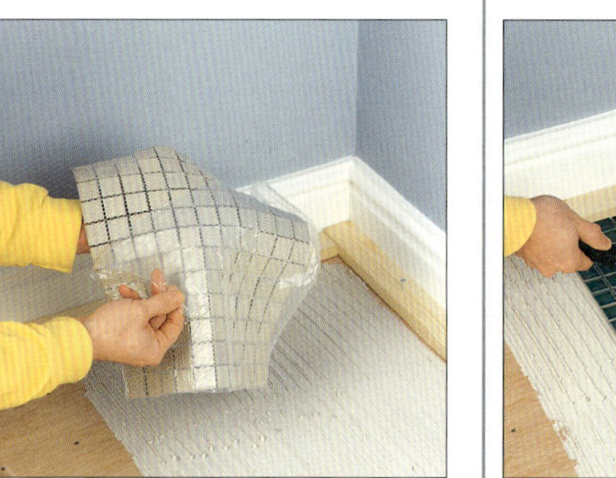

5 Lay the next sheet of tiles in the same way, inserting pieces of cardboard as spacers between each sheet to maintain a consistent gap between them.

6 As mentioned before, the flexible nature of a mosaic sheet can allow single tiles to move slightly out of position. Rather than checking and repositioning individual tiles one at a time, use a grout spreader to maintain consistent and straight gaps between rows of tiles. Where tiles appear out of position, simply press the blade of the spreader into the gaps between them to straighten any tile edges that are not aligned.

7 Once the central floor area is complete, apply tiles around the edge of the room. It is best to leave the full mosaic sheets to dry overnight before tackling the edges, in case you dislodge them from position. Remove the wood strips, then cut tile sheets to the desired size to fit in the gap between the full sheets and baseboard edge.

8 Apply adhesive along the gap in the usual way and carefully position the strips of tiles. Again, use a mini roller to make sure that they are embedded sufficiently and level with the surrounding tiles. Check that they are aligned correctly with the tiles that have already been laid.

9 You may need to use single tiles cut to size to follow the curved profile of obstacles such as a sink pedestal or the base of a toilet bowl. Single tiles are too small to be cut with a tile cutter, so use tile nippers to trim the unwanted portion of the tile before putting it in position.

10 Grout the floor with a grout spreader, pushing the grout firmly into all the joints and making sure that they are all evenly filled. Try to keep the level of the grout level with the mosaic tiles rather than raised above them. This will provide a smoother feel underfoot. Wipe away excess grout from the tiled surfaces using a damp sponge, then allow to dry overnight.

COLORED GROUT

Try finishing mosaic tiles with colored grout for a different finish. The color itself is normally supplied as a powder and mixed with white grout to achieve the required intensity. Matching the wall color can create a good effect.

ALL-OVER MOSAIC

For an all-over effect, use the same type of tiles on the walls as those used on the floor.

MOSAIC BORDER

Mosaic tiles may be used selectively on floors rather than as an overall design. For example, using large tiles in the center of the floor with mosaic tiles around the edge can be extremely effective.

CHANGING PATTERNS

Although mosaics are supplied in sheet form, patterns can be created by using a selection of different colored sheets or cutting single tiles from sheets and replacing them with another color.

laying carpet

The choice of carpet colors and patterns is virtually limitless, so it is easy to coordinate a carpet into the chosen decorative scheme of a room. Carpets made from artificial fibers are now suitable for high-traffic areas and rooms once considered inappropriate, such as bathrooms and kitchens. Often considered a professional job, carpet laying can in fact be undertaken by a skilled amateur.

First you will need to estimate the quantity of carpet, padding and tackless strips you will need (see pages 136–7). Carpet and padding are usually sold by the square yard, and are generally made in widths of 12 and 15ft. Tackless strips have different-length pins for different depths of carpet pile, so seek your supplier's advice. Carpet comes in different weights—the heavier the weight, the greater the wear.

tools for the job

- tape measure & pencil
- pruning shears or hand saw
- hammer
- caulk gun
- utility knife
- staple gun
- protective gloves
- knee kicker
- edge trimmer
- flooring chisel
- screwdriver

1 Fit tackless strips all the way around the room, cutting to length with pruning shears or a small hand saw. On chipboard and wooden floors, nail it down so that the slanted pins point toward the wall. Leave a gap two-thirds the thickness of the carpet between the back of the tackless strip and the wall.

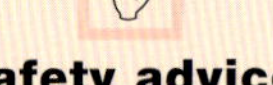

safety advice

The pins on tackless strip are extremely sharp—always wear gloves and safety glasses when working with it.

tips of the trade

To fit tackless strip the correct distance from the wall, make a spacer two-thirds the thickness of the carpet and use this when nailing it down.

2 On hard floors such as concrete use a special adhesive designed for sticking down tackless strip. Work fast, as the adhesive generally only stays workable for ten minutes.

3 Special tackless strips, often called napplocks, are fitted at doorways for a neat appearance. Nail the strip to the floor so that it will be covered completely by the bottom of the door when it is closed.

4 Cover the floor inside the tackless strip with padding, cutting to fit with a utility knife. Leave no gaps but do not overlap, as this will cause a bulge. Fix the padding to the subfloor using a staple gun.

5 Lay the carpet with the nap sloping away from the main source of light. Trim off excess with the utility knife, leaving 6in turned up the wall at each edge.

tips of the trade

The "nap" of a carpet refers to the way the pile slopes. Make sure that the nap all faces the same way when two pieces are joined together.

6 Press the carpet onto the tackless strip along the straightest wall with the ball of your hand. Wear gloves to avoid friction burns.

7 Position a knee kicker about 6in from the opposite wall and kick the carpet forward with your knee so that it is stretched and held by the tackless strip. Stretch out the whole width of the carpet.

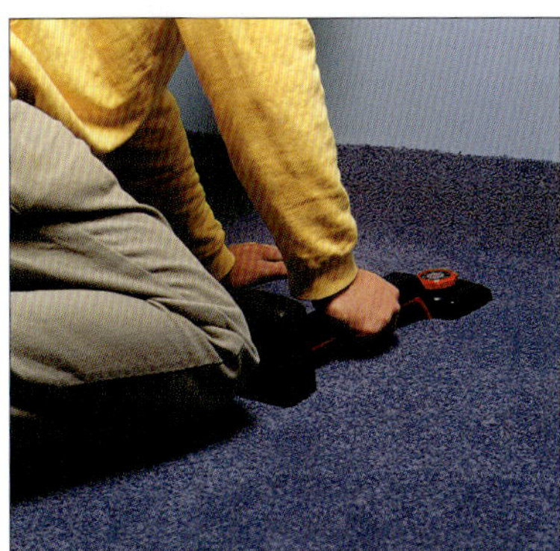

8 Cut the carpet to size with a carpet edge trimmer. Use the utility knife to get into the corners of the room. Stretch and fit the carpet to the other wall in the same manner.

9 Force down the edge of the carpet between the tackless strip and the wall/baseboard with a flooring chisel. Hand pressure is usually fine, but if the tackless strip is tight to the wall you may have to tap the chisel.

10 To fit carpet around pipes and other obstructions, cut a slit in the carpet the distance from the wall to the obstruction with a utility knife, then make small cuts across the edges of the slit. Use a screwdriver to tuck the carpet down around the pipe for a neat finish. Unless the pipe is larger than about ¾in, it is unlikely that you will have to cut out a circle of carpet.

Carpet can add color and warmth to a room. Deep-pile carpets are the most luxurious, but more durable varieties are available where strength is important.

altering a staircase

There can be a variety of reasons for wishing to alter a staircase, and a staircase can be altered in a variety of ways. For example, you might want to fit a balustrade for reasons of safety and appearance, or to convert the area underneath a stairway into a cupboard, or you may have decided that a cosmetic change is all that is needed and would like to paint or stain the stairs a different color. Before any such projects can be undertaken, you must first check that the basic structure of the staircase is sound and make any necessary repairs. Once you have satisfied that requirement, you may proceed with any number of projects for altering the staircase.

Spandrel paneling may be fitted underneath these stairs to create extra storage or closet space for minimal investment.

installing a handrail

Handrails are an essential aid for climbing and descending a stairway in safety and with ease. During the 1970s there was a trend towards doing away with handrails altogether, but while this is fine for the young and agile, it can be dangerous and difficult for children and senior citizens. Handrails are traditionally built on top of the balusters, but if you want to do away with tradition you can fix a handrail directly to an adjoining wall with the use of brackets. Alternatively, you may want to add another handrail to complement an existing balustrade, as shown here.

The instructions on these pages refer to a solid wall. If you are attaching the handrail to a hollow stud wall with plasterboard or drywall paneling, then you must modify the position of the brackets so that they can be screwed into the studs. Alternatively, use one of the many fastening mechanisms designed especially for hollow walls. Handrails come in a variety of styles and can be purchased from most DIY stores or builder's suppliers.

safety advice

A handrail is more than decorative, and should be chosen as much for its strength and security of fastening as for its style and appearance. It should be strong and sturdy enough to take the weight of someone falling against it, and should provide a secure hand hold that is easily grasped. For thinner handrails, stairs higher than average, or weak walls, consider installing additional support brackets.

tools for the job

- tape measure & pencil
- cordless drill/driver or hammer
- string or chalk line
- level
- awl
- hand saw

1 Measure up plumb 2ft 10in from the top and bottom tread and make a pencil mark at both points on the wall. Insert a nail or screw temporarily into the wall at these marks—do not nail or screw them all the way in, but make certain that they are secure.

2 Stretch a string or chalk line tightly between these two fastenings. Check the height at some of the intermediate treads. You may have to adjust one of the fastenings up or down if the measurements are not all the same.

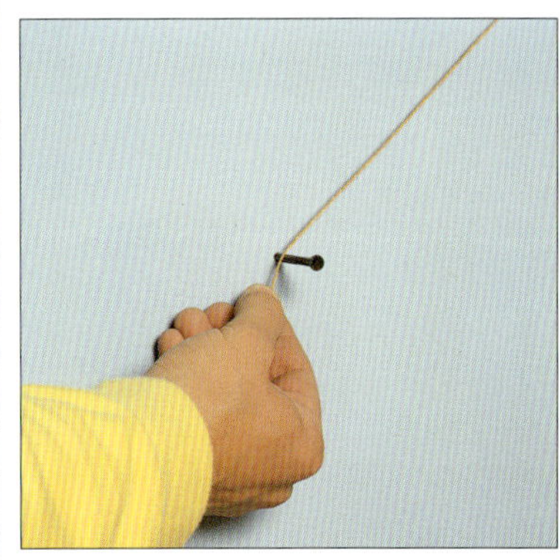

3 Mark plumb lines up from the front of the second riser at the bottom of the staircase and the penultimate riser at the top of the staircase. Draw a line at both points where the level bisects the string line.

4 Fasten brackets at the points just marked. Align the top plate of the bracket level with the underside of the string line, keeping the wall fastening plate centrally over the plumb reference line.

5 Mark the wall through the holes on the fastening plate with an awl. Remove the bracket and drill the fixing holes, making sure you fit the correct size of bit for the screws. Screw the bracket to the wall, double-checking that the top plate is still in line with the string. With the top and bottom brackets fitted, divide the gap between them into three and fit two more brackets, giving four in all.

6 Remove the string line and temporary fastenings and place the handrail on top of the brackets. Get a helper to hold it in position, or wind painter's tape around each bracket to keep it in place temporarily. With the handrail secure, use a level to mark level cuts in line with the first and last riser.

7 Remove the handrail and cut through the pencil marks with a fine hand saw. Smooth down the cut ends using abrasive paper. Place the handrail back into position and drill pilot holes up into the underside of the handrail, before finally screwing it in place on the bracket.

tips of the trade

While the handrail is in position to mark the level cuts, you can also mark on the screw positions. This makes it possible to insert the screws without having to use a drill upside down, while the holes will provide reference marks to be sure the handrail is repositioned correctly.

safety advice

After the handrail is installed, carefully remove any sharp edges on the surface of the wood, which could otherwise cause injury or give splinters, with abrasive paper. Once you have sanded any obvious edges, put on a thick pair of gloves and run your hand up and down the rail several times to make sure nothing catches on the glove material. If it does, sand over the surface once again.

ROPE HANDRAIL

Although not as sturdy as wooden or metal varieties, a rope handrail is a handy option for curved stairways. To install, screw the brackets to the wall as described. If you are fitting it to a curved stairway, measure the plumb height from each tread to find the correct bracket location. Thread the rope through the brackets and tie a decorative knot at the top and bottom to prevent it being pulled out. Leave 2in of slack between each bracket to avoid straining the screws.

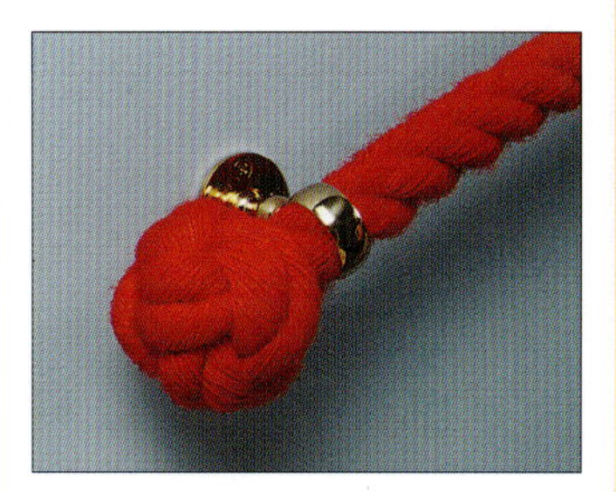

Once the handrail is fastened securely to each of the brackets, it provides a vital support that will make the stairs safer and more comfortable for all who use them.

installing handrail bolts

Handrail bolts represent the traditional method for jointing together two sections of handrail. Although, to a certain extent, their use has been superseded by other methods, when properly executed handrail bolts remain an unsurpassed jointing mechanism. Requiring no glue, they are ideal for jointing a straight section of handrail to a curve at the junction of a landing, or at the junction between different flights of a staircase.

Jointing sections of handrail together using the bolt method requires a high degree of skill, and accuracy is essential for best results both in the marking and cutting. Therefore this project should only be attempted if you are confident of your abilities, and this is certainly not a job for a beginner. You are unlikely to be able to find handrail bolts in your local general DIY store. These will most probably need to be bought from a specialist hardware retailer.

tools for the job

- hand saw
- miter box
- tape measure & pencil
- square
- cordless drill/driver
- ¼in chisel
- nail set

1 Take the two sections of handrail and, using a hand saw, cut the ends to be joined so that they are precisely square. Make the cuts in a miter box using a right angle cut guide, then check how the ends butt together. Rest the sections on a flat surface and bring together the two ends. There should be no gaps, and if there are you will need to recut the joints until perfect.

2 Establish a center line on the flat underside of one handrail section. Draw a neat pencil mark down this line to approximately 4in from the cut end.

tips of the trade

A trick for finding the center line of anything is to measure across at an angle until the measurement is easily divisible by two, then make a pencil mark at this point. This will give the exact center, irrespective of the actual half measurement.

3 Transfer this mark from the underside onto the cut face using a square, continuing the pencil mark until you reach the top surface. Accurately measure up half the height of the handrail and mark on this point square to the guideline.

4 Repeat steps 2 and 3 for the other section of handrail, then briefly put the sections to one side. Now take the handrail bolt and screw both nuts onto either end, screwing them so that a couple of threads are projecting past the nuts at either end. Carefully measure the distance between the inside edge of both nuts, divide this by two, and mark the dimension onto the underside of the handrail along the center line.

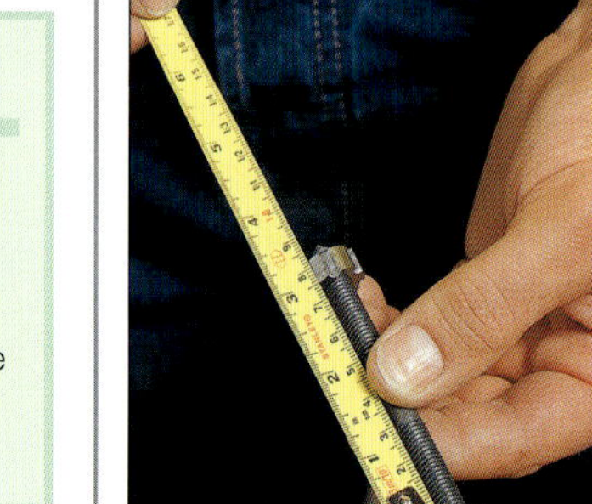

5 Drill into the end face of each handrail section at the center point marked in step 3. Use a drill bit $\frac{1}{16}$in larger than the diameter of the bolt and ½in deeper than half the overall length of the bolt.

6 Use a ¼in chisel to cut out a pocket in the underside of one of the handrail sections, into which the square nut will be dropped. Chisel out the wood at the point marked in step 4. Note that the pocket should be on the side of the line furthest from the end of the handrail. Once the pocket is complete, drop the square nut into it, allowing the bolt to poke through the hole and enter the thread.

7 In the same way, cut the pocket for the round serrated nut on the other handrail section. The pocket should be slightly larger, to allow the nut to turn on the bolt.

8 Use a small nail set to tighten the serrated nut so that the two halves of the handrail are pulled up tight. Do not overtighten, or you may split the wood. To prove that you have been accurate, the two sections should form a perfect fit.

9 Use a sanding block and abrasive paper to sand across the completed joint in order to blend any slight irregularities. Finally, fit the handrail into position on the stairs. Should the joint open up in the future, gently retighten the serrated nut.

A reef is the section of handrail that goes around a corner and connects one straight section to another. A handrail bolt is ideal for joining these sections together.

changing a newel post

Replacing a newel post can alter the overall appearance of just about any staircase. This project is much less drastic and expensive than replacing all the balusters and handrails. Swapping, for example, a contemporary square post with a classic turned newel can soften what might otherwise be seen as a box-like design.

Changing newel posts is a popular project and is often accompanied by changing baluster spindles (see pages 190–1). Larger DIY stores now offer a wide selection of newel posts that are specifically manufactured to replace existing posts.

tools for the job

- tape measure & pencil
- hand saw
- wood chisel & mallet
- cordless drill/driver & bore bit
- square

1 Measure the vertical height of the existing handrail adjacent to the existing newel. It is important to do this before you start work on removal of the old newel, as you will need this measurement at a later stage.

2 Cut the top off the old newel squarely, about ½in above the level where the handrail enters the post. You should be able visually to estimate where to cut. If not, draw a line as a guide around the newel and cut along the line.

3 Do the same below the handrail, but leave 1in on the inside of the newel post, to cut later.

4 Use a wood chisel and mallet to split away the wood carefully on either side of the newel post in order to expose the tenon.

5 Do a little at a time and be careful not to damage the tenon as you get closer to it, since you will need to slot it into the new newel post.

6 Square a line around the remaining newel post 1in above where the stringer enters, and cut at this point. Be accurate, as the new post will sit on top of this cut stump.

7 Use a sharp chisel or plane to flatten the stump of the existing newel post. Check the surface is flat with a square so that the new newel post will fit properly on top of the old base. If the stump is perfectly flat, this will make the job of drilling for the dowel a lot easier. Draw diagonal lines across the top of the stump and bore

a hole 1in in diameter about 3in deep at this center point. Make sure the drill bit goes in upright.

8 Mark and chisel the mortise for the handrail tenon from the new newel post. Transfer measurements from the existing tenon to the newel.

9 Measure the height you took in step 1 and transfer this to the new post less the distance left on the stump. Before cutting off the waste from the bottom of the new newel, double-check your markings by holding the new post up against the stump. Measure across the diagonals and drill.

tips of the trade

If you are at all unsure about your marking out, tape the new post alongside the old one while it is still in position, and transfer the positions of the handrail, stringer, and 1in high cut line prior to removal.

10 Fit a 1in dowel 5½in long to hold the base of the newel. Carry out a dry run to make sure that all the parts fit together. Take it apart, and glue the newel in position with wood glue or epoxy resin. Once the job is completed, sand the new newel post and apply your chosen finish. If you are replacing the newel post, then the finish should match as closely as possible the balusters and handrails. For additional information about finishing see pages 212–13.

safety advice

The strength and durability of epoxy resin is unsurpassed. However, some people may experience allergic reactions to certain products. To avoid this problem, wear latex gloves or apply barrier cream when handling these materials.

tips of the trade

If you plan to paint or stain your newel post, it is wise to sand it before it is installed, as the shape of the post makes it difficult to sand once it is connected to the handrail.

It is important to ensure a close match between the finish on the replacement newel post and the existing finish on the rest of the balustrade.

installing balusters

It is often the case that balusters are changed at the same time as the newel posts, to alter entirely the look of the stairs. The style of balusters you ultimately go for will depend on personal preference and your budget. You should consider which type of balusters will contribute best to the overall style that you are trying to achieve. Buying the most expensive hardwood balusters could be a waste of money if you are going to end up painting them, when cheaper softwood balusters would have given the same result for less money.

You will need to fit two spacer blocks and two balusters for each stair tread, plus the stringer capping and a new handrail, if this is being replaced at the same time (see also pages 184–7). All the parts should be available from good DIY stores.

tools for the job

- tape measure & pencil
- hand saw
- nail set
- hammer
- level
- sliding bevel
- sanding block

1 Place the capping that houses the bottom of the balusters on top of the stringer, and slide it down until it touches the newel. Holding a piece of waste wood against the newel, mark and cut the bevel.

2 Repeat the process at the top of the stairs, then nail through the capping into the top of the stringer, setting the nails below the surface of the capping with a nail set.

3 Mark a plumb line with a level on both the handrail and stringer capping. The position of this line does not matter, as it is simply a guideline to help you mark the length of the balusters. Draw equivalent lines across the top of the capping and underside of the handrail.

4 Use two lengths of thin wood strip to act as a guide for measuring the height of the balusters. Hold the two sections together and then slide them apart until they touch the plumb line marks made on the capping and handrail. Tape together the two pieces to preserve the measurement.

5 Hold the guide against one of the balusters and transfer the height measurement. Set a sliding bevel to the angle between the newel post and stringer capping, and transfer this bevel to the baluster. Note that the top and bottom bevels slope in the same direction.

tips of the trade

Store the balusters inside for a few days so that they can acclimatize to the temperature and humidity of the home prior to fitting. This will ensure they do not shrink subsequently, which will cause them to rattle.

6 Cut the bevels onto each end of the baluster and then place it between the handrail and capping to check for fit. Hold a level against the baluster when in position to make sure that it is plumb. If you are happy with the fit, use this first baluster as a pattern for cutting all the others.

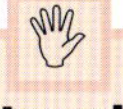

safety advice

Make sure that the balusters are not spaced too far apart, as this could allow a child to fall through.

7 Starting at the bottom of the staircase, nail the first two spacer blocks, one to the underside of the handrail, and the other to the stringer capping. Use a nail set to push the heads below the surface.

8 Add the first baluster, then follow this with the next spacer block, and so on until you reach the top of the stairs. No fastenings are made through the balusters themselves. Only the spacer blocks are fastened in place, as these are sufficient to hold the balusters.

9 When all the balusters have been installed, rub them over lightly with a sanding block and abrasive paper, then apply your chosen finish.

tips of the trade

If you have chosen barley-twist-style balusters, make sure that the twists all start in the same position at the bottom. This makes for a neater and more professional appearance.

Combined with a decorative handrail and newel post, balusters provide an ornate finish to a staircase. They also represent a safety option, especially if you have children.

blocking in the underside of a staircase

In smaller homes it may not be appropriate to fit spandrel paneling underneath a staircase if this would cause a portion of the main living space to be blocked off. You may instead want to consider leaving the side of the stairway open and disguising the architecture and construction details on the underside with the addition of a flat panel. If your needs change or you feel more confident in your DIY abilities, there is always the option to add spandrel paneling at a later date.

Plasterboard or drywall are commonly used to form the panel, although heavy and difficult to handle, and other materials will do just as well. For the project demonstrated on these pages, the panels have been cut from thin plywood. Working with lightweight and easy-to-handle plywood means it is perfectly feasible for a person of average skill to undertake this project single-handed and easily complete it over a weekend. Wooden strips form the framework for fixing the panels, and since these are small and thin it is important to use good-quality wood.

tools for the job

- tape measure & pencil
- hand saw
- screwdriver
- hammer
- nail set
- wallpaper brush & roller

1 Cut small sections of 1 x 1in wood strip to act as set-backs, against which cross pieces will be fixed at 8in centers to form the framework for the panels. You will need to cut two for each cross piece —make a template to save having to measure each individual piece when cutting. When you have cut enough pieces, measure and mark midway between each step the distance these pieces will need to be set back from the edge of the stringer to accommodate the cross pieces. Since the cross pieces are cut from the same strip of wood, this will be 1in. Glue and screw each set-back in the marked positions.

2 Measure and cut sufficient cross pieces to provide supports at 8in centers. Fasten these into position by angle-nailing or screwing through each end at an angle into the set-back sections of wood strip.

3 Cut ¼in plywood to fit across the width of the stairs, from stringer edge to stringer edge, so that any joints meet on the cross pieces.

4 Mark the center lines of the cross pieces a little way onto the sides of the stringers. Spread wood glue onto the face of each cross piece and fasten the panels into position on the stringers with ¾in brads. Join up the pencil marks across the face of the panels with a straightedge. These will act as guidelines for fixing brads into the cross supports.

tips of the trade

On older stairs, where access might be needed later, omit the glue and fasten the panels with small screws.

5 Push the nail heads just below the surface of the plywood with a nail set. Disguise the holes left by the nails by smoothing in enough wood filler so that it protrudes slightly. Leave to dry, then sand smooth.

6 Nail on some trim to cover the exposed joints between plywood and stringer. This helps to cover the slots left by the router for the treads and risers when the stairs were built.

tips of the trade

When fixing delicate trim use veneer nails instead of brads, as they are thinner and less obtrusive, and require less filler to disguise the nail heads.

7 Finally, paint or paper the surface of the finished paneling to match or blend with the existing decoration in the room for a unified look. If applying wallpaper, as shown, buy good-quality wallpaper to ensure an adequate bond with the plywood.

tips of the trade

If you plan to wallpaper the plywood paneling, it is a good idea to apply a coat of latex paint to the side of the panel that will face the back tread of the stairs prior to fastening. This may seem like an unnecessary job, as it will never be seen; however, it will prevent the wood from warping, and this in turn ensures the panel remains flat, and the wallpaper does not peel.

UNDERSTAIR LIGHTING

If the underside of the stairs could do with some additional illumination, one idea is to fit recessed lights. You will need to run the necessary wiring before you fit the panels. Use a jigsaw to cut the hole into the plywood panel as instructed by the manufacturer. Installing electrical lighting is a complicated procedure, and you must not take chances with electricity—employ a qualified electrician to wire the lights and final connection.

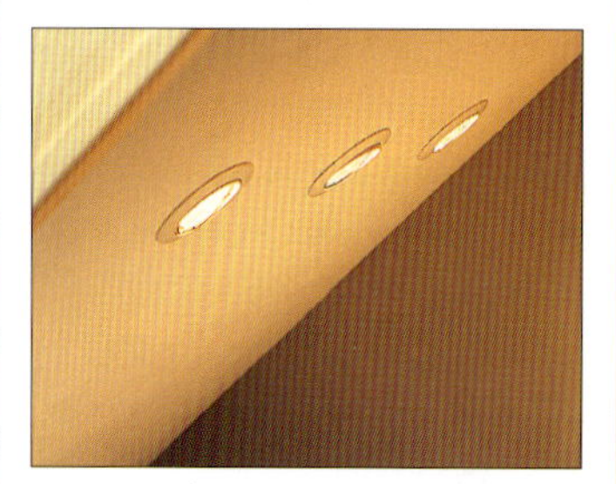

Finished appropriately, blocking in both conceals the underside of a staircase and incorporates the stairs into the overall decor of the room or hall.

installing spandrel paneling—1

Spandrel paneling is really just another name for the panels that can be fitted to fill in the area below the stairs and create cupboard space. Once common in older houses, it often does not feature in modern properties because of cost considerations. Although this is probably one of the more complex projects featured in the book, you will find that the attractive finish and extra storage space created ultimately make the effort worthwhile.

Before starting on this project it is advisable to clear as far as possible the room of furniture and other items, in order to give yourself enough space to work comfortably. Also remove any floor covering in the vicinity and check and repair the subfloor, if necessary before starting on the paneling. Use high-quality dressed wood for all the studwork, both to give a neater appearance on the inside of the cupboard, and because warped or twisted wood makes the job of getting the panel to stay flat impossible.

tools for the job

- tape measure & pencil
- plumb bob & line
- fine handsaw
- cordless drill/driver
- stud finder
- level
- sliding bevel
- claw hammer
- small hammer

1 Hold a plumb bob and line against the open stringer of the staircase and, with the bottom of the bob resting just clear of the floor, mark reference points with a pencil at two or three places along the floor between the newel post and the wall. Join up the marks with a straightedge to form a reference line for the sole plate of the paneling. At the same time, plumb a line up the wall between this sole plate guideline and the outside bottom edge of the stringer where it bisects the wall.

2 If baseboard is fitted around the back wall of the stairway, as here, it must be removed. Use a fine hand saw to cut the baseboard at the pencil mark you have just made and discard the section from under the stairs. Sometimes you can cut the baseboard in place by prying it away from the wall. To avoid uneven cuts it is neater and easier to remove the section completely. You may then cut it to length and replace.

3 Decide upon the position of the cupboard door and mark this on the sole plate reference line on the floor. As a guide, an opening about 2ft 6in wide and 10in from the wall is about right.

4 Cut sections of wood to form the sole plate, using 2 x 2in wood. Screw these sections to the floor with a cordless drill/driver, leaving a gap for the door at the point marked in step 3. Before screwing into the floor, check with a stud finder that there are no plumbing or electricity services directly underneath. The wooden sections will need to be set back slightly from the sole plate reference line made in step 1 to allow for the thickness of the paneling. Use a waste piece of $^{7}/_{16}$in plywood or MDF as a guide to ensure a consistent gap.

5 Screw a wooden stud to the wall below the open stringer. Again, keep this back $^{7}/_{16}$in from the

reference line. You will need to fasten the stud to the wall at three points 1ft 6in apart, and fasten it at the bottom to the sole plate, screwing at an angle down into the wood.

6 Screw another piece of 2 x 2in wood onto the back of the open stringer, making sure that the bottom edge is level with the bottom of the stringer. Onto this last piece of wood screw on another piece of 2 x 2in wood, set back the same 7/16in from the edge of the open stringer as for the sole plate. This will be the stringer plate to which the studs of the framework will be nailed at the top. Check with a level that it is fitted straight.

7 Cut further studs from 2 x 2in wood and nail them at 8in centers to the stringer plate at the top and sole plate at the bottom. Make sure the outside edges of the studs are aligned with the edge of the stringer and sole plates. Fit studs on both side of the door opening, checking with a level that these are fastened plumb. To draw the correct angle at the top, use a sliding bevel set to the same angle as that between the wall plate and underside of the stringer.

8 To form the head of the cupboard door frame, measure down 8in from the open stringer on the longest of the studs that comprise the sides of the door opening, marking this point with a pencil. Cut and fasten a piece of wood to form the head across at this point, checking with the level that it is level. Fasten the head section in place, screwing it to the stud and into the stringer plate at an angle. As you look at the door opening, you should have a rectangle with one corner cut off.

9 Cover the outside of the frame with either 7/16in plywood or MDF. Screw it to the framework with 1in screws. Use a countersink bit to sink screw heads below the surface. Make sure that plumb joints meet on a stud. Fit a block behind any unsupported horizontal joints.

10 Nail 2½ x ¾in wood around the inside of the opening to form a door frame, keeping it level with the paneling.

11 Fit baseboard and casing around the door frame, and a cover strip over the joint between the stringer and paneling.

tips of the trade

If there is room, you may find it easier to construct the whole panel flat on the floor, before lifting it up and screwing it into place on the framework.

installing spandrel paneling—2

With the basic panel below the stairs completed, you could just paint or paper it to match the room. However, adding a door, molded paneling, and other details will create a more finished appearance, and you can choose the look that best suits the overall style of your home.

tools for the job

- tape measure & pencil
- fine hand saw or jigsaw
- sharp plane
- hammer
- C-clamps
- nail set
- screwdriver

making the door

1 Check the opening is square and plumb. If the frame is not perfectly upright, withdraw the nails and adjust. Take accurate measurements from the door opening and transfer these to thin plywood or MDF—1/8in thick is ideal, otherwise use 1/4in. Cut around the door outline using a fine hand saw or jigsaw with a fine-tooth blade. Use a sharp plane to create a 1/8in gap all round.

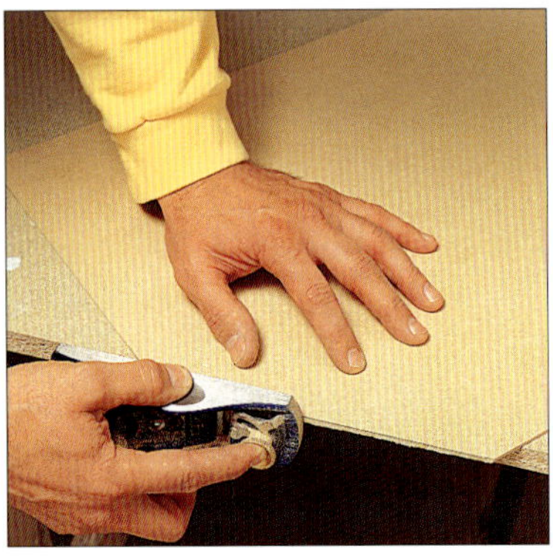

2 Check against the door opening that the first panel is a correct fit. Then make an exact copy using the panel as a template. Make sure both panels are identical, as differences may impart a twist to the final door.

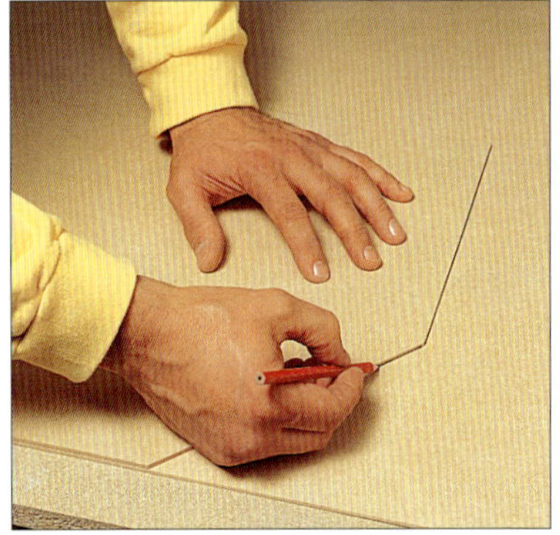

tips of the trade

When trying for fit, to prevent the door falling through the frame hammer two nails partway in either side of the door, leaving about 1/2in to support the leaning door.

3 Using one of the door panels as a guide, cut pieces of 1 1/2 x 1in wood to form an inside framework for a door 2in thick. Run the strips for the two long edges first and cut the cross pieces to meet these. If your woodworking skills are good, cut miters at the top corners. Spread wood glue around the edges of one of the panels and nail the wooden sections in place, holding them in position with C-clamps.

4 Spread wood glue around the edge of the wood, then nail the second panel into position, again holding the wood in place with C-clamps as you hammer in the nails. Push the nail heads below the surface with a nail set.

5 Fasten a hinge on the high side of the door, 6in down from the top and 8in up from the bottom. Surface-mounted hinges, as shown here, are the easiest to fasten. You can use traditional hinges that are let into the edge of the door and frame, but these are harder to fit and require a greater degree of skill.

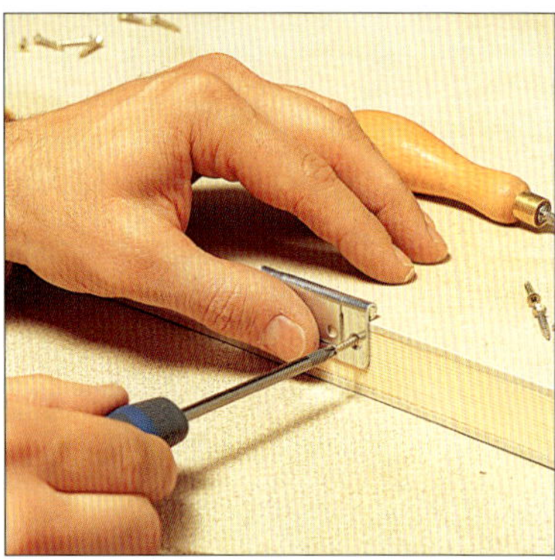

6 Attach a magnetic latch at the inside top edge of the door to retain it in the closed position. Then

fasten your chosen door handle no more than 3ft from the floor and 4in in from the opening edge.

adding molding

Adding molding will take some of the blandness out of what might otherwise be a rather flat panel. Correctly executed and tastefully applied details can enhance your work. Try to pick up from existing details and decor in the room or hallway. Matching baseboards or shoe molding along the bottom of the panel will tie everything together. Similarly, you may choose to match up nearby casing and use this to frame your doors.

1 One option to break up the expanse of flat panels is to add some faux fielded panels. First cut some ¼in thick MDF 4in smaller all round than the overall size of the door and panels. Plane a small bevel all around the edge before gluing and nailing it into position.

2 To give the appearance of molded panels, cut some pieces of small bolection molding to size, then glue and nail them so that they just cover the edge of the panel fastened in step 1. Be careful cutting the miters at the corners, as they will show up badly if poorly executed. Finally, check the finished door fits into the opening, planing the edges if required, then paint or paper the door as desired and screw it into position.

tips of the trade

It can be difficult to measure the gap between the door and frame. Try using a slim coin as a gauge for maintaining a consistent gap around the door.

UNDERSTAIR STORAGE

Many DIY stores stock metal shelving systems that are both lightweight and sturdy. These systems are ideal for areas like the underside of stairs since they can be easily adapted as storage needs change. Stores also offer a great variety of wooden shelving, but these are often quite expensive and with very little effort you can create your own at less than half the cost. If you intend to install coat racks or shelving, do this prior to hanging the door so you do not block access.

Painted to match the surrounding area, spandrel paneling will smarten the look of a staircase and can provide additional storage space if fitted with a door opening.

repairing floors & stairs

Every home, whatever its age, will need some degree of regular maintenance – the amount will usually depend on how well and how often repairs were carried out in the past. It is well worth taking your time to ensure the job is done effectively, as there is nothing more irritating than having to carry out the same repair for a second time just a few months later. Carrying out repairs will in itself breathe new life into older floors and stairs, but if you also wish to alter the look, this chapter offers several easy renovation ideas.

Old floorboards can be made to look good as new by replacing any damaged boards and stripping and varnishing the wood surface.

recognizing problems with floors & stairs

A house is probably the biggest investment that you will ever make so it pays to look after it. Major repairs are always more costly than catching a problem before it goes too far—as the saying goes, an ounce of prevention is worth a pound of cure. Cracks, moisture, and squeaking stairs are all things that should be investigated immediately. If caught early enough, repairs are often straightforward, but when ignored they can lead to structural failure.

problems with floors

cracks

Most cracks in the plaster of a room, especially in newer homes, will be due to the natural settlement of materials, or, in older houses, due to plaster that has been poorly mixed and applied. Such cracks often appear at the corners of the room or around door frames and should be no larger than hairline. Some cracks, however, especially ceiling cracks, are caused by slight movement in the floorboards rather than general settlement or poor plastering. These are usually no cause for alarm and may simply be patched, as a certain amount of seasonal movement is normal in solid wood floors. If the house is new, floor movement can probably be attributed to natural shrinkage once the property starts to dry out and the moisture content of the wood is reduced.

In older properties, however, ceiling cracks accompanied by springy flooring in the room above may signal rotten joists or boards that have come loose from joists due to rusted nails. Persistent cracks under baseboards may also indicate floor problems or even subsidence, and cracks in subfloors made from manufactured boards are generally indicative of more serious problems. If you cannot easily find the root cause of a crack or it continues to widen, this may indicate serious structural problems and you should seek professional advice.

moisture

Wet and damp baseboards are a sure sign of rising moisture in the fabric of the wall, which could be caused by a bridged or missing foundation coating. Such moisture is far more noticeable on walls facing the prevailing wind, especially after heavy rain when moisture is driven through the wall. If the wall is noticeably damp on these occasions, it may be that the joists are absorbing water. If this is allied to blocked air bricks and poor ventilation in the floor space, rot could soon follow. On upper stories a damp spot in the center of the ceiling is a good indicator of leaking plumbing.

Although most damage is likely to be to the ceiling itself, moisture may also be seeping into the joist timbers.

Cavity-wall houses built after 1920 are less prone to damp since their structure is designed to channel any water that penetrates the outer wall down its inner face to ground level.

problems with floorboards

Gaps between floorboards are most often caused by wood shrinkage. Insert wider boards or lift all the boards, close up the gaps, and re-lay the floor. Alternatively, insert small wedges coated with glue to seal gaps. If a board is badly split, remove and replace, but if the split is minor, simply apply extra fasteners to prevent further movement. If a floorboard has sprung up, then the fastening has failed or is missing, and the problem can be solved with new fasteners.

EMPLOYING A SURVEYOR

Surveyors do not just exist to assess properties when they are about to be bought or sold, but may also be contacted to examine suspected problems in your current home and offer advice on how to treat them. The services of suitably qualified surveyors are often quite expensive, but they will be able to take a professional look at the structure of your house, carry out specialist tests, and provide you with a written report on the condition of your property—much as a doctor might give you a health check. If you do choose to employ surveyors, make sure that they are members of an accredited professional association, who will be able to supply you with a list of members in your area.

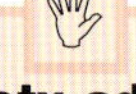

safety advice

Floors and stairs are major structural elements in a house and are often the site of domestic accidents and injuries. If you notice sudden changes or are at all concerned seek professional advice from a surveyor or structural engineer.

problems with stairs

stairs

Internal stresses in wood can cause a tread to split. If the split is bad, then remove and replace the tread, otherwise patch from below or inject epoxy resin into the gap. Squeaking stairs are most often caused by loose or missing glue blocks and wedges below stairs. Investigate the cause from below, and renew or replace any missing components. Alternatively, fastening a strengthening block of wood between the inside joint of tread and riser will often cure the problem. Broken nosing is usually just caused by general wear and tear, with no structural ramifications. Simply cut off the damaged area and let in a new section of wood to match the original. Damage to staircase risers is relatively rare, as these do not get wear in the same way that treads do. If a riser has split or become loose, then there may be something seriously wrong with the overall structure of the stairs. If further investigation indicates no other damage, the split riser can be fixed in the same way as a split tread.

stringers

If gaps start to form between the stringer and the wall, the fasteners holding the stairs back to the wall may have failed. To replace the fastenings, drill through the stringer and use a screw and wall plug to pull the stringer tight to the wall. A gap in the joint between stringer and tread usually indicates a failed wedge. Replace the wedge from beneath the stairs, making sure it is coated with glue.

balustrade

Open joints between a handrail and the newel post are often caused by glue failure in the joint, or a dowel through the joint may have failed. Drill out the old dowel, squirt in some wood glue, and replace with a new dowel. Newel posts on older stairs are held in place by a wedged mortise-and-tenon joint that goes through to the joists below the floor. It is common for the wedge in this joint to fall out. To cure the problem, remove a section of floorboard adjacent to the newel and replace the missing wedge. Loose, broken, and missing balusters are usually caused by broken joints at the top and bottom. Clean off the old glue and recoat the joint with new adhesive, taping the baluster into position until the glue sets.

identifying the problem

You should inspect the state of floors and stairs in your home on a regular basis, perhaps every six months or so. Such inspections are best made when the floor coverings have been removed and the subfloor and stair structure is exposed. It can also be helpful if another person slowly walks up and down the stairs and across the floor while you listen for creaks.

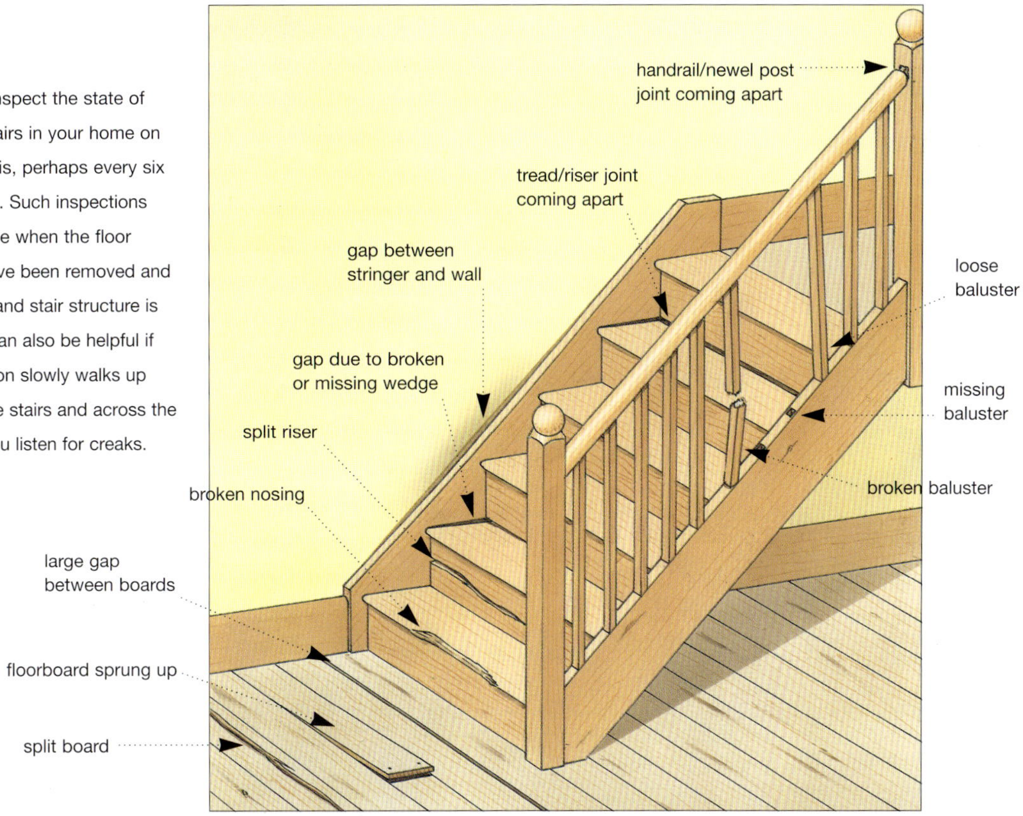

dealing with infestation & rot

A house is under constant threat from infestation and rot, and even in the best-maintained homes such pests can sometimes turn up. Being able to identify which pest has caused the damage, how they have been able to flourish, and what effective treatment can be used to eradicate them is essential. Some infestations are more a nuisance than a danger to structures, but others have the ability to destroy your home if left unchecked.

wood-boring insects

Over half of all homes suffer some sort of infestation from wood-boring beetles. It is not the beetles themselves that do the damage but their larvae, which bury into the wood, creating elaborate labyrinthine tunnels. The best way to treat the problem is to treat the wood with a woodworm solution. If you are at all unsure, then professional help should be sought.

wet & dry rot

Dry rot thrives in warm and stagnant areas caused, for example, by dripping pipes under a bathtub or blocked air bricks that prevent the air circulating under a floor. Once dry rot has taken hold it can attack perfectly good wood, and can even penetrate walls. At the center of dry rot is a large fruiting body, white in appearance, from which long, spindly, white/gray strands radiate. In the right conditions dry rot can spread at an alarming rate, quickly destroying hitherto healthy wood. If you find dry rot when working on the floor, all the infected wood must be removed and burnt to prevent the spread of the disease.

Wet rot is far less serious and does not have the capacity to spread as quickly as dry rot. Wet rot only occurs in wood with a high moisture content —the rot will cease to spread once moisture levels are lowered.

TYPE	SYMPTOMS	CAUSES	TREATMENT	TELLTALE SIGNS
Furniture beetle A brown beetle no more than ⅛in in length.	Destruction of wood caused by the grubs boring through the interior of a section of wood.	Beetles lay small lemon-shaped eggs in cracks and crevices, which then hatch. Woodworm can be introduced into the home by bringing in old furniture that is already infested. Most active in the early summer, it may enter your home at this time looking for a suitable nesting site.	Spraying or brushing the surface of the infected wood to kill the grubs and eggs. If the outbreak is serious, then contact a specialist.	Flight holes of about 1/16in in diameter and traces of what looks like very fine sawdust on the wood surface.
Deathwatch beetle Brown beetle often with white spots about ¼in in length. The grubs are white and about the same length when fully grown.	Destruction of wood caused by the grubs boring through the interior of a section of wood. Much more destructive than the more common furniture beetle.	Beetles lay eggs in cracks and crevices, which then hatch. Deathwatch beetle favors wood that is already well matured, and oak is a favorite habitat—it rarely attacks softwood.	Spraying or brushing the surface of the infected wood to kill the grubs and eggs. If the outbreak is serious, contact a specialist contractor. You must also notify the local authority.	The grubs cause great destruction with innumerable tunnels about ⅛in in diameter, converting the wood to dust in the process.

TYPE	SYMPTOMS	CAUSES	TREATMENT	TELLTALE SIGNS
Powder-post beetle Brown to black beetle about 1/4in in length. The grubs are white and about the same length fully grown.	Destruction of wood caused by the grubs boring through the interior of a section of wood. Unlikely to attack mature wood found in buildings, more likely to infect wood that is stacked at a lumber yard waiting to be transported.	Bad conditioning of wood tor using wood that has a high proportion of sapwood (the wood immediately below the bark).	Treatment is as for other forms of woodworm, using a suitable brush or spray treatment.	Holes of about 1/16in in diameter in the surface of the wood. Grubs do not burrow to the same depth as deathwatch or furniture beetle, so the whole surface of the wood may fall away when touched, exposing the holes.
Dry rot Consists of minute silky threads covering the surface of the wood in early stages. If conditions are right, this will change to what looks like cotton balls. In very advanced stages, this will further develop into dark red, sponge-like bodies.	Musty smell that does not go away. Often working out of sight below flooring and carpets in damp areas, the strands will spread to infect perfectly sound wood. Ultimately leads to total breakdown of joists and floorboards.	Moist, stagnant air with poor ventilation. Blocking up air bricks and under-floor vents. Leaking pipes and waste systems below flooring also promote ideal conditions for dry rot to thrive.	Curing the condition that caused the outbreak. Removal of infected wood at least 3ft beyond in all directions from the last visible signs of the rot or strands. Scorching of brickwork to kill spores in order to prevent reinfection. Specialist treatment is advised.	Often very few, the greatest indication being a musty smell. Visible surface of wood may change color, followed by the appearance of small mushrooms.
Wet rot Discoloration of the wood surface, with floorboards often turning black in the advanced stages. When the surface of the wood is broken away, the interior will be brown and fibrous.	Soft, crumbling wood with no strength and wet to the touch. Bubbling paint on the surface of the wood.	Leaking pipes and rainwater are the main causes. In the case of floor joists it could be where they are in contact with damp brickwork. Also moisture rising up a wall and being soaked into the ends of the flooring due to bridged foundation coating.	Fix the source of the problem before replacing any affected wood. Brush or spray on wood preservative to both new and remaining wood. Provide adequate ventilation.	Black spots on paintwork and wallpaper near the affected area, which, even when cleaned away, return after a few days. Moisture in the carpet or floor covering. Where floor tiles have been fitted, moisture may cause these to lift.

solving problems with older floors

Older floors will inevitably need repairs as ordinary wear and tear over the years takes its toll. Maintenance is usually straightforward and, since older floors are likely to have been laid before the advent of cheap large sheets of manufactured board, problems will tend to be confined to the solid wood floorboards. Most areas that require attention will be easy to spot once any floor covering is removed, and can be dealt with using a few basic tools.

tips of the trade

- **When to inspect**—The ideal time to inspect and correct problems is when the carpet or other floor covering is being replaced. At this time the boards will be completely exposed and can be given a thorough overall investigation.
- **Removing baseboard**—If you are renovating the floor, consider removing the baseboards before you start the work. This makes it far easier to re-lay the floor, as you do not have the problem of tucking new floorboards underneath baseboard.

safety advice

Wear knee pads when working on a wooden floor to protect your knees from splinters and projecting nails.

repairing loose boards

One of the main reasons for creaking floors is that floorboards have become loose over time.

tools for the job

- hammer
- nail set

Nail down any loose boards using flooring nails, which are specially designed for this use. Push any heads below the surface with a nail set.

closing up gaps

Over time floorboards will shrink so that gaps begin to appear between them. Gaps will make carpets more dirty and cause a room to feel colder as drafts blow up the gaps into the living area. There are two methods for sealing up these gaps—either the gaps are filled or the entire floor is taken out and laid again.

tools for the job

- tape measure & pencil
- hand saw
- hammer
- floorboard jack

filling the gaps

Regular gaps between floorboards can be filled with a strip of wood. Cut a strip the width of the gap and as thick as the adjacent board, coat it with glue on both edges, then tap it into the space with a hammer.

re-laying the floor

Another option is to lift and re-lay all the floorboards in the room. Fit the first board tight to the wall and, using a floorboard jack, butt each one up against its neighbor as it is fitted. Fit new boards into any remaining gaps.

tips of the trade

Tattered edges will often prevent nails from properly securing the boards. By ripping a strip off either side, though this narrows the boards, you will gain fresh edges to ensure a secure hold.

laying masonite

Laying sheets of manufactured board, in this case masonite, over existing floorboards is a worthwhile project. It instantly seals any small gaps, preventing dirt and drafts from coming up from below, and provides a smooth floor over which to lay carpet or other flooring. However, laying masonite should not be seen as a cure-all. Although it will successfully cover minor flaws and undulations in the existing floorboards, it is essential that any missing floorboards are replaced and any broken or damaged boards are repaired before the masonite is laid on top.

tips of the trade

- **Preparing the masonite**—Before being installed, masonite needs to be sprinkled with water to remove internal stresses. This prevents the masonite from bubbling or puckering up later, which could otherwise damage the floor covering laid on top.
- **Rough side up**—Laying masonite with the rough side uppermost will provide more grip for the carpet padding and prevents it slipping. If the floor covering is to be stuck down, the rough surface also helps to provide a key for the glue.

tools for the job

- tape measure & pencil
- staple gun
- safety glasses
- hammer
- coping saw
- handsaw

1 Start in one corner of the room, and lay a sheet of masonite smooth side down. The traditional method for laying masonite is with brads to fasten it to the floor at 4in centers in every direction. To reduce the chance of ripples forming, nail from the center of the masonite sheet toward the edges.

2 Work out from the first sheet, butting the edges of adjacent sheets against it. However, to avoid a ridge forming you must leave a small gap of approximately 3/16in between each sheet. If the room is particularly small or you are working alone, you may find that whole sheets of masonite are difficult to handle, and you may need to cut them down to a more manageable size. If you are using smaller sheets, remember that you will still need to leave a 3/16in gap all around the edge.

3 To fit the masonite around such obstacles as radiator pipes, first cut out a 4 x 4in piece in the adjacent sheet so that it clears the pipe. Then make a paper template that fits neatly into this cut out and around the pipe. Trace the shape onto a scrap piece of masonite before cutting it out and nailing it into place.

LAYING WITH STAPLES

An alternative and quicker method of laying masonite is with a heavy-duty staple gun. If you are using a staple gun, make sure you protect your eyes with protective goggles or safety glasses, as a misfired staple can fly up at your face at high speed and do serious damage.

TURNING OVER THE FLOOR

One way of rejuvenating an old floor without going to the expense of buying all new floorboards is to lift the existing boards and turn them over. Often the underside has no sign of the wear and tear you might find on the original side. If the floorboards are very damaged this may not work, but often it is worth investigating as a cost-saving measure.

FURTHER PROBLEMS

While you are inspecting and repairing the floorboards it is a good idea to investigate the supporting structure of the floor at the same time. Make sure that all joists, struts, and associated woodwork are sound, and repair and replace if necessary.

replacing a section of floorboard

Just about every home will include an area of wooden flooring, whether in the form of wooden floorboards or manufactured boards such as chipboard. Wooden floors generally require little in the way of maintenance, but there are times when individual boards need attention. For example, you may need to replace a wooden floorboard that has split or been irreparably damaged on its surface, or if access is required to pipes underneath the floor, boards may need to be cut out and new ones fitted. Replacing a section of flooring is a relatively straightforward task.

wooden floorboards

The procedure for replacing wooden floorboards described below applies to boards fitted with a tongue-and-groove mechanism. These are slightly more difficult to remove, and some of the stages mentioned can be omitted if the floor is constructed from straight-edged boards, which makes the job slightly less taxing. In some rooms, especially those that are fairly small, the boards tuck under the baseboard along the edges of the room with no intermediate joints. In this case, simply prying up the board in the center of the room and slipping a piece of waste wood underneath will allow you to cut it in half. If you are at all unsure about a section of floorboard, then it is wise to replace the whole length.

tools for the job

- stud finder
- circular saw
- flooring chisel
- square
- fine-tooth handsaw
- tape measure & pencil
- hand saw
- cordless drill/driver or hammer

1 Here, the board to be replaced is split down the middle. It is unlikely to be split along its entire length, so first inspect the damage to assess whether you can just replace a small section of the board.

2 Identify joist positions, either with the use of a stud finder, or alternatively by following the line of nails. Mark with a pencil if any joists run below the board to be replaced. Locate the joist just beyond the end of the split, and mark this too. For safety reasons, it is also vital to find out whether any plumbing or wiring runs under the boards before cutting.

3 Set a circular saw so that it will cut to a depth of approximately $^{5}/_{8}$in. Run the blade along both sides of the split board to cut through the tongues. If the floor has been constructed using square-edge boards, this step can be omitted.

safety advice

Circular saws are safe if used correctly, but not everyone is comfortable with them. If you are unsure, a floorboard saw (a special hand saw with a curved blade) may be used instead.

4 Insert a wide flooring chisel into the cut side and gently pry up the board. Start near the joint and work your way along the board. Hold up the board with a piece of waste wood and draw a line across with a square, ensuring any joint will be over the center line of the joist. Cut this line with a fine-tooth hand saw.

5 Measure and cut a new section of floorboard to fit neatly into the space left by the broken section. If you are using tongue-and-groove board, you will need to cut off the tongue with a hand saw before laying.

6 Once the new board has been cut to a precise fit, either nail or screw it in position. You may prefer to use screws if access to the underfloor area is likely to be required at some future date.

chipboard floors

It is highly unlikely that a section of chipboard floor will split in the same way that a wooden floorboard might, but you may still encounter situations where a section will need to be replaced. For example, you might have to replace one or more boards after cutting through to gain access to the underfloor services, or you might need to cut out and replace boards that have become unsound due to moisture damage.

tools for the job

- tape measure & pencil
- circular saw
- flooring chisels (wide)
- claw hammer
- clamps
- handsaw
- cordless drill/driver

1 Set a circular saw to a ¾in depth of cut and saw all around the edge of the board to remove the tongue. Be careful not to cut into adjacent boards.

2 Gently pry up the board using wide flooring chisels. Do not pry in just one position, but work all around the perimeter. The nails should come up with the board, otherwise pull them out with a claw hammer.

3 Install blocks between joists to support any board edges that do not join on a joist.

4 Saw off the tongues of the replacement board with a hand saw, so that it will fit into the gap.

5 Finally, fit the new board into the hole and fix it in position. Nails can be used as fastenings, but it is better to screw the board in place.

tips of the trade

A screwed board will allow easier access to underfloor services in the future, and screwing avoids the heavy vibrations of hammering, which can cause cracks in the ceiling below.

installing bridging

Bridging provides extra stiffness to upper floors in homes. Made from either wood or metal, it serves several purposes—to stop a floor from twisting out of shape, damp down vibration, and keep the joists uniformly spaced apart from one another. It is important to fit bridging properly, otherwise it will cause the floor to squeak.

Unless you are constructing an entirely new suspended floor, it is unlikely that you will have to completely fasten the floor with bridging. More often than not, you will find that there are just one or two parts loose or missing when the floorboards are lifted. For new floors, fitting bridging is a relatively straightforward job that has been made simpler in recent years with the introduction of ready-made metal struts. Both types of bridging should be fitted to joists prior to the installation of floors or ceilings.

safety advice

When fitting bridging there will not be any existing flooring in place. To make the job more safe and easy, lay scaffold boards or temporary flooring across the joists to create a working platform.

wooden bridging

tools for the job

- tape measure & pencil
- chalk lines
- guide
- sliding bevel
- miter saw
- cordless drill/driver
- hammer

1 Measure the length of the joists at each end of the room and divide this into three. Snap a chalk line at both points across the bottom of all the joists.

2 Make a guide from two thin strips of wood about 3/16 x 5/8in thick and about 1ft 4in long. Use the guide to measure the distance between the top of one joist and the bottom of the next joist. Wrap painter's tape around the guide to hold it at this setting.

3 Hold the guide diagonally across a piece of 1 x 2in wood and transfer the measurement by marking with a pencil at either end. Set a sliding bevel to a shallow angle and use this to mark the same bevel across the face of the wood at both ends of what will be the strut. Make sure the measurements are correct at this stage, as this will act as a template for future struts.

4 After checking for fit, cut the struts using a miter saw to achieve the bevel—you will need four struts for each joist. Since all bevels are the same, the cut edge of one forms the end cut on the next strut.

tips of the trade

If you have many struts to cut and install, it might be cost- and time-effective to rent an electric chop saw. This tool will help you to do the job in half the time.

5 Position the struts where the chalk lines cross each joist and angle-nail them between the joists, first drilling pilot holes with the aid of

a cordless drill. Leave a small gap between each strut to prevent any squeaking as the floor moves.

tips of the trade

The biggest mistake you can make when installing wooden or metal struts is to have them touch at the crossing points. This can cause annoying squeaks to develop once the floor is completed. To avoid this problem, use a piece of waste plywood as a guide to maintain an even gap between struts when fastening them in position.

metal struts

Metal struts have now largely taken the place of wooden struts in most new construction. Requiring no cutting, they are faster to fit and can be bought to suit the spacing of floor joists—which are typically at 1ft 4in, 1ft 6in, or 2ft centers.

tools for the job

hammer

chalk line

1 Set out two chalk lines as described above. Starting at one end of the room, nail through the hole in the top of each strut, using glavanized nails to fix them securely to each joist. Work your way along the length of the room.

2 Working from the room below, bend the struts until they touch the opposite joist. Nail these in position, again with galvanized nails, taking care to maintain a small gap where the struts crisscross to avoid any possible squeaking.

tips of the trade

Use a set of long-nosed pincers to hold the nails as you get them started into the joist. This will help to protect fingers from accidental hammer blows.

Bridging provides additional support to joists. It can be constructed from either wood or metal, but steel bridging is the easiest to fit.

renovating a woodblock floor

Solid woodblock flooring is seldom fitted in homes today, as the cost is often prohibitive, but it is relatively common in larger, older houses. Resilient and durable when properly laid, it will last for several lifetimes. Major repair is usually not required—if it is, this really is a specialist repair best left to the experts. Having said that, it is not beyond the competent DIY enthusiast to replace a few wood blocks or refinish a badly worn floor.

sanding

To sand a woodblock floor effectively you will need to rent specialist machines from tool rental shops. Start with a coarse paper on the sander, and finish with a finer grit to remove scratches, after vacuuming the floor surface. A special edging sander is needed to reach those parts that cannot be sanded with the large machine. Sanding can be dirty work, and you will almost certainly create a lot of dust. Before you start, remove all furniture and make sure that the floor is clear. Tape up any doors to the rest of the house, and open a window to ensure good ventilation. Wear a good-quality dust mask and ear protectors when using the machines.

tips of the trade

Any protruding nails or staples will tear the sanding sheets, which are expensive to replace, and rental shops often charge extra for the number of sheets used. Examine the entire floor and pull out or punch in anything that could catch on the sanding drum.

sanding procedure

Always turn on the machine tilted back so the drum is off the floor surface. Start at one wall and sand across the room with overlapping passes. If you allow the sander to remain in one spot too long, it will cut grooves into the floor.

1 Use floor sander at 45-degree angle to direction of floorboards, sweeping across the whole floor.

2 Repeat 45-degree angle sweep with sander in opposite direction.

3 Sand across entire floor surface following direction of floorboards and grain.

4 Use edging sander to finish perimeter of room next to baseboard or wall surface.

5 Use special corner sander to get into tight corners.

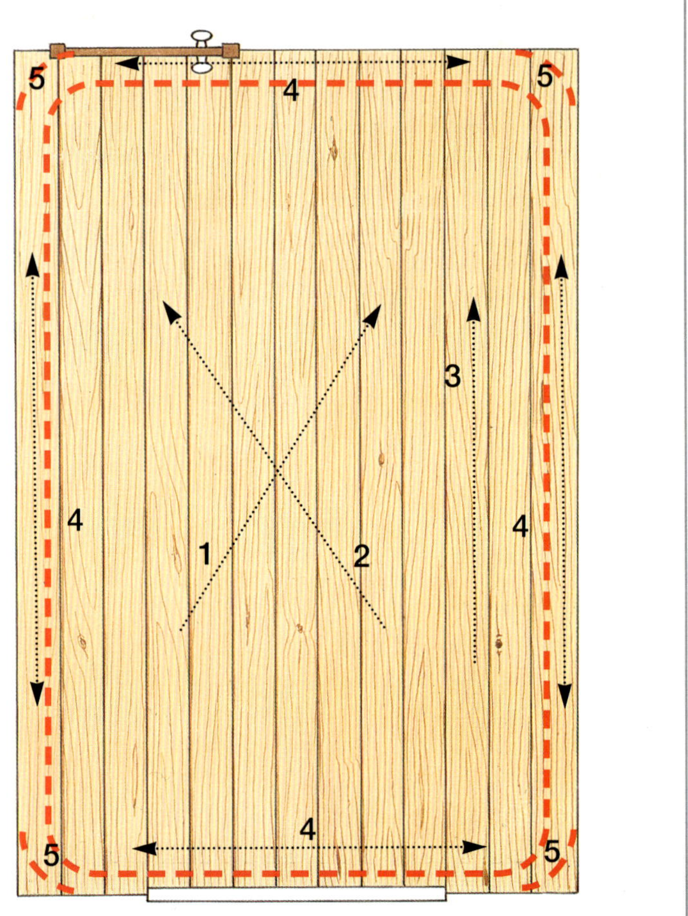

re-laying blocks

Blocks are usually laid onto a sand or cement screed with black pitch, but to replace just a few blocks use a ready-mixed latex compound. If blocks are missing, a local joinery manufacturer can make replacements, or you might find them in a reclamation yard.

tools for the job

- old chisel
- paint scraper
- old paintbrush
- electric sander

1 Remove the loose blocks and scrape off the old pitch from the back of the blocks with an old wood or bolster chisel. Do not use heat, as this may set the pitch alight.

2 Spread a layer of latex adhesive into the gap in the floor with a paint scraper, keeping it to a thickness of approximately $^{3}/_{16}$in.

3 Spread a thin layer of latex on the back of the blocks with an old paintbrush, then immediately lay the blocks onto the wet latex in the floor, following the original pattern of the surrounding blocks. In some cases, there will be a tendency for the wood blocks to float on top of the adhesive layer.

4 Sandwich a sheet of polyethylene between the floor and a piece of waste plywood, which should be slightly larger than the area of the floor being repaired. Then place several bricks on top of the ply to weigh down the blocks until the adhesive has set.

5 When the adhesive has set, fill any small cracks with a two-part wood filler. Finally, sand the blocks to the same level as the rest of the floor, before finishing to match.

With careful finishing to make sure the relaid blocks match the color of those surrounding them, the woodblock floor will look as good as new.

painting & varnishing floors

When the budget for home improvement is tight, there can be a tendency to leave the floor until you are better able to afford your ideal floor covering. A good way to give a room a finished feel without spending a fortune is by painting or varnishing the floor. As long as the floor is in a reasonable condition, you will be surprised how striking this can look for little cost. If you have a large expanse, including one or two rugs into the finished scheme can soften the effect.

tools for the job

- hammer & nail set
- putty knife
- power floor sander
- vacuum cleaner
- broom
- tack rag
- paint roller
- paintbrushes

varnishing

1 Go over the floor and push any raised nails below the surface. If the floor is screwed down, make sure the screws are well below the surface. You may have to withdraw all or some of the screws and re-countersink the holes if the heads are any less than ⅛in below the surface.

2 Use a putty knife and flexible filler to cover all nail and screw heads. If the floor is to be painted, the filler color will not matter. If you are varnishing, select a tone that blends in with the surrounding flooring.

tips of the trade

Almost all fillers change color when varnish is applied, so it is best to choose a shade slightly lighter than the surrounding wood. Test a discreet section before tackling the whole floor.

3 Once the filler has dried, sand the floor with power sanders, cleaning off the excess filler as you go. Follow the method for sanding a wooden floor described on page 210.

4 Vacuum the floor with an industrial sweeper. Use a soft, clean broom to dislodge any stubborn dirt and then vacuum once more.

5 Close all windows and doors, then go over the surface with a tack rag to pick up any remaining dirt that might otherwise spoil the finish.

6 Thin down the first coat of varnish by adding about 30 percent by volume of the recommended thinners. Apply the varnish using a roller with an extension arm. Work back from the main source of light so that you can see those areas that you have missed.

safety advice

Paint and thinners can be dangerous if ingested, so never leave open cans unattended near children.

7 Let the first coat harden, then apply the next coat without thinning the varnish. Again, use a paint roller, but keep a paintbrush handy so that you can cut in around the edge of the room and apply varnish to those areas you are unable to reach with the roller. Before you apply the third and final coat, sand any rough spots using fine abrasive paper and wipe up any dust with a clean tack rag. Water-based varnishes in particular will raise the grain to quite an extent, so this light sanding will pay dividends in the final finish.

painting

There are special durable paints designed for floors in garages and workshops. Although only available in a limited range of colors, they do provide excellent coverage and can be used in kitchens, bathrooms, and play areas. Latex paints are quick drying and will last several years, provided they are overcoated with a suitable varnish.

stenciling

A colored base can be livened up by painting or stenciling a border around the room. Either buy ready-made stencils, or cut your own from special stencil paper. Tape the stencil to the floor with painter's tape, then stipple a little paint with a stencil brush. Remove the stencil immediately.

applying kiln-dried sand

A simple yet highly effective technique for making the floor surface more safe in bathrooms and kitchens is to sprinkle a little kiln-dried sand onto wet paint to create a non-slip finish. When the paint has dried, sweep up the excess sand and seal the surface with a coat of varnish.

Dramatic decorative effects are possible when painting a floor. Colorful painted floorboards such as these will make any room feel warmer and brighter.

solving problems with older stairs

Stairs need very little in the way of maintenance, and a new staircase should function for years without any major problems. Fortunately, when problems do occur they tend to be relatively minor and simple to resolve, and basic maintenance is usually easy to accomplish. A squeaking stair or shaky handrail is often more of an irritation than a danger, but small problems such as these should be fixed promptly, for if left untreated, more extensive repairs will be required.

Almost all problems related to stairs can be fixed with a basic set of tools—the hardest part is often finding the problem. Squeaking stairs are caused by two pieces of wood rubbing against each other, so if a tread makes a noise when you step on it then it is almost certainly due to the tread being split or a loose wedge on the underside. When there are several problems with a staircase, try to work systematically, rectifying each one before moving onto the next.

tips of the trade

Get a helper to walk up and down the stairs while you carefully watch and listen for trouble spots.

tools for the job

- tape measure & pencil
- hand saw
- cordless drill/driver
- wooden or plastic mixing stick
- hammer
- jigsaw
- jack plane
- rubber mallet
- syringe

split treads

1 Split treads are common in older stairs, and if the stairs are fitted with carpet a sure sign will be a squeaking tread. They can be easily fixed in two different ways. First remove floor covering to expose the split.

2 If the underside of the tread is accessible, a patch can be fitted over the split. Cut a piece of plywood 6in wide and as long as will comfortably fit between the stringers. Coat the piece with wood glue and screw it in position. Make sure the screws are not too long, or they will cut through the face of the tread.

3 Epoxy glue is a good alternative when the only access is from above. Scrape out any dust and dirt from the crack, then force epoxy into the joint with a wooden or plastic mixing stick. Allow it to harden overnight, then sand level.

safety advice

Many people are sensitive to the components in epoxy resins. Wear disposable gloves or barrier cream to protect your hands.

tips of the trade

Mix epoxy resin with some sawdust for a stiffer mix to make troweling into wider joints easier. The glue has quite a runny consistency, and this will also prevent it from dripping out.

missing glue blocks

Another major cause of squeaking stairs is missing glue blocks. These triangular blocks reinforce the corner joint between the riser and tread and are fitted to the underside of the staircase. Replace any missing glue blocks by cutting a piece of wood to the correct size. Coat the replacement glue block with wood glue, then knock it into the appropriate channel in the stringer with a hammer, holding it in position with brads until the glue has set.

split or worn nosing

1 To repair a split or worn nosing, use a straightedge to draw a straight line 1/2in back from the original line of the front edge. Then cut a 45-degree splay 4in in from each end of the tread down to this line, with a panel saw. Having made these initial cuts, remove the rest of the waste wood using a jigsaw.

2 Cut replacement wood, slightly oversize. Glue this in position, holding it with painter's tape until the glue dries. When the glue has set, use a jack plane and abrasive paper to replicate the original nosing shape.

loose wedge

A gap between tread and stringer means a loose wedge. Remove the original wedge or cut a new one. Brush wood glue in the groove and tap home.

shaky newel

1 To tighten a shaky newel, measure up 2in from the base of the newel. Find the center line and mark where they meet. Drill a 7/16in hole 1/2in deep at a 45-degree angle down to the tread.

2 Continue to drill with a 1/8in bit from the center of this hole down as far as the tread. Then insert a 2 3/4in 8-gauge wood screw into the hole and firmly tighten it up. Shape and glue a small wooden pellet to fit the 1/2in hole and cover the screw head.

loose baluster

To refasten a loose baluster, detach it from the underside of the handrail by tapping it with a soft mallet and pulling it from the mortise in the tread. Clean off all the old glue and brush on new adhesive before renailing it to the underside of the handrail.

tips of the trade

If the problem requires a repair that involves removing some part of the stair but this cannot be done without extreme difficulty, a good repair can be achieved by squirting epoxy glue into a loose joint with a small syringe.

mending a broken stair tread

Stairs suffer inevitable wear and tear, but they usually remain structurally sound for a very long time. However, if a broken tread is suspected it should be repaired immediately to avoid a potentially serious accident. Replacing a stair tread is an easy enough job for the average DIY enthusiast, but if the fault looks more serious you may need to consult a professional builder.

There are several methods of repairing broken stair treads, but even the simplest will require access to the underside of the stairs. Stairs fitted with spandrel paneling are easy to repair because the underside is readily accessible. For newer stairs that have been blocked in, you may have to remove the board to gain access and refit it afterwards (see pages 192–3).

safety advice

When working on stairs, tie a ribbon or a bright piece of tape across the top and bottom of the staircase to prevent it being used. A nasty accident could occur if someone were to put their foot through where a tread is missing.

tools for the job

- tape measure & pencil
- hand saw
- cordless drill/driver
- hacksaw blade
- wood chisel
- claw hammer
- rubber mallet
- keyhole saw
- hammer

quick fix

If the stair tread is split along its length a quick repair is to glue and screw a plywood patch to the underside. Cut this from 7/16in plywood, making it as large as possible to keep it just clear of glue blocks and wedges.

replacing the tread

Two methods are used to join treads to risers. Some stairs employ a simple butt joint reinforced into the riser to hold the tread secure. The other, more common, approach is for the riser to be tongued or housed into the tread. To check which type you have, try to insert a hacksaw blade between the tread and riser joint. If you cannot work it through, then you have the latter type of joint, which must be cut before the tread can be removed.

1 Pry off the molding fitted under the nosing with a wood chisel. Keep the nosing for refastening later. Pull out any nails left behind.

2 From the underside of the stairs use a chisel and mallet to remove any glue blocks fitted into the corner of the joint between tread and stringer. Do not try to save these, as new ones will have to be fitted later.

3 Drill three or four small holes of about 1/8in diameter into the riser and through to the tread joint below the damaged tread—these will enable you to insert the blade of a keyhole saw. Start making the cut with the saw, then when it is long enough use a hand saw to finish off the cut, keeping the blade flat to the underside of the tread. Employ the same procedure to saw through the joint between the tread and the next riser, which you will need to do from under

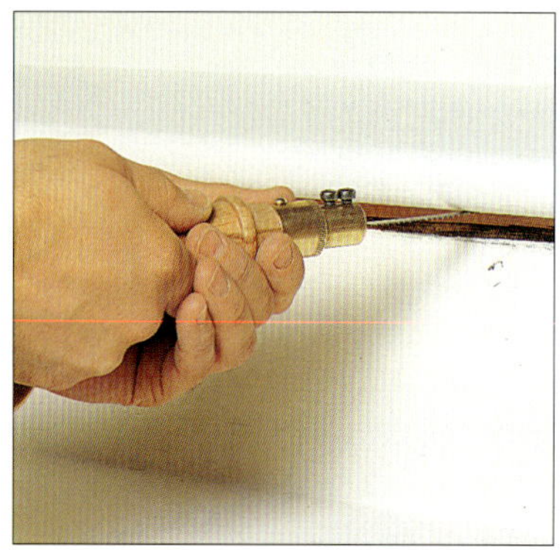

the stairs. Again, make sure that you keep the saw blade flat on the surface of the stair tread.

4 Chisel out the wedges that hold the tread in place. If your staircase is of the closed-stringer variety, free the tread by giving it a sharp tap with a hammer and block of wood right above and adjacent to the string. With the tread free, drive out to the rear again by tapping the nosing with a block of wood and hammer.

5 If you have an open-stringer staircase, the approach is slightly different. Pry off the return molding on the end of the tread, then remove the balusters by tapping them sideways from the shallow mortises before knocking out the tread from the rear.

6 Cut a replacement tread from wood, using the old tread as a template for the new one. Make sure that it has the same dimensions as the existing tread and that the nosing is identical to the original, otherwise it will not fit correctly.

7 Reattach the tread following the same procedure for removing it, only in reverse. Cut new wedges and glue blocks, coat these with adhesive, then fit by tapping the wedges firmly home. Finally, replace the balusters and return molding, and shoe molding if it was removed earlier.

tips of the trade

If your staircase is old or there is any evidence of infestation or rot, both new and old wood must be treated with a suitable preservative before sealing in the underside of the stairs.

Having made the repair, it is a simple matter to return the new tread to the same finish as the others, and the staircase will be good as new.

dealing with squeaking stairs

Irrespective of the quality of their construction, there will inevitably come a time when the treads of a staircase will start to squeak. The main causes of squeaking stairs are simply general wear and tear, coupled with the natural shrinkage and movement of wood, which means that sooner or later almost every staircase made from wood will develop squeaks. In many cases, this is annoying rather than anything to worry over, and by spending a little time you should be able to eradicate just about every squeak.

In most cases, the best results are obtained if as many of the repairs as possible are made from underneath the stairs. While this is the ideal scenario it is not always a practical option. However, many effective smaller repairs can still be carried out from the front. Several different repairs can often be employed to deal with the exact same problem, and most of the options available are demonstrated on these pages.

tools for the job

- hammer
- cordless drill/driver
- saw
- screwdriver
- wood chisel

tips of the trade

It will help to identify where repairs are needed if someone else walks slowly up and down the stairs while you watch and listen to each step in turn. If you have a cupboard under the stairs you may also be able to find open joints by standing inside with the light off to spot any chinks of light filtering in from outside.

loose tread—nailing

One of the simplest of all repairs, which is ideal if you are unable to gain access to under the stairs, is to nail down through the tread into the riser below. Be careful that the nails do not come through the front of the riser and spoil the appearance. The nails will have better grip if they are inserted in dovetail fashion as shown.

loose tread—screwing

A better method for fixing down a loose tread, again without needing access under the stairs, is with a row of screws rather than nails. You will first need to drill holes level with the riser just through the surface of the tread, and then insert the screws. Use 1½in 8-gauge screws, and make sure that any heads are countersunk below the surface of the tread. For the ultimate finish use a screw sink and matching plug cutter. The special drill bit drills the correct size of pilot hole for the screw and cuts a straight counterbore that sits below the surface. Pellets are then cut from matching wood, glued over the screw head, and cut off level.

replacing wedges

A gap between the upper surface of the tread and the stringer indicates a loose or missing wedge. If loose, remove the wedge from under the stairs, clean off the old adhesive, brush on glue, and reposition. If missing or damaged, cut a new one from hardwood, then glue and reposition.

strengthening joints

To strengthen the joint between an open stringer and tread, cut a block of wood 1⅜in square and the width of the tread. Access under the stairs and, at the back of the step in question, screw the wood block into the corner at the joint between tread and stringer. First coat the block with glue and drill holes for 2in 8-gauge screws. If you can, get a helper to stand on the tread from above to close up the gap between block and step as you drive the screws home.

loose riser joint

Gluing on a section of a quadrant can sometimes reinforce a loose riser joint at the back of the tread. If the stairs are exposed, you may want to give each tread the same treatment to match.

injecting adhesive

You may be able to pry open a joint with a wood chisel and inject adhesive. Clamp the joint until the glue has set. This is effective combined with other repairs, such as replacing glue blocks.

where to insert wedges

Driving in small slip wedges coated with glue is an effective method for tightening joints between tread and riser. Make the wedges about 1/4in long, tapering from about 3/16in down to nothing. After the glue has dried use a sharp chisel to cut off the end of any protruding wedges.

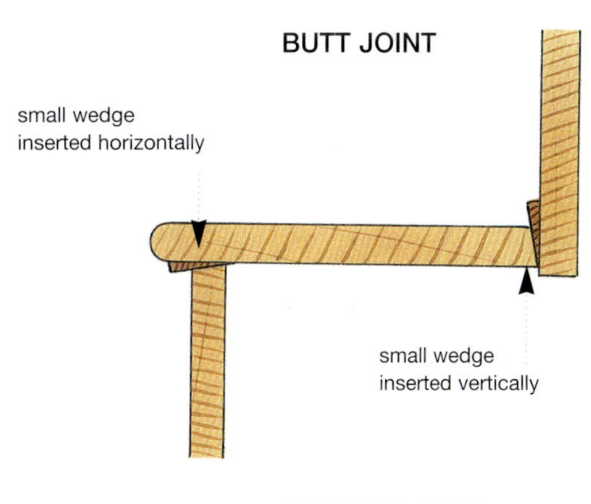

MORTISE & TENON JOINT

small wedge inserted vertically at front

small wedge inserted horizontally

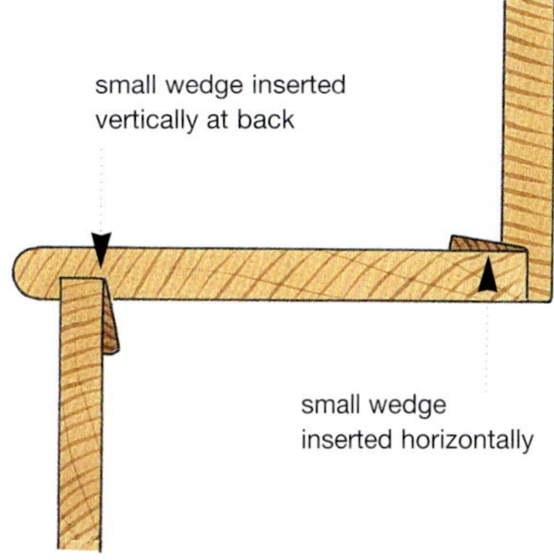

windows & doors

As with any structure in your home, the design and makeup of doors and windows will vary according to a number of factors. The age of your house, decisions taken by previous owners, your own particular preferences regarding appearance, and the specific function of the door or window will all affect the types of doors and windows you have in your home. Before making changes or restoring doors and windows, it is necessary to have some understanding of the different structures that are available and how these relate to your personal requirements. It is also important to determine how door and window structures relate to the walls they are fitted into, so that when you make changes, you will have a good understanding of the work that is required to carry out particular tasks.

door types & construction

There are many types of door design, but they all have functions and features in common. Much of the structural variation derives from the materials used. This in turn is related to cost and so to a certain degree, structure and quality are common denominators in the design of doors. The examples given here provide a cross section of door types and help towards understanding the differences in door design.

solid panel doors

Wooden panel doors are very common and manufactured in a wide range of qualities. Softwood varieties are much less expensive than hardwood doors, the latter commonly being used for front doors.

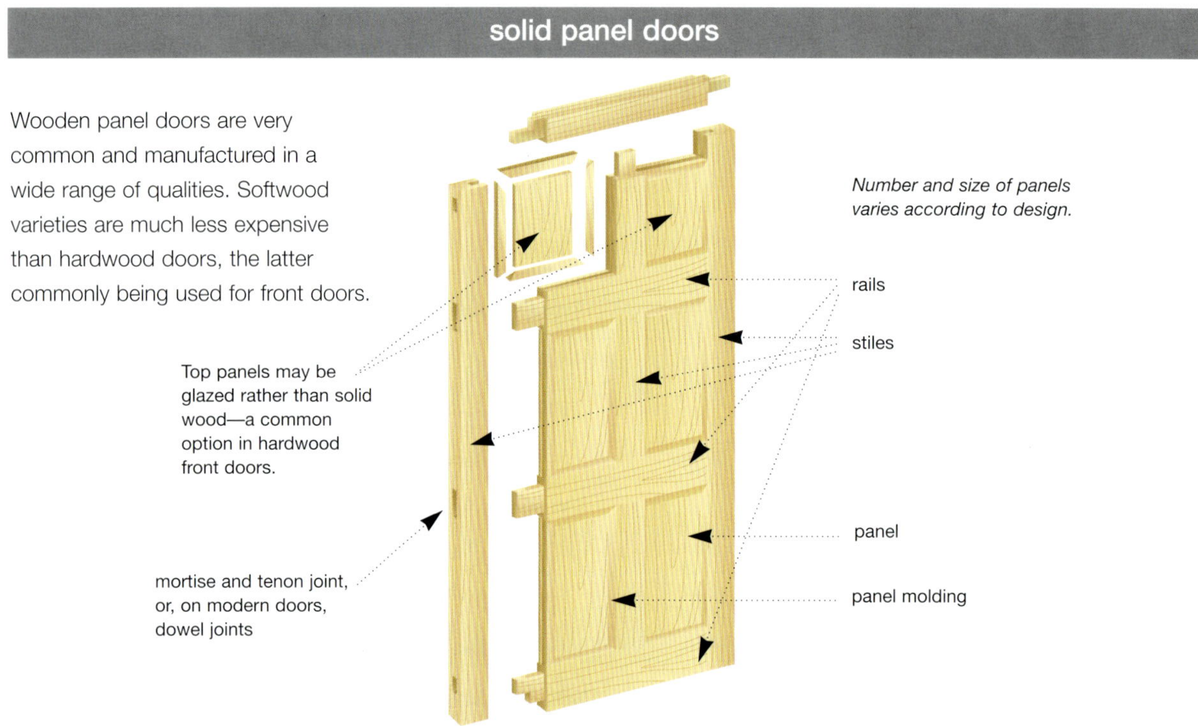

ledge & brace doors

This more traditional and rustic door design offers a completely different look. The construction is based on a number of different wooden sections attached vertically and braced by horizontal and diagonal rails.

Sometimes ledge and brace doors are framed with rails and stiles to make a more substantial structure.

Hinges are surface-mounted on ledges. Those used are not butt hinges but T-hinges (for example, see antique iron hinge page 234).

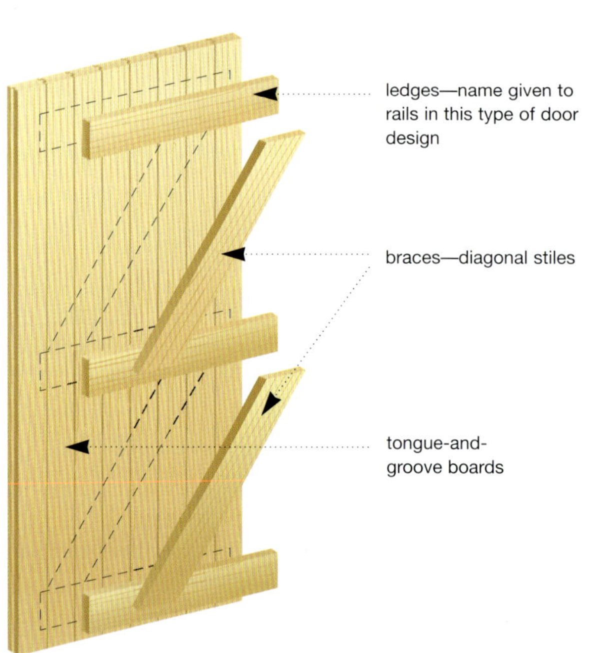

flush door (solid)

Solid flush doors have plain, flat surfaces without any sort of panel features. The materials used in their construction do vary, but the framework of the door is usually made from softwood, and the door's surface from plywood.

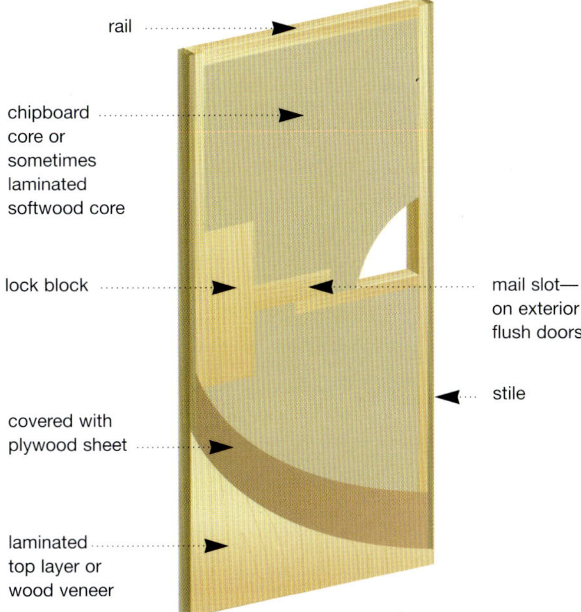

flush door (hollow)

These cheaper versions of solid flush doors tend to be used only on interior doors and offer an economical option for replacing doors throughout your home. Though less substantial, they can be used very effectively.

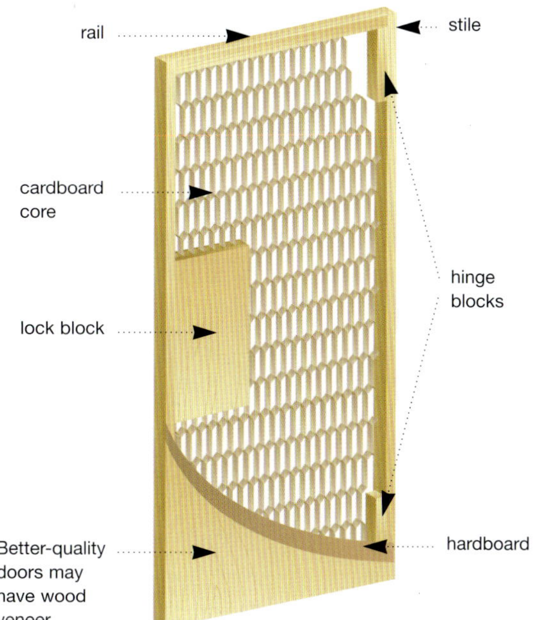

vinyl and fiberglass doors

These doors tend to be used in homes where double glazing and good insulation are a priority. They are molded and supplied with a fitted frame, ready for installation into a wall opening. Generally used only as exterior doors.

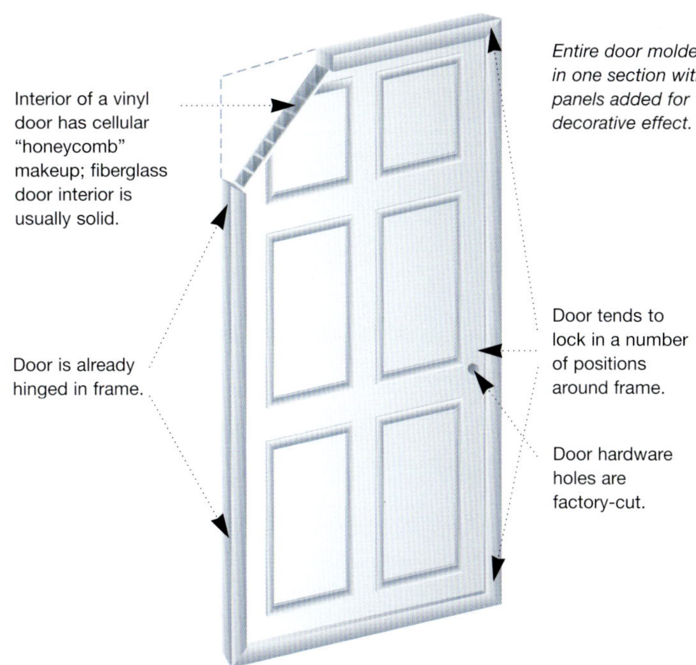

tips of the trade

Softwood—Most warping problems tend to occur with softwood doors. Therefore, the majority of exterior wooden doors are made of hardwood. Although softwood doors can be used on the exterior, be sure to buy good-quality paint or stain in these cases to make sure that the wood is treated with the best possible exterior finishing materials.

safety advice

Fire considerations—Before purchasing a new door it is worth considering what regulations the door conforms to. This is especially important when you are considering its performance in the event of a fire. Some doors are specifically supplied as fire doors because retardant materials are built into their design. It is therefore important to check these issues and consider their relevance to your needs before making a final choice.

how doors are installed

All doors are installed into some form of frame or jamb, and differences tend to lie in the hinge mechanism and how it works in relation to the frame. Door hardware also tends to be slightly different for interior and exterior doors, and can vary according to the door structure. The illustrations provided identify many of the characteristics that differentiate doors, and show how this affects their relationship to the frame or jamb.

interior doors

In this example, a solid wood panel door has been used for illustrative purposes. However, most of the features and hardware referred to can be related to other kinds of interior doors. For example, although many flush doors have hollow areas in their structure, the actual door perimeter is solid, enabling hinges and opening hardware to be fitted.

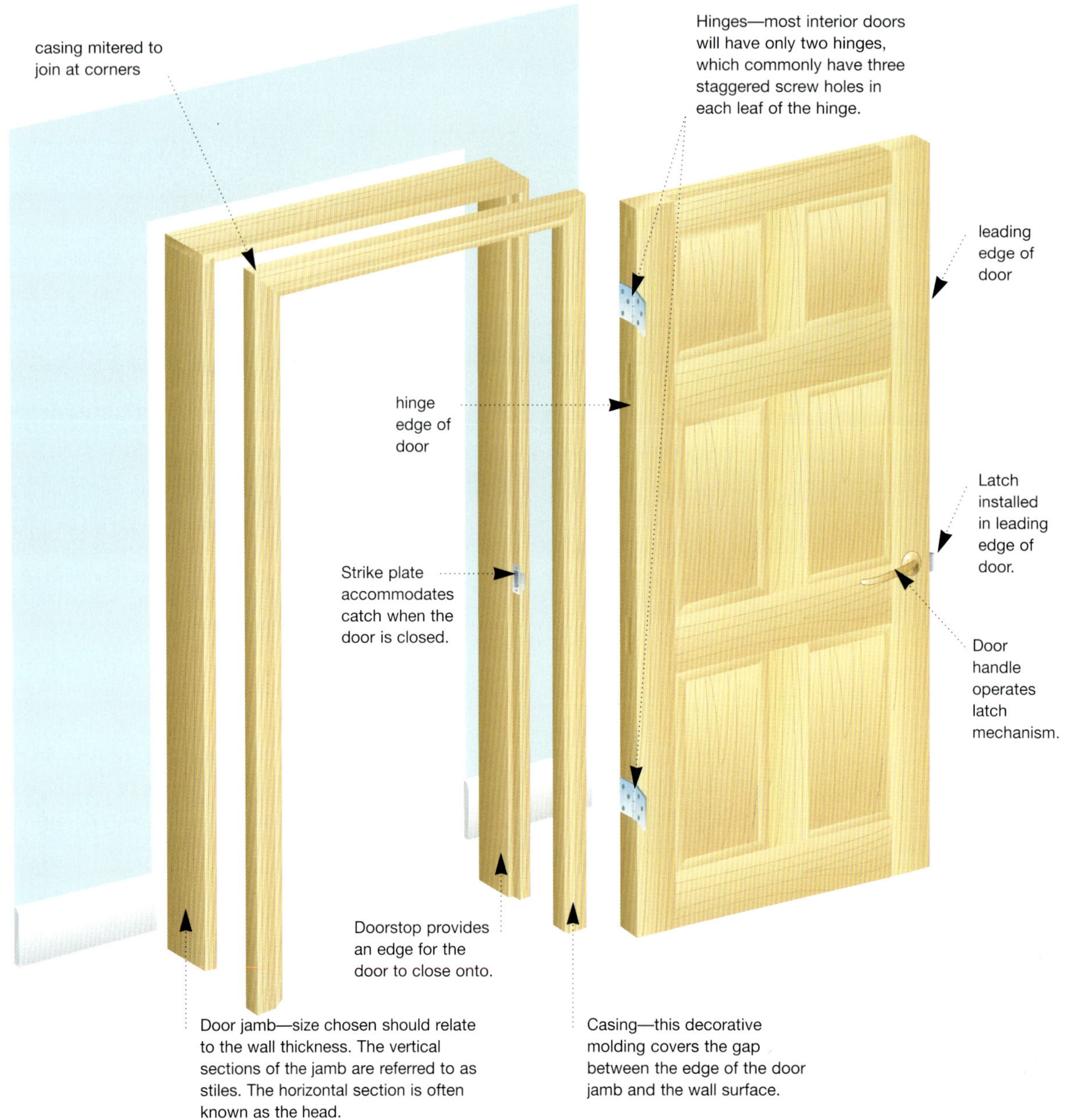

exterior doors

Exterior doors tend to have slightly more features than interior doors, as security is more of an issue and the door incorporates structures aimed at counteracting the weathering process.

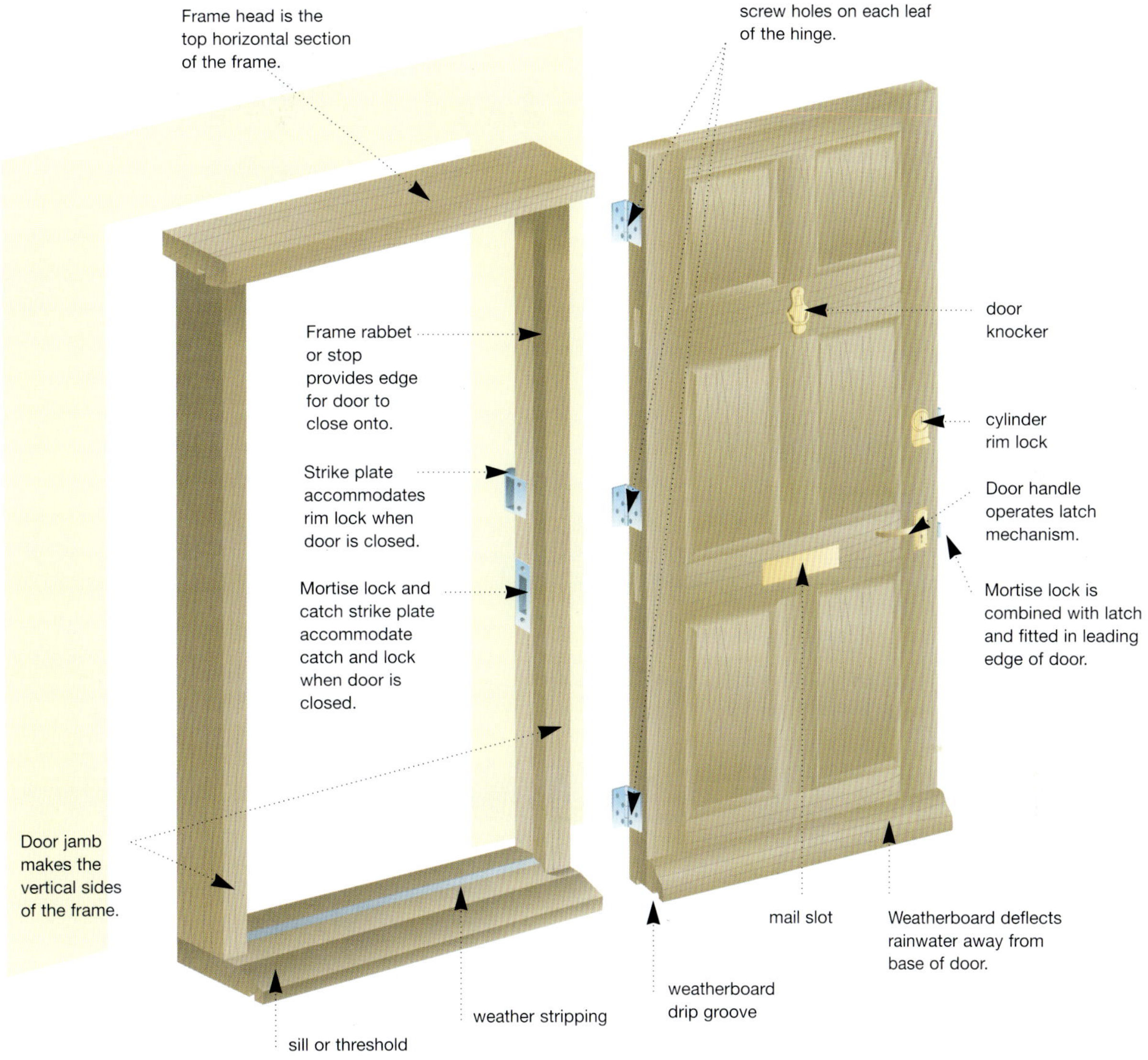

Frame head is the top horizontal section of the frame.

Hinges—the extra weight of an exterior door usually requires three hinges, which tend to have four staggered screw holes on each leaf of the hinge.

Frame rabbet or stop provides edge for door to close onto.

Strike plate accommodates rim lock when door is closed.

Mortise lock and catch strike plate accommodate catch and lock when door is closed.

Door jamb makes the vertical sides of the frame.

door knocker

cylinder rim lock

Door handle operates latch mechanism.

Mortise lock is combined with latch and fitted in leading edge of door.

sill or threshold

weather stripping

weatherboard drip groove

mail slot

Weatherboard deflects rainwater away from base of door.

patio doors

Other common varieties of exterior doors include patio doors. These are sometimes hinged or in many cases are positioned in tracks and are therefore opened and closed by a sliding mechanism. In both cases the frame of the door itself is fitted into the wall in a similar manner to any exterior door. In other words, the frame is installed in the wall opening and then the doors are added. Before purchasing, check that any patio doors you choose have good security features.

garage doors

Garage doors, although completely different in terms of size and style to other forms of exterior door, still follow similar installation principles, with the frame being installed before the door is hung. It is at the later stages where variations can occur, because although many garage doors are hinged in a similar position to normal exterior doors, others have automatic opening mechanisms which require completely different installation techniques.

window types & construction

Much of the variation between window types relates to style and period. There is also a need to consider window function in terms of insulating properties and to what extent opening lights and casements are required in the window structure. The examples provided here help to demonstrate many of the variations available, and to show the major differences in the construction of each type of window.

casements

Casements generally refer to windows with hinged opening sections combined with fastened sections. The design within this category can thus vary considerably.

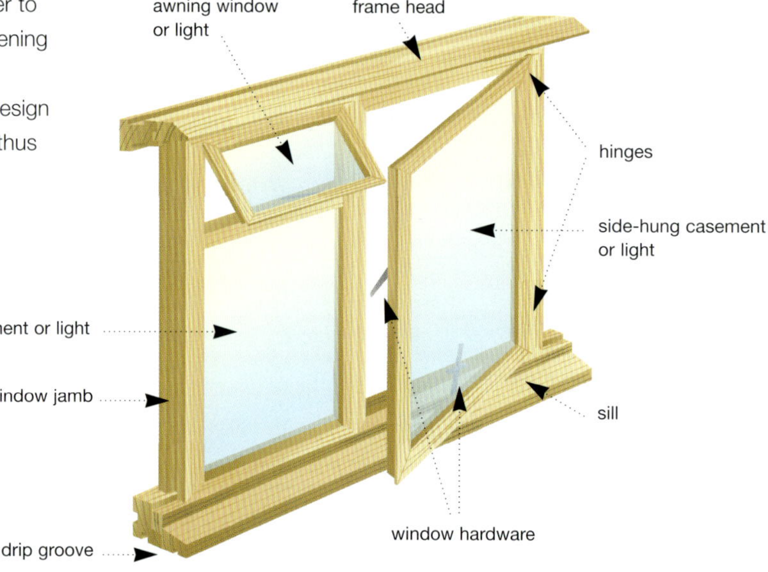

sashes

These are traditional-looking windows, which involve the movement of casements or lights in the window frame by means of a cord and pulley mechanism. Modern variations may use chains or have spring balances.

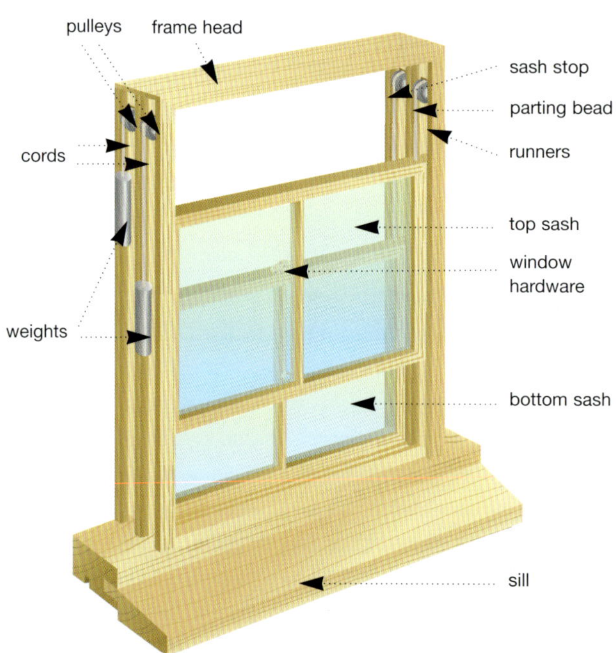

roof windows

These vary considerably in design from normal windows and are based on the principle that they fit into a roof situation. Tiles are removed and the window is positioned or cut into the roof framing or rafters, with the addition of some extra support.

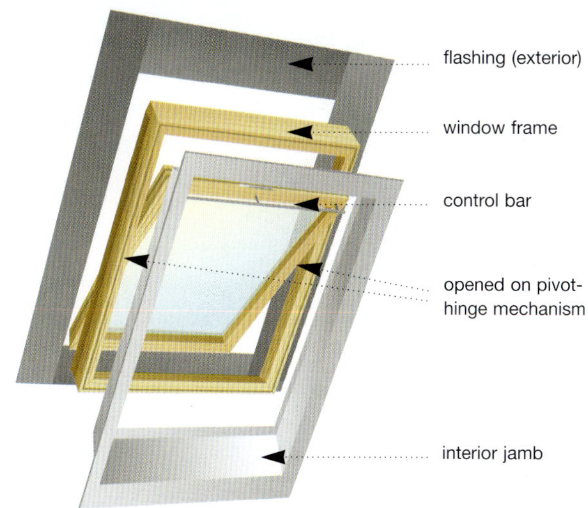

bay windows

Bay windows are large windows that extend beyond the exterior wall, often positioned on either side of the front door or entrance. Structure tends to take the form of a casement window that has been stuck together in a number of sections.

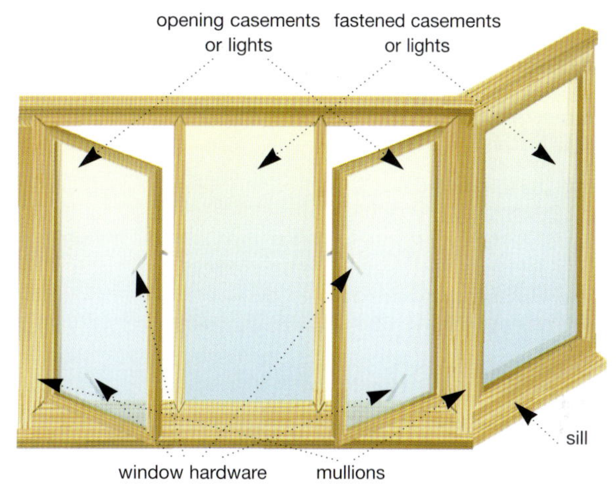

vinyl windows

These windows provide by far the best insulation and can take the form of either casement or sash, depending on the manufacturer's design. As a result of its thermal efficiency and low maintenance requirement, this structure has become increasingly popular for homeowners.

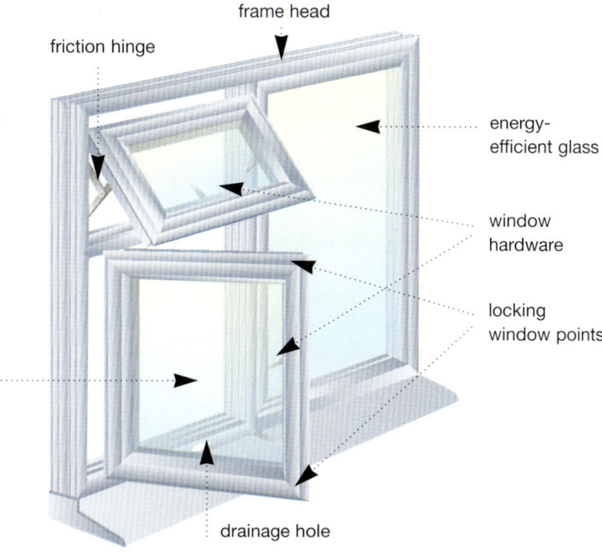

how windows are installed

Broadly speaking, the main determining factor in the positioning of windows is whether the wall in which they are to be installed is of a solid or cavity structure. The former situation tends to apply to older houses where solid walls are more prevalent, while a cavity wall situation is far more likely to be found in modern houses. The general issues for both are outlined here, showing the most important features relevant to the fitting of windows in these two common wall structures.

solid walls

Most new houses are built with a cavity wall structure, but if you need to replace windows in older properties it is necessary to understand how they are installed so that replacement may be carried out using the correct technique. The main difference here relates to the fact that in older properties, where there is no cavity, it is unlikely that foundation coating was used around the window. Therefore replacement merely requires positioning the window in the same place as the previous one. Once the window is in place, the junction between frame and masonry is sealed with mortar or sealant.

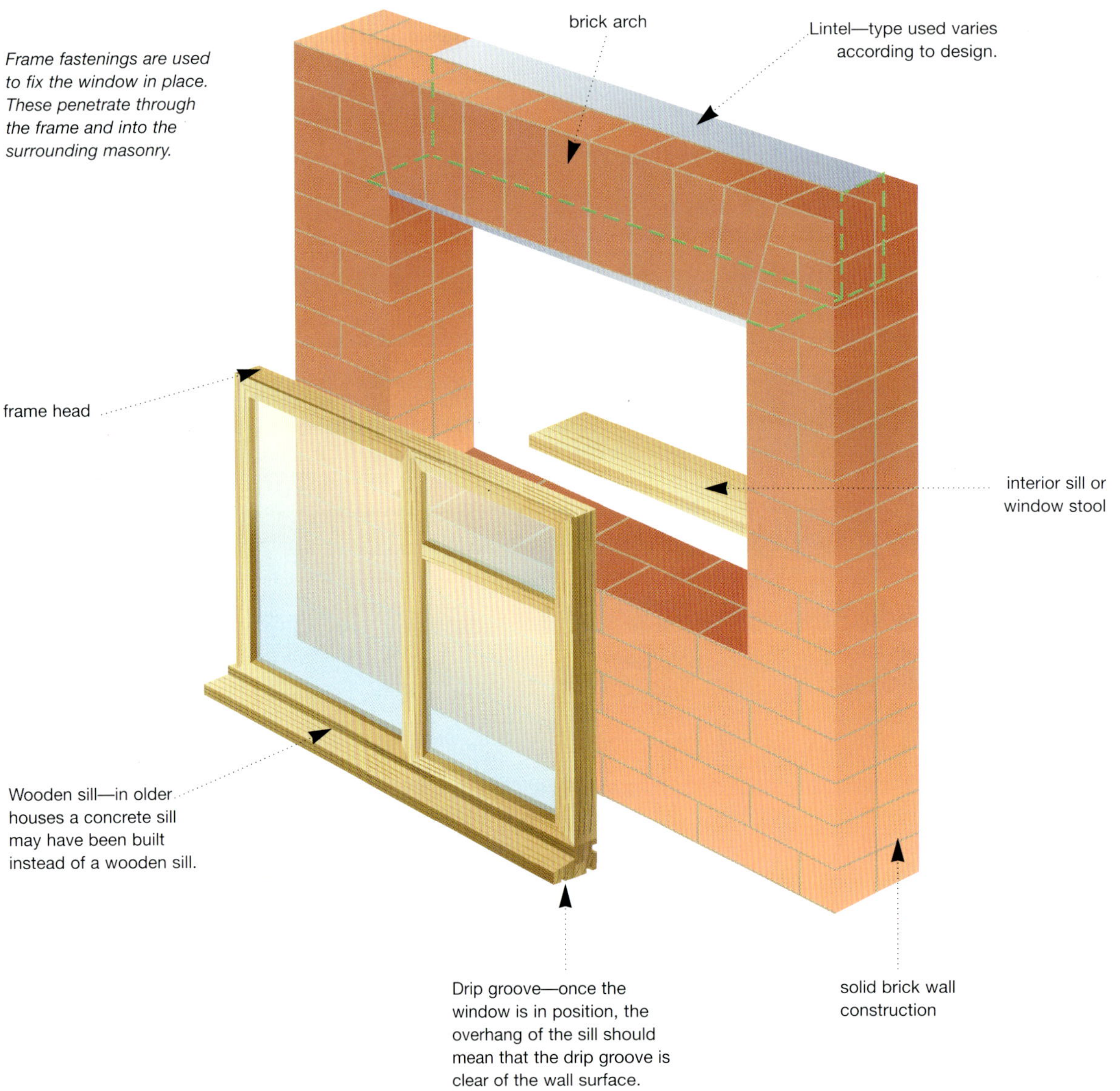

Frame fastenings are used to fix the window in place. These penetrate through the frame and into the surrounding masonry.

cavity walls

With cavity walls, positioning is slightly different and other factors need to be taken into account when looking at how the window is to be installed. There will inevitably be slight variations depending on window type, but this illustration helps demonstrate the main principles involved. Whether the window is wooden, vinyl, or metal, similar principles of fixing apply.

Frame fastenings are used to secure the window in place. These penetrate through the frame and into the surrounding masonry.

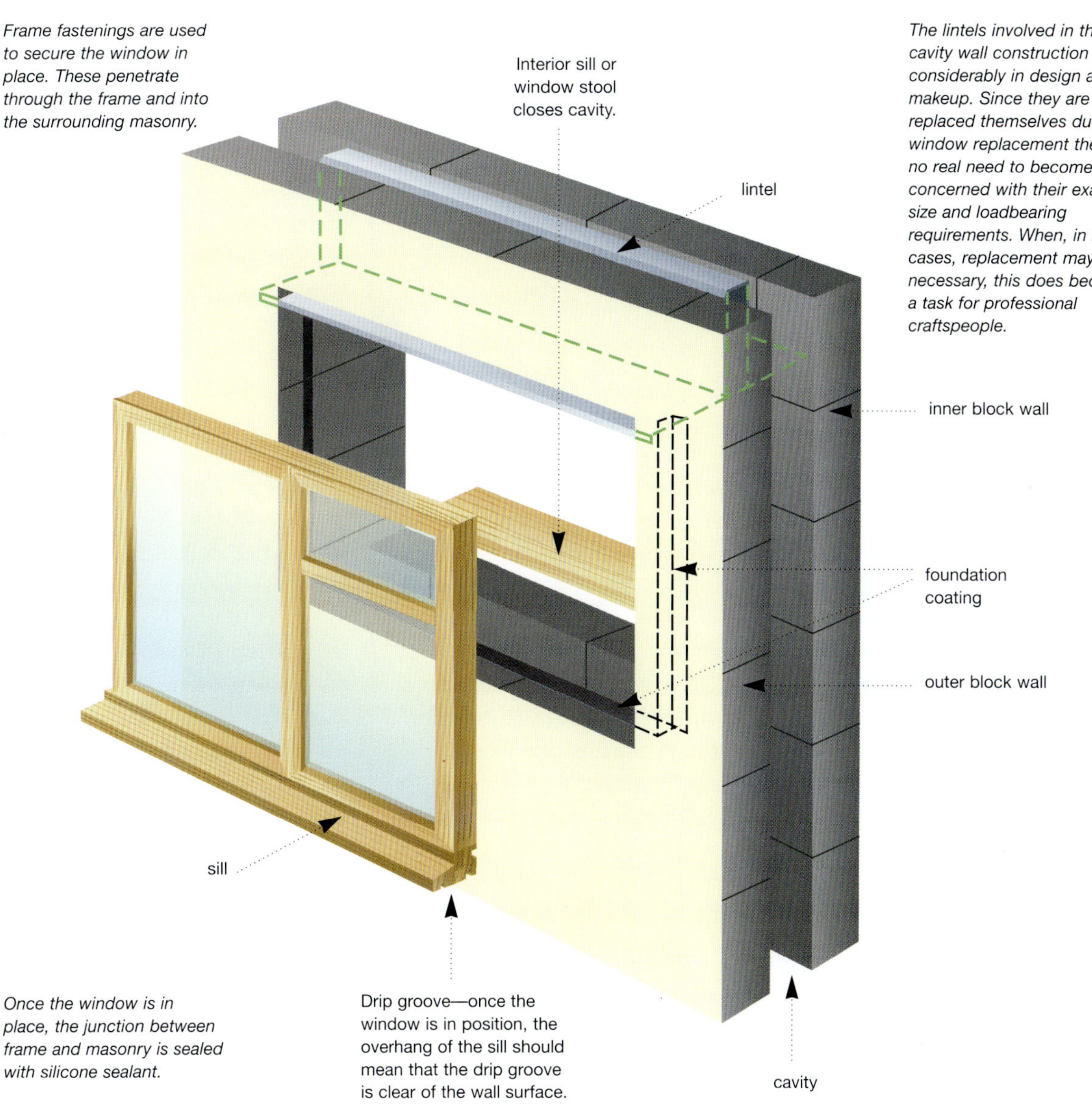

The lintels involved in the cavity wall construction vary considerably in design and makeup. Since they are not replaced themselves during window replacement there is no real need to become concerned with their exact size and loadbearing requirements. When, in rare cases, replacement may be necessary, this does become a task for professional craftspeople.

Once the window is in place, the junction between frame and masonry is sealed with silicone sealant.

Drip groove—once the window is in position, the overhang of the sill should mean that the drip groove is clear of the wall surface.

bay windows

Although bay windows display many similar characteristics in the way they are fitted, it is important to realize that in some situations the bay window itself does have a weight-supporting and therefore loadbearing part to play in house structure. Simply taking out an old bay window and replacing it with a new one should only be undertaken once the relevant checks have been made. Therefore, if you are thinking of replacing a bay window, it is always best to seek some professional advice, to make sure that you take the necessary measures needed to support the wall structure, if required.

forms

In modern houses it is not uncommon to find an extra part to the framing structure of a window. This extra piece is called a form and is inserted, or, more accurately, built, into the wall structure to create the correct size of opening for the window.

glass & glazing options

Glass options need a certain amount of consideration, because all windows contain some sort of glass, along with many part-glazed or totally glazed doors. Modern invention and innovation has allowed for a range of different types of glass to become available, with differing properties of both their finish and function. Decisions, therefore, need to be made on what type of glass is suitable for your needs in relation to the door or window in question.

clear glass

By far the most common type of glass used in houses is clear, to allow the maximum amount of light into the house and to ensure the view outside is made as clear and open as possible. However, clear glass is available in a number of categories which are difficult to pick up instantly with the naked eye.

thickness

Glass thickness is often difficult to spot when it is in position; only when you see the edges of glass panes does it become apparent that there can be considerable variation. In general, thinner clear glass is used for windows and thicker versions are used in doors. This tends to relate to safety considerations, as thinner glass is naturally easier to break, and a child mistakenly running into a glass door is less likely to break the glass, causing injury. As well as being thicker, glass used in doors and low-level areas in the home should also be safety glass or tempered, so that if it is broken it shatters into relatively small granular sections, which tend not to cause injury compared to the sharper shards common in normal glass breakages.

laminated glass

Laminated glass is in fact two or more panes of glass that have a clear plastic layer fused in between them. This plastic layer binds the panes together as one solid structure. It is available in many different thicknesses and varieties such as clear, patterned, and tinted. Laminated glass is difficult to cut, and it is therefore advisable to get glass cut to size by your supplier. Although laminated glass is an expensive option, it is an excellent choice in security terms as well as for safety purposes—in glazed doors, for example. It can absorb greater impact than most alternatives and is relatively strong. If it does break under severe impact, the plastic layer holds the glass pieces in position so that it remains in one piece and splinters of glass are not scattered around.

double-glazed units

Double-glazed units are two panes of glass separated by a void filled with inert gas and then totally sealed off from the surrounding atmosphere. Glass thickness tends to increase according to pane size and so the larger the panes, the thicker the glass. Double-glazed units may be fitted into vinyl- and aluminum-framed windows as well as new wooden ones. However, if you wish to change single panes for double-glazed units in an existing window, you will need to check that the rabbets in the frame are wide enough to accommodate the new unit. If they are too narrow, it will be necessary to fit units with a stepped edge to allow for the difference. Double-glazed units significantly improve insulation and can reduce condensation as well as noise pollution.

patterned clear glass

Patterned clear glass is often for privacy. For example, bathroom windows or doors may contain such glass to provide the required privacy while still allowing maximum light into the room. The variety of designs available is wide, so there is considerable room for choice and thus for finding a suitable option for your personal requirements.

patterned colored glass

Patterned colored glass offers a further design option and is often used in conjunction with clear patterned glass when maximum light is not a priority.

leaded lights

Leaded lights provide a traditional-looking window and are often supplied using different colored glass in varying designs. They can be fitted into appropriately designed casements or are common features in part-glazed front doors. Many companies will provide a "self-design" service, allowing you to decide which you require.

etched glass

Etched glass can be considered a more exclusive version of patterned glass and is more commonly used in part-glazed front doors. As well as adding privacy, light is still let in, and the availability and attractiveness of designs makes this option a real addition to the overall look of windows or doors.

wired glass

Wired glass has a mesh inside the glass pane to increase its strength, even though the glass itself may still shatter when broken. It is not particularly attractive and tends only to be used in fire doors because of its retardant properties. The wire binds the glass together during a fire and maintains a retardant barrier.

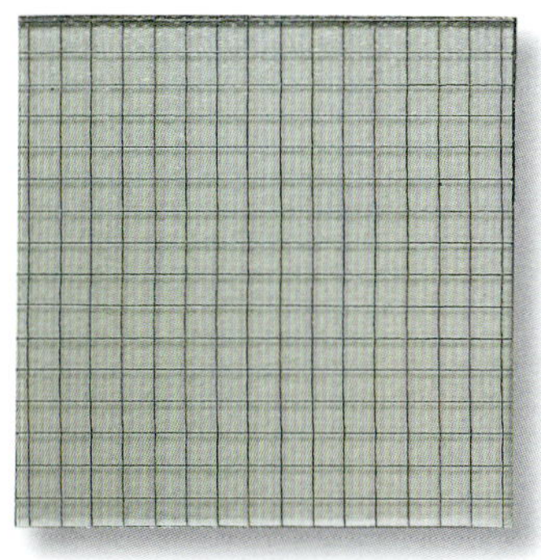

installing doors

Installing a door requires a methodical technique that can be adapted to take into account variations in door design and function. The actual principle and method remains similar with all doors, but it can be necessary to make variations during installation, depending on such factors as whether the door is interior or exterior, and what type of hinges are being used. This chapter looks at many of these variations in door design and use, and demonstrates the most common procedures for installing not only the door but all the accessories required for its correct functioning. This includes such items as the handles needed for opening and closing, and the relevant security hardware that has become an essential requirement in modern everyday life. Doors are crucial components in how your home functions, and therefore close attention to detail will ultimately be rewarding.

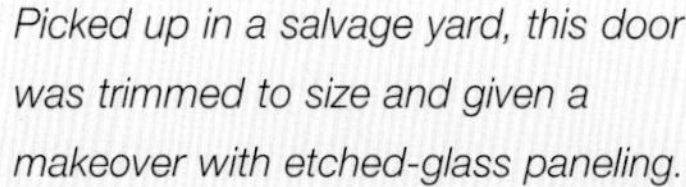

Picked up in a salvage yard, this door was trimmed to size and given a makeover with etched-glass paneling.

door hardware & security features

Doors clearly need the appropriate hardware in order to function properly. Although this is a mainly practical concern, there is considerable choice in terms of style and design when it comes to purchasing door hardware. Add to this the relevant security features that may be needed and the options expand even more. It is, therefore, necessary to look at some examples of what is available so that you can make the right choices for your particular needs.

handles

Door handles can broadly be placed into two categories—those that have a basic knob design and those that operate in a lever fashion. Nearly all operate the closing and opening mechanism of a door, or the latch, by means of a spindle joining the two handles on a door through the latch mechanism. On doors that do not have a latch mechanism, for example on cupboard doors that may use a simple spring-loaded ball catch, a spindle is not required, and the handles merely act as a secure gripping point to open the door. Shown on the right are some examples of common door handles and the latch sets they may operate in conjunction with. Owing to the fact that there are many different designs available, it is possible to combine their style with the relevant security features that may also be used on the door.

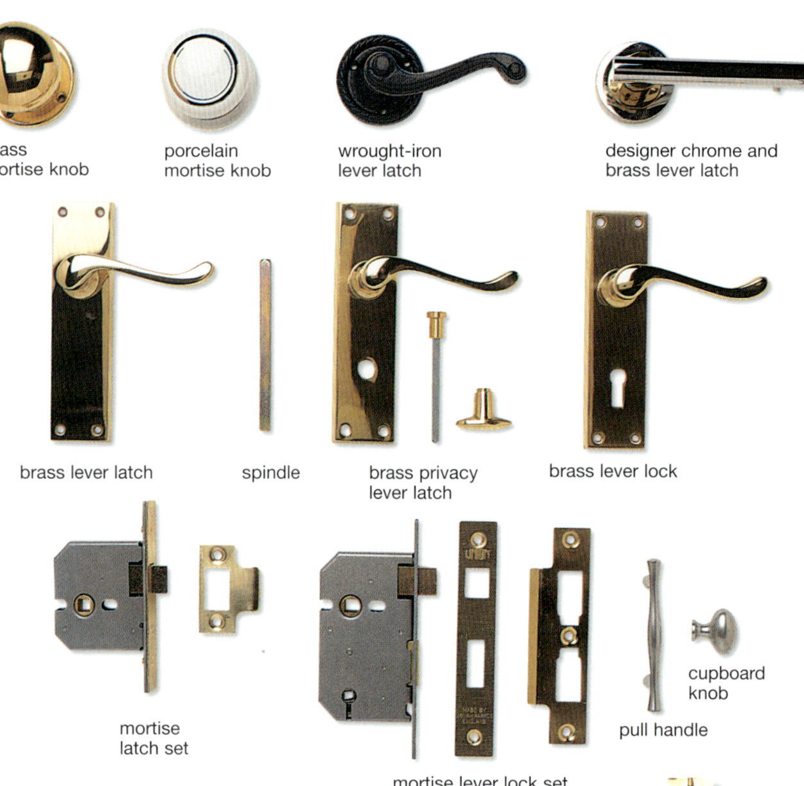

brass mortise knob

porcelain mortise knob

wrought-iron lever latch

designer chrome and brass lever latch

brass lever latch

spindle

brass privacy lever latch

brass lever lock

mortise latch set

mortise lever lock set

pull handle

cupboard knob

hinges

Straightforward butt hinges are used as the hinge mechanism on most entrance and cupboard doors in the home. Even though most of the hinge is concealed when the door is shut, there are still some designs that have decorative appeal. Exposed hinges, such as the antique iron one shown, are used most commonly in conjunction with traditional door designs such as a dutch door or ledge and brace. Piano hinges are also an option for cupboard doors.

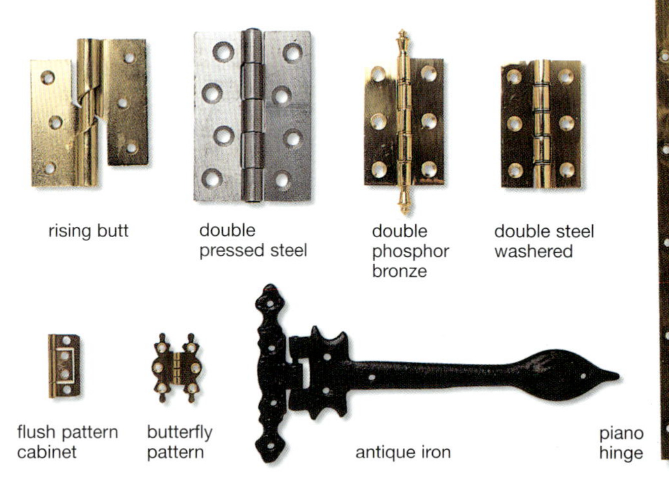

rising butt

double pressed steel

double phosphor bronze

double steel washered

flush pattern cabinet

butterfly pattern

antique iron

piano hinge

door security

Door security features are mainly concerned with exterior doors, although some items are used in conjunction with rooms of privacy such as bathrooms. Most devices either interact directly with the handle latch mechanism, or are separate to this and used as extra security devices on other areas of the door. Because security is such an important issue in modern society, system designs vary considerably. On the right are examples of the security mechanisms available, that cater to many different requirements.

peephole

peephole with cover

cylinder pull

door limiter

security chain

knob side flush bolt

door bolt

mortise door bolt

cylinder rim lock

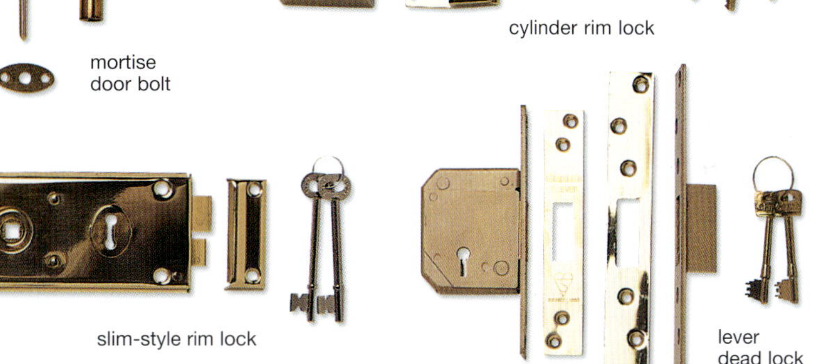

slim-style rim lock

lever dead lock

tips of the trade

It is worth remembering that although good security products can be expensive, this expense is usually balanced by peace of mind and the possibility of lower insurance premiums. Higher prices usually also guarantee that the product will be long-lasting and function correctly throughout its working life.

accessories

Aside from the essential opening, closing, and security aspects of door hardware, there are other items that can be applied to a wide range of door surfaces, either to complement those already mentioned or to fulfill another specific function. Fire doors, for example, will definitely require door closers. Most of these items have a highly decorative aspect to their makeup and so need to be chosen with this aesthetic requirement in mind. All these features are generally less complicated to install compared with other door hardware. It is therefore worth making these additions to improve the look and function of the door.

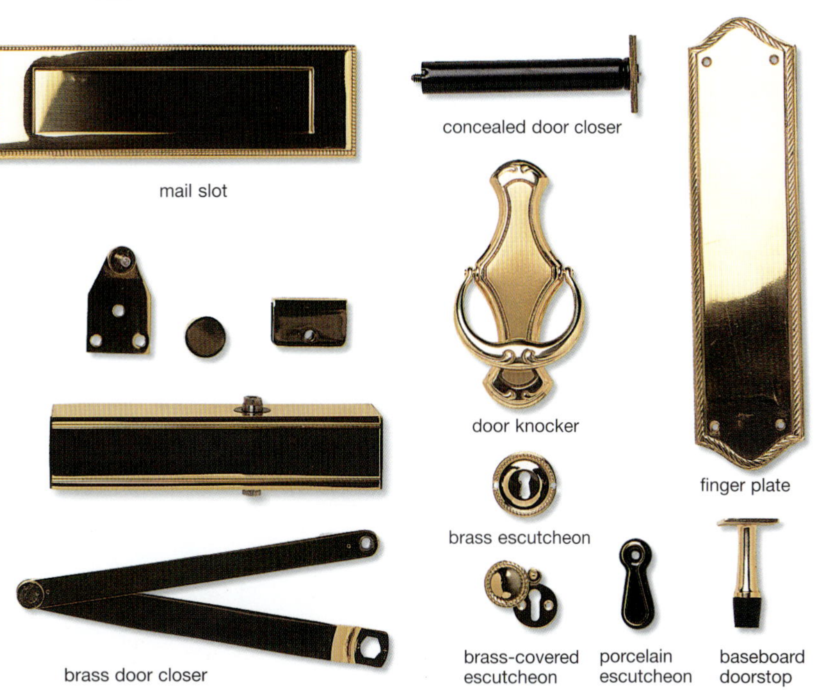

mail slot

concealed door closer

door knocker

finger plate

brass escutcheon

brass door closer

brass-covered escutcheon

porcelain escutcheon

baseboard doorstop

cutting to size

It is unlikely that a door will fit perfectly into the door jamb or frame, and so some cutting to size will probably be required. Trimming a door too much, though, may weaken its structure. This is particularly true of hollow doors that are based on a simple wooden frame. Most doors can be cut down using saws and planes, but for doors that are steel-faced or made of fiberglass or carbon fiber, the manufacturer's guidelines for installation should be observed.

interior panel door

Fitting a solid panel door provides an ideal demonstration of the best technique for cutting a door to size. If you have fitted a new jamb, then trimming the door to size should be straightforward. Installing a new door to an old jamb can be more complicated, but the same basic technique can be followed in both cases. First, the door must be trimmed to less than the size of the aperture. Once this is achieved, precise installation can be carried out.

tools for the job

- hammer
- pencil
- tape measure
- level or straightedge
- wood plane or power plane
- board or door lifter

1 Insert two nails into the head of the jamb. Their distance from the front of the head should be equal to the depth of the door. In this way, when the door is placed in position in the jamb, it will not fall through and will be supported securely enough to carry out the installation procedure.

2 Fit the door in the jamb, and mark around the edge of the door to provide a ⅛in clearance, or reveal, between the two vertical door stiles and the lining stiles. Depending on the squareness of the jamb, this may require more wood to be trimmed in some areas than in others.

POWER PLANES

Power planes are excellent tools for trimming down doors quickly, and are especially useful when there is more than just a small fraction of an inch to be shaved off.

tips of the trade

Excess trimming—Where the amount of wood to be shaved off a door edge is more than can be done with a plane, it may be necessary to use a jigsaw with a fine cutting blade.

3 Join the marked points along the door edge using a straightedge or level.

4 It may also be necessary to trim the height of the door, depending on whether the jamb is square, and/or if the floor is level. Adjust your measurements to account for the required floor clearance.

5 Use a pencil to join markings, so that a precise guideline for trimming purposes is achieved.

6 Plane along the edge of the door to remove wood down as far as the pencil guideline. Clamp the door in a workbench for this procedure—this will hold it steady during the planing process.

7 Plane along the leading edge of the door at a slight angle, so that a little more wood is being taken off the edge, which will eventually be the closing edge of the door. This fractional extra wood removal will make the door clearance slightly larger on the back of the leading edge than on the front. This makes the clearance between door and jamb much more even and reduces the risk of the door sticking in the future.

8 Once the door edges have been trimmed to fit and are checked in the entrance for size, trim down the top and/or bottom of the door as required. A plane may also be used for this process. Since this will mean working the plane over the end grain of the vertical stiles, work the plane only in a direction into the door and not towards its edge, which may cause the grain to split and damage the look of it.

9 A board or door lifter is the ideal tool to hold the door in place whilst clearances and preciseness of fit are measured. It also allows you to support the weight of the door, lifting or lowering it into the desired position. It is best to position the door lifter below the central stile and bottom rail.

10 Wedge the door in place at the top and bottom, butting it up tightly against what will be the hinge side. Measure the distance between the leading edge and the door jamb to check that it is exactly ¼in, which will allow for a clearance of ⅛in on both edges of the door once it is accurately hung in position.

EXTERIOR DOORS

The installation process for an external door is very similar to that for an interior one, except that an exterior door will always be fitted into a frame rather than into a jamb. Apart from this, the same principles of cutting to size are employed. It is also likely that you will need to cut a rabbet into the bottom of the door in order to accommodate the weather stripping on the door sill. This can be achieved using a router. Some doors will come with "horns" extending from the ends of the vertical stiles. This elongation of the stiles is simply a measure to protect the end grain before installation. Accordingly, they should be cut off just prior to installation.

Exterior doors are generally much more expensive than interior doors, mainly because they are built to withstand prolonged exposure to the elements. Mistakes may therefore be costly, and so it is wise to take extra time in your measuring process to make sure that you do not waste any materials.

cutting in hinges

The accuracy of cutting in hinges is the vital factor that ensures the ease and efficiency with which a door opens and closes. Exterior doors should always have three hinges because they are heavier than interior ones. Three hinges also lessen the chances of a new door going out of shape and are a wise choice if you have purchased relatively cheap doors. However, most interior doors may be hung successfully using two standard butt hinges.

tools for the job

- tape measure
- combination square
- wooden mallet
- chisel
- cordless drill/driver
- door lifter

1 Mark the hinge positions on the door edge, 6in from the top of the door and 9in up from the bottom of the door.

2 At the top mark, position the hinge wrong side up and directly below the 6in measurement.

Holding the hinge wrong side up allows the hinge barrel to be held flush against the door edge, which will ensure that the hinge position is marked off in the correct place. Draw a guideline around the edge of the hinge.

3 To measure the depth of the hinges you are using, hold one against a combination square. Adjust the rule on the square to the depth of the hinge and lock it in position.

4 Hold the combination square perpendicular to the door edge so that the depth measurement for the hinge may be drawn accurately on the face of the door.

5 Use a wooden mallet and sharp chisel to remove the wood to the marked depth by making chisel indentations for the top and bottom edge of the hinge. This keeps the wood from splitting when you chisel a guideline along the vertical length of the hinge mark.

6 The wood needs to be removed gradually to ensure accuracy and depth of the cut. Make a number of chisel cuts horizontally along where the hinge position will be, allowing the chisel to penetrate only as far as the depth measurement on the face of the door. Knocking the chisel in too far will cause an uneven surface once the recess wood is removed.

7 Now position the chisel so that its blade can be inserted beneath and at right angles to the horizontal cuts. Carefully pry up and remove the wooden sections, taking care not to allow the chisel to extend over the hinge guidelines.

8 Repeat steps 2–7 at the base of the door for the bottom hinge, but hold the hinge above the 9in measurement. Then put the door in position in the door jamb and place an open hinge between the top of the door and the door jamb. This gives the measurement for the door clearance at the top and allows you to mark off the hinge positions accurately on the door jamb. Mark at the top and bottom of the hinge position for both the top and bottom hinge.

9 Remove the door and—in a similar way to marking on the door edge—again hold a hinge wrong side up on the door jamb and mark around it with a sharp pencil. Measure hinge depth and chisel out as required in the same manner as used for the door edge. Carry out this process for both the top and bottom hinge.

10 Hold a hinge, right side up and in position, on the door edge. Make pencil marks for the screw positions, allowing the pencil point to move fractionally away from the screw hole center and toward the back edge of the hinge.

11 Remove the hinge and drill pilot holes for the screws. Be as accurate as possible, making sure that the drill bit is inserted directly at the marked pencil points.

tips of the trade

Rising butts—Instead of installing standard butt hinges, you may need to fit rising butts. These lift the level of the door as it is opened. Cutting in rising butt hinges is similar to cutting in standard butt hinges but you must determine whether you have right- or left-handed hinges, depending on the way the door opens. Also, bevel the top corner edge of the door (nearest to the hinges) so that it will shut properly.

12 Reposition the hinge and insert screws into the pilot holes. Do not tighten the screws until all three are in place and the hinge is in the correct position. Repeat steps 10–12 for the bottom hinge.

13 Hold the door open but in position in the door jamb. Be sure that each hinge fits exactly into the chiseled-out positions. Mark with a pencil and pilot drill, before screwing the hinges in place. The door should open and close into the jamb with a perfectly smooth action.

installing handles—1

Handles are installed in three stages, which correspond to the main components required for handles to work. First, it is necessary to install the latch; second, the handles themselves; and third, the strike plate has to be installed in the door jamb. Although a mortise lever lock has been used in this example, the principles are the same for a simple mortise latch.

tools for the job

pencil
combination square
cordless drill/driver
chisel

installing the latch

1 Hold the latch on one face of the door at the required height. Allow the latch plate to overlap onto the edge of the door, so that the main latch casing sits level against the door surface. Make a pencil mark along the top of the latch, one at the bottom, and two at the sides to show the height of the spindle position and the height of the keyhole.

2 Using a combination square, make horizontal guidelines to the marked points on the door face. Be sure that the combination square is held tight against the edge of the door so that the guidelines are accurate. Continue these lines onto the edge of the door and round to the other face, thus making a mirror image of the guidelines.

3 Measure the exact width of the door edge and lock the combination square to half this measurement. Use it to draw a centered guideline vertically through the horizontal guidelines on the edge.

4 Use the combination square again to measure the distance between the front of the latch plate and the center of the spindle hole. Lock the square in position at the correct measurement. You may allow a fraction extra to this measurement in order to compensate for the depth of the latch plate, as it will be recessed into the door edge.

5 Transfer this measurement to the door edge, lining up the square with the pencil guideline, which denotes the spindle height on the door face. Make a vertical line through the horizontal one to provide a pinpoint cross. Repeat this on the other side of the door. Repeat steps 4 and 5 to mark the exact position of the keyhole on the appropriate horizontal guidelines on the door. Double-check both measurements as mistakes are difficult to rectify later.

tips of the trade

Accuracy is key when installing latches, so it is essential that the chisels you are using are razor-sharp. Before you start installing the handles, make sure that you have serviced these tools, as it will certainly help to ensure that the job is completed to a high standard. See also the General Tool Care section on page 19.

6 Use an auger or spade drill bit to bore into the edge of the door along the vertical pencil guideline. The size of the bit should correspond to the width of the latch casing, not the width of the latch plate. Measure the depth of the latch and transfer this length to the drill bit, marking it with a piece of tape. This way, it is possible to drill accurately to the required latch depth. Work down the vertical guideline, making a series of overlapping drilled holes. Be sure that the drill bit enters the door edge at right angles to the door so that the depth of holes remains consistent.

7 At the marked crosses for the spindle and keyhole, drill through the door using the correct size of auger or spade bit. It may be necessary to drill two overlapping holes to accommodate the keyhole. To avoid splitting the wood, drill from the marked points on both sides of the door, since drilling all the way through from one side can cause damage to the face of the door when the bit breaks through the surface.

8 Use a chisel to straighten the edges of the overlapping drilled holes along the door edge. Work methodically to produce clean and accurate cuts. Make safety cuts horizontally against the grain at the top and bottom of the hole. This will prevent the splitting of the wood.

9 Push the latch into the hole and carefully draw a precise pencil guideline around the latch plate on the edge of the door. There is little room for error at this stage, so take time to make sure that the latch is perfectly vertical, with the spindle and keyhole exactly aligned, before doing any marking.

10 Take out the latch and chisel around the guideline, removing a depth of wood equal to that of the depth of the latch plate. Take care not to split the wood, by again using safety cuts to slice across the grain at the top and bottom horizontal guideline before making cuts along the vertical guideline, and therefore along the grain of the wood. Carefully remove the loosened wood until the correct level has been achieved and the plate sits flush.

11 Reposition the latch, allowing the chiseled-out area to accommodate the latch plate. The plate should be vertical and sit level with the door edge. Drill pilot holes for the screws.

12 Finally, screw the latch in place, securing it in position with screws at top and bottom of the plate. Ensure the screws are done up well, but do not overtighten and risk distorting the face of the latch plate.

installing handles—2

With the latch in position, the next step is to attach the handles to the door. Most handles are made to fit on a standard spindle, which in turn is inserted through the door and latch. This allows you to choose handles according to your own taste. In this case, a lever lock handle has been used to demonstrate the general technique required for installation.

tools for the job

- awl
- cordless drill/driver
- screwdriver
- tape measure
- pencil
- combination square
- chisel

installing the handles on the door

1 First, position the spindle through the door and latch, to check that it fits precisely. If the position is slightly off, the spindle movement may be hindered, therefore it is essential to check that its positioning is free from obstruction of any kind.

2 Fit one handle onto the spindle and hold it in the correct position, vertical to the door surface. This can be checked with a torpedo level, but it is usually possible to check its position by eye, by judging the distance at the top and bottom of the handle plate relative to the door edge. Use an awl to make marks or indentations on the door surface through the handle plate screw holes.

3 Remove the handle and use a small drill bit to create pilot holes in the marks. Do not penetrate the surface much, as the holes are just a starting point for the screw insertion.

4 Reposition the handle and carefully screw it in place. It is best to insert the screws in a particular order to ensure that the handle stays level. Start at the top, inserting a screw in one corner, and then fix the second screw in the opposite diagonal corner at the bottom of the handle plate. Finish with the other top screw followed by the final bottom one. This makes it easier to ensure that the handle is precisely aligned throughout the process of screw insertion.

THE OTHER SIDE

Repeat steps 2–4 on the other side of the door to fix the other handle in place. If, when you first position this handle, the length of the spindle prevents the handle plate from sitting level against the door surface, it will be necessary to remove the spindle and cut it down to size. Because spindles are supplied as multi-purpose items to fit all depths of door, it is often the case that spindle cutting will be required. This is a simple process, which can be achieved with the use of a standard hacksaw. Once trimmed down, reposition the spindle and fit the handle.

tips of the trade

When screwing handles in place, it is always best to use a handheld screwdriver, rather than a power driver. You have greater control to ensure that the handle is positioned vertically, and there is less chance that the screwdriver head can slip and scratch the surface of the brass. Such scratches are irreparable.

attaching the strike plate

Once the latch and handle have been installed, you can attach the catch mechanism, or strike plate, to the door jamb.

1 In a locked position, close the door onto the door jamb, allowing the latch and lock to rest against the jamb. Then make pencil marks on the jamb edge to denote the top and bottom positions of the latch and lock. Make these guidelines as clearly as possible—accuracy is very important.

2 Open the door and continue the marked pencil lines on the jamb edge around and onto the face of the door jamb.

3 Holding the door in an open position, it is now necessary to measure the precise depth of the latch and the lock and along the door edge in order to gauge the correct position of the strike plate. Lock the combination square at this depth measurement by tightening the rule-retaining screw.

4 Transfer the depth measurement, making a vertical guideline for the front of the latch and the lock respectively, between the appropriate horizontal jamb guidelines.

5 Hold the strike plate in position. Mark around the strike plate to give its exact position.

6 Chisel out inside the latch and lock guidelines and the exterior guideline for the strike plate. Position the strike plate, drill pilot holes, and then screw it in place.

Once door hardware, doorstop, and casing have been installed, the entire area may be painted, creating an attractive finished product.

finishing the frame 

A door should be finished off with a doorstop and casing. The doorstop prevents the door from closing further than level with the wall surface. Failure to fit one will mean the door can be closed too far and you will risk damaging the hinges. The casing, however, fulfills a purely decorative role, adding a finish to the jamb and an overall frame to the door.

tools for the job

- hand saw
- hammer
- pencil
- torpedo level
- miter saw or miter block
- tape measure
- nail set

exterior doors

Most exterior doors do not require a doorstop, since there is one already built into the frame. Similarly, the exterior of the frame does not need an casing, but the interior can be surrounded with one if required.

attaching the doorstop

Doorstops vary in dimension, but are normally about 1½ x ⅜in in cross section. Sizes vary according to the door dimensions and between manufacturers. In most cases, a doorstop is supplied as part of the door jamb kit.

1 Close the door so that you are on the side from which you can see the entire door jamb. Draw a pencil guideline on the jamb at the position where the door meets the jamb. Open the door, and cut lengths of doorstop to fit the head of the jamb and down the two stiles. Position the doorstop at the head of the jamb. Check that it fits precisely before proceeding to fix it in position using wire finish nails.

2 Nail the head doorstop in place so that its front edge aligns precisely with the pencil guideline. Do not hammer the nails all the way in at this stage—simply insert them far enough to be secure, but so the nailhead is still protruding. This allows for easy removal and repositioning if necessary.

3 Cut and attach the length of doorstop on the strike plate stile. Then cut and attach the doorstop on the hinge side of the jamb. Instead of positioning this length along the pencil line, fix it slightly back from the line. This will allow the hinge edge to shut and prevent it catching on the doorstop. Finish by tapping the nails in after opening and closing the door to check the action.

installing the casing

Once you have chosen the casing style, installation is relatively simple as long as cuts are accurate and a miter saw or miter block is used during this process. Remember that, for the best decorative effect, the casing should be chosen to match with the other moldings in the room, such as the baseboard and chair or picture rails, if appropriate.

1 Use a scrap of casing to determine corner positions. Hold the piece in place above the door, approximately $^3/_{16}$in to ⅜in away from the jamb edge. This distance is often decided by aesthetic preference and is a matter of personal choice.

However, once you have chosen it, you must ensure that it remains consistent around the entire door jamb. Draw a pencil guideline along the top of the casing, which extends out onto the wall surface to the side of the door, as this will help you to do this.

2 Hold the scrap vertically along the hinged side of the jamb, keeping the same distance between the casing edge and the door jamb edge as the distance that you used at the top of the door. If you draw another pencil guideline along the outer edge of the casing, it will then cross over the horizontal pencil guideline. Next, repeat steps 1 and 2 at the other corner of the jamb. These pencil lines will now provide you with the precise guidelines for what will be the outside corners of your casing.

3 Measure the length requirement for the top section of casing by measuring between the two points where the pencil guidelines cross above each corner of the door. Mark off this distance along the back edge of a piece of casing. Then use a miter saw to cut your casing accurately to size.

4 Position the casing above the door jamb and nail it in position. Ideally, attach the length so that the nails protrude into the edge of the door jamb and into the studwork around the jamb. For block or brick walls, some masonry nails may be required.

5 Continue by measuring the vertical casing requirements. This can be done very precisely by holding a length of the casing, that is slightly longer than the door height, wrong side out and butted against the edge of the top length of fixed casing. Then make a mark with a sharp pencil where the vertical length meets the horizontal one, and use this as an accurate guideline when you use the miter saw to cut the length to the required size.

6 You can now nail the vertical lengths in position. Add one further nail into each casing corner joint, inserting the nail through one section of the casing and into the adjacent piece. This helps to hold the mitered joints tightly together and reduces the risk of them splitting open at a later date.

7 Finally, use a hammer and nail set to be sure that nailheads are hammered in below the surface level of the casing.

tips of the trade

- Although a miter saw has been used to cut the casing in the example shown here, an alternative method is to measure the distance required and use a hand saw and miter block to achieve a clean 45-degree cut.
- When preparing a finished door frame for painting, use a flexible filler to seal the gap along the outside edges of the casing and the mitered joins, to allow for any slight movement in the door frame once it is in use.

adding front door accessories

Front doors often need accessories that are not necessary on interior doors. Although these fittings have a functional job to perform, they also add a decorative aspect to the front door and exterior of the house as a whole.

tools for the job

tape measure
pencil
combination square
cordless drill/driver
jigsaw
pliers
hammer

adding a mail slot

The positioning of a mail slot is to a large extent determined by front door design. Installation can take place when the door is hung in position, but it is often easier to carry it out with the door laid flat on saw horses.

1 On the outer side of the door, mark out a rectangular guideline slightly larger than the plate of the mail slot on the middle of the central rail. Then mark crosses far enough in from each corner to accommodate the diameter of the drill bit. The drill hole should be large enough to accommodate a jigsaw blade.

2 Drill through the door at each cross with an auger or spade drill bit, making sure that the hole does not extend outside the guideline. When drilling through, hold a block of scrap wood tightly against the other side of the door where the drill point will emerge. This will prevent any wood being split or blown out on the other side.

3 Cut along the pencil guideline with a jigsaw, beginning each cut from one of the drilled holes. Remove the block of wood, then smooth any rough edges with fine-grit sandpaper. Next, mark the position of the retaining bolts.

4 Drill holes for the retaining bolts, holding a wooden block on the opposite side of the door to prevent splitting. Often mail-slot design requires holes on the exterior of the door to be widened slightly at, and just below, surface level in order to accommodate the mail-slot plate, so two sizes of drill bit may be required.

5 Attach the retaining bolts to the mail slot and thread them through the holes to the other side of the door.

6 Turn the door over and screw the retaining nuts onto the bolts. (Tighten with pliers if necessary.)

installing a knocker

A door knocker is installed using a similar principle as for a mail slot, again with bolts that extend through the door and are secured by nuts on the inside face. Positioning is again affected by door design, but for panel doors, a central position where the top door rail crosses the vertical central stile is always a suitable place for a knocker.

1 Measure out the central position for the knocker and strike plate, making a clear pencil cross to act as a guideline for drilling.

2 Drill through the door, holding a wooden scrap on the other side to prevent damage to the wood. You may need to use a second, slightly larger drill bit to open up the entrance holes in order to accommodate the knocker and strike plate design.

3 Screw the supplied bolts into the retaining holes of both the knocker and strike plate, making sure that the bolts are inserted straight, so that the risk of crossthreading is thereby reduced.

4 Insert both the knocker and strike plate through the appropriate holes, turn the door over, and tighten the retaining bolts to secure the door knocker in place. When positioning the knocker, a tap with the butt end of a hammer or a wooden mallet may be required, as the knocker is often designed with a small point behind its face that pierces into the door surface and adds to the security of the fastening. It is best to cover the face of the knocker with a cloth when carrying out this process, to keep from scratching or damaging the knocker surface finish.

The practical and aesthetically pleasing combination of exterior door hardware can add tremendous decorative appeal to the overall look of a front door.

installing cylinder rim locks

Cylinder rim locks are among the most common types of lock for exterior doors. From a security standpoint they are very effective, but are always best when combined with other door security features (see pages 250–1). Designs do vary, but the basic principle of cylinder rim locks remains the same, in that a locking barrel extends through the door and combines with a latch to form a closing mechanism operated by key from the outside and with a lever from the inside.

tools for the job

- pencil
- combination square
- cordless drill/driver
- screwdrivers
- hammer
- mini hacksaw
- chisel

1 On the inside of the door, draw a horizontal pencil guideline across the closing stile of the door. Use a combination square to continue this line around the edge and onto the front of the door. The exact height positioning for a cylinder rim lock is not standardized, but it should be on the upper half of the door—4ft 3in from the floor is generally an acceptable height.

2 Use the combination square to measure the distance between the lock edge (closest to the latch) and the hole that will accommodate the flat connecting bar. Lock the combination square in position at this exact point. Then transfer this measurement to the door, opening it slightly and resting the edge of the combination square against the door edge, as you mark the position on the horizontal pencil guideline.

3 Use an auger or spade bit to drill through the door at the marked point. The size of bit required will normally be suggested on the lock packaging and relates directly to the size of the cylinder for the lock. It is best to drill from both sides to make the holes because otherwise the emerging drill bit can make splits in the wood surface. Alternatively, as you drill, hold a wood scrap tight against the other side of the door, where the drill bit will appear.

4 On the exterior of the door, insert the cylinder through its brass ring and the drilled hole, so that the flat connecting bar extends through to the other side of the door.

5 Attach the mounting plate to the cylinder and the inside of the door, making sure that it is level, and that the edge of the plate is aligned precisely with the door edge. It may be necessary to make pilot holes for the screw fastenings, especially if you are using a hardwood door, which is what is shown here. When drilling the pilot holes, be sure that you are extremely accurate, and also make certain that the drill bit goes into the door surface absolutely level.

6 Depending on door thickness, the flat connecting bar may be too long to allow for the easy positioning of the lock. You may have to trim the bar back so that the lock may be fitted. A mini hacksaw is the ideal tool for this purpose. Double-check your cutting measurements because you will not be able to rectify mistakes later.

7 Push the lock case onto the mounting plate, shifting it along until it catches firmly in position. This precise installation procedure may vary slightly between different designs, and although the fit itself is very tight, there is normally a simple procedure for sliding the casing in place. Once in position, insert the two retaining screws to secure the lock casing firmly on the door.

8 Next, close the door and draw a straight guideline above and below the lock casing on the door frame. A torpedo level can be used for this process, but space is very often confined, and therefore you may find that it is actually easier to use the straight edge of the strike plate itself to aid you in this marking process.

9 Open the door and hold the strike plate in place, following the guidelines you have just made. Continue the guideline round onto the inside facing of the door frame.

10 Measure the recessed part of the strike plate and transfer the measurement to the frame. This shows what wood must be removed. Use a chisel to cut the area, taking care not to damage the surrounding wood.

11 Finally, position the strike plate in the recess and screw it in place on the frame. Test the door to make sure the rim lock closes and opens correctly, making any minor adjustments as required.

RIM LOCK GUIDELINES

- **Standards**—Use only a rim lock that is supplied in packaging and displays the relevant approval logos and assertions. Also check that the lock comes with a guarantee.
- **Dual use**—Although rim locks are a common front door feature, they are ideal for any other exterior door.
- **Decorative choice**—Security features such as this are never going to be attractive, but do consider that, like most hardware, locks can be bought in different finishes.
- **Stile check**—Check the dimensions of the door stile to make sure the lock casing will fit into it. Otherwise, a slimmer lock than that shown here will be required.
- **Dead bolt**—The rim lock shown here has a dead bolt so that, once it has been locked with the key, it is not possible to open the door. This is essential for doors with glass panes, so if thieves break a pane and reach the lock, they will still be unable to open the door. For safety reasons, key-operated dead bolts must not be used when people who do not have a key are inside the home.

adding extra security

Security hardware for doors, and front doors especially, includes more than just rim locks, and there are a number of other systems that may be used to add to the security offered by a rim-locking mechanism. It is not necessary to use all the features shown here on a single door, but a combination of these items will make you feel safer in your own home.

tools for the job

- pencil
- tape measure
- cordless drill/driver
- chisel
- awl
- screwdrivers
- torpedo level

mortise door bolts

Mortise door bolts are straightforward to fit and offer an excellent security mechanism for exterior doors. They are operated by a specially shaped key that extends the bolt between the door and frame when moved to the locking position. These door bolts can be installed on a hanging door or before it is hung, as shown here.

1 Holding the barrel of the door bolt, draw a guideline around its faceplate on the door edge. Be sure that the rectangular guideline drawn is centered on the edge of the door.

2 Using the correct size auger or spade drill bit (size should be on the packaging), drill vertically down into the door edge. Make sure that the drill remains completely vertical, otherwise operation of the bolt will be hindered. Drill to a depth equal to that of the door bolt.

3 Chisel out inside the rectangular pencil guideline to a depth equal to that of the door bolt faceplate. Make cuts with the chisel along the shorter dimensions of the rectangle (across the grain) before making cuts along the longer dimensions (with the grain). This will help to keep the wood from splitting.

4 Hold the door bolt on the face of the door, aligning it with the drilled hole in the edge. Use an awl to mark the face of the door at the position on the bolt where the key will be inserted. Drill into the door at this point, allowing the drill to extend only as far as the door bolt hole in the edge of the door. Make sure you do not continue to drill through to the other side of the door.

5 Fit the door bolt in place in the edge of the door, securing it with the retaining screws. It may be necessary to drill pilot holes for the screws before inserting them.

6 Finally, attach the key plate on the face of the door so that its hole aligns directly with the one in the door. Another mortise door bolt may now be fitted at the bottom level of the door, before it is rehung on the door frame. Both bolts will need holes and cover plates positioned in the door frame. A similar technique to that for installing a door latch strike plate is used here, where the position for the

plate is marked and the appropriate amount of chiseling out is done to accommodate the slide bolt.

slide bolts

Simple slide bolts offer another option to the mortise door bolt. These are surface-mounted and are even simpler to fit. Again, it is wise to have slide bolts positioned at both the top level and bottom of the door.

1 Hold the bolt in position on the door, using a torpedo level to make sure that the bolt is perfectly horizontal. Use an awl to mark the positions for the screws on the face of the door.

2 Pilot drill holes and then screw the bolt in place. The same marking procedure can be used to position the catch plate for the bolt on the door frame. Take care when using screws with solid brass hardware, because a simple slip with the screwdriver may scratch the brass surface and therefore detract from the finished look of the job once it has been completed.

peepholes

Door security does not necessarily have to involve a lock or mechanical barrier of some nature, as the use of peepholes demonstrates. These security items are simply used to check the identity of a caller even before opening the door.

1 Peepholes are normally supplied with both sections screwed together. Undo the two components and select a drill bit slightly larger than the size of the thread in the peephole.

2 Drill a hole in the door centrally at eye level on the middle door stile. On the outside of the door insert the correct piece of the peephole.

3 Turn the door over and insert the other section of the peephole, screwing it in position into the other section. The flat edge of a screwdriver may be required for tightening purposes. Although this peephole has been installed with the door off its hinges, these security devices can also be installed with the door still hung in place.

door chains

These useful fasteners allow the door to be opened slightly, so that visitor identity can be checked before the door is opened fully. Door limiters are another version of this system.

1 Position the chain at an appropriate height around the middle section of the door. Just below the rim lock is ideal. Use an awl to mark the position, and then screw the main chain plate onto the door.

2 Attach the chain and retaining plate to the door frame, positioning it so that the chain can be conveniently slipped in place on the main chain plate.

changing door appearances

From time to time, it can be desirable to change the appearance of doors in your home without going to the effort and expense of full replacement. Decorative changes are outlined on pages 410–15, but it is possible to renovate doors, or change their appearance to something more appealing, in ways other than simply painting. These pages explain how to make and fit decorative panels to a flush door, adding simple but attractive texture to the door surface.

renovating a flush door

Flush doors can be considered relatively featureless examples of door design. In some cases, this may be the minimalist look required. There is always the option, however, of adding panels to an existing flush door, which provides greater character at half the cost of full replacement with authentic panel doors. You can also save money by adding panels to a relatively inexpensive new flush door.

panel considerations

Before starting you should first consider how many panels are going to be required on the door surface. Choices are normally either four panels of a similar size or six panels with the top two being around half the size of the lower four. Bear in mind that the greater the number of panels, the larger the amount of molding and the greater the number of cuts that will be required. This is a particularly important consideration if you are paneling throughout your home and on both sides of doors, because the expense can escalate rapidly.

The choice of molding also varies in style as well as price. The most ornate varieties can be expensive, and often the cheaper, simpler designs are all that is required to achieve an effective panel door. Since molding is normally painted, wood quality is not an essential consideration, so long as the molding is not split.

tips of the trade

If the molding is to be used in a different color from the rest of the door surface, it is best to apply primer and top coat to the molding before it is cut to size, and to paint the flush door surface with primer and top coat as well. This done, the molding can be attached so that the only paint requirement will be a touch-up of the coats already applied. Thus the very exacting cutting-in requirement of the two differing colors on the door will be avoided, speeding up the time taken to complete the task by a considerable margin.

tools for the job

- paintbrush
- combination square
- pencil
- tape measure
- level
- miter saw
- scissors or utility knife

1 On a new door, it is always best to prime the surface before attaching the panels. The primer improves adhesion between the molding and the door when the double-sided tape is applied and the molding is positioned.

2 In addition to the door itself, it is also worth priming the molding lengths before they are cut to fit. This saves time later, and also improves adhesion for the same reasons as explained in step 1.

3 Once the primer has dried, accurately measure the door size and begin by marking what will be the outer corner points of the panels. A combination square is an ideal aid for this process and helps to keep measurements precise.

4 Use a level to draw the pencil guidelines. Keeping these lines plumb and level as required makes the paneling process much easier to achieve. Once all the panels are marked out on the door surface, measure each panel dimension separately and use a miter saw to cut lengths of molding to size. Accuracy at this stage will help to eliminate the need for any filling on miter joints once the panels are in place.

5 Apply double-sided tape to the back of the molding. Make sure that the tape runs all the way, centered, along its length, and that there are no wrinkles or unevenness in the tape surface. Remove the backing from the tape once positioned, so that it may then be stuck to the door surface. The double-sided tape can be cut using scissors or a utility knife.

6 Attach the molding so that its outside edge runs along the pencil guidelines. The adhesive properties of the tape should allow for some adjustment of position when first placed on the door surface, though the glue will soon set, creating a tight bond between molding and door surface. Continue to apply lengths until all panels are complete.

PANELING TIPS

- **Filling**—As long as measurements are accurate, there should only be limited filling needs on the molding before painting can take place. Use flexible filler or caulk to fill any slightly open miter joints and along any open joints between the molding edges and the door face.
- **Nailing alternative**—Instead of using double-sided tape, it is possible to attach the molding using finish nails. However, the heads will require filling and sanding once they are hammered in place. Apply a small amount of wood glue to the back of the molding before it is positioned, to ensure that a good bond is achieved.
- **Ready-made panels**—Some manufacturers produce completed panels that can be attached directly to the door surface, eliminating the need for you to make miter cuts. However, while these kits are very useful, they can be expensive.

Combining color can help to enhance the appearance of a panel door and draw attention to its texture and design.

installing door closers

Door closers are primarily used for fire doors, where the automatic mechanism shuts the door to maintain a fire barrier at all times. Door closers may also be used on standard doors, and can either be visible or concealed from view.

tools for the job

awl
cordless drill/driver
chisels
tape measure
combination square
pliers

installing a hydraulic door closer

These are the most common of the visible variety and are generally positioned at the top of the door and frame. The hydraulic mechanism is enclosed in a housing that is attached to the top of the door and joined to the frame by a pivoting bar. As well as pulling the door shut, the mechanism also controls the speed at which the door closes. Designs can vary slightly, but most are based on principles similar to those demonstrated here.

1 Most such door closers will come supplied with a paper template to help position the housing. Attach the template to the door, securing it in place with some painter's tape. Be sure the template is the right way round for the way the door is opening, and that its edges are perfectly aligned with those of the door. Use an awl to mark the fastening positions for the housing, making slight indents through the template and into the door surface. At the same time, mark the positions for the retaining bracket for the door closer arm on the casing.

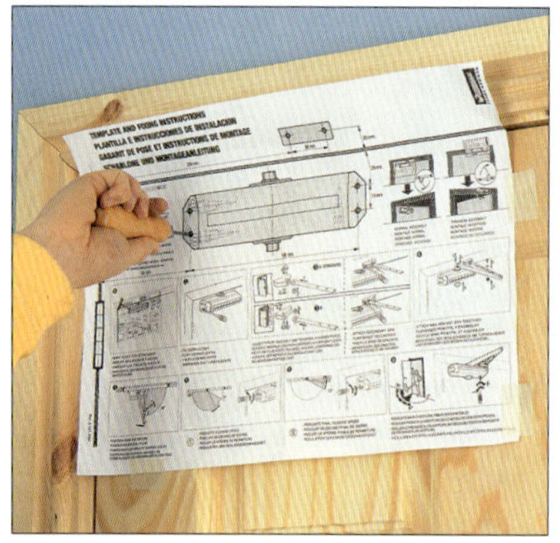

2 Drill pilot holes for the housing and screw it in position on the door surface. Take extra care to ensure that the door closer housing is the right way up and accurately positioned using the template hole guidelines.

3 Depending on the casing design, it may be necessary to cut out a small section of wood from the casing, so that the door closer arm bracket can be fixed flush in position. Draw an outline for the bracket and drill pilot holes, so that once wood has been chiseled out it will still be possible to see the holes for screw insertion.

4 Attach the first section of the closer arm to the bracket and screw it in place on the casing. Again, check that the bracket and arm are positioned the right way up, as subtle differences may hamper you from determining this.

5 Attach the other section of arm to the door closer housing and join it to the first arm with the nut and bolt supplied. Small adjustments may be necessary for exact positioning.

6 Open the door and allow it to close. It may be necessary to adjust the tension to suit your requirements. Most such door closers can be adjusted with a slot-head screwdriver, inserted at a special point on the side of the door closer.

concealed door closers

With the function and workings hidden whilst the door is closed, this variety of door closer can be considered far more aesthetically pleasing than the type shown opposite. However, depending on door weight and its overall dimensions, more than one concealed door closer may be needed to fulfill the automatic closing function.

1 Open up the door and mark a cross in the middle of the door edge, central to the door's middle rail.

2 Drill at right angles and perfectly horizontally into the door at the point of the cross just marked. Use an auger or a spade drill bit equal to the size of the barrel of the door closer. (Drill bit size will normally be printed on the packaging.) Only drill in as far as the length of the door closer itself.

3 Insert the door closer in the hole and use a pencil to mark around the edge of the face plate. Be sure that the face plate is precisely vertical for the pencil guideline.

4 Chisel out a recess to accommodate the depth of the face plate. Working close to the door edge like this means that extra care is required not to split the wood.

5 Use the face plate of the door closer to draw another guideline on the door jamb surface. Chisel out this area to the depth required for the door closer anchor plate.

6 Use pliers to pull the anchor plate away from the face plate, and insert the retaining bar across the chain to prevent it closing. Now insert the door closer in the door.

7 Finally, screw the anchor plate in place. Carefully remove the retaining bar from the chain and allow the door to close automatically. Tension may be adjusted if necessary.

weather-stripping doors

Most doors suffer from draft problems, especially given that the opening and closing mechanism will not function efficiently without gaps around the door edges. Fiberglass and double-glazed doors offer the best insulation, but with wooden doors it is often necessary to take further measures to improve insulation and reduce unwanted drafts. Such insulating techniques may be applied to both exterior and interior doors, although the materials used tend to differ.

exterior strips

An effective option used on many exterior doors is to attach weather stripping to the door frame. When the door is closed, a slight overlap of the strip from the door onto the frame effectively closes the gap that a draft may otherwise penetrate through. Designs vary, but most weather stripping is fitted using the technique shown below.

tools for the job

- tape measure
- utility knife
- hammer
- nail set

1 Cut the strips to size so that you have one for each upright of the door frame and one length for the top of the frame. Mitered corners provide a good join between the strips. Position them so that the flexible edge of each section touches and follows the profile of the door surface.

2 Nail the strips in place, making sure there is contact between them and the door surface when the door is in a closed position. Since the nails used are so small, it is often easier to position them using a nail set. This also reduces the risk of damaging the strip with the hammer.

insulating tape

An alternative to the exterior strips is to use insulating tapes that are positioned on the internal part of the frame or on the doorstop. The advantage of these is that they are not visible when the door is in a closed position, and they are also particularly easy to apply. Always read the manufacturer's guidelines to determine their recommended positioning: tape design varies, and they may be used in slightly different positions on the frame or door surface.

Most insulating tapes are self-adhesive and are secured in place by peeling away the backing and pressing the strip into position. The adhesive used on these tapes is fast-acting, so take care to position the tape correctly on first application—later adjustment is not always possible.

frame/wall junctions

Another area for draft penetration can be between the door frame and surrounding masonry or framing. It is particularly important to close up such gaps, as these are also areas where damp or moisture can penetrate, leading to further problems.

tools for the job

- caulk gun
- painter's tape

1 In order to make a neat finish, it is best to use painter's tape, or masking tape on an unpainted surface. Apply separate strips of tape along the length of the junction on both the wall and frame. Try to smooth the tape into all

depressions and recesses, while still maintaining a precise vertical edge to it.

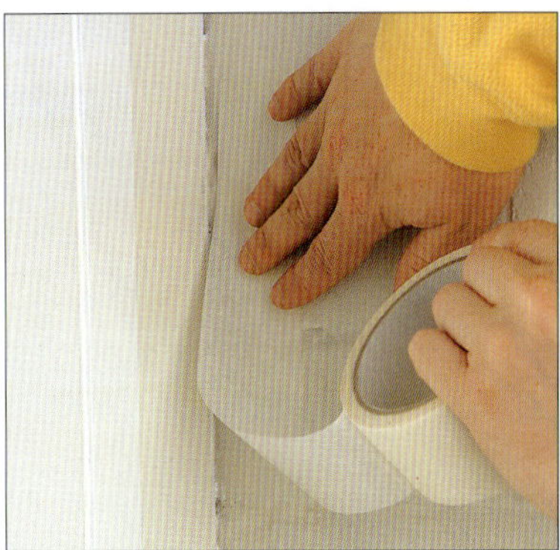

2 Load the caulk gun with a tube of silicone sealant. Cut the nozzle so that its diameter is slightly wider than the gap between the two lengths of masking tape. Depress the trigger and expel an even bead of sealant along the junction.

3 Smooth the sealant with a wet finger and proceed to remove the masking tape. The tape must be removed immediately after application, before the sealant dries.

interior options

A common and inexpensive measure to reduce drafts and improve insulation is to use door sweep on interior doors.

tools for the job

- tape measure
- mini hacksaw
- awl
- screwdriver

1 Strips are supplied in lengths greater than standard door size so it is necessary to cut them down to size before screwing in place. Measure the width of the base of the door and cut down the metal section of the door sweep using a mini hacksaw.

2 Insert the supplied brushes into the strip and position at the base of the door. Make pilot holes for the screws using an awl. Make sure the strip is positioned so that when the door is in a closed position the brushes rest on the floor, thereby cutting out any draft penetration under the door.

3 Screw the strip in place, again to making sure that the brushes make good contact with the floor surface. If necessary, make adjustments before tightening the screws.

SOUND INSULATION

As well as insulating for draft reduction, it is possible to insulate with sound reduction in mind. All the measures shown here will certainly help with sound insulation, but there are other methods that can be employed.

- **Door quality**—If sound insulation is a priority, then door quality must be a consideration. As a general rule, doors of higher quality will tend to be more solid, and so their sound-insulating properties are enhanced. This door replacement is always an option.
- **Increasing depth**—Door depth can sometimes be increased to improve sound insulation. Simply attaching plywood sheets to the surface of the door will help reduce sound transference between rooms.
- **Sound-insulation strips**—Manufactured sound-insulation strips can be purchased and installed in a similar way to that shown here for weather stripping.

installing windows

Installing windows involves both the interior and exterior, so there are many areas to be considered when working on their installation. In many cases the projects may involve replacing more than one window, and therefore planning your work and adhering to a timetable becomes a crucial factor. Remember that aesthetic considerations are just as important on the outside as they are on the inside. Furthermore, with exterior windows you have added concerns of making sure that the best security is employed, and that the window is able to deal with all manner of attack from the elements, through weatherproofing techniques such as insulation and weather stripping. This chapter looks at all these concerns and explains the best techniques for installation of both full window units and the various accessories that are used to complete the window function.

This window has been installed with wooden beads to leave a neat finish between the framework and panes.

window & security hardware

Most new wooden windows are supplied with window hardware, but it is often relatively cheap and simple in design, and there is always the option to change it for something more decorative. Security fittings will also need to be added to wooden windows to make sure they are easy to lock through and safe from intruders. Vinyl and metal windows tend to be supplied with window furniture as part of the window design and therefore options should be chosen at the same time as the windows.

security hardware

Security hardware is required for both casement and double-hung windows, and in a growing market there are many options to suit particular needs and window designs. Some are combined with window opening and closing mechanisms, such as locking casement fasteners or locking sash window fasteners. Other hardware operates independently of the main hardware and represents a supplementary mechanism.

sliding sash window lock

sliding sash window bolt with plate casement

casement locking stay pin

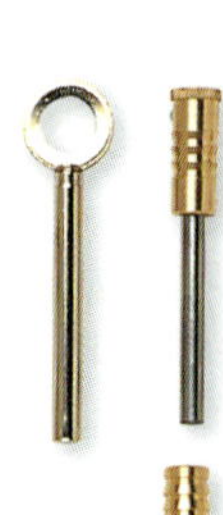

sliding sash window bolt

casement window lock (automatic locking)

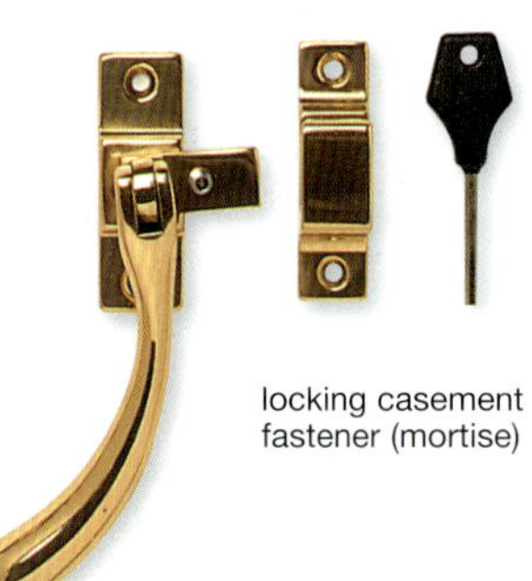

locking casement fastener (mortise)

locking casement fastener (wedge)

INSURANCE

It is worth bearing in mind that many insurance companies will specify the lock type to be used on windows and doors. You should therefore check your policy to see if there is any stipulation before going ahead and installing security systems.

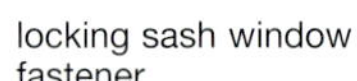

locking sash window fastener

casement window lock

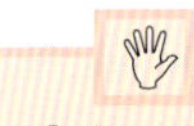

safety advice

Make sure that all members of the household know where window keys are kept. Ideally, there should be one in each room, since in the event of an emergency, quick access may be vital.

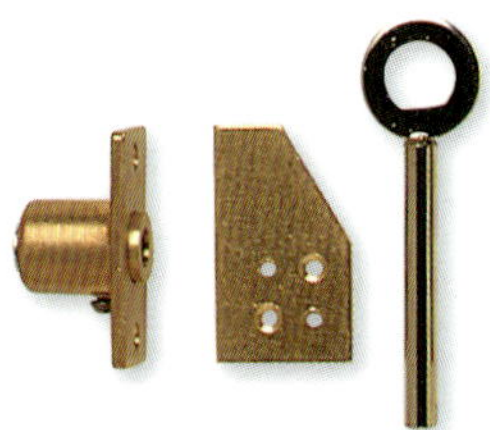

sash window stop

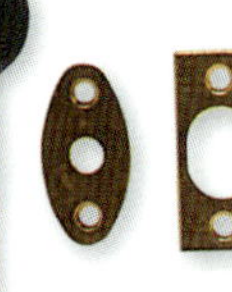

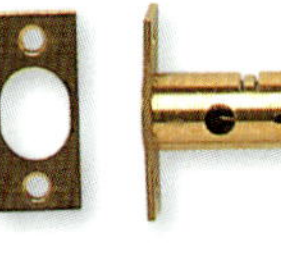

mortise window bolt

casement hardware

Casement hardware is based on fasteners and stays, primarily because these are the tried and true mechanisms for both closing and opening windows and allowing them to be opened and locked at a certain distance. Trickle vents are also now installed in new windows to increase room ventilation. When choosing window hardware, make sure that the dimension of window rails is suitable for the hardware you choose, as the size of the fixing plate for fasteners and stays does vary.

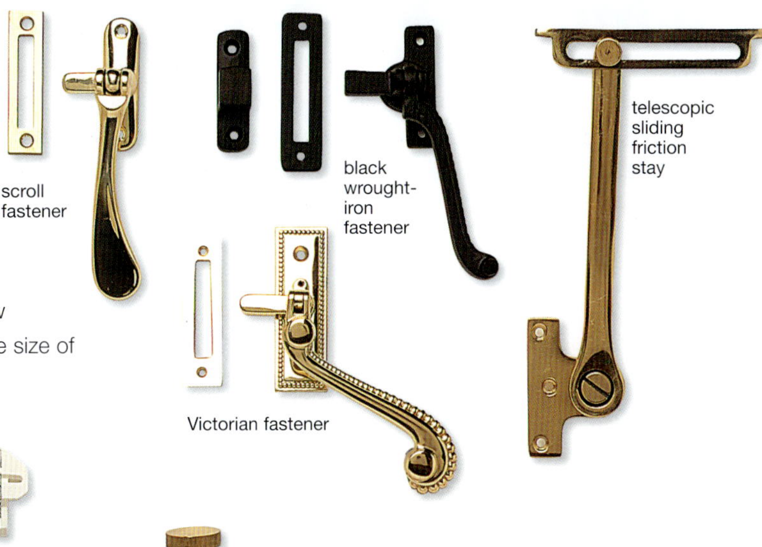
scroll fastener
black wrought-iron fastener
telescopic sliding friction stay
Victorian fastener

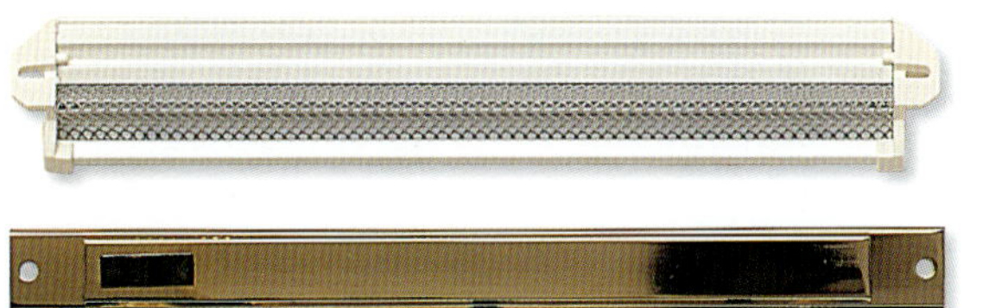
trickle vent

screw stay for casements

black wrought-iron stay and pins

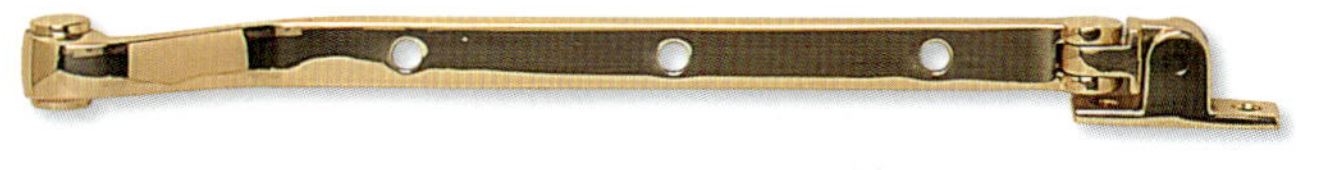
brass casement stay and pins

sash hardware

Sash hardware has to operate in a completely different fashion to casement equivalents, as the opening and closing mechanism for the window is very different. Since the distance a double-hung window can be opened is secured in position by the sash cord balance mechanism, the main function of such hardware is to fasten the window when shut, or to provide an area to grip onto for opening or closing. There is a wide selection of options available.

sash lift

sash eye

sash pulley with nylon wheel

sash lifting handle

ring sash lift

FANLIGHTS

Fanlights require a catch mechanism similar to sashes, and this has no involvement in the distance a window stays open. These catches normally fall into two categories:

fanlight—catch plate

fanlight—catch box

sash stop

sash fastener—unsprung

sash fastener—fitch

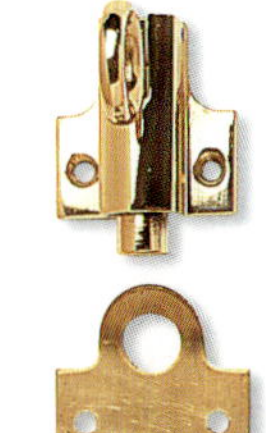
sash fastener—quadrant arm

installing a window—1

Replacing an old window with a new one is a two-part process of removal followed by installation. Always check that the new window is the right size before you remove the old one, or you have to board up the opening temporarily.

window removal

Removing a window is the most arduous part of the project. Before starting work it is best to check the weather forecast, since opening your home to the elements is an inescapable consequence of window replacement. In this example, an old metal window is being removed from a brick wall. Wooden windows tend to be much simpler to remove, since they can be sawn or cut out much more easily than metal, which requires the use of heavy-duty cutting equipment. However, in both cases the aim must be to remove the entire existing window and frame.

tools for the job

- protective equipment
- grinder
- hammer
- old chisel or screwdriver
- nail set
- hacksaw
- pry bar
- dusting brush

1 Remove any opening casements from the window. On wooden windows, this can be achieved by unscrewing the hinges to release the casements. On metal windows, the hinges are normally on the exterior and cannot be undone in the same manner as for wooden ones—they must be physically cut away from the main frame. The best tool for this is a grinder, whose rotating blade can be used to cut though the metal hinge. Grinders can be rented quite cheaply from your local rental store. Follow all the manufacturer's instructions and guidelines for use.

2 Once all opening casements have been removed, apply masking tape over the glass in the remaining fastened casements. Proceed to remove the glass panes by initially knocking away any loose putty around the edges of the panes, using a hammer and old chisel or screwdriver. At the same time, you should be looking for the screw or bolt heads on the horizontal rails that join the various sections of the metal window. Look for screws on the outer side of the window frame as well—these are for attachment to the wall surface. Generally, most of the glass has to be removed to expose these fastening points.

3 When fastenings are found, use a hammer and nail set to punch the screw or bolt out of the frame. A few firm taps with the hammer should loosen it.

4 Once the head of the screw or bolt is exposed, it can be easier to use the claw of the hammer to pry it out of the frame. Alternatively, you can use the claw end of a pry bar to do this.

5 Almost invariably, the fastenings around the edge of the window, which are attached to the wall, are not so easy to shift. This is mainly because they are longer and more heavy-duty in order to secure the

window in place. You may therefore need to use a grinder to cut off the screw or bolt heads. Once the heads are off, a few hits with a hammer and nail set on the fasteners should free them from the frame, releasing the window edge from a fastened position.

6 The fastened sections of the window may be further broken down by once more using the grinder to cut through the uprights of the vertical rails.

7 If vibration of the rail or window unit as a whole becomes too intense to make use of the grinder effective, it may be easier to finish these cuts using a normal hacksaw.

8 The removal of the fastenings in the horizontal part of the window frame, combined with the cuts in the vertical framework, now makes it possible to pull the sections of the window frame apart. A pry bar is the ideal tool to help with this job of separation.

9 Once the central areas have been broken down, it now becomes easier to pry the frame away from the surround of the window. Again, a pry bar is ideal for this job. You may find frame fasteners that you missed during the initial removal process. Simply use the grinder to remove screw or bolt heads as necessary and pull the frame from the wall surface.

10 Check around the edge of the window opening to be sure that no remnants of frame fasteners are still attached. Remove with a claw hammer, at the same time taking care not to cause damage to the surface of the surround. Any fasteners that might remove large portions of masonry when pried out should be removed using the grinder instead.

11 Once the entire window framework has been removed and the opening is totally clear, brush and then dust around the entire frame to remove any debris and loose material. A standard painter's dust brush may be used to provide a clean surface for the installation of the new window.

safety advice

Taking out windows requires caution, as some glass will almost certainly be broken. Wear gloves and goggles for protection against glass and other flying debris. Also, hang a dust barrier close to the window inside the house to keep mess to a minimum, and always make sure to tidy away any broken glass as soon as possible, both inside and outside.

installing a window—2

Whether you have masonry (shown here) or stud walls, installing wooden or vinyl windows is very similar. The most important part of installation is to make sure that the new window is positioned in exactly the same place as the old one.

installing a vinyl window

In houses that have cavity walls, it may be necessary to renew the foundation coating around the edge of the window opening before installing the new window. You may also need to attach the windowsill to the new window frame before you attempt installation.

tools for the job

- level
- cordless drill/driver
- caulk gun
- hammer
- mini hacksaw

1 Windows will almost certainly be supplied covered with protective tape to prevent any damage in transit and prior to installation. This can be removed either before or after the window is fitted—the protective layers should simply peel away from the main vinyl frame.

2 Position the window in the opening and use a level to be sure it is vertical and horizontal. For large windows two people may be required for this process, with one checking the level while the other makes minor adjustments. Once you are satisfied that the positioning is correct, use small shims to hold the window in place.

3 Secure the window in position with frame fasteners that will penetrate at least 1½in into the surrounding brick, block, or stone. Drill a pilot hole for the fasteners directly through the window frame, using the correct size of drill bit.

4 Insert the frame fastener and, using a caulk gun, place a dab of silicone in the fastener hole—this will provide a seal once the fastener has been secured in place. Frame fasteners will normally require one or two blows with a hammer to position them in the hole. Stop using the hammer once the wall plug is level with the surrounding frame.

5 Drive the screw into place, making sure that the thread bites firmly into the wall plug and therefore the wall surface. Be careful not to overtighten the screw because this can cause the frame to bow and distort its shape. As you apply more frame fasteners, keep checking with the level that the window has not moved out of place—it must be maintained in a vertical position.

6 Once all frame fasteners have been inserted, if the glazing is in place, proceed to step 8. Otherwise, you can begin installing the glazing now. This will generally require the use of packers in the rabbets of each

casement. These will be supplied with the window and should be positioned as the manufacturer's guidelines.

7 With packers in place, the glazed units can be slotted into place. A little pressure is often required to position the units. Also, if the unit has integral glazing bars, as the example here shows, be sure that they are straight. Snap the interior glazing beads into position once you are happy with the positioning of the glazed unit.

8 Once the whole window is glazed, it is necessary to deal with the junction between the window frame and masonry. To hide any rough edges, apply a bead of silicone around the sides of the frame, and press a vinyl cover strip along the bead to secure it firmly in place. Cut the vinyl cover strips to size using a mini hacksaw. Fill the recesses inside the house with a bead of silicone around the frame.

9 Some windows may have drainage holes to let out any moisture from around the frame. Caps can be snapped in position on these holes to provide a more attractive finish to the window frame.

10 Finally, seal around the outer edge of the window frame and cover strips with a further bead of silicone sealant. The surface of masonry is generally undulating, so it can be difficult to maintain an even and continuous line of sealant. The process can be aided by ensuring that the nozzle of the sealant tube is cut to the correct size, and if possible you can use painter's tape to prevent excess sealant from spreading across the frame or masonry surface. Take plenty of time for this task, as it affects the finished look of the window.

Vinyl windows are a practical alternative to traditional wooden varieties, and since they are maintenance-free, they have become a good option for many homeowners.

measuring & cutting glass

In most cases, it is advisable, and often more convenient, to have glass cut by a supplier, especially if a considerable number of panes are required. Some varieties of glass, such as tempered or laminated, should always be cut by a professional. However, situations may arise where it is necessary to make glass cuts of your own, so it is important to understand the right principles and techniques for carrying out this procedure.

measuring glass

It is vital that any measurements you take are extremely accurate, since glass has no flexibility and cannot easily be trimmed to size. Nor is it possible to join glass if a mistake in measurement has been made. A few simple guidelines must therefore be followed when obtaining measurements for cutting needs.

Bear in mind that glass is always bedded into a window or door frame, whether this be into putty or silicone (vinyl windows are clearly excluded from this category). Any measurement must therefore leave a $^{1}/_{16}$in tolerance around the edge of the glass for this purpose. In openings that have never been glazed, it is a simple case of measuring dimensions and subtracting the tolerance allowance.

For old windows where a cracked pane may need replacing, measurement is made more difficult since putty may obscure the exact edge of the opening, and therefore some estimation is required for accuracy. It is also worth remembering that, in older windows especially, the frame or apertures may not be totally square, so be sure to measure all the separate dimensions in order to reach the correct size requirements.

Since accuracy is so important, take extra care when measuring glass requirements and double-check everything before any cut is made. Some extra vigilance at this stage may save a great deal of time later in the project.

tools for the job

- cutting board
- felt tip or china marker
- combination square
- standard glass cutter
- circular glass cutter
- tape measure
- scissors

cutting a simple pane

Cutting down a large pane of standard clear glass to a smaller size is a very straightforward process, provided you use a good-quality glass cutter. Make sure that you have a firm, totally flat surface to work on—a piece of MDF board is ideal.

1 Use a felt tip or china marker to mark the dimensions of the cut on the glass. A simple mark on the edge of the glass is all that is required, and always double-check the measurement—mistakes cannot be rectified. A combination square is an accurate measuring tool.

2 Holding a straightedge across the pane—again a combination square is an ideal tool here—score the surface of the glass with a glass cutter. Score the surface only once, making a precise line from one edge of the pane to the other.

3 Wear goggles during the cutting process to protect against flying splinters of glass. Pick up the pane and position it on top of the combination square, so that the scored line runs precisely along the edge of the rule of the square. Apply downward pressure to either side of the scored line, causing the glass to crack precisely along the line. The pane is now ready for installation.

safety advice

Handling glass can cause severe personal injury and requires extreme caution. When working with glass, be sure to observe safety precautions and wear protective equipment when necessary.

cutting circles

A circular cut can often be required in such instances as vent installation in a window pane. Although this may sound difficult, cutting a circle uses the same principles as for cutting a straight line, except that the type of glass cutter used is slightly different. To achieve a circle, the head of the cutter needs to be fixed at a right angle to the shaft, and there must also be a suction cup on the other end of the glass cutter to secure and pivot the cutter when in use.

1 Measure the radius requirement of the circular hole and transfer it to the glass cutter. It will be possible to adjust the position of the suction cup accordingly before securing it in place at the position required on the glass.

2 Secure the cup in the center of the pane and carefully rotate the cutter around this position to provide a scored outline. Again, this should only be done once, applying even and constant pressure to the glass cutter head. You may also need to apply downward pressure to secure the suction cup in position.

3 Fasten the glass cutter head into a position perpendicular to the shaft, and make further scores in the glass surface inside the bounds of the scored circular guideline.

4 The scored glass circle will rarely come free in a single piece, so weaken the glass further, enabling it to be removed in smaller pieces. To do so, use the butt end of the glass cutter and tap in the central area until sections of glass begin to break free.

dealing with awkward shapes

The design of a window or door will sometimes demand glass panes of an irregular shape. This can make measurements for glass installation slightly more difficult. For such awkward shapes, the best technique is to make paper templates and then use them as a guide for cutting purposes.

1 Tape a piece of stiff paper or cardboard over the opening and draw a guideline around the edge of the opening to provide a replica of the required shape.

2 Cut out the shape accurately, making allowances for the glazing compound. Position the template in the frame opening to check that it fits. When correct, take the template to a glass supplier who will have the specialist equipment to make such a complex cut. Do not try to cut a shape like this yourself.

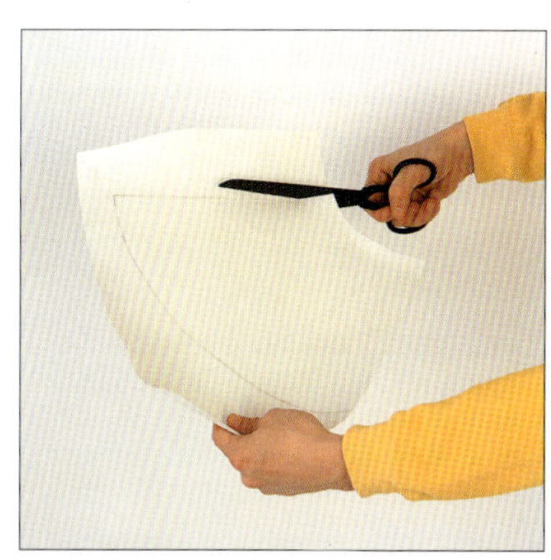

installing glass

Installing standard glass panes is a straightforward procedure which usually falls into one of two categories—installation that either uses putty or wooden beads. The former method is demonstrated in more detail on page 290, where a broken pane of glass is being replaced. The latter method is shown below and demonstrates the best technique for securing wooden beads.

safety advice

Take care to keep your hands away from the very edge of the glass as the edges are sharp and can cut you. Also, never apply pressure in the center of the pane when positioning it. Instead, keep to the face of the pane, but near the edges.

installing glass with beads

For new windows, manufacturers will often supply beads with the window, but in some cases you may have to cut your own. The essential point to remember is that the beads must have a chamfered edge, so that when they are positioned water is taken away from the glass surface and prevented from collecting on the window rabbets. Aside from this design necessity, the bead can be hardwood or softwood, which should generally be determined by the make-up of the window itself. Beads may also be used to secure double-glazed units into wooden frames or openings.

tools for the job

- tape measure
- caulk gun
- cloth
- miter saw
- hammer
- cardboard
- nail set

1 Even on a new window, check the dimensions of openings to ensure that they are square. On a window with multiple panes, it is often the case that not all will be of the same size. Often, those on the smaller opening casement are of a different size to the rest of the window, so be sure to check this situation before ordering or cutting glass. Once the

glass has been cut or supplied, check that the panes fit before proceeding any further.

2 With a caulk gun, run a bead of silicone around the complete rabbet of the opening. Make sure that the bead is continuous and there are no gaps. Silicone is supplied in a large range of colors—the clear variety is the most suitable for glazing purposes.

3 Take a pane of glass and position it in the opening, by firstly embedding the bottom edge of the pane in the silicone sealant along the bottom rabbet. From this starting

point, move your thumbs up the face of the pane, but close to its edges, gradually pressing it into place.

4 Carefully press the pane of glass in place, making sure that it fits correctly. Use a dry cloth to remove any excess silicone sealant.

tips of the trade

Silicone sealant is a notoriously sticky substance that can create a mess when an excessive amount is used. For large areas of overspill, use white spirit on a cloth to clean it away before it can dry.

5 Use a miter saw with a fine blade to trim any beading as necessary. Apply another bead of silicone around the glass opening rabbet, and position the first wooden bead along the bottom edge. Push the bead into position, so that its face is flush against the glass surface and its base is sitting level on the bottom wooden rabbet.

6 Secure the top wooden bead followed by the side ones. The side beads may be a slightly tight fit, and you might need to tap them in place using the butt end of a hammer. However, take care not to force the beads as this could crack the glass (if they are simply too tight, saw off a sliver and refit them). Once the beads are secured, use a cloth to remove any excess sealant from the glass.

7 The beads should be secured in place using some finish nails. Two on each bead is all that is required. Protect the glass surface from the edge of the hammer with a piece of cardboard.

8 Finally, be sure that the finish nails are level with the wooden bead surface by using a nail set for the final taps with the hammer.

prepainting

In the example shown here, a natural wood finish means that there is no need to think about paint when installing the glass. Where a window requires painting, it is worth considering painting the beads before installation to reduce the time otherwise taken to cut in paint next to the glass. It may also be advisable to paint the rabbets before glass insertion. Depending on the thickness of glass used, it may be possible to see the bare wood at the bottom of the rabbets through the edge of the glass once it has been installed. Painting the rabbets with the same color as the window can help to avoid such an unsightly edge to the finished product. Also, it is worth bearing in mind that paint will not adhere to silicone, so it may be worth prepainting the beads before application. This means that any overspill of silicone will not affect the finished look of the final painted surface.

Wooden beads create a neat finish for wooden windows, making a clear and defined line between glass and frame.

installing window hardware

Clearly, for windows to function correctly they require some sort of window hardware to operate the various opening and closing mechanisms. Some new windows come with window hardware installed, and there is the option to use these or to change them to suit your personal tastes. A large selection of different types is shown on pages 260–1, but always check the hardware before making your final selection, since not all window hardware is suitable for every type of window.

installing casement fasteners

Decide whether the fastener closes by means of a hook or mortise action. The former only requires surface mounting, whereas the latter needs to be cut into the window frame's central upright. This is shown below.

tools for the job

- awl
- screwdriver
- utility knife
- chisel

1 Old hardware or, as in this case, the window hardware supplied with the new window, may simply be unscrewed and set aside before installing new hardware. Hold the arm of the new fastener in the center of the vertical casement rail. Use a pencil to mark through the screw holes onto the wood below. The height up the window will depend on window design—at least halfway, but below two-thirds is generally suitable.

2 Use an awl to make pilot holes at the pencil marks, then screw the fastener arm into position. Use a handheld screwdriver, since a cordless driver has less control, and you risk allowing the driver head to slip off the head of the screw and scratch the brass fastener surface.

3 Bring the window to a closed position and hold the mortise plate of the fastener in place on the vertical casement frame. Position it so you can tell that the fastener arm will be able to close into the mortise, once the frame has been chiseled out. Draw around the plate with a sharp pencil, making sure that the plate is in a vertical position.

4 Cut around the pencil guideline with a utility knife, taking care not to allow the blade to slip. Cut to a depth equal to that of the fastener mortise plate. Use a chisel carefully to remove wood down to the depth of the mortise plate. This should be easily achieved by hand and not require the services of a hammer. Then hold the plate in place and draw a guideline inside the central area of the plate. Remove it once more and chisel the area out down to a depth that will allow the insertion of the fastener arm end.

5 Finally, place the mortise plate back in position, use an awl to make pilot holes once again, and screw it in securely.

hook fasteners

The main alternative to using mortise fasteners is to use hook fasteners. A similar technique is used to fit hook fasteners, except that the hook point of the fastener is surface-mounted and does not need to be cut into the casement surface, unless the fastener design requires it to be the case. It is still important to position the hook point vertically on the central part of the casement frame and check that the fastener will close securely before screwing the hook point in place.

attaching stays and pins

As well as fasteners, most casements require stays to complete the opening and closing mechanism. Again, old or unwanted new window hardware should be removed, so that chosen stays and pins may be added.

tools for the job

- pencil
- awl
- screwdriver
- cordless drill/driver

1 Close the window, securing it in place with the fitted fastener. Hold the stay in place along the bottom rail of the casement, marking the rail with a pencil through the screw holes in the stay securing plate.

2 Use an awl to make pilot holes and then screw the stay in place, again by hand rather than cordless driver to avoid the risk of scratching the stay surface.

Mark the positions of the stay pins with a pencil. It may be necessary to hold the stay in a closed position to find the exact location required for fastening the pins in the correct place.

3 Make pilot holes at the pencil marks using an awl or fine drill bit as shown here. Screw the pins in position by hand and check the completed opening and closing mechanism of the window. It is still possible, even at this late stage, to adjust the pin position slightly to make sure that the stay closes onto the pins securely.

Although window hardware has a primarily functional role, it can also add a decorative edge to the finished look of a window.

adding security locks

Security locks are additional window hardware, yet they are as important as the usual opening and closing mechanisms. Issues of security should be considered for all varieties of window, not simply wooden casement windows (shown here). Again, there is a wide selection of locks, and you should choose according to the design of your windows and the finish of the other window hardware.

adding casement locks

Some casement fasteners are supplied with an integral locking system (see page 261), but whether or not your windows have these, casement locks further enhance the overall security setup. Normally, two casement locks should be attached to each casement, with one at the bottom and one at the top of the vertical rail.

tools for the job

- awl
- cordless drill/driver
- screwdriver

1 Hold the two sections of the lock mechanism in place on the window casement and frame. Use an awl to mark the fixing points for the lock on the casement.

2 Use a cordless drill to drill pilot holes accurately in the casement. Ensure that the drill bit used is smaller than the diameter of the screw shafts used for fitting the casement lock.

3 Screw the first part of the lock in position on the opening casement. Use a handheld screwdriver to provide better control than the cordless driver equivalent and reduce the risk of scratching the lock fastening.

4 Hold the second part of the casement lock in position on the vertical rail of the frame. Check its correct position by opening and closing the lock and, using an awl to mark its position, drill pilot holes and screw the plate in place.

5 Finally, shut the window and use the supplied lock key to check that it closes correctly. Employ the same procedure to attach a further casement lock at the top level of the window.

installing stay locks

There are many different designs of stay lock available today, but one of the more common and most simple to fit is one that involves locking pins. In this situation, the original pins are being replaced by locking varieties, thus making the window more secure once it has been shut and locked.

tools for the job

awl

screwdriver

1 Release the stay from its closed position and unscrew the pins.

2 Hold the new locking pins in place and use an awl to mark new holes if necessary.

3 Screw the locking pins in place, making sure they are secured firmly in position on the frame.

4 Close the stay and screw the locking barrels onto the threaded pins, securing them in place with the key supplied. These barrels will now rotate in position, unless a key is used to release them.

Vinyl windows

Vinyl windows are usually supplied with both the standard hardware and security mechanisms built into the window design. Most vinyl windows have locking fasteners, which in many designs have a number of locking points around the edge of any opening casements. These points are released or locked by the handle opening mechanism. So although security is, in general, already taken care of with vinyl windows, there are few, if any, alternatives for changing window hardware after initial installation.

sash windows & security

Most sash window fittings have security built into their design, as demonstrated by the variety of fasteners and options shown on page 261. However, the illustration below helps to demonstrate how sash window fasteners act together to form a security system aimed at preventing or discouraging forced entry.

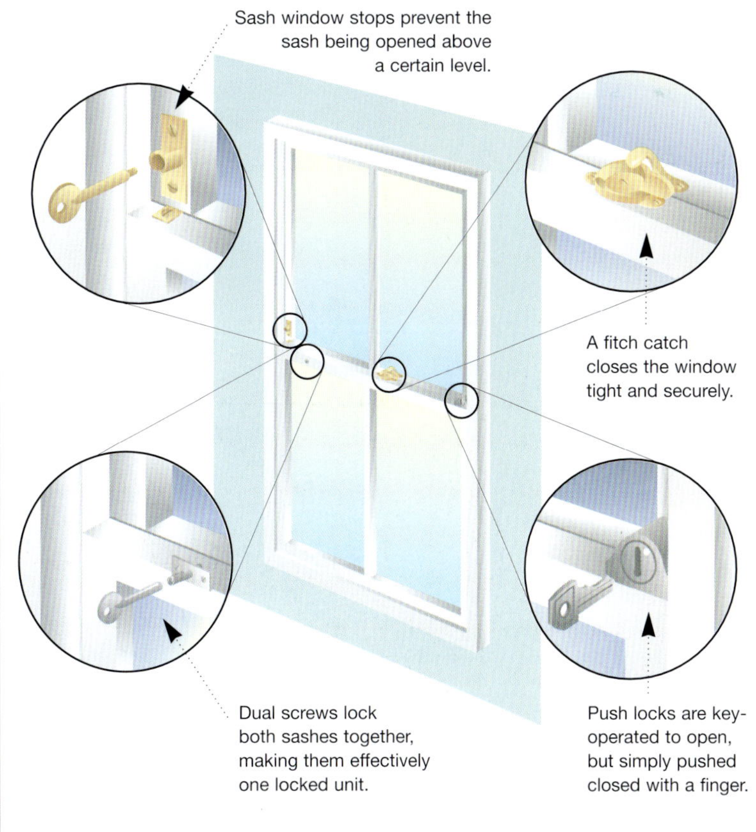

insulating windows

The most effective form of window insulation is clearly to choose the vinyl option and have new window units installed. In many cases, however, this can prove too expensive, and other ideas need to be considered when looking at the best way of improving insulation in your home. Fitting a further window layer or insulation barrier to an existing window offers a cheaper form of insulation than full double-glazing, and is therefore often referred to as secondary double-glazing.

adding secondary double-glazing—sliding sashes

Sliding secondary double-glazing tends to be installed in window recesses, and its design still allows access to the main window so that it may be opened and closed as required. These units tend to be supplied in a kit form by manufacturers, which is then cut to size and installed to your particular requirements.

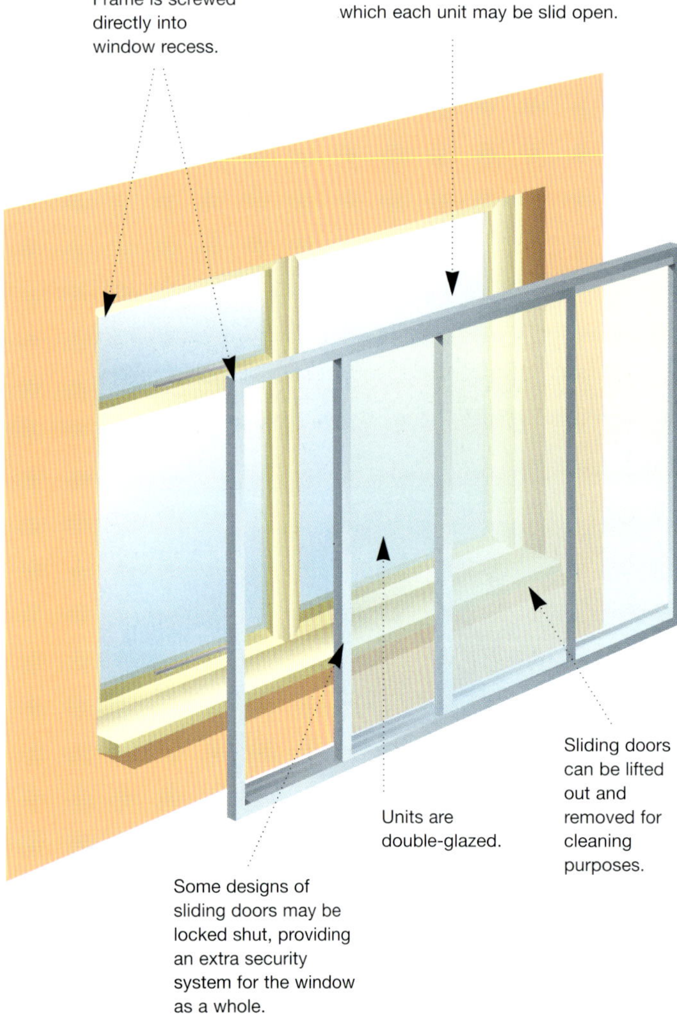

OTHER INSULATION OPTIONS

- **Polyethylene sheets**—One of the most economical ways of providing insulation is to use thin polyethylene sheets, secured across the window or recess. This can be bought in kit form, and the sheet is initially secured around the window frame with tape. A hairdryer is then directed at the sheet, which tightens the polyethylene and provides an insulating barrier. The obvious drawback is that it is not possible to get to the window without breaking the sheet of polyethylene, but as a seasonal option or for windows that are rarely opened or do not open, this easy method is ideal.

- **Double-glazed panes**—On existing wooden windows, insulation may be improved by replacing the panes of glass with double-glazed units. Since these units are much thicker than normal panes, it is important first of all to check that the rabbets of the windows are large enough to house the panes.

- **Weather stripping**—Another, very economical option for existing windows is to use one of the many freely available designs of weather stripping. Different manufacturers provide different products and designs. The two most common systems are self-adhesive foam-based strips, or more substantial plastic brush strips. The latter are mitered at the corners of the frame and fastened in place using finish nails. Different designs are suited to different types of windows.

A simpler system than the sliding doors can be found by using single acrylic sheets fastened across the entire window surface. This provides an effective insulating system, which is much simpler to fit than the sliding sash mechanism shown opposite. Access is also possible in terms of opening windows if required. This is a cost-effective and simple option that can either be applied on a seasonal basis or on windows that do not require frequent opening.

tools for the job

- tape measure
- mini hacksaw
- utility knife
- screwdriver

1 Accurately measure the dimensions of the whole window frame, as these will form the measurements for the plastic retaining track used to hold the acrylic sheet in place. In this instance the sheet is being fitted directly onto the window frame inside the recess, but it may also be fitted on the wall surface outside, thus covering the whole recess. Before adding the secondary double-glazing, it is worth cleaning the window on both the inside and outside, since access is more limited once the acrylic glazing sheet is positioned.

2 Cut the track to size with a mini hacksaw or utility knife, mitering the ends to form neat joints in each corner of the window. Remove the backing of the adhesive tape on the back of the track.

3 Press the track firmly in position on the window frame, making sure there is good contact between the tape and frame surface. There is normally a short period of time before the adhesive secures the track permanently in position, so minor movements or adjustments should be made quickly.

4 Once the track is in position all around the frame, carefully pry it open. A screwdriver may be needed to help open up the track initially, but once it has opened it can normally be finished by hand. Measure the exact dimensions of width and height required for the glazing sheet. Transfer the measurements onto the acrylic sheet and use a mini hacksaw to cut it to the required size.

5 Insert the glazing sheet into the retaining track, sliding it carefully into position. Again, it is worth cleaning the sheet before positioning it, since access is limited to the inside face once it is fastened in place.

6 Finally, snap the retaining track closed onto the acrylic surface, creating effective insulation.

repairing doors & windows

Doors and windows are expensive yet essential elements in the makeup of your home, and therefore need to be looked after to as great a degree as possible. You must understand how normal issues of wear and tear affect doors and windows in order to determine how problems occur and which are the best techniques for repair and restoration. Many of these problems are simple and fall into the category of nothing more than general servicing to make sure doors and windows continue to function well. However, other repairs may be more extensive, requiring more detailed measures when it comes to restoration. The following chapter covers a wide range of topics in this area, and helps to demonstrate the best and most suitable techniques for dealing with the most commonly occurring problems.

These window panes feature a small section of stained glass, which adds to the finish of the bathroom.

recognizing problems

An accurate diagnosis is the first step to addressing any problems with windows and doors. Because they almost always include an opening and closing function and mechanism, many of their problems relate to the various ways in which this function is either hindered or prevented. Although many problems are caused by general wear and tear affecting all types of doors and windows, most problems occur in those that are constructed from wood.

problem areas on doors

There are a number of areas on doors where problems may occur, with some being far more serious and more difficult to fix than others. This example shows many of the areas and points where problems may occur.

CAUTION

- **General sticking**—Sometimes sticking doors can point to more serious problems, as wall subsidence may knock a door frame out of line, creating a misshapen opening for the door to close into. If in any doubt, therefore, seek professional advice on this matter, but remember that this sort of problem is relatively rare, and sticking doors are more likely to result from the other explanations provided.

- **Warping doors**—This can occur with relatively cheap doors soon after installation. To avoid it happening, be sure that the doors are stored flat before installation and are left in the room they are to be put in for a number of days before being hung. This enables them to get used to the prevailing atmospheric conditions.

- **Sticking latch**—Gradual movement over time, or an old door which has slowly been planed and planed to fit the frame, may eventually reach a point where planing cannot continue because the latch plate is raised above the door edge. It is therefore necessary to recess the latch plate further into the door edge.

- **Hinge bound**—Where hinges have not been recessed into the door jamb and/or door edge, a situation arises where the door is unable to close onto the doorstop. As a result, pressure is put upon the hinges, which may eventually cause the door jamb or door edge to split or damage. Resetting the hinge position is therefore necessary.

problem areas on casement windows

Due to the fact that casement windows work on a hinge mechanism, many of their problems can be seen as similar to those suffered by doors. The reasons for sticking casements are therefore often similar to those given for doors. However, windows will always have an exterior aspect, and the diagram below illustrates some other problems that may occur.

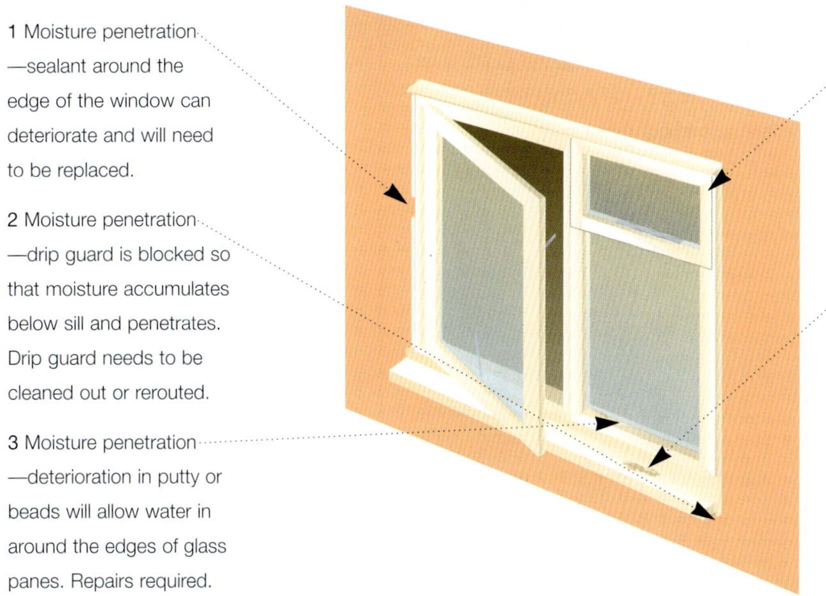

1 Moisture penetration—sealant around the edge of the window can deteriorate and will need to be replaced.

2 Moisture penetration—drip guard is blocked so that moisture accumulates below sill and penetrates. Drip guard needs to be cleaned out or rerouted.

3 Moisture penetration—deterioration in putty or beads will allow water in around the edges of glass panes. Repairs required.

Sticking casements can be caused by paint buildup or swelling during damp conditions, or sometimes hinging problems. Normally a little planing will fix the problem, but in some cases rehinging will be required.

Sometimes moisture and/or insect attack can cause problems with wooden windows. If caught early enough, small, localized areas can be treated, filled, or partially replaced with new wood. Failure to carry out repairs quickly may lead to total window replacement being necessary.

problem areas on double-hung windows

Many of the problems found with double-hung windows are the same as those illustrated for casement windows. In other words, dry rot and moisture problems are just as likely to occur. However, there are some other problems that relate specifically to double-hung windows, as shown in the illustration below.

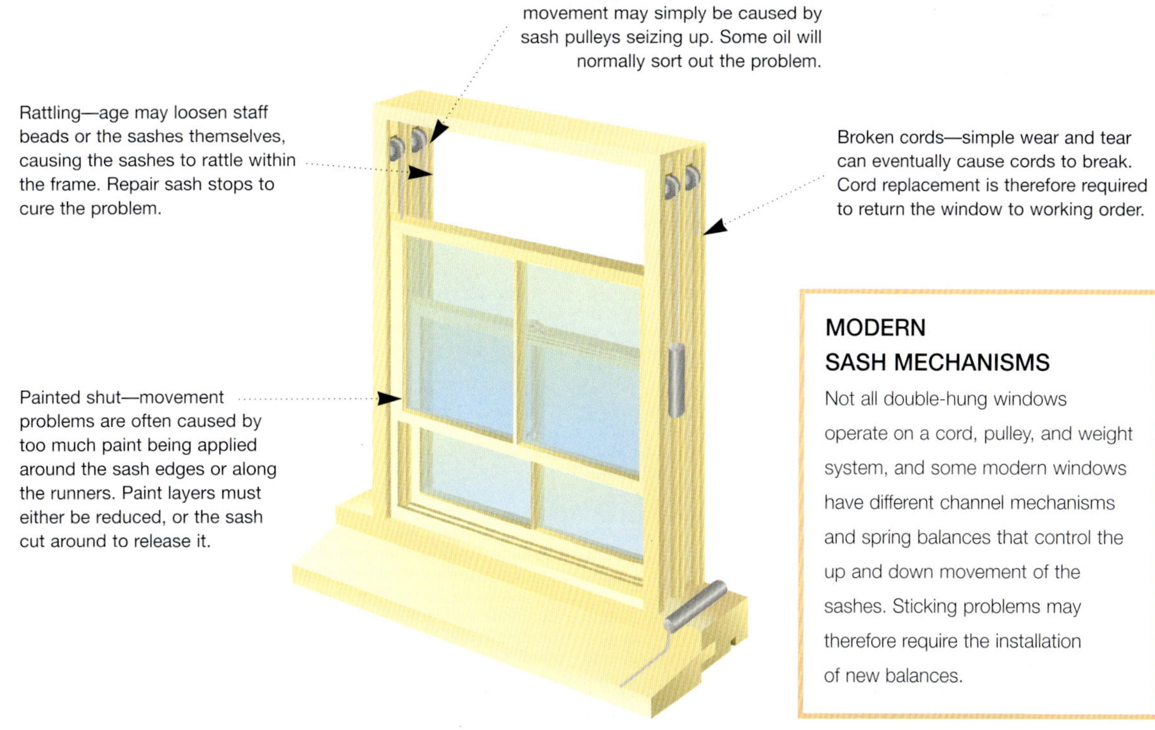

Pulley problems—hindered sash movement may simply be caused by sash pulleys seizing up. Some oil will normally sort out the problem.

Rattling—age may loosen staff beads or the sashes themselves, causing the sashes to rattle within the frame. Repair sash stops to cure the problem.

Broken cords—simple wear and tear can eventually cause cords to break. Cord replacement is therefore required to return the window to working order.

Painted shut—movement problems are often caused by too much paint being applied around the sash edges or along the runners. Paint layers must either be reduced, or the sash cut around to release it.

MODERN SASH MECHANISMS

Not all double-hung windows operate on a cord, pulley, and weight system, and some modern windows have different channel mechanisms and spring balances that control the up and down movement of the sashes. Sticking problems may therefore require the installation of new balances.

releasing sticking doors & windows

Once diagnosed, sorting out window and door sticking problems becomes the comparatively straightforward task of choosing the right technique to deal with the particular problem at hand. As in all instances, it is best to start by trying easy cures before moving on to more complicated ones.

simple solutions

With sticking doors, especially along the sides, it is best to begin by trying the simpler solutions before taking more dramatic action, which may entail extensive wood removal from the door edge. Sometimes the slight seasonal changes in response to atmospheric conditions can cause minimal expansion and contraction of door surfaces, and minimal easing is all that is required.

tools for the job

- candle
- sandpaper or sanding block
- wood plane
- jigsaw
- utility knife

1 Rub a candle down the leading edge of the door. Sometimes, this small transfer of wax to the door edge can help to ease its operation, allowing the door to open and close more easily.

2 If this does not work, use sandpaper or a sanding block down the edge—use the rough side of the block and then the smooth side.

3 If still more easing is required, resort to using a wood plane and gradually shave off sections of wood along the door edge. Take care not to work all along the door edge as it may only be sticking in one localized area. It is normally possible to see where the door is sticking by closing it and making a mark with a pencil to show the obstructing areas.

4 Set the plane so that only small amounts of wood are shaved off each time. Keep opening and closing the door to monitor the situation until ease of function is restored. The door edge may then be repainted.

tips of the trade

Sometimes paint buildup on a door edge must be reduced to help the opening and closing of the door. A heat gun can be used to remove excess paint initially, before employing a wood plane to smooth the surface. Paint may otherwise clog up the workings and blade of the plane, making it difficult to move along the door edge, so removing the paint first is a good option. Remember when using heat guns to adhere to all safety rules and guidelines, and never to leave a heat gun unattended when switched on.

bottom of door sticking

When a door is sticking at the bottom it is best to use a scribing technique to measure how much wood needs to be removed. Put the door in a closed position. Cut a block of wood with a height equal to the required clearance between the bottom of the door and the floor. Hold a pencil tight on top of the block, with its point resting on the block edge. Draw the block and pencil along the floor surface at the base of the door, leaving a pencil guideline along the bottom of the door. Remove the door from its hinges and trim to this guideline. For small cuts, a wood plane may be used. For larger sections, a jigsaw is the ideal tool. Once the wood has been removed, reseal the bottom edge of the door.

sash sticking

Sticking sashes is a common problem, and before attempting to take any mechanisms apart it is worth checking whether the window has simply been painted shut.

If a window has been painted without allowing any movement of the sashes, it is likely that as the paint dries it will form a bond between the sashes and runners and therefore prevent the window from being opened. To cure this situation, simply use a utility knife to run around the edge of the sash, thus breaking the bond or seal and freeing up the window so that it may freely be moved up and down once more.

door hardware

On occasion, the door hardware itself may be responsible for preventing doors from opening and closing easily. This is usually due to the latch mechanism sitting higher than the door edge and catching the door frame or catch plate as it closes.

tools for the job

screwdriver
chisel

1 Remove the door handles and unscrew the latch plate. With some latches this may be a two-stage process, with a second cover plate actually covering the main latch.

2 It can be tricky to pull the latch out of the door, for if it has been installed correctly it should be held tightly. Position a screwdriver where the door handle spindle would normally be, and pull on both the handle and the shaft of the screwdriver simultaneously, to pop the latch out of its recessed position.

3 Use a sharp chisel to remove more wood from the recess, gradually scraping the recess surface back and taking care not to remove too much wood. If a lot of wood removal is required, you will need to reposition the hole for the handle and lock, since any adjustment in latch plate position will push the handle position away from the door edge and across the door surface.

4 Once you are happy with the amount of wood removed, replace the latch and check that the door closes before putting it back in place. Remember that because the handle is not yet in position, once the door is shut it will not be possible to open it unless you have a flathead screwdriver available to insert into the latch and act as a temporary handle, while you check that the door opens and closes.

repairing loose doors & windows

As irritating as sticking doors or windows can be, there are also problems of equal inconvenience when doors or windows are loose and do not function properly. Whereas sticking problems tend to require removal of wood or recessing of hardware, loose doors or windows require the opposite remedy, with additional material needed to restore function.

adjusting a strike plate

As explained below, adding wood strips is an extreme measure, and, for a door that is loose, a simpler solution is to adjust the position of the strike plate. Bringing the plate fractionally away from the door frame is usually all that is needed to allow the latch to hold in position once the door is shut.

ADDING WOOD

Where there is a huge difference between the width of a door and its frame, there is clearly a need to actually add wood to the edges of the door. This situation may only arise in extreme circumstances, or where a door that is obviously too narrow is moved to fit into a wider frame. In these cases, it literally becomes a procedure of cutting strips to the depth and width requirement, and screwing them to the door edges. It may be necessary to screw strips to both edges to maintain the balanced look of the door, especially if it is a paneled design. For smaller additions, jointing on one side may be all that is required. If attempting this technique, remember that accuracy is vital in order to keep joints unnoticeable, and it is likely that the door will require a painted finish, because a natural wood coating may highlight the jointed strips and make the repair too obvious.

tools for the job

screwdriver
scissors
utility knife

1 Unscrew the strike plate from its fixed position. It may require a little persuasion by prying it free with the end of a flathead screwdriver.

2 On a piece of cardboard, draw a pencil guideline around the edge of the strike plate itself.

3 Cut out the strike plate template precisely using scissors, but do not worry about cutting away the extended front section, since this is an area which is not required when you fit the cardboard in the recess itself.

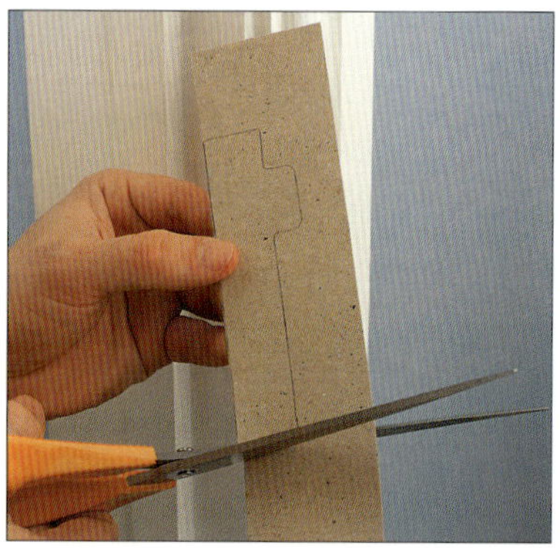

4 Position the cardboard template in the strike plate recess, trimming as necessary to make any final adjustments for fitting precisely and tightly in place.

5 Screw the catch plate back in place, through the template and into the screw fixing holes below.

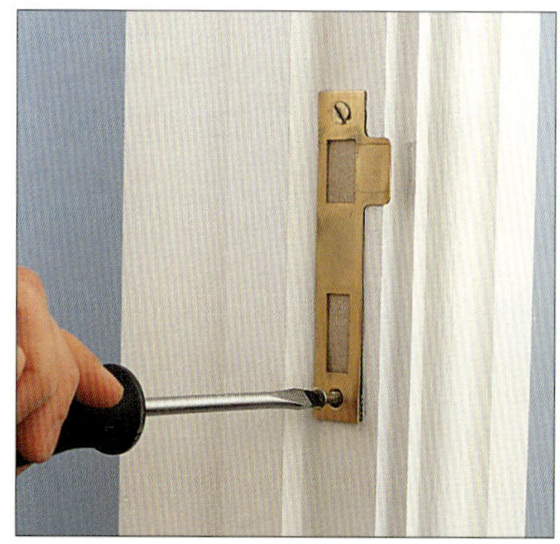

6 Use a utility knife to cut out the holes for housing the latch and lock. Try closing the door to see if the movement of the plate has affected the closed position. If the door is still loose, remove the strike plate and add a further piece of cardboard to increase the skimming. Continue to test until the door closes properly.

rattling doors

Rattling doors are another example of how a door may be loose-fitting, but in this case the door itself may be a perfect fit in terms of its position in the frame, with the actual problem relating to the position of the doorstop. In other words, the doorstop has been positioned too far from the latch, so that even small gusts of wind or drafts cause the door latch to rattle rather than being held firmly in place by the latch position and doorstop combined. Conversely, the door may not close properly because the doorstop is positioned too far forward or too close to the strike plate, and therefore the door cannot physically be shut in place. The remedy for this problem is fortunately very simple.

tools for the job

- old chisel
- pencil
- hammer

1 Remove the doorstop by carefully prying it out of position, using an old chisel to assist you.

2 Close the door and mark a line on the door jamb to show where the ideal position for the edge of the doorstop will be—one that allows the door to close tightly but easily. Simply reopen the door and nail the doorstop back in place according to the new guidelines.

It may also be necessary to move the doorstop on the head and hinged side of the frame, so check for this once the first piece of doorstop has been repositioned.

loose casements

The opening casements in windows may also rattle or become loose, often as a result of warping slightly or losing shape through age and weather attack. This situation may often be helped by adjusting the window closing mechanism and, more specifically, the position of the window stays. The fastening plate of a window stay is usually positioned closer to the hinging edge of the casement than the opening edge. This allows the window to be opened further. However, where a window has warped, by moving the fastening plate closer to the opening edge greater leverage is gained when closing the window, and therefore the stay helps to pull the casement back into shape.

tools for the job

- screwdriver
- awl or pencil
- cordless drill/driver

1 Unscrew the stay fastening plate from its position near the hinged edge of the casement.

2 Reposition it, using an awl or pencil to mark the new fastening position. Drill pilot holes and screw the stay in place. There is normally no need to reposition the stay pins.

repairing hinges

Many of the problems associated with doors and windows failing to open and close efficiently are caused by faulty hinging mechanisms, such as hinges not positioned correctly or not working in the appropriate manner. Outlined here are some common remedies for malfunctioning hinges on both doors, as shown, and casement windows.

tools for the job

- hammer
- utility knife
- screwdriver
- cordless drill/driver
- wooden mallet
- chisel
- pencil
- scissors
- saw
- wood plane

loosening stubborn screws

When dealing with hinge problems, the first obstacle to overcome can in fact be removing the screws from their position. When hinges have not been painted removal tends to be relatively simple, but for painted ones the process can be much more difficult.

1 Begin by using the head of a flat-head screwdriver to scrape out paint from the slot in the screwhead. A utility knife may also be used here.

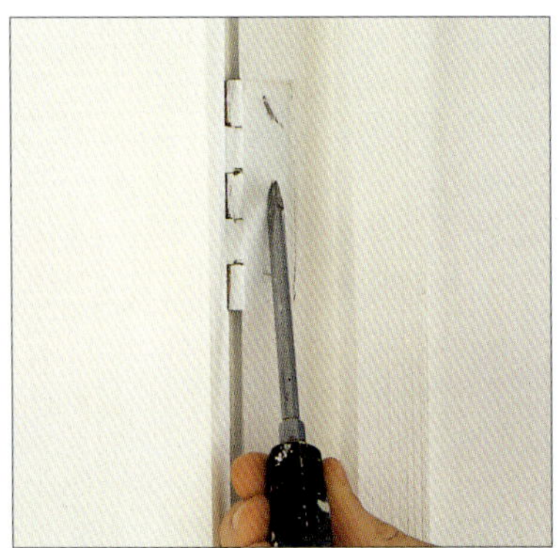

2 As further encouragement to moving the screws, give each one a few blows with a hammer on the screwdriver to dislodge it fractionally from its painted solid position. If the screwhead is too corroded to make undoing possible, it may be necessary to drill out the screw and use a new fastener.

strengthening a hinge

Through general wear and tear, hinges can become worn and their fasteners can loosen, which results in a door moving out of position in its frame. Retightening screws may fix this situation, but usually the holes have become too large for the screws to bite firmly. It is therefore necessary to fill the holes and drill new ones.

1 Remove the door from the frame. Make the existing screw holes much larger by using a large drill bit to bore into the door lining at each screw position. The size of the drill bit should be similar to that of the diameter of the wooden dowel which will be inserted into the holes.

2 Insert lengths of wooden dowel into the bored holes, making sure that the dowel is a tight fit. Apply some wood glue around the dowel before putting it in position.

3 Tap each dowel in place using a wooden mallet, tapping carefully until the dowel extends a good distance into the hole. Avoid using a hammer for this process, since it is likely to split the dowel. Use a cloth to wipe away any excess wood glue from around each dowel.

4 Leave the dowels to dry overnight so that they are glued firmly in position. Then, using a sharp chisel, cut off the dowel ends so that they are level with the surface of the door jamb.

5 Holding the hinge in position, use a pencil to mark the exact points for the screw fasteners. This stage is important if you have changed or renewed the door hinges.

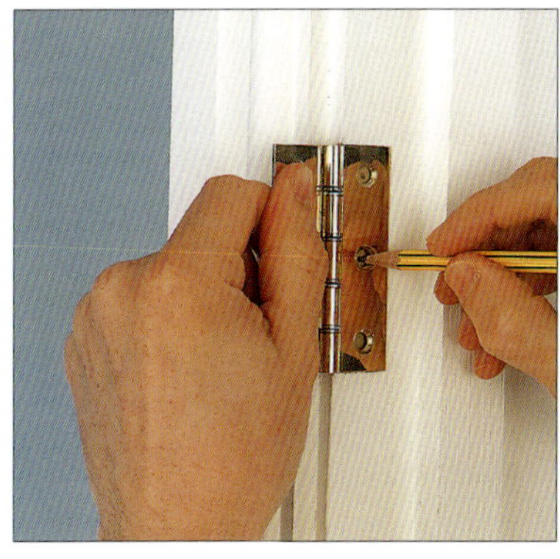

6 Using a fine bit, drill pilot holes at each newly marked position. Finally, reposition the hinges and rehang the door.

skimming a hinge

In a similar way to skimming a catch plate as shown on page 282, hinges may also be skimmed to adjust the door position to close more efficiently. Instead of introducing cardboard behind the strike plate, the hinges are removed and cardboard is positioned behind them.

1 Remove the door and hinges and cut some thick cardboard to the size of the hinge recess. Be as accurate as possible to be sure that the cardboard fits snugly into the hinge recess. Try adding different thicknesses to aid this process. As an alternative to cardboard, thin plywood may also be used.

2 Position the cardboard in the recess before screwing the hinges and door back in position. Test the door to see if closing has improved. If not, add more cardboard. You may find that the other hinge on the door will also require skimming.

patching a removed hinge

For many reasons a door may be removed from an entrance, or the side it hinges on the frame may be changed. Whatever the reason, the recesses of the old hinges in the door frame need to be repaired so that the frame may be painted. This is achieved by a simple patching technique that fills the recess and repairs the frame.

1 Having removed the hinge and cleaned up the hole with a chisel, cut a piece of softwood as close to the dimensions of the hinge recess as possible. Test it fits before applying some wood glue to it and positioning it in the frame.

2 Once the glue has dried, use a wood plane to smooth the surface of the patch and bring it level with the surrounding door frame. Finally, some fine filling may be required before repainting the area to blend in with the rest of the frame.

repairing double-hung windows—1

The opening mechanism of double-hung windows is based on a cord, pulley, and weight system, which balances the weight of the window as it is opened and closed. The repair process is fairly complex, but relatively simple to do if tasks are undertaken in the right order.

removing the sash & replacing the cord

The balance of a double-hung window is such that the frame really only acts as a guide for moving the sashes. The sashes themselves are free-running, using the pulley and cord mechanism as its only attachment to the frame as a whole. In other words, there is no solid or hinged attachment between a sash and the frame. However, releasing sashes from their operating position can be tricky.

tools for the job

old chisel or screwdriver
hammer

1 Pry the sash stop away from the main part of the frame using an old chisel or screwdriver. The stop is normally fastened with relatively small nails, so moving the position of the chisel up and down the junction should gradually loosen the fastenings and the stop can be removed. It is important to try not to damage the stop, which will be repositioned once the window repair is complete.

2 Remove the sash door that hides the weights inside the frame of the window. These are sometimes metal plates that unscrew, but in this case the door is made from a wooden panel. Again, use an old chisel or screwdriver to pry and ease the door out of the frame.

3 Pull the top of the weight from inside the frame and remove the broken section of sash cord. In some cases it may be necessary to reach down inside the frame to locate the weight.

4 Remove the sash from the frame, remembering that when you pull the side of the sash (with the damaged cord) away from the frame, the other side of the sash will still be attached to the frame. It can thus be tricky to move the sash into a position that is clear from the frame and allows access for repairs. It is best to maneuver the undamaged cord so that the sash can be rested on a workbench in front of the window.

5 With the sash out of the way, this is a good chance to service the pulley and confirm that it is in good working order. Apply oil to the pulley mechanism to be sure that its moving parts are lubricated.

6 Take a piece of string and tie it onto a nail. Instead of using a straight nail, ensure that the one you use is slightly curved. This can be achieved with a few hammer blows.

7 Holding the untied end of the string with one hand, thread the end with the curved nail over the pulley. If the nail does not go through on the first attempt, because it is still too straight—increase the curve of the nail until it threads through easily.

NEW SASH SYSTEMS

Double-hung window design has been varied slightly in modern times with the introduction of different mechanisms to balance the sashes, but the opening principle remains the same, with the sashes still sliding along runners. Modern double-hung windows have vinyl jambs for the runners and spring balances in place of the traditional mechanism, but cords and weights are still the most common sash-opening mechanism.

8 Once the nail appears in the hole revealed by the removal of the sash door, turn your attention to the other end of the string and tie a new section of sash cord to it.

9 Now thread the sash cord end, while tied to the string, over the pulley and into the window frame. It is important that the end of the cord is trimmed, because if it is in any way frayed it will be difficult to thread over the pulley mechanism.

10 Pull on the other end of the string (the end with the nail on it), thus pulling the cord down to the sash door hole. Once you can grab the end of the cord, pull it out from the hole and remove the string.

11 Thread the cord into the securing hole on the weight and tie it off tightly. Weight design will vary slightly, but generally the cord must be threaded through a hole in the top of the weight, pulled through a hole in the side of the weight, tied off and then pushed back into the side hole to wedge the knot in place.

12 In some cases, if the weight is designed to drop down into the window frame, it will be necessary to tie a knot at the other end of the cord to prevent the weight pulling it over the pulley and down into the window frame, which will oblige you to start the threading process again. Make a simple knot which can be untied easily when it is time to attach this end of the cord to the sash. Alternatively, tie off the cord onto a screwdriver, which may then be positioned next to the pulley and will prevent the cord pulling through.

repairing double-hung windows—2

With the sash removed and the new cord threaded over the pulley and into the frame, attention can be turned to reattaching the sash to the cord and getting it back into a running position. Once again, it is best to follow a particular order of tasks, so that the window is reassembled properly and runs smoothly.

tools for the job

needle-nose pliers
pencil
marking pen
scissors or utility knife
hammer
caulk gun

attaching the cord and replacing the sash

It may be worth checking the running mechanism of the other part of the sash window, to be sure that the interior parting stop allows the sash to run freely. If not, reposition it while the other sash is out of its place before tackling the broken sash.

1 Remove the remaining part of the broken sash cord. The method required will depend on the exact type of sash design. In this case, a pair of needle-nose pliers is ideal to pull the old knotted section of cord out of its position in the side of the sash. If the cord is nailed or stapled, use pliers or a claw hammer to pry out any fasteners.

2 Use a pencil to mark on the front of the sash (being repaired) the exact position of the cord-retaining hole located on the side of the sash.

3 Reposition the sash in the frame, so that it is in its totally open position, with the top of the sash up close to the pulley mechanism. Untie the new section of sash cord and hold it in the appropriate position, feeling the tension of the weight balance on the cord, and use a marking pen to mark on the cord next to the position of the cord-retaining hole (marked in step 2).

4 Pull the sash out of its position in the frame once more and thread the cord through the top of the sash and out through the cord-retaining hole, until you see the marked point on the cord. This task may be better suited to two people, so that one can take the weight of the sash window while the other threads the cord.

5 Tie a secure knot in the cord at the marked point and allow it to position itself inside the retaining hole. Check your measurements again before cutting off the excess cord with a pair of scissors or a utility knife, once the knot has been securely tied. Once again, two people may be required for this process, with one holding the sash window while the other ties off and cuts the cord.

6 Reposition the repaired sash back in the frame. Be sure that the running mechanism is working correctly by opening and closing the sash a few times, checking that the movement is smooth and that the window does not jam or become caught in the runners. It may sometimes be necessary to readjust the sash cord length slightly to reach optimum levels of movement.

7 Once you are happy with the smooth-running system, the sash door can be replaced. Wooden ones often simply be pushed back in position, and may require one or two taps with the butt end of a hammer. Take care not to damage the cover even though the fit may be tight, because making an exact replacement is a difficult task.

8 The sash stop may now be replaced in its original position and part-nailed in. This is a suitable time to test the running of the sash in relation to all the front sash stops. If the sash has tended to rattle, for example, it may be necessary to take out and move the stops slightly closer to the sash surface. Conversely, if the sash has generally been too tight in the runners, the stops may need to be moved away from the sash by a fractional amount. The stops can now be fully nailed in.

9 Finally, refill any nail holes in the sash stop with all-purpose filler and sand to a smooth finish once the filler has dried. Run a bead of flexible filler or caulk between the bead and the frame, and smooth with a wet finger before it dries. The window frame may now be repainted.

Double-hung windows are both attractive and efficient, as long as the running mechanism is kept in good order so it moves freely up and down.

replacing a broken pane

Broken panes are probably the most common window problems in most households. Correcting the situation comes down to a straightforward case of glass replacement, though the technique required for this task will be dependent on the way in which the glass pane is secured in the window. Glass is held in position by wooden beads or putty, which is demonstrated below.

tools for the job

- hammer & old chisel
- hacking knife
- pliers
- paintbrush
- putty knife
- tape measure
- protective gloves
- goggles

broken pane in a puttied window

1 Tape up the outside of the broken pane with painter's tape, keeping the tape only on the glass surface and not encroaching onto the putty or wooden frame of the window. Take care not to apply too much pressure on the glass surface and risk shattering the glass further at this preliminary stage.

2 On the inside of the broken pane, tape a folded plastic bag to the wooden rails of the window frame. Make a total seal around the edge of the tape, making certain that there are no gaps or holes. The bag will prevent glass splinters from being scattered inside the house when the old pane is removed.

3 From the outside of the window, use the butt end of a hammer to tap the glass pane, knocking it inward and allowing it to break away from the rabbets of the frame. Always wear protective goggles when carrying out this process to shield your eyes from any flying glass or debris.

4 Remove the largest sections of broken glass and place them in a bucket for safe disposal later. Some putty on the window rabbets may also come away during this process, and should also be disposed of. Remove only the loose material by hand and leave the more secure pieces until later.

5 Use a hacking knife to scrape around the edge of the window rabbets to remove any last pieces of glass and debris. If you do not have a hacking knife, a hammer and old chisel may be used to equally good effect. Remove old glazing points in the rabbets with a pair of pliers.

6 Remove the plastic bag and dust off the rabbet to remove any debris. Seal the surface by priming all the bare wood in the rabbet and on its

edges. Allow this to dry before continuing. The paint seals the surface and provides a base for the putty.

7 Apply a small amount of putty around the rabbet. Make sure that the putty has been well kneaded in your hands to mix it up and remove any lumps before application. The putty should have a similar texture to very pliable plasticine.

CHOOSING GLASS

Measuring size requirements is considered on pages 266–7, but it is also important to consider what frame the glass is being fitted into. Although the example here shows a window, a similar technique is used for doors. The glass used in doors, however, must be thicker, and sometimes tempered, compared to the thinner glass specified for windows. So whether cutting your own glass or leaving it to a supplier, remember to choose the correct thickness for the particular replacement pane required.

safety advice

Replacing a pane will require access to both the inside and outside of the window. Therefore if the window is higher than ground-floor level, be sure to use the appropriate access equipment for safe work on the exterior. Broken glass is extremely sharp and dangerous to handle, so wear protective gloves and goggles.

8 Press the glass into position in the frame, inserting the base first and applying pressure only near the edges of the pane. Allow the edges to become well embedded into the putty, squeezing excess out onto the interior rabbet.

9 Hammer a few glazing points into the rabbet, next to but not touching the glass surface. This prevents any possibility of the pane falling out before the putty dries. Use a piece of cardboard to protect the glass surface from the edge of the hammer during this process.

10 Apply another putty bead around the glass/frame junction. This bead should be of more generous proportions than the first, covering the entire rabbet area.

11 Use a putty knife to finish the putty surface. Rest the edge of the knife on the glass on one side and rabbet edge on the other. Applying a little pressure on the blade, drag the knife across the putty surface. It may take more than one run of the knife to achieve a smooth finish. Finally, trim any excess putty from the interior rabbet of the pane. Allow it to dry before repainting.

REPLACEMENT OPTIONS

For wooden beads, you need to remove the beads and broken glass before following installation guidelines as detailed on pages 268–9. Double-glazed units in wooden frames require a similar process, but seek professional advice if a pane or unit replacement is required for vinyl windows.

restoring leaded lights

Leaded lights usually involve different-colored glass being used in a pattern. Some windows may be composed entirely of leaded lights, while others have sections. Repairing broken panes is an exacting job, which in some cases is best left to the professionals. However, as long as there is easy access to the damaged area, it is more than possible to make the repair yourself. If it's feasible, remove the damaged casement section first so that it can be treated on a flat surface.

repairing hairline cracks and leaking panes

Small cracks in panes are often relatively inconspicuous to the naked eye, but will become worse unless attended to. The pane can be fully replaced, but this is generally not required as weatherproof properties can be restored by simply using some silicone sealant to seal any such problem areas.

tools for the job

- dusting brush
- caulk gun
- cloth

1 Dust out any loose material from the glass/lead junction and apply a small but continuous bead of sealant around the junction.

2 Use a clean cloth to remove any excess sealant from the glass surface and smooth the sealant to a finish. Turn the entire casement over, and repeat steps 1 and 2 before repositioning the casement in the window as a whole.

replacing a broken pane

tools for the job

- utility knife
- chisel
- goggles
- putty knife
- cloth

1 The method for knocking out a broken pane shown on page 290 cannot be applied to leaded lights, since this will almost certainly damage the lead, and access is required right into the lead groove. First of all, cut the putty seal between the lead and the glass, using a utility knife.

2 The pliable nature of lead allows you to fold it back away from the glass surface to reveal the glass edge. A chisel is the ideal tool for this purpose, but take care only to fold the lead back and not to cause it to tear.

3 Turn the casement over and repeat steps 1 and 2, followed by a further cut around the edge of the glass with a utility knife.

4 Turn the casement once more and tap out the broken pieces of glass. A little pressure with a scrap of wood is a good tool to dislodge areas that do not come away easily. Wear protective goggles, just in case any splinters of glass are propelled from the broken pane.

5 Apply a small bead of putty around the lead groove. Ensure that it covers the entire groove.

6 Carefully position the new pane in the light, pressing gently to form a good contact between the glass and the putty.

7 Use the chisel to fold the lead back in place (on both sides of the casement), using the flat face of the chisel over the lead strips and molding it back to its original finish.

8 Use a putty knife to trim away the excess putty, providing a neat finished edge to the glass/lead junction. Finally, clean the glass with a clean cloth.

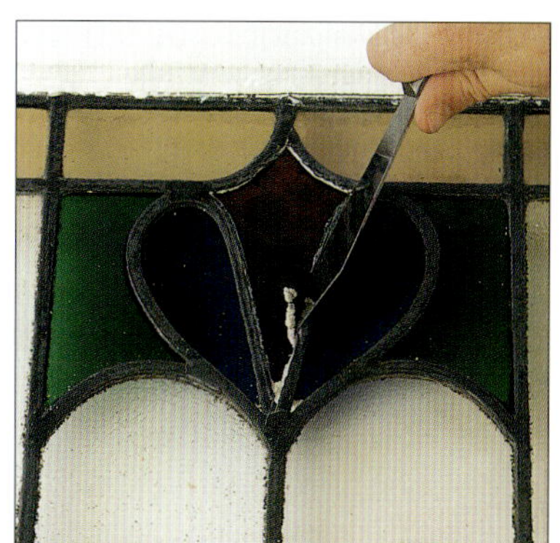

Leaded lights, whether in doors or windows, are an attractive option for a simple casement structure. Color variations and designs add to the look of this finish.

renovating metal

There are a number of areas on windows and doors that may require repair or renovation. Many different kinds of metal are featured in designs for doors and windows. Some are meant to be left simply with a metallic finish, such as the brass in door or window fittings, while others are meant to be painted.

repainting metal windows

Traditional metal windows have always required painting, but more modern versions that are normally incorporated in double-glazed designs should not be painted and only require simple cleaning for restoration purposes. However, in order to obtain a satisfactory finish on metal windows that are designed for paint, it is important to follow a simple but necessary preparation procedure.

tools for the job

scraper
sanding block
wire brush
dusting brush
paintbrush

1 Remove as much flaky paint as you can from the window surface using a scraper. Applying pressure with the blade will remove much of the loose material on the rail surfaces.

The corner of the scraper blade may also be used along the joints of the window for further paint removal from these more inaccessible areas.

2 Use some coarse-grit sandpaper or a sanding block to further smooth the surface of the window and further remove traces of old coats of paint.

3 For preparing metal windows, a wire brush is also useful in areas that are not flat—such as around the edge of the window casements, which often demonstrate a curved profile and can render the use of a scraper ineffective.

4 Prime the bare metal with a metal primer immediately after scraping and sanding has been finished. If you do not prime the metal quickly, exposure of the metal surface to the open air, even for a short time, may encourage corrosion of the surface to begin again. Once primed, the window may be top coated and finished as desired.

replacing putty

Where putty has decomposed or come loose from the glass/rabbet junction, remove the affected area and replace with a new section of fresh putty. Before reapplying the putty, make sure that the window rabbets are free from dust and debris, and that they are primed with a metal primer. This will improve the adhesion between the putty and the window rabbets. Putty should be applied using a similar technique to that for wooden windows shown on pages 290–1.

using a heat gun

The flat surfaces of metal windows are ideal for stripping using a heat gun, and so this is an option or addition to the methods described above. If you do choose to use a heat gun, remember to follow the manufacturer's guidelines and obey all safety instructions.

metal window security

As part of a general metal window renovation, it is worth introducing security systems if they are not already in place. There are locking mechanisms available for metal windows that cover both the stays and pins, and fasteners as shown in the diagram below.

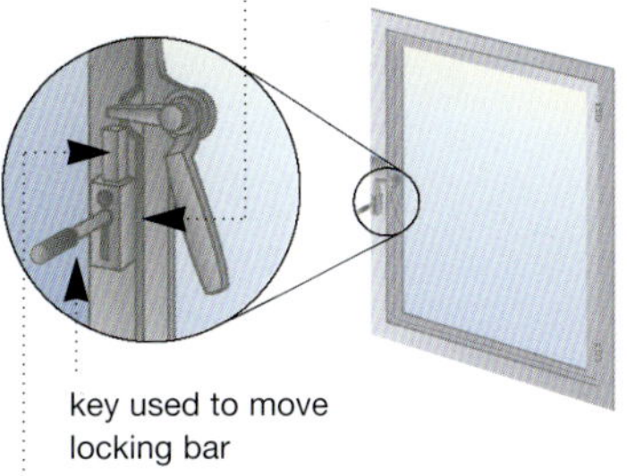

Other systems may also be purchased to lock window stays in position. These are similar to the locking stays for wooden windows shown on page 273. Remember to keep keys in a safe place so that you have easy access in the event of an emergency. Ideally, there should be a key in every room.

repainting window hardware

The window hardware on wooden windows is generally metal-based. Brass fasteners or those that have a brassed finish should not be painted, but it can be possible to revive the look of other metal window hardware by painting it. Some fasteners may have a type of paint finish on them already, and the way that a new coat of paint takes to a particular surface is variable. It can therefore be worth testing a piece of window hardware first before committing yourself to painting it all. However, in most cases paint can be applied to these surfaces with good effect. The best method for application tends to be using aerosol paints.

tools for the job

- screwdriver
- steel wool

1 Always remove the window hardware from the window, and clean it down using some fine-grade steel wool.

2 Place the stays and fasteners on a board, and holding the aerosol nozzle at 6–8in away from the window hardware, spray it with several thin coats of paint.

3 A good way of painting the screwheads for the window hardware is to insert them in an old sponge, so that the heads point up, and spray them in the normal way. Once dry, all the window hardware may be reinstalled.

brass accessories

Many door accessories are brass or given a brass effect. For a thorough cleaning it is always best to remove the particular article from the door or window, since commercial polishes can damage the finish on other parts of the door or window surface. Always use a soft cloth when buffing the brass to a finish.

wrought iron

Many door and window accessories are made from wrought iron and finished in a matte black coating. They can be revived by simple preparation and repainting. For particularly corroded pieces, immerse in an appropriate paint stripper overnight before thoroughly rinsing and repainting the following day.

repairing a windowsill

As well as being exposed to all the elements, sills are under particular attack because of their function of collecting all water runoff from the window and diverting it away from the exterior walls of the house. Due to this more concentrated exposure to dampness, decay is often more prevalent in sills. Unless damage is dealt with quickly, dry rot can spread to other parts of the window, necessitating extensive repair or even total window replacement.

minor repairs

tools for the job

- hacking knife or chisel
- dusting brush & paintbrush
- cordless drill/driver
- protective gloves

1 Cut away loose material from the sill with a hacking knife or chisel. Clean the area with a dusting brush.

2 Apply a generous coating of wood hardener to the bare wood of the sill, ensuring that you apply good coverage. Be sure to flood the area, and allow the wood to soak up the hardener.

3 Once the wood hardener has dried, mix up some two-part (polyester/resin) wood filler and apply it to the hole concerned, making sure that it is pressed into every crevice. Wood filler is difficult to work with and dries very quickly. It is therefore worth making more than one application, to build up layers to the level of the sill.

4 Directly adjacent to the filled area, in the sound part of the sill, drill some holes into the sill using a drill bit of equal diameter as some preservative pellets.

5 Insert the preservative pellets into the holes so that they are pushed deep into the sill. Wear protective gloves to do this—the pellets are normally very toxic, so you must avoid all contact with your skin.

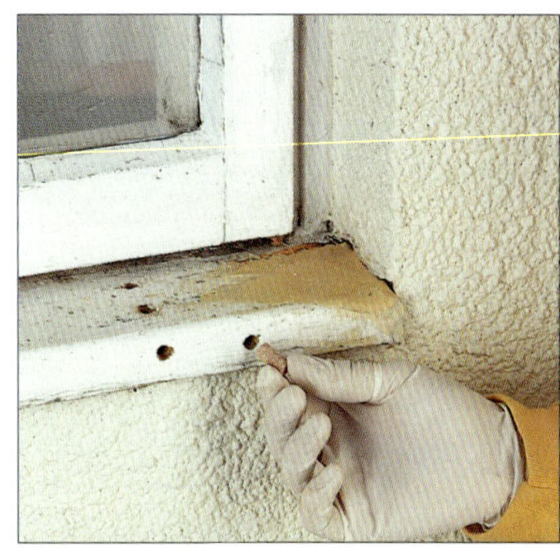

6 Mix up some more wood filler, and fill over the pellet holes. Once all the wood filler has dried, it may be sanded to a smooth finish and the sill repainted. Over time, the preservative pellets will break down and secrete a preservative solution into the sill. Therefore the combination of wood hardener and preservative pellets acting together will provide double protection against further wood decay.

major repairs

In some cases, sill damage becomes so extreme that the use of filler and preservatives is ineffective, and more drastic action is required.

tools for the job

- old screwdriver
- pencil
- combination square
- hand saw
- cordless drill/driver
- paintbrush
- wood plane

1 Decide on the boundaries of the decaying area by inserting a screwdriver into the sill. If the sill has rotted, the screwdriver will penetrate the wood easily. If it is sound, the screwdriver will not break the sill surface.

2 Mark the limits of the rotted area, extending your guideline slightly farther onto the sound wood.

Draw the guideline so that the section you produce cuts into the sill at a 45-degree angle.

3 Beginning at the front of the sill, saw along the angled guideline back to the other guideline on the sill. Keep your cut as vertical as possible.

4 Saw along the back guideline to join the other cut. The saw will usually be very close to the wall surface, which can make sawing quite difficult. Be sure that the cut is as straight as possible.

5 Use the cutout section to mark the replacement requirement on a new piece of prepared wood. The

wood should be of a dimension slightly larger than the cutout section, so that once it has been installed, it may be planed and sanded to the shape of the sill.

6 Saw down the new piece of wood to the marked size and predrill holes in the new front side of the sill. Also, use a countersink drill bit to open up the entrance point for the screws. Use wood preservative on the cutout area on the old sill, and be sure that the new section of wood has been treated with preservative before it is attached to the windowsill.

7 Glue and screw the new section in place, using exterior glue and making sure that the screws bite deep into the existing sound section of the sill. Complete any final fitting requirements by planing the section to size. Use wood filler to cover joints and screw holes. You will need more than one application of filler followed by sanding and wiping with lacquer thinner before repainting.

repairing a doorway 

Exterior doors clearly experience more punishment and wear and tear than interior doors, with much of this being due to normal weathering processes. It is therefore important to keep them in a good state of repair. Ensuring that surfaces are well painted, and therefore preserved, is one of the best methods of preventing problems, but there are also other more structural ways in which doors may be protected.

attaching a weatherboard

Weatherboards are sloped sections of wood designed to increase runoff away from the base of an exterior door. If exterior doors do not have weatherboards as part of their original design, they may be attached later.

tools for the job

- pencil
- tape measure
- level
- chisel
- mallet
- hand saw
- cordless drill/driver
- paintbrush

1 With the door in a closed position, hold a cut section of the weatherboard up against the door frame. Use a pencil to draw a guideline along the profile of the board and onto the hinge side of the frame. Repeat this procedure at the leading or opening edge of the door.

In each case, be sure that the base of the board is held slightly above the door threshold strip.

2 Draw a level guideline across the door, joining the top mark of each profile guideline. There may have to be some adjustment here, especially if the door is out of shape or was not hung properly. However, any adjustment must still ensure that the base of the weatherboard guideline is above the threshold strip.

3 Along each guideline on the door frame, chisel out the section of wood back to the main stiles of the frame. A small chisel is ideal for this particular job as the

size of the blade will allow you to follow the curved guideline as accurately as possible.

4 Saw the weatherboard to the length required and hold it in position, with the door still closed. Drill pilot holes through the board and into the door. Visually, it is best to place the holes in the concave part of the molding. Five to six pilot holes should be drilled equidistant along the weatherboard length.

5 Before attaching the weatherboard, paint the underside with a good-quality primer. The priming must be done first, for once the board is fitted access to this

part of it will be impossible, and the underside is also a particularly vulnerable area for dry rot.

6 Once dry, reposition the board and fasten it in place. Be sure that each pilot hole has been countersunk so that when screws are inserted, their heads will sit below the surface level of the molding. The holes may then be filled and sanded before painting. Check the action of the door—you may need to shave a bit of wood off the leading edge of the weatherboard, so that it opens and closes smoothly into the frame.

frame problems

tools for the job

tape measure
pencil
hand saw
pry bar
paintbrush
cordless drill/driver
hammer

Decay problems on exterior doors tend to occur more often in the frames than in the doors themselves. This is normally caused by mold and dry rot spreading up through the main body. It then becomes necessary to cut out the affected area and replace it with a new section of wood.

1 Determine how far the rot has progressed up the frame and make a diagonal cut slightly farther along, into a sound section of wood.

2 It is likely that the section of frame to be discarded is held in position with frame fasteners, and so a pry bar may be required to lever the section free.

3 Use the old section as a template to draw a guideline on a new piece of wood of equal dimensions to that of the door frame. Ensure that the new wood has been well treated with preservative.

4 Saw the section to the correct size and position it in the frame. Drill pilot holes, making sure that at least one screw will penetrate through the diagonal joint made by the new section and old part of the frame.

5 Glue and then screw the new section in place—use exterior glue and concrete anchor screws with wall plugs for a masonry wall like this one.

6 Cut to size and reattach the missing section of doorstop. Nail this in place. Fill, sand, and prime the entire section before repainting.

kitchens & bathrooms

Kitchens and bathrooms are working rooms in the home where specific tasks are performed—as a result, many of the features found in these rooms, whether they are kitchen sink units and worktops or bathtubs and bathroom sinks, are common to all kitchens or bathrooms. It is important to understand how these features interact so that they can be positioned to be sure that best use is made of the available space. This section considers the vital components that make up the majority of kitchens and bathrooms and shows how design is tailored to meet those requirements.

the basic shape of a kitchen

The size and dimensions of a room obviously set constraints on the shape of a kitchen, but how space is utilized will also determine both its look and efficient operation. Kitchen design is based around three main areas: food storage and preparation, cooking, and washing. All three need to be positioned to enable the efficient and safe preparation of meals. The working triangle of kitchen design reveals how these three areas interact, showing the ideal positions for refrigerator and preparation areas in relation to the range and the sink. The illustrations on these pages demonstrate how this working triangle applies to three common kitchen shapes.

U-shaped kitchens

This type of kitchen shape provides probably the most satisfactory example of all for a working triangle. Distances between all three points are kept almost equal, which allows for optimum movement and access. The U-shaped design is most commonly found in large kitchens, although the same principles may also be applied to smaller kitchens where floor space is much more limited, and a similar working triangle shape can still be maintained.

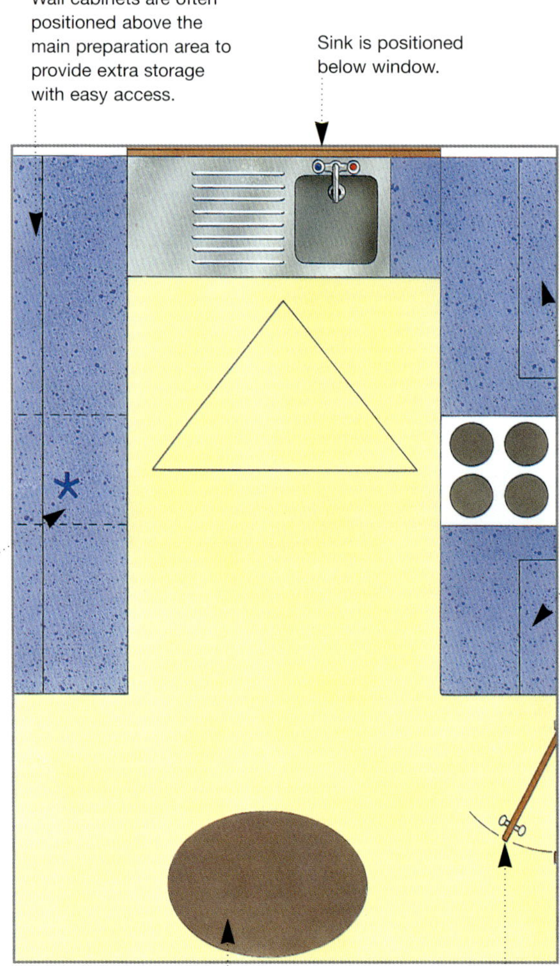

Wall cabinets are often positioned above the main preparation area to provide extra storage with easy access.

Sink is positioned below window.

Wall cabinets may be used in these areas as long as they do not extend over the range.

Refrigerator is centrally positioned beneath the main worktop area.

Eating area is away from the main working triangle, but within easy access of the food serving area next to the range.

Door can be opened without danger of hitting anyone working in the kitchen.

GALLEY KITCHENS

A galley-style kitchen is another popular design, similar to the U-shaped kitchen but more suitable for a narrow room. Galleys have cabinets on the opposing longer walls but not on the opposing shorter walls. The working triangle in this situation still bears similarities to that of the U-shaped kitchen—some U-shaped kitchens are often referred to as galley kitchens, especially when the U is particularly elongated and floor space between the two opposing longer runs of wall cabinets is limited. In a traditional galley kitchen, however, the sink would be moved onto one of the longer walls, while still ensuring that a good working triangle, with fairly even dimensions, is maintained.

L-shaped kitchens

As the name suggests, the units in an L-shaped kitchen cover the majority of two adjacent walls in the room. The working triangle can still be maintained, although distances between the three points are no longer equal. Depending upon room size, it should still be possible to include an eating area in the kitchen.

Storage space is above preparation area—this may block off some light, but it is a good compromise when extra storage space is needed.

Sink is positioned below window.

Extra wall cabinets provide storage but must not extend over the range, which is positioned in the center of the worktop and has plenty of space on either side for serving meals.

Door can be opened without danger of hitting anyone working in the kitchen.

Eating area makes the best use of available space and is still close to the food-serving area of the worktop.

tips of the trade

Sink position—In most kitchens the sink tends to be positioned underneath a window. The main reason for this is to provide a view when menial tasks are being carried out at the sink. However, positioning a sink below a window also guarantees that it is on an outside wall, and this makes it much easier to link the waste pipes to an outside drain.

single-run kitchens

These are simple in design and are often used in long, narrow kitchens where the inclusion of double-facing cabinets is impossible due to space limitations. In some cases, however, this choice of kitchen shape is used when a simple, limited, inexpensive stretch of units is all that is required. Although the wall cabinets and accessories are on one wall, it can still be possible to maintain a working triangle, although the dimensions of the triangle will have to be considerably elongated to fit in with the kitchen design.

Range is positioned with room on either side for serving meals.

Refrigerator is beneath center part of food preparation area.

Sink is positioned to share natural light with food-preparation area. Butting the sink against the wall leaves a larger continuous food-preparation area.

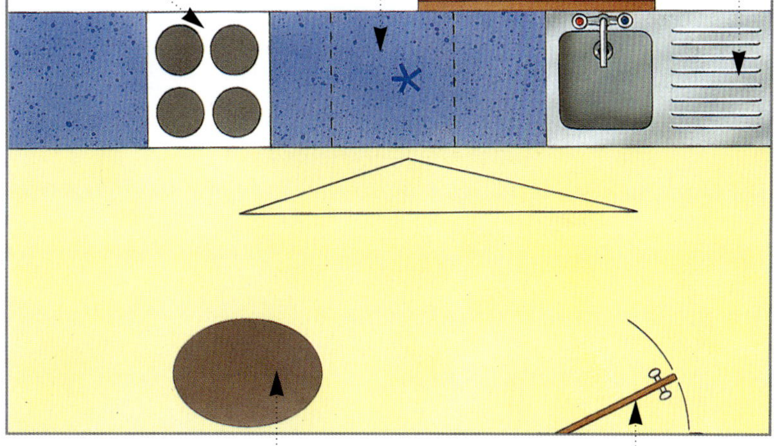

Eating area is positioned so as much access as possible is made available, while still being close to the serving area.

Door can be opened without danger of hitting anyone working in the kitchen.

built-in kitchens

The term "built-in kitchen" is used to describe a type of kitchen where the units are fixed in place to create the impression they are built into the room. Most modern kitchens are of the built-in variety. Naturally, the appearance and function of individual units will vary between manufacturers, but all units can be categorized according to whether they are handmade or standard, and whether they are fixed to the floor or attached to the wall above a worktop.

handmade cabinets

Handmade items are traditionally more expensive than standard items, as labor costs are greater and the materials used tend to be of higher quality—kitchen units are no exception to this rule. All the doors, drawers, and carcasses of handmade cabinets are constructed using traditional jointing methods, such as dovetail jointing, and tend to be made from solid soft- or hardwoods, which guarantees durability, rather than particle board and laminate. Installing handmade kitchens is a highly specialized job, and most people do not attempt to undertake it themselves.

standard units

Standard kitchen units are much cheaper than handmade varieties because they are mass-produced and usually made from particle board with a laminated finish, although quality and price do vary considerably. As well as aiming to achieve a pleasing appearance, modern designs are increasingly aimed toward specific needs in the kitchen.

kit cabinets

Commonly known as "knockdown furniture," kit cabinets are supplied broken down into their constituent parts, and it is up to the individual to put them together. Kit cabinets tend to occupy the lower end of the price scale, but there are some exceptionally good-quality units available, and by choosing carefully you can produce a very fine kitchen. Greater time will be needed for installation, but this can be set against the financial gains.

rigid

The main difference between rigid units and knockdowns is that rigid units are supplied factory-assembled to reduce the time for installation. As a rule, however, only the carcass is supplied ready-made from the manufacturer, and you will still need to fit the doors, drawer fronts, and other accessories to the carcasses. This allows the manufacturer to supply general carcass units that can be adapted to suit the finished look of any style of kitchen.

combination

Combination cabinets are supplied semi-assembled, so that part of the unit may be considered rigid, while the other part is in effect self-assembly. Corner cabinets and carousels are often combination, as well as carcasses that are used to house accessories such as refrigerators or ranges. These carcasses can be adapted to fit different types of accessories and to house a greater variety of appliances, offering more choice to the customer.

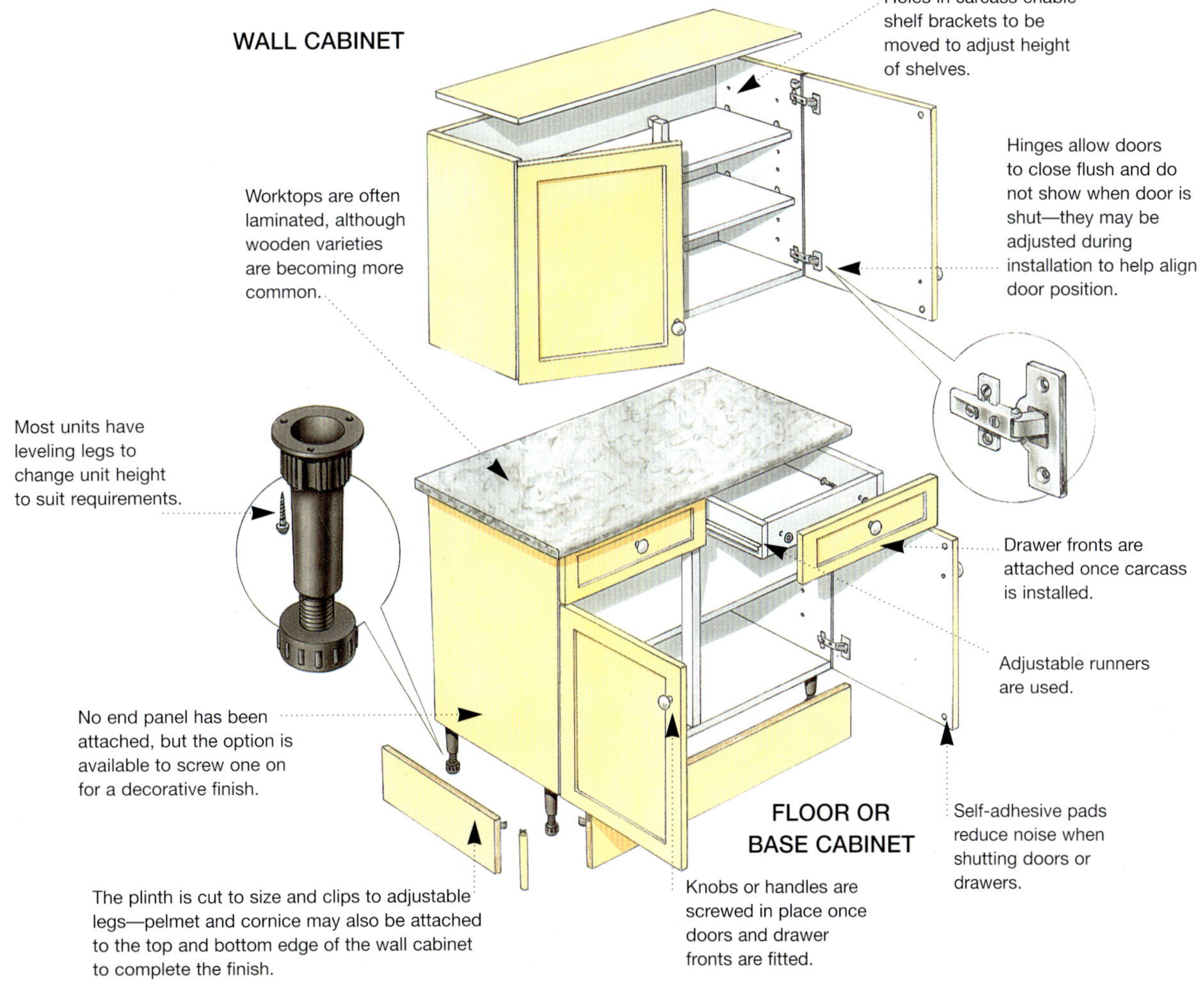

freestanding kitchens

Freestanding kitchens offer a more traditional look, since they refer back to an era when kitchen furniture and worktops were separate items not permanently attached to walls or ceilings, with individual dressers and sideboards comprising the main utility items in the kitchen in addition to sink units. This look has enjoyed something of a revival, with many manufacturers now offering semi-built-in units that imitate this type of traditional kitchen design.

freestanding units

The main visible difference between freestanding units and standard kitchen units is that the former tend to resemble more closely the look of everyday furniture found elsewhere in the house. Thus a storage unit may have a closer connection in terms of appearance to a wardrobe or cabinet than to modern base and wall units. However, the actual way in which freestanding units are now constructed and fitted is similar to that of standard kitchen units. For example, the doors and drawers in freestanding cabinets will have been constructed using exactly the same method as their built-in counterparts, even though the sizes may be slightly more unusual, and they will still need to be attached to the cabinet carcass once it is in place. The diagram below provides an example of a freestanding cabinet, and also points out the various features it shares with a standard kitchen unit.

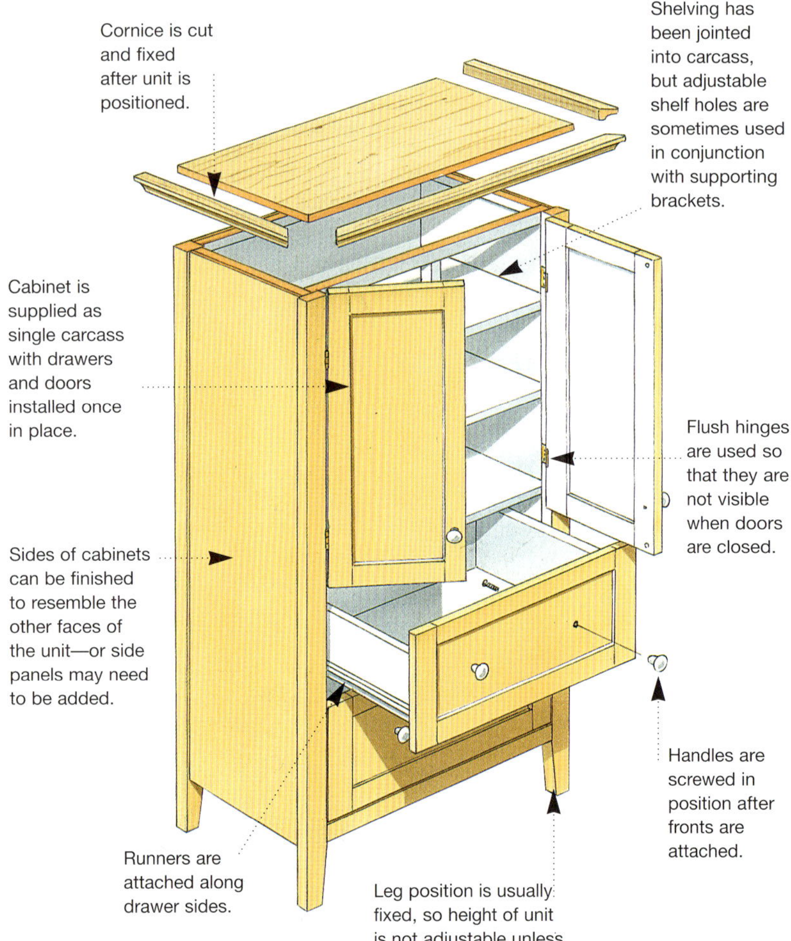

ACCESSORY UNITS

It is also possible to purchase freestanding accessory units, such as units for holding sinks, although it is likely that the unit will be supplied still requiring a substantial amount of assembly, and the worktop will also require cutting to fit the sink. So although the freestanding look is now being catered for by manufacturers, it must be understood that there will still be a fair amount of fitting and assembling in order to achieve the finished unit look.

TRADITIONAL IDEAS

It is also possible to achieve a freestanding look by using more traditional pieces of furniture, such as sideboards or dressers. New reproductions may be purchased or older items can be painted to suit your style. This is an attractive option, especially when using a distressed paint effect, as older items lend themselves well to creating this type of look. You can combine new units with old to create a more haphazard look, which can provide a pleasing design.

Provided that access is not hindered, positioning an island unit in the central floor area of a kitchen is a sensible use of space. The simple kitchen table represents the most traditional and basic form of island unit, and this type has always been popular due to the variety of functions it can fulfill—acting equally well as a food-preparation area, a dining area, and more often than not an activity area for the whole family. The only difference with modern kitchens is that a greater choice of designs is now available, with additions being made to enhance utility and aesthetic appeal. Island units usually do not need to be attached in place owing to their weight, which means that they are also still moveable. The diagram below shows a typical island unit that incorporates a hanging rack to provide a further storage area in what would otherwise simply be redundant ceiling space.

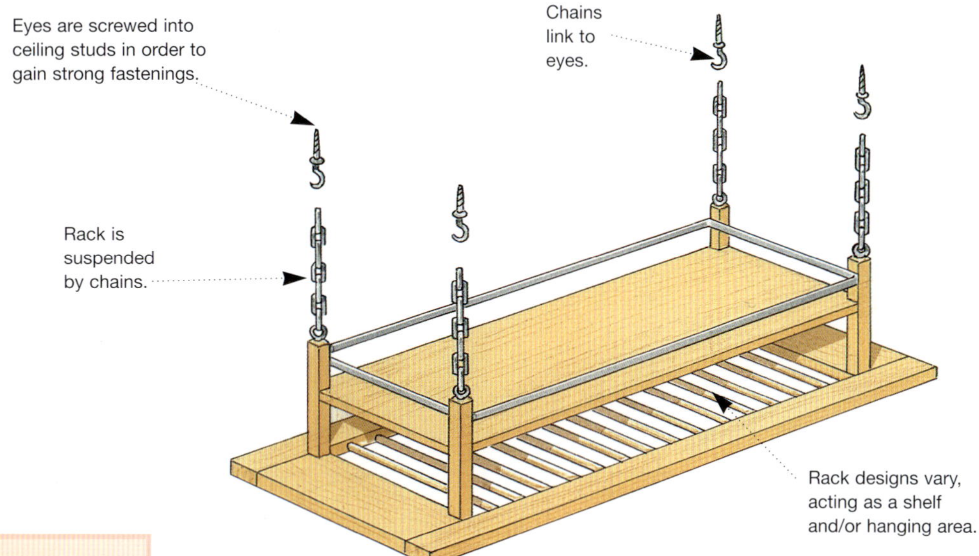

safety advice

When deciding on the position for hanging racks it is important to use a stud finder. This will ensure that fastenings are inserted into joists to provide adequate support, while avoiding any wiring or plumbing that runs across the ceiling space.

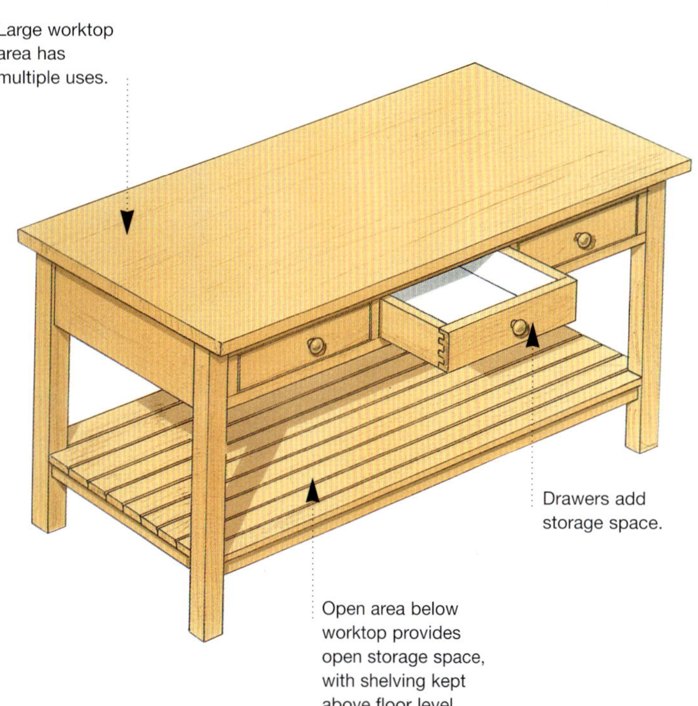

ALTERNATIVE ISLANDS

Standard kitchen units can also be used to create islands in the center of a room. These are attached in place and have the characteristics of standard unit design. It is also possible to fit sinks or cooking areas into island units, but this will require water or gas and/or electricity supplies to be fed to these areas, which can be a difficult job. However, in the right size of kitchen the effect of such units can be well worth the work involved.

basic bathroom shape

The basic shape of a bathroom is primarily affected by the size of the room and the number of items comprising a chosen suite. The number of bathrooms in a household, and the extent to which each bathroom is used, and by how many people, will also have an influence. The bathroom is a very functional part of the home, and it is important to position appliances so that they may function with optimum efficiency. The ideal area for ease of use of a particular item is referred to as "standing room" or the "working area," and these are demonstrated by the red boxes in the diagrams below. However, a bathroom is also a room for relaxing in, and it is important to incorporate a degree of comfort and aesthetics into the overall design.

spacious bathrooms

The larger the bathroom, the greater the choice available for design, but this still means that careful planning is essential. In fact, smaller bathrooms are often easier to design because options are limited. In general, where there is a large bathroom the available space tends to be filled with as many fixtures as possible, which is satisfactory, provided working areas are available for each particular fitting. Large bathrooms can be used by more than one person at the same time, and it is therefore necessary for standing areas to be as separate as possible.

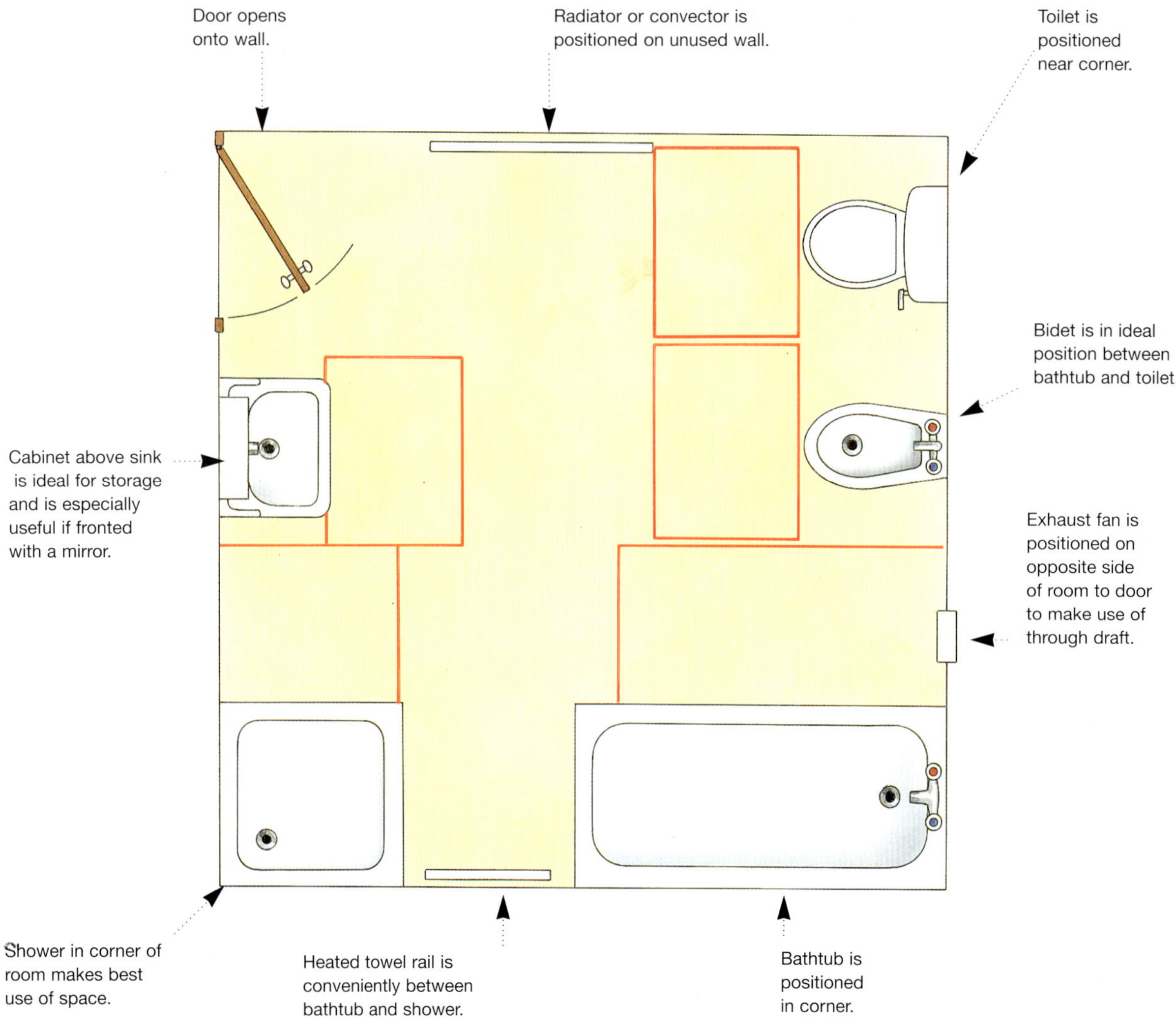

family bathrooms

In households with a single bathroom used by the entire family, there may need to be some compromises depending upon the available space. There are opportunities to choose installing designs aimed at space saving, such as quadrant shower trays and a heated towel rail that also acts as the heater in the room. Working areas may need to overlap in family bathrooms, but this can be limited to a certain extent, so that efficiency is maintained and the bathroom can still be used by more than one person at a time.

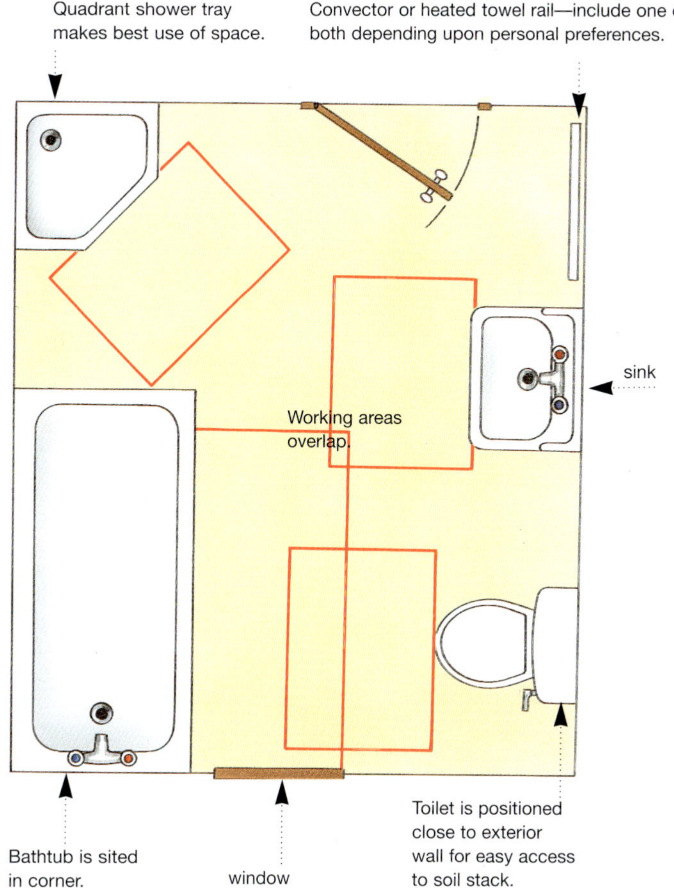

tips of the trade

Toilets should ideally be located on external walls, or close to external walls, so that the plumbing required to get from the toilet to the exterior soil stack is kept to a minimum.

en-suite bathrooms

En-suite, or connected, bathrooms tend to be small, and as such many design choices will be dictated by the space available. Since this type of bathroom is not as busy as others, the idea of working or standing areas tends to become redundant. Instead, a single central space becomes the working area for all items in the bathroom. Attention is more focused on providing easy access to the fixtures in the bathroom by one person at any one time, so the bathtub working area can become the sink working area, depending upon which item is in use. Fitting a shower cubicle instead of a bathtub will allow for more space.

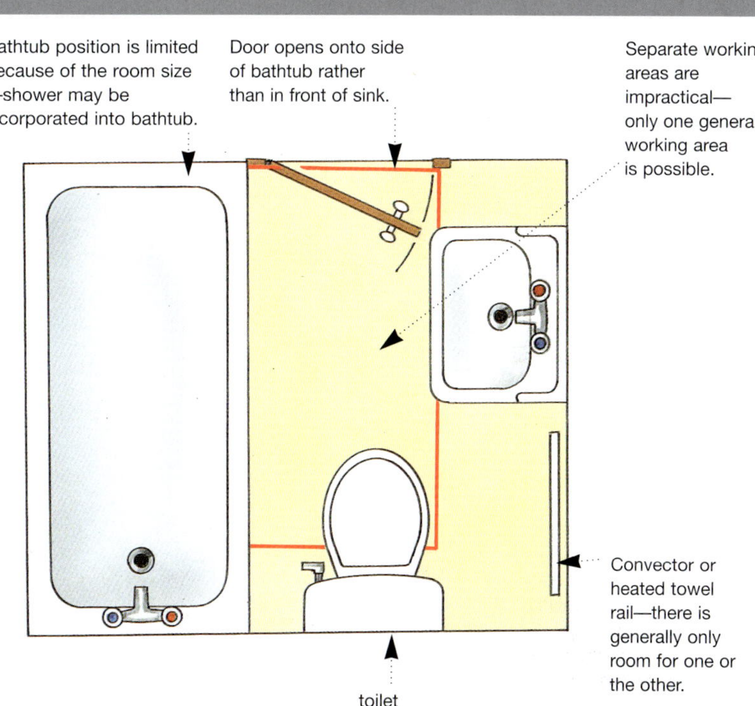

built-in bathrooms

All bathrooms are built-in, in that the main items are permanently plumbed in and fastened in position. When the term "built-in" is applied to bathrooms, therefore, it usually indicates that those items are housed in specially designed units. The units usually have a collective finish and produce a continuous visual link that gives the bathroom a pleasing overall look. The term is also used to indicate that pipes are boxed in and hidden from view.

bathroom units

You can build your own units if you wish, or purchase custom-made versions. Manufacturers produce many different designs that can be fitted into most bathroom layouts. Although quality and price can vary dramatically, there are a number of common features in the way that units are designed and constructed. The example below shows the way in which a sink cabinet—sometimes called a vanity unit—is constructed.

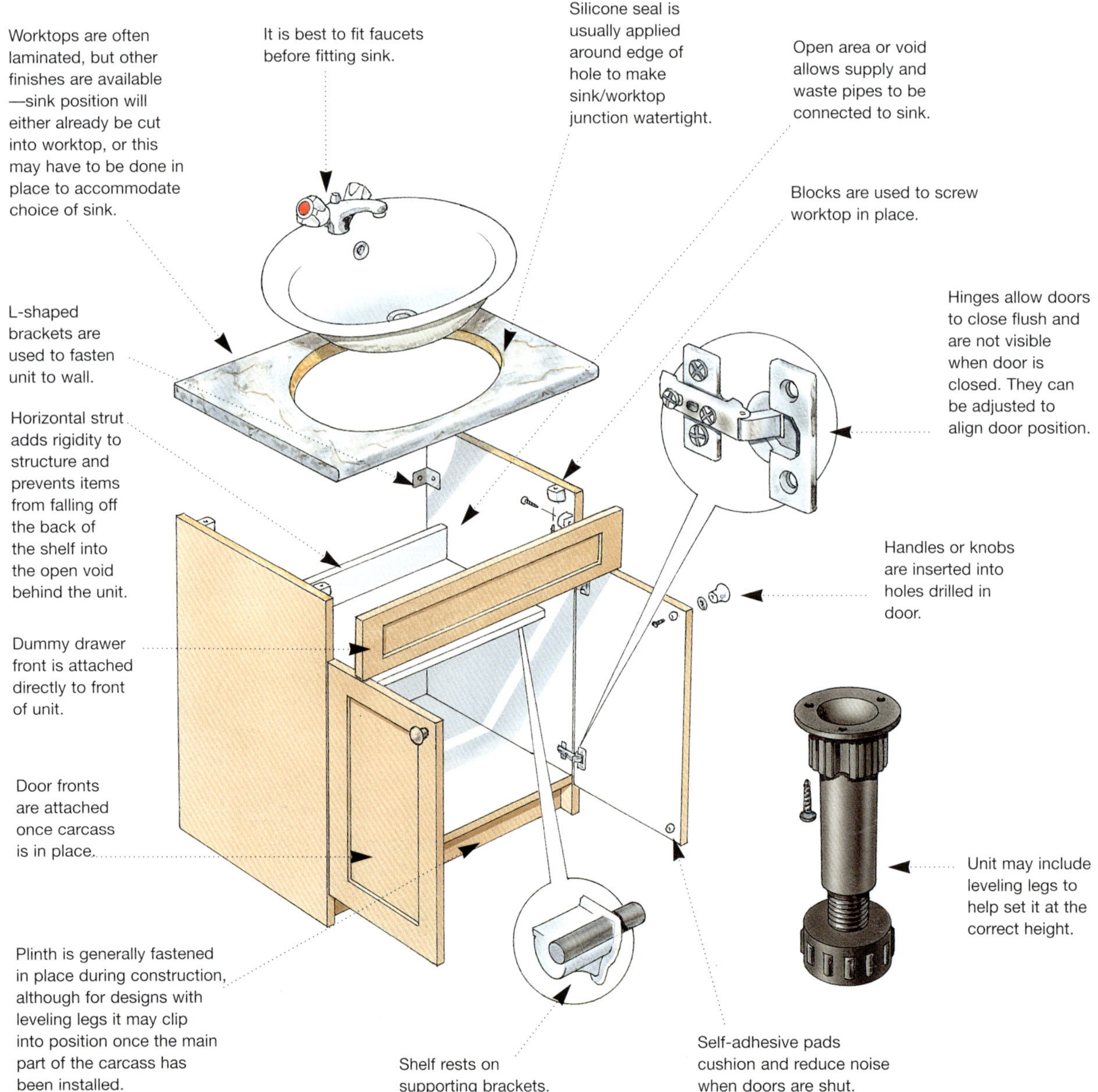

It is possible to achieve a built-in look in one of two ways. One method is to house all the bathroom fixtures, such as the sink and toilet, within carcass units, and to connect these units with extra storage and display units so that units run from wall to wall. Paneling can be applied around the bathtub to match the unit finish. The bathtub is the largest fixture in the bathroom, so paneling is an effective way of incorporating it into the decoration of the rest of the room, rather than allowing it to dominate. The aim of this type of bathroom design is to hide all the pipes and connections within the runs of units, while still maintaining maximum practicality and a modern and attractive appearance.

RIGHT *Unit design may be linked with other decoration in the room to enhance the built-in look. The blue color of some of the door and drawer panels of the units in this bathroom is repeated in the color of the walls.*

The other method for achieving a fully built-in look is to box in all unsightly elements. As well as disguising or hiding areas of pipes from view, the boxes can also be designed to provide extra shelving that is useful for both storage and display purposes. As long as the frameworks are well constructed, boxes can be just as pleasing to the eye as manufactured units. You can also apply a decorative finish to box-frameworks, such as tiling, in order to produce a well-integrated and built-in effect. Full instructions on boxes are given on pages 354–5.

LEFT *Decorating the boxed areas with the same tiles used for the floor enhances the built-in look and gives the impression of a custom-built overall bathroom design.*

plumbing & electricity

Installing a new kitchen or bathroom with all the relevant fixtures requires a certain amount of skill with plumbing and electricity. There will probably be some areas where you need to seek professional advice, but as far as the basic tasks are concerned, most jobs are relatively straightforward as long as the correct order of work is followed and appropriate techniques used. This chapter shows the best techniques for installing a selection of fixtures. Be sure to plan jobs thoroughly so that you have all the right connections for a particular installation before you start.

Bathroom fixtures, such as the toilet and bathtub shown here, must be assembled, then positioned and plumbed.

preparing plumbing & electricity

When new fixtures are to be positioned in a different place from old ones, you will need to reroute supplies. It is therefore important to have some understanding of the different types of pipe available and the various ways in which they can be jointed. Before embarking on any pipework, always turn off the water supply and drain the pipes. In terms of electricity supplies, major overhauls are not usually required, although some cables may need rerouting.

cutting copper pipes

tools for the job

pipe cutter

steel wool

1 Clamp the pipe cutter around the pipe and rotate it in the direction designated by the arrow until it cuts all the way through. You can use a hacksaw to cut the pipe if you wish, but a pipe cutter gives a cleaner cut.

2 Clean the pipe using steel wool before making any connection.

connecting copper pipes

There are several ways of making a connection or joint between copper pipes. The simplest is to insert a compression fitting. However, this may be unsightly if it is in a position that can be easily viewed. The other methods involve using solder and a gas torch. They are slightly more difficult, but produce a neater finish.

compression fittings

Compression fittings are easy to attach because the process does not require the use of a gas torch.

tools for the job

adjustable wrenches

1 Separate the compression fitting and slip it in place on the two ends of the cut pipe. To begin with, position it hand tight with the compression rings situated on the pipe inside the fitting.

tips of the trade

Pipe connectors are made in many different shapes, for example elbow joints and T-connectors, so that it is possible to reroute most pipes.

2 Use adjustable wrenches to tighten the joint, allowing the threaded section to tighten onto the rings to create a watertight seal.

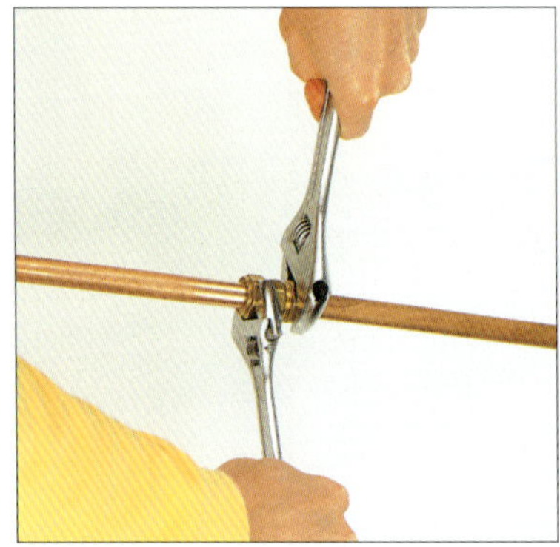

solder ring joints

Solder ring joints are the easiest type of joint to make because the solder itself is already inside the connector.

tools for the job

gas torch

heat-resistant mat

1 Apply flux to the ends of the pipes and inside the connector. The flux helps to clean the copper and achieve a watertight joint.

2 Slot both ends of the pipe into the connector. Holding the pipe over a heat-resistant mat, use a gas torch to heat the joint gently, allowing the solder ring inside it to melt and form a watertight seal.

safety advice

When using a gas torch, always read the manufacturer's guidelines to be sure of safe use. Gas torches should never be left burning unattended, and a heat-resistant mat should be positioned next to the joint to avoid burning or singeing adjacent surfaces.

end feed joints

The other type of solder joint is referred to as an end feed joint. It does not contain a ring of solder inside, so the solder must be applied during the heating procedure with the gas torch. Flux is still used to clean pipe ends, but solder wire must be applied around the joint to create a watertight seal.

connecting plastic pipes

Plastic pipes are usually very easy to connect since many have instant fittings or are threaded with rubber washers. However, in some cases solvent weld joints have to be formed using a special type of cement to fasten the pipes together.

tools for the job

hacksaw or hand saw
cloth

1 Cut the pipes to the required size with a hacksaw or hand saw, and clean the ends thoroughly.

2 Apply solvent weld cement around the end of the pipe. Push the end of the pipe into the required connector. Remove excess cement with a cloth and allow the joint to dry before continuing with the next section.

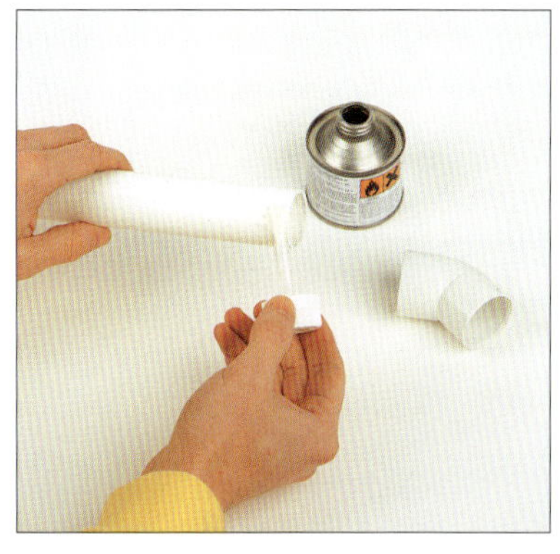

rerouting cables

In hollow walls or ceiling voids, cables can be fed into place, but with solid walls the procedure is more laborious. Leave the actual electrical work, such as wiring, to professionals.

tools for the job

hand sledge
brick chisel
hammer
protective equipment

1 Draw pencil guidelines where the cable will run. Use a hand sledge and brick chisel to cut through the wall, removing material to a depth of around 1in.

2 Position the cable well below surface level. Cover it with an impact-resistant plastic channel held in place with galvanized nails, then apply a surface finish such as plaster.

plastic pipes

Although copper pipe is still used as the main type of water supply pipe in the home, plastic pipe is becoming much more commonplace because the way it is jointed makes it incredibly easy to work with. Pipe and installation designs can vary slightly between manufacturers, so it is best to use the same type of plastic pipe throughout your home. However, all manufacturers produce adaptors to join their plastic pipes with traditional copper pipe systems.

tools for the job

- pipe cutter or mini hacksaw
- adjustable wrenches
- screwdriver
- cordless drill/driver

cutting & jointing plastic

Before you can build up any sort of plastic supply pipe system, you need to understand how to form a simple joint or connection between two lengths of pipe.

1 Plastic supply pipe can be cut with any fine-toothed saw—a mini hacksaw is ideal. Alternatively, you can buy pipe cutters. Whatever you use, try to make the cut as square as possible. Remove rough edges with fine-grit abrasive paper.

2 Push both ends of the pipe into the ends of the connector. Push each pipe in as far as it will go, making sure they have both been grabbed by the rings inside the joint.

3 Pull the pipes away from the joint to create a watertight seal.

4 If you need to undo the joint for any reason, push the end collar on the joint to loosen it and pull the pipe free from the connection.

jointing copper & plastic

Jointing a section of copper and plastic pipe together can be achieved using a specially designed transition fitting. This is fitted in a similar way to a compression fitting.

1 Attach one section of a copper compression fitting onto the end of the copper pipe and remove the securing nut from the other end of the fitting.

2 Attach the transition fitting onto the compression fitting, and use adjustable wrenches to tighten the joint and make it watertight.

3 Insert and secure the plastic pipe as shown in steps 2 and 3 of "cutting & jointing plastic" on the opposite page.

attaching a shutoff valve

Shutoff valves are available for both copper and plastic pipes. Designs vary—the one shown here is operated by a slot-head screwdriver.

inserting a stop cap

It is sometimes necessary to close off the end of a pipe. For example, when changing bathroom fittings there may be a time delay between removing the old fitting and installing the new one. The water may have to be turned back on in the meantime to provide a supply for other areas in the house. Whatever the reason, the method used is to push a stop cap into the opening of the pipe and then pull it back to secure it in place.

using reducer couplings

When a larger bore of pipe needs to be joined to a smaller bore, use reducer couplings to connect them. These are manufactured in all sizes to cope with a variety of needs.

1 Insert the end of the coupling into a connector for the larger pipe bore. Pull it back to lock it in position.

2 Insert the small bore pipe into the reducer coupling and pull it back to lock it in position. Insert the larger bore pipe into the large bore.

supporting pipes

All supply pipes have to be supported at intervals along the course of their route. However, because plastic pipe is more flexible than copper pipe, more straps are needed to provide adequate support to the pipe once the water supply is in use.

1 Position pipe straps along the route of the pipe at intervals of no more than 1ft.

2 Make sure that the pipe is strapped firmly in place before the water is turned on, so that there is no danger of the pipes sagging and thereby placing joints under unnecessary stress.

tips of the trade

To be sure that straps are aligned, use a level to draw a pencil line along the joists to act as a fastening guideline.

installing a bathroom sink 

Most of the hard work involved in installing a bathroom sink is concerned with making sure that the water supply pipes and waste pipe are appropriately located for easy connection. If you are merely replacing a sink, you will usually be able to reuse the existing supplies and waste when it comes to reconnection. However, if the new sink is situated in a different area to the original sink position, it will be necessary to adjust the lengths of the supply and waste pipes, as discussed earlier in this chapter (see pages 314–15).

faucets & pop-up stoppers

Whatever the type of faucet or stopper installed, the basic technique for installing a bathroom sink remains the same. It is best to attach the faucets and stopper to the sink before fixing the sink to the wall, as it is much easier to gain access. In this case, a compression faucet and pop-up stopper are being installed.

tools for the job

- slip-joint pliers
- screwdriver
- level

1 Position the sealing washer at the base of the faucet, so that a watertight seal will be formed when it is positioned on the sink. If the faucet you are using is not supplied with a washer, apply silicone sealant around the base of the faucet before attaching it in place.

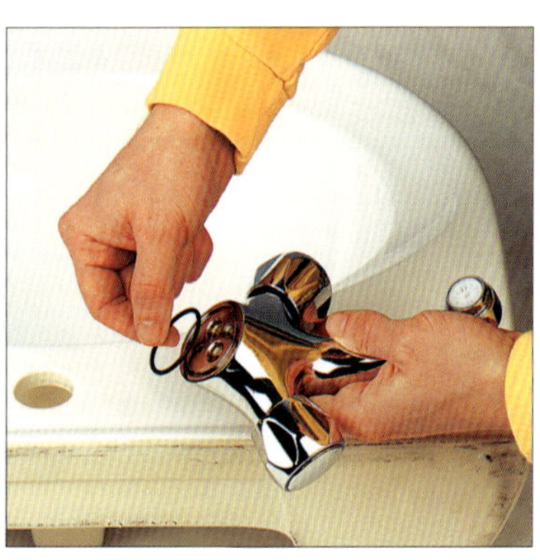

2 Attach the copper supply pipes by screwing them into the base of the faucet. A rubber washer is generally supplied to form a tight seal between the threaded part of the supply pipe and the faucet. Insert the threaded bolt, which is used to hold the faucet in position.

3 Thread the supply pipes and threaded bolt through the hole in the sink. Position a rubber flange on the underside of the sink hole, followed by a retainer ring, threading both over the threaded bolt. Secure them with a locknut, which can be done by hand but may need tightening with pliers. Do not overtighten.

tips of the trade

Sinks can easily be chipped or cracked, especially when working on a concrete floor, so you should always protect the sink by laying a drop cloth on the floor.

4 Attention may now be turned to the stopper. A pop-up stopper system is constructed from a number of components. Thread the top section of the waste outlet through the outlet in the sink, making sure that the correct flange has been fitted over the outlet tail. If a flange is not supplied with the outlet, the waste may be seated on silicone sealant. If using sealant, be sure to wipe away any excess before it dries.

5 Screw the bottom section of the stopper on the underside of the outlet. Once again, ensure the correct flange has been positioned between the stopper section and the underside of the sink outlet. Do not overtighten, just make sure the stopper is securely attached and watertight.

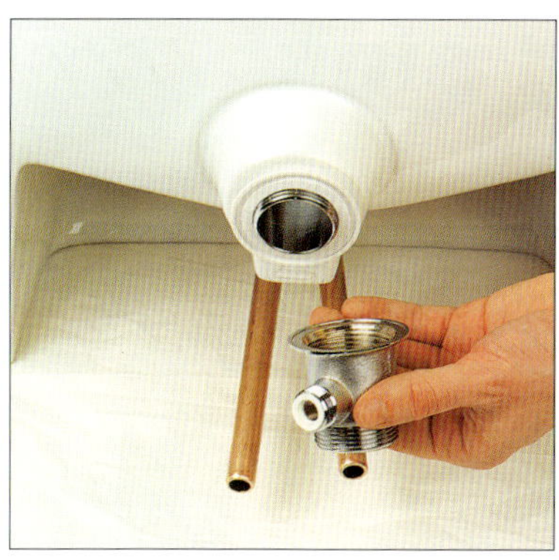

6 Insert the pop-up stopper rod and screw the stopper lever into the base of the stopper outlet. Fasten the stopper lever with a threaded nut, which is secured handtight.

7 Join the lever and pop-up stopper rod with the supplied clamp by threading the rod and lever into two retaining holes in the clamp. Fix the rod and lever firmly in place with two well-tightened screws.

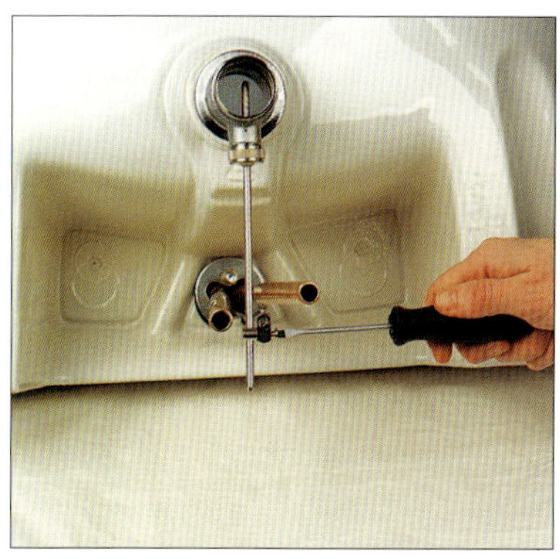

8 Position the sink base in front of and covering any supply pipes. Until the basin is in place and leveled, you will not be able to position the base exactly. However, positioning the base before the sink will make sure of a good contact between the two, making the overall placement as secure as possible.

9 Carefully lift and position the sink on top of the base, adjusting base position to make sure the basin sits correctly. Use a level to check the sink is level, with its back face flush against the wall.

10 Fasten the sink in place with retaining screws inserted through the back of the sink and into the wall surface. If it is a solid wall, you may need to use wall plugs. Overtightened screws may crack the sink, so use a hand-held screwdriver for greater control.

11 Secure the base through the holes inside the base. Do not overtighten, and make sure the screws are long enough to hold firm in the floor, but not so long that they damage underfloor services.

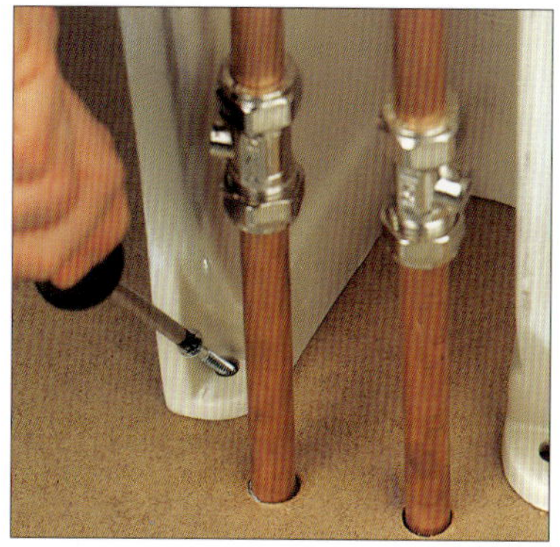

12 Position the stopper, adjusting the level so it will provide a watertight seal. Connect up the outlet and water supply pipes, before turning on the water supply.

ALTERNATIVE FAUCETS

Some faucets have tails that connect to the water supply with braided steel supply tubes. These tails are secured in place with locknuts on the sink before the supply tube is attached. You will still require a flange and/or washer barrier between the metal surfaces of the faucet and the sink.

installing a wall-mounted sink

There is little difference between a wall-mounted sink and a sink and base in terms of connections and function. The different installation processes center around the way in which the sink is fastened to the wall, and the manner in which supply and drainage pipes are either hidden or made more attractive. This need to hide supplies can make installing a wall-mounted sink awkward because access to connections is more limited.

solid walls

You need to provide an appropriate route for the required pipes to reach the sink. In a solid wall, this involves cutting out a channel.

tools for the job

- tape measure
- pencil
- level
- hand sledge
- brick chisel
- protective equipment

1 Mark the sink position on the wall and draw pencil guidelines down the wall to demarcate a channel to accommodate pipes. Allow space for connecting with existing supplies.

2 Use a hand sledge and brick chisel to remove this channel. Wear gloves and goggles to protect from flying debris. Once the channel is deep enough, supply pipes may be routed to the correct position.

hollow walls

Pipework can be routed through the cavity in hollow walls. However, access holes often need to be so large to accomplish this that cutting out a section of plasterboard or drywall may be the easiest option. In addition, you may need to fix extra blocking in the studs to provide adequate support for the sink.

tools for the job

- tape measure
- cordless drill/driver
- pipe cutter
- adjustable wrenches
- hand saw
- hammer
- plastering or dry-lining equipment

1 Check height measurements to be sure of the exact position of the sink and where brackets will need to be fastened to support it. Attach one or more extra blocks in place at the correct height for the brackets.

2 You may have to drill holes through studs to provide space for pipe rerouting.

3 Position the pipes and add appropriate connections as required (see pages 314–17).

4 Insert an insulation blanket between the studs. Nail a drywall or plasterboard sheet over the area, then dry-line or plaster as required. Make access holes for the pipe tails to protrude into the room.

installing the sink

tools for the job

- level
- tape measure
- pencil
- cordless drill/driver and/or screwdriver
- hacksaw
- adjustable wrenches

1 Draw a level pencil guideline where the brackets require fastening to the supporting points on the back of the sink. Screw the brackets directly into the wooden stud in hollow walls, or use wall plugs and screws in solid walls.

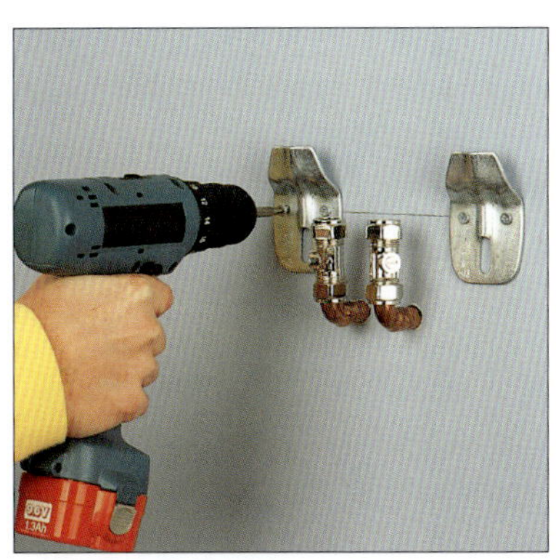

2 Attach the faucets and waste pipe to the sink before hooking it in place over the supporting brackets. Screw the sink in place through the predrilled holes on its underside. Sometimes a plastic washer is supplied to produce a barrier between the screw and sink. Do not overtighten the screw.

3 Hold the waste assembly in place and measure the length of pipe required to connect between the sink and trap. Cut the pipe to the appropriate length and make the necessary connections. You can now connect the faucets to the hot and cold water supplies, and the sink is ready for use.

Wall-mounted sinks provide a compact and elegant finish. The chrome waste system matches the faucets so that it does not detract from the effect.

installing a bathtub ⚒⚒⚒

Before installing a bathtub, make sure that the necessary provision has been made for supply pipe and drainage pipe connections. In many cases, the existing pipework will be sufficient, but if the new bathtub is to be in a different place from the old one, pipe adjustment will be required. Installation tends to be a two-part process—first, the feet and supporting frame are put in place, then the faucets and waste system are connected.

tools for the job

- screwdriver and/or cordless drill/driver
- adjustable wrenches
- level
- pencil
- tape measure

attaching the feet

Most bathtubs have feet and supporting legs so that the underside is raised from the floor. The legs can be leveled to take into account any unevenness across the floor surface. Most manufacturers supply bathtubs without the feet attached.

1 Lay the bathtub upside down on a drop cloth to protect its surface. Most new bathtubs are coated with a protective plastic film, but this is meant to protect against dirt and cannot prevent scratches or scrapes. Position the bathtub legs in the sockets situated around the rim. These are generally secured in the socket by a grub screw, which passes through the outside of the socket and into the leg.

tips of the trade

Older bathtub designs may not have leveling feet, and the feet that they have may already be attached to the main bathtub body. In such instances, you may need to insert wooden shims below the feet to ensure that the bathtub is perfectly level. A level bathtub is important for the safety of users as well as a good finish.

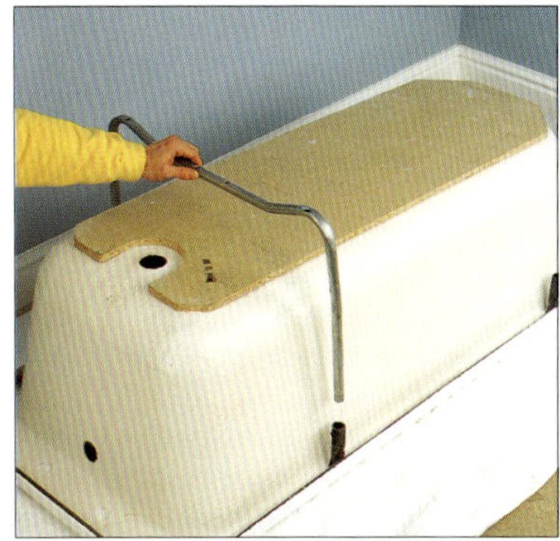

2 Position the feet in the holes at the base of the legs using a nut on either side of the leg framework to hold them in place. Adjust the position of each foot to approximately the same height—these can be adjusted more accurately when the bathtub is in place. Most leg frames can also be screwed into the base of the bathtub through pre-drilled holes in the center of the leg framework. Take care to use screws of the correct length so that they penetrate the chipboard base but not the bathtub itself.

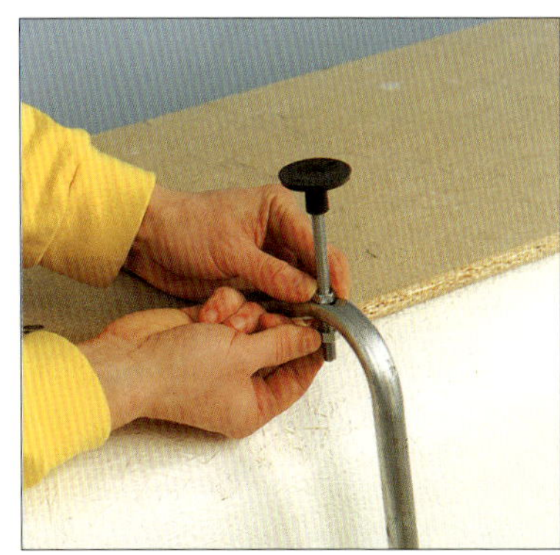

3 Most bathtub designs have a central leg to provide extra support. This is much smaller in size and is screwed, with a foot attached, in the middle of the bathtub base. Again, take care to use the correct length of screw.

installing & leveling

Once the legs and feet are attached, turn the bathtub right side up. Two people are needed for this because even very light bathtubs are awkward to handle on your own. The next step is to fit the faucets and waste pipes before finally leveling the bath once it is in position.

1 First attach the waste and overflow system to the bath. Pop-up stopper designs for bathtubs differ slightly from sinks in that the stopper is operated by a circular handle above the overflow outlet. A cable runs from the handle to the stopper so that the plug hole can be opened and closed as required. Fit the supplied flanges to both the waste outlet and overflow.

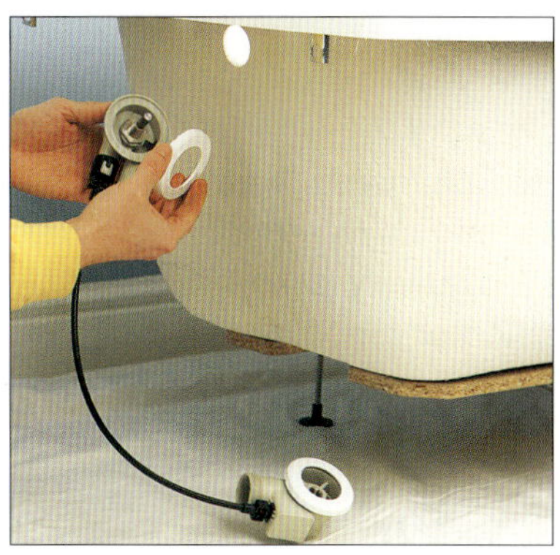

2 Holding one part of the stopper outlet in one hand, screw the second part into the underside section through the outlet in the bathtub. Make sure that the appropriate flange is positioned on this side of the outlet, otherwise apply a bead of silicone sealant.

3 Hold the back section of the overflow outlet in place in the same way, screwing the visible section of the assembly into position on the inside of the bathtub. Again, a flange is generally supplied to create a watertight seal on this side of the assembly. Otherwise, apply sealant.

4 Attach the overflow pipe between the overflow outlet and the underside of the waste assembly. Screw fitting collars with rubber washers are generally used for this.

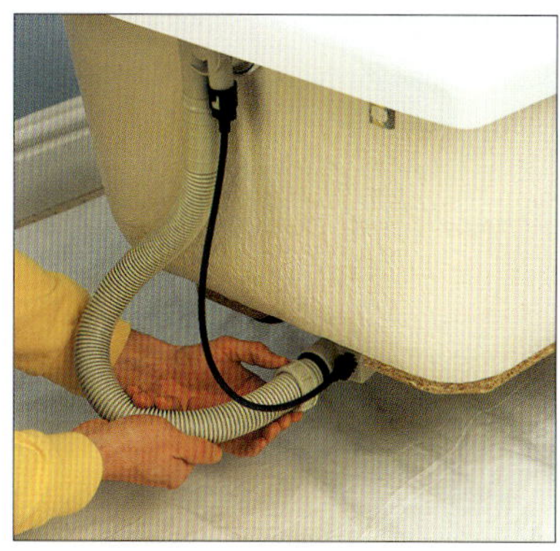

5 Lower the faucets through the precut holes in the bathtub and secure them in place with a locknut. Most faucets are seated on a flange (as here), but if one is not supplied, silicone sealant can be used.

6 Ease the bathtub toward its final position, using a level to help adjust leg heights to be sure that the bathtub is completely level.

7 The bathtub must be held securely in position. You can do this by cutting a channel in the wall and allowing the extreme edge of the bathtub to be supported in this channel. Alternatively, as shown here, fasten supportive brackets into the wall and corresponding brackets on the bathtub rim, then fit the rim over the brackets. Always double-check that the two halves of the brackets align before screwing them in place.

8 Connect the faucets to the water supply and connect the drainage system (see pages 314–15), then screw the feet to the floor.

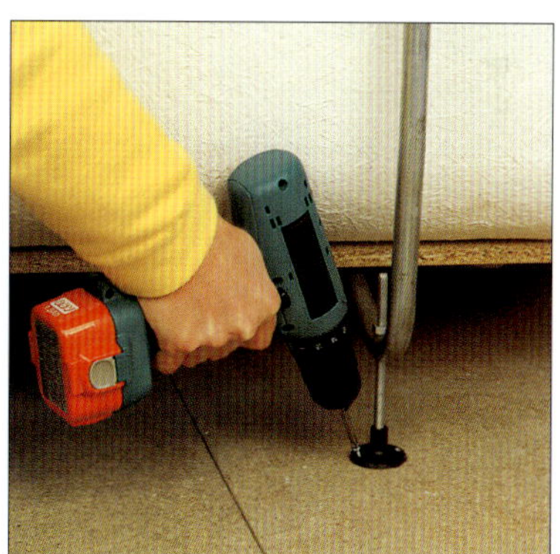

tips of the trade

It is important that bathtubs are stable in order to avoid accidents. You can add extra support by inserting blocks of wood between the floor and underside of the bathtub. Weight can also be spread more efficiently if the feet are positioned on top of planks of wood. In many cases, the extra height this produces is advantageous.

installing a toilet & tank

A cursory glance at a toilet and tank tends to suggest more complicated plumbing than is actually the case. Supply and drainage systems are in fact fairly simple and, as long as the toilet is not being moved too far from the original position, a changeover is a relatively straightforward process. Problems only tend to occur if soil stacks need to be lengthened or repositioned to accommodate a completely new toilet location.

close-coupled toilets

Most modern toilets follow a close-coupled design, where the tank sits directly on top of the bowl. This type of design is the easiest to fit and provides fewer complications than low-level or high-level toilets. The instructions provided here show the general principles involved in the fitting of a close-coupled design.

tools for the job

screwdriver

slip-joint pliers

1 First, assemble the internal tank mechanism. Position the inlet-valve assembly inside the tank by allowing the bottom threaded section to pass through the hole in the base of the tank.

2 Fit the supplied rubber flange over the threaded section, then position the connecting plate.

3 Secure the tank connecting plate in position with a large threaded collar, then insert bolts in the holes on either side of the plate.

4 Insert the flushing-valve mechanism or water control assembly into the tank, again allowing the threaded end of the water inlet pipe to pass through the hole at the bottom of the tank.

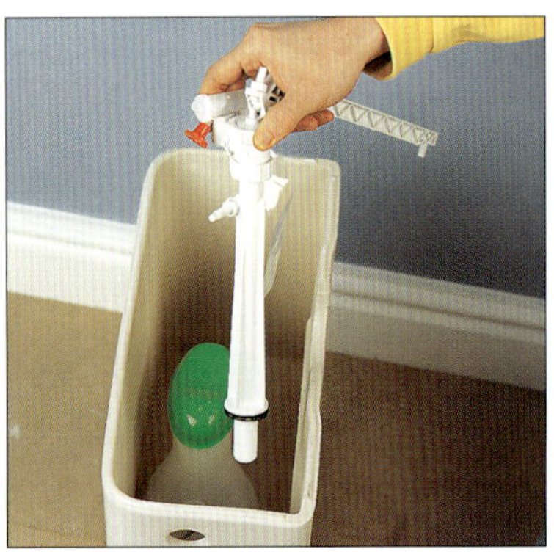

5 Secure it in place using the supplied washer/flange and threaded collar. It is usually only necessary to tighten by hand the collars for the inlet pips and the flush valve. Take care not to crossthread either collar during the tightening process.

6 Fit the flushing handle to the tank, holding it in place with a threaded collar. Make sure that the handle is linked to the flushing-valve assembly.

7 Ease the toilet bowl into position, allowing the outlet pipe to marry with the soil stack.

8 Lift the tank onto the bowl so that the connecting bolts thread through the retaining holes on the pan. Position a rubber flange at the flush entrance so that the threaded section of the inlet-valve assembly is inserted through the flange.

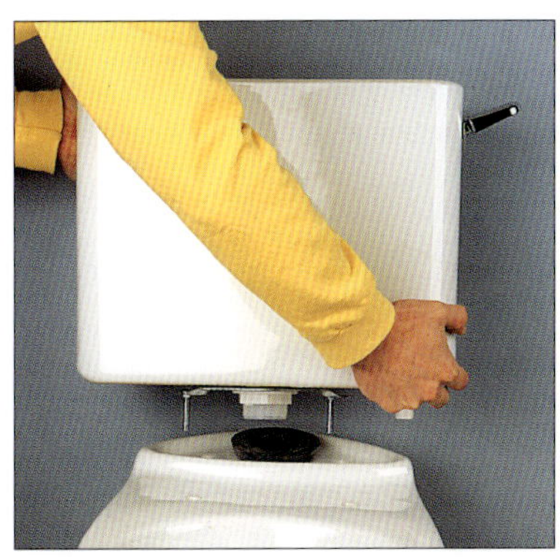

OTHER TYPES OF TOILET

- **Low-level toilets**—These have tanks mounted on the wall above the bowl, with a connecting pipe from the bottom of the tank to the bowl. The tank must be attached to the wall with substantial fasteners because, unlike a close-coupled toilet, the bowl does not support any of its weight.

- **High-level toilets**—The tank is fitted high up the wall so the flush pipe needs to be much longer. Again, wall fasteners must be sturdy enough to support the tank weight.

9 Fasten the nuts supplied by the manufacturer to the tank connecting bolts using both rubber and metal washers to hold the tank securely in place. This will provide a barrier between the metal and ceramic surfaces.

10 Connect the inlet pipe for the cold-water supply to the tank using slip-joint pliers.

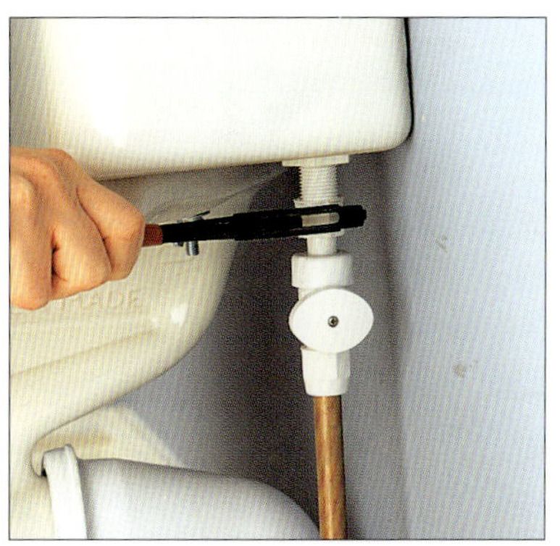

11 If the tank has pre-drilled holes in its back, next to the wall, insert screws to secure the tank in place. Again, use both metal and rubber washers.

You should also insert retaining screws through the holes at the base of the bowl in order to hold it securely in position.

12 Finally, install the toilet seat by securing it in place through the pre-drilled holes at the back of the bowl. Turn the water supply back on—the toilet is now ready for use.

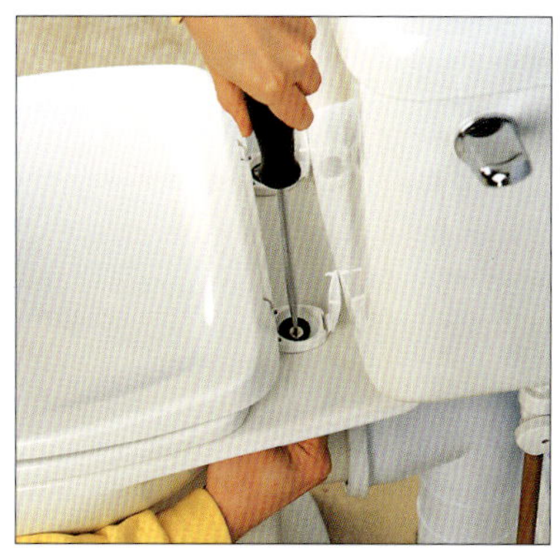

REPOSITIONING A TOILET AGAINST AN INTERIOR WALL

Complications will occur if a toilet is to be moved from an exterior wall to an interior one. The reason that toilets are usually located on or close to an exterior wall is because there is easy access to the soil stack, which tends to run down exterior walls and into the sewer system. Having the toilet on an interior wall necessitates extending the large drainage pipe from the toilet out to the soil stack. Clearly, the dimensions of the drainage pipe make routing difficult because it is unlikely to fit and have the required run if it is positioned below floor level. The alternative method of running the pipe around interior walls is unsightly and is also unlikely to provide the necessary run. As a result, keeping the new toilet position close to the existing one or at least situated on an exterior wall will always make installation procedures much easier.

installing a bidet

If you have the luxury of a spacious bathroom, a bidet is a very useful fitting. There are two types: over-rim and rim supply. The former is illustrated here, and has water coming from faucets above the bidet rim. A rim supply bidet fills from below the rim, and warms the seat as water is pumped into the bowl. This system has a risk of back siphonage, which means a dedicated hot and cold water supply is essential, making it a more complicated undertaking.

over-rim supply bidets

An over-rim supply bidet is installed in a similar way to a bathroom sink. First, make sure that both hot and cold water supplies have been routed for bidet connection (see pages 314–17). The waste pipe can be joined directly to the soil stack or connected to the sink or bathtub waste pipe. A simple T-connector can be cut into either one of these waste outlets for this purpose. However, consider waste heights carefully, because there can be a danger of water from a basin running back into the bowl of the bidet if the waste is much higher than the bidet. Also, waste from the bidet could run back into the bathtub if it is much higher than the bathtub waste. You need to adjust the run of waste pipes to account for this kind of potential problem.

tools for the job

- slip-joint pliers
- adjustable wrenches
- screwdriver
- tape measure
- pipe cutter

1 Thread the top section of the pop-up stopper through the outlet in the bidet, making sure that the correct flange has been installed over the tail. If a flange is not supplied with the outlet, it can be seated on a layer of silicone sealant to produce the necessary watertight seal. If you are using sealant, always be sure to wipe away the excess before it has a chance to dry.

2 Screw the bottom section of the stopper onto the top section underneath the bidet. Make sure that the correct flange is positioned between the stopper section and the ceramic surface of the bidet.

3 Turn your attention to the faucet for the bidet. Position a sealing washer at the base of the faucet—again, if the faucets you are using are not supplied with sealing washers, they can be seated on silicone sealant.

4 Fit the copper hot and cold water supply pipes to the base of the faucet assembly, screwing them firmly in place, but taking care not to overtighten them. Attach the threaded bolt that will be used to secure the faucet in position.

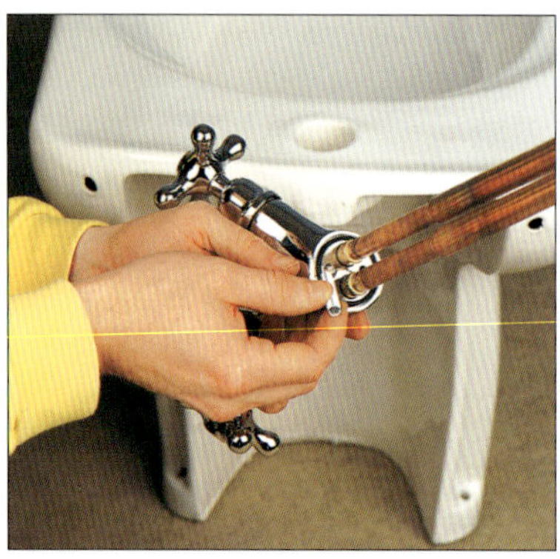

5 Thread the copper pipes of the faucet assembly through the hole in the bidet. Secure the faucet assembly in place using the supplied washers or locknuts. Fasten a locking nut onto the threaded bolt, tightening by hand. You may have to give the nut one or two turns with an adjustable wrench to ensure the faucets are securely in place. Take care not to overtighten.

6 Screw the pop-up stopper lever into the base of the waste outlet. Tightening by hand is usually sufficient, although you may need to use adjustable wrenches.

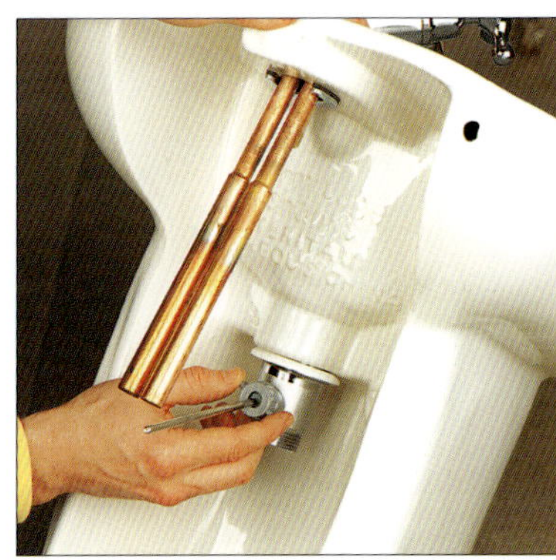

7 Insert the pop-up stopper rod into the stopper lever and join it to the lever with the supplied clamp. Fasten them in place, using a screwdriver to tighten the connection. Adjust the fastening if necessary so that the waste stopper sits correctly in the outlet. The pop-up stopper itself is also adjustable to ensure a watertight fit in the outlet, so make any necessary adjustments now.

8 Make sure that all the necessary inlet pipes and waste stacks are in place, ready for the bidet to be positioned and connected. In this case, a swept T-connector has been used to make the appropriate connection in an existing waste pipe. Shutoff valves have also been fitted to the inlet pipes so that water can be turned off in an emergency. See pages 314–17.

9 Position the bidet, connecting the inlet pipes and waste outlet and trap. Secure the bidet in place by inserting screws at the base of the bidet through the predrilled holes. Take care not to overtighten these fastenings, and use washers if these have been supplied by the manufacturer. The water supply may now be turned on and the bidet can be used.

Providing an extra dimension of hygiene and comfort, bidets can also be a highly ornate element of a bathroom design.

installing a shower

Showers are convenient and efficient bathroom fixtures that consume a fraction of the water used by baths. Shower types vary, as do the mechanisms by which they are controlled—our main concern here is the installation procedure. A shower that is sunk into a wall tends to create a more aesthetically pleasing finish, but surface-mounting the shower is easier to implement. In this example, a shower unit is being fitted into a stud wall.

recessed shower units

tools for the job

- tape measure
- cordless drill/driver
- slip-joint pliers
- adjustable wrenches
- plasterboarding & tiling equipment

1 You will need to install an extra block inside the wall to act as a mounting position for the shower. If it is a new wall, do this during the construction process. If it is an existing wall, strip the drywall or plasterboard and fasten a block at the required height and at a depth that will allow the shower unit to sit behind the wall surface, with the controls standing proud beyond it. Route hot and cold water inlet pipes to the correct position in the wall.

2 Secure the shower unit in place on the supporting blocking so that the connections for the water supply match the unit. Cut the pipe length with a pipe cutter if necessary. Use an adjustable wrench to tighten the connections between the inlet pipes and shower unit.

3 In many cases you will need to connect an additional length of pipe from the unit to the shower head. Follow the guidelines provided by the manufacturer.

4 You should now complete the wall. Marine plywood makes a good background for a tiled shower enclosure, but drywall or plasterboard can be used if it is sealed and/or plastered. Screw the decorative part of the shower head inlet pipe onto the recessed part of the pipe.

5 Fit the appropriate collars and/or washers over the unit and inlet pipe. These generally push into place.

6 Fit the shower head retaining bracket on the wall and connect the hose to the inlet pipe.

installing a bathtub screen

If a shower is being installed above a bathtub, you must fit a screen to protect the room from water spray.

tools for the job

- tape measure
- level
- cordless drill/driver
- screwdriver

1 Use a level to fasten the channeling for the frame vertically above the edge of the bathtub. If fastening into tiles, use the correct type of drill bit to make pilot holes so that you do not damage the surface.

2 Fix the hinge mechanism to the channeling. Designs vary, but in many cases the hinge is a two-part assembly. The first part is used to create a secure wall fastening, to which a second section is added.

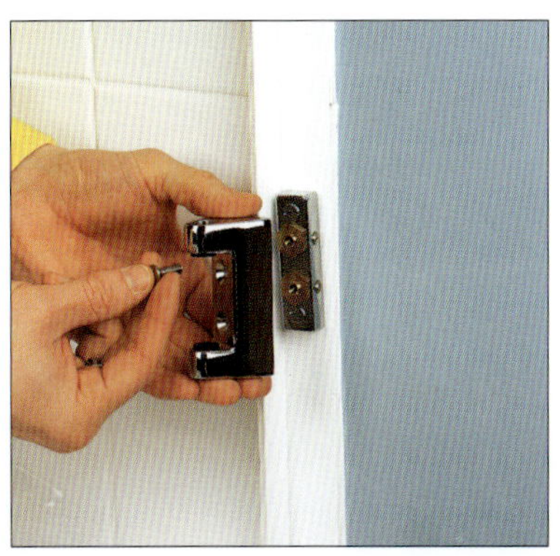

3 Fasten the corresponding hinge sections onto the screen. These are normally of a decorative design. Take care to place any gaskets or protective barriers between the metallic part of the hinge and, in this case, the glass surface.

4 Here, a retaining bolt is pushed through the hinge barrel. It holds the door in place while allowing the hinge mechanism to push the door backward and forward from the bathtub edge. Fit rubber sealant strips to the underedge of the screen.

Simple bathtub screens provide a physical barrier that prevents water overspray. Different shapes and designs can be chosen to match your bathroom layout.

installing kitchens & bathrooms

To a greater or lesser extent, most modern kitchens and bathrooms are based on a built-in design that makes the best use of the available space, while still being functional and attractive. This chapter demonstrates the techniques used for constructing and combining units to produce a built-in kitchen and bathroom. There are always slight differences in unit design between manufacturers, which means techniques will need to be refined. However, this chapter helps to demonstrate that most of the general principles involved in installing kitchens and bathrooms remain constant, irrespective of manufacturing variations. For those instances where unit design does require a change in technique the different options available are also explained.

This stylish kitchen was constructed by building up carcasses, installing a worktop, attaching fronts, and finishing.

assembling knockdown units

Knockdown, or flatpack, is the name given to a unit or carcass that requires assembly before being installed, the latter because of the way they are delivered. Methods for construction will always vary slightly between manufacturers and for different types of unit, but general principles of assembly do remain constant. This chapter demonstrates how to construct a large base cabinet and covers almost all the techniques you are likely to come across.

There can be a surprising number of components in knockdown. It is best to lay out all the carcass sections and panels first, then check the fastenings pack to ensure you have the correct number of sections and the correct choice and quantity of fasteners.

tools for the job

standard-tip screwdriver
Philips-tip screwdriver
cordless drill/driver
hammer

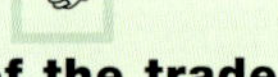

tips of the trade

It can be worth undertaking one or two dry runs putting the unit together without fastenings. This helps to work out how each section relates to the other once the whole unit is complete. Always check each new section has been positioned the right way up.

1 Many knockdowns are assembled following a system of cam bosses and screws in predrilled holes. This offers an efficient connection, as the holes are drilled with great accuracy in a factory. Position bosses according to the guidelines and screw them by hand into the predrilled holes. Some bosses may need a few turns of the screwdriver to fit securely.

2 Attach drawer runners to the side panels, following the marked positions. Only attach a runner on each side panel if the unit includes two drawers. Choose correct screws for the runners—if they are too long, you risk going right through and damaging the outer surface.

3 Position plastic threaded dowels in predrilled holes on the base section and the ends of connecting sections. These dowels simply push into place and will make joints much stronger when the unit is assembled. Some manufacturers use wooden dowels, which will require gluing (see drawers in step 10).

4 Insert cam screws in the appropriate holes indicated (these will eventually correspond with the holes that have had the cam bosses already inserted into them). Again, you should be able just to press these screws into position by hand. Make sure the open side of the cam screw faces the edge of the section, so that it will be possible to join the section to the side panel with the corresponding cam boss. Make sure that the head of the cam screw fits level with the surrounding panel surface.

5 Use the central strengthening vertical piece as the starting point for full assembly. Connect the base of the vertical to the base section, and screw the top strengthening rail in place on top of the vertical. Check that each section is being positioned the right way up.

6 The side sections of the cabinet can now be put in place using the position of the dowels, and cam bosses and screws, as a guide. Tighten the cam screws to produce a rigid structure. To encourage the cam fastenings and dowels to align, you may need to make one or two gentle blows with the butt end of a hammer on the outside of the side sections.

7 The back panel may now be added. This normally slides into position in purpose-made channels in the side panels. You will find that back panels are more often than not thinner than the other section, since they provide no structural strength to the unit as a whole. Secure them in place by nailing brad nails along the bottom edge of the back panel into the edge of the base section. Make sure that the brads are inserted perpendicular to the base panel edge rather than at an angle—if you make an angled insertion, this can cause the brads to break through the surface of the base panel, resulting in a weak fastening and unsightly blemish.

8 Clip the shelf supports in place. These should push in by hand, but you may need to apply one or two knocks with the butt end of a hammer. Now insert the central shelf, allowing it to come to rest on the supports. The shelf will either be held in position by the force of gravity or it will have a clip design, resting both below and on top of the shelf to hold it in position.

9 Screw the central drawer runner(s) in position. Two central runners will be needed for a cabinet with two drawers (one either side of the central vertical piece), otherwise only one will be required.

10 Drawers are usually assembled with dowels, often made of wood, and these need to be glued before the drawer unit is assembled. If no glue is supplied, wood glue will suffice. Wipe away any excess with a cloth before it dries.

11 Allow the doweled joints to dry before attaching the runners. Screw them in position perpendicular to the drawer edge.

12 Finally position the drawer(s), and the cabinet is ready for the first stage of the kitchen-installation process.

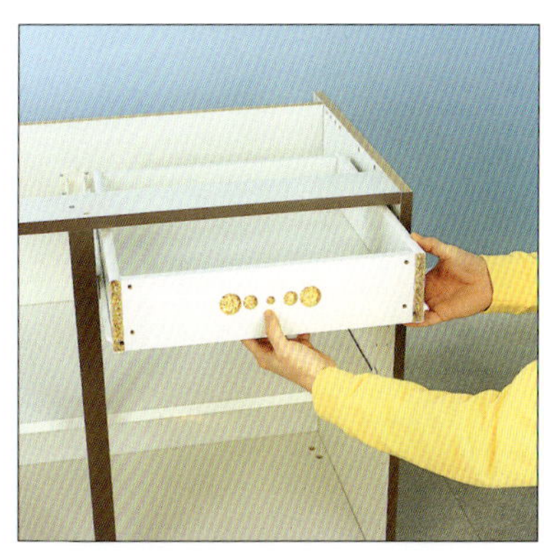

getting level

When installing a new built-in kitchen, it is vital that work begins from a level starting point. From this point the whole kitchen is developed, and any inaccuracy at this stage will be magnified as work continues. The importance of taking time to get a level starting point cannot be emphasized enough.

measuring & marking

The aim is to mark a horizontal level guideline at a height corresponding to the top of the base units, which should always be fitted first. If the units are rigid with no feet to allow height adjustment, the guideline will be equal to unit height. Where units have adjustable feet, a good height is 34–5in. To make the guideline you will need to measure up the highest point in the floor level. Not all floors are perfectly level, and you will need to make adjustments at this stage to counteract the situation.

tools for the job

level

tape measure

pencil

1 In most kitchens at least one unit will be installed in or around a corner (see pages 338–9). This makes an ideal starting point, and you should try to fix the level guideline from one of the corners. If you have a choice of corners, take your level line from the highest. If there are no corner units, simply find the highest point along the floor. Lay a long length of furring strip on the floor against the baseboard, then position a level on top to gauge which way the floor is "running."

2 Mark at the desired unit height, measuring from the floor up the wall surface.

3 No further measurements need be taken up the wall surface, but simply use the level to draw a horizontal guideline on the wall. This will represent the height at which the kitchen cabinets will be fitted.

4 Make an accurate plan of the position of cabinets by marking along the guideline where one ends and the next will begin. Refer to your kitchen plan in order to gain accurate measurements.

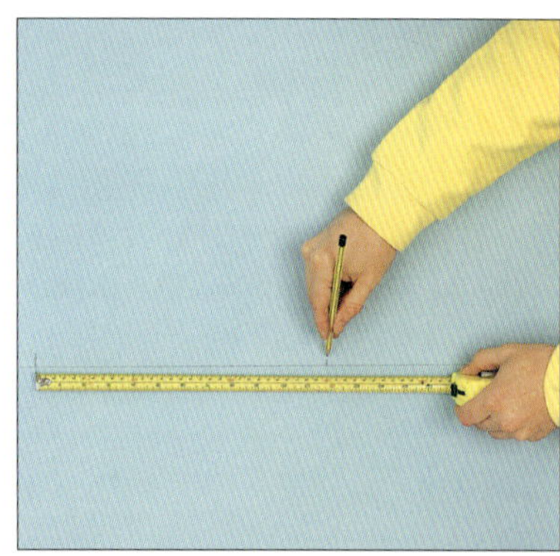

using a furring strip

Attaching a furring strip along the level guideline will facilitate the process of installing units, but is not always specified by manufacturers. However, the strip method creates an excellent fastening point for units and provides extra support for the worktop once installed. If the cabinets are not particularly deep, and as such will be set away from the wall, you will definitely need to attach furring strips to support the worktop. With deeper units personal choice comes into play. Techniques for attaching units to a wall with or without strip are discussed more fully on pages 336–7.

tools for the job

hand saw

cordless drill/driver

power drill

hammer

using concrete anchors

For solid walls, concrete anchors are the ideal choice, as they offer by far the quickest method and create exceptionally strong fastenings.

> **safety advice**
>
> Before knocking in any fastenings, always check the wall surface using a stud finder.

1 Cut a piece of furring strip to length, then drill through it directly into the wall surface below. Drill bit size should correspond to that of the concrete anchor screws being used.

2 To create a solid fixture, simply screw the concrete anchors directly through the wood and into the solid wall below. Continue to make fastenings about 12–18in apart along the length of the furring strip.

using wall plugs

Wall plugs can be used for making fastenings in both solid and hollow walls. A different type of plug is required for each type of wall surface, and you will need to check the packet. Here, a solid wall is shown.

1 Drill into the wall through the strip. In some cases an electric power drill may be a more suitable choice than a cordless drill/driver, especially if the wall is made from particularly strong material.

2 Press a wall plug into the hole and then insert a screw into the plug. Use a hammer to gently tap the screw and plug further into the wall, until the screw will go no further without a considerable increase in the force applied with the hammer. You will need to tighten up the screw after hammering it in to make absolutely sure the fixture is solid. Employ a cordless drill/driver for this. Continue to add further wall plug fixtures along the strip as required.

fitting legs

Whether you have purchased a knockdown or solid-carcass kitchen, the manufacturer will almost certainly have left you with the job of attaching legs to each cabinet.

> **tools for the job**
>
> cordless drill/driver

1 Screw the legs so that they are in the halfway position along the adjusting thread.

2 Position the legs in the pre-drilled holes on the underside of the cabinet.

3 Attach them in place with the screws supplied. The units are now ready to be installed.

positioning base units

Having gained a level guideline, attention may now be turned to the job of positioning and installing the actual units. A level is again the most important tool here, for although the back edge of the units can be aligned against the furring-strip guideline, the front edge must also be resting at the same level. Positioning the units before installation thus becomes a methodical process of adjusting leg height to ensure the unit is level across all dimensions.

unit fastenings

As a final preparation before the units are positioned, any fastening brackets supplied will need to be attached to the units. There are usually just two types of bracket—those for the worktop and those for the wall.

tools for the job

- hammer
- cordless drill/driver or screwdriver

worktop brackets

These are small plastic blocks that are knocked into pre-drilled holes in the side of the unit. To form the fastening mechanism between the unit and worktop, a screw is inserted through the bracket into the worktop.

wall brackets

These are L-shaped brackets that are fixed to the back corner of the side panels on a unit. Their L-shape means that once the unit is in position against the wall, a further screw is inserted through the bracket to hold the unit in place.

NONADJUSTABLE UNITS

For units without adjustable legs, small shims should be used to adjust the height as necessary. You can cut your own wedges from 1 x 2in furring strip.

positioning & leveling

The kitchen design featured is of a single run of units along one wall. It is best to begin in the corner of the room if possible, and although kitchen units are not too heavy, you might want to employ a helper to lift the larger ones into position.

tools for the job

- level
- cordless drill/driver
- clamp

1. Lift the first unit into place in the corner, addressing the back edge to the furring-strip guideline.

2. Adjust leg height by unscrewing or screwing the legs as required. This will raise or lower the unit as a whole, thereby bringing it to the correct height for leveling with the furring-strip guideline.

3. Hold a level across the top of the unit to make final adjustments on height. The top of the unit should sit flush with the top edge of the strip. Check the position of the unit by holding the level across all directions on top of the unit, adjusting leg height as required.

4 Move the next unit into position, adjusting leg height as required and repeating the leveling procedure. Be sure to hold the level across both units to check they are positioned at the same height.

5 Continue to add further units until the entire run is complete, checking they are all level with each other. Clamp adjacent units together for fastening purposes. If the design of your unit does not include pre-drilled holes for jointing, then make your own by drilling through the unit at a point that will be hidden by the hinge plate once it is attached.

6 Screw all the units together to form a tight fastening. Provided they are all level, this will turn single units into a rigid, seamless row.

7 Attach the units to the furring strip by firmly inserting screws through the wall brackets and into the furring strip on the wall.

wall fastening alternatives

The method demonstrated above is not the only way of fixing units to a wall, and some manufacturers may specify their own particular guidelines. Much of this will be due to the depth of the units. The technique shown will work for most unit types. It is vital, however, to check that the depth of worktop you have will not be too shallow if the units are brought forward from the wall surface using only the furring-strip technique. For kitchen cabinets that are either relatively shallow or particularly deep, you may need to consider applying the following alternative techniques.

shallow units

For shallow units, follow the steps described on pages 334–5 for attaching furring-strip guidelines to the wall. In order to account for standard worktop depth, however, the units will have to be set slightly farther away from the wall. Use the technique described on the left to gain the correct height of the units. Then attach additional, shorter lengths of wood to provide a solid fastening between the unit and the wall.

deep units

For deep units it is very likely that the depth of the worktop will be only slightly larger than the actual depth of the unit. As a result, it is essential that the units themselves are positioned as closely as possible to the wall. In this case, simply refrain from using a wooden furring strip to act as a guideline, and instead attach the units directly to the wall, still using wall brackets but carefully following a pencil guideline.

assembling corner units

On pages 336–7, beginning in the corner of a room was demonstrated using a straight run of base units. However, it is often the case that kitchen layout will require cabinets to extend around an inside corner. In this situation it is still best to begin in the corner of the room, but clearly the unit used will be a corner base cabinet rather than a standard base unit. The technique for installation will therefore need to be modified slightly to account for this variation in design.

Corner units can be supplied ready-made, but they are more often supplied part-assembled and require further assembly and leveling, as shown here. Some corner units are designed to have a simple shelf storage system. Another storage option, however, is a carousel system that facilitates access once the unit is fitted. Although a carousel system can be more complicated to install, the space-saving possibilities make it very worthwhile.

tools for the job

- cordless drill/driver
- hammer
- Philips-tip screwdriver
- level

1 Add an extra leg to the assembled part of the base unit carcass. This leg is generally positioned directly below the pivotal point for the carousel unit, and will provide extra support for both the unit and carousel when loaded. Adjust leg height to a similar level to that of the other four legs on the unit.

2 Before the unit carcasses are transported they will often be fitted with an inside temporary support to maintain their shape and reduce the risk of damage. Once the extra leg has been added and the unit is turned up the correct way, this temporary support may be removed. Following the guidelines provided by the manufacturer, use a hammer to knock in shelf connectors along the edge of the carcass. These will correspond to the attachment of the self-assembly part of the unit.

3 Install the carousel brake ring into the predrilled section at the base of the carcass. Make sure the ring is the correct way around.

4 Thread the top shelf of the carousel onto the supporting pole. Position a supporting dowel or pin through the pole to stop the shelf from slipping down the pole. Then take the second (lower) carousel shelf, and thread it into position. If required, attach a supporting dowel to prevent slipping, as for the first shelf. Attach the lock roller to the underside of the lower shelf, making sure that the arm of the roller is in the correct position as indicated by the manufacturer's guidelines.

tips of the trade

A particularly useful tool to use when you are attempting to align and position kitchen units is a 2yd (6ft 6in) spirit level. The length makes it much easier to check the level of a number of units at the same time once they are in position. This is especially useful in L-shaped kitchens, where you may wish to allow the level to span from one wall of units across to the other. Although these extended spirit levels are quite expensive, if you are a home-improvement enthusiast this tool will prove invaluable for both kitchen installation and future projects.

5 The secured carousel shelves may now be positioned inside the corner unit carcass. Thread the pole up through the top of the carcass before allowing the base of the pole to rest inside the carousel brake ring. Once in position, knock the securing holder in place through the top of the unit. This will hold the pole and carousel securely in place, while allowing it to rotate fully for ease of access.

6 With the carousel securely attached inside the pre-assembled unit, attention may now be turned to assembling the knockdown section of the corner unit. Before making a start, however, it is important to take a little time to lay out the pieces in front of you on the floor. This will allow you to identify the different sections as required and make sure each section is around the right way. Once you are familiar with the layout, use a hammer to knock in connectors along the edges of the sections that correspond to the connectors inserted in step 2.

7 Where indicated in the manufacturer's instructions, use corner-connecting blocks to join the back section of the unit to what will become the side section of the corner unit as a whole. You will probably find it easier to use a hand-held screwdriver rather than a cordless driver in this situation, since it allows you to maintain greater control while holding the relevant sections in position.

8 Added strength is often given to the joint in the floor sections of these units by creating a doweled join between the floor and side sections. Glue and insert dowels, making sure that when the floor section is positioned it joints neatly with the side panel. Use a damp cloth to wipe away any excess wood glue before it dries.

9 To complete the self-assembly section of the corner unit, add two further legs to supply support for the unit as a whole once it is assembled. Screw these in place in the usual way.

10 Stand the assembled corner section up on its legs and match the connectors positioned in steps 2 and 7. Corresponding connectors should simply screw into each other. Again, a hand-held screwdriver is often the best tool for this purpose.

11 Position the finished unit in the corner of the room, leveling the legs to gain the correct level. Use the spirit level across all angles on top of the unit to ensure precise positioning, as all the other cabinets will take their lead from the position of the corner unit.

installing wall units

As with base units, wall units must also be installed exactly level to achieve the best possible appearance and in order to function properly, allowing the doors to be opened and closed smoothly. Wall cabinets rely on wall fastenings to secure them in position, so it is vital that these fastenings are correctly installed. Most units are hung on wall brackets and for further strength tend to come already fitted with a fastening rail, where screws can be inserted directly through the back of the unit and into the wall surface. This combination of brackets and rail provides the best method for securely positioning wall cabinets.

tools for the job

- cordless drill/driver
- tape measure
- pencil
- level
- screwdriver
- clamp

1 Before taking measurements for wall bracket position, drill some pilot holes in the fastening rail on the back of each of the wall units —two or three holes per unit should be adequate.

2 Measure up from the top of the base units to what will be the bottom edge of the wall units. This distance can vary according to personal preference, but you should bear in mind certain safety issues. Where a wall unit is directly above a range, the distance must be at least 2ft. Where units are either side of a range, a minimum distance of 1ft 6¼in is required. Therefore a good base height for wall cabinets is somewhere between 1ft 6in and 1ft 8in. Remember to adjust your measurements to account for the depth of the worktop. The height is measured from the top edge of the worktop, so you will need to add worktop depth on top of unit height.

WALL UNIT HEIGHT

To determine the position of wall units you will need to decide what height best suits your needs. A key factor is the stature of the person or persons who most frequently make use of the kitchen facilities—they should not need to overstretch when reaching into cupboards or bang their head when preparing food. Issues of safety should, however, be accounted for. As discussed in step 2, cabinets above and either side of a range must have a minimum height. This minimum often then dictates the height of the other units, as it is better to have an even run of units rather than incorporating a step for the range.

3 Use the mark made to indicate the height of the units to draw a level pencil guideline. Use a spirit level as a straightedge so that you do not need to make farther marks along the wall—simply ensure the bubble remains level. This guideline identifies the base position of all the wall units.

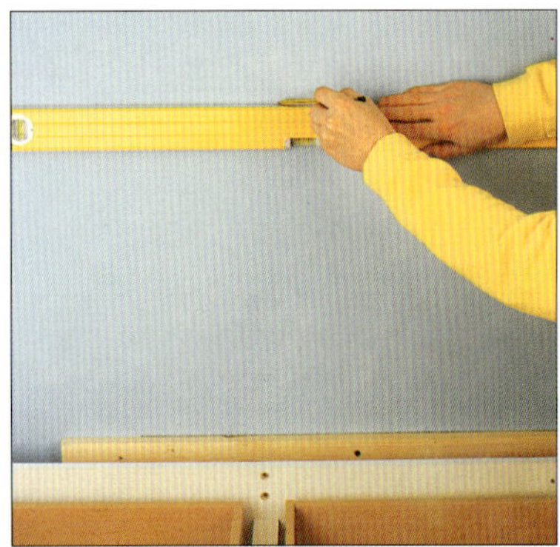

4 Measure up from the base guideline a distance equal to the height of the wall units and draw a further level line to denote what will be their top edge once in place. Paying close attention to the kitchen plan, draw plumb lines to separate the positions of the different wall units.

Follow the manufacturer's guidelines to gain the correct distance between the plumb and horizontal guidelines and the edges of each bracket. Mark this position with a pencil.

5 Hold the brackets in place and attach them to the wall with suitable fastenings. Remember to choose the correct type of wall plug depending on whether it is a solid or hollow wall. Continue to attach wall brackets—most units will require two brackets, one for each corner.

safety advice

When drilling and fastening into walls, take care not to coincide fastenings with supply pipes or cables. Use a stud finder to help avoid this.

6 Hook the wall cabinet over the brackets to hold it in position on the wall. For larger units it may be worthwhile employing a helper to lift the cabinet into place.

7 Once all the units are in place, some minor adjustment may be required for final leveling purposes. In the top inside corner of the units, there is normally an adjustment block that has two functions: one screw can be tightened or loosened to adjust the height of the unit, the other is used to tighten the unit against the wall bracket once you are satisfied that it is totally level. In order to gain access to these screws, it may be necessary to remove a shelf from inside the unit.

8 Wall cabinets should always be mechanically jointed together to be sure they create a rigid storage structure. To make a fastening, clamp together adjacent units and drill directly through the side panel of one unit into the next. Position the hole close to the front edge, in line with the hinge fastenings.

9 Use two-part steel connection screws to joint the units, inserting two fastenings along each unit edge. Tighten with a screwdriver.

10 As an extra precaution to be sure the unit structure is solid, fasten directly through the back of the unit by inserting screws through the holes drilled in step 1.

tips of the trade

The methods recommended in order to achieve a strong fastening with screws inserted in the fastening rail will vary according to the type of screw and wall surface.

- If the wall has to be plugged, you will need to predrill holes in the wall surface, so that the screw may be inserted once the wall unit is in place. To make this plugged fastening, after step 7 mark through the drilled hole in the fastening rail, remove the wall unit and then drill and plug the wall before repositioning the unit.
- On solid walls, use concrete anchor screws so that plugging is not necessary.
- Where the drilled hole in the fastening rail coincides with wooden studs in a hollow wall, there is no need for plugging as a standard screw will fasten directly into the stud.

attaching doors & drawer fronts

Doors, drawer fronts, and handles add the finishing touch to a kitchen cabinet. Although the fastening procedure for all these items is very straightforward, because they contribute to the finished look of a kitchen it is important to take the time to be sure correct technique is employed.

tools for the job

cordless drill/driver

screwdriver

cupboard doors

Most manufacturers precut holes on the inside of doors to indicate the exact hinge position, and predrill holes on the cabinet for the hinge plate. Nevertheless, precision is still vital when inserting screws to make sure the door functions smoothly.

1 Position hinges on the inside of the door and screw them in place securely.

tips of the trade

Always select the correct size of screw for each item. If the screws are too long, they will penetrate through to the front of the drawer or door front.

2 Fasten hinge plates in the predrilled holes in the carcass. A cordless drill/driver is the ideal tool to use so that the screws bite firmly, but set it on a low speed to maintain good control with the driver.

3 Position the door so the hinges slip over the hinge plates, then tighten the retaining screws.

4 If the door height needs to be adjusted to level up the edges, this can be done by loosening off the hinge plate screws that allow the door to be moved up or down.

5 Tightening or undoing the hinge screw allows further adjustment of door position to gain a level when the door is closed. One screw may require tightening while the other screw needs loosening.

attaching handles

Manufacturers generally make a small indentation on the inside of doors as a guide for attaching handles.

1 Using the correct-size drill bit —it should match the shank of the handle screw—drill through the

door from the inside to the front. Hold a block of wood against the door front at the point where the drill bit will break through. This will prevent the surface of the door splintering. You may need to drill more than one hole, depending upon your chosen handle design.

2 Insert the handle-retaining screw(s) through the hole(s) just drilled.

3 Secure the handle in place by tightening the screw(s).

corner unit doors

The door fronts of corner units tend to require slightly different fastening techniques, due to the many designs that facilitate access to the awkward storage space. Technique will also vary according to whether the doors are full-height, in that they make up the total height of the unit, or whether dummy drawer fronts need to be attached before installation.

full-height option

With corner units, a post is attached to the inside edge of one of the doors for a seamless appearance when the doors are closed. Secure the post in place by attaching fastening plates to the back of the door to overlap onto the corner post. Use the procedures described above for attaching doors and handles to the corner unit.

170-degree opening option

Alternative hinges are available for corner units. These are slightly more complex in design in that they can be opened to 170 degrees, making access inside the unit much easier.

dummy drawer option

In this situation, more fastening plates are used to overlap between the door and drawer front. Thus when the cabinet is in a closed position it appears to function like separate cupboards and drawers, where in fact the corner unit is only a cupboard.

attaching drawer fronts

Check the manufacturer's guidelines as to whether handles need to be attached before the drawer fronts are screwed in, or afterward.

1 Match the predrilled holes and double-check the drawer front is the right way around.

2 Screw through the predrilled holes inside the drawer into the drawer front to secure it in place. Hold the front in position to ensure a good, tight fastening.

installing wooden worktop

Most varieties of worktop are installed using similar techniques, although these can vary in particular cases. For example, wooden worktop is not always supplied with a molded edge, so if you want one, choose carefully or you will have to create it yourself on your worktop. You may also need to take into account variations in cutting techniques and plan so that the best use is made of the factory edges on the worktop material.

deciding on cut positions

Factory-cut edges on a worktop will be much more accurate than those cut at home, so the best use should be made of them. The diagram opposite shows the ideal arrangement of cut edges for a typical worktop formation. The ends you cut yourself should form junctions with the walls, so that their edges will be covered by final finishing on the walls. In this design, only one cut end is exposed as a visible edge, and with further finishing the cut will, in effect, be hidden. It is best to join the sides to factory-cut ends in order to achieve a precise fit.

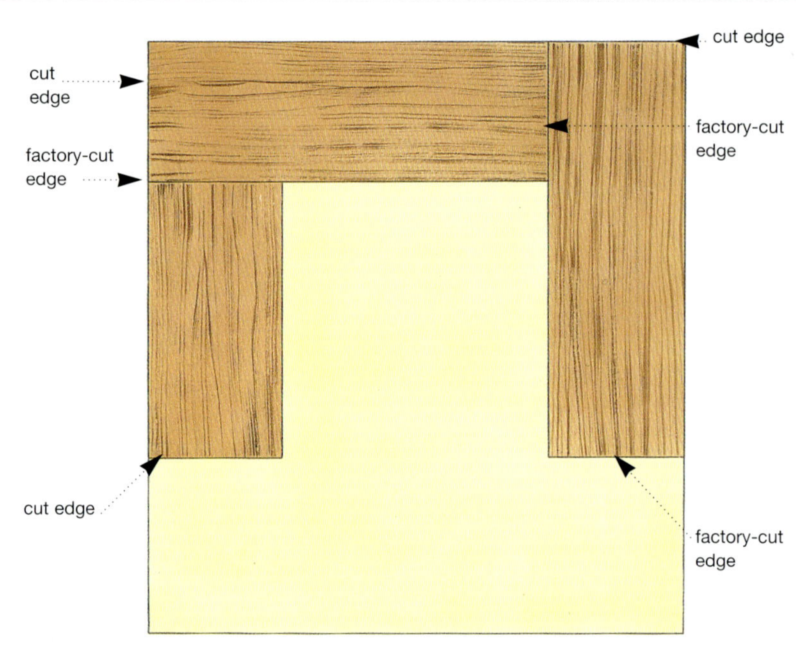

tools for the job

- hand saw or jigsaw
- tape measure & pencil
- clamp
- router

installing a straight run

A straight worktop run is easiest to install, but the same techniques can be used for more complex designs.

1 Cut the worktop to length and position it approximately on top of the units. Measure the overhang at the front. If the units have been installed correctly, this distance should be slightly more than the required overhang. Normal overhangs are between ⅛ and ¾in, measuring from the door or drawer front. Ridges or waves in the shape of the wall may cause the initial overhang to vary slightly along the length of the worktop. Rather than simply trimming a specific length off the back of the worktop, therefore, you may need to cut away a more graduated portion. To do this, first position the worktop so that its front edge overhangs by the same amount along the entire run of cabinets, while making sure that the back edge is touching the wall in at least one place.

tips of the trade

Cutting to length—Wooden worktop can be cut with a jigsaw or hand saw. Make sure the correct blade has been fitted if you are using a jigsaw, as anything too coarse will splinter the edges of the cut. If using a hand saw, keep the angle of the blade shallow in relation to the worktop surface to produce the cleanest possible cut.

2 The next step is to make a scribing block to help work out how much of the back edge requires cutting away. The size of the scribing block will be equal to the distance between the front edge of the work surface and the carcass, less whatever distance you wish for the finished overhang of the worktop. Cut a small block of wood to this exact size. Hold a pencil next to the block and draw a guideline by sliding the block along the back wall. You may wish to clamp the work surface in position to ensure it does not move during this procedure.

3 Cut along the guideline using a jigsaw or hand saw. Accuracy is important, but any small splinters caused by the jigsaw can be sanded away and will, in any case, be hidden when the worktop is installed against the wall surface.

4 Reposition the worktop so that the cut back edge is tight against the wall, with the front edge forming an even overhang along the front of the unit. Clamp the worktop in position, screwing through the brackets if supplied. Also fasten into the underside of the worktop through the front fastening rail of the units.

dealing with corners

Corners should not present too many problems, provided that the ideal positioning for cut edges has been taken into account—follow the layout indicated by the diagram opposite. Separate lengths should be cut to size and scribed as required, before jointing together.

1 At the corner joint, apply a generous amount of wood glue along the joint.

2 Move the sections into position, creating a strong bond. Wipe away excess glue with a cloth before it dries. Some manufacturers supply fastening plates that can be attached on the underside of the joint to help hold it firmly in position.

finishing the edge

A router is the ideal tool to add a decorative edge to the worktop. Choose the cutter according to the type of finished edge you require.

1 Follow the manufacturer's guidelines for the router, and lock the cutter in position.

2 Run the router along the edge of the worktop to create a molded edge. Work in smooth, continuous motions—by staying in particular areas you can singe the wood.

installing other worktop

In addition to the many wooden varieties, there are a number of other types of worktop available in a range of materials, including laminate and synthetic or natural stone. Installing natural and synthetic stone worktops should really be left to the professionals, but laminated worktop can be installed using a similar technique to wooden worktop, with only slight changes in terms of planning and procedure.

deciding on cut positions

The arrangement of cut edges for laminated worktops is similar to that indicated for wooden worktops on page 344. It equally follows that cut ends should, if possible, be positioned against wall junctions so that their edge will be covered by whatever finish is applied to the wall. However, since laminated worktops cannot be sanded and their edges are not finished by routing, it is even more important to position factory cut edges at the exposed ends. Jointing strips can be used to neaten the effect of inaccurate cuts in corners.

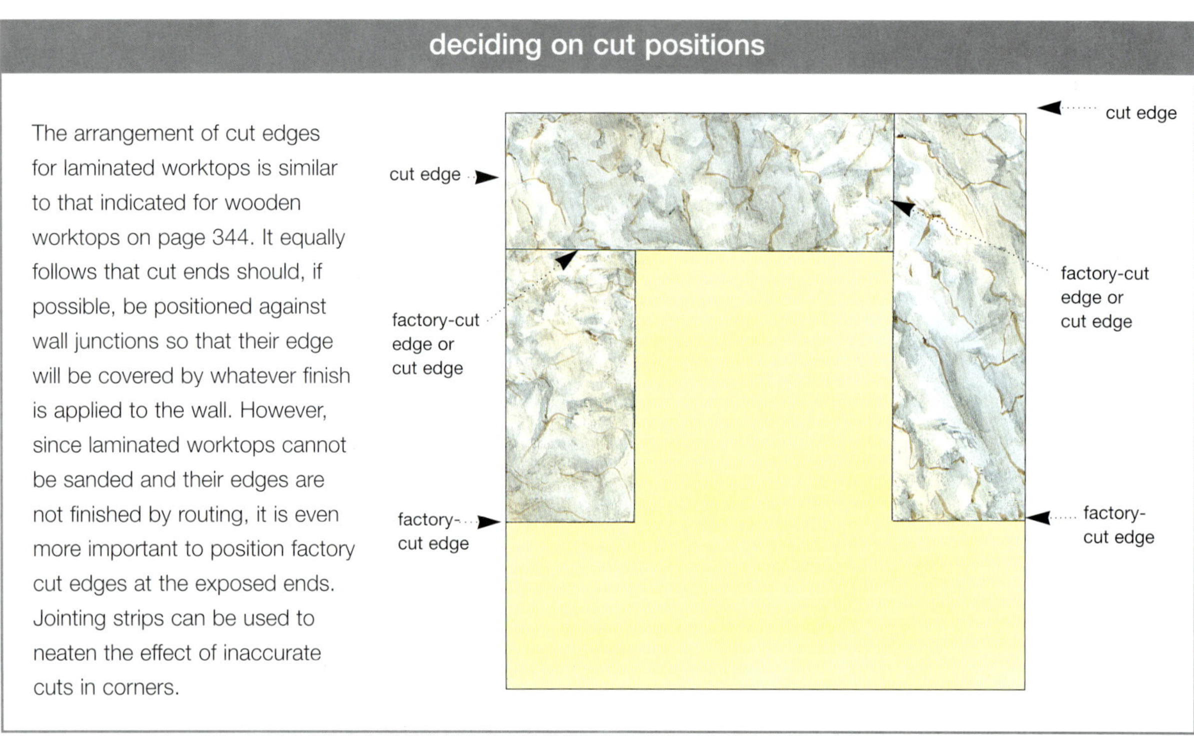

tools for the job

- tape measure & pencil
- wooden straightedge
- hand saw or jigsaw
- hacksaw
- cordless drill/driver

cutting worktop

Laminated worktops may be cut with either a hand saw or jigsaw. If using a jigsaw it is vital to choose a blade designed for cutting through laminate, otherwise the surface of the worktop can splinter. Cutting the worktop with the underside uppermost reduces the risk of splintering even more.

1 Mark the required length and draw a precise guideline across the width of the worktop using a length of wood as a straightedge.

2 Move the wood to one side of the guideline, a distance equal to that between the edge of the jigsaw and its blade. Screw the wood in place, securely but temporarily, at this point on the underside of the worktop. Cut through the worktop holding the jigsaw against the wood. This method produces a perfectly straight cut. Make sure the worktop is well supported when cutting, as any shift in position will risk splitting the laminated surface.

dealing with corners

It is extremely difficult to make an accurate cut across the laminated worktop so that it can be glued and installed in the same way as for wooden worktop. Even the slightest blemish in a cut or unevenness in positioning will magnify any problems. To overcome this problem, jointing strips are commonly used to create a strong joint between sections.

1 Cut the jointing strip to the exact width required for the laminated worktop—strips are usually made from aluminum, which can be cut using a hacksaw.

2 Apply some silicone sealant along the cut edge of the worktop, and then screw the jointing strip in place along the edge.

3 Add a further quantity of silicone sealant along the facing edge of the adjoining worktop section, which should already be in place on the unit. Then slide the section with the jointing strip into position level with the edge covered with sealant.

4 Screw through the fastening rails in the carcass into the underside of the worktop. Pay special attention at the corner. Wipe away any excess silicone, then allow it to dry and create a watertight bond.

tips of the trade

Attaching straight lengths—For straight lengths of laminated worktop, follow the same technique described for wooden worktop on pages 344–5. Check the correct jigsaw blade is installed for cutting laminated finish.

finishing edges

The manufacturer will have provided laminated strips to finish the worktop ends. These are applied using a warm iron, which melts and activates an adhesive on the back of the laminated strip to stick it securely in place.

tools for the job

- iron
- scissors
- utility knife

Heat the iron to the temperature specified by the manufacturer. Cut the laminated strip to size with scissors and hold it against the worktop edge. Gently run the iron across the surface of the strip until it bonds. Once the adhesive has dried and the strip is securely positioned, trim the edge of the strip to ensure a neat and precise finish—a utility knife is ideal for this purpose.

WORKTOP OPTIONS

- **Natural stone**—To fit a natural stone worktop, such as granite, create a template of the area required first and give this to the factory to cut to the correct size and polish. The worktop is fitted in large sections, and this is best carried out by professional craftspeople. An epoxy-based resin is normally used for dealing with joints. Since the stone has no elasticity, it is vital that the units are exactly level, since any undulations will cause the stone to crack under its own weight.
- **Synthetic stone**—This type of worktop also needs to be templated for installation, which is best done by professionals. A level surface is similarly crucial for installation.

attaching cornice, pelmet, & end panels

Cornice, pelmet, and end panels provide finishing touches to cabinets and are used as embellishments to improve the overall appearance of the kitchen. These items have no structural role to play, and are primarily concerned with hiding fastenings and rounding the edges and sides of cabinets, to create a pleasing finished appearance.

tools for the job

- tape measure & pencil
- miter saw
- cordless drill/driver
- caulk gun
- clamp

attaching cornice

Cornice is the decorative edging fitted around the top edge of wall cabinets to provide a molded and framed finish to the run, enhancing the built-in look. Fastenings are hidden from view when inserted through the cornice top into the cabinet tops. Attaching cornice is a process of careful measuring and fastening, and accuracy is important for installing cornice round a corner.

1 Note how the design of the cornice will relate to the fastening process, then measure the required length and cut the two pieces to size. Mark on the end of each piece the 45-degree angle cut required to form the miter joint. You will usually need to align the cornice with the 90-degree angle made by the corner of the wall unit carcass. However, if the cabinet includes an end panel and/or door extending slightly from the carcass, this should be taken into account.

2 Make the angled cut on the cornice using a miter saw for accuracy. Make sure the saw is well supported to prevent tearing the cornice surface as the cut is made.

3 Screw the first section of cornice in position, allowing the screws to bite firmly into the cabinet. Be sure to use screws of the appropriate length so that they do not penetrate through to inside the cabinet.

4 Apply some wood glue to the end of the fastened section before attaching the next piece.

5 Position the next cornice piece, forming the miter joint by hand initially, and allow the glue to produce a tight bond. Continue by screwing the cornice in place, employing the same technique described in step 3.

6 In some cases a tiny gap may appear in the miter joint. Fill this gap with silicone sealant of a similar

color to the cornice. Wipe away excess with a cloth before it dries.

attaching pelmet

Many manufacturers produce one shape of molding that can act for both cornice and pelmet, such is their similarity. The main difference is that pelmet is attached to the bottom, rather than the top edge of the cabinet. The technique for installation is very similar. Measure and cut the pelmet as for cornice; however, you will need to clamp the pelmet in place to allow it to be fastened to the underside of the cabinets.

attaching end panels

End panels are an optional fixture attached to the ends of both wall and base cabinets. They are chosen to match the door and drawer fronts.

1 Cut the panel to height, then position it at the end of the unit, overlapping the front edge. Pull the drawer out to allow access for a tape measure, and measure the distance required for the panel to overhang the front of the unit. Cut away any extra from the back edge. Most walls are not totally level, so it is best to scribe the back edge of the panel to create a neat fit. While measuring the overhang at the front, therefore, allow the panel to touch the wall in at least one place. Then measure and cut a scribing block, which will produce the required overhang.

2 Draw a guideline along the back edge of the panel, using the scribing block to maintain distance.

3 Cut away the unwanted section of panel with a jigsaw using a blade suitable for laminate. Position and clamp the panel at the end of the cabinet, then insert screws from inside the unit into the back of the panel. Screwing from the inside makes sure no damage is visible.

tips of the trade

As an alternative method, apply bonding adhesive or silicone sealant to the end panel before screwing it in place. Thus you will only need one or two screw fastenings while the adhesive or sealant dries.

End panels, cornice, and pelmet help to lift the appearance of what are essentially functional units in a kitchen design.

attaching plinth

As cornice and pelmet provide a finished edge to wall cabinets, so plinth provides the finished edge to the bottom of base units. For units with legs, plinth is fitted by means of clips attached to the back of the piece of plinth and then clipped in place on the legs.

tools for the job

- tape measure & pencil
- miter saw
- hand saw or jigsaw
- combination square
- cordless drill/driver
- iron
- scissors
- utility knife

1 Plinth is generally supplied in standard lengths of a set height. In most cases, the height will not need to be cut down, as units tend to be manufactured so that the plinth fits comfortably underneath. A slight gap between the top of the plinth and the underside of the unit should not cause a problem, since this area is not in general view. Before cutting plinth to the correct length, check to see whether you will also need to reduce the height at the same time. Remember this gap may not be consistent under all units, especially if the floor has a slope. You should therefore check the height measurement in several positions.

2 Cut the plinth to the correct length and, if necessary, reduce in height. You can use a hand saw or jigsaw to cut the plinth across its width, but a miter saw set to a 90-degree angle will provide a cleaner and more accurate cut for the best possible joints with other sections. Use a hand saw or jigsaw to adjust plinth height.

3 Lay out the cut length of plinth in front of the base units, allowing its bottom edge to rest against the unit legs (the front of the plinth should be facing down). Use a combination square and pencil to draw a series of lines on the back of the plinth to correspond with the center of the base legs.

4 Attach clip brackets in the center of each guideline. Make sure the screws being used are not too long, otherwise they will penetrate through to the front face of the plinth and cause unsightly damage.

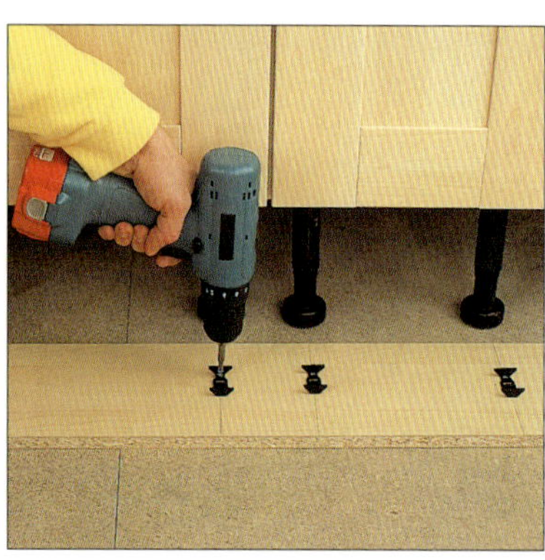

5 Position the clips in each of the brackets so they are still aligned with the base unit legs.

6 If a sealant strip is supplied, turn the plinth upside down and attach the strip to the bottom edge. The purpose of a sealant strip is to create a neat, watertight seal that facilitates cleaning.

7 Having applied the sealant strip—if applicable, otherwise after the clips have been positioned—turn the plinth back up the right way and clip it in position on the base unit legs.

8 Once again check the plinth height. If flooring is yet to be laid, bear in mind it is best for the flooring material to extend under the units, with the plinth fitting neatly on top. Use a piece of cardboard or board similar in height to your choice of flooring to check for adequate tolerance. If you find there is not enough, unclip the plinth and cut down the height further.

inside corners

Inside corners present a slight problem when dealing with plinths, as it is unlikely that a leg will fall precisely on the point where the plinth needs to be jointed. You will therefore need to use another type of bracket, which joints the two plinths together to form a connection rigid enough to hold both ends securely in place.

1 Cut the two lengths of plinth so that one length extends slightly farther under the units than would be the case for an exact corner joint. Lay this longer length on the floor so that the front is facing up. Secure a fastening bracket on the front face in a central position, slightly back from the point where the two sections of plinth will ultimately joint.

2 Attach the connecting clip for the corner bracket at the end of the shorter length of plinth on the back face. When the two lengths are positioned, the clip on the back edge of the shorter length will joint with the bracket on the longer length, clipping together to form a tight inside joint in the corner.

dealing with cut ends

In some cases the cut end of a length of plinth may be visible, for example, on outside corners where there is often no option but to have an exposed end. If this situation arises, employ a similar technique for dealing with the cut ends of a worktop, and cover over the end with a thin strip of laminate (see also page 347).

1 Measure and cut the laminated strips to size with scissors.

2 Position the strip on the end of the plinth, then smooth over the strip with a warm iron—the heat from the iron causes the adhesive to bond with the cut end. Since it is a contact adhesive, there is no need for clamping. Once it is secure, trim the strip with a utility knife for a neat finish.

PLINTH OPTIONS

Although built-in kitchens normally include specially manufactured plinth, it is possible to make your own using either MDF or prepared softwood planks. The same procedure is used for fixing the plinth in place, but the main benefit with this method is that more options for finishing are available—for example, planking can be stained to provide a natural look.

installing breakfast bars

Breakfast bars are becoming an increasingly popular addition to kitchen design. They can be built separate and freestanding or integrated into a run of built-in units, thus transforming a worktop into a multipurpose area that can be used for both food preparation and eating. What fundamentally changes a worktop into a breakfast bar is the ability to sit comfortably at the worktop so that meals may be taken.

separate bars

Separate breakfast bars are ideal for individuals or couples, and are a good way of using scrap pieces of worktop.

tools for the job

- tape measure & pencil
- hand saw or jigsaw
- cordless drill/driver
- level
- hacksaw

1 Cut 1 x 2in furring strip to a length equal to what will be the back edge of the breakfast bar. Chamfer the ends of the strip so that they will not be visible when the worktop is in position. Screw the strip to the wall at a suitable height. This need not be standard worktop height—the ability to sit comfortably should be the deciding factor.

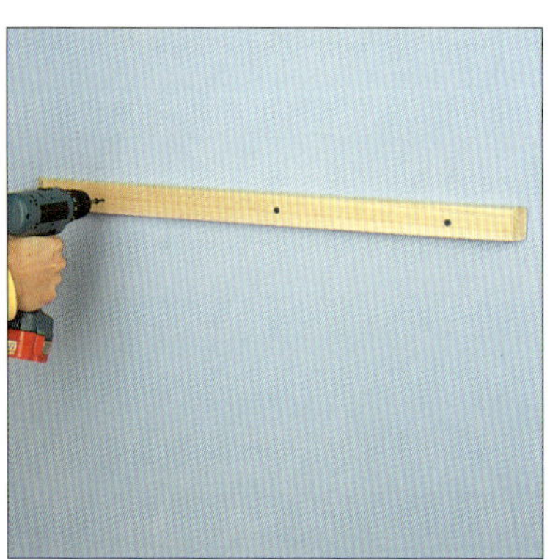

2 Attach L-shaped fastening brackets along the furring strip at roughly 8in intervals. Make sure that the top section of the brackets extends horizontally and level with the top edge of the furring strip.

3 Cut a section of worktop to size. Adding a curved edge to the corners will help soften its appearance. To form the curved edge, make a guideline—you can use the base of a paint can for a template—then cut along the guideline with a jigsaw.

4 Hold the worktop in position, sitting on the furring strip, and rest a level on the surface. Make any adjustments needed to get the worktop level, then measure the distance from the underside of the worktop to the floor.

5 Using a hacksaw, cut a length of stainless steel tubing to this measurement. With suitable brackets, attach the pole to the underside of the worktop and floor. Fasten the worktop securely through the L-shaped brackets along the back edge. The edge may now be routed for final finishing (see page 345).

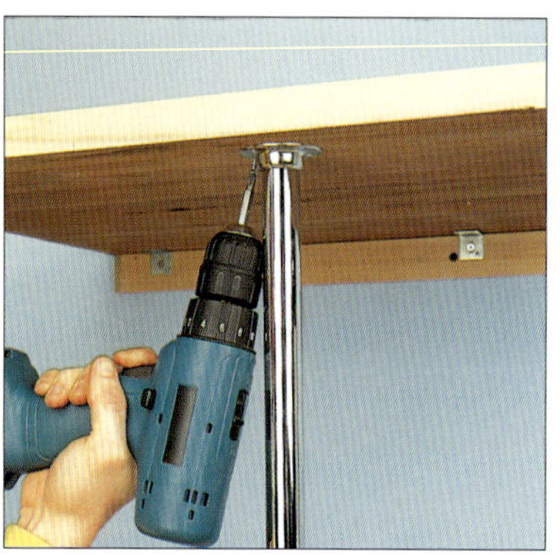

integrated bars

An integrated breakfast bar is basically a continuation of the kitchen worktop, but it can be much deeper or wider than standard size. As such, much of the installation procedure is similar to that demonstrated on pages 344–7.

tools for the job

- tape measure & pencil
- hand saw or jigsaw
- cordless drill/driver
- level
- hammer

1 It is always best to install a breakfast bar before the rest of the kitchen worktop, because of its greater size, even though it may not be attached as the first section. Breakfast bars are often supplied in a specific size, although wooden ones may be cut down and the edge finished yourself. Measure the worktop to work out the different overhangs. As with a worktop, the non-seating edge should have an overhang of between ⅛in and ¾in. The opposite overhang should be deep enough for people to sit comfortably.

2 On the seating side of the bar, it will be necessary to provide some sort of finish to the back of the kitchen units. Tongue-and-groove paneling offers an attractive and durable option. You will need to build a framework to attach the paneling—a length of 1 x 2in or 2 x 2in furring strip is ideal for this purpose. Gain a secure fastening by the wall and continue to build the framework.

3 Horizontal struts will need to be included in the furring strip framework to provide additional strength and extra fastening points for the tongue-and-groove paneling.

4 Once the framework is complete, build up the panels by fastening through the tongues of each board into the horizontal strips below. Joint each new length over the previous panel to hide the fastening points.

tips of the trade

Breakfast bars with a considerable overhang may need to be fastened with extra support. To do this, screw a length of furring strip at the wall junction underneath the overhang.

Here, a run of floor units has been fitted with a worktop that overhangs on one side so that it may be used for both dining and food preparation.

boxing

One of the attractive features of a built-in kitchen or bathroom is that most of the exposed cables and pipes are hidden by the units themselves. Sometimes, however, a small amount of boxing may be required to cover unsightly features still exposed after the units have been installed. There are two main types of boxing—one that covers over permanently, and one that incorporates a built-in access hatch of some kind.

without access

Boxing without access is by far the easiest to build of the two types, as it is simply a case of making the most unobtrusive boxing design possible. The most versatile materials for building any type of boxing are sheet MDF used in combination with 1 x 2in furring strip.

tools for the job

- tape measure & pencil
- hand saw or jigsaw
- cordless drill/driver
- hammer

1 Pipes are one of the most common obstacles to be dealt with by boxing, and are often found in the corners of rooms. First of all, attach cut furring strip to the wall surface on both sides of the pipes.

2 Measure the dimensions required to make a box with two pieces of MDF. Remember that one piece will have to overlap the other in order to create a right-angle joint.

3 Cut the MDF to size using a jigsaw or hand saw. If using a hand saw, remember to keep the angle of the blade shallow in relation to the surface of the MDF—this will improve both the ease of cutting and the accuracy of the cut.

safety advice

MDF creates more dust when sawn than other fiberboards, so whether cutting with a jigsaw or hand saw, always wear a dust mask.

4 Nail the MDF sheets in place with brad nails. Start off the brads by knocking them along the edge of the MDF before it is in position. This makes final nailing much easier and reduces the chance of damaging the wall with the hammer.

5 Nail the second piece in place, then add further brads along the edge of the overlapping sheet to form a strong corner joint. The boxing can now be painted or tiled as required.

tips of the trade

Cracks along the junction made by the boxing can be filled with flexible caulk before painting. Flexible filler reduces the risk of cracking, especially important when boxing over hot-water pipes where temperature changes cause the boxing to expand and contract slightly.

with access

Access is generally required when a shutoff valve is present in a section of pipework. Whatever the situation, access panels can be hinged, fastened with magnetic catches, or can even be built as freestanding units that are positioned without any permanent fastening. Freestanding units are a common type of boxing for below boilers in kitchens, where access is required—a small free-standing boxing unit is placed over the pipework to shield it from view.

tools for the job

- tape measure & pencil
- hand saw
- cordless drill/driver
- jigsaw
- screwdriver
- hacksaw
- hammer

hinged access

1 Having cut an MDF panel to fit your boxing framework, mark the size of door required in the face of the MDF. A tile makes an excellent template and is an ideal size for a hatch that needs to be large enough for hand access.

2 Using a flathead drill bit, drill through the MDF at each corner of what will be the access panel opening. Be careful not to allow the edge of the drill bit to extend over the pencil guidelines.

3 The drilled holes will act as an access point for a jigsaw to cut out the panel.

4 Cut a door to fit in the hole in the panel from another piece of MDF. Then use a hacksaw to cut a length of piano hinge and screw it into the hinging edge of the panel door.

5 Fit a small handle to the door before finally screwing it in place on the hinge edge of the panel. The entire panel may now be attached to the boxing framework following the method described opposite.

freestanding access

1 Cut pieces of MDF to size and fasten them together along one edge to create a right-angle unit.

2 On the inside of the unit, glue additional blocks to the right-angle junction, thus enhancing the structural strength. The unit can now be tiled over or painted and positioned on a worktop, covering pipework that needs periodic access.

installing shelves

Shelves are usually fitted to provide storage in addition to wall cabinets. Where budgets are limited, however, shelves can be used as a straight alternative to cabinets, and in small rooms where space is at a premium and wall cabinets would create a cramped atmosphere, simple shelves are a suitable option. Whatever your reasons may be for choosing to install shelves, it is vital to employ adequate fastening techniques to ensure the shelves are level and secure enough to support the weight of whatever you place on them.

making use of worktop

A good way of making use of the inevitable scrap pieces of worktop is to make extra shelves. Moreover, the width and depth of worktop material allows for hidden fastenings.

tools for the job

- tape measure & pencil
- jigsaw or hand saw
- cordless drill/driver
- router (optional)
- hacksaw
- disposable resin applicator

1 Mark the outline of the shelf on the worktop. Then cut around this guideline—a jigsaw is ideal for this purpose, but you can also use a hand saw. Using a flathead bit, drill holes at a point outside the guideline to accommodate the jigsaw blade. A router may be used to shape a decorative molded edge around the front of the shelf if desired (see page 345 for further instructions).

2 Firmly clamp the cutout shelf to a workbench and use a drill with a flat bit to make two holes in the back edge of the shelf, relatively close to either end. The holes need to be just wider than the circumference of a threaded bolt, which will be used as the wall fastening mechanism.

3 Cut the two bolts to length using a hacksaw. The bolts should penetrate inside the shelf to a depth of at least half the shelf width, and should penetrate into the wall to an equal distance. Measure and mark the position of the holes on the wall, checking they are aligned, and drill the holes required.

4 Insert resin into the holes in the wall with the disposable applicator. Push the threaded bolts into the holes and allow the resin to dry out. Once the bolts are secured, use the applicator to insert resin into the bolt holes in the shelf itself.

5 Lift the shelf into place, with the holes in the back edge over the threaded bolts in the wall.

tips of the trade

Resin drying times will vary. Follow the guidelines to get the timing right when you make the fastening.

hidden brackets

The more traditional approach to installing shelves involves a visible bracket, but it is possible to hide the fastenings. Discarded worktop may be used to create the shelves.

tools for the job

- tape measure & pencil
- jigsaw or hand saw
- cordless drill/driver
- mini level
- awl
- hammer
- torpedo level

1 Again, measure and mark the outline of the shelf on the worktop. Use this guideline to cut the worktop to size, ideally using a jigsaw, but otherwise a hand saw will be adequate. Drill holes outside the guideline for initially inserting the jigsaw blade. Having cut the shelf, you may turn your attention to attaching the hidden brackets. Hold the housing section of one of the brackets against the wall and employ a mini level to be sure that it is precisely vertical. Then mark the fastening position with an awl.

2 Drill the correct size of hole in the wall and insert wall plugs. They may push in by hand, or require some additional encouragement with one or two taps of the butt end of a hammer.

3 Now reposition the housing section and screw it securely in place. Check it once more with a torpedo level to be sure that it has not shifted out of position.

4 Position the second housing section on the wall next to the section already fastened in place. It will need to be positioned at the correct distance to accommodate the shelf. Place a level across the top of both sections to ensure that they are precisely level and aligned. Once again mark with an awl through the second section to indicate where you need to screw.

5 Screw the section in place, then slide the support brackets into both the housing sections.

6 Finally, position the shelf and secure it in place by using a hammer to knock one or two brad nails through the top of the shelf and into the brackets below.

ALTERNATIVE SHELVING SYSTEMS

In both the examples shown, scrap wooden worktop has been used to create extra shelves, thereby helping to create an overall integrated look in the kitchen. However, most DIY outlets will stock a wide selection of shelving systems, and you may prefer to choose a material or design that provides a contrast with the other kitchen surfaces. Whatever system you ultimately choose, the secret of successful shelves remains the same —make sure the shelves sit level and that the brackets and fastenings can bear the weight requirements.

installing built-in bathroom units

Built-in bathroom units are becoming increasingly popular. They are sometimes supplied ready-assembled but, in many cases, they are knockdown and need to be assembled before being installed. Some units are designed to form part of a run, while others, such as vanity units, are used as separate features. Whatever the case, the principles for assembly are similar. Many knockdowns are put together using cam bosses and plastic connecting blocks, as shown here.

tools for the job

hammer

screwdriver

cordless drill/driver

1 Organization is the key to assembling units, so lay out all the relevant sections to make sure you have the required number of components and the correct fastenings to put them together. Follow the manufacturer's guidelines for assembly—in most cases, the first step is to hammer plastic connectors into predrilled holes along the edges of the panels. In this case, the connectors are being inserted in the two side panels of the unit.

2 Insert wooden dowels into the appropriate holes on the edges of the shelving sections. Insert cam screws into the predrilled holes, pushing them in position by hand and making sure the open end of the screw thread is pointing towards the edge of the shelf or unit section. Insert the cam bosses that will attach to the screws in the corresponding part of the unit. Some may need a turn of the screwdriver to fit them securely in place. Since the pre-drilled holes have been accurately made in a factory, cam bosses and screws offer connection mechanisms that make sure of precision and eliminate the chance of errors.

3 Assemble the unit by matching the corresponding sections at the appropriate fastening points. The cam bosses connect with the cam screws by inserting the boss into the screw, then turning the screw to lock the fastening in place. Continue to add sections of the unit until the basic carcass is complete.

4 Now work on the cabinet doors. Most manufacturers use recessed hinges that are hidden from outside view when the door is closed. Their exact positions are generally premarked and cut into the back of the doors, so installation is a simple process of positioning the hinge and screwing it in place.

5 Hinge plates may also be attached to the carcass of the unit, again using the predrilled holes made in the manufacturing process. Most hinge plates are reversible, but in some cases there is a right and wrong way up, so always check before attaching them to make sure that the door hinges will fit.

6 Fasten the doors in place by hooking the hinges onto the hinge plates and tightening the central retaining screw to hold them in position. These types of hinges are always adjustable, so once the unit is in place it is still possible to move the door position slightly to make sure they are level and open and close correctly, although it usually takes a little trial and error to get them right.

7 Now fit the basin section of the unit. In this case, the molded basin section is screwed in place using the plastic connecting blocks on the edge of the carcass. Screws are inserted through the blocks into a chipboard section that is an integral part of the sink unit. There will inevitably be variations between manufacturers regarding how the sink is fitted, so it is important to follow their guidelines.

8 With this unit a drawer front is used to finish the front section, which is held in place with connecting blocks.

9 You will need to make some sort of provision at the back edge of the carcass for fastening the unit to the wall. L-shape brackets are ideal for this purpose and are usually supplied by the manufacturer. Screw them into position along the back edge of the unit.

10 Attach door handles by drilling through the door at the marked points. Be sure to use an appropriate size drill bit or the handles will be loose. To prevent splitting or damaging the doors, hold a block of wood at the position where the drill bit will emerge from the door.

11 Screw the handles in place, using one hand to hold the handle while the other hand operates the screwdriver.

LEVELING A RUN OF UNITS

In many cases it will be necessary to connect a number of units in a row. In such circumstances, assemble the units separately and position them along the wall, using a spirit level to check that they are correctly aligned horizontally and/or plumb, according to the planned layout of the room. A 2yd spirit level is a particularly useful tool for this job, because it can span several units, making this procedure much easier.

FINISHING TOUCHES

Once the unit is assembled, it can be positioned against the wall. If necessary—for example, for a vanity unit, as shown here—make sure that the relevant water inlet and drainage outlets are ready for connection. You will also need to install the fastenings for the sink (this is covered in greater detail on pages 318–21). It is often best to fit faucets to a unit before it is installed in its final position so that you can gain easy access to the underside of the sink. When you have completed all of the above, final installation is a case of doing up connections and securing the unit in position against the wall.

MAUGHAM DYNASTY

using adhesive

Another way of attaching a mirror to a wall surface is to use mirror adhesive or a strong bonding adhesive, available in tubes and expelled with the aid of a caulk gun. You will need to support the weight of the mirror while the adhesive dries.

tools for the job

- tape measure & pencil
- hand saw
- mini level
- cordless drill/driver
- caulk gun or dispenser

1 Cut a length of wood strip equal to the width of the mirror. Fasten it to the wall at the position where the base of the mirror will be. Use a mini level to check that the strip is level.

2 Apply adhesive generously to the back of the mirror.

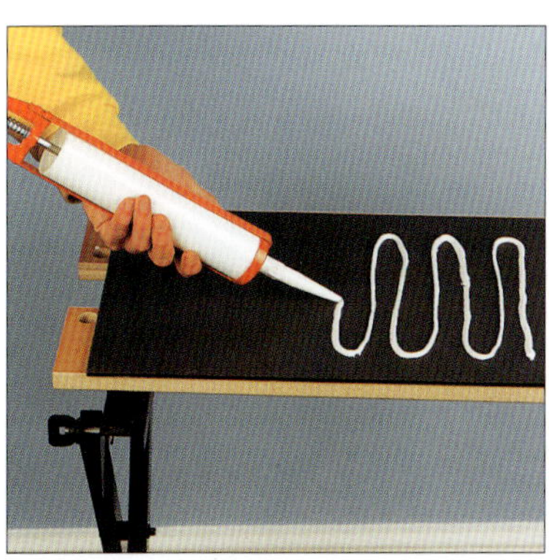

3 Position the mirror with its bottom edge on top of the wood strip. Once the adhesive has dried, remove the strip, fill the screw holes with filler, and decorate the wall.

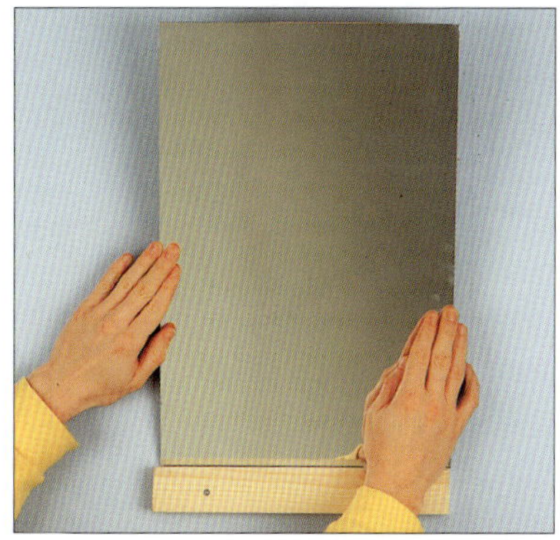

mirror tiles

tools for the job

- pencil
- tape measure
- level

1 Use a level to draw a pencil guideline on the wall at the point where the bottom edge of the first row of tiles will sit. Draw a plumb guideline to help you position the first column of tiles precisely. Attach self-adhesive pads to the backs of the tiles. One on each corner is usually sufficient, but you should read the manufacturer's guidelines because some heavier or larger tiles may need more pads to support them.

2 Use the pencil guideline you have drawn to position the tiles on the wall, gradually building up your chosen design. In most cases you can butt the tile edges up against each other, although some manufacturers may recommend leaving a small gap.

MIRROR SCREWS

Mirror screws are the best option for fastening mirrors with predrilled holes in their surface. The screws are specially designed so that decorative caps can be fixed over the screw head once the mirror is in place. Like many fastenings, different manufacturers produce different designs, so you are likely to find variations in the types of mirror screw available. Some designs include a rubber grommet that should be positioned in the mirror hole before the screw is inserted. This helps to minimize the risk of the mirror cracking when the screw comes into contact with the edge of the hole (although you still need to be careful when inserting the screw to make sure that you do not overtighten it). In the same way that screw designs vary, so do the actual caps that fit over the screw heads. Designs range from round domes to more flattened, square shapes. Some caps actually screw in place onto the mirror screw, while others are snapped or clipped in position like a popper fastening.

installing accessories

All the small accessories in a bathroom, such as soap dishes, toothbrush holders, and non-heated towel racks, supply additional storage areas that make the best use of space. They also provide the finishing touches to the overall look of the bathroom, which will make your decorative scheme look complete and the room welcoming. Many of these accessories are available as sets so that you can achieve a coordinated finish.

safety advice

Always check for pipes and wiring using a stud finder before you start to drill into walls.

The fastening mechanisms on accessories vary, but it is usually the case that specially designed brackets are attached to the wall surface first, then the fastening is attached to the bracket and held in place with a discreetly positioned grub screw. This two-part process can be difficult because you need to make sure that brackets align correctly with fasteners. Alternatively, the fastening bracket is integral to the fastening and, once in place, a cover or cap is placed over the bracket for an attractive finish.

Installing accessories on tiled surfaces requires a specific technique to make the appropriate pilot holes for wall plug and screw fastenings.

fastening into tiles

Fastening accessories to plaster walls, whether solid or hollow, can be achieved using the correct wall plugs and screws, and the same is true for tiled surfaces. However, you need to use a specially designed drill bit that is strong enough to penetrate a tile accurately. Accuracy is the key point here, because a hole drilled in the wrong place cannot simply be filled and repainted in the way that you would with plaster walls. Also, even though tiles have a very strong surface, they can shatter or crack if the wrong technique is used. A standard masonry drill bit may well go through some tiles, but it is often the case that while piercing the tiled surface, the coarseness of the bit can break away glazed sections of tile around the hole.

tools for the job

- fiber-tip pen
- tape measure
- cordless drill/driver
- screwdriver

1 Take your time when deciding on the precise position for the fixture—in this case a towel ring—because mistakes are not easy to rectify on a tiled surface. The bracket for the accessory should be fastened in as central a position on the tile as possible. The closer you move toward the edge of a tile, the more likely that drill vibrations will cause it to crack. Hold the fixture in place with one hand and use a fiber-tip pen to mark through the screw holes onto the tile surface below.

2 Remove the fixture from the tile surface and cover the marked points with painter's tape. It should still be possible to see the marks through the tape, but if they are not obvious, renew them on top of the tape. The reason that painter's tape is applied over the drilling points is that the shiny surface of the tile can cause the drill bit to slip, which makes accurate drilling impossible and can lead to scratching. The painter's tape adds some grip and keeps the point of the bit in place.

3 Insert the tile drill bit into the drill, making sure it is securely held in place. A tile drill bit looks like a miniature javelin or spear.

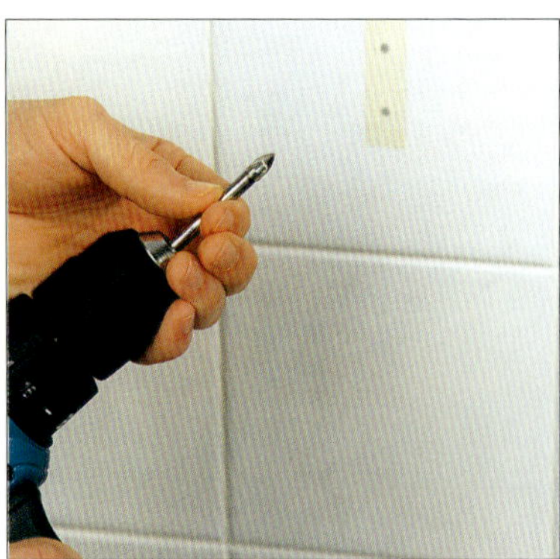

4 Holding the drill bit against the marked point on the tile, start the drill at a low speed. This will create a tiny indentation in the tile surface that will allow the bit to gain a good grip before the speed is increased. Once this initial break is made, use the drill in the normal way to penetrate through the tile surface and into the wall behind. Holding a vacuum cleaner nozzle below the hole while you drill will improve the aesthetic finish of the tiled surface, because it prevents the dust produced when drilling through tiles from falling down and resting in grout joints or sealant beads at the base of the wall. Even if this dust is wiped off, there is often unsightly staining of the grout or sealant. By using the vacuum to remove dust as you drill, there is no need to clean up afterward, and the grout or sealant cannot become stained.

5 Once the holes are drilled, remove the painter's tape from the tile surface. Insert wall plugs into the holes. These are usually supplied with the fixture—if not, choose some suitable ones from your supply or buy some if you do not have any already. The plugs will generally slip into the holes, easily tightening as the head of the plug becomes level with with the wall surface. In some cases, you may need to use the butt end of a hammer to knock the plug into position. Be sure to use only the butt end of the hammer, because using the other end will risk breaking the tile.

6 Reposition the fixture and screw it in place. It is always best to use a hand-held screwdriver for this because it offers greater control regarding the amount of pressure exerted. If a cordless screwdriver is used, there can be a danger of overtightening, which could crack the tiled surface so that the tile will need to be replaced.

7 Finally, screw the covering cap in place to obscure the fastening mechanism. This may attach with a grub screw or simply a threaded fastening that is screwed into place by hand.

tips of the trade

• **Leveling**—Sometimes, on final viewing, the accessory you have just installed may not appear to be precisely level. Most manufacturers take this into account and design their accessories so that small adjustments can be made after installation. Where two screws are used to secure a fixture, one of the holes is often of a slightly elongated shape, which allows the screw to be loosened and the fixture rotated to a different position. This is usually enough to rectify it.

• **Waterproofing**—By drilling a hole in a tiled surface, you are in effect piercing the watertight barrier created by the tiles and grout. It can, therefore, be worth applying a small amount of silicone sealant to the end of screws before they are inserted so that this watertight barrier is maintained.

INSTALLING TWO OR MORE BRACKETS INTO TILES

In the example shown here, only one bracket is required to hold the fixture in place. However, for larger fixtures such as horizontal towel racks, more than one bracket will be needed. When two brackets are required, it is vital that they are positioned perfectly level so that when the rail, or other accessory, is installed in the brackets you achieve the best possible finish. In such instances, always use a level to draw a horizontal pencil guideline along the tiles, and measure along this line to mark the exact positions where holes need to be drilled for the fixtures. You can then use the drilling technique shown in steps 3 and 4. Once the holes have been made, erase the pencil line with a putty eraser and then finish fastening the brackets in place. The way that accessories are inserted into the brackets varies between manufacturers, so always pay close attention to their specific instructions to ensure that all fixtures are secure.

installing ventilation

Ventilation is important in bathrooms because of their moist atmosphere. This type of environment suffers from condensation, which can damage decoration and finishes unless adequate ventilation systems are installed. The advent of double-glazing has increased the problem and made ventilation systems essential, since the somewhat drafty nature of older windows and doors did at least allow some flow of air.

mechanical ventilation

Mechanical ventilation is usually in the form of exhaust fans. These fixtures remove the moist air from the room and help to produce a less humid atmosphere. They can be positioned in either walls or ceilings—the latter is particularly common in shower stalls. Most are operated by an electricity supply that switches the fan on automatically when the light is turned on in the room. This mode of operation varies according to the manufacturer, and many designs incorporate automatic cutoff switches after a set period of time. It is worth bearing in mind that building regulations in new properties specify that an exhaust fan must be fitted in a bathroom.

WALL-MOUNTED EXHAUST FAN

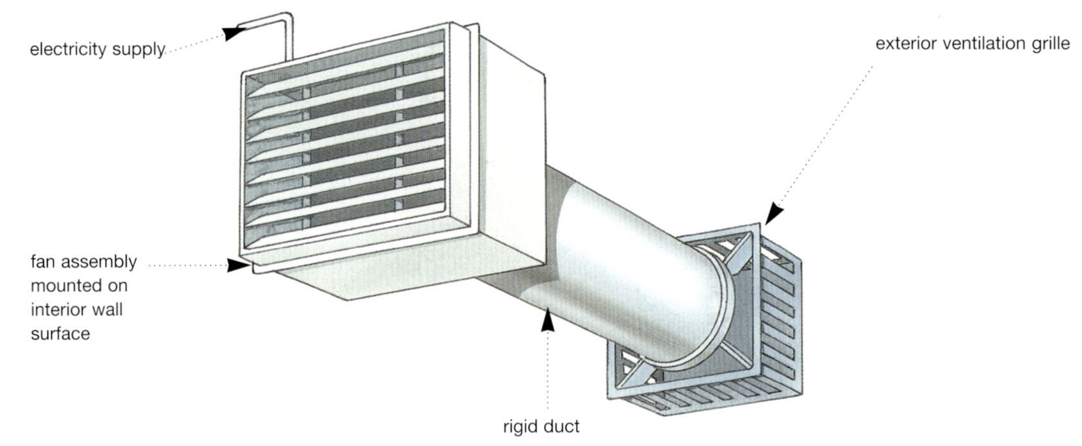

CEILING-MOUNTED EXHAUST FAN

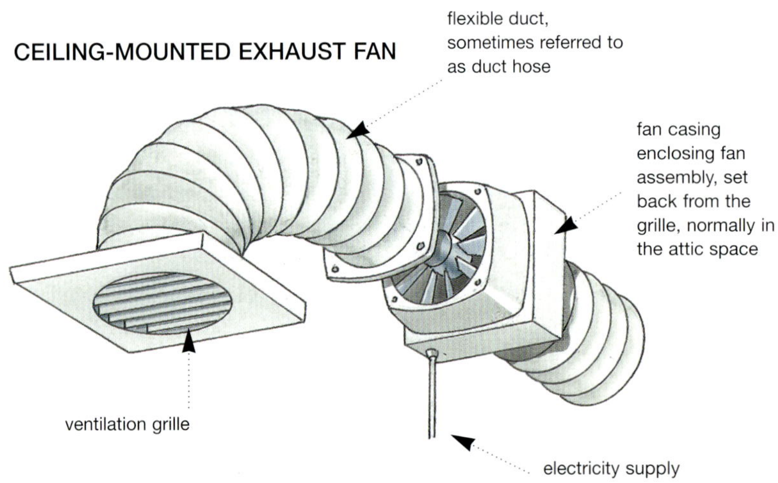

WINDOW-MOUNTED FANS

Fans that can be fixed into a circular hole in a windowpane are readily available. You will need to cut the hole using the correct type of glass cutter, although it may be easier to get your local glass supplier to perform this task. You should never attempt cutting holes in double-glazed windows. The actual fan assembly is fitted on the inside of the pane, with an inner casing covering the moving parts. An exterior grille is used to finish the outer part of the assembly.

making access

For wall-mounted fans, a hole must be cut through the wall to the exterior of the house. In order to cut a hole through masonry with any degree of accuracy, you will need to rent a core drill bit and drill. It is not worth buying this type of equipment, because it is extremely expensive and will only be needed for very occasional use—it is much more cost-effective to rent from a local supplier. For ceiling-mounted fans, the equipment required is not as heavy-duty since there is no masonry work involved. The simple technique for making an access hole in a plaster ceiling is demonstrated here.

tools for the job

- pencil & tape measure
- stud finder
- keyhole saw
- screwdriver

1 Work out the position of the fan, using a stud finder to check that there are no supply pipes or wiring cables in this area. These will obstruct the fan and could be dangerous if cut. There should also be no ceiling joists because they would make it impossible to install the fan. You may, therefore, have to make a small compromise when deciding on a position. Hold the grille in place on the ceiling and use a pencil to draw around the circumference of the circular section of the grille. This provides a cutting guideline.

2 When you have determined the position of the fan, use a keyhole saw or drywall saw to cut out the circular section of ceiling.

3 Secure the first part of the grille assembly in the hole with retaining screws. Clip the grille in place, then install the duct hose and exhaust above the grille assembly.

passive vents

Passive vents are an alternative type of bathroom ventilation that do not involve any mechanical parts. They simply allow air to flow in the room, using natural drafts to create the circulation. Some examples of passive-vent systems and covers that are used to neaten the finished look are shown here.

Louver vents act as the interior covers for ventilation holes or ducts in exterior walls. Different designs and finishes are available. Plastic and aluminum examples are shown here. Plastic vents can be painted to blend with wall finishes. As with the air brick, the grille is permanently open.

Hit-and-miss vents are interior covers for holes or ducts that have an opening and closing mechanism.

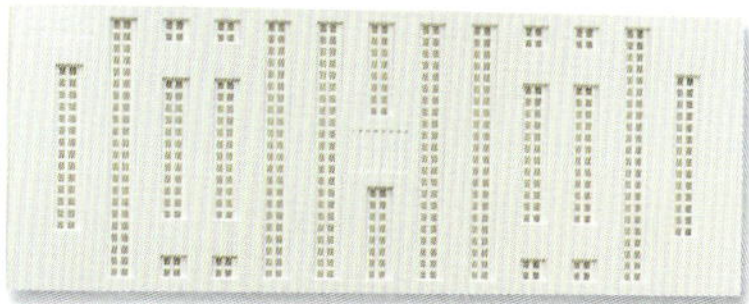

Air bricks are positioned in the wall structure and are permanently open.

repairs to kitchens & bathrooms

No matter how fine the quality of fixtures and finishes in the kitchen and bathroom, you will almost certainly need to make repairs at some stage. In most cases the incidence of repairs is determined by frequency of use, but that said, it is not uncommon to find that faucet washers need to be changed, door handles fixed, or worktops resealed in even relatively underused kitchens and bathrooms. This chapter demonstrates how to make all these repairs—and remember, it is important to make repairs as soon as the need arises, since regular maintenance helps to extend the life of the room and will save you money in the long term.

All kitchens need repairs over time—with this kitchen, for example, you may need to replace a broken tile on the worktop.

reviving worktop

Worktops are invariably the most used of all kitchen surfaces, and as a consequence will probably require frequent repairs to maintain their condition. Outlined below are a number of common problems experienced with different types of worktop and guidance on the best techniques for returning them to good order.

wooden worktop

Wooden worktop should receive occasional reoiling, but you may also need to make localized repairs caused by spillages that have been allowed to soak and stain, or through surface scarring caused by knives or other cutting implements.

tools for the job

electric sander (optional)
cloth

1 Sand the affected area until the stain has been removed. An electric sander is ideal for this, but take care not to dig the edge into the worktop, which will make undulations in the wood surface.

2 Apply a small amount of oil to a dry cloth and gently rub it into the sanded area. You may need to make two or three applications to blend the area back in with the existing worktop.

laminated worktop

Damage to a laminated finish cannot be simply sanded away—it is more a case of effective camouflaging.

repairing edges

tools for the job

glue applicator
painter's tape

1 If the edge has chipped, glue the broken piece of laminate back, if possible, using neat wood glue.

2 Use painter's tape to hold the section securely in position while the glue dries.

scratches

tools for the job

artist's brush
dry cloth

To deal with surface scratches, simply dust and clean the area then paint along the groove with a fine artist's brush using an oil-based paint such as eggshell. Try to match the worktop color as closely as possible. For a patterned worktop, it is best to choose one of the darkest colors in its design. Wipe away any excess.

repairing the front edge

Where damage to a laminated worktop is so extreme that minor repairs would have little effect, you may need to consider replacing the front edge with an alternative finish. In this example, wood molding has been used to create a new edging on the front of the worktop.

tools for the job

clamps

combination square

jigsaw

hammer (optional)

1 Clamp a section of wood strip along the front edge of the worktop. It needs to be positioned so that a jigsaw can rest against the side, then use the strip for a guide as it is moved along the worktop, producing a straight cut along the edge.

2 Remove the damaged worktop edge with a jigsaw. Keep the blade tight against the wood strip to make sure of a dead straight cut.

3 Cut and glue a length of molding along the newly cut edge of the worktop. Fix the molding with wood glue. Nail one or two brad nails through the molding to hold it in place while the glue dries, if necessary. Stain and varnish the wood strip to seal the surface and provide a decorative finish.

tiling

If damage to the worktop is excessive, then a further option is to tile the entire worktop surface to provide a complete new look.

tools for the job

tiling equipment

Attach molding along the front edge of the worktop, and stain and varnish it to your preference. Then apply tiles directly on top of the worktop (see pages 420–1 for further instructions). Remember that sink or cooktop height may have to be adjusted so that the tiles can be lipped under the edges of such appliances.

resiliconing

The overall appearance of a worktop can often be let down simply by staining or damage over time to the silicone seal. By periodically replacing the seal, you will not only revive the look of the worktop, but also renew the waterproof seal between the worktop/wall junction.

tools for the job

paintbrush

window scraper

utility knife

caulk dispenser or gun

1 Paint a proprietary sealant removal solution onto the silicone, and allow it to soak in as much as possible.

2 Use a window scraper to ease the old seal away, then clean the area thoroughly before reapplying a new silicone bead.

repairing doors & drawers

Hinges and handles on drawers and doors are the areas that most commonly suffer damage on kitchen units. As moving parts, it is inevitable that hinges will eventually wear out, and the daily tugging on handles will similarly loosen the fastening or even pull off the handle altogether. In some cases, once these sort of breakages occur it can signal the time for a new kitchen. Generally, however, only the most frequently used doors or drawers in a kitchen will experience any major problems. Repairing such one-time problems can therefore return the kitchen to optimum working level, and does not have to signal the need for a complete kitchen refit.

repairing a hinge

tools for the job

- cordless drill/driver
- pencil
- combination square
- hinge-cutting bit
- mini level

A sagging or off-level door will often indicate that there is a problem with hinges. The movement of the hinge is likely to have caused the fastening holes of the hinge plate to widen, so that the plate comes away from the side of the carcass. The best way to fix this problem is to relocate the hinge plate to a slightly higher position on the door, which will require refastening both the plate and hinge mechanism itself.

1 Unscrew the door from the unit and remove both the loose hinge plate from the carcass and the hinge mechanism from the door.

2 Use a combination square to measure up from the original hinge position to a new location further up the door. Mark the central point for the new recess required to house the hinge.

3 The next stage is to cut the new hinge recess in the door. This can be done using a cordless drill with a hinge-cutting bit attached. Make sure that the point of the hinge cutter is precisely inserted at the marked point for the center of the new recess. Gradually cut into the door taking care to drill to the exact depth requirement for the hinge.

4 Thoroughly dust out the hole and then screw the hinge into the new recess, making sure that it is correctly aligned with the door edge. Before rehanging the door, fill the old recess with matching wood filler.

5 Use the same measurement to mark on the inside of the carcass the change in position of the hinge plate. Then reattach the hinge plate by screwing it securely in place. Rehang the door and screw together the hinge and plate. Finally, fill the old holes on the door and unit and, if necessary, paint over them for a finish almost as good as new.

quick repair

As an alternative to cutting a new hinge, it may sometimes be possible to refasten a hinge plate with the aid of some resin.

1 Remove the loosened hinge plate and then carefully press some resin into the old holes.

2 Reposition the hinge plate and screw it back in place, holding it in position until the resin sets. Some excess resin will probably squeeze out around the edge of the hinge plate when it is screwed in place. Remove this with a cloth before it has the chance to dry. Rehang the door once the resin has fully hardened.

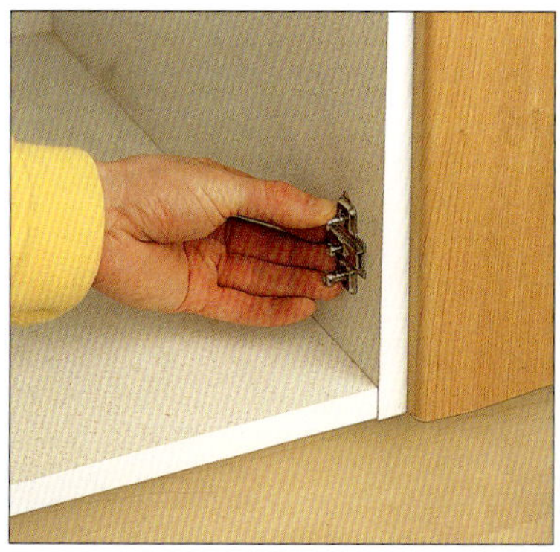

drawer problems

Although hinge problems are common for unit doors, the main problems encountered with drawers tend to relate either to the loosening of screw fastenings for the handles, or the drawer fronts themselves. In either case, adhesive can be used to reinforce fastenings and return the drawers to good working order.

tools for the job

- cordless drill/driver
- clamps (optional)
- screwdriver

repairing fronts

1 Drawer fronts often become loose, as the effectiveness of the screw fastenings lessens with constant use. To remedy this problem, simply unscrew the drawer front and apply a generous amount of wood glue to the back face.

2 Screw the front back onto the drawer carcass. It is important for the back face of the drawer front and the front face of the carcass to be pressed together very tightly, in order to ensure proper adhesion.

You may therefore need to attach some clamps to hold the front firmly in position. Although the screw fastenings for the drawer front will remain slightly loose, the combined effect of the glue and screws will hold the drawer front in position.

repairing handles

1 Again, the daily opening and closing of drawers will take its toll on the screw fastenings for handles, which may become loose or fall off completely. For obvious aesthetic reasons it will not be possible to reposition the handle and make new fastenings altogether. To repair a loosened handle, therefore, you will need to unscrew it and apply a small amount of resin to the thread of the fixing bolt.

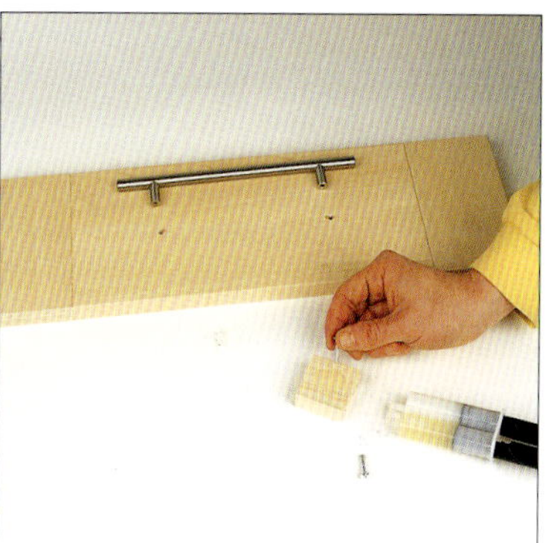

2 Screw the handle in position, using washers to help spread the force put on the handle when the drawer is opened. This technique can also be applied to door handles and handles with only one fastening point.

changing doors & handles 

The style of a kitchen is often created by the types of doors, drawer fronts, and handles that have been used in its design. The carcasses themselves have little to do with the look of a kitchen, so in order to change style, as long as the carcasses are in a good state of repair, it only becomes necessary to make changes to the more obvious areas, such as cupboard fronts and/or handles. Changing handles is clearly a very economic way of altering a kitchen look—door and drawer front replacement is certainly more dramatic, but will greatly increase the cost.

design options

There are always many options to choose from when making such changes, and personal preference will be the determining factor in the choice you make. Below are just a few examples of cupboard fronts and handles, showing slightly different designs and finishes. Remember when making choices, especially with doors, to make sure that the new ones will fit the existing units in your kitchen. Subtle differences in size may not be immediately obvious when choosing between manufacturers, and you should always double-check that dimensions will be suitable.

DOORS

wooden panel door

laminated wood-effect panel door

painted finish panel door

solid wood flush door

KNOBS

brass

wood

ceramic

porcelain

HANDLES

brass

wood

antique brass drawer pull

brass drawer pull

brushed steel

tools for the job

cordless drill/driver
screwdriver
combination square
pencil
wood block

changing doors

Replacing doors is a simple process where the old ones may be unscrewed at the hinges and the new ones fitted. In some cases, it may be suitable to reuse the old hinges, but if there is a difference in manufacturer's designs, you may need to fit new ones. Likewise, the hinge plates themselves may need changing on the carcass unit.

changing handles

Nearly all kitchen handles are interchangeable in that manufacturer's differences tend not to create too many problems. If you are changing a knob to a handle, however, you will need to drill an extra hole, and if you are changing a handle to a knob, you will need to fill the leftover hole and repaint the unit to conceal it.

simple changeovers

1 Firmly hold onto the knob or handle while you undo the retaining screw(s).

2 Position the new knob or handle, and screw it in place. Start this process by hand before using a screwdriver for final tightening.

changing from knob to handle

1 Use a combination square to measure from the existing hole to a position that mirrors the distance between the threaded fixing points on your chosen new handle.

2 Mark this position accurately—if it is out of place, the thread of the screw may not engage correctly with the thread of the handle.

3 Drill through the marked point. Be sure to position a block of wood on the other side of the door so that when the drill bit emerges it cannot split or blow out the hole and damage the door side.

4 Line the new handle over the drilled holes and tighten the fastenings securely with a screwdriver.

DRAWER FRONTS

When you are replacing a drawer knob or handle, you may encounter a separate set of problems. Replacing one knob with another is a simple changeover, but it is more difficult to change a knob to a handle, as two new holes will need to be filled, leaving a central hole in the drawer front. This creates another scenario where the drawer front must be painted in order to cover the old fastening holes. Even with a simple changeover of one handle for another, you must check that the distance between the holes is the same.

unit makeovers 

As an alternative to replacing doors, handles, or drawer fronts, it is possible to work on or add other finishes to existing units and fronts in order to change their appearance. As for all unit makeovers, it is important that the existing units are in a sound condition so that your efforts will be long-lasting, and that adequate preparation is put into these tasks so that the finish itself is durable. Ideas and materials for unit makeovers are constantly being updated by manufacturers, and below are just some examples of the options available.

adding panels

tools for the job

- pencil
- tape measure
- combination square
- cordless drill/driver

To increase interest on a flat or flush cupboard front, panels may be used to produce a more textured or three-dimensional finish. Moldings may be bought and cut to length or, as shown here, readymade kits may be purchased where the panels are already made up and simply require installing. This latter technique adds a little expense, but it saves a lot of time and makes sure that the mitered corners of the panels are precise.

1 Use a pencil and combination square to measure the ideal position for attaching the panels to the doors. It is easier to remove doors and lay them out flat for this purpose.

2 Most panels are fastened with double-sided tape. Peel the tape off the back of the moldings.

3 Position the moldings so they are aligned with the pencil guidelines. The adhesive is very strong, but you can make any necessary minor adjustments in positioning before it finally sticks.

4 It is likely that the new molding position may make it necessary to move handles. Simply remove the existing ones and fill in the screw holes. Then measure for an appropriate position to drill through the door and fix a new handle.

tips of the trade

- In order to get the best possible adhesion between the molding and door, make sure that the door surface has been both thoroughly cleaned and well dried before you apply the panel.
- If you are using moldings that are not fixed with self-adhesive tape, brad nails can be used to secure the moldings in place. It can also be worth using a little white glue on the back of the moldings to add further strength to the fastening. The heads of the brads will need to be punched in and filled before you go on to paint.
- Normally, the newly paneled door will require painting. Be sure to use a suitable preparation on the door surface if it is of a laminated or melamine finish. A varnished wooden door should be sanded back and primed before painting. If your preference dictates that panel color is to be different to the background door color, it is worth painting the panels and the doors separately before positioning the panels. In this way, the dividing line between each will be as sharp as possible, and no time-consuming and fussy cutting in will be required.

MOLDED UNITS

Instead of adding panels to flush doors, another method for producing a paneled effect is to use a router. By fitting the correct type of cutter, the router can be used to channel a molded pattern in the front of doors. This technique is for the more advanced woodworker.

covering doors

An alternative to adding moldings to a flush door is simply to cover the whole face with a decorative wallpaper. There are companies that specifically manufacture for this purpose. Such paper is self-adhesive, and the technique for fitting is similar to that of general wallpapering.

tools for the job

- tape measure & pencil
- scissors
- utility knife
- sanding block
- cordless drill/driver

1 Remove the handles and sand down the door surfaces to provide a key for the adhesive.

2 Use a damp sponge to wipe away any dust from the door surface, and allow the surface to dry.

3 Use scissors to cut the paper to a size slightly longer than that of the door. (The width of the paper roll should be slightly greater than the door.) Peel back a small amount of the self-adhesive backing paper and position the roll at the top of the door.

4 Gradually unroll the paper, pull the backing away, and allow the paper to stick to the door. Use the factory-cut edge of one side of the length to follow the door edge.

5 Smooth the surface of the paper to remove any air bubbles, and use a utility knife to trim off excess.

6 Use fine-grit sandpaper to sand the edges of the door gently to make sure that the paper edges will not lift away from the surface.

7 Screw the handles in place. If you are changing handle design, fill the original holes before applying the paper, then drill new holes.

DRAWER UNITS

In both these examples, a door has been used for illustrative purposes. The same techniques may also be applied to drawer fronts in order to blend in the whole finish.

repairing a bathtub

Bathtubs can be given a new look by simply changing the panels or choosing a new design of faucet to update the style. In addition, the bathtub surface can be repaired to hide scratches or defects, as long as the correct materials and techniques are used. Re-enameling kits are easy to apply, and can make an old bathtub look like new. Replacing the sealant around the edges of the bathtub is also very effective in brightening up its general appearance.

re-enameling a bathtub

Although enamel bathtubs are very durable, they eventually tarnish, with their surface becoming stained or losing its enamel finish in places. Professional re-enameling is expensive, but there are now kits available that have some success returning old enamel bathtubs to their original condition. They are easy to use, but careful application is necessary to achieve a reasonable finish. Often these kits can be used on more than just enamel surfaces—sometimes ceramic, iron, or plastic bathtubs can be recoated using the same procedure—however, the kits cannot be used on acrylic bathtubs. Read the manufacturer's guidelines carefully to make sure that the kit is suitable for your particular bathtub surface. In this example, an old enamel bathtub is being renovated using one such kit.

tools for the job

- sponge
- cloth
- re-enamelling kit
- cordless drill/driver

1 First, clean any dirt or grime off the bathtub surface using a mild detergent and allow it to dry thoroughly. Cover the faucets and waste outlets with painter's tape, or remove these items temporarily while re-enameling takes place.

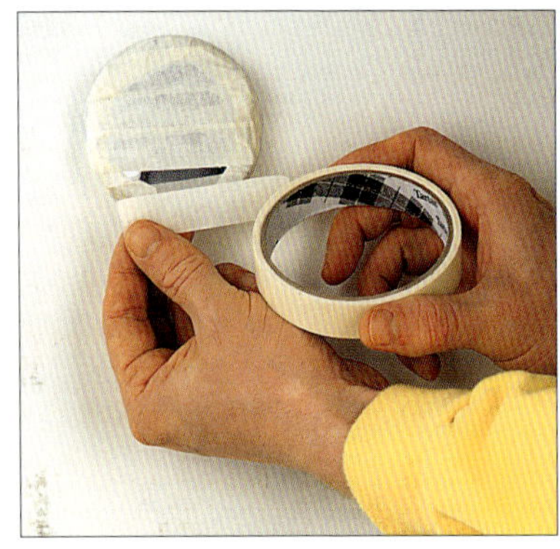

2 Clean the bathtub using the cleaner and sponge supplied with the kit. Rinse and allow to dry.

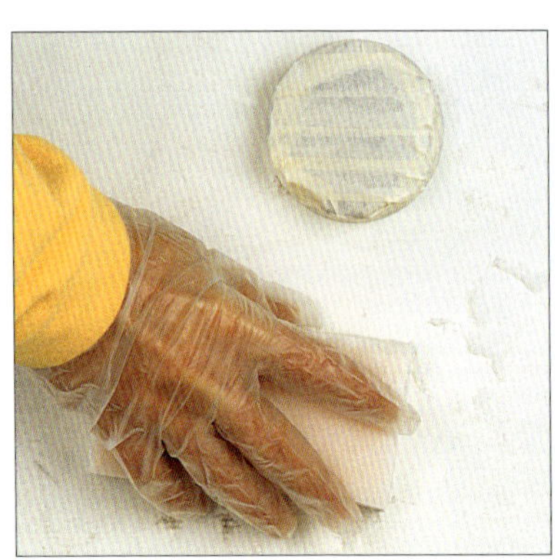

3 Sand the bath surface using fine-grit abrasive paper. Rinse with warm water and allow to dry.

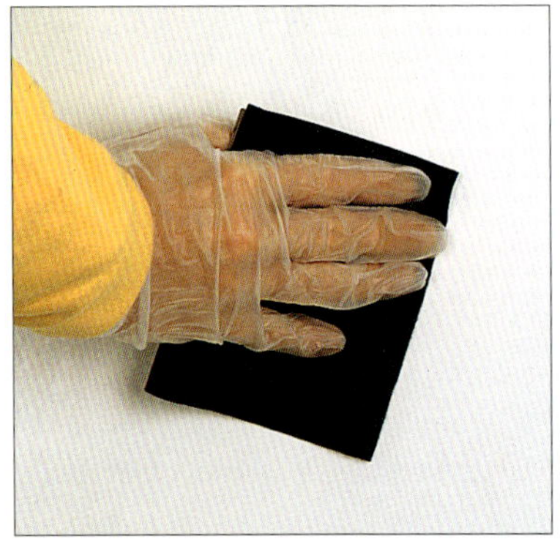

safety advice

Make sure that the bathroom is adequately ventilated when using re-enamelling kits, because the fumes can be quite overpowering.

4 Most kit systems involve mixing a hardener with the coating prior to application. Follow the manufacturer's guidelines.

5 Use a brush to paint all the detailed areas around outlets and faucets, and those places where a roller would be unable to gain access. Take care to apply the coating as evenly as possible.

6 Pour some of the coating mixture into a roller tray or the tray supplied with the kit, and distribute the coating evenly over the roller surface.

7 Apply the coating to the bathtub as evenly as possible, reloading the roller at appropriate intervals. Try to cover any unsightly brushmarks.

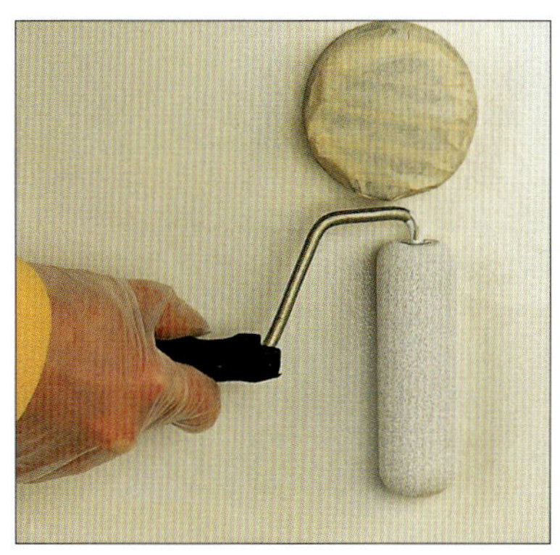

8 Once the coating is dry, apply another coat. Again, try to cover previous brushmarks and roller marks in order to produce an even finish. When the surface is dry, remove the painter's tape.

tips of the trade

- **Sealant removal**—Where the bathtub is in contact with wall surfaces, remove sealant so that the new coating extends to the edge.
- **Drying time**—Coatings may need to dry for 48 hours before the bathtub can be used, so make sure you read the manufacturer's guidelines for any specific instructions.
- **Future cleaning**—After the bathtub has been coated, only use liquid, non-abrasive cleaners on its surface, applied with a sponge or cloth.
- **Further protection**—As a further protective measure, apply a coat of car wax to the bathtub once or twice a year to help maintain its finish and keep it as clean and bright as possible.
- **Change sleeves**—Use a different roller sleeve for each coating, because it is not possible to clean the roller between coats. If you attempt to use the same roller sleeve for the second coat, it will produce a very rough and unsatisfactory finish.

USING SILICONE SEALANT

First, apply painter's tape along each side of the joint to be sealed, then press the sealant along the joint. Smooth it with a wet finger. Remove the tape while the sealant is still wet, smoothing the edges of the sealant if necessary with a wet finger.

replacing seals

The sealant around the edge of a bathtub will need to be repaired at some point during its lifetime. Removing the old seal and replacing it with a new one is a simple process.

tools for the job

- small paintbrush
- window scraper
- caulk gun or dispenser

1 Use a small paintbrush to apply a sealant removal solution along the sealant bead. Allow this to soak into the sealant according to the manufacturer's guidelines.

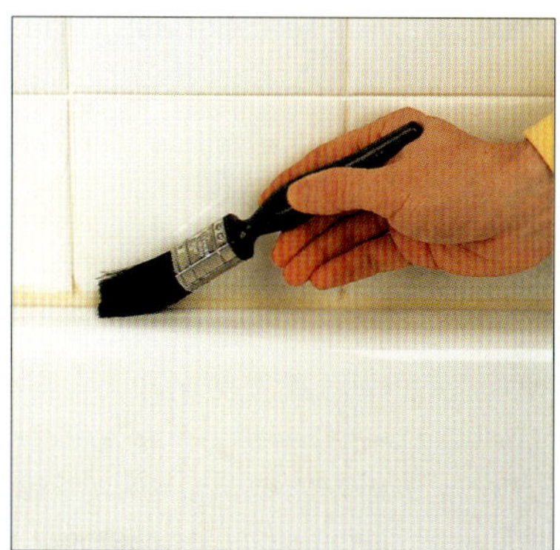

2 Use a window scraper to ease the sealant away from the wall and bathtub surface, taking care not to scratch the surface of the bathtub.

3 Use a cloth to clean away any remaining sealant. Dampening the cloth with denatured alcohol will help to prepare the surface for reapplication of sealant to give a watertight finish.

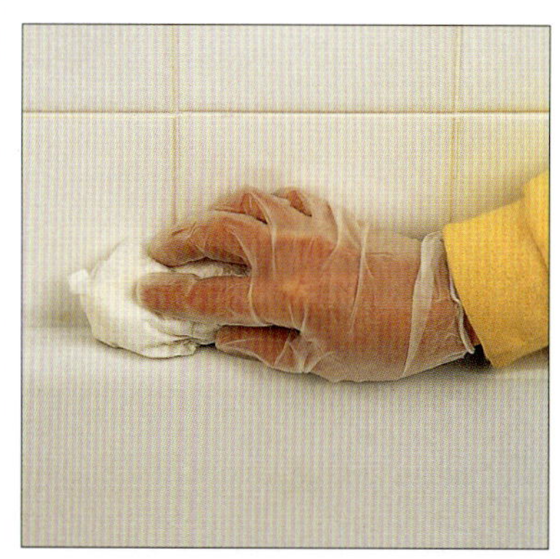

making tile repairs

It is almost inevitable that the tiles in a bathroom will become damaged and that their appearance will deteriorate over time. Rather than completely retiling, you may prefer to carry out some sort of repair or renovation to restore a good finish to the existing tiled surface. The degree of damage may vary in seriousness, from broken or cracked tiles to simple grout discoloration. Whatever the damage done, carrying out a repair is a relatively straightforward process.

Condensation, general moisture levels, and wear and tear over time, are all factors that contribute to the gradual deterioration of grout joints between tiles. Often the main reason people choose to change tiles in their bathroom is because the old grout has become discolored and detracts from the overall appearance of the tiled surface. However, it is not always necessary to retile, and often tiles can look good as new by either reviving or replacing the grout.

regrouting

tools for the job

- grout raker
- vacuum cleaner
- grout spreader
- sponge

1 Employ a specially designed grout raker to remove old grout from joints. The serrated, roughened edge digs out the grout as you apply pressure to the surface. Take care not to scratch the edge of the tiles.

2 Once you have raked out all the joints from around the tiles, it is important to remove any dust or debris from both the tile surface and within the joints. Wipe the surface down and use a vacuum cleaner to remove debris from the tile joints.

3 With the old grout completely removed from the joints, regrout the tiles using the usual techniques (see page 421). However, for a slightly different look you might like to consider using a colored grout as a change to the standard white varieties. Grout coloring is usually supplied in a powdered form, which is mixed with white grout until the desired color intensity is achieved.

grout reviver

Reviving grout is in many ways a simpler and quicker way of restoring grout to a clean finish when compared to regrouting. Total regrouting does tend to last longer, and is the more durable option, but because the task of grout revival is quick, it can be performed on a more regular basis. Grout reviver tends to be supplied in kit form.

tools for the job

- grout-reviving kit
- sponge

Make sure the tile surface has been thoroughly cleaned and is completely dry. Apply the reviver along all the grout joints in the same way that you would apply paint. Wipe away any excess reviver using a damp sponge. There is normally a critical timing between application and wiping away excess, so you should always refer to the manufacturer's guidelines in order to attain the best finish.

replacing a tile

Tiles can be broken by accident, or they can simply crack over time due to weaknesses in their manufacture. Whatever the reason, the process for replacing a broken tile is the same. It can be difficult to find an exact match for the tile being replaced, and even small color variations are noticeable in the finished product, so choose carefully. This is a good reason for always keeping a few tiles when you finish any new tiling project.

tools for the job

- cordless drill/driver
- scraper
- hand sledge
- cold chisel
- protective gloves
- goggles
- adhesive spreader
- grout spreader
- sponge

safety advice

When drilling into tiles and removing them, always wear goggles to protect your eyes from any flying pieces.

1 Drill a number of holes into the broken tile surface to weaken its structure. Use a tile drill bit if possible, but since accuracy is not paramount, a masonry bit should break through the tile just as well. Make sure the drill does not slip onto surrounding tiles and damage them.

2 The next step is to loosen the grout around the edge of the broken tile with a grout raker.

3 Remove the damaged tile with a hand sledge and cold chisel. Again, take care to position the point of the chisel so that it cannot slip and damage the surrounding tiles.

4 Use a scraper to remove any remaining tile adhesive from the wall surface.

5 Apply adhesive to the space left by the old tile, and position the new one. Use spacers to maintain a consistent gap around the edge of the tile for the grouting joints. The spacers will have to be applied at a right angle to the tile surface.

6 Hold a wood strip across the tile surface to check that the new tile sits level with the surrounding tiles. If necessary, adjust adhesive levels until the tile sits level.

7 Once the adhesive has dried, remove the spacers and grout the tile joints in the usual way.

repairing dripping faucets 

Dripping faucets are a common problem, but repairs are usually simple to carry out. Leaving a faucet that is dripping is not only a waste of water, but can also lead to stained fixtures, so it is best to deal with the problem immediately. Although manufacturers regularly update faucet designs, the way in which leaks and drips are repaired remains relatively unchanged. Rubber washers are the most common type of seal—the more modern alternative is ceramic cartridges.

Rubber washers are situated at the base of the body deep inside the faucet design. In order to gain access to the washer, you must disassemble the faucet. There will always be slight variations in the dismantling procedure, depending on the faucet design. This usually relates to whether the handle is held in place with a retaining screw or simply push-fit. Retaining screws may also be covered with caps, so gaining access to them may not be instantly obvious. The example below shows a standard faucet design and demonstrates the main principles of gaining access to washers and the way in which they are replaced.

Before beginning work, you will need to turn off water from the supply or by closing the shutoff valve below the relevant faucet. Make sure that you allow any water left in the pipes to run off before dismantling. If you forget to do this, it will spill out when you remove the packing unit from the faucet base.

replacing washers

tools for the job

- screwdriver
- adjustable wrenches
- long-nose & slip-joint pliers
- utility knife

1 Remove the faucet handle. In this case, it simply pulls away from the main body of the faucet.

2 Unscrew the retaining screw at the top of the plastic cover that is fitted over the faucet sleeve.

3 This cover acts purely as a mounting for the faucet handle, so simply pull it off the sleeve.

4 Use an adjustable wrench to undo the sleeve from its position in the main faucet body. You may need to clamp another wrench or some slip-joint pliers onto the faucet base to hold it in place while you apply the necessary pressure to undo the sleeve. If this extra support is required, either tape the jaws of the pliers or wrap a cloth around the faucet base to prevent scratches.

5 With the sleeve removed, you can gain access to the washer. In this case, it is secured in position with a nut. This can be removed with a pair of long-nose pliers or a small adjustable wrench, as shown here.

6 Remove the old washer. You will probably find it easiest to do this by using a standard-tip screwdriver to flick it off. Replace it with a new washer before assembling the faucet.

tips of the trade

- **Avoiding losing parts**—Make sure the sink stopper is in place when changing a washer, because the various small screws and parts of the faucet can easily be dropped in the sink and disappear down the drain.
- **Easing washers**—In many cases, the washer will not be held in place with a nut but simply pushed onto the end of the sleeve. The old washer can be cut away using a utility knife if it is difficult to remove. Soaking the new washer in hot water can make it more pliable and easier to press into place.

OTHER TYPES OF LEAK

Replacing washers will deal with leaks from the spout of the faucet. However, leaks that occur further up the faucet base are more likely to be caused by the failure of a different type of seal. This seal is referred to as an O-ring and can be found in a number of places in the faucet, on both the sleeve and within some spout designs. If leaks become apparent around the shrouds that cover the faucet sleeve or at the base of the spout on a dual faucet, the O-ring seal usually needs to be replaced.

replacing ceramic disc cartridges

This modern type of water-control system is very efficient, and it is unusual to have to replace a disc cartridge because of leakage. In fact, it is so rare that there are no small parts such as washers that can be changed. Instead, the whole cartridge must be exchanged for a new one. There are many different designs of cartridge, so it is important to know the correct type for your particular bathroom before purchase.

Before beginning work, make sure that the water is turned off from the supply, or that the shutoff valve below the relevant faucet has been closed. Run any water left in the pipes before you start work.

tools for the job

- screwdriver
- adjustable wrenches

1 Remove the faucet handle. In this case, a cap is unscrewed off the top of the handle to gain access to the retaining screw below. The escutcheon can then be unscrewed. This will often come away by hand, but adjustable wrenches or pliers can be used if greater pressure is required. Protect the surface of the escutcheon to prevent it from being scratched, if using wrenches or pliers.

2 Unscrew the cartridge from the main faucet base using an adjustable wrench. You may need to grip the faucet base in order to provide the necessary leverage.

3 Pull the old cartridge out of the faucet base and replace it with a new one. The faucet may now be reassembled.

OTHER FAUCETS

The repairs shown here relate to two different types of faucet design. However, there are other mechanisms used to control water flow. Some modern faucets are controlled with a ball-type mechanism in which one handle is used to control the flow of both the hot and cold faucets. Washers and O-rings are still used in their design, however, so methods of repair are similar. There are sometimes small differences between designs from different manufacturers, who often produce specific repair kits for each type of faucet.

dealing with shower problems

Showers can suffer damage to both their functioning and finish. In terms of finish, most damage is caused by the constant action of water hitting wall surfaces, combined with the humid atmosphere. Whether the shower is enclosed in a separate stall or positioned in a bathtub, steam can have a marked effect on surrounding painted surfaces. As far as function is concerned, there are a few simple maintenance procedures that will ensure the best performance from your shower.

installing a vinyl ceiling

The ceiling directly above the shower is the area that suffers most from water damage. Moisture accumulates there and can lead to a breakdown of the decorated surface (normally paint). To prevent this, a sheet of vinyl or polyvinyl chloride (PVC) can be installed to form a waterproof area.

tools for the job

pencil
tape measure
hand saw
caulk gun or dispenser

1 Measure the dimensions of the ceiling area above your shower. For an enclosed shower, this will be the entire ceiling inside the stall—otherwise, you will have to judge what size area you need to cover.

2 Mark the dimensions on the sheet of vinyl and cut it to size using a panel saw.

3 Apply a generous quantity of silicone sealant across the back of the vinyl sheet.

4 Hold the sheet securely in place, and the sealant should adhere quickly.

5 Once the sealant has dried, apply a further bead of silicone around the edge of the sheet to create a neat seal (see box on page 391). You may wish to use painter's tape to help you achieve a neat sealant line. Once this has dried, the shower may be used, after leaving this last application of sealant to dry for 24 hours.

FIXING VINYL WITH SCREWS

If the vinyl sheet does not adhere easily to the ceiling, you may need to hold it in place with some sort of mechanical fastening. Drill pilot holes through the sheet and into the ceiling, then insert screws to hold it in position. Ideally, snap some vinyl caps onto the screw heads to disguise them and make the sheet more pleasing to the eye. To ensure a good seal around the screws, apply a small quantity of sealant to the screw head before inserting it. In this way, as the screw is driven into place, the sealant wraps around the thread of the screw and creates a watertight seal.

painting the ceiling

Problems with peeling paint, build-up of mold, and staining are often the result of the type of paint used and the fact that the area is not often wiped. Wear protective gloves when carrying out this process.

tools for the job

- protective gloves
- cloth or sponge
- paintbrush

1 Sand the area, then wipe with a fungicidal solution to kill mold. Allow it to dry, then rinse with water.

2 Oil-based eggshell paint is more durable and resistant to moisture and condensation than standard latex paint, and because of this it is the preferred paint for use in a bathroom. Apply two or three generous coats and allow to dry thoroughly.

maintenance

Many of the problems associated with shower fixtures are related to the shower head itself or the hose. These elements of the shower are in frequent use, so regular maintenance should be undertaken.

head cleaning

Shower outlet holes can often become blocked with limescale, and this is particularly true if you live in a hard-water area. If this happens, you should disassemble the head and descale the holes. Always wear protective gloves when handling descaling fluid.

tools for the job

- screwdriver
- toothbrush
- protective gloves

1 The way in which shower heads are dismantled varies between manufacturers, but in most cases there is an obvious screw fastening that is simply undone in order to gain access to the inside of the shower head.

2 Clean the outlet holes with a descaling fluid. Use an old toothbrush to apply the fluid to all of the intricate parts of the shower head. Be sure to read the manufacturer's guidelines carefully for the solution you are using, and check that it is suitable for plastic- or metal-based shower heads.

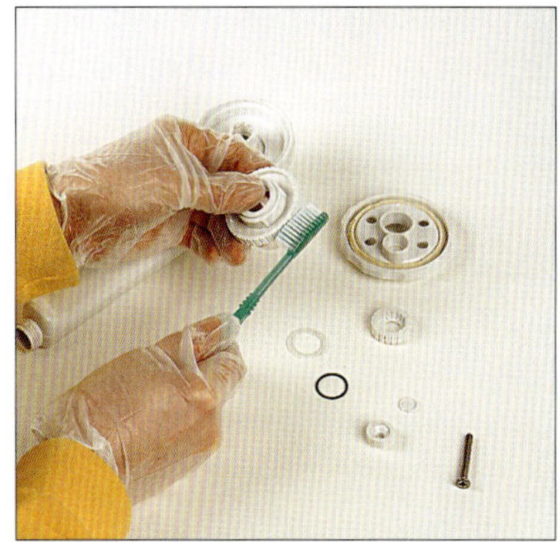

tips of the trade

Some blockages in shower holes can be removed using a pin (although take care not to prick yourself while doing so). However, you should avoid this method if your shower head contains plastic diaphragms, because these can be damaged by the pin.

hose replacement

Another common problem with showers is when the hose begins to leak around the connection with the head itself. In some cases the problem can easily be fixed with a washer, but in general a new hose is required. Be sure to get the correct size of replacement hose, then simply unscrew the old one and screw the new one in place.

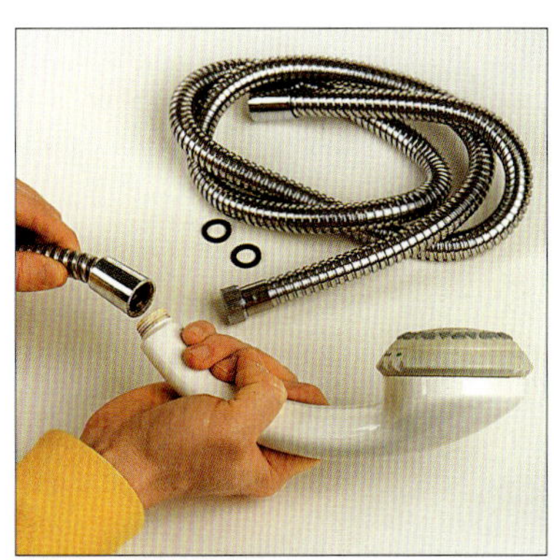

dealing with clogs & leaks

Many problems in bathrooms and kitchens are hidden from view, but their effects can be devastating if not acted upon quickly. Clogs of any nature should be dealt with as soon as they are noticed, because any delay could lead to repairs that incur a much greater cost. Likewise, any leaking pipes should be repaired immediately, because once water does begin to drip from a joint or hole, it will not stop unless an adequate repair is made.

simple sink solutions

There are two methods of dealing with sink clogs, both of which are outlined here.

using chemical cleaners

There are various chemical cleaners available. Most are caustic (generally containing sodium hydroxide), and as such, protective gloves should always be worn. They are best used when the first signs of a clog become apparent. Read the manufacturer's guidelines carefully, but in general one or two spoonfuls of the cleaner need to be poured into the drain opening in the sink. Run a small amount of water to ensure that none of the granules are allowed to rest on any exposed part of the sink bowl. Leave the cleaner to work for 20–30 minutes, before flushing the system with more water. One further application may be required to clear the clog. Make sure there is adequate ventilation when carrying out this procedure, because the fumes can be quite strong and overpowering.

safety advice

For homes with a septic tank as part of their drainage system, chemical-based caustic cleaner cannot be used. Instead, a bacteria-based treatment must be employed. As usual, always follow the manufacturer's instructions.

using plungers

When chemical cleaners are ineffective, the next option to try is a plunger. First, you must create an airlock in the drainage system. This can be achieved by inserting a rag or cloth in the overflow outlet. When you have done this, position the suction pad of the plunger over the sink drain. Move the plunger handle rhythmically up and down, which should put enough pressure on the clog to loosen it. In this example, a modern design of plunger has been used that works on a similar principle to traditional designs, except that here, water is sucked into the plunger cylinder and forced at high pressure into the clog below, thus dislodging it.

unclogging toilets

Toilets can be unclogged using a plunger in the same way that you would unclog a sink, as long as the head of the plunger is large enough to cover the outlet in the toilet bowl. Alternatively, use a closet auger, as demonstrated below.

1 Pull out the spring section of the closet auger to a suitable length for extending around the trap of the toilet.

2 Push the spring section into the trap of the toilet and turn the handle on the back.

removing traps

If the options for dispelling a clog at sink level are not successful, it may be necessary to turn your attention to below sink level and consider the waste pipes and sink trap. It may, therefore, be necessary to undo the trap and clean it out by hand in order to remove a clog.

1 Most traps simply unscrew by hand. For particularly stiff or solid joints, however, it may be necessary to use some slip-joint pliers to provide a good grip and extra leverage to unscrew. Before you start this unscrewing, always position a bowl below the trap to catch any excess water inside.

2 Flush out the trap with water, and use your fingers to remove any large pieces of material that could be contributing to the clog. This can be a bit of a messy business, so you may wish to wear some gloves to protect your hands.

3 Before you replace the trap, you could take the opportunity to replace any washers in order to renew the seals.

using a closet auger

Closet augers are extremely effective tools for dealing with all manner of clogs, and where a sink is clogged, or rather a sink drainage system is clogged, a closet auger might be the best piece of equipment for rectifying the situation. The long spring and handle mechanism give you good access to the clog, and provide the force you will need to break it up and release it.

1 Remove the trap on the sink to leave access to the waste pipe. Pull out the sprung section of the closet auger to a length that can be inserted into the waste pipe. When removing the trap from the sink, remember to have a bowl close at hand to catch the excess water that will be released.

2 Insert the sprung section into the pipe and turn the handle of the closet auger so that it screws into the pipe void and eventually comes into contact with the clog. Keep turning the closet auger handle to allow the sprung section to burrow into the clog, gradually breaking it down and making it much easier to wash down the pipe.

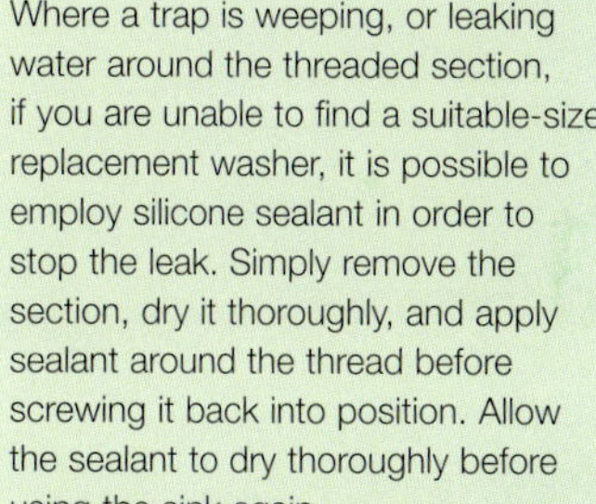

tips of the trade

Where a trap is weeping, or leaking water around the threaded section, if you are unable to find a suitable-size replacement washer, it is possible to employ silicone sealant in order to stop the leak. Simply remove the section, dry it thoroughly, and apply sealant around the thread before screwing it back into position. Allow the sealant to dry thoroughly before using the sink again.

MACHINE MAINTENANCE

Clothes washers and dishwashers require little general maintenance, other than occasionally checking to ensure that the inlet and waste pipes are in good working order, and that there are no visible leaks or drips. However, it is worth referring to the manufacturer's guidelines for the particular appliance as, for example, in some situations filters may need cleaning or replacing to enable the clothes washer or dishwasher to function at optimum levels.

decorative finishes

However well constructional tasks have been carried out, the decorative aspect of any renovation work is the deciding factor in determining how good the finished product will look. Attention to detail at this stage of a project will turn an ordinary finish into an outstanding one. This section provides options and instruction on many decorative processes while supplying the crucial information on how to achieve good finishes through preparation and planning. Take time to choose decorative schemes, and use this section as a guide for selecting the most appropriate materials and techniques.

choosing finishes

Decoration is very much an issue of personal preference. In general, most people tend to have particular opinions on certain finishes—for example, many people have wallpaper in every room, while others cannot bear the thought of wallpaper anywhere. Some use strong colors in every room scheme, while others shy away to more neutral shades. There is no right or wrong, and it can be worth trying out a range of options.

design aspects

When considering any decorative option, design or period features may influence the type of decoration you use. Both period homes and ultra-modern apartments are similar in this respect, because both have some limitations on the types of materials that can be used, if the home is to retain its style or design. Therefore, some research or thought gathering on authenticity should take part in your final decision-making process.

Knocking two rooms into one, or widening entrances between rooms is a way of creating a more open-plan layout. While providing a lighter, more spacious atmosphere, consideration needs to be made of the feasibility of removing whole or partial walls, especially if they are loadbearing. However, this sort of renovation can dramatically change the look of your home, and totally transform a cramped, rather gloomy atmosphere into a design with far greater appeal.

RIGHT *Period design features, such as fireplaces, help to create extra interest in the decorative scheme.*

wallpaper

The modern DIY revolution has also increased the range of options open to people who wish to use wallpaper. Manufacturers now produce papers in a greater range of designs, colors, and textures than ever before. Wallpaper has an instant effect, which often makes it an attractive option for many people, but it is important to paint any surrounding woodwork or surfaces in colors that will complement the paper. It's also important to ensure that furnishings in the room will make a suitable contrast or complement to the paper design. Different wallpapers may have markedly different effects on the atmosphere of a room, so choose your pattern carefully.

LEFT *Stripes are a particularly effective wallpaper design, and can help to create the impression of height within the room by making the ceiling appear higher.*

ABOVE *Tile designs can be used effectively on both walls and floors to create a well-integrated scheme.*

RIGHT *Large, open-plan room designs provide a broad canvas for atmospheric color schemes.*

BELOW *Strong colors are a particularly effective way of picking out the different types of surfaces and features in a room.*

tiles

Tiles form part of the decorative scheme in most bathrooms or kitchens, even if their primary use is for practical purposes. Design choices may be influenced by a desire to tie in colors with other wall decoration, or you may opt for neutral colors that will complement any number of alterations to the surrounding decor.

paint

Paint is the most versatile of all decorative products, and is used in most rooms on at least some surfaces. Color availability stretches through every imaginable shade, which means that all tastes are catered for—to the point that there can sometimes be so much choice that it is difficult to decide between closely matched colors. This vastness of range presents plenty of options for co-ordinating colors and producing complementary or contrasting schemes to suit personal choice.

painting details

Contrasting colors can enliven surfaces, particularly when they are used to pick out certain details or features in a room. The right combinations can create greater texture and add interest to various architectural features. However, the greater the range of colors used, the greater the amount of time that should be spent planning the scheme to ensure that the correct blend is chosen.

choosing materials

Having made decisions on the type of finish you require, it is necessary to choose the best materials for that particular finish. The best materials are those that have the most suitable properties and the right decorative attributes—some finishes are suited to some surfaces more than others, and these factors should be considered before materials are purchased and used.

tiles

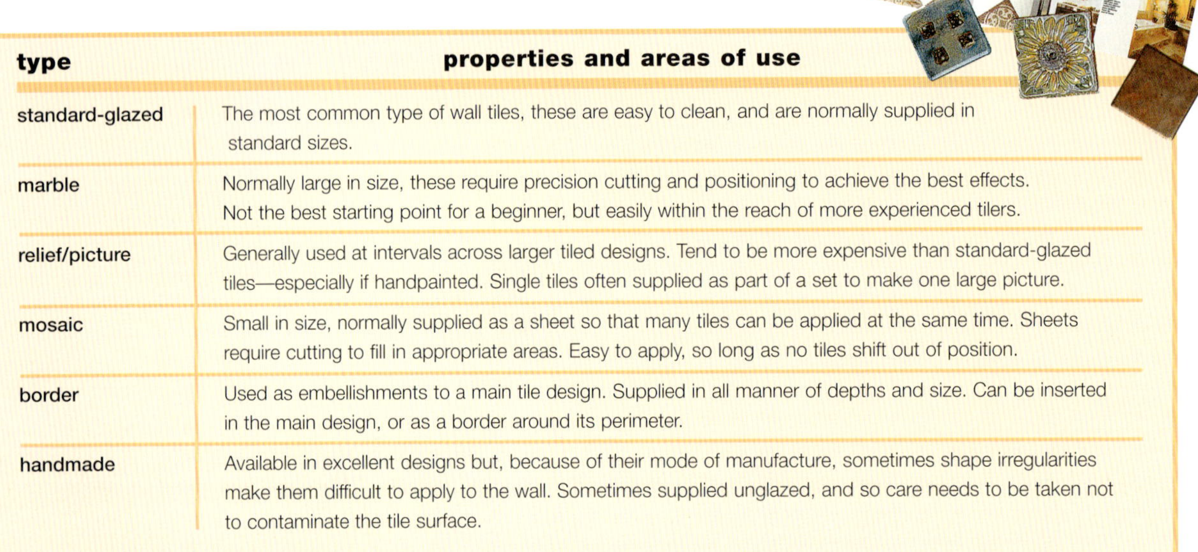

Tiles are the most durable of decorative materials, making them suitable for most areas in the home. Able to withstand knocks and regular cleaning, they are most commonly used in kitchen and bathroom areas.

type	properties and areas of use
standard-glazed	The most common type of wall tiles, these are easy to clean, and are normally supplied in standard sizes.
marble	Normally large in size, these require precision cutting and positioning to achieve the best effects. Not the best starting point for a beginner, but easily within the reach of more experienced tilers.
relief/picture	Generally used at intervals across larger tiled designs. Tend to be more expensive than standard-glazed tiles—especially if handpainted. Single tiles often supplied as part of a set to make one large picture.
mosaic	Small in size, normally supplied as a sheet so that many tiles can be applied at the same time. Sheets require cutting to fill in appropriate areas. Easy to apply, so long as no tiles shift out of position.
border	Used as embellishments to a main tile design. Supplied in all manner of depths and size. Can be inserted in the main design, or as a border around its perimeter.
handmade	Available in excellent designs but, because of their mode of manufacture, sometimes shape irregularities make them difficult to apply to the wall. Sometimes supplied unglazed, and so care needs to be taken not to contaminate the tile surface.

wallpaper

Different wallpapers have surprisingly varied properties, which means that they can be used in a range of areas around the home. When choosing a design, make sure that the actual paper makeup is also suitable.

type	properties and areas of use
lining	Dead flat and available in various thicknesses. Either used as an underlayer for patterned wallpaper, or can simply be painted over. Smooths wall surfaces, and provides a softer texture than cold plaster walls.
textured	Relief is built into the paper structure in order to provide pattern and/or texture. Excellent for covering over rough wall surfaces. Some varieties can be painted, while others have a vinyl finish already applied.
standard-patterned	Machine-patterned, and made in vast quantities and ranges of designs. Ideal for most wall surfaces. Often requires lining first, though not on drywall. Available as ready-pasted or paste-the-back varieties.
vinyl	Durable paper designed to be easily cleaned or wiped down. The vinyl layer makes it suitable for bathrooms and kitchens.
natural	Composed of natural fibers such as silk or hessian. Difficult to hang and best left to the professionals. Provides an outstanding finish, but not particularly durable.

paint

This table contains some of the most common finishing paints for walls and ceilings, and explains their relevant properties. In addition to these common varieties, it is possible to choose specialized finishes.

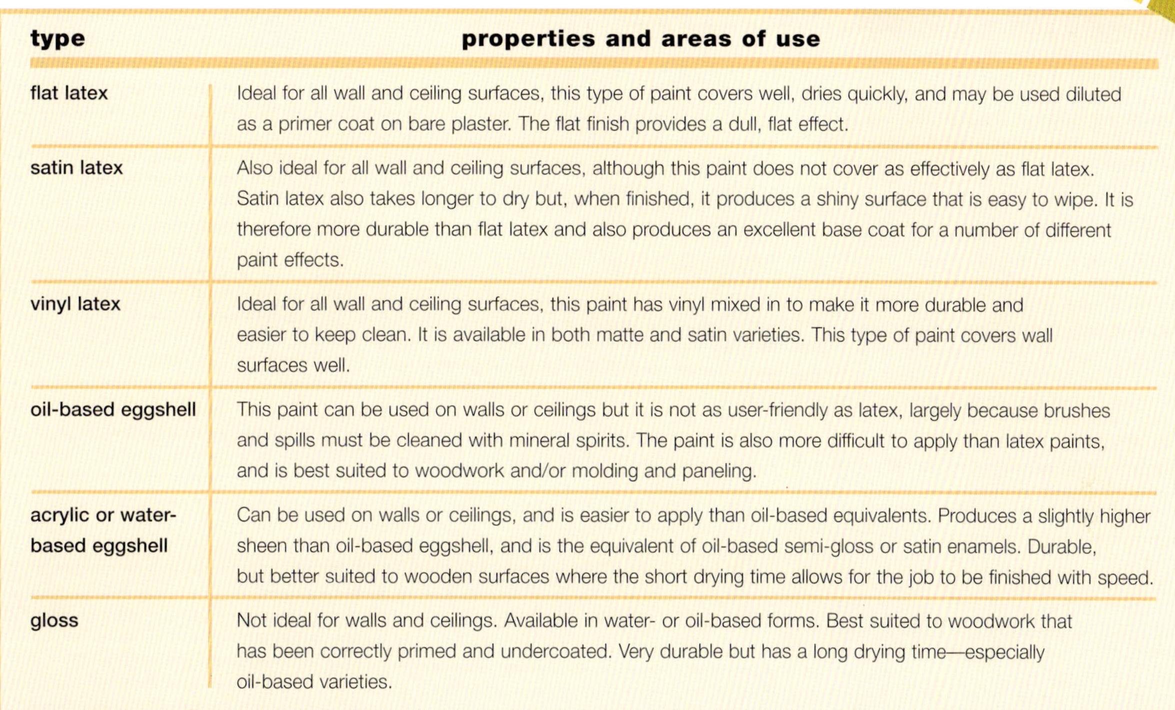

type	properties and areas of use
flat latex	Ideal for all wall and ceiling surfaces, this type of paint covers well, dries quickly, and may be used diluted as a primer coat on bare plaster. The flat finish provides a dull, flat effect.
satin latex	Also ideal for all wall and ceiling surfaces, although this paint does not cover as effectively as flat latex. Satin latex also takes longer to dry but, when finished, it produces a shiny surface that is easy to wipe. It is therefore more durable than flat latex and also produces an excellent base coat for a number of different paint effects.
vinyl latex	Ideal for all wall and ceiling surfaces, this paint has vinyl mixed in to make it more durable and easier to keep clean. It is available in both matte and satin varieties. This type of paint covers wall surfaces well.
oil-based eggshell	This paint can be used on walls or ceilings but it is not as user-friendly as latex, largely because brushes and spills must be cleaned with mineral spirits. The paint is also more difficult to apply than latex paints, and is best suited to woodwork and/or molding and paneling.
acrylic or water-based eggshell	Can be used on walls or ceilings, and is easier to apply than oil-based equivalents. Produces a slightly higher sheen than oil-based eggshell, and is the equivalent of oil-based semi-gloss or satin enamels. Durable, but better suited to wooden surfaces where the short drying time allows for the job to be finished with speed.
gloss	Not ideal for walls and ceilings. Available in water- or oil-based forms. Best suited to woodwork that has been correctly primed and undercoated. Very durable but has a long drying time—especially oil-based varieties.

paint effects

Paint effects are produced by the use of a colored glaze that allows for the creation of broken-color finishes on a wall surface. So the materials used are more concerned with achieving pattern and effect, rather than actually containing finishing properties in their own right.

type	properties and areas of use
acrylic or latex glaze	This is water-based, and makes an ideal base for the majority of paint effects. It dries quickly—helping to speed the process, but also necessitating speedy application. User-friendly and easy to clean tools after use.
transparent oil glaze	This is oil-based and has similar properties to acrylic or latex glaze, but it may need the addition of turpentine to achieve the correct medium—this varies between manufacturers. It requires a long drying time and is less user-friendly than the acrylic equivalent.
colorizers	Used to add color to glazes. Some colorizers are universal, in that they may be added to either medium, while others are only appropriate for use with one or the other. Only small quantities are required, as the pigment is very strong.
varnish	This is used to cover finished effects for protective purposes, and allows the surface to be wiped clean. Flat or gloss finishes are available.
glaze coat	Similar to varnish, except that it is always water-based. Easy and quick to apply, it produces a surface that is easy to clean. Provides a slight sheen to the finish.

ceiling & wall preparation

The quality of a decorative finish depends on thorough surface preparation. This stage of the renovation procedure is one of the most important in terms of ensuring that the building work you have carried out will be shown off to its best possible potential. It is important not to rush surface preparation and to be sure that any defects are corrected before proceeding, in order to prevent their appearance in the final surface.

filling

Filling cracks, joints, or holes in wall and ceiling surfaces can be considered a relatively uncomplicated task, and you will achieve the best results by following a methodical order of work. There are three main types of filler: all-purpose filler, flexible filler, and expandable foam. Each type is designed for a particular kind of task, and all products currently on the market are based on one of them.

all-purpose filler

Manufacturers describe this type of filler as all-purpose, and although it can physically be used for most things, it is still best suited to particular types of hole. It can be bought ready-mixed, or as a powder to which water is added and a smooth, creamy filling paste created. It is most effective in small divots and dents on open wall or ceiling surfaces.

1 Remove any dust in the hole and dampen it slightly to improve the filler's adhesion. Use a putty knife to press the filler into place, applying pressure with the knife's flexible blade. Leave the filler slightly proud of the hole—it shrinks slightly as it dries—but remove excess from around the outside.

2 Once dry, sand to a smooth finish, level with the surrounding wall. For deep holes, a second application of filler may be necessary, because excessive shrinkage can pull the first application down below the hole surface. Be careful if using a power sander on drywall, because it is easy to damage the surface.

flexible filler

Although some all-purpose fillers claim to have flexible qualities, they tend not to achieve the standards set by tubed flexible filler or caulk. This type of filler is used along corner or ceiling junction cracks where slight movement is always prevalent. Although all-purpose filler can be used in these areas, it tends to crack after time, while flexible filler or caulk tolerates more stress through movement. However, take care to smooth the filler before it dries, as it is not possible to sand it.

safety advice

Always wear a dust mask when using an electric sander, and preferably hook it up to a vacuum that has an HEPA filter.

1 Use a caulk gun to apply sealant along the corner cracks, allowing the filler to bead over and cover the crack beneath.

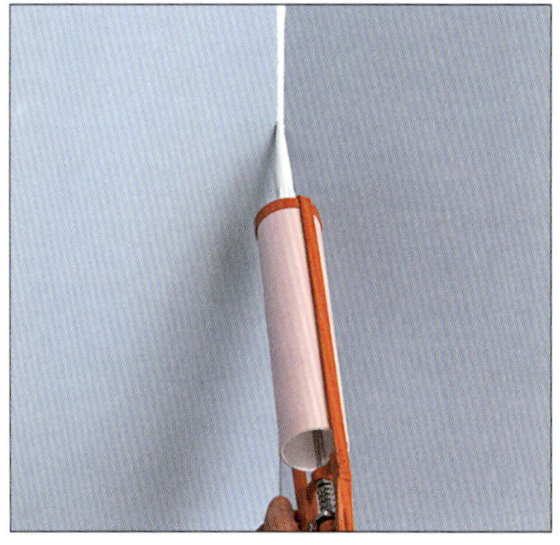

2 Before the filler dries, use a wet finger or a sponge to smooth the filler into the junction. Keep a cup of water handy to wet or clean your finger as you work on shaping the filler.

3 For storage purposes, insert a nail or screw into the nozzle of the filler tube to prevent it hardening in the nozzle and making it difficult to use when next required.

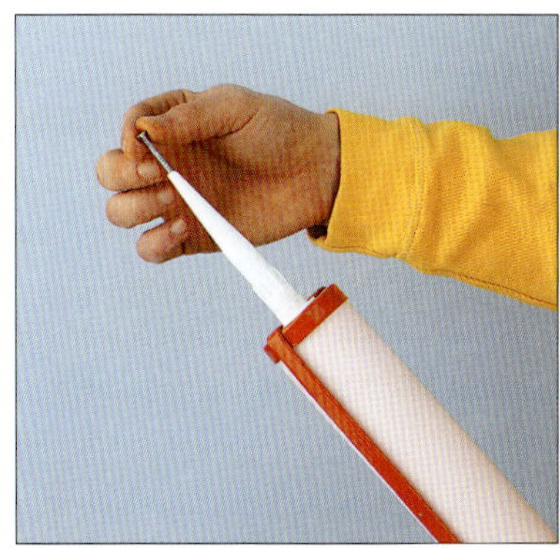

expandable foam

In large gaps or holes, especially around awkward-shape inlets such as pipes, the use of flexible or all-purpose filler is neither suitable nor economic. Expandable foam is ideal as it gets into all the small crevices, adheres well, and makes a neat finish. However, it is best to use it with all-purpose filler because expandable foam has a rough texture. So, once the major filling process is complete, finish off the surface with a final skim of all-purpose filler.

Expandable foam is aerosol-based, and is guided into a hole using an extended nozzle. As its name suggests, once out of the aerosol the chemical makeup of the foam expands and takes up the entire area that requires filling. This leads to the foam protruding from the hole. Once dry, this can be trimmed back with a utility knife to a neat finish and then skimmed with all-purpose filler, following the safety guidelines.

caulking blade

A caulking blade or caulker (not to be confused with caulk in terms of flexible filler) is ideal for speeding up the all-purpose filling process. On walls with a number of small holes, draw the wide, filler-loaded blade of the caulker across the surface. This enables you to fill several holes simultaneously, rather than having to attend to each one separately with a small putty knife.

tips of the trade

Although it is important not to jeopardize the quality of the finish by rushing the job, there are a number of practical, time-saving measures that can be taken. Various tools have been designed to speed up DIY tasks, and electric sanders, in particular, are useful pieces of equipment. Sanding is never the most inspirational or invigorating of tasks, and so using an electric sander helps to speed up the process. Be wary, however, of using it directly on drywall—it can damage the surface, and the dust can be a health hazard.

cleaning and sealing surfaces

Once the necessary filling and sanding of surfaces has been completed, it is important to clean surfaces with warm water and mild detergent to remove dust and impurities. Finally, rinse the surfaces with water and allow to dry. Depending on their condition and the decorative layers to be applied, it may also be necessary to seal the surfaces before painting or decorating. In the chart shown on the right, the solution referred to comprises a mix of 5 parts water to 1 part white glue (PVA). Mix the solution thoroughly before application.

type	surface treatment
surfaces that have been stripped of paper	Must be sealed with a white glue primer
drywalled	Bare drywall primer must be applied to the surface before painting or papering
new plaster	Must be sealed with a primer specified for plaster before painting or papering
old painted	Ensure the surface is completely clean. Sizing is required if paper is to be applied
old papered	Inadvisable to paint over an old papered surface unless you are sure the paper is firmly stuck down
wood paneling	Prime and paint as required, or apply a natural wood finish

painting techniques

The quality of a painted finish is dependent on both the type of paint used and the method of application. Therefore, having purchased quality materials, you should develop a good painting technique in order to achieve the best possible finishes. There are a number of different tools that may be used for applying paint, and many are suited to particular surfaces and tasks, but a certain amount of personal preference can also influence your choice.

tools for the job

ceilings

Painting ceilings always tends to produce the initial problem of gaining the best access. Although using a stepladder and brush is an option, there are far more efficient and easier ways of going about this task.

1 Attach an extension pole to the roller so that the ceiling can be painted with your feet on the floor. An extension pole is also useful for walls, as it helps gain access to the top area of a wall and reduces the need to bend over for lower wall areas. Using an extension pole also produces a more even pressure during paint application, and improves the quality and evenness of the finish.

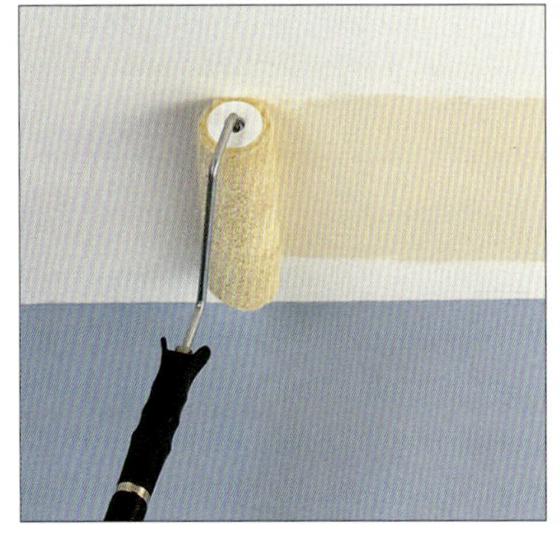

2 Having used a roller, you need to finish or cut in around the edges of the ceiling. A brush is the best tool for this purpose. If the walls in the room are to be painted, allow the ceiling color to extend slightly down on to the wall surface—when the wall is painted, you may then paint over the excess ceiling color and cut in precisely into the wall/ceiling junction. This technique ensures you do not waste time cutting in the ceiling color.

tips of the trade

New equipment is always being devised and, while some prefer traditional tools, it can be worth experimenting.

improving technique

There are a number of factors that can affect the final appearance of a painted surface. Practicing your painting technique will always help to ensure a good ceiling or wall finish, as will considering the following points.

number of coats

Probably one of the key factors in producing a good finish, it is always best to have a flexible attitude when deciding on coat requirement. As a rule, no surface should receive fewer than two coats of paint and new plaster surfaces should get three. The quality of paint you are using will also determine requirement—hence the false economy of buying cheap paint. Refreshing a previously painted room with the same color as before will only require one coat. So flexibility is the key but, as a general rule, the greater the number of coats, the better the finish.

wet edges

The chemical makeup of modern paints often includes such substances as vinyl (making them easily washable), which can be a problem when painting. The slight sheen that the vinyl produces can cause highlighting of areas where paint layers are greater than in other areas. This occurs when the central areas of a wall are painted, left to dry and then the edges cut in later. So as coats are applied, the slight overlap between the edge of the central wall areas and the cut-in edges acquire a buildup of paint layers, which can cause a noticeable color difference. To prevent this, paint one wall at a time so that both the edges and central area of the wall are painted and therefore dry at the same time. This is especially important for dark colors, which can be more noticeable than lighter shades.

roller trails

The texture of rollers leaves a slight imprint in the paint and surface finish. Make sure you avoid paint buildup at the ends of rollers, as this can lead to thicker paint lines or trails on the ceiling or wall surface.

priming

Prime areas that have been filled with an all-purpose filler using your chosen wall color. Otherwise, the varying

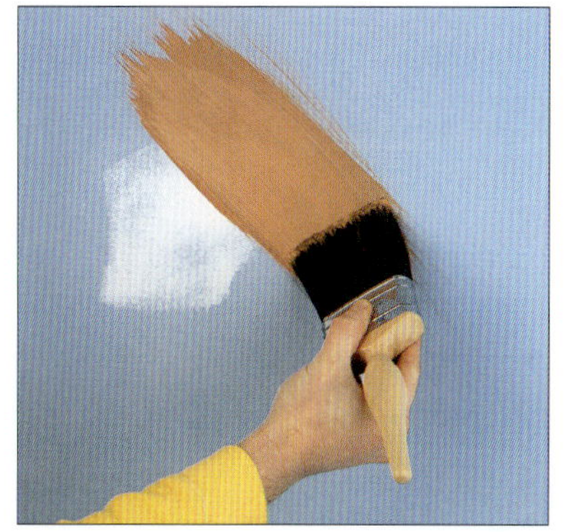

absorption properties of the filler and the wall can cause shading differences when further coats of paint are added.

For troublesome stains on an older painted surface area, it is best to use a stain sealer to coat the area before continuing with finishing paint.

Where flexible filler or caulk has been used, it is always best to prime it with an oil-based undercoat, as water-based latex applied directly to the caulk can sometimes crack as it dries.

spraying

In some circumstances, a spray gun is a useful tool for painting large open areas. However, always mask off areas that do not require painting, and wear goggles and a respiratory mask. Apply a number of thin coats rather than a few thicker ones, as this will help to prevent runs in the finish.

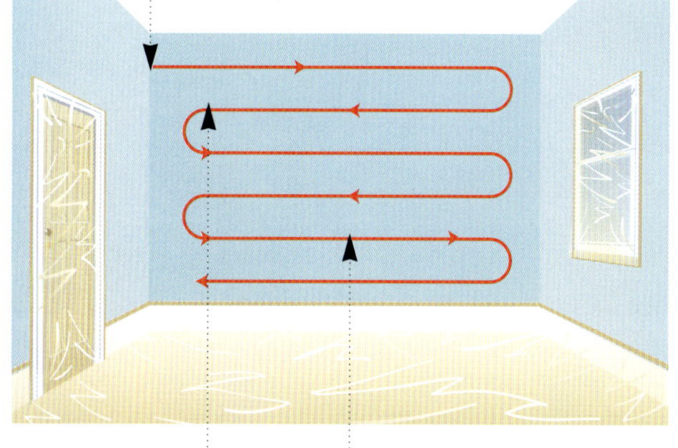

Start the gun slightly to the side of the section to be painted, and then progress on to the area.

Start at the top of the wall and work down to the bottom.

Allow each level of paint to overlap slightly as you progress.

painting doors

Quite simply, there is a right and a wrong way to paint any item, and doors are no exception. You must refine your technique so that the best possible quality of finish is achieved. Once preparation and priming have been completed, application of top coats, and perhaps a finishing coat, follows the same system or order of work. Doors vary in design, but one of the more common varieties is the panel door, and the best way of achieving a good finish is demonstrated below.

tools for the job

1½in paintbrush

1in paintbrush

painting a panel door

Panel doors vary in design from two large panels making up their surface to as many as eight panels. However, the best system for painting them stays the same and here a six-panel door has been used. Choice of brush size is very important, and a 1½in brush is ideal in most cases.

1 Begin by painting the panels themselves, starting at the top. As well as painting the central flat area of the panel, also complete the molded area and try not to allow paint to encroach onto the rails or stiles.

2 Continue to work down the door, completing all the panels, using the bristles of the brush in line with the direction of the wood grain. Even if you are painting a pressed-panel door that does not have any grain as such, still direct the brush in the direction of what would be the perceived grain.

3 Once the panels are complete, move on to paint the center vertical stile down the middle of the door. Try not to allow the paint to extend on to the horizontal rails, and if any excess encroaches on the painted panels, be sure that you brush the paint out to prevent a paint buildup.

4 Move on to coat the horizontal rails to complete the center portion of the door. Take care when creating the joint between these rails and the painted vertical stiles to be sure of a precise defining line. This will maintain the principle of painting in line with the grain and therefore provides the neatest possible finish.

5 Finish the face of the door by painting the two outer vertical stiles on the hinge and opening edge of the door. Again, make precise divisions at the point where the vertical stiles cross the edges of the horizontal rails while still brushing the paint out in the usual manner.

6 Paint the leading edge of the door using a 1in brush to avoid overlap. Take care to paint precisely down the edge of the door only, and not on the door face.

7 Now that the door itself is complete, turn your attention to the door casing. The hinge edge of the door in this instance need not be painted, as it should be the same color as the other face of the door. Begin on the casing by painting the edge.

8 With the casing edges complete, paint the face of the moldings, returning to the 1½in brush for quicker coverage.

9 Paint the inner doorstop and remaining side of the frame, and check for any areas that you have missed. Finally, turn attention back to the face of the door to make sure there are no drips on the paint surface. Brush in such areas as required.

flush doors

Flush doors do not have the complicated surface of panel doors. Hence they may be treated more as an overall open surface, which is best painted by mentally dividing the door area into eight equal-sized sections, beginning with two at the top and three further rows of two areas as you go down the door surface. It is important to maintain a wet edge in the paint as you move from each area to the next, so that there is no visible join between each of the eight areas. The casing and door frame may be painted as for panel doors.

glazed doors

When painting a glazed door, it should be treated more like a casement window than a solid door surface.

A well-painted door forms an integral part of any room decoration. Attention to detail and precise dividing lines help to enhance its look and provide a good-quality finish.

painting windows

As with doors, achieving the best possible finish for windows requires a particular order of work. Accuracy is even more important, because it is vital to prevent paint transfer or overspray from reaching any glass surface. Therefore windows must be broken down into different sections and painted systematically, according to the order listed below.

tools for the job

1in paintbrush

casement windows

Casement windows provide a good example of how all window painting should be approached. Casements themselves vary in design, with different types and sizes of opening sections, but a similar principle regarding the order of work applies. Remember to continually look back to painted areas so you can brush out any drips or runs that you find before the paint dries. Make sure to pay particular attention to the numerous joints and corners, which provide areas where paint could build up.

1 Initially, attention should be aimed towards the smallest opening casement. Begin by painting the rabbets using a 1in brush. Take care to bead the paint directly along the rabbet/glass junction, creating a precise edge.

tips of the trade

- **Preparing the sill**—Before painting a windowsill, wipe over it with a cloth dampened in lacquer thinner and allow it to dry before applying paint. This removes dust particles and improves the overall finish.
- **Window guards**—If you find producing a precise edge between rabbet and glass particularly difficult, it may be worth using a window guard. These specially designed pieces of metal or plastic can be held along the junction of glass and wood, positioned to shield the glass surface so that paint is applied only to the wood. However, after painting each rabbet, the edge of the window guard or shield should be cleaned with a cloth to remove excess paint and prevent it being transferred to the glass surface when it is next positioned.
- **Drying time**—Always allow sufficient drying time for paint. Closing the window too early will almost certainly lead to its sticking shut.

2 Move on to complete the rest of the small opening casement, first painting the horizontal rails, and then the vertical ones. Remember always to keep the brush bristles in line with the direction of the wood grain, depending on which section of the casement is being painted. This creates a neat finish between vertical and horizontal rails.

3 Now move on to the larger opening casement, beginning once again with the window rabbets. Start painting the top panes and work down the window rabbets to the bottom level of the pane.

4 You can now finish painting the opening casement by completing the central horizontal and vertical rails. The very last parts that are left to be painted are the outer vertical rails on the hinged side and the leading edge of the casement.

5 Then paint the fixed casements, starting on the rabbets first before finishing with the open faces of the rails.

6 Next, paint around the inside rabbets of the main window frame, between the outer edge of the frame and the casements themselves. When working next to the opening casements, be sure to paint a precise dividing line so that there is no untidy overspill on the window edges.

7 Finally, complete the main face of the window by painting the outer frame. Similar accuracy is required here for painting the rabbets next to the glass. Always produce a precise dividing line between the window frame and the wall surface.

8 With the window complete, the sill may be painted to provide the overall finished product.

It is worth noting that painting the exterior of a window is very similar to the interior, except the rabbets may be putty or wood. The technique used will remain very much the same.

double-hung windows

Painting double-hung windows follows similar principles as for casements, starting next to the glass and working out towards the frame being the best method. The main problem with sashes is when painting the runners, as this tends to be the area where sticking may occur and hinder the mechanism of the window. It is therefore worth inspecting the runners closely before beginning to paint—if they do not require recoating, it is not worth painting them purely for the sake of it. Bear in mind that the runners are obscured most of the time, and it is better to have them functioning easily than stuck fast because of layers of paint buildup. From an aesthetic point of view, efforts should be concentrated on window parts that are most visible.

A well-painted window provides clean, crisp lines that show off detail work, enhancing the overall look of the room decoration.

paint effects

The popularity of paint effects has never been greater, and manufacturers are responding to this demand by producing various tools, equipment, and materials. One of the most important materials is the glaze—quality paint effects tend to be as dependent on this as they are on the technique or correct equipment. Some techniques are slightly more difficult than others, so it is worth bearing in mind the level of skill required when choosing which effect to have.

tools for the job

mixing colors

Most paint effects are created using transparent glaze. This is the medium that provides the textured or three-dimensional effect that makes paint effects appealing. Traditionalists would argue that the glaze should be oil-based, but by far the most user-friendly are acrylic-, latex-, or water-based equivalents. These can simply be bought off the shelf so that mixing color becomes a basic process of adding pigment or tints to the glaze in order to achieve the shade you require.

However, some caution and instruction is required for this process, in order to avoid waste and be sure that the color you mix will actually be the color you require on the final wall surface.

adding tints

Before adding color to the glaze, mix tints to produce the shade you require. It is unlikely that your perfect color requirement will be that of a particular tube of tint, so mixing is nearly always necessary. When you are happy with the shade you have mixed, add some of it to a small quantity of glaze on a mixing palette, so that you can test it on a discreet area or scrap of wood. Skipping this process and adding tint directly to large quantities of glaze can lead to a glaze being mixed to the wrong color, which then cannot be mixed back and leads to unnecessary waste of materials.

dilution considerations

Remember that the strength of tint in a small area will be considerably diluted when added to a large quantity of glaze. Therefore, bear in mind that although the pigment of tints is very strong, once applied to the wall there will be some dilution of the effect.

quantities

Directions will vary between manufacturers in terms of how much pigment is required and how much coverage the glaze will provide on the wall surface. Remember, however, that although glaze does go a lot further than traditional paints, if you run out it will be nearly impossible to remix a glaze exactly the same. Therefore, always mix up more than you need, to make sure that this situation cannot arise. Any leftover mixture can always be stored in an airtight container for future projects.

techniques

Most paint effects are categorized by whether they involve "on" or "off" techniques. The former involves using a tool to apply the effect directly to the wall, whereas the latter involves applying glaze to the wall with a normal paintbrush before using a tool to apply an effect in the glaze. The same tool may be used in both techniques, but with a completely different finished effect. For example, the finish produced by sponging on is markedly different to that of sponging off. However, not all tools can be used for both methods, and some are more clearly suited to one technique or the other.

sponging on

Dip a dampened natural sponge into wet glaze and remove any excess before lightly applying the sponge to the wall surface. Change your wrist angle and sponge direction as you progress across the wall in order to achieve a totally random effect. Wash out the sponge periodically.

ragging off

Apply glaze to the wall with a paint brush and use a crumpled, dampened rag to make impressions of the rag in the glazed surface. Change your hand angle and the position of the rag to maintain a random effect. Work only in areas of 1yd^2 at a time, otherwise the glaze will dry before you get a chance to make the impressions. Use a new rag (or wash the old one) when it becomes clogged with glaze.

stippling

This is really an "off" technique. Apply glaze to the wall before using a stippling brush to make fine, textured imprints in the glaze surface. Keep the bristles of the brush at right angles to the wall surface at all times. Again, only work in areas of 1yd^2 at a time, and remove excess glaze from the bristles at regular intervals.

color washing

Probably the most simple of "off" paint effects, color washing involves brushing on the glaze and using the texture of the brush to produce the finished effect. Brushstrokes can be used randomly or in a uniform manner, depending on taste. Also, more than one coat may be applied to build up the overall depth of finish.

STAMPING

Stamps (like stencils) provide a method of applying a definite image to a wall surface. The design can be anything decorative and may be combined with other types of paint effects—used over the top of them—or applied directly onto plain, painted walls.

- Apply paint to the back face of the stamp using a specially designed foam roller. Test the stamp on scrap paper before applying it to the wall, in order to check for the correct amount of paint for the depth of finish you require.

- Apply the stamp to the wall, ensuring that it does not slip on the wall surface and therefore smudge the image. Remove the stamp at a right angle from the wall surface, and then move on to the next position. Paint can be reapplied between each stamp application or between, every two to three applications, which helps to produce a softer, more random effect.

wallpapering techniques

Wallpapering requires a methodical approach, with close attention to detail. It is important to take time when choosing your paper, making sure that it suits aesthetic requirements and that you will feel confident applying it. Some papers are easier to use than others, and subtle patterns can make accurate lining up difficult, but careful practice should make the process easier.

tools for the job

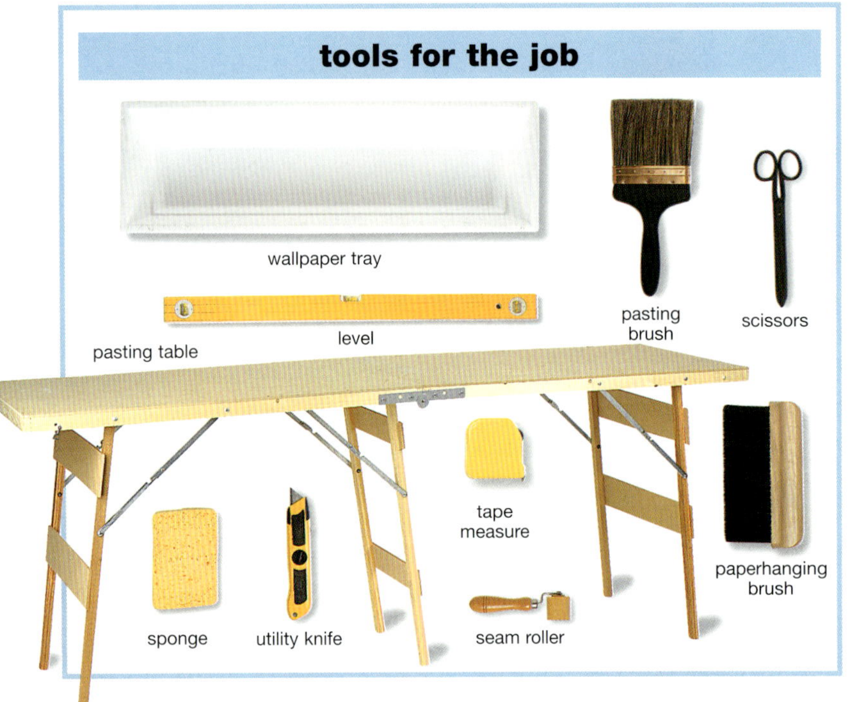

Try to decide on a starting point that allows the first length of paper to be a full one—that is to say, the only trimming required will be at the top and bottom edges. The exact starting position will depend on the particular room's shape. With most papers it is best to start near a corner, because if a joint is required it is least noticeable when positioned on a corner junction. With large patterns, the design should be centered on any prominent walls such as a chimney breast, so that a balanced effect will be created.

1 Use a level to draw a vertical line from the ceiling to the floor—this will provide a guideline for positioning the first length.

2 Apply paste to the back of the first length of paper (if required) and position it so that the edge runs down the vertical guideline. Use a paperhanging brush to remove air bubbles, brushing the paper out from the center toward the edges.

3 Use a utility knife to trim lengths at both ceiling and floor level. For the best results, trim slightly on to the ceiling and baseboard respectively, so that when the paper is brushed into place, the best-looking finish is produced.

4 Always butt-joint the lengths and make the pattern meet at eye level. It normally follows that the pattern will match along the entire length, but occasionally "pattern drop" does occur. In these instances, it is better to have the best match where the paper is most seen, in other words, at eye level.

ceilings

Ceilings are sometimes lined to improve their finish, or they may be wallpapered as an additional decorative option. In both cases, it is important to begin in the correct place and to paper across the longest dimension, thus minimizing the number of joints. Obstacles, such as light fixtures, must also be taken into account. You will need at least two pairs of hands and should pay extra attention to safety:

- Construct a safe access platform from which to work, with planks over stable trestles.
- Turn off electricity at the main panel when working around electrical fixtures.

Ideally, paper across the longest dimension of ceiling, thereby reducing the number of joints.

direction of papering

When papering a ceiling without obstacles such as light fixtures, start against the wall and work across the surface area.

When papering a ceiling with obstacles such as light fixtures, start in the center of the room and work away from the pendant in both directions.

invisible joints

In some circumstances, butt-jointing lengths may be impossible. On an outside corner, for example, the length of paper becomes slightly creased because it cannot round the corner and still remain vertical.

1 Allow the length to overlap on to the previous one, matching the pattern on the overlap.

2 Using a utility knife and straight-edge—a level is ideal—cut through the center of the overlap from ceiling to floor.

3 Peel back the edges of the full lengths and remove the two strips of excess paper. Then brush the edges back into place to reveal a perfect joint between the two lengths.

PREPARING TO PAPER

Before applying paper to the walls, it is necessary to run through a few standard checks and procedures.

- **Paper type**—Determine whether the paper is prepasted or whether the back requires paste application. Although the technique for hanging both is similar, the tool and material requirements vary slightly.
- **Lots**—Always check that the rolls display the same lot numbers. This is because there may be a slight shading difference between manufactured lots.
- **Cutting**—When cutting paper, always allow for the size of the pattern repeat and a small excess for trimming purposes at each end.
- **Lining**—Walls should generally be lined with lining paper before wallpaper is applied. Check the manufacturer's guidelines on the particular wallpaper you are using for their recommendations.

applying embossed wall coverings

Embossed wall paneling offers a lightweight alternative to wooden paneling such as tongue and groove. The application procedure is more similar to that of wallpaper than wooden paneling, although the panels are supplied in specific sizes and are generally designed to cover only the chair-rail level in a room.

planning

The predetermined size and patterning of this type of paneling means that you will need to plan its positioning quite carefully. The aim should be to keep joins in discrete areas, so try to join full panels in corners that are seen every day, and seam half panels in corners that are less obvious.

tools for the job

- level
- pencil
- tape measure
- pasting brush and table
- sponge
- paperhanging brush
- utility knife
- hammer

1 Decide on the best starting position and draw a vertical guideline on the wall with a level.

2 The back of the panels must be soaked with water and left for approximately 20 minutes before paste can be applied. A systematic approach therefore needs to be developed so that while one panel is soaking, another is being applied. It can be a good idea to pencil the timings on the back of the panels, so that you can gauge accurately when each one is ready for pasting.

3 Use the recommended paste on the back of the panels, taking care to ensure that the entire surface has an even coverage of the paste.

Work the brush from the center out to the edges of the panel, and try to avoid getting any paste on the table. Any overspill should be removed with a damp sponge.

4 Apply the first panel to the wall using the pencil guidelines for positioning. Use a paperhanging brush to remove air bubbles as you run the brush across the entire panel. The bottom edge of the panel should sit level along the top of the baseboard.

5 Join subsequent panels using the same technique, butting the edges tightly together. However, take care not to allow any overlaps because these will show up clearly in the finished effect—a slight gap is actually preferable to an overlap.

tips of the trade

Once in position, panels must be primed with an oil-based undercoat before additional coats of paint and decorative effects can be applied.

site-made paneling

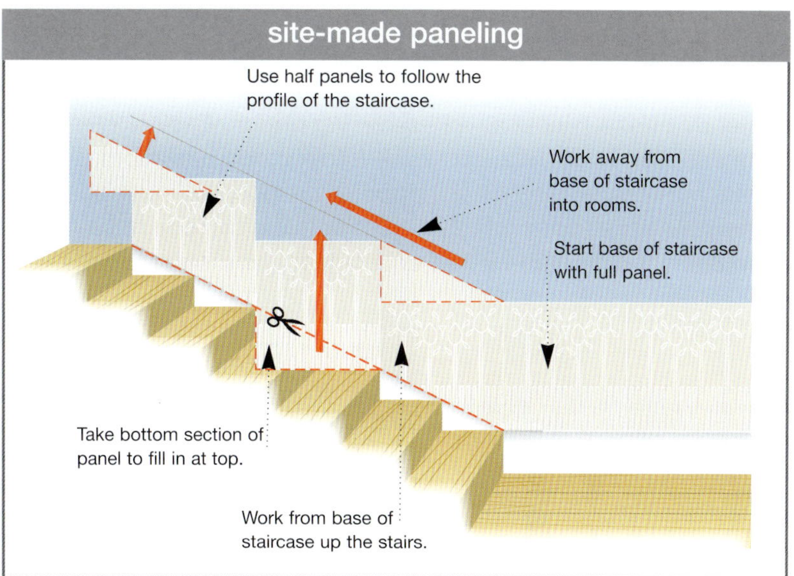

6 At the stairwell, cut panels vertically in half and continue to apply them up the staircase. Use the paperhanging brush to mold the bottom section of the panel into the staircase profile. Trim any excess along the junction with a utility knife.

7 Take the trimmed excess from the bottom section of the panel and butt it at the top of the same

panel. The angle of ascent of the paneling edge should relate directly to the angle of ascent of the staircase. (The diagram above illustrates how panels should be cut and installed.)

8 To finish the top edge of the paneling, apply a chair rail (see pages 428–9). The rail should slightly overlap the paneling, so that a neat, precise finish is produced.

9 Finally, caulk all the joints in the paneling to produce a smooth finish and prevent edges lifting at a later date. Remove excess caulk with a damp sponge.

Decorative wall paneling makes an attractive finish in any room, and looks particularly effective when used on stairwells with a matching chair rail.

tiling techniques

In addition to being decorative, tiles clearly offer a practical wall-covering option. Easy to clean and durable, their use tends to be concentrated in areas such as the kitchen and bathroom. In terms of applying tiles to the wall, in much the same way as wallpapering, emphasis must be put on keeping the tiles level or plumb to ensure a balanced effect. Actual application requires a methodical technique combining meticulous planning as well as accurate measuring and cutting.

PREPARING TO TILE

Before tiling, it is important to be fully prepared, organizing your order of work, to minimize mistakes and confusion.

- **Checking tiles**—Always open boxes of tiles before purchasing to ensure that there are no breakages.
- **Shuffling**—When using single-colored tiles for the entire or major part of a design, mix up or shuffle the tiles between boxes so that any slight color variations will be evenly spread across the tiled surface and therefore invisible to the naked eye.
- **Tile gauge**—To help decide on starting points, make a tile gauge from a piece of scrap wood. Lay a line of tiles out dry on a flat surface (allowing for the spacers) and hold a piece of wood strip along their length. Use a pencil to mark the joints between the tiles on the strip. Now hold the strip against the wall and use it as a gauge to determine the most suitable position for the tile layout. It also allows you to plan cuts in the most suitable places and for a balanced effect to be achieved.
- **Spacers**—You can buy bags of individual spacers or sheets of spacers that need to be broken up before use. It is best to break up a number of sheets before you begin to tile, so that time isn't wasted when applying tiles to the wall surface.
- **Keeping clean**—Tiling can be messy, so always keep a bucket of clean water close to hand so that surfaces and tools can be kept clean at all times.

tools for the job

There are a few simple guidelines that may be applied to most tiling projects you will undertake.

1 The top of a baseboard is rarely precisely level, nor is it the best point to apply the first row of tiles. Therefore, nail a piece of wood strip in position above the baseboard using a level as a guide. This will support the tiles and prevent them from slipping down the wall surface. Once the main body of tiles is complete and dry, you can remove the wood strip and fill the area above the baseboard with cut tiles.

2 Spacers must be used to maintain the distance between tiles, but remove them before grouting

tiling sequence

Although each room differs, there is a basic order of tiling that will help to achieve the best finish.

1 Apply full tiles.
2 Fill in around obstacles.
3 Complete corners.
4 When main design is dry, fill in cut tiles at bottom of wall.
5 Apply border tiles if required.

1 Lay full tiles.

2 Fill in around obstacles.

5 Apply border tiles if required.

4 Use cut tiles at the bottom of the wall.

3 Complete corners.

or the grout may crack. At the bottom level, they can be positioned flat on the strip and remain in position until the tile adhesive has dried. They may then be removed along with the wood strip.

3 When grouting, always use a grout spreader or float (never your fingers), moving it in all directions across the tiles to press the grout into every joint. Remove the excess from the tiles as you progress.

4 Wipe down the tiled surface with a damp sponge before using a grout shaper to tool the joints and provide a neat finish. Run the shaper

along the joint to smooth the grout between each of the tiles.

cutting tiles

Cuts can be divided into two simple categories—those that are straight and those that have a curve.

straight cuts

1 Although hand-held tile cutters can be used for this purpose, a tile-cutting machine is the ideal tool for accuracy and ease of use. Measure the size of the required cut and score along this line to produce a definite

scratch through the glazed surface of the tile.

2 Design varies between tile cutters, but the general principle of breaking the tile along the scored line involves applying weight to either side of the line, causing it to crack along the cut.

curved cuts

Cutting curves involves the use of a specially designed rod saw. Clearly mark the curved guideline on the tile and clamp it in a workbench before cutting through the tile using the saw.

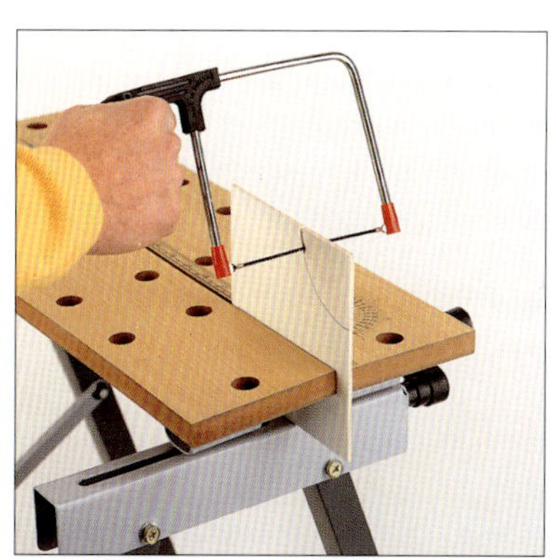

tiling a backsplash

If bathroom or kitchen walls are not fully tiled, a backsplash may be necessary behind a bathroom sink, cooktop, or kitchen sink. The key to achieving a good result is to make sure that the backsplash is centrally positioned in relation to the sink. You can then center the first tile on this point and tile out from there, or use the center point as a joint between the first two tiles, again working out.

tools for the job

- tape measure & pencil
- torpedo level
- notched spreader
- power tile-cutting machine
- grout spreader (optional)
- protective gloves
- sponge
- caulk gun or dispenser

1 Measure the back edge of the sink and mark the center point.

2 Draw a pencil guideline up from this point. Use a torpedo level to make sure that the line is plumb.

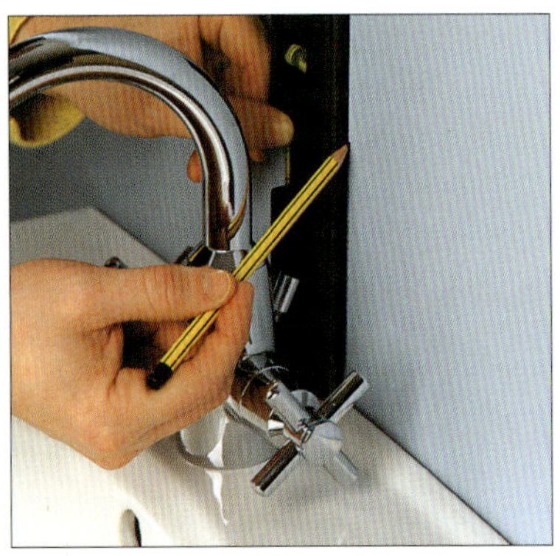

3 Mark the middle of the first tile along its top edge. This mark is required for positioning purposes only, so it can be wiped off later. Apply tile adhesive to the back of the tile using a small notched spreader.

4 Position the tile by making sure that the pencil mark corresponds exactly with the plumb pencil guideline on the wall.

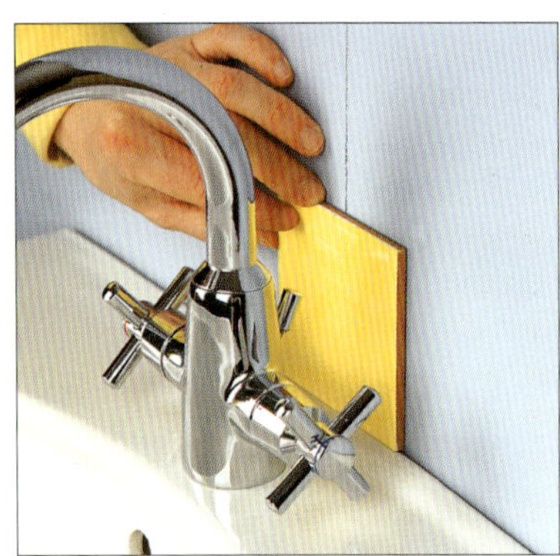

5 Continue to apply tiles to the wall, using spacers in joints to maintain a consistent gap between tiles. The back edge of many sinks is curved. This makes tiling slightly more difficult, because you will need to place cardboard beneath the edge of the first row of tiles to maintain the correct level for the tiles. The amount of cardboard used at a particular point depends on how much is required to keep the row level. When border tiles are added, you will also need to use cardboard under the first ones on either side of the design in order to maintain the correct height.

6 You usually need to cut border tiles at the corner of the backsplash. A good effect is achieved by making mitered joints. For relief border tiles, as shown here, it is best to use a power tile-cutting machine. Again, wear protective goggles and follow the manufacturer's instructions.

7 Once the first mitered tile has been positioned, measure the next tile by holding it in place and marking the points at which the tile needs to be cut.

8 Position the tile, judging a joint between the miter that is equal to the gaps between the tiles in the main part of the design.

9 Once the design is complete, allow to dry, then apply grout. It can be easier to use your fingers, rather than a spreader, to push the grout into place on tiles with a raised surface, but wear protective gloves.

10 When you have finished grouting, apply a silicone sealant strip along the back edge of the sink. Use the technique described on page 391.

tips of the trade

- **Full tiles**—Ideally, you should only use full tiles in a backsplash design because there is no way of hiding from view cut tiles that can mar the overall look of the sink. It does not usually matter if tiles overhang the edge of the sink slightly, and in many cases, a row of border tiles can provide an attractive frame.
- **Spacers**—When using spacers with relief border tiles, it is not possible to insert them into joints flat against the wall. Instead, insert them at right angles to the wall surface, and remove them once the adhesive has dried.

A tiled backsplash provides a practical and decorative feature that highlights and complements a sink design.

adding to existing tiles

An easy way to change the look of your bathroom or kitchen is to alter the existing tile layout. In many instances, even if tiles still look new and bright, a slight update in appearance can work wonders. The examples shown here should only be carried out on existing sound tile surfaces. If tiles are coming away from the wall or are poorly fitted, then you should remove the old ones and start from scratch (see also pages 392–3 for how to remove tiles).

tile transfers

A bank of clean white tiles may look good in some bathrooms, but using tile transfers to add pattern to a bland tile surface can be an attractive option if you wish to brighten up the room. The exact method of application can vary slightly between manufacturers, but the principles of soaking and positioning transfers remains similar.

tools for the job

- sponge
- bucket
- cloth

1 The first job is to make sure that the tile surface is completely clean by wiping away all traces of dirt or grime with a sponge.

2 Soak the transfer in a bucket of clean warm water, making sure that the entire sheet is immersed. Read the manufacturer's guidelines for the required soaking time.

3 Remove the transfer from the bucket and shake off excess water. Position the transfer on the tile.

4 When happy with the position, slide off the backing paper to leave the transfer image on the tile.

tips of the trade

Do not position transfers in areas that are prone to abrasion. Although they are quite robust once dry, they cannot withstand regular rigorous cleaning. It is a good idea to buy a few extra transfers so that you can replace any that may get damaged, although this problem will not arise if you choose to apply a selection of designs.

5 Dab the image with a dry cloth to remove excess water and smooth away air bubbles.

painting tiles

A simple way of changing tile appearance is to paint them a new color or a combination of colors. Tile primers that make this process possible are now available and allow a durable finish to be achieved.

tools for the job

- sponge
- paintbrush

1 Sand the tiled surface to provide a key for the paint. Clean any dust or grime with a mild cleaner, and rinse with clean warm water. Allow the surface to dry completely.

2 Paint tile primer over the entire tiled surface. When dry, you can apply your chosen latex, eggshell, or gloss paint.

tips of the trade

If you use latex paint, varnish over the top to increase its durability.

adding picture tiles

Another way to liven up an existing area of tiles is to remove some of them and replace them with picture or patterned tiles. The technique for removing tiles is shown in more detail on pages 392–3, where broken tiles are removed before new ones are put in their places.

tools for the job

- grout raker
- cordless drill/driver
- protective gloves & goggles
- hand sledge
- cold chisel
- notched spreader
- grout spreader

1 Use a grout raker to scrape away as much grout as possible from around the edges of the tiles that are to be removed. Drill a number of holes through the surface of the tiles to weaken their structure, then use a hand sledge and cold chisel to knock out the broken sections of tile. Remember to wear protective gloves and goggles.

2 Apply tile adhesive to the wall and press the new tile into position. Use spacers to maintain the gap around its edge while the adhesive dries. When dry, remove the spacers and grout the joints.

tile sheets

A quick, inexpensive way of changing the appearance of a tiled surface is to use plastic tile sheets. These are easy to apply and can be used over existing tile surfaces.

tools for the job

- notched spreader
- scissors
- grout spreader

1 Use a notched spreader to apply tile adhesive to the back of the sheets, making coverage as even as possible.

2 Press the sheets into position. The number of tiles on each sheet means that a large area can be covered very quickly. The sheets can be cut with scissors to fill in gaps around the edge of a design. Once the adhesive has dried, apply grout.

installing tongue-&-groove paneling

Tongue-and-groove paneling is an extremely effective way to transform a wall surface and make a room feel warm and inviting. The paneling can be applied across entire walls or just up to chair-rail level, as in the example demonstrated here. To apply paneling, you need to build a framework onto which the boards will be applied, then cut the boards to fit the space and attach them.

safety advice

Always check for hidden cables or supply pipes with a stud finder before drilling into walls to fix the furring strips and paneling in place.

tools for the job

- pencil
- tape measure
- level
- hand saw
- cordless drill/driver
- hammer
- nail set
- miter saw

building the framework

Tongue-and-groove paneling should be attached to a furring strip framework. Although 1 x 2in strips are often ideal, it can be advantageous to use slightly larger strips such as 2 x 2in so that a shelf can be formed across the top of the paneling for extra storage. Another advantage is that furring strips produce deep paneling, which means that pipes attached to the wall can often run beneath the framework.

1 A good height for chair-rail paneling is about 1yd above floor level. For these dimensions, three horizontal strips should be fixed to the wall surface, one at floor level, one at the required height for the top of the paneling, and one about halfway between the two. Draw guidelines for these furring strips using a level to make sure that they are horizontal.

2 Fix the strips to the wall surface using the guidelines for positioning. In this case, concrete anchors are inserted directly through the strips into the masonry wall below. For hollow walls, use the correct wall plugs and screw fasteners to hold the strips in place.

3 To deal with any pipes, cut furring strip lengths so that a gap is left to allow the pipe to run down through the framework.

attaching the paneling

The structure of tongue-and-groove paneling allows it to be fastened in place so that the actual fastening points are hidden from view. Small nails or brad nails (depending on the thickness of the paneling) are inserted at a 45-degree angle through the tongue of a board to hold it in place. The groove of the next board covers this tongue and, therefore, the fastening. When applying boards, it is best to start at an inside corner and have a number of boards cut to size before you begin, so that progress is swift. However, be aware of the fact that small waves or slopes in the floor may mean that you need different heights of board if the top of the paneling is to be neat and level.

tips of the trade

Remember to make access hatches in the paneling for any shutoff valves, so that the water supply from the mains can be turned off easily in the event of an emergency.

1 Position the first board, using a level to check that it is completely plumb.

2 Attach the first board to the strips through the top, middle, and bottom of its face. Only hidden fastenings should be necessary with all subsequent boards.

3 Knock nails through the tongue of the board, and use a nail set to make sure that the head disappears below wood surface level.

tips of the trade

- **Selective paneling**—On walls that have a number of kitchen or bathroom fixtures, building a framework and paneling can be a complicated procedure. It is often worth paneling only those walls that are relatively free from obstacles.
- **Decoration**—Tongue-and-groove paneling can be finished with paint, or coated with a natural wood stain or varnish to complement the existing decoration in the room.

4 Keep adding boards, slipping the groove of the new length over the tongue of the previous one, and inserting nails along the tongue of the new board.

5 You will need to add a decorative molding at outside corners to cover the joint. This can either be glued or nailed in position.

6 To finish the top of the paneling, cut 1 x 3in furring strip, mitering the joints neatly at the corners. This produces a much more attractive and professional finish than butting the straight edges.

7 Fix the 1 x 3in furring strip in place by inserting screws or nails through the strip into the 2 x 2in furring strip beneath to secure it in position.

8 Attach a decorative molding around the underside of the 1 x 3in furring strip to produce a more attractive result.

ALTERNATIVE EDGING

Instead of using molding, you can achieve a simpler finish by routing the edge of the top furring strip.

installing decorative rails

Decorative rails offer another way of adding character to walls. The rail shape tends to be determined by its function—a picture rail usually has an upturned top edge to provide a stable base for the hook, while chair rails are traditionally used to prevent chairs from damaging the wall surface, and so have a rounded surface. Generally, chair rails are fitted about 3ft from floor level, and picture rails are positioned between 8in and 20in from the ceiling.

fitting a chair rail

Chair rails tend to be the most popular choice of molding, as many modern houses do not have the height to accommodate picture rails. Chair rails can be applied in rooms with low or high ceilings, and will produce an excellent effect.

tools for the job

- tape measure
- pencil
- level
- miter saw
- hammer or cordless drill/driver
- nail set
- caulk gun
- sponge

1 Draw a horizontal guideline around the wall perimeter using a pencil and level. Measure the wall dimensions and calculate the required lengths for each wall. Be sure to get the end of the tape measure right into the corners of the wall.

2 Clamp the molding into the miter saw (to ensure a precise cut) and cut the required lengths.

3 Apply bonding adhesive to the back of the molding. Allow the adhesive to run down the central portion, so that when it comes into contact with the wall it will spread from the center toward the edges.

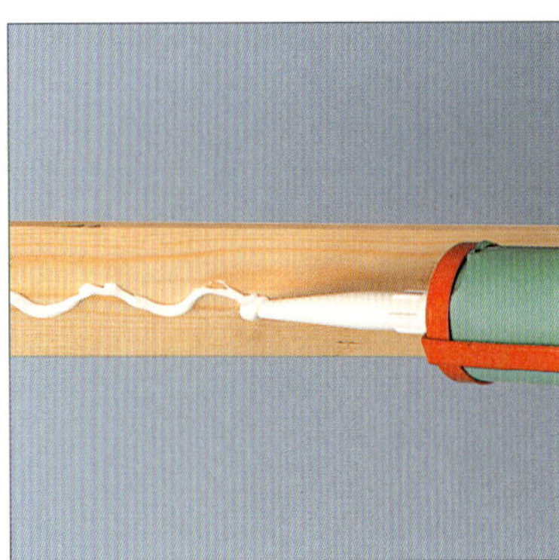

4 Press the molding in position, allowing the pencil guideline to run along either the top or bottom edge. Continue to press in position along the molding's length, so that total contact between the rail and wall is achieved. Use a sponge to remove any excess adhesive.

5 Nail or screw fastenings along the length of the molding to hold it firmly in position, and push in the nail heads below the molding surface level. Continue to attach lengths around the rest of the room.

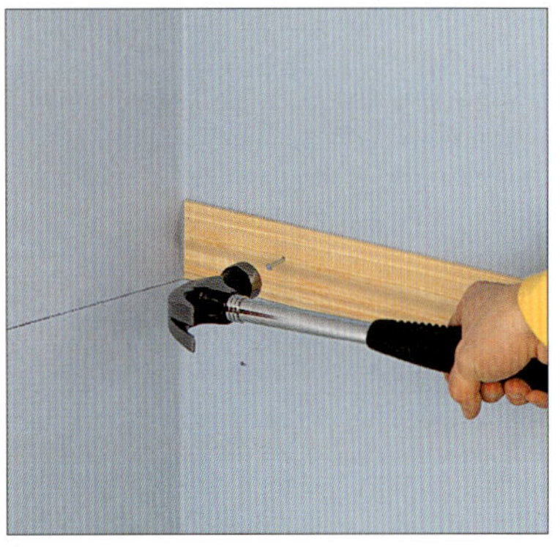

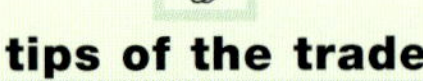

tips of the trade

When a chair or picture rail is to remain unpainted, avoid using permanent nail fastenings, which will be easily visible. Instead, just apply a strong contact adhesive that will hold the molding permanently in position while it dries. Some extra support may be given during the drying process by taping over the molding—the tape will help to bear the molding's weight.

6 Apply a bead of caulk along the top edge of the chair rail, smoothing it into the joint with a wet finger. This will help to cover any small cracks and produce a better surface finish for painting.

7 Also apply caulk to corner joints, especially where miter joints are not totally tight. Nail heads may then be filled with an all-purpose filler and carefully sanded to a smooth finish before staining or painting.

Decorative rails provide an attractive feature which divides wallspace while adding character to a room design and decoration.

tips of the trade

Using strongly colored wall surfaces or rails can eliminate the need for caulking along the edges of the rail/wall junction. This is because the strong color should overshadow any slight cracks along the joint.

DECORATION

- **Wallpapering**—If the decorative rail is to be used to divide two types of wallpaper, or there is to be a particularly strong contrast between the rail color and the wall, it may be better to paint or stain the rail before it is fastened in position.

  Apply wallpaper to the surface before attaching the rail. Even if the rail is to divide two different papers, it is possible to use only rough joints, as the rail will cover this area.

- **Staining**—For a natural or stained wood finish, apply two coats to the rail before cutting and attaching it, so that there is no need to encounter an exacting staining process along the edge of the rail. This early staining means that you should not have to cut in too closely to the paper when applying a final top coat. This method may also be used with paint.

- **Painting**—If you plan to paint the rail in a strong color, mask both sides of the wall surface with painter's tape.

Remember that applying rails after wall decoration does make repairing any scrapes or wall damage more difficult, so take extra care when installing the rail.

creating a textured ceiling finish

Various types of finish may be added to flat ceiling surfaces to produce a textured or patterned effect. These coatings can be used on drywalled or plastered ceilings, or even over rougher, wavy surfaces, helping to create a more attractive finish. However, textured coatings should never be applied over the top of wallpaper or lining paper, and they must only be applied to ceilings that have been sealed and are therefore stable enough for this type of coating.

tools for the job

There are specific tools available for creating a textured finish. Not all of these pieces will be required—the tools you use depend upon the the type of texture or pattern you are planning to create (see below).

stippling a ceiling

Once the coating has been applied to the ceiling, a specific tool is required to create the finish. Combs or trowels may be used, but in this case a stippler has been employed to produce a stippled ceiling effect.

tips of the trade

If possible work from a sturdy platform, moving gradually across the ceiling surface. Stepladders may be used, but this will involve a lot of effort getting up and down.

1 On plasterboard or drywall ceilings, make sure that all the joints between the separate boards are taped with self-adhesive jointing tape. Check that the tape is firmly stuck down and that there are no ripples or creases, as imperfections will affect the ability of the textured finish to adhere to the ceiling properly.

2 Mix the textured coating in a bucket. Follow the manufacturer's instructions regarding the amount of water required to add to the powder. Although the coating can be mixed by hand, it is much easier to use a mixing tool attached to a drill.

TRADITIONAL TAPING

Instead of using self-adhesive tape, you can use standard jointing tape, which needs to be soaked in water before use, then applied to the joints between the drywall sheets in a similar way to the tape above. Some tapes can be embedded in wet compound and smoothed on with a drywall knife.

3 Use a caulking blade or drywall knife to apply a band of textured coating over the drywall joints and any nail heads in the ceiling surface. Allow this area to dry thoroughly before coating the rest of the surface.

4 Use a block brush to apply the main coating to the ceiling surface. Apply a thick, even coat to ensure total coverage and a consistent depth. Work in areas of approximately 1yd^2 at a time, in order to prevent the mixture from drying.

tips of the trade

It is a good idea to have two people working on the surface at any one time—as one person applies the coating, the other can use the stippler. This helps to ensure the coating always has a wet edge and that the job is finished at one time, without dried, patchy areas. It may also pay to practice the technique on a scrap piece of drywall, before beginning work on the ceiling. This is especially important when using combs, as the technique can take time to master.

5 Take the stippler and press it into the surface coating at a right angle to the ceiling. Lift away, again at a right angle to the surface, and move to the adjacent coated area. Overlap the stippled impressions slightly to produce a random effect. Change the angle of the face of the stippler on the surface for an even greater random effect. Repeat steps 4 and 5 across the ceiling surface until the whole area is complete.

6 Finish off around the ceiling edge by dampening a 1in brush and drawing it through the wet coating. This provides a neat border to the coating.

tips of the trade

Once dry, textured coatings can be left uncoated, but you can add a flat or satin finish if you prefer.

These coatings provide an effective finish on a ceiling, giving depth and texture to what is normally a flat, rather two-dimensional area in a room.

installing curtains, shades & blinds

Your choice of window dressing will depend on the decorative style you want for your room, as well as the amount of space you have available for the window dressing. You will also need to consider the amount of light and privacy required.

The type of room in which the window dressing will hang also requires some thought. Voluminous, billowing curtains can be very attractive in a living room or bedroom, but would not be a practical option in a kitchen or bathroom. They are particularly unsuitable over a worktop, unless the hanging system and length of curtains is considered very carefully. In those situations shades and blinds that fit into the window recess and can be adjusted to provide light and privacy are more practical.

tools for the job

- tape measure & pencil
- straightedge &/or level
- cordless drill/driver
- screwdriver

curtains

When choosing fabric for curtains also consider practicality. For kitchens, bathrooms, and other rooms subject to variable humidity, durable and washable fabrics are essential. Curtains may be hung on either a traverse rod or a pole.

traverse rods

Traverse rods tend to be regarded as the less attractive type of curtain hanging, and are normally kept discreetly hidden by ensuring that the head of the curtain covers the rod as much as possible. Traverse rods are a good choice where space is limited, however, since they hold the curtain tight against the wall or window.

1 Draw a level guideline above the window to indicate the position of the traverse rod. Using a level for a straightedge is the easiest way to ensure a level line. Traverse rods require frequent fastening points in order to support the curtain weight. Mark equidistant points along the line, and drill and plug these positions.

2 Screw in the brackets along this line, making sure the brackets are the right way up and that they bite firmly into the plugged holes.

3 Once all the brackets have been attached, clip the traverse rod onto the front of them. You will need to position the traverse rod so that it overhangs either side of the window by an equal amount. Now simply fit the slides and hang the curtain.

curtain poles

A curtain pole offers a more ornate hanging system than traverse rods. You will usually find that the ends of the pole are decorated with finials, and in many cases the curtain head is deliberately made to hang below the pole so that its decorative qualities are always in view. A major drawback is that a pole will cause the curtain to encroach further into the room, but as long as space is not a problem in your room, then poles can be an ideal choice for hanging curtains.

Attach a bracket at each corner of the window to hold the pole in place. For large windows you may need to attach a central bracket as well, to

support the weight of the curtain. The curtain is usually hung with rings, with a finial attached to both ends of the pole in order to prevent the curtain from falling off.

shades & blinds

Types of shades include simple roller shades and pulley blinds that can be raised or lowered to control light. There are also venetian (or slatted) blinds and vertical blinds, both of which are ideal for privacy.

Shades and blinds are normally made from easy-to-clean material. They are generally supplied in a kit form that involves attaching brackets to the window frame.

1 Measure the width of the window before buying your shade or blind to make sure of the correct requirement. It is important to take measurements all the way down the window, not just at the top, as distortions in the recess may result in the window being narrower at the bottom. With significant distortion, the shade or blind must be bought with the narrowest measurement in mind so that it will fit comfortably within the window recess.

2 Attach the brackets in the top corners of the window, screwing into the wooden frame. Make sure that each bracket is positioned the correct way up and at the right corner for each end of the shade or blind.

3 Position a roller shade and then insert each end into the correct bracket. One bracket is of a different shape to the other, as the fastenings on each end of the roller are made to fit with only one of the brackets. Finally, attach a cord pull to the shade or blind so that it may be put into operation.

tips of the trade

Shade and blind kits are sometimes supplied with the material separate from the roller. Join the material to the roller with staples, double-sided tape, or double-sided Velcro, which is useful for taking the shade down for cleaning.

A shade was the ideal choice of window dressing for this kitchen, as it rests tight against the window frame and does not intrude into the working area of the sink.

making exterior changes

While your scope for executing masonry projects indoors is fairly limited, in the yard or garden you can build walls to your heart's content—along boundaries, around a patio, as barriers to retain soil in terraces on a sloping site, or simply to hide an unattractive feature. You can add features such as a garden arch, and link different levels with flights of steps. You can build in brick or stone, creating formal or informal structures to suit the style of your garden. The two key points you need to remember are that every garden structure needs good foundations, and because you are building outside, everything you construct must be thoroughly weatherproof. Make sure you consult local building-code regulations before embarking on exterior building projects.

planning exterior masonry projects

Whatever you plan to build in your garden, you need to do some planning and preparatory work first, even if you are just building a straight stretch of wall. This involves deciding what you want to achieve, where to site the various components of your scheme, what materials to use, and how to organize the job into practical and achievable stages. You can then estimate and order materials with confidence, and tackle the job in an orderly fashion. You can also prepare the foundations that are essential for any garden structure.

making drawings

If you have a clear idea of what you want to create, buy some graph paper and pencils and start measuring things so that you can make a detailed scale drawing to work to. Begin with a plan so that you know where walls, steps, and other features will be built. Add elevations to help you estimate materials accurately. Work to a sensible scale—1:20 is suitable for most gardens—and make sure you know the sizes of the various materials you will be using, so that you can use your drawings for estimating the quantities when you order the materials.

preparing the site

When you have decided what to build and where to site it, you must do some basic site preparation. Mark out the area of the work with mason's line tied to marker stakes. Remove all plants, grass, weeds, and other vegetable matter, and dig away the turf, moving it to another part of the garden for redistribution. Cut back the roots of any large trees or shrubs well clear of the working area. As you dig, keep your eyes open for any buried services. Professionally laid cables and pipework should be buried at least 18in down, but amateur supplies to garden buildings may have been laid at a far shallower depth.

laying foundations on a sloping site

The foundations should be laid as linked and overlapping steps. Each step should be a whole number of bricks in length, and the step height should be equal to a maximum of three courses of brickwork or one of blockwork (9in). The upper step should overlap the lower one by the length of two bricks or one block (about 18in). Fasten a board across the trench at the step position to form the edge of the upper step and lay each concrete step in the same way that you would lay a concrete slab on a flat site (see opposite).

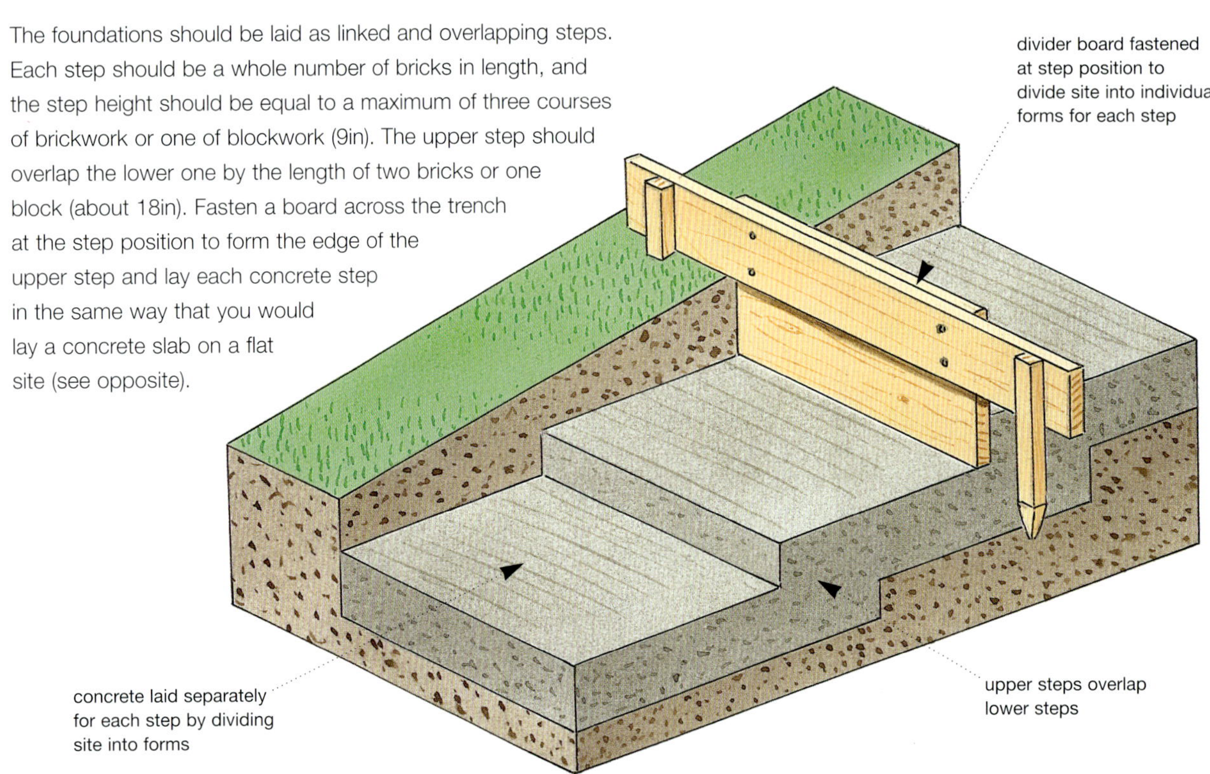

laying foundations on a flat site

For most garden walls, a concrete strip foundation is all that is required, but its size and positioning are important. It should be a minimum of 6in thick, and up to 8in thick on clay soils because of the tendency for clay to shrink and swell. The strip should be placed in a form 14 to 16in deep, with its top one course of blockwork or three courses of brickwork below ground level. This allows soil to be placed right up to the foot of the wall, and helps protect the foundation from frost or accidental damage from digging close by. The width of the foundation strip should be twice the thickness of the wall you are building, up to a height of about 30in. For higher walls, make sure to increase the strip width to three times the wall thickness.

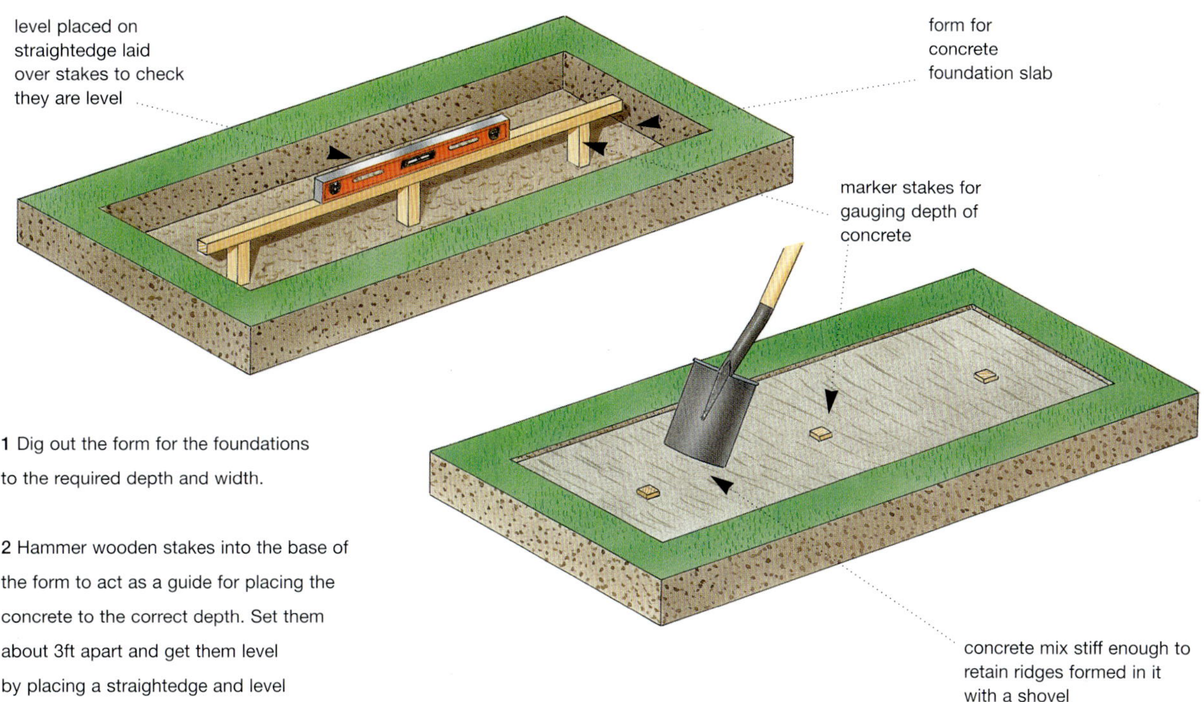

1 Dig out the form for the foundations to the required depth and width.

2 Hammer wooden stakes into the base of the form to act as a guide for placing the concrete to the correct depth. Set them about 3ft apart and get them level by placing a straightedge and level on adjacent pegs.

3 Estimate how much concrete you need for the foundation. For example, the strip for a wall 13ft long and 5ft high, built in 9in thick brickwork on sound subsoil, should be 15ft long, 27in wide, and 6in thick. Its volume is 15 x 2.25 x 0.5 cubic feet—that is, 16.87cu ft. To make this quantity, you will need about two-and-a-half 110lb bags of cement and just under 2000lb of mixed aggregate.

4 Mix the concrete (see pages 470–1 for more details). For in-ground foundations you should use a mix of 1 part cement, 2.5 parts sharp (concreting) sand and 3.5 parts of ¾in coarse aggregate (gravel). If you are buying mixed aggregate (mixed sand and gravel), mix 1 part cement to 5 parts aggregate. Use a bucket to measure the quantities accurately by volume, mix them thoroughly by hand or in a cement mixer, and add water until the mixture is stiff enough to retain ridges formed in it with a shovel.

5 Move the concrete to the form in a wheelbarrow, tip it in, and tamp it around the marker stakes. Use a piece of fence post or similar wood held lengthwise in the form to tamp it down, and add more concrete as necessary to get the surface level with the tops of the stakes. Do not worry about any slight irregularities in the surface—you can compensate for these when bedding the first course of masonry on the foundation.

6 Cover the concrete with a polyethylene sheet if rain or frost threatens, and allow it to harden for at least three days before starting to build on it.

FOUNDATIONS FOR STEPS

If you are building a flight of steps against a retaining wall, start by calculating its overall size. Then lay a concrete slab 4in larger all around than the size of the flight and 4in thick (6in thick on clay soils). See pages 470–3 for more details about laying concrete slabs. Alternatively, if you are building steps in a bank, only the bottom step requires a foundation strip. This strip should be 12in wide, 6in thick and 8in longer than the width of the steps.

garden walls

Garden walls can mark property boundaries, act as dividers between different levels of the garden on sloping sites, or form self-contained planters and other garden features. Their method of construction varies according to whether their purpose is structural or merely decorative, and whether you are building in brick or blocks. If you are building a garden wall from the start, its foundations below ground level are as important as its structure above.

foundations

Even the lowest garden wall needs proper support in the ground. In most cases this means excavating turf and sod, and laying a concrete strip foundation using a mix of 1 part cement to 5 parts combined aggregate (mixed sharp concreting sand and ¾in gravel). The strip should be twice as wide as the wall for masonry up to 30in high, and three times the width for higher walls. It should be at least 6in thick on all soil types except clay, in which case it should be 8in thick because clay is prone to subsidence. Its top surface should be about 9in below ground level, so that three courses of bricks or one of blocks can be placed below ground level and planting or turf can be laid next to the wall.

brick walls

The simplest brick garden walls are built as a single wythe or layer of brickwork, one brick (4in) thick. The bricks are laid in stretcher bond, with each brick overlapping those in the course below by half its length. The maximum safe height for this type of construction is six courses of bricks, unless it is supported by piers one brick square at the ends and at 10ft intervals in between, when a further three courses can be added. A taller wall needs brickwork twice as thick—this time the length of a brick (8½in) instead of the width of one. You can build a wall of this type to a height of 4ft without piers, and to 6ft if you construct end and intermediate piers one-and-a-half bricks (about 11in) square. Building a thicker wall in this way means that you are required to adopt a different way of arranging the bricks (see box).

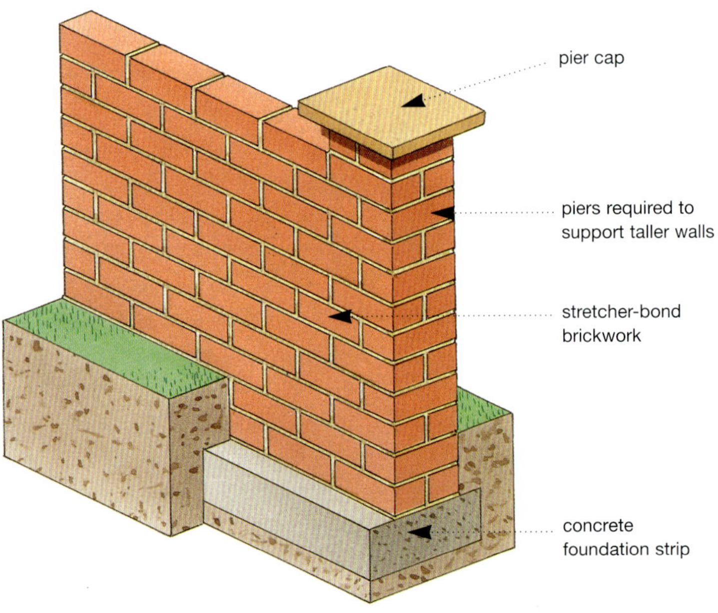

TYPES OF BOND

Three different bonding arrangements are commonly used for garden walls.

- **English bond**—The first course has two rows of parallel stretchers, the second course is formed by headers (bricks laid end-on to the face of the wall). Alternate stretcher and header courses build up the wall. In header courses, a brick split lengthwise (closure) is used at corners.

- **Flemish bond**—Each course has two parallel stretchers followed by one header. The headers are centered over the pair of stretchers in the course below. Closures are used at the ends and corners in alternate courses.

- **English garden wall bond**—The first three, four, or five courses are laid as parallel stretchers, followed by a single course of headers. This type of bond is similar to English bond, but it is not as strong because there are not so many courses of headers.

block walls

Two types of concrete blocks are commonly used for garden walls. The first is reconstituted stone. These blocks have one face and one end molded to resemble natural stone, while the other faces are smooth so the blocks can be laid just like bricks in level courses. Some ranges include blocks of different lengths and heights, creating the appearance of random stonework when laid. The same height restrictions apply as for brickwork, with the provision of piers being necessary for high walls.

The second type is the screen wall block. This is a square block pierced with a variety of simple designs. They are commonly 12in square and 3½in thick, and are designed to be laid in stack bond —in columns and rows with no overlap between the blocks, which obviously cannot be cut to size. The resulting wall is comparatively weak unless piers are built at 10ft intervals and metal lath reinforcement is used in the horizontal mortar joints. Piers can be of brick or solid block, or can be constructed using special matching end, corner, and intermediate pier blocks that are 8in high and have hollow centers so that they can be erected around lengths of vertical or horizontal rebar set in the foundation concrete. The maximum wall height is 24in (two blocks) without reinforcement, and 6ft with it.

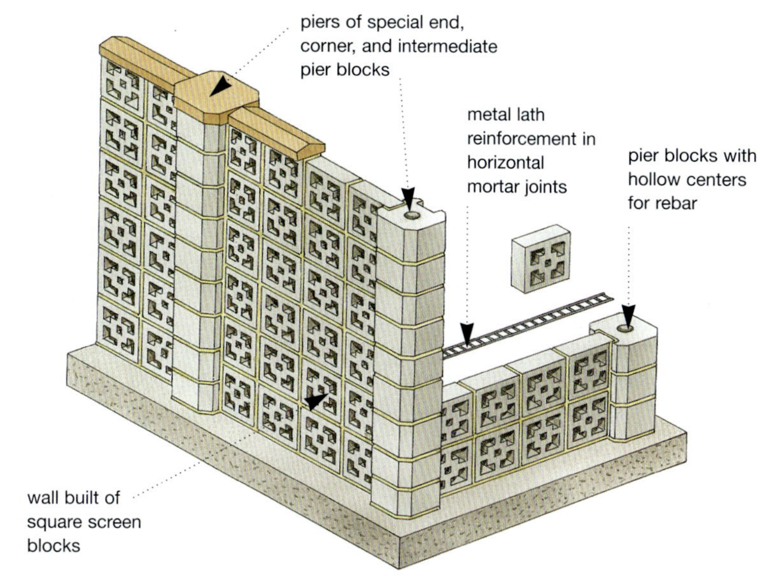

retaining walls

Walls used to enclose a sloping garden have to be strong enough to hold back the weight of earth. A low brick wall up to 24in high can be built in 8½in thick brickwork, without reinforcement, in one of the bonds described opposite. For a wall up to 4ft high, the wall is built as two wythes in stretcher bond, with rebar set in the foundations and sandwiched between the two walls. For extra strength, the walls are bonded together with cavity wall ties, and the cavity is filled with fine concrete. Walls higher than 4ft must be built by professionals to ensure that they are strong enough to withstand collapse. For this reason, it is better to enclose a sloping site with several low walls forming a series of shallow tiers, rather than to have a single high retaining wall.

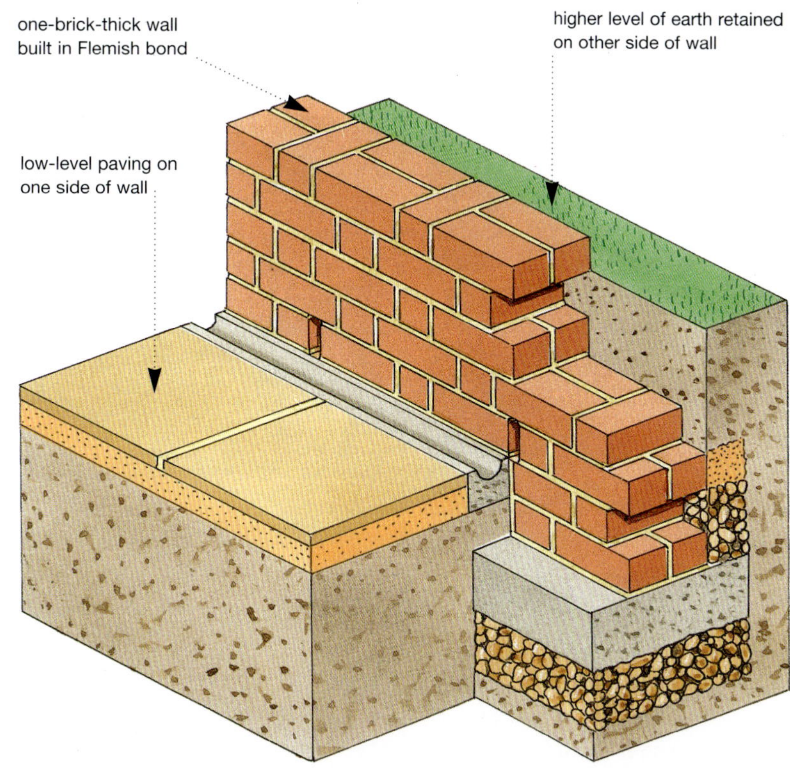

building a brick wall—1

For your first attempt at bricklaying, it is best not to be overambitious. Plan to build a straight section of wall no more than about fifteen bricks long and about eight bricks high, with the bricks laid end to end in stretcher bond. This will enable you to practice laying bricks level and in line, handling mortar, getting even joints, and building to plumb. When you have mastered that, you can progress to forming corners and piers and building thicker walls.

tools for the job

- mason's line & markers
- hammer
- bricklaying trowel
- level
- brick chisel
- hand sledge
- story pole (see box page 441)
- line pins
- pointing trowel

1 The first step is to lay a foundation strip (see page 437). When you have done this, hammer a marker into the ground just beyond each end of the strip and tie mason's line between the two to act as a guide for aligning the faces of the bricks in the first course of the wall. Position the line so that the bricks will sit centrally on the foundation.

2 Mix some mortar and trowel a strip about 6in wide onto the foundation or patio. Level it roughly with the tip of a bricklaying trowel. Place just enough mortar to enable you to lay three or four bricks.

3 Working from one side of the foundation, set the first brick in place (some bricks have a recess, called a frog, which some people prefer to bed into the mortar, while others position it uppermost). Tamp the brick down into the mortar with the handle of the bricklaying trowel until it looks level. You can check this and adjust the level once you have laid several bricks.

4 Butter a generous amount of mortar onto the end of the next brick, pressing the mortar on firmly with the trowel held at 45 degrees to the edges of the brick. If the mortar keeps falling off, dip the end of the brick in a bucket of water first.

5 Lay the second brick in line with the first, butting it up to the first brick so that the mortar on its end is compressed to a thickness of about ½in between the two bricks. You may need to hold the first brick in place as you do this so that it cannot move. Tamp the second brick down level with its neighbor and check that the two bricks are in line. Continue in this way until you reach the end of the first course. Lay a level along the top and against the faces of the bricks, and tap any that are high or projecting back into line. Then turn the level through 90 degrees and check that each brick is level across its width.

6 To ensure that the vertical joints are staggered in subsequent courses, you need to start the second course of the wall with a brick cut in half. To cut a brick, score a line across the flat side and place the brick on a soft surface (a bed of sand or the lawn will do). Align the edge of a brick chisel with the scored line and strike it firmly with a hand sledge. The brick should cut cleanly with a single stroke.

7 Spread some mortar onto the first course of bricks and set the half brick in place to start the second course. Lay as many whole bricks as needed to complete the course, finishing it off with the other half brick that you cut in step 6. Trim off excess mortar from the joints as you work, then check the line and level with a level as before.

8 Add bricks at one end of the wall to start the third, fourth, and subsequent courses, building up until the wall is eight bricks high. You will have to lay four bricks in course three, three and a half in course four, and so on, up to one and a half bricks in course eight. After laying each course, use a gauge rod to check that the horizontal (bed) joints are the same thickness (see step 10). The bricks now form even steps half a brick long running down from the end of the wall. This process is called racking back, and the object of the exercise is to build the wall by working from the ends toward the middle. Repeat the process at the other end of the wall.

9 Before proceeding any further, use a level to check that the ends of the wall are plumb and that the face of the wall is flat. To check that the vertical joints are a standard width, rest the level on the sloping brickwork. It should just touch the corner of every brick.

10 Hold the story pole against each end of the wall to check that the joint thicknesses are even all the way up. If not, knock down the faulty section and rebuild.

MAKING A STORY POLE

To check that mortar joints are the same thickness, make a tool called a story pole from a length of softwood. Mark lines on it to indicate the bricks or blocks and the mortar joints between them. In this project, for example, you should mark alternate brick widths (2½in thick) and joints (½in thick).

11 Push a line pin into the mortar between the third and fourth courses at each end of the wall, and tie a mason's line between them. Use this as a guide for laying the rest of the bricks in course three. Move it up a course at a time and complete another course of bricks, finishing with the eighth and final course laid with the frog down. You do not need a mason's line to lay this course. Once again, use a level to check line and level, and make sure that all the vertical joints in the wall line up from course to course. You have just built your first wall.

building a brick wall—2 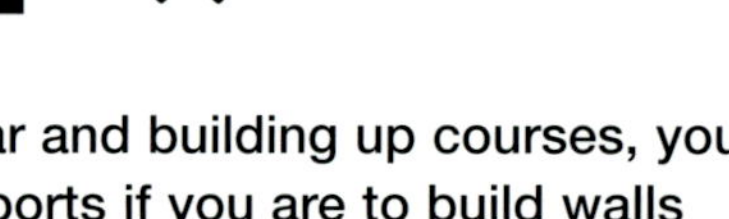

Once you have mastered the basics of handling bricks and mortar and building up courses, you can move on to turning corners and adding piers—essential supports if you are to build walls longer or higher than the one on the previous pages. As with building a straight wall, the object of the exercise is to maintain the bond—the overlap of half a brick's length from course to course—to be sure that corners and piers do not form weak points in the wall structure.

tools for the job

- mason's line & markers
- hammer
- bricklaying trowel
- level
- builder's square (see box below)
- brick chisel
- hand sledge
- rubber mallet
- story pole (see box page 441)
- line pins
- pointing trowel

MAKING A BUILDER'S SQUARE

Cut three lengths of 1 x 2in softwood —16, 20, and 24in long. Glue and screw the two shorter pieces together at a right angle with a corner lap joint (formed by crossing the two lengths of wood and removing half the thickness of the wood from each piece to form a flush joint). Make a mark on the outside edge of the shorter length 12in from the corner and on the longer one 16in from the corner.

Check that the distance between the marks is exactly 20in. Lay the 24in length across the angle with its outer edge in line with the pencil marks. Glue and screw it to the other pieces, then cut off the overlaps at each end level with the shorter pieces.

A simpler alternative is to cut a large triangle from the corner of a machine-cut sheet of plywood.

turning corners

If you build walls in stretcher bond, turning corners is straightforward. You simply place each corner brick at a right angle to the one beneath it. This ties the two sections of the wall together and maintains the bond pattern in each course. The only cut bricks needed are in alternate courses at the open ends of the two sections, as for a straight wall.

1 Lay two foundation strips at a right angle to each other (see page 437), then lay the first course of bricks forming one section of the wall (see page 440). Place the first brick of the second section at a right angle to the corner brick of the first section, after buttering some mortar onto its end, and tamp it down level.

2 Place several more bricks in the first course of the second section of wall, and use a level to check that they are horizontal and in line. Hold a builder's square in the inside angle between the two sections to check that they are at a right angle to each other, and adjust them if they are not. Complete the rest of the first course.

3 Start the second course by laying two bricks in place at the corner, laid the opposite way around to the two in the first course. Tamp them down and get them level in both directions—along their length and across their width.

4 Build up the brickwork on both sides of the corner until the wall reaches its final height and you have just a single brick in the top course. This is the same process of racking back that you used in building a straight section of wall.

5 Hold a story pole against the corner to check that the joints are even, rebuilding the affected section if they are not (ideally you should check after each course). Build up the brickwork in the same way at each open end of the wall, and check the courses there as well.

6 Place a level or story pole on the sloping steps of brickwork to check that the racking back is even and the joints between the bricks are uniform—the level or pole should just touch the corner of each brick. Build up each section of wall as shown in step 11 page 441.

building piers

Piers are also bonded into the wall structure for strength. In stretcher bond brickwork they can be one brick square and projecting from one face of the wall or, for maximum strength, one and a half bricks square and centered on the wall. For walls built in stretcher-bond brickwork more than 18in high, you need a one-brick pier at the end of the wall and at 10ft intervals along it. Position the larger piers in exposed locations. The maximum safe height for a stretcher bond wall with piers is 26in—nine courses. Higher walls should be built 8½in—one brick length—thick. This can be used up to 4ft without piers and up to 6ft with two-brick (18in square) piers.

projecting piers

To build piers one brick square at the end of a stretcher bond wall, place a brick alongside the last whole brick laid at the end of the first course. Place the first brick of the second course at a right angle to them, then lay bricks in the second course as usual. Complete the pier with a half brick in this and every alternate course.

To build intermediate piers one brick square, place two bricks side by side at a right angle to the wall face in the first course. To avoid the vertical joints aligning in the second course, center a half brick over the two whole bricks in the first course, then lay a three-quarter brick at either side of the half brick. Complete the second course of the pier with a whole brick. Repeat this arrangement for alternate courses.

centered piers

You can build centered one and a half brick piers in one of two ways. The first uses whole bricks for all courses of the pier, and the wall is tied to the piers with strips of metal lath embedded in the mortar every two or three courses. The second, stronger method bonds each course of the wall into the pier. This requires the use of half and three-quarter bricks in the pier structure to maintain the bond pattern.

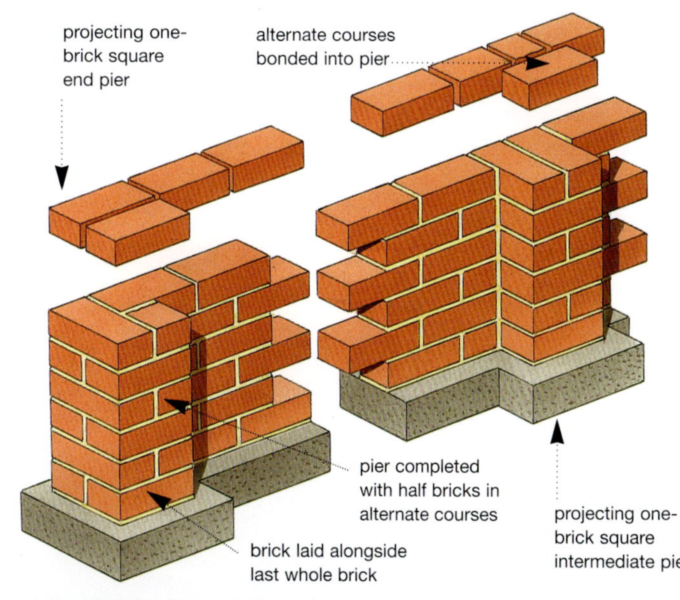

building a stone block wall

Manufactured stone walling blocks allow you to build natural-looking stone walls just as easily as if you were laying bricks. The blocks have faces and ends shaped to look like rough-hewn stone, but the tops and bottoms of the blocks are flat so that they can be laid in level mortar courses. Most ranges of blocks offer a choice of different lengths and heights, enabling you to build walls with the appearance of random stonework.

Visit suppliers such as garden centers and builders' stores to select the blocks you want to use for the stone wall. There you will find the range of blocks available on display, giving you the opportunity to look at color, texture, and size options before deciding on your choice. The next stage is to plan the wall layout and estimate how many blocks are required. Accurate estimation is important if the wall is to include a mixture of block sizes. Design the wall on paper first and then count up how many blocks of each size will be needed to create the arrangement. Blocks tend to be sold in complete packs, but most suppliers will split packs if necessary. The smallest quantity they will supply is generally enough to build about 10sq ft of wall. Most suppliers will deliver direct.

tools for the job

- bucket & mixing equipment
- hawk
- rubber mallet
- bricklaying trowel
- level
- story pole (see box page 441)
- line pins
- builder's square (see box page 442)
- pointing trowel

1 Lay the foundation strip (see page 437), then lay out the blocks dry. This enables you to check that the drawing translates correctly into three-dimensional reality, and provides an opportunity for correcting any errors before actual construction begins. You can then pick up the blocks course by course as you build the wall.

2 Prepare a standard mortar mix, made from 1 part cement to 5 parts soft (building) sand. Then set up mason's line guidelines as for building in brickwork, and trowel enough mortar onto the foundation slab to lay the first three or four blocks. Lay the first block in place on the mortar and tamp it down until it looks level. Butter mortar onto the end of the next block and lay it in the same way. Repeat for the next two blocks, then check with a level that they are horizontal and aligned.

tips of the trade

Whatever the mix, there is a correct method for preparing mortar. Measure the proportions by volume, using separate buckets for cement and sand. Always mix the ingredients dry before adding water, and make sure the mortar is not too sloppy or it will run and stain the faces of the stones.

3 Complete the first course by spreading more mortar on the foundation and laying further blocks. Start laying the second course, placing any double- or triple-height blocks according to your sketch plan and checking that all the blocks overlap those in the first course to maintain the correct bonding pattern.

4 Place smaller blocks alongside the larger ones. There will inevitably be some alignment of the vertical joints where two or three smaller blocks butt up against a larger one. Use a story pole to check that the mortar joints between the stacked blocks are the same thickness. Add further mortar to the joints if required.

5 Continue building the wall course by course, mixing large and small blocks according to your sketch plan. Make frequent checks with a level as you build to be sure that the courses are horizontal and that the face and ends of the wall are both rising straight and not leaning or sloping too much. Complete the main part of the wall by adding the final course. The maximum recommended height for manufactured stone block walls built with piers every 10ft is 2ft in 4in thick blockwork and 6ft in 8¼in blockwork. It is advisable not to build any higher, or the wall will become structurally unsound.

6 Now turn your attention to the pointing. Use a fairly dry mix for the pointing mortar in order to avoid staining the faces of the blocks. Take a sausage link of mortar off the hawk with a pointing trowel and press it well into the joint. Clean the surface with the point of the trowel and leave to harden. Remove any droppings from the faces of the blocks with a stiff brush when they have dried. Finish the wall by adding a layer of coping stones. These protect the top courses of the wall from rain and frost damage, and help to throw water clear of the faces of the blocks below. Set the coping stones in a generous mortar bed, tamping them down level with each other, then fill the joints with a further quantity of mortar.

BLOCKWORK WITHOUT MORTAR

Some manufacturers offer manufactured stone blocks that are designed to be laid without mortar in low walls up to 2ft high. The blocks have grooves on their undersides and ridges on their top surfaces, which interlock as the wall is built. Other blocks are molded to imitate dry stone walling, with each manufactured block having the appearance of several interlocking stones. These can be laid with special thin-bed walling adhesive instead of mortar to give the appearance of a wall handbuilt using individual stones. Matching coping stones are also available, molded as stones set on edge so that you can finish the wall in the traditional way.

Coping stones add the finishing touch to a stone block wall, and protect the blockwork from frost and damp. Simply tamp them down on a thick bed of mortar.

building a retaining wall

If you have a sloping garden or you want to create raised planters, you will need to build walls that hold soil behind them, called retaining walls. These obviously have to be stronger than a freestanding wall because they act as a kind of dam, holding back not only the soil but also the considerable amount of moisture that it can contain after wet weather. This means building in 8½in thick masonry, making provision for trapped groundwater to drain away.

When you are planning the design and siting of retaining walls to enclose a sloping site, it is better to construct several shallow terraces rather than one or two tall ones (if you do build tall ones, they will need reinforcing; see box opposite). Smaller walls will be under less stress, and building steps to link the levels (see pages 452–3) will be much simpler. If you are creating several terraces, build the retaining wall that is furthest from the house first, so that you do not have to move materials from one terrace to the next. Retaining planters are unlikely to be higher than about 3ft, and their box-like structure gives them more than enough strength to contain the soil to be held within them, so reinforcement is unnecessary. Ask for professional advice before building retaining walls that are higher than about 4ft.

bonds for retaining walls

It is possible to build a retaining wall with two parallel skins of stretcher-bond brickwork—known as double-thickness running bond—but the wall will not be very strong, even if the two wythes are tied together with cavity wall ties in the mortar beds. A stronger structure results if some of the bricks are laid end-on as headers, when they act as ties to hold the wall together. Two bonding arrangements commonly used for walls 8½in—one brick length—thick are English and Flemish bonds.

In English bond the wall is built with different alternate courses, the first of stretchers laid side by side in running bond, the second of headers. At corners, a course of stretchers becomes a course of headers in the return wall, and vice versa. At ends and corners, a brick cut in half lengthwise (a closure) is fitted before the last header to maintain the bonding arrangement. A variation called English garden wall bond has from three to five courses laid as stretchers, followed by a single course of headers. It is sometimes used instead of pure English bond to reduce the amount of pointing required in the header courses, but is marginally less strong.

In Flemish bond, each course consists of a pair of stretchers followed by a single header, so that on the face of the wall each header is centered on the stretcher below. Again, closures maintain the bond at ends and corners. The finished wall is a little stronger than English bond because every course contains headers as through ties. A variation known as Flemish garden wall bond has a header after around three pairs of stretchers in each course, again to reduce the amount of pointing required.

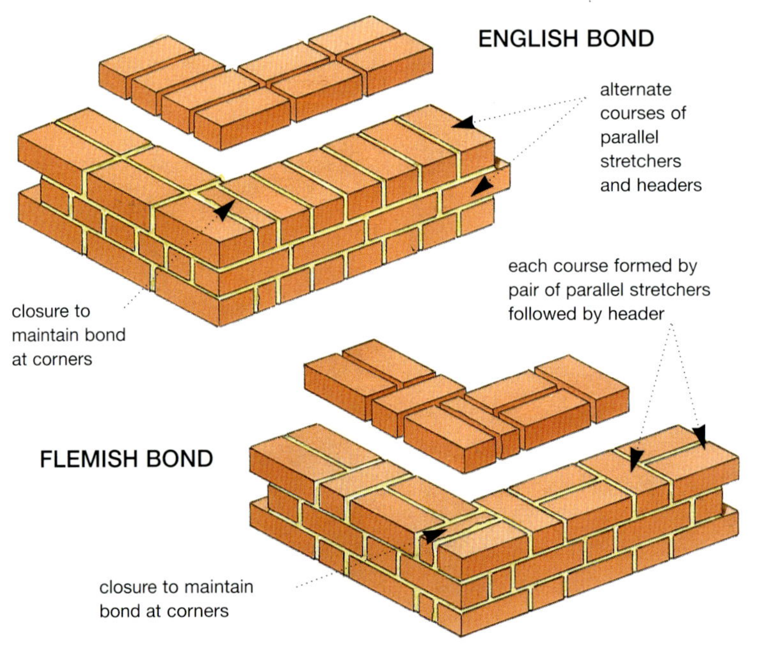

building a retaining wall

Any retaining wall needs solid, secure foundations. Excavate a form to a depth of about 18in and pack down a 6in layer of rubble using a fence post as a ram. Then hammer in wooden marker stakes to act as a depth guide for the foundation strip, and place a 6in thick layer of concrete (1 part cement to 5 parts mixed aggregate) over the rubble. Tamp it down with a beam held lengthwise in the form, level it, and cover it with polyethylene sheet. If you have clay soil, dig deeper so that you can put in a 12in thick concrete strip. Allow the concrete to harden for at least three days.

tools for the job

- spade
- wheelbarrow
- mason's line & marker stakes
- hammer
- bricklaying trowel
- level
- rubber mallet
- brick chisel
- hand sledge
- story pole (see box page 441)
- line pins
- builder's square (see box page 442)
- pointing trowel

1 You need to use special-quality frost-proof bricks for retaining walls—manufactured stone wall blocks are naturally frost-resistant. Lay the first course of brickwork, adjusting the thickness of the mortar bed to correct any unevenness in the foundation. Begin with a course of stretchers laid in running bond if you are building in English bond, as shown here, or pairs of stretchers followed by a single header if you are building in Flemish bond.

2 If the wall turns a corner, lay the first course of the return section of wall next. Place a closure behind the last stretcher at the face of the wall to maintain the bonding arrangement in the return wall. In English bond, the course continues along the return wall as a course of headers. In Flemish bond, place a pair of stretchers next to the closure, then a header and another pair of stretchers alternately along the rest of the course.

3 To allow water trapped behind the wall to drain away, either leave every other vertical joint open in the bottom two courses of the wall to act as weepholes, or build short lengths of copper or plastic drainpipe into the mortar bed above the first, second, or third course of bricks—the first course is usually best.

4 Continue building the wall up to its required height in your chosen bond. Line the back of the wall face with heavy-duty polyethylene sheet, or give it two coats of liquid damp-proofing solution. This will prevent the masonry from becoming saturated, causing white efflorescence to appear on the exposed face of the wall—a problem that spoils the appearance of many retaining walls. Fill behind the wall with gravel to a depth of at least 12in to assist with drainage behind the foot of the wall. Allow the mortar to harden for a week before filling with soil.

REINFORCING WALLS

Walls higher than about 3ft should be built around vertical steel rebar set into the foundation or footing concrete. Build the wall in double-thickness running bond with the rods between the two wythes of the wall. Tie the two wythes together with cavity wall ties placed 18in apart in every alternate bed joint, and in every course at wall ends and corners. Fill the space between the wythes with fine concrete.

building a screen block wall 

Pierced screen wall blocks allow you to build walls that act as a screen rather than a solid barrier. You can use them on their own or incorporate them as decorative panels in brick or block walls. Unique among building blocks, they are laid in vertical columns—an arrangement known as stack bonding—which means that a screen block wall is inherently weak unless it is reinforced during construction to compensate for the lack of bonding between the individual blocks.

Screen wall blocks are made to a standard size of 12in square, giving a modular unit 12in square with a ½in thick mortar joint. This means that any wall you build with them must be a multiple of 12in in length and width. The maximum height for a wall built solely using screen walling blocks is 6ft—six courses. The blocks are usually 3½in thick, and are white or off-white in color.

Block manufacturers also make matching hollow pier blocks. These are 8in high, so that three pier blocks coordinate with two wall blocks. They are made in four types—to form end piers, intermediate piers, corners and T-junctions—and, depending upon the type, they have one or more recessed faces into which the wall blocks fit. Any wall that is built with pier blocks must therefore have an even number of courses. Matching pier caps and 2ft long wall coping slabs complete the range.

tools for the job

- bricklaying trowel
- hand sledge
- rubber mallet
- level
- pointing trowel

1 To build a freestanding wall, lay a foundation strip (see page 437), then spread a bed of mortar on it long enough to embed three blocks. Set the first pier block in place at one end and tamp it down with the handle of a hand sledge. Use a level to check that it stands square.

2 Butter some mortar onto one face of the first block and rest it on the mortar bed so that you can lower the mortared edge into the groove in the pier block. Tap it along gently until it engages, then tamp it down gently into the mortar bed. The blocks are not strong, so try to tamp them close to the corners so that the force of the blow is transmitted down through solid material.

3 Butter the edge of the next block and embed it against the first, again tapping it horizontally until the vertical joint is ½in thick. Tamp it down level with its neighbor and trim off any excess mortar to avoid staining the block surfaces. Continue placing blocks in this way to complete the first course of the wall, finishing off with an end pier block. If the wall is longer than 10ft—ten blocks—incorporate intermediate piers at a maximum of 10ft intervals.

4 Spread some mortar on top of the first pier block at one end of the wall. Place the second pier block on it, tamp it down to a joint thickness of ½in, and check with a level that it is level in both directions and that the pier is plumb.

5 Repeat the process to place the third pier block. To reinforce the pier, fill its hollow central section with mortar, tamping it down inside the pier with a softwood scrap.

6 Place the second course of blocks on top of the first. Make sure that the first block engages fully in the groove in the pier blocks, and that subsequent blocks are aligned with the ones below. The top of the second course should be level with the top of the pier.

7 If you intend to build a wall higher than two courses, the pier blocks must be built around a steel rebar that is set in the foundations. Tie the wall blocks to the pier with a strip of expanded metal lath embedded into the mortar in alternate courses and hooked over the rebar.

Add pier and screen wall blocks as necessary to complete the wall. If the finished wall will be more than four courses high, add two more courses now and allow the mortar to harden overnight before adding the next two.

Finish the wall by placing pier caps and coping slabs on top of the wall. These could be matching or contrasting in color, depending on taste. Check that the coping slabs are level and that they overlap the wall blocks by an equal amount on each side of the wall. Mortar the joints between the coping slabs.

tips of the trade

- **Matching mortar**—Since screen wall blocks are white or cream in color, ordinary mortar will look much darker and will spoil the appearance of the wall. To get around the problem, order white portland cement and the palest sand available from your building supplier, and use these to make a matching mortar. If these materials are not available, the only alternative is to paint the wall with masonry paint or exterior latex paint when the wall is complete.
- **Filling panels**—If you intend to use screen walling blocks as filling panels in solid masonry walls, remember that one block coordinates with four courses of brickwork. The blocks are a little narrower than a brick, so center the blocks on the brickwork if the wall will be viewed from both sides, but fit them level with the face of the brickwork if only this face of the wall is visible.

Use a rubber mallet to tap the pier caps and coping slabs into the mortar on top of the wall, and check with a level to make sure that they are level.

building a brick arch

A brick arch is a striking way of framing a gateway or an opening in a high boundary wall (although building the latter is best left to the professionals). The structure is self-supporting once built, but you need the help of some wooden formwork to support the arch bricks while the mortar sets. A two-ring arch is the best choice for a freestanding archway. A one-ring arch is weak and looks insubstantial, while a three-ring arch is too overpowering, and looks better in a wall.

An arch works by transferring its weight down into the wall or piers that support it. If the arch is freestanding, the piers must be at least 8½in—one brick—square, and it is generally best to err on the side of safety and build the piers measuring 13 x 8½in with three bricks in each pier course. Each pier should have its own concrete foundation pad, 18in square and 6in thick.

tools for the job

- bricklaying trowel
- level
- tape measure & pencil
- jigsaw
- hammer
- arch form (see step 2)
- pointing trowel
- raking tool or small cold chisel

1 Build the two piers, checking after each course that they are rising at the same level. Continue until you reach the springing point—the level at which the arch will begin. For an archway 3ft wide, piers consisting of twenty-two courses of brickwork will give adequate headroom.

2 Measure the width of the opening at the springing point and cut two semicircles of plywood to that diameter with a jigsaw. Nail them to scrap pieces of wood to make an arch form measuring about 8in from front to back. Set the form on bearing posts so that it sits level with the tops of the piers.

3 Place some mortar on top of each pier, next to the form, and set a brick in place on each one. Butt it up against the form and tamp it down in the mortar.

BUILDING A SEGMENTED ARCH

You can use a variation on the brick arch technique to build a flatter arch, known as a segmented arch because its curve is a smaller segment of the circle's circumference than a semicircle. Use a pencil, some string, and a thumbtack as improvised compasses to draw the curve you want on a sheet of board. Cut it out, check its appearance across the opening and use it to mark and cut a matching piece for the other side of the form. Remember that the flatter the arch, the more upright the bricks will be at either side of the opening. You will probably have to build the tops of the piers level with the end bricks to improve their appearance.

4 Add bricks to each side of the form one by one, making sure that each one is butted against the former and that the wedge-shape mortar joints between the bricks are the same width—around ½in thick on the inside of the curve, and about ¾in on the outside.

KEYSTONE ALTERNATIVES

Instead of using a brick as a keystone, you could use pieces of slate, plain clay roof tiles, or quarry tiles. Simply fill the keystone position with mortar and push the pieces down into it one by one (you will probably need four or fives pieces).

5 If you have spaced your bricks carefully, there should be room for a single brick—the keystone—at the top of the arch. Butter mortar on both sides of it and slot it into place.

6 When the keystone is in place, hold a level against the face of the arch to check that all the bricks are aligned.

7 Spread mortar on top of the first ring of bricks and build up the second ring in the same way, with wedge-shape mortar joints. The second ring will have a slightly larger radius than the inner one, so the brick joints will not align after the first brick. You will need more bricks for the second ring—typically twenty-three (compared with nineteen for the inner ring) for an arch 3ft wide. When you have added the second keystone, clean all the visible mortar joints.

8 Leave the form in place for 48 hours to give the mortar time to set hard (if rain or frost threatens, cover the top of the arch with polyethylene sheet). Then remove the bearing posts carefully and let the form drop out without disturbing the brickwork. Point the joints on the underside of the arch to complete the job. Finally, rake out the dried mortar to a depth of ⅛in and replace it with fresh mortar using a pointing trowel.

When the arch is built, rake out the dried mortar from the joints and fill them with fresh mortar, either level with the face of the bricks or recessed slightly, for a perfect finish.

building steps on a slope

In a steeply sloping garden, the safest way to get up and down sloping lawns is via a flight of steps, and the simplest way to build them is to use the slope to provide the step's foundations. As long as the sod is firm and has not been disturbed recently, careful cutting of the step shapes will provide a stable base for the flight. All you need is a single concrete foundation base slab to anchor the lowest tread.

Garden steps should have treads at least 1ft from front to back and 2ft wide. Increase this to at least 4ft to create enough room for people to pass each other on the steps. The height of the risers will be governed by the bricks or blocks you use—two courses of brick or standard wall block topped by a paving slab will produce a step height of just under 8in. The treads should overhang the risers by about 1in. If the flight will be more than ten treads long, look to incorporate a wide landing that is situated halfway up the flight.

safety advice

Treads and risers should be the same size throughout the flight and the treads laid with a slight slope from back to front so that rainwater drains off them and cannot freeze there.

tips of the trade

To count the number of treads you will need, use a horizontal mason's line and a long garden cane stuck in the ground at the foot of the bank to measure the bank height. Divide this by the height of each tread to calculate how many steps you will need. Divide the length of the mason's line by the number of steps to check that the tread depth will be at least 12in.

preparing the site

1 Use marker stakes and mason's lines to mark the sides of the flight and the positions of the tread nosings on the slope. Remember that treads need to be at least 12in from front to back. Using paving slabs 18in square gives a tread about 14in deep, allowing for the depth of the riser that will be built off its rear edge.

2 Remove the transverse mason's lines and use a spade to cut out step shapes in the slope. The stakes will act as a guide to where the front of each tread should be. Work from the top of the slope down, so that you do not break down the edges of the treads you have cut by standing on them.

3 Dig a form at the foot of the flight and cast a 4in thick concrete strip foundation about 12in longer than the width of the flight and about 12in wide (see page 437). Allow the foundation slab to set for three days before starting to build the flight of steps.

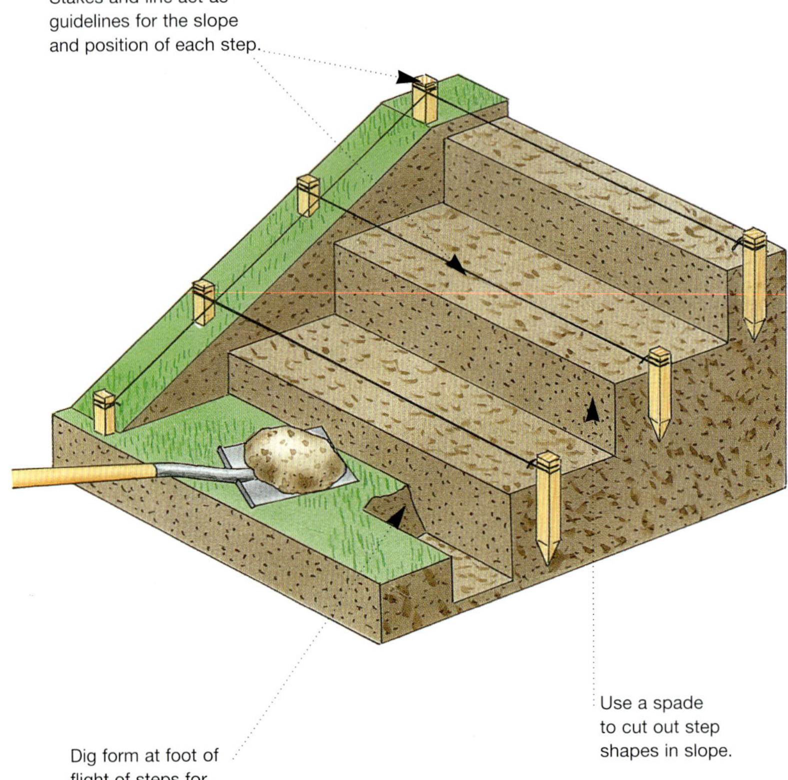

Stakes and line act as guidelines for the slope and position of each step.

Dig form at foot of flight of steps for concrete foundation base slab.

Use a spade to cut out step shapes in slope.

building the steps

1 Spread a bed of mortar across the center of the concrete foundation strip and embed the first course of bricks or blocks in it. Four bricks laid in stretcher bond make a flight of steps that is 36in wide, ideal for paving with two 18in square slabs per tread. Then cut a brick or block in half to start the second course of the riser. Embed it in place at one end of the riser, and then complete the second course.

2 Fill behind the brick or blockwork of the first riser with crushed aggregate, which compacts better than rubble because it contains a mixture of large and small pieces. Tamp it down well with a fence post or a similar sturdy, thick piece of wood, taking care not to disturb the bricks or blocks that you have just laid.

3 Spread a line of mortar on top of the first riser and over the filled area below where the edges of the paving slabs that are to form the treads will be. Embed the first slab in place, checking that it is level from side to side and has a slight slope toward its front edge to allow rainwater to drain off. Set the second slab of the tread alongside it, tamp it down level with its neighbor, and trim off excess mortar from beneath the fronts of the treads.

4 Build the brick or blockwork of the second riser up at the rear of the first treads. Spread a mortar line and set the bricks or blocks in it as before. Fill behind the riser and embed the next two treads in place, using the same method as before. Continue to build risers and place treads until you have completed the flight of steps. Finally, clean the pointing and brush dry mortar into the gaps between the treads.

5 If the cut edges of the treads show signs of crumbling, build dwarf brick walls at each side of the treads to contain the soil.

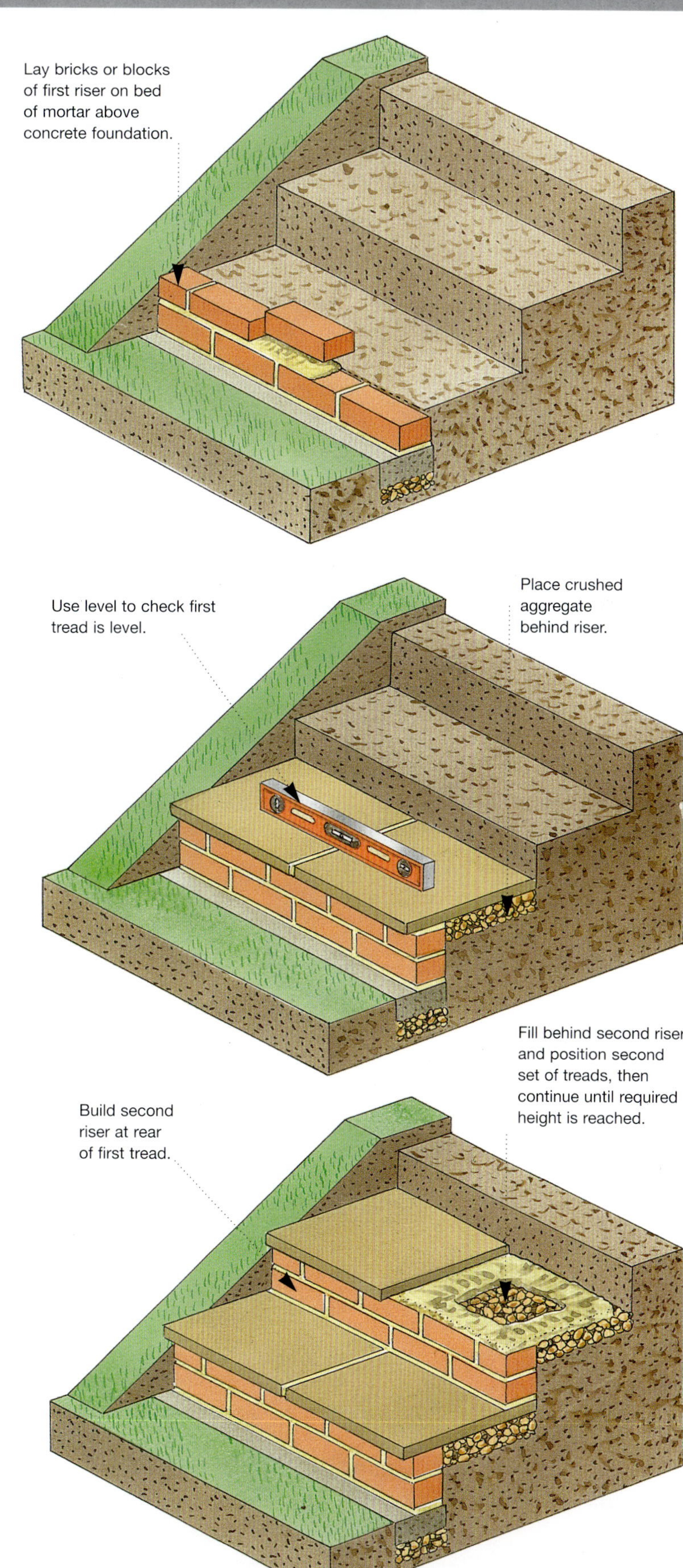

building freestanding steps 

If you are creating different levels in your garden through the use of retaining walls, you will need to build some steps to give you easy access from one level to the next. The easiest way to do this is to build a flight of freestanding steps between the two levels. This is more complex than building steps on a slope, since you have to create the entire structure yourself instead of letting the slope do the work of supporting the steps.

Plan the shape and dimensions of the new steps around the pavers and walls you intend to use. It makes sense to match the bricks or blocks to those used for the existing retaining walls, and to choose pavers that match what you have elsewhere in the garden. Most paver ranges offer slabs in several different sizes, so you can choose whichever best suits the dimensions of your steps.

A freestanding flight of steps needs foundations to support the perimeter brickwork and the interior brickwork that supports the edges of the treads. Clear the site for the steps of vegetation and turf, and excavate to a depth of about 8in. Ram in a layer of rubble about 4in deep, and use sand to fill in the voids. Then place and level a 4in thick concrete foundation base slab about 14in larger in each dimension than the flight of steps. Refer to pages 470–3 for more information on laying concrete slabs.

The flight of steps in the example illustrated here is built against a brick retaining wall four bricks high. It is four bricks wide, has risers two bricks high, and treads formed of two 18in square paving slabs. The top tread sits on the wall and the earth that is retained behind the wall.

safety advice

The height and width of a flight of steps, as well as the materials used, contribute to their safety. Refer to pages 452–3 for advice.

tools for the job

- marker stakes & mason's line
- garden spade
- wheelbarrow
- bricklaying trowel
- level
- builder's square (see box page 442)
- brick chisel
- hand sledge
- wooden straightedge

1 Spread a bed of mortar along the line of the perimeter brickwork and lay the first course. Tamp them down with the handle of a trowel. Use a level to check that they are level, and a builder's square to check the corners. Finish each course with a half brick.

2 Start the second course with a whole brick. On flights more than 18in high, you need to tie the steps to the wall to prevent cracks from developing between the steps and the wall as time goes by. You can either cut out a half brick in the wall and bond a whole brick from the steps into the recess, or alternatively you can use metal wall extension profiles.

3 Complete the second course of bricks. Once again, use a level to check that the course is level, with all the bricks correctly aligned, and that the face of the brickwork is plumb.

4 Build transverse walls inside the brick box to support the second riser brickwork and the meeting edges of the slabs that will form the first tread. These can be of honeycomb construction (that is, the vertical joints do not need pointing).

5 Add two more courses of brickwork to form the second riser and the sides of the flight, and build up the rear interior support wall to the same height to support the meeting edges of the slabs that form the second tread. Use a level to check that the wall is level.

6 Spread some mortar on top of the brickwork that forms the first step. Position the two slabs that will form the tread of the steps. Tamp them down level with each other, and with a slight fall towards the front of the step. Once again, use a level to check the position.

7 Point the joints between the slabs and along their rear edges, and trim off excess pointing between them and the brickwork below. Place the slabs that form the second tread in the same way. If this tread is at the top of the flight, as in this example, rest the rear edges of the slabs on the wall behind.

POSITIONING HIGHER FLIGHTS OF STEPS

The picture sequence illustrated on these pages shows steps ascending at a right angle to the face of the wall. If the retaining wall is more than six courses of brickwork in height, however, extra steps will be needed, and the flight will have to extend farther away from the wall as a result of this. If this is not acceptable, either because you do not have sufficient space for them, or simply for aesthetic reasons, turn the flight of steps through 90 degrees so that the flight rises parallel to the wall face. Such a flight will then project onto the lower level by just the width of the treads.

Use the point of a bricklaying trowel to scrape away excess mortar from all the joints. The quality of the pointing can make a big difference to the finished look of the steps.

creating & repairing exterior surfaces

Most householders want to do more than just admire the garden from the house. They want to walk around it without getting their feet wet, sit outside without chairs and tables sinking into soft grass, and perhaps create decorative features with gravel or cobblestones. They may even want areas of concrete to provide foundation slabs for garden buildings, or just to provide an inexpensive parking bay for the car. The most popular materials for creating patios, paths, and other outdoor surfaces are paving slabs and interlocking pavers. Both come in a wide range of styles, shapes, and colors, and are very easy for the amateur landscape gardener to lay. All you have to decide is which to choose and where to lay them. Consult local building-code regulations before embarking on exterior building projects.

For areas with light traffic, such as patios or paths, slabs may be laid on sand rather than a mortar base.

patios, paths, & driveways

Apart from walls, garden landscaping also requires hard surface areas for traffic and to take garden furniture. Patios, paths, and driveways can be surfaced in a variety of materials, including individual slabs or blocks laid on a sand or mortar bed, and areas of concrete, cobblestones, or gravel. The key requirements of any hard surfaces outside the house are that they should provide a stable, firm surface that drains freely in wet weather and is laid on a solid base so that it does not subside and become uneven as time goes by.

slab paving on sand

Pavers come in a range of shapes and sizes, and sets are available that build up into circular features with up to three concentric rings around a central stone. Slab texture may be smooth, molded to simulate split slate or stone, or finished with a fine gritstone or coarser aggregate surface. Colors range from buff and gray through various shades of terra-cotta to red. For areas that will get only light traffic, such as patios and garden paths, the slabs can be laid on a raked and compacted sand bed about 2in in depth. This provides continuous support for the undersides of the slabs, accommodates any unevenness in the soil beneath and makes it easy to get neighboring slabs level. The sand bed can be laid directly over well-compacted soil, but if it is unstable or has been dug recently, a 3in thick layer of well-rammed broken rubble or crushed rock will be required below the sand to provide a firm base that will not subside. The joints between the slabs are filled with brushed-in sand or soil.

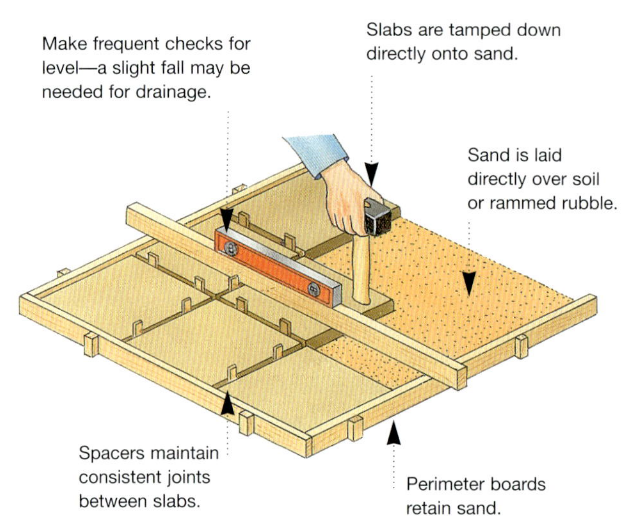

slab paving on mortar

For areas such as driveways and parking bays that have to take vehicles, slabs must be laid on mortar, otherwise the weight of the vehicle will make individual slabs subside and crack. The mortar bed needs a firm and stable sub-base —either a 4in thickness of well-rammed rubble or crushed rock, or an existing concrete driveway. The slabs are laid on lines of mortar placed beneath their edges and across the center, leaving space for the mortar to be compressed and squeezed out sideways into an almost continuous bed when the slab is placed and leveled. Joints between slabs are filled with a very dry, stiff mortar mix to avoid staining the slabs when they are placed.

Irregular or crazy paving is a form of slab paving laid with the same method as for normal paving, but with irregular-shape slabs laid on a continuous bed of mortar, rather than mortar being applied under each one.

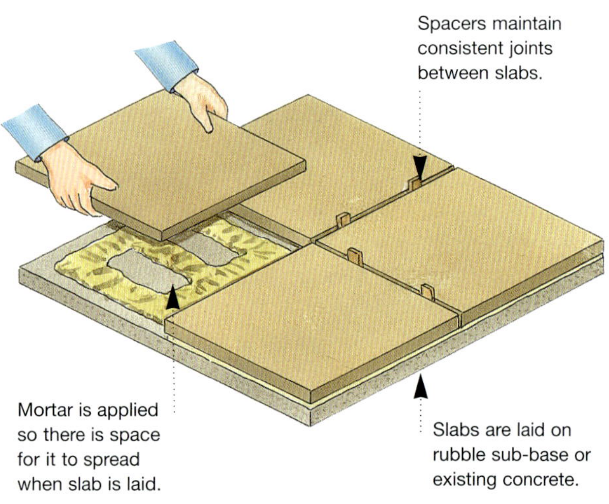

concrete

Concrete is a mixture of cement, coarse sand, and fine aggregate—stones up to ¾in across —which makes an ideal surface for patios, paths, and driveways where the emphasis is on economy and durable properties, rather than a grand appearance. When formed into strips and slabs, the concrete is contained in a timber mold called formwork. This ensures that the cast slab will have clean vertical edges, and also acts as a leveling guide when pouring in the final layer of concrete. The correct mix for exposed slabs is 1 part cement to 3.5 parts combined sand and aggregate.

Once the form has been dug and formwork established, a firm sub-base of compacted rubble or crushed rock is laid, followed by a thin layer of sand or ballast to fill in gaps in the rubble, with the concrete laid on top. The combined depth of the two sub-base layers should be approximately 3in for a path or patio, and 4in for a driveway, rising to 6in on clay soils. Similarly, the concrete layer should be 3in thick for paths and patios, 4in thick for driveways, and 6in on clay.

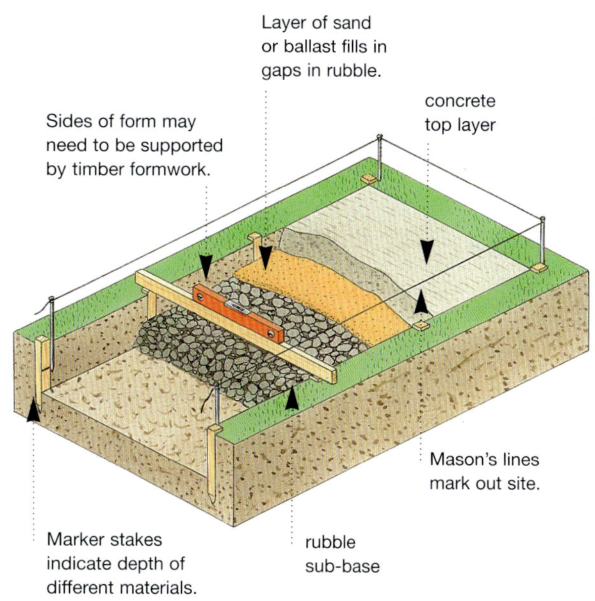

gravel & cobblestones

Gravel is river stone typically sieved to a diameter of ¾in. It is loosely laid over a firm sub-base of well-rammed soil or crushed rock (rubble is too coarse), ideally with a weed-proof membrane laid under the sub-base. A depth of 2in is required for a garden path, and 4in for a driveway. The area will need some form of edge restraint, such as kerbstones or embedded wooden boards, to prevent the gravel from transferring to adjacent lawns or flowerbeds.

Cobblestones are larger rounded pebbles up to 3in in diameter. They can be laid loose, but are more commonly set to around half their depth in a continuous mortar line. They make an attractive surface but one that is relatively uncomfortable to walk on, so they are usually laid only as small feature areas within other paving, or as a trim.

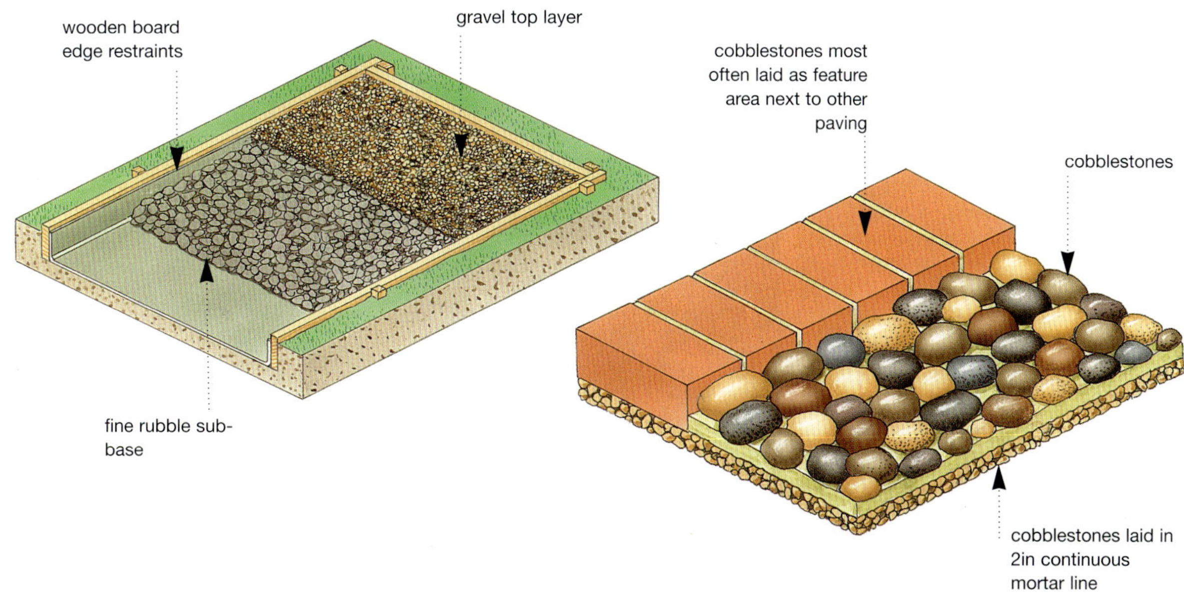

laying slabs on sand

The simplest way to create hard surfaces in your garden, such as patios and paths, is to lay paving slabs on a sand bed. Sand is easy for embedding and leveling, and will provide a firm support for slabs as long as they are subjected only to pedestrian traffic. As the individual slabs are quite large, you can cover a sizeable area quickly once the site is cleared and sand bed prepared. However, large slabs are heavy, and anyone with back trouble should avoid laying them.

SLAB SIZES & FINISHES

Most pavers are square or rectangular in shape, but wedge-shape sets are also available that build up to form circles. Square slabs range from 9 or 12in up to 24in in size, while rectangles start at 9 x 18in and go up to 24 x 36in. This last size is often used for laying sidewalks, but is perhaps too large for a small garden, and is certainly too heavy for one person to lift and lay on their own. Finishes available include smooth, textured, and riven—which is an imitation of split natural stone. Colors range from off-white and buff to red, granite, and slate. Cheaper slabs are simply formed from cast concrete. These are relatively brittle and are very difficult to cut accurately. More expensive slabs are hydraulically pressed, which makes them stronger and more easy to cut.

tips of the trade

You need to plan the number of slabs you will need. To avoid unnecessary and time-consuming cutting, plan an area that is a whole number of slabs in length and width. Take approximate measurements of the site, select the slabs you want to use, and note the sizes in which they are manufactured. It is then a simple job to plan the layout in squares, rectangles, or a mixture of the two, using graph paper to produce a scale drawing of the arrangement. Not only will this help when it comes to laying, it will also enable you to order precisely the right number of slabs in each size and so avoid unnecessary wastage.

tools for the job

- tape measure
- marker stakes & mason's line
- spade
- hammer
- wheelbarrow
- shovel & rake
- leveling board (homemade)
- level
- mallet
- brick chisel & hand sledge
- stiff-bristle broom

1 Mark and clear the site, then excavate to a depth of 4in. Compact the soil if it has not been disturbed recently. If it has, dig down a further 3in, then spread and compact a 3in layer of gravel or crushed rock over the site. Tamp it down firmly with a length of fence post. Unless the pavers will finish level with an existing grass area, edge the area with 4in wide perimeter boards to retain the sand bed. Use sawn preservative-treated 1in thick wood, nailed to wooden markers hammered into the soil.

2 Bring the sand to the site in a wheelbarrow and rake it out to a thickness of 2in. Use a piece of perimeter board as a leveling board to smooth over and level off the sand. Rest a level on top of the board as you work, to check that the sand bed has a slight fall away from the house for drainage purposes. Kneel on a scrap piece of board as you work so that you do not disturb the sand.

tips of the trade

To estimate how much sand to order, measure the length and width of the paved area in yards and multiply the two together to get the area in square yards. Then divide this by 20 to get the volume in cubic yards for a layer 2in thick. Add 10 per cent to the total volume to allow for uneven soil and filling joints.

3 Place the first slab at one corner of the area and tamp it down into the sand bed using either a mallet or the handle end of a hand sledge. Check that the slab is level in one direction and has the correct slope in the other.

4 Lay the next slab, either butting it up to the first one if you want close joints, or use wooden spacers if you prefer wider joints. Tamp it down and check that it is level with its neighbor, with the same fall away from the house. If the slab sits too low, lift it and add a little more sand underneath, then reposition.

5 Continue laying slabs along the first row, removing the spacers as soon as each slab is surrounded by further slabs on either side. Follow your plan unless you are laying only square slabs in a checkerboard pattern of rows and columns.

6 Once each row is complete, lay the leveling board along the row to check the slabs are lying level. Then check the fall down each row and make any adjustments.

7 If your design is such that you need to cut a slab, mark the cutting line in pencil or chalk and use a brick chisel and hand sledge to make a shallow cut across the slab. Then place the slab on the sand and strike the slab harder so that it snaps along the cut line. If you have a lot of cutting to do, it is a good idea to rent an angle grinder, which will make the cuts quickly and cleanly. When you have laid all the slabs, remove the last spacers and shovel some sand onto the surface. Use a soft-bristle broom to brush the sand into all the joints between the slabs, then brush off the excess.

tips of the trade

If you are laying pavers in an area that has an access hole, do not simply pave over it. The sand will enter the drains, and you will have an awkward job of lifting slabs to gain access. Get a builder to raise and reposition the frame so that the cover will be level with the new paving (or tackle the job yourself by adding a course of bricks around the top of the chamber).

There is no need to fill the joints with mortar when laying slabs on sand—it is enough to brush more sand into the joints.

laying block pavers

Block pavers are the most popular choice for outdoor surfaces. Their advantages are that they are small, easier to handle than slabs, they are designed to be laid on a sand bed, and there is no pointing to be done as they are butted together. In addition, unlike other dry-laid paving materials, they will withstand the weight of an automobile. The drawbacks are that it takes longer to cover an area with blocks than slabs, and the paved area must have edging to retain the sand bed.

Block pavers are generally rectangular and 2–2½in thick. The most common size is 4 x 8in, but many other sizes are available. They also come in a wide color range. The surface of block pavers is slightly textured, with the block edges beveled to emphasize their outline when laid. Either the blocks themselves or matching kerb blocks may be used as perimeter edging—these will need to be set in mortar.

Block pavers can be laid in various designs, from simple basketweave to intricate herringbone patterns. Most designs are laid square to the edge restraints, but you can also lay the blocks at an angle—generally 45 degrees—running across the site. Note that the sand used for the embedding layer should be coarse (concreting) sand, not fine (building) sand, which does not compact as well and may also stain the blocks.

tools for the job

- garden spade
- tape measure
- marker stakes & mason's line
- wheelbarrow & shovel
- rake & tamping beam
- leveling board
- rented plate compactor (driveways)
- level
- bricklaying trowel
- rubber mallet
- brick chisel
- hand sledge
- rented block splitter (optional)
- broom

1 Clear the site of vegetation and mark the area to be excavated. Dig the area to a depth of about 4in for patios and paths, and compact any disturbed subsoil—a thick fence post is used here. For a driveway, excavate an additional 4in, then add a 4in layer of rubble or crushed rock. Compact this layer using a rented plate compactor (see box below right).

2 Position the edge restraints around the area to be paved. Set block or kerbstone edging in a mortar bed or nail preservative-treated wooden edging to strong markers. Allow mortar to harden for 24 hours before laying the blocks.

3 Fill a wheelbarrow with sand and tip the sand into the area to be paved. When all the sand is in place, rake it to a uniform depth of about 2in. Use a leveling board to smooth and level the sand across the area, working from a board so that you do not compact the sand bed by treading on it. Form stacks of blocks at intervals around the perimeter of the site.

LAYING BLOCK DRIVEWAYS

If you are laying block pavers as a driveway, you need to settle them into place to prevent them from subsiding under the weight of vehicles. To do this, rent a power tool called a plate compactor. This vibrates as you run it over the laid blocks, settling them into the sand bed and also compacting this so that it cannot itself subside. You should make one pass of the machine after placing the blocks, and another after brushing sand into the joints. This tool is also ideal for compacting any rubble and crushed rock that is being used as a sub-base for any paving project.

4 Place the first blocks against one edge restraint, following whatever laying pattern you have chosen. If you are laying a patio or path, tamp them down into the sand bed using a rubber mallet. If you are creating a driveway, simply set them in place. Make sure the blocks are butted closely together.

5 After laying about 10 sq ft or so of blocks, lay a level on the leveling board and place it across the blocks in various directions to check that they are level and sitting at the same height as each other. Tamp down any that protrude above their neighbors.

6 Carry on laying blocks across the area, checking regularly that you are maintaining the pattern correctly. Depending on the pattern chosen and the shape of the site, you are likely to have to cut some blocks to finish the surface. Lay as many whole blocks as you can first of all, then insert the cut blocks, tamping each one into place.

7 You can cut block pavers with a brick chisel and hand sledge, as shown here, but you will save time and effort (and spoil fewer blocks) if you rent a hydraulic block splitter for the day. Mark the cutting line in chalk, position the block in the cutter, and pull down on the handle to split the block.

With all the cut blocks in position, lay a level across them to check the levels once more and tamp down any that protrude above their neighbors. When you are satisfied, spread some fine, dry sand liberally over the surface and brush it this way and that until all the joints are filled. Sweep off the excess sand.

Make sure that you move the brush across the whole paved area, bending the bristles into all the joints to ensure that they are filled with sand for a perfect finish.

laying slabs on mortar

If you want to use paving slabs for a driveway or another area that will get more than just pedestrian traffic, you need to bed them on mortar over a concrete sub-base to ensure that the slabs have a continuous solid support and will not crack under the load. You can also lay slabs on mortar rather than sand for patios and paths. In this instance, a concrete base is not required, but the soil beneath the slabs must be firm and well compacted.

Laying concrete from the beginning in order to place slabs on top to create a driveway is an expensive way of creating this type of outdoor feature, but if the concrete is there already the job becomes a more feasible one. As long as an existing concrete base is sound—in other words, not riddled with cracks and subsiding in places—and is at least 4in thick, it will make the perfect foundation for a paved driveway.

As with laying slabs on sand (see pages 460–1), the secret of success lies in careful planning. Take time choosing the slabs you want—you will have to live with the results for some time—and work out the layout to avoid having to cut slabs unless it cannot be avoided. On an existing concrete base you may have to mix slab sizes to ensure that you have whole slabs along all open edges of the base. Increasing or decreasing the spacing between the slabs may also help you avoid having to cut slabs.

tools for the job

- tape measure
- shovel
- bricklaying trowel
- hand sledge & rubber mallet
- level
- wooden straightedge
- watering can
- pointing trowel
- stiff broom
- brick chisel
- safety goggles
- work gloves

patios & paths

After planning (and if necessary sketching out a scale drawing) the slab layout, clear and mark out the site. If laying onto subsoil, make sure it is well compacted. Mix a mainly sloppy mortar mix in the proportions 1 part cement to 6 parts soft (building) sand. Compact the subsoil thoroughly and place five mounds of mortar in the place where the first slab will be positioned, one under each corner and one in the center. Lay the slab in place on the mortar and tamp it down with the handle of a hand sledge or a rubber mallet so that it is perfectly level. Then repeat the process to lay other slabs across the area, checking the level from time to time with a level resting on a wooden straightedge. When you have laid all the slabs, brush a mixture of cement and sand into the joints and sprinkle water onto the paving with a watering can to dampen the mortar and make it set hard between the slabs. Once dry, the mortar locks the slab in place and ensures that it does not move.

driveways

1 If you are laying a driveway on a concrete base, brush the surface of the concrete with a stiff broom to remove any loose material, and treat it with a chlorine bleach solution to kill any weeds, lichen, and algal growth. This should prevent any weeds or other plant growth from emerging through the joints in the paving for some time, though you will have to take measures to control this problem in the future. Spread a thick square of sloppy mortar where the first slab will be positioned, and add two lines of mortar at a right angle across the center of the square —this is called box-and-cross embedding by craftspeople.

2 Place the first slab on the mortar and tamp it down well with a hand sledge. This will compress the layers into a continuous layer of mortar and bond the slab securely to the concrete. Use a level to check that the slab is level (assuming that the concrete base beneath it is level, of course).

3 Place more box-and-cross mortar for the next slab, position it and put two ½in wood spacers between it and the first slab. This makes sure that the pointing gap remains constant across the whole paved area. Then tamp the slab down and check that it is level and aligned with the first slab.

4 Lay the rest of the slabs in the same way with spacers between them, working your way across the area row by row. You can remove the spacers as soon as each slab is surrounded on all sides by other slabs.

5 Allow the mortar to harden overnight. Mix a mainly dry mortar mix so that it does not stain the slabs, and work it into the joints with a pointing trowel. Use a scrap piece of wood to pack the mortar down well. Allow mortar drops to dry on the slabs, then brush them off.

cutting slabs

1 If you have to cut just a few slabs, do it by hand. Wearing safety goggles and gloves, mark the cutting line and cut a shallow groove along it with a brick chisel and hand sledge. Alternatively, score the line with repeated passes of the corner of the brick chisel.

2 Place the scored slab on a bed of sand and position the brick chisel in the center of the line. Strike it firmly with the hand sledge, and the slab should split along the scored line. If you have to cut a lot of slabs, consider renting an angle grinder for the day.

ACHIEVING EFFICIENT SURFACE DRAINAGE

With mortar-pointed slabs, rainwater will not drain away between the slabs in the way that it does when slabs are embedded and pointed with sand. You should therefore build the slabs on a slope in order to prevent puddles from collecting and standing on the surface after it has rained. The slope should be of a continuous uniform gradient across the paved area.

If the paved area is situated next to the house, lay the slabs so that the slope falls away from the house. Aim for a slope of about 1 in 40—that is, a 1in drop for every 3ft of patio or driveway width.

tips of the trade

- **Seal the concrete**—If the existing concrete slab is dusty, treat it with a solution of polyvinyl acetate (PVA) building adhesive, diluted as recommended by the manufacturer for use as a sealer. Not only will this bond the concrete surface together, but it will also help the mortar to bond well to the concrete, making sure that the slabs do not work loose as time goes by.
- **Plant the gaps**—If you want your paving to have an informal look, lay the slabs with wider than usual joints and fill them with soil rather than mortar to encourage grass, moss, and low-growing plants. Using slabs in a mixture of different sizes also looks less formal than same-size slabs laid in regimented rows.

laying crazy paving

Crazy, or irregular, paving is a paved surface created by bedding irregular-shape pieces of stone in mortar and then pointing the gaps between the pieces. The stone is usually broken paving slabs, although natural stone can also be laid as crazy paving in the same way. It may have got its name from the crazing that affects the glaze on old pottery. The stones have to be well fitted and the pointing carefully detailed to avoid a ragged finish.

The main attraction of crazy paving, apart from its rustic and informal look, is that the paving is cheap—broken slabs are widely available in large quantities from local demolition contractors. As an approximate guide, 1 ton of broken slabs will cover an area of 100sq ft, but this will depends on the thickness of the slabs. Ask your supplier for advice when ordering. You may be offered a choice of stones in one predominant color and texture, or as a random mixture. For the most part, crazy paving looks better if all the pieces are more or less the same shade.

When the delivery arrives, separate the stones into groups. Pieces with two square adjacent edges will form corners, while those with one straight edge will serve as perimeter stones. Separate what is left into large irregular pieces for the center of the paved area, and smaller piece for filling gaps. Stack the groups around the paving site so that you have them to hand while you work.

The best base for crazy paving is an old concrete slab in need of a makeover. The alternative is a layer of crushed rock or rubble, laid over well-rammed subsoil. Brush old concrete to remove loose bits from the surface, treat it with a chloride bleach solution if it is covered in lichen and green algae, and seal its surface with diluted polyvinyl acetate (PVA) building adhesive if it is very dusty. Clear a new site of vegetation, skim off the topsoil, and bed down a 3in layer of crushed rock ready for the mortar bed that will take the paving.

tools for the job

- shovel
- wheelbarrow
- rented cement mixer
- bricklaying trowel
- rubber mallet
- level
- wooden straightedge
- hand sledge
- brick chisel
- pointing trowel
- mortar board
- stiff broom

1 Mix your first batch of mortar using a rented cement mixer—you will need so much mortar for embedding and pointing that hand mixing is not really an option for this job. Use a mix of 1 part cement to 5 parts coarse (concreting) sand, and make it quite sloppy. Start work at one corner of the site, shoveling enough mortar onto the area you are paving to cover about 10 sq ft at a time. Trowel it over the area to a thickness of approximately 2in.

2 Select a corner stone and tamp it down into the mortar bed using a mallet or the handle of a hand sledge. Use a level to get it level, and make sure it is aligned with the edges of the slab if you are laying on concrete. Otherwise, use mason's lines to help you keep the edge stones accurately in line.

3 Choose a large perimeter stone that fits well against the corner stone—aim for a pointing gap of no more than 1in in width, or your crazy paving will look very gapped. Set it in place and tamp it down, using a mallet or the handle of the hand sledge, then check that it is level and in line with the corner stone.

4 Continue to lay perimeter and corner stones all the way around the site until the edge is complete. As you embed the stones, mortar will squeeze up between them. Leave it, as this will reduce the amount of pointing needed later, but make sure it does not protrude above the surface of the stones.

5 Shovel in more mortar, spread it out, and start embedding large irregular stones in the center of the area, working from one end to the other. Use a brick chisel and hand sledge to trim stones to improve their fit. Check that each stone is level as you tamp it down, by placing a wooden straightedge across the paving with its ends on the perimeter stones. Kneel on a board as you work across the site to avoid disturbing the pieces you have already laid.

6 Use smaller pieces of stone to fill in the remaining gaps, again trimming them to size first if necessary. Use any remaining mixed mortar to fill the gaps between the stones to within about ¼in of the surface of the paving. Allow the mortar to harden overnight before starting on the pointing—the most time-consuming part of the job.

7 Make up a pointing mortar of 1 part cement to 5 parts fine (building) sand. It should be somewhat drier than the embedding mortar to prevent the stone surfaces from being stained. Trowel it into the joints from a mortar board, then draw the side of the trowel blade along the edge of each stone to recess the mortar about ⅛in below it and leave two sloping bevels meeting at a central ridge.

8 Allow any loose mortar that you have dropped to dry on the stones—lifting this when it is wet will leave stains. Once the pointing mortar has dried hard, brush the paving surface to remove the debris.

Crazy paving has a rustic, informal look that is perfectly enhanced by a busy planting scheme, with flowers and shrubs allowed to overlap onto the paving.

laying gravel & cobblestones

A gravel path or drive makes an attractive contrast to flat paving materials, especially if the aggregate is chosen with care. Strictly speaking, gravel is made up of small water-rounded pebbles and is available in a range of natural earth shades. Crushed-stone aggregates have rough-edged stones and are available in colors ranging from white and gray, through reds and greens, to black. These can be laid as a single color, or can be mixed if preferred.

tools for the job

- tape measure
- spade
- handsaw
- hand sledge
- claw hammer
- bricklaying trowel
- shovel & wheelbarrow
- garden roller or tamping beam
- rake
- wooden straightedge

using cobblestones

Cobblestones are large, rounded river stones. They make an uncomfortable surface to walk on, but can look very attractive when used in the garden to provide a visual counterpoint to flat surfaces—perhaps as a border to a path. They can be loose-laid, but are better embedded in mortar.

1 To create a cobblestone feature, complete the surface that it will complement—a brick or block border, for example. Then spread a bed of quite sloppy mortar about 2in deep and place individual cobblestones in it to about half their depth.

2 Use a scrap piece of wood and a hand sledge to tamp them down into the mortar bed until they are reasonably level. This will make sure that they do not work loose later. When the mortar has dried, brush away any excess and apply a coat of clear silicone masonry sealant to the stones to give them a permanent wet look and enhance their colors.

using gravel

Gravel surfaces are satisfyingly crunchy to walk on or to drive over, and are an excellent burglar deterrent —you cannot cross gravel quietly, even on tiptoe. However, they do have several practical drawbacks. For a start, they need some form of edge restraint, such as embedded boards or concrete kerbstones, to stop the gravel from migrating onto lawns or into flowerbeds. You also have to rake them regularly to keep them looking neat and tidy, and they need to be treated with weedkiller from time to time. Another drawback is that they can attract local cats and dogs, who regard gravel as an ideal outdoor litter tray. Last of all, pushing a laden wheelbarrow across gravel is like wading through quicksand.

If you decide to create a gravel feature in your garden, you need to first choose which type of aggregate to use. Then measure the area you intend to cover and the depth to which you want to fill it, so that you can calculate the volume you require. A depth of 2in is usually adequate for gravel on a path, but 3in is better for a driveway.

You will need to arrange bulk delivery for all but the smallest projects. 35cu ft of gravel or aggregate will cover about 215sq ft to a depth of 2in, and 140sq ft to a depth of 3in. If your supplier delivers by weight, 1 ton will cover about 80sq ft. Bulk loads are delivered loose or in large canvas slings—these are preferable to a big heap because the gravel is contained better while you move it to its final destination. For small projects, you can buy gravel and other aggregates in 45, 90, and 110lb bags.

1 Measure out the site and clear vegetation and topsoil. Compact the subsoil thoroughly. Put the edge restraints in place, either nailing preservative-treated wood to strong markers or embedding kerbstones in a fine concrete mix. If you are using boards, secure them with stakes every 3ft or so to prevent them from bowing.

2 Lay a weedproof membrane over the site to discourage deep-rooted weeds from growing through the gravel. Overlap these strips of membrane by at least 4in, and trim the edges.

3 You can lay the gravel directly over the membrane, but if the subsoil is soft it is best to put down a layer of crushed rock or fine rubble first. Shovel it onto the membrane to a depth of at least 2in.

4 Compact the crushed rock with a heavy garden roller if you have one. Otherwise, use a heavy wooden tamping beam, such as a length of fence post, to pack down the layer of rock. To test whether you have tamped it down sufficiently, walk on the surface—if you do not leave footprints, then the rock has been tamped down enough.

5 Use a wheelbarrow to transport the gravel to the site and tip it out in heaps. Then spread out the gravel shovelful by shovelful up to the level of the edge restraints. Take care not to disturb the compacted base layer. Rake the gravel out level, then place a wooden straightedge on the edge restraints and draw it across the site to identify any high or low spots. Rake off the former and fill the latter with more gravel. Once the gravel is level, roll or tamp it to embed it well, and leave the finished surface about 1in below the tops of the edge restraints.

It is important to rake the gravel level in order to achieve an attractive finish, and it is a good idea to do this regularly to keep your gravel feature looking as good as new.

placing concrete—1

Concrete can be used to create driveways, patios, or paths, but suffers by comparison with paving slabs and blocks as far as appearance goes. It can also form bases for lightweight garden buildings, such as summerhouses, sheds, and workshops, and is the material used to create foundations for all sorts of garden structures, including walls, arches, and steps. Its main advantage over other materials used for creating exterior surfaces is that it is very economical.

ingredients

Concrete is a mixture of coarse and fine aggregates—stones up to about ¾in in diameter with smaller stones and coarse sand—that is bound together into a solid matrix by cement. You can buy the ingredients separately from builders' stores and mix them yourself, buy dry ready-mixed bags of cement and aggregate (ideal for small jobs), or order ready-mixed concrete (best for large areas).

Ready-mixed concrete may be delivered by a large truck mixer with its familiar slow-turning drum, or by a smaller vehicle that carries dry cement and aggregates plus a cement mixer, which can mix the amount you need on the spot. Truck mixers can deliver up to about 200cu ft of concrete directly to the site. Smaller vehicles mix by the wheelbarrow load, which you then have to move from truck to site.

The ingredients of a concrete mix depend on the use to which the material will be put. The three standard formulae are given in the table below, along with the quantities you need to make 35cu ft of concrete. Mixed aggregate is a mixture of coarse sand and ¾in aggregate.

Always mix ingredients by volume, using separate buckets or similar containers of the same size for cement and aggregate. Mix batches based on 1 bucket of cement plus the relevant numbers of buckets of sand and aggregate.

USE	MIX	PROPORTION	AMOUNT PER 35.3CU FT
General-purpose cement (most uses except foundations and exposed paving)	cement	1	6.4 bags (700lb)
	coarse sand	2	1500lb (15.8cu ft)
	¾in aggregate	3	2600lb (23.6cu ft)
	OR mixed aggregate	4	4100lb (34.6cu ft)
Foundations (strips, slabs, and bases for paving)	cement	1	5.6 bags (615lb)
	coarse sand	2.5	1600lb (17.6cu ft)
	¾in aggregate	3.5	2560lb (23.6cu ft)
	OR mixed aggregate	5	4150lb (35.3cu ft)
Paving (exposed slabs, especially driveways)	cement	1	8 bags (880lb)
	coarse sand	1.5	1320lb (14.8cu ft)
	¾in aggregate	2.5	2640lb (24.7cu ft)
	OR mixed aggregate	3.5	3960lb (33.5cu ft)

mixing your own concrete

For hand mixing you will need a hard, flat surface. A sheet of exterior-grade plywood is ideal for protecting driveways or patios, which should not be used unprotected because the concrete will stain them, however promptly you hose them down. Plastic trays 3ft across may be bought for mixing small quantities.

tools for the job

- shovel
- clean bucket
- wheelbarrow
- rented cement mixer

by hand

1 Measure out the sand and aggregate into a compact heap. Make a shallow depression in the center with a shovel and add the cement. Mix the ingredients dry until the pile is uniform in color and texture. For dry ready-mixed concrete, pour out the sack and mix thoroughly.

2 Make a depression in the center of the heap and add water. The aggregate will contain a certain amount of water already, so the amount you need to add will be guesswork at the start. After two or three batches, you will be better able to gauge how much to add.

3 Turn dry material from the edge of the heap into the central depression. Keep on mixing and adding a little more water in turn until the mix reaches the right consistency —it should retain ridges formed in it

with the shovel. If it is too sloppy, add dry ingredients, correctly proportioned as before, to stiffen it again.

with a mixer

If you are using a cement mixer, set it up on its stand and check that it is secure. Put some aggregate and water in the drum and start it turning. Add most of the cement and sand, then water and solid material alternately, to ensure thorough mixing. Run the mixer for two minutes once all the ingredients are in, then pour out some of the contents into a wheelbarrow. The mix should fall cleanly off the mixer blades.

preparing formwork

Concrete foundations for walls can generally be poured straight into a prepared form, since they will be hidden once the wall is built. However, surfaces such as paths, patios, and bases for buildings need to have straight, plumb edges, and the way to provide these is to lay concrete within what is known as formwork or shuttering —lengths of form board supported by strong stakes to form a mold. The top edges of the formwork provide a leveling guide, while its inner faces give the finished slab a neat molded edge.

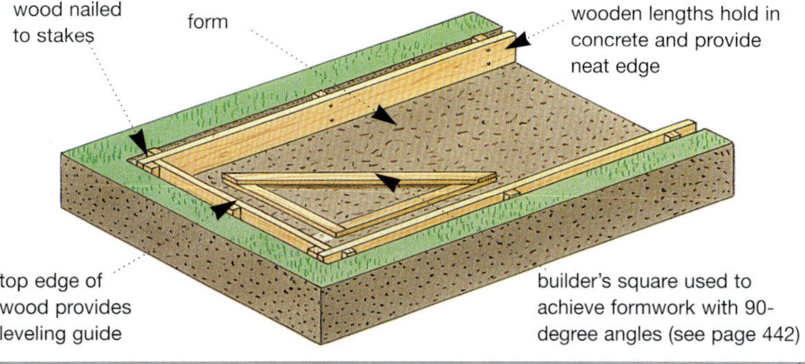

placing concrete—2

With the concrete mixed and the formwork in place, you are ready to start placing your concrete feature. Make sure that you have excavated the site to the correct depth and that you have placed and compacted a layer of crushed rock or rubble if this is required—see pages 458–9 for details. Check that the formwork is square and level, or has a slight fall if drainage of rainwater is needed away from the house.

Large areas of concrete cannot be laid as continuous slabs or they will crack due to expansion and contraction. You must therefore divide the work into bays, each separated from its neighbor by an expansion joint of masonite or similar material, if the concrete is being laid as a continuous operation. Where the area being concreted has a curved edge, make sure that expansion joints meet the curves at a right angle. If you are using the alternate bay technique (see opposite page), an expansion joint is not necessary—simply remove the formwork between filled and unfilled bays before concreting the unfilled bays. The recommended maximum size of each bay is around 13 x 13ft. On paths less than 6ft 6in wide, you should incorporate an expansion joint every 6ft 6in.

tips of the trade

It is best not to place concrete if frost is forecast, because permanent damage will be caused if the water in fresh concrete freezes. If frost sneaks up on you, lay polyethylene sheets over the concrete and cover them with a layer of earth or sand. Leave this in place until a thaw sets in. Never place concrete on frozen ground.

compacting the concrete

The most important part of concreting is compaction. For a concrete slab, the ideal compacting tool is a screed, a length of 2 x 4in sawn wood used on edge, long enough to span the formwork. If you wish, add angled wooden handles to each end of the screed so that you and a helper can operate it together.

Shovel concrete into the formwork, then rake it out level. Make sure that corners and edges are well filled. Add more concrete until the level is about ½in above the top edges of the formwork.

Set the screed in place across the formwork at one end of the slab and start tamping the concrete down. Use the beam with an up-and-down motion until the concrete is level with the top edge of the formwork, moving it along by half the screed's width after each tamping stroke—do not simply scrape the screed along the formwork. Continue tamping in this way until you reach the far end of the concrete slab, then repeat the process using a side-to-side sawing action to remove excess concrete. If the surface of the concrete still contains small voids, spread a thin layer of extra concrete and use the screed to tamp it again.

Compact the concrete by moving the screed across its surface with an up-and-down motion, then with a side-to-side sawing action.

using expansion joints

Cut strips of masonite to match the thickness of the concrete and set them on edge with mounds of concrete against their sides. The top of the strip should be level and just below the top edges of the formwork. Then place concrete up to the strip, working from both sides at the same time so that placing and compaction do not push the strip out of position. Incorporate similar joints where concrete slabs meet buildings. If there is an inspection chamber within the area being concreted, first place formwork around the chamber so that you can place a box of concrete around it. When it has set, remove the formwork and fit expansion strips all around it before concreting the rest of the slab. For concreting irregular-shape areas, set formwork boards across the area to divide it into bays. These boards should always be at a right angle to the perimeter boards.

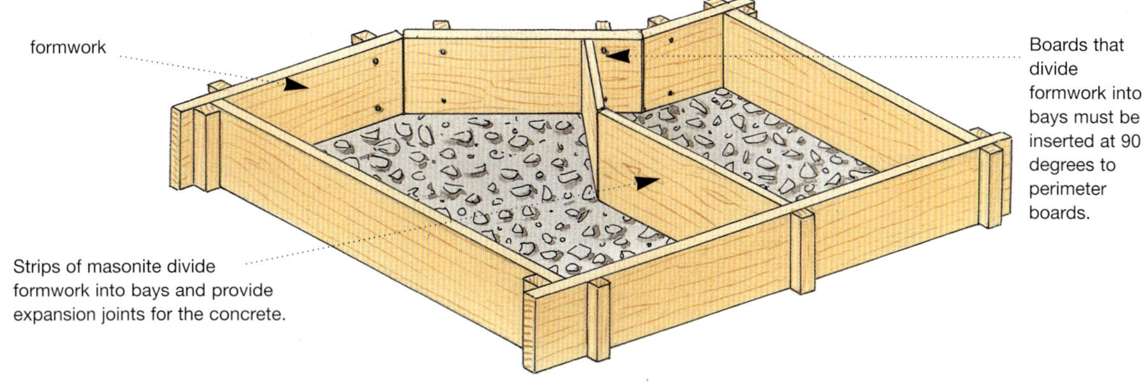

alternate bay technique

If a slab adjoins a wall, you will not be able to use the screed at a right angle to the wall. Instead, you will have to lay alternate bays along the wall. Set up formwork as usual, with wooden divider boards separating the bays. Place an expansion joint next to the wall and fill alternate bays, tamping the concrete parallel to the wall. Remove the divider after 48 hours and concrete the remaining bays, using the hardened concrete edges of the first set of bays to guide the screed. There is no need to fit expansion joints between the bays.

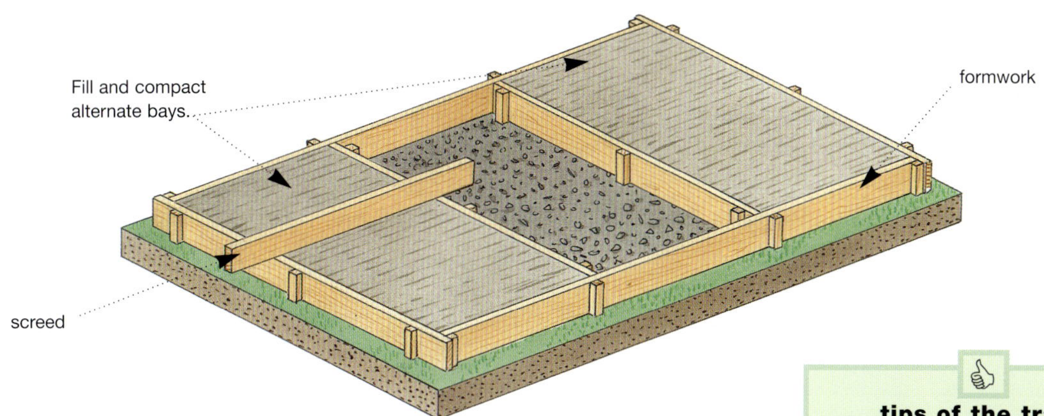

FINISHES FOR CONCRETE

You can leave concrete with the rippled finish created by tamping, but this is not very attractive. You can create a finer rippled finish if you do the final tamping by working the screed backward and forward with a sawing motion at a right angle to the formwork. Brushing the tamped surface with a soft broom will flatten the ridges and leave a fairly smooth finish. A wood plasterer's trowel will give a fine sandpaper texture, while a steel float will create a fine, flat finish.

tips of the trade

Fresh concrete will weaken and crack if it dries too quickly, and this is a particular risk with thin slabs of large surface area. As soon as the concrete slab is placed and finished, cover it with polyethylene sheet weighted all around with bricks or baulks of wood to stop wind from blowing under it. Leave the sheet in place for about three days.

patching concrete

Concrete is the most widespread—and economical—material for laying driveways, paths, patios, and other surfaces around the house and garden. Although it produces a highly durable surface, it can crack if overloaded by heavy vehicles, or if the ground subsides or swells beneath it. These cracks let in water that then freezes, widening the crack and opening up further cracks that can eventually lead to the complete breakup of the surface.

If you have a concrete surface that is looking the worse for wear, inspect it more closely to get an idea of the true extent of the damage. Cracks, holes, and broken edges are all relatively straightforward to repair using the techniques outlined in the step-by-step sequence below, but if the surface has cracked and partly subsided, you will probably be better off breaking the sunken section and laying new concrete in its place (see the box on the opposite page for advice on how to deal with subsidence).

tools for the job

- safety goggles
- work gloves
- brick chisel
- cold chisel
- hand sledge
- pick
- spade
- bucket & mixer
- pointing trowel
- screed (for larger repairs)
- plastering trowel
- stiff broom
- rake

1 Break away all loose material from the site of the damage, using a cold chisel, a brick chisel, or even a pick if necessary. Always wear protective safety goggles and thick work gloves to do this kind of work. Pick the debris out of the hole or crack piece by piece. Do not disturb any crushed rock or rubble that was beneath the concrete. If there is none and the slab was laid directly on the earth, excavate the concrete to a depth of about 4in.

2 If you had to dig out the subsoil in step 1, pack some rubble (pieces of broken brick, flints from the yard, or similar solid material) into the hole and tamp it down firmly with the handle of the hand sledge.

3 Mix some concrete using 1 part cement to 3.5 parts mixed aggregate (combined coarse sand and gravel). For small jobs, buy a dry ready-mixed bag of concrete and just add water. Shovel it into the hole, or place it beside a crack.

4 Tamp the concrete into the hole using a piece of wood that is long enough to span it on edge. By moving this from side to side as you work your way across the patch, you will automatically rule off excess concrete. Fill cracks using a pointing trowel, pressing the concrete well down into the crack and finishing it level with the surrounding surface.

5 Tamping with a wooden straightedge will leave the repair with a ribbed surface finish. Flatten this with a plastering trowel if you want a smooth finish, or use a stiff-bristled broom to create a more definite textured effect. Cover the

repair with polyethylene sheet weighted with bricks. Allow to harden for 24 hours before walking on it, and for 48 hours before driving over it.

6 If an edge of the concrete has broken away, remove all loose material and cut the concrete back to a sound vertical edge. Cut a piece of wood or board deep enough to match the thickness of the concrete and long enough to span the patch, and hold it in position against the edge of the concrete with a couple of bricks or with wooden stakes driven into the ground.

Pack concrete into the mold, tamping it well with a wooden straightedge to make quite sure that the mold is completely filled and well compacted. Finish the surface of the patch to match the surrounding concrete, cover it with polyethylene sheet, and allow it to harden for 24 hours. Before removing the wood the next day, run the blade of a pointing trowel between the wood and the edge of the concrete.

Use a wooden straightedge to tamp the patch of concrete down well in order to achieve a level, even surface that is safe to walk on and attractive to look at.

DEALING WITH SUBSIDENCE

If an area of concrete has cracked and subsided slightly, you cannot simply lay more concrete on top of it to bring it back level with the rest of the slab, because a thin layer will always be prone to break up and delaminate. Break up the area that has subsided using a pick or a rented concrete breaker, then excavate to a depth of at least 6in and pack in a 6in thick layer of rubble or crushed aggregate. The latter is better than rubble, because it compacts more fully and provides a denser and more stable base for the new concrete. Stake some wooden formwork around the area you are replacing, and add more aggregate to fill the edges and corners of the mold, making sure that you tamp it down well. Mix some concrete using 1 part cement to 3½ parts combined aggregate, shovel it into the mold, and rake it out. Overfill the mold slightly, then rest a wooden screed across the formwork and tamp the concrete down level with it. This will also remove any high spots. Fill any hollows that appear, and tamp again. Then finish the concrete surface to match the rest of the slab, cover it with polyethylene sheet, and allow it to harden for 48 hours or more.

leveling uneven paving

Paving slabs and interlocking concrete pavers are very popular for giving hard surfaces around the garden a decorative finish. Even when they are level when first laid, slabs and blocks can become uneven due to ground movement, subsidence of the base on which they were laid, or overloading by heavy traffic. Once this occurs, every raised edge is a trip hazard, and the whole area soon begins to look unsightly, with weeds starting to grow through cracked joints.

Uneven paving is often the result of inadequate preparation and incorrect techniques when the slabs or pavers were first laid, especially if they were placed dry on a sand bed with joints also filled with sand. Water running off the surface of paving slabs can slowly erode the sand beneath, allowing the paving to settle. Settlement is also a common problem with concrete pavers that were laid by hand, rather than being embedded into its sand base with a plate vibrator. The solution to this problem is to lift and relay the affected slabs or pavers.

tools for the job

- safety goggles & work gloves
- pointing trowel
- brick chisel & scrap wood (for lifting slabs)
- shovel
- hand sledge
- bucket & mixer
- bricklaying trowel
- level
- long wooden straightedge
- chalk
- rake & stiff broom
- cold chisel

dealing with uneven paving slabs

1 If a paving slab has subsided, rake out any sand or mortar pointing between the affected slab and its neighbors. Alternatively, use the tip of a pointing trowel to do this.

2 Drive a brick chisel into one of the gaps, lay a piece of scrap wood on the edge of the adjacent slab to protect it, and use the wood as a fulcrum to lever the slab up. Slide the wood underneath the raised edge so that you can get a grip on the slab and lift it out. Wear a pair of thick work gloves to give your fingers some protection while lifting out the heavy slab.

3 If the slab was laid on sand, add a little fresh sand to the bed and replace the slab. Stand it on edge at one side of the hole in which it fits, lower it horizontal, and slide it slightly so that it drops into place without disturbing the sand line. Tamp it down with the handle of a hand sledge until it sits level with the neighboring slabs. If it still sits a little low, repeat the process to add more sand.

If the slab was laid on mortar mounds, chip the old mortar off the back of the slab with a brick chisel and hand sledge. Take care not to crack the slab—it does not matter if a little mortar stays stuck to it. Then mix a small amount of bricklaying mortar (a bag of dry, ready-mixed mortar is ideal for this sort of job) and use a bricklaying trowel to place five mounds on the bed of the hole—one near each corner and one in the middle. Drop the slab back into place and tamp it down with a hammer to the required level.

4 Lay a level across the relaid slab and its neighbors to check that they are correctly aligned, then fill the joints around the relaid slab with sand or dryish mortar to match the rest of the area. If you are using mortar, lay strips of cardboard alongside the joint to prevent mortar from staining the slabs while you fill the joint.

dealing with uneven concrete pavers

1 Identify the extent of the subsidence by laying a long wooden straightedge across the paving in different directions. Mark any pavers that have sunk below the straightedge with chalk.

2 Wearing protective gloves, pry up several pavers at the edge of the area of sunken paving. Work your way paver by paver toward the area that has subsided, and lift these pavers too.

3 Shovel some fresh sand onto the affected area and rake it out evenly, then start to replace the pavers one by one. Tamp each paver down firmly into the sand bed so that it is flush with the neighboring blocks. Use the straightedge to check that you have eliminated the subsidence after replacing every four or five blocks.

4 Finish replacing the paver, check they are level once again, and complete the job by brushing fine, dry sand into the joints. This will help to lock the pavers together and prevent subsidence from recurring.

repointing crazy paving

Crazy paving is usually embedded in mortar, so it is not generally prone to subsidence. However, the pointing between the individual stones can crack and break out, leaving unsightly paving that can also be a trip hazard. The solution is to repoint the joints with fresh mortar.

If the individual pieces of stone have begun to crack and break up, lift them and replace them with new pieces of stone, trimmed to fit.

1 Wearing safety goggles and a pair of thick protective work gloves, cut out all the failed pointing with a cold chisel and hand sledge. Take care not to disturb the individual stones of the paving when you do this, unless you are planning to replace damaged pieces. Brush away the debris.

2 Place new pieces of stone on a mortar bed and tamp them down level with their neighbors. Point the joints with a dryish bricklaying mortar, taking care not to get any on the faces of the stones. Fill the joint almost level with the surface, then draw the tip of a pointing trowel along each edge of the joint in turn, letting it follow the contours of the stones. The aim is to highlight the edges of the stones and give the pointing a raised V-shape profile.

glossary

Access hatch—section cut out of a floor, wall, or ceiling and made into a hinged door or removable panel.

Acrylic (or water-based)—describes the makeup of paint or glaze used for open areas such as walls or ceilings.

Aggregate—broken stone, pebbles, gravel, or similar material that forms the largest part of compounds such as concrete and mortar (finest aggregates are better known as sand). Aggregate is also referred to as ballast.

Air brick—brick containing a number of holes, used for ventilation into a room or under a floor.

Angle-fastening—nailing or screwing at an angle through wood or masonry in order to provide a fastening. Also called toenailing.

Awning window—a top-hinged casement window.

Backsplash—an area on a wall surface subject to splashes from basins, sinks, or cooktops, covered with an easily wipeable material, such as tiles, stainless steel, or glass.

Baluster—part of a balustrade, the correct term for stair spindles between stringer and handrail.

Base coat—the first coat of plaster or paint, also known as the undercoat. A top coat of finish plaster or paint is added to it.

Base unit—a kitchen or bathroom unit that is sited at floor level.

Baseboard—decorative and protective wooden molding fitted at the junction between floor and wall.

Bathtub panel—a decorative panel attached to the side of a bathtub. Normally removable for access to area under the bathtub.

Bearing post—an adjustable telescopic steel tube used to support needles or the floor above when removing all or part of a wall.

Blinding—sand spread over rubble layer in concrete floor to prevent the damp-proof membrane being pierced.

Block—masonry unit, usually larger than a brick, used to build house and garden walls. Also a short, horizontal piece of wood fastened between wall studs or ceiling joists to stiffen the structure.

Blocking in—filling in a space (e.g. to disguise the construction details under a staircase) by adding flat panels of masonite or drywall.

Bond—the way in which bricks are arranged in a wall. Different bonds are used for different types of walls.

Bonding agent—all-purpose adhesive used to bind and/or stabilize surfaces. Used in concentrated and dilute forms.

Boxing—technique of employing a framework to cover up unsightly items, such as pipes. Usually constructed as a frame of wooden furring strips and covered with building board.

Breakfast bar—a length of worktop used for both food preparation and serving meals. Incorporates a seating facility created by an overhang on one or more sides.

Brick—a masonry unit made from burnt clay and other materials that is used for building house and garden walls and other structures. A standard brick measures 8½ x 4 x 2½in.

Bridging—wooden or metal diagonal braces that are attached between joists to prevent movement in floors.

Built-in—term used to describe a kitchen or bathroom that consists of similar units fastened in a permanent position, usually integrated together in runs.

Bulkhead—partial wall that often hangs over a stairwell or to one side of the staircase, and which is not directly supported by a floor.

Carcass—the basic structure of a bathroom or kitchen unit where no embellishments, such as doors or drawer fronts, have been added.

Carousel—a circular shelving system used in corner units. Rotates in order to aid access.

Casement—name given to a section of window or used to refer to an entire window made of a number of casements. Normally, casement windows contain both opening and fixed sections.

Casing—decorative strips of molding fastened around a door frame to create a finish over the joint between frame and wall. Also called crown molding.

Caulk—latex, acrylic, or water-based flexible filler supplied in tube and dispensed from a caulk gun. Must be smoothed to finish before it dries.

Cavity wall—wall consisting of two layers, or skins, of masonry held together with metal or plastic wall ties, and with a gap (the cavity)—commonly 2in wide—between them. Common in construction of exterior walls of modern homes.

Ceiling center—ornamental plaster or foamed plastic molding fixed in the center of a ceiling for decoration.

Ceiling unit—A kitchen unit that is fixed to the ceiling.

Cement—binder in powder form that bonds sand or aggregate together to form mortar for bricklaying or concrete.

Chair rail—a wooden rail or molding that denotes the top of the dado and therefore divides up the wall surface into a lower and upper area. Sometimes referred to as a dado rail.

Chipboard—manufactured board made of compressed wooden fibers and supplied in sheets that are normally joined with a tongue-and-groove mechanism.

Cladding—name given to a material that covers the main structural element below it.

Cleat—small, short length of wood that supports another larger piece.

Closed tread—the type of stairs that includes a riser in each step. The opposite of open tread.

Closure—a brick cut in half along its length and used to maintain the bond pattern in English and Flemish bond.

Cobblestone—rounded pebble, up to 3in in diameter, laid loose or in a mortar bed.

Colorizer—concentrated color that is supplied in small tubes or containers, designed to add color to paint or glaze for paint-effect purposes. Some can be added to either latex, acrylic, and solvent-based paints, or glazes.

Concrete—building material made from cement, sand, aggregate, and water that sets to a hard, stone-like mass and is used for floors and subfloors, wall foundations, and as cast slabs for laying patios, driveways, and the bases for outbuildings.

Concrete anchor—screw designed to fix into masonry without the need for a wall plug.

Condensation—moisture that forms when the air is completely saturated and unable to absorb any more. Most likely to collect on surfaces that are colder than the surroundings, such as cold windows.

Coping—a brick, stone, or concrete strip, usually overhanging, set on top of a wall to protect it from the weather.

Corner bead—a molding made from galvanized steel and expanded metal mesh that is used as reinforcement for plaster on outside wall corners.

Cornice—decorative molding fastened around top or bottom edge of wall units, or along wall/ceiling junction. Generally more ornate, and greater in depth than cove.

Cove—a plain molding, generally concave in cross-section, fitted in the angle between a wall and ceiling for decorative purposes. A cornice is a more ornate type of cove.

Crazy paving—a paved surface created by bedding irregular-shaped pieces of stone or paving slab in mortar and then pointing the gaps between the pieces. Also called irregular paving.

Cutting in—term used to describe painting in the corners, or at the different junctions on a wall surface, or between walls and wooden moldings.

Dado—the lower area of an interior wall. *See also* chair rail.

Damp-proof course (DPC)—a continuous layer of impervious material (formerly slate, now usually plastic) built into a house wall just above ground level to stop ground water soaking into the wall and causing rising damp. Concrete ground floors incorporate a damp-proof membrane (DPM).

Damp-proof fluid—means of repairing a failed DPC or substitute if none exists. Liquid is injected at numerous points into an exterior wall at the level of a damp-proof course in order to form an impermeable layer.

Damp-proof membrane (DPM)—a sheet material laid between subfloor and flooring to prevent moisture from rising up through concrete and screeds.

Datum mark—a mark on a wall, or other immovable part, of a known height, from which all other measurements are taken.

Dead bolt—locking system that requires a key to open. Some require a key to be put in the locked position, while others may be locked without a key but still require one for opening.

Distressing—paint effect that is designed to give surfaces an aged look.

Door jamb—the wooden lining (the inside part) of a door frame.

Doorstop—a strip of wood that runs around the inside part of a door frame or jamb and acts as a barrier for the door edge to close on to.

Double-hung window—two sash windows that open vertically within the same window frame, usually by means of a cord, pulley, and weight system. Modern versions may use a chain or spring balance version.

Dry rot—type of fungal attack to wood and other building materials. Starts as minute silky threads covering the wood surface, then changes to what looks like cotton balls and finally dark red, sponge-like bodies.

Dry-lining—a wall lining formed from tapered-edge sheets of drywall or plasterboard fastened to a framework of wooden furring strips. The joints are taped and filled, but the board does not require plastering.

Drywall (or wallboard)—a gypsum layer that is compressed and enclosed or sandwiched between thick paper and manufactured in sheets to be used as standard building board for plaster surfaces. *See also* plasterboard.

Drywall finishing—technique combining drywall and joint compound to create wall or ceiling surface ready for painting or papering. Joint compound is used between sheets of drywall or plasterboard.

Dummy drawer front—a drawer front that is not attached to a drawer but is fastened to a unit carcass to imitate a drawer, in order to maintain the decorative finish of a run of units.

Efflorescence—powdery white salts left on a wall surface as it dries out after construction or plastering. (They should be brushed, not washed, off.)

Eggshell—durable paint that has a dull, flat finish. Available in latex acrylic or solvent-based forms.

Enamel—a durable decorative coating for bathroom fixtures that is traditionally used on old iron bathtubs.

End panel—decorative panel attached to the exposed sides of wall and base units at the end of a run of units. Often matches finish of door fronts.

English bond—an arrangement of bricks in a wall with alternate courses laid as headers and stretchers. The wall is one brick (8½in) thick.

Ensuite—term normally applied to a bathroom directly adjacent to, and serving, one particular room.

Escutcheon—a small plate used as decorative finish to a keyhole. May have a cover for insulation or privacy.

Expanded metal lath—perforated metal sheet or strip used to support plaster when patching holes in partition walls and ceilings.

Factory-cut edge—a cut edge that has been produced as a result of the manufacturing process and is therefore cut with precision. Exposed edges should be factory-cut edges rather than those cut by hand.

Fan—mechanical ventilation system, either ceiling- or wall-mounted.

Filler—plaster powder used to fill small holes and indentations, and to cover nail and screw heads before painting.

Fire door—a type of door that has fire-retardant materials built into its design.

Flemish bond—an arrangement of bricks in a wall where each course consists of a header followed by a pair of stretchers. The wall is one brick (8½in) thick.

Floor grille—a metal cover fitted over a hole in the floor to allow air into the room and the area under the floor. Can be rigid or with a shutter design.

Floor unit—a bathroom or kitchen unit that is installed at floor level.

Flush door—type of door, available in both hollow or solid forms.

Flush lighting—lighting systems that are recessed into a surface, such as recessed spotlights on a ceiling.

Flux—cleaning material used on joints prior to soldering.

Formwork—wooden boards attached to stakes in the ground to form a mold for a cast concrete ground slab. Removed when the concrete has set.

Foundation—a strip of concrete cast in a trench to support a wall or other masonry feature. Sometimes referred to as a footing.

Furring strip—a thin piece of wood used for boxing and other construction requirements. Also known as cleat.

Galley kitchen—a long, narrow kitchen with units on opposing walls. Similar to a u-shaped kitchen.

Glaze—medium to which colorizers are added to create paint effects. Latex, acrylic or solvent-based alternatives can be referred to as scumble.

Gloss—a highly decorative, durable, and shiny paint finish.

Glue block—triangular wooden block fitted at the back of the stairs between tread and riser.

Glue wedge—wooden wedge fastened to stairs so that the tread is held tightly into the stringer.

Gravel—washed river stone typically sieved to a maximum diameter of $^{3}/_{4}$in.

Grout—waterproof compound that fills the gap between tile joints.

Handrail—rail fixed either to wall or open side of staircase that may be gripped to provide support as you climb and descend the stairs.

Hard tiles—ceramic wall or floor tiles as opposed to softer varieties, such as cork or vinyl.

Hawk—a metal or plywood square with a handle underneath that is used to carry small amounts of mortar or plaster to the work area.

Head plate—a horizontal wooden stud that creates a ceiling fastening for stud wall framework.

Header—a brick laid in a wall with only its ends visible. Also wood around a fire surround to support cut joists.

Headgear—term denoting the internal mechanism of a faucet.

Hearth—area in front of, and at the base of a fireplace.

Housing—shallow groove into which another section of wood may be fastened.

I-beam—a rolled-steel joist that is in essence a heavy-duty lintel. Used mainly over an opening when a loadbearing wall is removed and two rooms are converted into one.

Inside corner—a corner that extends out into the room. Also called interior corner.

Island unit—a single unit or run of units positioned in the center of a room, separate from the units around the perimeter of the room.

Jointing compound—similar to plaster or filler. Used to join gaps between plasterboard or drywall when dry-lining.

Jointing tape—tape used to join plasterboard or drywall sheet prior to dry-lining or plastering. Self-adhesive varieties are available.

Joist—a wooden or steel beam supporting a floor and, in upstairs rooms, the ceiling below.

Joist hanger—a metal bracket used to support the ends of floor joists at wall junctions, with varieties specifically designed for attaching to masonry or timber. Some joist hangers can be built-in.

Joist socket—a hole in a wall, or a heavy beam to support joists when joist hangers are not used.

Keystone—the central brick or stone at the top of an arch.

Knockdown—also known as self-assembly, a unit supplied in sections that needs to be assembled before fastening in place.

Laminate—a term used to describe the process whereby a thin layer (plastic or wood veneer) is bonded to another surface, such as fiberboard, to create one solid piece.

Landing—the area halfway up a staircase that links different flights of stairs, usually to allow flights to change direction. Also commonly used to refer to the area of the upper hallway immediately at the top of a staircase.

Latch—a retractable lever that allows doors to open and close into a frame.

Latex—acrylic or water-based paint used for open areas such as walls and ceilings.

Lath and plaster—a older lining for ceilings and stud partition walls, consisting of plaster applied to closely spaced wooden strips (lath) that are nailed to the ceiling joists or wall studs.

Leading edge—the vertical edge of a door or window that is farthest from the hinges.

Level—where two or more surfaces create a seamless join.

Lever handle—a handle designed in the shape of a horizontal bar. Pushed down to operate the latch in a door.

Lever latch—the latch mechanism of a door operated by a lever handle.

Light—another word for casement when referring to a window section. Normally used to describe small parts of a window, either fixed or opening (e.g. "the small light in a casement window" would be a small opening section); also used in conjunction with leaded-light windows.

Lighting track—lighting system where a number of lights are positioned along a track. Light position is usually adjustable along the track.

Lining—the application of lining paper to wall surfaces.

Lintel—a steel, wood, or concrete beam that spans the opening of a door or window.

Locking lever latch—latch mechanism with separate locking system built into overall latch casing.

Low-level lighting—lighting system where lighting position is well below ceiling level.

L-shaped—term used to describe the layout of a kitchen that resembles the shape of an L. The units extend from one wall around to the adjacent one.